The

Oxford

Book

of

STORIES
BY
CANADIAN
WOMEN

in

English

The
Oxford
Book
of

STORIES
BY
CANADIAN
WOMEN

in
English

Edited by

ROSEMARY SULLIVAN

OXFORD
UNIVERSITY PRESS

OXFORD
UNIVERSITY PRESS

70 Wynford Drive, Don Mills, Ontario M3C 1J9
www.oupcan.com

Oxford University Press is a department of the University of Oxford.
It furthers the University's objective of excellence in research, scholarship,
and education by publishing worldwide in

Oxford New York

Athens Auckland Bangkok Bogotá Buenos Aires Calcutta
Cape Town Chennai Dar es Salaam Delhi Florence Hong Kong Istanbul
Karachi Kuala Lumpur Madrid Melbourne Mexico City Mumbai
Nairobi Paris São Paulo Singapore Taipei Tokyo Toronto Warsaw

with associated companies in Berlin Ibadan

Oxford is a trade mark of Oxford University Press
in the UK and in certain other countries

Published in Canada
by Oxford University Press

Canadian Cataloguing in Publication Data
Main entry under title:
The Oxford book of stories by Canadian women in English
Includes index.
ISBN 0-19-541426-8
1. Short stories, Canadian (English – Women authors.* 2. Canadian fiction
(English) – 20th century.* I. Sullivan, Rosemary

PS8321.0936 1999   C813'.01'089287   C99-931720-2   PR9197.32.095 1999

1 2 3 4 - 02 01 00 99
This book is printed on permanent (acid-free) paper ∞
Printed in Canada

CONTENTS

❧

ACKNOWLEDGEMENTS

EDNA ALFORD. 'The Late Date' from *The Garden of Eloise Loon* (Lantzville, BC: Oolichan Books, 1986). Reprinted by permission of Oolichan Books.

MARGARET ATWOOD. 'Bluebeard's Egg' from the short story collection *Bluebeard's Egg* by Margaret Atwood © 1983 McClelland & Stewart. Reprinted with permission of the author and McClelland & Stewart, Inc. The Canadian Publishers.

HIMANI BANNERJI. 'On a Cold Day' from *Her Mother's Ashes*, ed. Nurjehan Aziz (Toronto: TSAR Publications, 1994). Reprinted by permission of the author.

JUDY FONG BATES. 'My Sister's Love' from *China Dog and Other Tales from a Chinese Laundry* (Toronto: Sister Vision Press, 1997). Reprinted by permission of the publisher.

SANDRA BIRDSELL. 'Night Travellers' from *Agassiz Stories* (Winnipeg: Turnstone Press, 1982). Copyright © Sandra Birdsell 1982. Reprinted by permission of Turnstone Press.

DIONNE BRAND. 'Photograph' from *Sans Souci and Other Stories*. Copyright © 1988 by Dionne Brand. Reprinted by permission of Firebrand Books, Ithaca, NY.

BETH BRANT (Degonwadonti). 'A Long Story' from *Mohawk Trail* by Beth Brant. Copyright © 1985 by Beth Brant (Toronto: Women's Press, 1990). Reprinted by permission of Firebrand Books, Ithaca, NY and the author.

BONNIE BURNARD. 'Crush' from *Casino & Other Stories* by Bonnie Burnard. A Phyllis Bruce Book, Published by HarperCollins Publishers Ltd. Copyright © 1994 by Bonnie Burnard. Reprinted by permission of HarperCollins Publishers Ltd and Westwood Creative Artists.

SHARON BUTALA. 'Fever' from *Fever* by Sharon Butala. Published by HarperCollins Publishers Ltd. Copyright © 1990 by Sharon Butala. Reprinted by permission.

ANNE CARSON. From '*The Anthropology of Water*' from *Plainwater* by Anne Carson. Copyright © 1995 by Anne Carson. Reprinted by permission of Alfred A. Knopf Inc.

JOAN CLARK. 'The Train Family' from *Swimming Toward the Light* (Toronto: Macmillan Canada, 1990). Reprinted by permission of the author.

LYNN COADY. 'A Great Man's Passing' copyright © by Lynn Coady 1994 from *Play the Monster Blind*, to be published by Doubleday Canada in Spring 2000. Reprinted by permission of the author.

SARA JEANNETTE DUNCAN. 'The Pool in the Desert' from *The Pool in the Desert* (Toronto: Penguin Books, 1984).

MARIAN ENGEL. 'Anita's Dance' from *The Tattooed Woman* (Toronto: Penguin Books, 1985). Reprinted by permission of Russell & Volkening as agents for the author. Copyright ©

1985 by Marian Engel. Copyright © 1985 by the estate of Marian Engel. Reprinted by permission of Penguin Books Canada Limited.

CYNTHIA FLOOD. 'My Father Took a Cake to France' from *My Father Took a Cake to France* (Burnaby, BC: TalonBooks, 1992). Reprinted by permission of Talon Books Ltd.

MAVIS GALLANT. 'The Moslem Wife' from *The Moslem Wife and Other Stories* by Mavis Gallant. Used by permission, McClelland & Stewart, Inc. The Canadian Publishers. 'The Moslem Wife' from *The Fifteenth District* by Mavis Gallant (New York: Random House, 1979). Copyright © 1979 by Mavis Gallant. Reprinted by permission of Georges Borchardt, Inc. for the author.

CONNIE GAULT. 'Inspection of a Small Village' reprinted from the collection *Inspection of a Small Village* by Connie Gault, published by Coteau Books, with permission of the publisher.

SHREE GHATAGE. 'Deafness Comes to Me' from *Awake When All the World is Asleep* (Concord, ON: House of Anansi Press, 1997). Copyright © 1997 by Shree Ghatage. Reprinted by permission of House of Anansi Press Limited.

MARGARET GIBSON. 'The Butterfly Ward' by Margaret Gibson is reprinted from *The Butterfly Ward* by permission of Oberon Press.

KATHERINE GOVIER. 'The King of Siam' from *Before and After* by Katherine Govier (Toronto: Penguin Books, 1990). Copyright © 1989 by Katherine Govier. Reprinted by permission of the author and Penguin Books Canada Limited.

BARBARA GOWDY. 'Ninety-three Million Miles Away' from *We So Seldom Look on Love*. © 1992 by Barbara Gowdy. Reprinted by permission of the author.

ELISABETH HARVOR. 'There Goes the Groom' from *Let Me Be the One* by Elisabeth Harvor. Published by HarperCollins Publishers Ltd. Copyright © 1996 by Elisabeth Harvor. Reprinted by permission.

ELIZABETH HAY. 'The Friend' from *Small Change* (Erin, ON: The Porcupine's Quill, 1997). Reprinted by permission of The Porcupine's Quill.

JANETTE TURNER HOSPITAL. 'Hear and Now' from *Isobars: Stories* by Janette Turner Hospital (Toronto: McClelland & Stewart, 1990). Copyright © 1990 Janette Turner Hospital. Used by permission, McClelland & Stewart, Inc. The Canadian Publishers and the author.

ISABEL HUGGAN. 'Celia Behind Me' by Isabel Huggan is reprinted from *The Elizabeth Stories* by permission of Oberon Press.

E. PAULINE JOHNSON (Tekahionwake). 'A Red Girl's Reasoning' from *The Moccasin Maker* (1913).

JUDITH KALMAN. 'The County of Birches' from *The County of Birches* by Judith Kalman, © Judith Kalman 1998, published by Douglas & McIntyre. Reprinted by permission of Douglas & McIntyre and St Martin's Press.

JANICE KULYK KEEFER. 'Going Over the Bars' from *Travelling Ladies*. Copyright ©1990. Reprinted by permission of Random House of Canada Limited.

MARGARET LAURENCE. 'The Rain Child' from *The Tomorrow-Tamer and other Stories* by Margaret Laurence (Toronto: McClelland & Stewart, 1970). Copyright © 1970 Margaret Laurence. Used by permission, McClelland & Stewart, Inc. The Canadian Publishers and the estate of Margaret Laurence.

LUCY MAUD MONTGOMERY. 'The Quarantine at Alexander Abraham's' from *Chronicles of Avonlea* (1912).

ALICE MUNRO. 'The Albanian Virgin' from *Open Secrets* by Alice Munro. Used by permission, McClelland & Stewart, Inc. The Canadian Publishers.

P.K. PAGE. 'Unless the Eye Catch Fire . . .' from *The Hidden Room* (Erin, ON: The Porcupine's Quill, 1997). Reprinted by permission of The Porcupine's Quill.

MARLENE NOURBESE PHILIP. 'Burn Sugar' from *Daughters of Africa* ed. Margaret Busby (London: Jonathan Cape, 1992). Reprinted by permission of the author.

JANE RULE. The story 'Lilian' by Jane Rule is reprinted from the collection *Outlander*, Naiad Press, 1981, with permission.

DIANE SCHOEMPERLEN. 'Five Small Rooms (A Murder Mystery)' from *Forms of Devotion* by Diane Schoemperlen. A Phyllis Bruce Book, published by HarperCollins Publishers Ltd. Copyright © 1998 by Diane Schoemperlen. Reprinted by permission of HarperCollins Publishers Ltd and Bella Pomer Agency.

GAIL SCOTT. 'Tall Cowboys and True', © Gail Scott, from *Likely Stories: A Postmodern Sampler* ed. George Bowering and Linda Hutcheon (Toronto: Coach House Press, 1992). Reprinted by permission of the author.

CAROL SHIELDS. 'The Orange Fish' from *The Orange Fish*. Copyright © 1989. Reprinted by permission of Random House of Canada Limited, Penguin Books USA, and Blake Friedmann, UK.

ELIZABETH SPENCER. 'I, Maureen' from *The Stories of Elizabeth Spencer* (New York: Doubleday, 1981). Reprinted by permission of the author.

LINDA SVENDSEN. 'White Shoulders' from *Marine Life* by Linda Svendsen. Copyright © 1992 by Linda Svendsen. Reprinted by permission of Farrar, Straus & Giroux, Inc. and Robin Straus Agency.

SUSAN SWAN. 'The Man Doll' from *Stupid Boys Are Good to Relax With* (Toronto: Somerville House, 1996). Copyright © 1996 by Susan Swan. Reprinted by permission.

AUDREY THOMAS. 'Local Customs' from *Goodbye Harold, Good Luck* by Audrey Thomas. Copyright © 1986 by Audrey Thomas. Reprinted by permission of Penguin Books Canada Limited.

CATHARINE PARR TRAILL. 'The Bereavement' from *Literary Garland* (1846).

JANE URQUHART. 'The Death of Robert Browning' from *Storm Glass* (Erin, ON: The Porcupine's Quill, 1987). Reprinted by permission of The Porcupine's Quill.

ARITHA VAN HERK. 'In Visible Ink' from *In Visible Ink: Crypto-Frictions* (Edmonton, AB: NeWest Publishers, 1991).

MEEKA WALSH. 'No More Denver Sandwiches' from *The Garden of Earthly Intimacies* (Erin, ON: The Porcupine's Quill, 1996). Reprinted by permission of The Porcupine's Quill.

EMMA LEE WARRIOR. 'Compatriots' from *All My Relations: An Anthology of Contemporary Canadian Native Fiction* (Toronto: McClelland & Stewart, 1990).

SHEILA WATSON. 'Antigone' from *Four Stories* (Toronto: Coach House Press, 1979). Reprinted by permission of the Estate of Sheila Watson.

HELEN WEINZWEIG. 'Causation' was first published in *A View from the Roof* (Goose Lane Editions, 1989). The story has been reprinted by permission of the publisher.

ETHEL WILSON. 'We Have to Sit Opposite' from *Mrs Golightly and Other Stories* (Toronto: Macmillan Canada, 1961).

RACHEL WYATT. 'The Day Marlene Dietrich Died' from *The Day Marlene Dietrich Died* (Lantzville, BC: Oolichan Books, 1996). Reprinted by permission of Oolichan Books.

Every effort has been made to determine and contact copyright owners. In the case of any omissions, the publisher will be pleased to make suitable acknowledgement in future editions.

INTRODUCTION

In 1984, Oxford University Press invited me to edit *Stories by Canadian Women*. Three years later, a second volume followed entitled *More Stories by Canadian Women*. These projects initially grew out of my frustration with the under-representation of women writers in anthologies. In those days, it always seemed to be the same few women writers who were accorded anthology status. One could find stories by Margaret Laurence, Alice Munro, Mavis Gallant, Audrey Thomas, and Margaret Atwood in most collections, but many other excellent women writers were excluded. Moreover, no effort had yet been made to offer a historical overview of the contribution of Canadian women to the short story genre.

Editing those books was exciting. In my research, I scoured nineteenth-century journals and found wonderful stories by writers like Isabella Valancy Crawford, Susie Frances Harrison, and Sara Jeannette Duncan. I also spent months searching through French-language journals, having decided to include stories by French-Canadian writers in both volumes.

Much has changed in the past fifteen years. Now an anthology of stories by women writers is no longer a political statement about exclusion. We have gone through a period of historical recovery so that writers who were rarely read before, like Duncan and Harrison, are now frequently anthologized. And the sheer number and diversity of new women writers is overwhelming. This present anthology is an effort to celebrate the vitality, quality, and range of current writing by Canadian women.

Selecting stories for an anthology is always fraught with problems since the inclusion of some seems inevitably to signal the exclusion of others. Let me say from the outset that I have come across wonderful writers whose stories I have had to exclude simply because of limitations of space. The principles for selection in this anthology have been as straightforward as I could make them. The authors represented here have published at least one collection of short stories. I have not included extracts from longer prose works, which, unfortunately, has meant the exclusion of fine writers like Joy Kogawa and Anne Michaels. I have chosen only stories written in English because an adequate representation of the richness of contemporary French-Canadian women writers is beyond the scope of this anthology. I have tried to select stories that reflect a wide range of styles, from documentary narrative (Catharine Parr Traill's 'The Bereavement'), romance adventure (E. Pauline Johnson's 'A Red Girl's Reasoning'), satiric social comedy (Lucy Maud Montgomery's 'The Quarantine at Alexander Abraham's'), science fiction (Susan Swan's 'The Man Doll'), to postmodern metafiction (Gail Scott's 'Tall Cowboys and True'). I have picked stories that I hoped would fit together to form a kind of collective narrative of women's experience. All the stories are about women: in childhood, adolescence, maturity, and old age; in relationships as daughters, sisters, lovers, mothers; in a variety of social and political contexts. I have selected authors to represent the many geographical regions of Canada, from Newfoundland to British Columbia, and also to reflect the racial and ethnic diversity of the country. Though all authors are Canadian by birth or choice, nationality and gender have different meanings for each of them.

This new anthology encompasses over a century and a half of writing by Canadian women, a time span that is only slightly longer than the existence of Canada as a country. Thus, as the anthology moves from the harsh pioneer life in the backwoods of Canada depicted by Catharine Parr Traill in 'The Bereavement' to portraits of modern urban life in stories like Barbara Gowdy's 'Ninety-three Million Miles Away' or Carol Shield's 'The Orange Fish', one of the stories it tells is the political evolution of Canada from colony to nation. This is not to suggest that these stories became increasingly 'Canadian' over the years. It may not be possible to identify a story as specifically Canadian, other than by its references to a particular geographic location or landscape. What I am referring to is the fact that most of the significantly Canadian writing has been done in the past four decades.

As with many other New World cultures, such as Australia, New Zealand, Chile, Mexico, or Argentina, the battle against cultural colonialism in Canada has been a protracted one. The Canadian critic, Northrop Frye, described the impact of a colonial mentality on literary production best when he called it a 'frostbite at the roots of imagination'. Nineteenth-century Canada did not provide a cultural climate accommodating to writers. Writing, if it was thought of at all, was thought of as something that was done elsewhere, mostly by Europeans. Canadian writers persisted against the odds, of course, and even a few, like E. Pauline Johnson and, later, Lucy Maud Montgomery and Mazo de la Roche, became famous in their day. Still, one of the greatest practitioners of the art of the short story, Alice Munro, who published her first story in 1953, has said that when she began her career, any young man or woman who thought to write in Canada was viewed with suspicion. It has only been relatively recently that Canadians have taken for granted the presence of great writers in their midst.

Literary historians have often noted that Canada, in comparison with other countries, has produced an unusual, even a preponderant number of women writers. Margaret Atwood once reflected that Canadian writers had 'foremothers rather than forefathers'. The first novel set in Canada was written by Frances Brooke in 1759, while the most colourful of pre-Confederation writers were the Strickland sisters. Atwood claims that when she started out as a writer in the late 1950s, she never felt excluded as a woman; the writing community was so small it welcomed anyone with talent, whether male or female. Perhaps it was just that being a colony—as women were then described—within the Canadian colony, women didn't have to feel peripheral to the national tradition. They were its definition. And women writers have kept in the vanguard ever since. Margaret Laurence, Alice Munro, Mavis Gallant, and the younger Margaret Atwood were among the first writers to achieve international reputations outside Canada.

In the 1960s, small presses burgeoned across the country and Canadian cultural institutions began to direct their attention to supporting indigenous writing. As the cultural infrastructures (magazines, publishing houses, etc.) developed, the number and diversity of writers increased dramatically. Of course there were many people who participated in this cultural revolution, but the Canadian short story tradition in particular owes a great debt to the editor and critic Robert Weaver. Shortly after joining the Canadian Broadcasting Corporation in 1948, he established the radio program *Anthology*. From 1954 through the next several decades, he commissioned original Canadian stories, edited innumerable short story collections, and helped to found the influential literary quarterly *The Tamarack Review*. Not only did he encourage Canadian short story writers, but he ensured that a Canadian audience existed that could appreciate their work. Two of the world's finest practitioners of the genre, Mavis Gallant and Alice Munro, were able to make their reputations on the basis of their short fiction alone. In Canada, short story collections competed easily with novels for the most important national prizes.

In the last twenty years, Canadian literature has undergone another sea change. Now, First Nations writers are publishing their work with mainstream presses. Among Native writers included here is Bay of Quinte Mohawk writer Beth Brant, whose 'A Long Story' records the effects of Canadian racism and colonialism on Native peoples. Of course, one of the effects has been silence. Brant only began writing in 1981 at the age of forty. Her anthology, *A Gathering Spirit*, published in 1988, was the first book to provide a forum for Native women writers.

The racial and ethnic diversity of current writers has dramatically expanded, reflecting the multicultural nature of contemporary Canadian society. This has, of course, had an impact on how Canadian writing is perceived, and has also brought new critical challenges. Issues of the construction of identity as well as the implications of the dispersal of people around the world, have become a primary concern for writers. Writers like Marlene Nourbese Phillip in 'Burn Sugar' and Dionne Brand in 'Photograph' turn back to roots outside Canada, paying homage to personal history and asking about the cost of cultural displacement. Himani Bannerji in 'On a Cold Day' and Judy Fong Bates in 'My Sister's Love' look at the often brutal tensions caused by assimilation or integration.

The variety and range of contemporary stories by Canadian women reflect a new sense of cultural authority. It is obvious that women can never be shunted to the margins again. They speak, from and beyond gender and cultural identity, to the heart of the human dilemma: have we achieved it? being human? At the end of the twentieth century our collective hold on our humanity is shaky. It is good at least to have stories that call us back to a sense of our failings and our shared possibilities.

In the process of compiling this anthology, I consulted a number of colleagues and friends. In particular, I would like to thank Richard Teleky and Mark Levene for their invaluable advice. I would also like to thank Branko Gorjup, Sharon van de Sande, Colleen Rae, and Patricia Cress, with whom I have had the pleasure of discussing and debating my selections; and Mildred Price who helped me with archival research. I would also like to thank Sally Livingston and express my gratitude to my editor Phyllis Wilson for her patience, kindness, and commitment to the project.

CATHARINE PARR TRAILL

❦

THE BEREAVEMENT

It was one of those soft warm mornings in April, that we not infrequently experience in this country during the melting of the snow, when the thermometer indicates a degree of temperature not less than summer heat. The air was filled with insects which had either revived from their winter torpor or been prematurely awakened to the enjoyment of a bright but brief existence. A few, sleepy, dusty looking flies had crept from their hiding places about the window—while some attenuated shadowy spider made vain attempts at commencing a web to entangle them. Without all was gay and cheerful—a thousand spring-like sounds filled the air—flocks of that pleasant warbler, the Canadian song-sparrow, mingled with the neat snow-bird (*fringilla nivalis*) flitted about the low wattled fence of the garden; at the edge of the cedar swamp, might be heard from time to time the rapid strokes of the small spotted wood-pecker, full of energy and animation, the mellow drumming of the Canadian partridge, (or ruffled Grouse,) mingled not unharmoniously with the wild cry of that bold but beautiful depredator, the blue jay. There too was the soft melancholy whispering note of the little chickadee, (*parus palustris*,) as it restlessly pursued its insect prey among the feathery branches of some old gnarled hemlock—the murmuring melody of the breeze stirring the lofty heads of the pines, with the 'still sweet sound of waters far away,' combining made sweet music to the ear.

Bright and blue as was the sky above, warm and genial as was the air around, and inviting as were the sounds of nature abroad, I yet found myself obliged to be an unwilling prisoner; the newly melted snow had rendered the surface of the ground porous as a sponge; half decomposed ice and pools of water made the roads and paths impassable. The luxury of India rubbers had scarcely at that time reached our settlement; they were among the rare things heard of but seldom seen. How I envied the more fortunate flocks of wild geese and ducks that were revelling in the azure pools, that lay so invitingly open to them, on the ice-bound lake in front of our log house. Sorely tempted as I was by the bright sunshine, and all spring's pleasant harmonies, to go forth into the newly uncovered fields— yet I dared not risk wetting my feet, having but recently recovered from a severe fit of illness.

I was still lingering at the open door, watching the graceful manoeuvres of the wild fowl on the lake, when my attention was attracted to a bare-footed, bare-headed, uncouth looking girl, who was hurrying towards the wicket, and panting from the speed which she had used. The little damsel, as soon as she could speak, told me she had been sent by her mistress (a nice young Scotchwoman, wife to the overseer of a neighbouring saw-mill,) to entreat me to go and see her baby, a lovely infant of eight weeks old—which lay dying as she feared. I hesitated. Of what use could I be in a case of such emergency? I asked myself. The road lay through a tangled cedar swamp, the mudholes would be opened by the soft air—and I cast a glance at the wide pools of water, and the honey-combed ice. The bare-legged little messenger seemed to read my thoughts.

'Ye'll no find the path sae vera bad, gif ye'll gang the same gait wi' me. The mistress is greeting, greeting sairly a' the time, about the sick wean—she'll weary till she sees ye coming.'

The simple entreaties of the little lassie prevailed over the dread of swamps and mudholes, wet feet and draggled garments. If I could afford no aid to the suffering child, I might yet support and console the afflicted mother—it was worth some little risk. Joy sparkled in the eyes of my little conductress as she watched me adjusting my tartan shawl; and as a reward for my compliance, she declared that I looked 'like a bonny Scotch leddy.'

My rough but warm-hearted little guide set off at a good round trot before me—heedless of mud or mire, stone or log; plunging most independently through the first, and scrambling fearlessly over the second—more than one high pile of logs she invited me to cross, after having set me the example with the agility, if not with the grace, of a squirrel—I might as well have followed a Will-o-the-Wisp, as little Maggie Freebairn.

Half an hour's quick walking brought me to the dwelling of the young mother and her sick infant. The babe had been ill several days, and many improper remedies had been successively adopted; among the most pernicious of these whisky punch, (the country people, by-the-bye, call all mixtures of spirits and water punch,) and bad port-wine had been forced down the babe's throat. It now lay, convulsed and evidently dying, on the lap of the weeping, sorrowing mother, a pale and wasted shadow of what had been so lovely only a single week before disease had seized it. The hand of Death had set its seal upon it—and 'life's young wings were fluttering for their flight!'

By the advice of my sister-in-law, who happened to call in a few minutes after my arrival, we put the babe into a warm bath, and applied gentle friction to its body and extremities; but alas! it was beyond the reach of human skill or human care. It seemed almost cruel to torment it with unavailing remedies. It was sad to see the anguish of the poor mother, as she hung in tearful agony over its pale unconscious face. It was her first-born—her only one, and the bare possibility of parting from it was too bitter a grief to be dwelt upon. With what tender solicitude did her sad eyes wander towards it continually, as it lay upon my knees, while she almost unconsciously performed those household tasks which her situation rendered imperatively necessary, having to cook for some ten or twelve workmen, belonging to the saw-mill. How often would she throw herself upon her knees beside me to take its cold damp hands and place them on her bosom, or bathe them with her scalding tears—and ask with despairing accents, if I thought it could yet recover—and with what eager looks did she listen to the assurances of the compassionate millwrights and lumberers, that the infant would surely live— they had seen many young children brought as low and yet grew up fine stout boys and girls. I felt as if it were cruel to deceive her.

Towards night, the convulsion fits became more frequent, and, yielding to the passionate entreaties of the poor young woman, not to leave her alone with her dying babe, I consented to take share in her painful vigil. The little Scotch lass was again set forth on a message to my household, and I prepared to act the part of nurse and watcher, while poor Jessy laid down to sleep—that heavy sleep, that the weary in heart and body alone know. Alone, in silence—I watched, by the flickering light cast by the pile of logs that had been carefully built up in the ample chimney (for candle there was none,) the last faint glimmerings of life in the unconscious form that lay upon my lap. No sound but the crackling and settling of the burning logs upon the hearth, the shrill chirp of the crickets, and the deep breathing of the tired slumberers in the loft above, met my ears within the dwelling; the ever moving waters of the river, as they rushed along their rocky bed, was the only sound abroad: and thus I passed the long night.

The first grey dawn found me still watching—I had not the heart to rouse the worn-out mother. I knew she could only waken to renewed anxiety. I felt the chill air of the early frosty morning blow bleak through the wide chinks of the imperfectly framed apartment. The infant appeared to have sunk into a tranquil sleep, and cramped with having maintained one posture for many hours, I now placed it in the cradle, and looked forth upon the face of Nature—and a lovely sight it was! The frosty earth was gemmed with countless diamonds—the mimic picture of those bright orbs above, which were still gleaming down from the clear blue sky; the saffron tint of early dawn was streaking the East. A light curling mist was gathering on the face of the rapid river, which lay before my eyes in all the majesty of its white crested waves, darkly shaded by the then unbroken line of forest on the opposite bank.

The little hamlet with its rude shanties and half erected dwellings and mill, lay scattered before me on the wide area in front—it was a scene of quiet and of freshness, save the rapid restless river rushing over its ledge of limestone rock, and hurrying away beneath the newly erected bridge in its downward course. It recalled to my mind Moore's lines written at the falls of the Mohawk river:

> From rise of morn till set of sun,
> I've seen the mighty Mohawk run—
>
> Rushing alike untired and wild
> Thro' rocks that frowned and flowers that smiled.

From the contemplation of things like these, I turned with a subdued and humbled heart to look upon human suffering and human woe. Without all was beauty and magnificence, for I gazed upon the works of God. Within was sorrow and death—the consequence of man's sin.

On my re-entering the house, I found Jessy sitting beside the cradle—her hopes had risen with the new day.

Her profound sleep had refreshed both body and mind, and she came to her labour of love with renewed spirits. She was anxious to get breakfast for me, but I preferred the reviving influence of the morning air to anything she could offer me, and promising to return in a few hours, I set forth on my solitary walk homeward.

There is no season when gratitude seems more naturally to fill our hearts, than at early dawn—it is the renewal to us of our existence, we feel that we have been cared for and preserved, and we lift our hearts to Him, from whom all blessings flow. How indeed, can we listen to the chorus of thanksgiving poured forth at sunrise, without being assured that an instinctive feeling of gratitude animates all things living—nay, even the very flowers, and trees, and herbs seem to rejoice in their freshness. Do not the Heavens declare the glory of God, and the firmament shew his handy-work!

The day was now risen, and the silent woods seemed suddenly to become eloquent with melodious notes, heard at no other time. The ground was white and crisp with frost, a comfortable change from the soft mud and half melted ice of the preceding day—the breeze blew sharp and cold from the river, but it seemed to revive my exhausted spirits and wearied frame. The wood-peckers were at their ceaseless work, hammering away at the pines and hemlocks—the red squirrels were out crossing my path in every direction, now stopping to regard me with furtive glance, now angrily erecting their beautiful feathery tails and darting up the stem of some rough barked tree, pausing from time to time in their ascent, to chatter forth some indignant remonstrance at my unseasonable intrusion on their privacy at such an hour—seldom, I ween, had lady fair been seen at dawn of day among the deep solitudes of these hemlock and cedar shades, through which I then winded my way. I was lost in a train of reflections to which the novelty of my situation had given birth, when a heavy tread upon the frozen ground near made me look round, and I perceived my husband advancing among the trees to meet me. He had risen thus early to escort me home.

I had not been home more than two hours, before the little Scotch maid came over to tell me that the babe was dead. The deep sleep, in which I had left it, was its last—it breathed its little life away so peacefully, that it might indeed be said, that it fell asleep and wakened in Heaven. The golden bowl was broken, and the young spirit, wearied with this earthly strife of pain, had returned to God who gave it!

It was evening when I renewed my visit to the house of the afflicted mother. Exhausted with weeping, she lay stretched upon her bed, fevered and ill at ease in body, and bowed down with the grief that belongs to human nature, when deprived of the object of its love. It was her first-born, her only one. It was piteous to hear her sad wailing, as she cast her eyes down upon her arm, and exclaimed:

'It used to lie here—just here, but it will never rest upon my arm again. It is gone—gone—gone!'

I did not then know the pangs of a bereaved mother, mourning for a dear babe, but I have often thought of poor Jessy, since that day—and felt how natural was her sorrow.

It was the third day, after this last sad visit, that I again re-entered the house of mourning. It was a day of sunny brightness. The sounds of business and labour had ceased—the axe no longer made the woods echo to its heavy strokes, the rush and whirl of the mill-wheels was stopped—it was the Sabbath morning, and silence and repose reigned over that busy spot. The door of the dwelling stood open, and I entered unbidden. A solemn feeling came over me, as I stepped across the threshold, from the broad glare of daylight into the dim religious light of the darkened room. In the centre was a table, decently covered with a snow white damask cloth; beside it sat the father of the child, his hat craped and tied with the simple white riband, symbol of the youth and innocence of the dead; his head was bent down over the big Bible, that rested on his knees; he was habited in decent mourning. As I entered, he raised his head, and bowed with an air of deep reverence, but spoke no word, and I passed on, unwilling to intrude upon his wholesome meditation. The father was gathering strength from the Book of peace and consolation.

At the further end of the apartment stood the mournful mother, her face bowed over the pale shrouded form of the idol of her heart. Her fair hair, gemmed with tears, fell in long soft ringlets over her face, and swept the pallid brow and tiny ice-cold hands of the dead infant; they were wet with the holy weeping of maternal love.

The sound of my steps made her look up, and forgetting all distinctions of rank, and alive only to the sympathy that had been shewn to her in her hour of deep distress, she threw her arms about my neck, and wept—but her grief was softened and subdued. She had schooled her heart to bear the sad reality, and she now sorrowed, as one not without hope.

Silently, she drew from within the folds of her muslin handkerchief, a small packet, carefully fastened with a thread of black silk—it was the fair hair of her lost treasure. She regarded it with a look of inexpressible tenderness, kissed it and replaced it in her bosom—then imprinting a last passionate kiss upon the marble brow and cheek of the dead babe, she suffered me to lead her quietly away, while the men approached to screw down the coffin, and throw the white pall over it.

With tearful earnestness did poor Jessy entreat of me to join in the procession that was about to form, but the burial ground was three or four miles off, on the opposite side of the river, and I was unequal to so long a walk.

I watched the funeral train, as it slowly crossed the bridge, and ascended the steep banks of the river, till the last waving of the white pall and scarfs of the mourners was no longer visible among the dark pines. I turned to retrace my steps, and felt that it was better to go into the house of mourning, than the house of mirth.

'Tis a sweet quiet spot, that burial ground in the woods. A few rudely sculptured stones—a heap piled here and there—a simple cross of wood, or a sapling tree planted by some pious hand, are the only memorials, to point out where rest the poor forgotten emigrant or his children. But the pines sigh above them a solemn requiem, the wild birds of the forest sing their lullaby, and the pure white lily of the woods and the blue violet, grow as freely on their green mossy graves, as though they slept within the holy shadow of the sanctuary. Their resting place is indeed hallowed, by the tears and humble prayers of their mournful relatives.

There is one that sleeps there among the children of the soil, unknown and uncared for, save by one who sadly remembers his guileless childhood, his early promise, and the bright example of a talented, but too indulgent father, and of a doting mother—

> 'But thoughtless follies led astray
> And stained his name.'

Cut off in the reckless levity of youth's mad career, he fills an early grave; and I might say of him in the words of the old Scotch ballad:

> 'Ah! little did thy mother think
> The day she cradled thee,
> Through what lands thou should's travel,
> And what death thou should'st die!'

E. PAULINE JOHNSON
(TEKAHIONWAKE)

❧

A RED GIRL'S REASONING

'Be pretty good to her, Charlie, my boy, or she'll balk sure as shooting.'

That was what old Jimmy Robinson said to his brand new son-in-law, while they waited for the bride to reappear.

'Oh! you bet, there's no danger of much else. I'll be good to her, help me Heaven,' replied Charlie McDonald, brightly.

'Yes, of course you will,' answered the old man, 'but don't you forget, there's a good big bit of her mother in her, and,' closing his left eye significantly, 'you don't understand these Indians as I do.'

'But I'm just as fond of them, Mr Robinson,' Charlie said assertively, 'and I get on with them too, now, don't I?'

'Yes, pretty well for a town boy; but when you have lived forty years among these people, as I have done; when you have had your wife as long as I have had mine—for there's no getting over it, Christine's disposition is as native as her mother's, every bit—and perhaps when you've owned for eighteen years a daughter as dutiful, as loving, as fearless, and, alas! as obstinate as that little piece you are stealing away from me to-day—I tell you, youngster, you'll know more than you know now. It is kindness for kindness, bullet for bullet, blood for blood. Remember, what you are, she will be,' and the old Hudson Bay trader scrutinized Charlie McDonald's face like a detective.

It was a happy, fair face, good to look at, with a certain ripple of dimples somewhere about the mouth, and eyes that laughed out the very sunniness of their owner's soul. There was not a severe nor yet a weak line anywhere. He was a well-meaning young fellow, happily dispositioned, and a great favourite with the tribe at Robinson's Post, whither he had gone in the service of the Department of Agriculture, to assist the local agent through the tedium of a long census-taking.

As a boy he had had the Indian relic-hunting craze, as a youth he had studied Indian archaeology and folk-lore, as a man he consummated his predilections for Indianology by loving, winning, and marrying the quiet little daughter of the English trader, who himself had married a native woman some twenty years ago. The country was all backwoods, and the Post miles and miles from even the semblance of civilization, and the lonely young Englishman's heart had gone out to the girl who, apart from speaking a very few words of English, was utterly uncivilized and uncultured, but had withal that marvellously innate refinement so universally possessed by the higher tribes of North American Indians.

Like all her race, observant, intuitive, having a horror of ridicule, consequently quick at acquirement and teachable in mental and social habits, she had developed from absolute pagan indifference into a sweet, elderly Christian woman, whose broken English, quiet manner, and still handsome copper-coloured face, were the joy of old Robinson's declining years.

He had given their daughter Christine all the advantages of his own learning—which, if truthfully told, was not universal; but the girl had a fair common education, and the native adaptability to progress.

She belonged to neither and still to both types of the cultured Indian. The solemn, silent, almost heavy manner of the one so commingled with the gesticulating Frenchiness and vivacity of the other, that one unfamiliar with native Canadian life would find it difficult to determine her nationality.

She looked very pretty to Charles McDonald's loving eyes, as she reappeared in the doorway, holding her mother's hand and saying some happy words of farewell. Personally she looked much the same as her sisters, all Canada through, who are the offspring of red and white parentage—olive-complexioned, grey-eyed, black-haired, with figure slight and delicate, and the wistful, unfathomable expression in her whole face that turns one so heart-sick as they glance at the young Indians of to-day—it is the forerunner too frequently of 'the white man's disease,' consumption—but McDonald was pathetically in love, and thought her the most beautiful woman he had ever seen in his life.

There had not been much of a wedding ceremony. The priest had cantered through the service in Latin, pronounced the benediction in English, and congratulated the 'happy couple' in Indian, as a compliment to the assembled tribe in the little amateur structure that did service at the post as a sanctuary.

But the knot was tied as firmly and indissolubly as if all Charlie McDonald's swell city friends had crushed themselves up against the chancel to congratulate him, and in his heart he was deeply thankful to escape the flower-pelting, white gloves, rice-throwing, and ponderous stupidity of a breakfast, and indeed all the regulation gimcracks of the usual marriage celebrations, and it was with a hand trembling with absolute happiness that he assisted his little Indian wife into the old muddy buckboard that, hitched to an underbred-looking pony, was to convey them over the first stages of their journey. Then came more adieus, some hand-clasping, old Jimmy Robinson looking very serious just at the last, Mrs Jimmy, stout, stolid, betraying nothing of visible emotion, and then the pony, roughshod and shaggy, trudged on, while mutual hand-waves were kept up until the Hudson's Bay Post dropped out of sight, and the buckboard with its lightsome load of hearts, deliriously happy, jogged on over the uneven trail.

She was 'all the rage' that winter at the provincial capital. The men called her a 'deuced fine little woman.' The ladies said she was 'just the sweetest wildflower.' Whereas she was really but an ordinary, pale, dark girl who spoke slowly and with a strong accent, who danced fairly well, sang acceptably, and never stirred outside the door without her husband.

Charlie was proud of her; he was proud that she had 'taken' so well among his friends, proud that she bore herself so complacently in the drawing-rooms of the wives of pompous Government officials, but doubly proud of her almost abject devotion to him. If ever human being was worshipped that being was Charlie McDonald; it could scarcely have been otherwise, for the almost godlike strength of his passion for that little wife of his would have mastered and melted a far more invincible citadel than an already affectionate woman's heart.

Favourites socially, McDonald and his wife went everywhere. In fashionable circles she was 'new'—a potent charm to acquire popularity, and the little velvet-clad figure was always the centre of interest among all the women in the room. She always dressed in velvet. No woman in Canada, has she but the faintest dash of native blood in her veins, but loves velvet and silks. As beef to the Englishman, wine to the Frenchman, fads to the Yankee, so are velvet and silk to the Indian girl, be she wild as prairie grass, be she on the borders of civilization, or, having stepped within its boundary, mounted the steps of culture even under its superficial heights.

'Such a dolling little appil blossom,' said the wife of a local MP, who brushed up her etiquette and English once a year at Ottawa. 'Does she always laugh so sweetly, and gobble you up with those great big grey eyes of hers, when you are togetheah at home, Mr McDonald? If so, I should think youah pooah brothah would feel himself terribly *de trop.*'

He laughed lightly. 'Yes, Mrs Stuart, there are not two of Christie; she is the same at home and abroad, and as for Joe, he doesn't mind us a bit; he's no end fond of her.'

'I'm very glad he is. I always fancied he did not care for her, d'you know.'

If ever a blunt woman existed it was Mrs Stuart. She really meant nothing, but her remark bothered Charlie. He was fond of his brother, and jealous for Christie's popularity. So that night when he and Joe were having a pipe he said:

'I've never asked you yet what you thought of her, Joe.' A brief pause, then Joe spoke. 'I'm glad she loves you.'

'Why?'

'Because that girl has but two possibilities regarding humanity—love or hate.'

'Humph! Does she love or hate *you?*'

'Ask her.'

'You talk bosh. If she hated you, you'd get out. If she loved you I'd *make* you get out.'

Joe McDonald whistled a little, then laughed.

'Now that we are on the subject, I might as well ask—honestly, old man, wouldn't you and Christie prefer keeping house alone to having me always around?'

'Nonsense, sheer nonsense. Why, thunder, man, Christie's no end fond of you, and as for me—you surely don't want assurances from me?'

'No, but I often think a young couple—'

'Young couple be blowed! After a while when they want you and your old surveying chains, and spindle-legged tripod telescope kickshaws, farther west, I venture to say the little woman will cry her eyes out—won't you, Christie?' This last in a higher tone, as through clouds of tobacco smoke he caught sight of his wife passing the doorway.

She entered. 'Oh, no, I would not cry; I never do cry, but I would be heart-sore to lose you, Joe, and apart from that'—a little wickedly—'you may come in handy for an exchange some day, as Charlie does always say when he hoards up duplicate relics.'

'Are Charlie and I duplicates?'

'Well—not exactly'—her head a little to one side, and eyeing them both merrily, while she slipped softly on to the arm of her husband's chair—'but, in the event of Charlie's failing me'—everyone laughed then. The 'some day' that she spoke of was nearer than they thought. It came about in this wise.

There was a dance at the Lieutenant-Governor's, and the world and his wife were there. The nobs were in great feather that night, particularly the women, who flaunted about in new gowns and much splendour. Christie McDonald had a new gown also, but wore it with the utmost unconcern, and if she heard any of the flattering remarks made about her she at least appeared to disregard them.

'I never dreamed you could wear blue so splendidly,' said Captain Logan, as they sat out a dance together.

'Indeed she can, though,' interposed Mrs Stuart, halting in one of her gracious sweeps down the room with her husband's private secretary.

'Don't shout so, captain. I can hear every sentence you uttah—of course

Mrs McDonald can wear blue—she has a morning gown of cadet blue that she is a picture in.'

'You are both very kind,' said Christie. 'I like blue; it is the colour of all the Hudson's Bay posts, and the factor's residence is always decorated in blue.'

'Is it really? How interesting—do tell us some more of your old home, Mrs McDonald; you so seldom speak of your life at the post, and we fellows so often wish to hear of it all,' said Logan eagerly.

'Why do you not ask me of it, then?'

'Well—er, I'm sure I don't know; I'm fully interested in the Ind—in your people—your mother's people, I mean, but it always seems so personal, I suppose; and—a—a—'

'Perhaps you are, like all other white people, afraid to mention my nationality to me.'

The captain winced, and Mrs Stuart laughed uneasily. Joe McDonald was not far off, and he was listening, and chuckling, and saying to himself, 'That's you, Christie, lay 'em out; it won't hurt 'em to know how they appear once in a while.'

'Well, Captain Logan,' she was saying, 'what is it you would like to hear—of my people, or my parents, or myself?'

'All, all, my dear,' cried Mrs Stuart clamorously. 'I'll speak for him—tell us of yourself and your mother—your father is delightful, I am sure—but then he is only an ordinary Englishman, not half as interesting as a foreigner, or—or, perhaps I should say, a native.'

Christie laughed. 'Yes,' she said, 'my father often teases my mother now about how *very* native she was when he married her; then, how could she have been otherwise? She did not know a word of English, and there was not another English-speaking person besides my father and his two companions within sixty miles.'

'Two companions, eh? one a Catholic priest and the other a wine merchant, I suppose, and with your father in the Hudson's Bay, they were good representatives of the pioneers in the New World,' remarked Logan, waggishly.

'Oh, no, they were all Hudson's Bay men. There were no rumsellers and no missionaries in that part of the country then.'

Mrs Stuart looked puzzled. '*No missionaries?*' she repeated with an odd intonation.

Christie's insight was quick. There was a peculiar expression of interrogation in the eyes of her listeners, and the girl's blood leapt angrily up into her temples as she said hurriedly, 'I know what you mean; I know what you are thinking. You are wondering how my parents were married—'

'Well—er, my dear, it seems peculiar—if there was no priest, and no magistrate, why—a—' Mrs Stuart paused awkwardly.

'The marriage was performed by Indian rites,' said Christie.

'Oh, do tell me about it; is the ceremony very interesting and quaint—are your chieftains anything like Buddhist priests?' It was Logan who spoke.

'Why, no,' said the girl in amazement at that gentleman's ignorance. 'There is no ceremony at all, save a feast. The two people just agree to live only with and for each other, and the man takes his wife to his home, just as you do. There is no ritual to bind them; they need none; an Indian's word was his law in those days, you know.'

Mrs Stuart stepped backwards. 'Ah!' was all she said. Logan removed his eye-glass and stared blankly at Christie. 'And did McDonald marry you in this singular fashion?' he questioned.

'Oh, no, we were married by Father O'Leary. Why do you ask?'

'Because if he had, I'd have blown his brains out to-morrow.'

Mrs Stuart's partner, who had hitherto been silent, coughed and began to twirl his cuff stud nervously, but nobody took any notice of him. Christie had risen, slowly, ominously—risen, with the dignity and pride of an empress.

'Captain Logan,' she said, 'what do you dare to say to me? What do you dare to mean? Do you presume to think it would not have been lawful for Charlie to marry me according to my people's rites? Do you for one instant dare to question that my parents were not as legally—'

'Don't, dear, don't,' interrupted Mrs Stuart hurriedly; 'it is bad enough now, goodness knows; don't make—' Then she broke off blindly. Christie's eyes glared at the mumbling woman, at her uneasy partner, at the horrified captain. Then they rested on the McDonald brothers, who stood within earshot, Joe's face scarlet, her husband's white as ashes, with something in his eyes she had never seen before. It was Joe who saved the situation. Stepping quickly across towards his sister-in-law, he offered her his arm, saying, 'The next dance is ours, I think, Christie.'

Then Logan pulled himself together, and attempted to carry Mrs Stuart off for the waltz, but for once in her life that lady had lost her head. 'It is shocking!' she said, 'outrageously shocking! I wonder if they told Mr McDonald before he married her!' Then looking hurriedly round, she too saw the young husband's face—and knew that they had not.

'Humph! deuced nice kettle of fish—poor old Charlie has always thought so much of honourable birth.'

Logan thought he spoke in an undertone, but 'poor old Charlie' heard him. He followed his wife and brother across the room. 'Joe,' he said, 'will you see that a trap is called?' Then to Christie, 'Joe will see that you get home all right.' He wheeled on his heel then and left the ball-room.

Joe *did* see.

He tucked a poor, shivering, pallid little woman into a cab, and wound her bare throat up in the scarlet velvet cloak that was hanging uselessly over her arm. She crouched down beside him, saying, 'I am so cold, Joe; I am so cold,' but she did not seem to know enough to wrap herself up. Joe felt all through this long drive that nothing this side of Heaven would be so good as to die, and he was glad when the poor little voice at his elbow said, 'What is he so angry at, Joe?'

'I don't know exactly, dear,' he said gently, 'but I think it was what you said about this Indian marriage.'

'But why should I not have said it? Is there anything wrong about it?' she asked pitifully.

'Nothing, that I can see—there was no other way; but Charlie is very angry, and you must be brave and forgiving with him, Christie, dear.'

'But I never did see him like that before, did you?'

'Once.'

'When?'

'Oh, at college, one day, a boy tore his prayer-book in half, and threw it into the grate, just to be mean, you know. Our mother had given it to him at his confirmation.'

'And did he look so?'

'About, but it all blew over in a day—Charlie's tempers are short and brisk. Just don't take any notice of him; run off to bed, and he'll have forgotten it by the morning.'

They reached home at last. Christie said good-night quietly, going directly to her room. Joe went to his room also, filled a pipe and smoked for an hour. Across the passage he could hear her slippered feet pacing up and down, up and down the length of her apartment. There was something panther-like in those restless footfalls, a meaning velvetyness that made him shiver, and again he wished he were dead—or elsewhere.

After a time the hall door opened, and someone came upstairs, along the passage, and to the little woman's room. As he entered, she turned and faced him.

'Christie,' he said harshly, 'do you know what you have done?'

'Yes,' taking a step nearer him, her whole soul springing up into her eyes, 'I have angered you, Charlie, and—'

'Angered me? You have disgraced me; and, moreover, you have disgraced yourself and both your parents.'

'*Disgraced?*'

'Yes, *disgraced*; you have literally declared to the whole city that your father and mother were never married, and that you are the child of—what shall we call it—love? certainly not legality.'

Across the hallway sat Joe McDonald, his blood freezing; but it leapt into every vein like fire at the awful anguish in the little voice that cried simply, 'Oh! Charlie!'

'How could you do it, how could you do it, Christie, without shame either for yourself or for me, let alone your parents?'

The voice was like an angry demon's—not a trace was there in it of the yellow-haired, blue-eyed, laughing-lipped boy who had driven away so gaily to the dance five hours before.

'Shame? Why should I be ashamed of the rites of my people any more than you should be ashamed of the customs of yours—of a marriage more sacred and holy than half of your white man's mockeries?'

It was the voice of another nature in the girl—the love and the pleading were dead in it.

'Do you mean to tell me, Charlie—you who have studied my race and their laws for years—do you mean to tell me that, because there was no priest and no magistrate, my mother was not married? Do you mean to say that all my forefathers, for hundreds of years back, have been illegally born? If so, you blacken my ancestry beyond—beyond—beyond all reason.'

'No, Christie, I would not be so brutal as that; but your father and mother live in more civilized times. Father O'Leary has been at the post for nearly twenty years. Why was not your father straight enough to have the ceremony performed when he *did* get the chance?'

The girl turned upon him with the face of a fury. 'Do you suppose,' she almost hissed, 'that my mother would be married according to your *white* rites after she had been five years a wife, and I had been born in the meantime? *No*, a thousand times I say, *no*. When the priest came with his notions of Christianizing, and talked to them of re-marriage by the Church, my mother arose and said, "Never—never—I have never had but this one husband; he has had none but me for wife, and to have you re-marry us would be to say as much to the whole world as that we had never been married before. You go away; *I* do not ask that *your* people be re-married; talk not so to me. I *am* married, and you or the Church cannot do or undo it."'

'Your father was a fool not to insist upon the law, and so was the priest.'

'Law? *My* people have *no* priest, and my nation cringes not to law. Our priest is purity, and our law is honour. Priest? Was there a *priest* at the most holy marriage known to humanity—that stainless marriage whose offspring is the God you white men told my pagan mother of?'

'Christie—you are *worse* than blasphemous; such a profane remark shows how little you understand the sanctity of the Christian faith—'

'I know what I *do* understand; it is that you are hating me because I told some of the beautiful customs of my people to Mrs Stuart and those men.'

'Pooh! who cares for them? It is not them; the trouble is they won't keep their mouths shut. Logan's a cad and will toss the whole tale about at the club before to-morrow night; and as for the Stuart woman, I'd like to know how I'm going to take you to Ottawa for presentation and the opening, while she is blabbing the whole miserable scandal in every drawing-room, and I'll be pointed out as a romantic fool, and you—as worse; I *can't* understand why your father didn't tell me before we were married; I at least might have warned you to never mention it.' Something of recklessness rang up through his voice, just as the panther-likeness crept up from her footsteps and couched itself in hers. She spoke in tones quiet, soft, deadly.

'Before we were married! Oh! Charlie, would it have—made—any—difference?'

'God knows,' he said, throwing himself into a chair, his blonde hair rumpled and wet. It was the only boyish thing about him now.

She walked towards him, then halted in the centre of the room. 'Charlie McDonald,' she said, and it was as if a stone had spoken, 'look up.' He raised his head, startled by her tone. There was a threat in her eyes that, had his rage been less courageous, his pride less bitterly wounded, would have cowed him.

'There was no such time as that before our marriage, for we *are not married now*. Stop,' she said, outstretching her palms against him as he sprang to his feet, 'I tell you we are not married. Why should I recognize the rites of your nation when you do not acknowledge the rites of mine? According to your own words, my parents should have gone through your church ceremony as well as through an Indian contract; according to *my* words, *we* should go through an Indian contract as well as through a church marriage. If their union is illegal, so is ours. If you think my father is living in dishonour with my mother, my people will think I am living in dishonour with you. How do I know when another nation will come and conquer you as you white men conquered us? And they will have another marriage rite to perform, and they will tell us another truth, that you are not my husband, that you are but disgracing and dishonouring me, that you are keeping me here, not as your wife, but as your—your *squaw*.'

The terrible word had never passed her lips before, and the blood stained her face to her very temples. She snatched off her wedding ring and tossed it across the room, saying scornfully, 'That thing is as empty to me as the Indian rites to you.'

He caught her by the wrists; his small white teeth were locked tightly, his blue eyes blazed into hers.

'Christine, do you dare to doubt my honour towards you? *you*, whom I should have died for; do you *dare* to think I have kept you here, not as my wife, but—'

'Oh, God! You are hurting me; you are breaking my arm,' she gasped.

The door was flung open, and Joe McDonald's sinewy hands clinched like vices on his brother's shoulders.

'Charlie, you're mad, mad as the devil. Let go of her this minute.'

The girl staggered backwards as the iron fingers loosed her wrists. 'Oh, Joe,' she cried, 'I am not his wife, and he says I am born—nameless.'

'Here,' said Joe, shoving his brother towards the door. 'Go downstairs till you can collect your senses. If ever a being acted like an infernal fool, you're the man.'

The young husband looked from one to the other, dazed by his wife's insult, abandoned to a fit of ridiculously childish temper. Blind as he was with passion, he remembered long afterwards seeing them standing there, his brother's face darkened with a scowl of anger—his wife, clad in the mockery of her ball dress, her scarlet velvet cloak half covering her bare brown neck and arms, her eyes like flames of fire, her face like a piece of sculptured greystone.

Without a word he flung himself furiously from the room, and immediately afterwards they heard the heavy hall door bang behind him.

'Can I do anything for you, Christie?' asked her brother-in-law calmly.

'No, thank you—unless—I think I would like a drink of water, please.'

He brought her up a goblet filled with wine; her hand did not even tremble as she took it. As for Joe, a demon arose in his soul as he noticed she kept her wrists covered.

'Do you think he will come back?' she said.

'Oh, yes, of course; he'll be all right in the morning. Now go to bed like a good little girl, and—and, I say, Christie, you can call me if you want anything; I'll be right here, you know.'

'Thank you, Joe; you are kind—and good.'

He returned then to his apartment. His pipe was out, but he picked up a newspaper instead, threw himself into an armchair, and in a half-hour was in the land of dreams.

When Charlie came home in the morning, after a six-mile walk into the country and back again, his foolish anger was dead and buried. Logan's 'Poor old Charlie' did not ring so distinctly in his ears. Mrs Stuart's horrified expression had faded considerably from his recollection. He thought only of that surprisingly tall, dark girl, whose eyes looked like coals, whose voice pierced him like a flint-tipped arrow. Ah, well, they would never quarrel again like that, he told himself. She loved him so, and would forgive him after he had talked quietly to her, and told her what an ass he was. She was simple-minded and awfully ignorant to pitch those old Indian laws at him in her fury, but he could not blame her; oh, no, he could not for one moment blame her. He had been terribly severe and unreasonable, and the horrid McDonald temper had got the better of him; and he loved her so. Oh! he loved her so! She would surely feel that, and forgive him, and— He went straight to his wife's room. The blue velvet evening dress lay on the chair into which he had thrown himself when he doomed his life's happiness by those two words, 'God knows.' A bunch of dead daffodils and her slippers were on the floor, everything—but Christie.

He went to his brother's bedroom door.

'Joe,' he called, rapping nervously thereon; 'Joe, wake up; where's Christie, d'you know?'

'Good Lord, no,' gasped that youth, springing out of his armchair and opening the door. As he did so a note fell from off the handle. Charlie's face blanched to his very hair while Joe read aloud, his voice weakening at every word:

'DEAR OLD JOE—I went into your room at daylight to get that picture of the Post on your bookshelves. I hope you do not mind, but I kissed your hair while you slept; it was so curly, and yellow, and soft, just like his. Good-bye, Joe.

'CHRISTIE.'

And when Joe looked into his brother's face and saw the anguish settle in those laughing blue eyes, the despair that drove the dimples away from that almost girlish mouth; when he realized that this boy was but four-and-twenty years old, and that all his future was perhaps darkened and shadowed for ever, a great, deep sorrow arose in his heart, and he forgot all things, all but the agony that rang up through the voice of the fair, handsome lad as he staggered forward, crying, 'Oh! Joe—what shall I do—what shall I do?'

It was months and months before he found her, but during all that time he had never known a hopeless moment; discouraged he often was, but despondent, never. The sunniness of his ever-boyish heart radiated with a warmth that would have flooded a much deeper gloom than that which settled within his eager young life. Suffer? ah! yes, he suffered, not with locked teeth and stony stoicism, not with the masterful self-command, the reserve, the conquered bitterness of the still-water sort of nature, that is supposed to run to such depths. He tried to be bright, and his sweet old boyish self. He would laugh sometimes in a pitiful, pathetic fashion. He took to petting dogs, looking into their large, solemn eyes with his wistful, questioning blue ones; he would kiss them, as women sometimes do, and call them 'dear old fellow,' in tones that had tears; and once in the course of his travels, while at a little way-station, he discovered a huge St Bernard imprisoned by some mischance in an empty freight car; the animal was nearly dead from starvation, and it seemed to salve his own sick heart to rescue back the dog's life. Nobody claimed the big starving creature, the train hands knew nothing of its owner, and gladly handed it over to its deliverer. 'Hudson,' he called it, and afterwards when Joe McDonald would relate the story of his brother's life he invariably terminated it with, 'And I really believe that big lumbering brute saved him.' From what, he was never known to say.

But all things end, and he heard of her at last. She had never returned to the Post, as he at first thought she would, but had gone to the little town of B——, in Ontario, where she was making her living at embroidery and plain sewing.

The September sun had set redly when at last he reached the outskirts of the town, opened up the wicket gate, and walked up the weedy, unkept path leading to the cottage where she lodged.

Even through the twilight, he could see her there, leaning on the rail of the verandah—oddly enough she had about her shoulders the scarlet velvet cloak she wore when he had flung himself so madly from the room that night.

The moment the lad saw her his heart swelled with a sudden heat, burning moisture leapt into his eyes, and clogged his long, boyish lashes. He bounded up the steps—'Christie,' he said, and the word scorched his lips like an audible flame.

She turned to him, and for a second stood magnetized by his passionately wistful face; her peculiar greyish eyes seemed to drink the very life of his unquenchable love, though the tears that suddenly sprang into his seemed to absorb every pulse in his body through those hungry, pleading eyes of his that had, oh! so often, been blinded by her kisses when once her whole world lay in their blue depths.

'You will come back to me, Christie, my wife? My wife, you will let me love you again?'

She gave a singular little gasp, and shook her head. 'Don't, oh! don't,' he cried piteously. 'You will come to me, dear? it is all such a bitter mistake—I did not understand. Oh! Christie, I did not understand, and you'll forgive me, and love me again, won't you—won't you?'

'No,' said the girl with quick, indrawn breath.

He dashed the back of his hand across his wet eyelids. His lips were growing numb, and he bungled over the monosyllable 'Why?'

'I do not like you,' she answered quietly.

'God! Oh! God, what is there left?'

She did not appear to hear the heart-break in his voice; she stood like one wrapped in sombre thought; no blaze, no tear, nothing in her eyes; no hardness, no tenderness about her mouth. The wind was blowing her cloak aside, and the only visible human life in her whole body was once when he spoke the muscles of her brown arm seemed to contract.

'But, darling, you are mine—*mine*—we are husband and wife! Oh, heaven, you *must* love me, you *must* come to me again.'

'You cannot *make* me come,' said the icy voice, 'neither church, nor law, nor even'—and the voice softened—'nor even love can make a slave of a red girl.'

'Heaven forbid it,' he faltered. 'No, Christie, I will never claim you without your love. What reunion would that be? But, oh, Christie, you are lying to me, you are lying to yourself, you are lying to heaven.'

She did not move. If only he could touch her he felt as sure of her yielding as he felt sure there was a hereafter. The memory of times when he had but to lay his hand on her hair to call a most passionate response from her filled his heart with a torture that choked all words before they reached his lips; at the thought of those days he forgot she was unapproachable, forgot how forbidding were her eyes, how stony her lips. Flinging himself forward, his knee on the chair at her side, his face pressed hardly in the folds of the cloak on her shoulder, he clasped his arms about her with a boyish petulance, saying, 'Christie, Christie, my little girl wife, I love you, I love you, and you are killing me.'

She quivered from head to foot as his fair, wavy hair brushed her neck, his despairing face sank lower until his cheek, hot as fire, rested on the cool, olive flesh of her arm. A warm moisture oozed up through her skin, and as he felt its glow he looked up. Her teeth, white and cold, were locked over her under lip, and her eyes were as grey stones.

Not murderers alone know the agony of a death sentence.

'Is it all useless? all useless, dear?' he said, with lips starving for hers.

'All useless,' she repeated. 'I have no love for you now. You forfeited me and my heart months ago, when you said *those two words*.'

His arms fell away from her wearily, he arose mechanically, he placed his little grey checked cap on the back of his yellow curls, the old-time laughter was dead in the blue eyes that now looked scared and haunted, the boyishness and the dimples crept away for ever from the lips that quivered like a child's; he turned from her, but she had looked once into his face as the Law Giver must have looked at the land of Canaan outspread at his feet. She watched him go down the long path and through the picket gate, she watched the big yellowish dog that had waited for him lumber up to its feet—stretch—then follow him. She was conscious of but two things, the vengeful lie in her soul, and a little space on her arm that his wet lashes had brushed. It was hours afterwards when he reached his room. He had said nothing, done nothing—what use were words or deeds? Old Jimmy Robinson was right; she had 'balked' sure enough.

What a bare, hotelish room it was! He tossed off his coat and sat for ten minutes looking blankly at the sputtering gas jet. Then his whole life, desolate as a desert, loomed up before him with appalling distinctness. Throwing himself on the floor beside his bed, with clasped hands and arms outstretched on the white counterpane, he sobbed. He sobbed. 'Oh! God, dear God, I thought you loved me; I thought you'd let me have her again, but you must be tired of me, tired of loving me, too. I've nothing left now, nothing! it doesn't seem that I even have you to-night.'

He lifted his face then, for his dog, big and clumsy and yellow, was licking at his sleeve.

SARA JEANNETTE DUNCAN

෴

THE POOL IN THE DESERT

I knew Anna Chichele and Judy Harbottle so well, and they figured so vividly at one time against the rather empty landscape of life in a frontier station, that my affection for one of them used to seem little more, or less, than a variant upon my affection for the other. That recollection, however, bears examination badly; Judy was much the better sort, and it is Judy's part in it that draws me into telling the story. Conveying Judy is what I tremble at: her part was simple. Looking back—and not so very far—her part has the relief of high comedy with the proximity of tears; but looking close-ly, I find that it is mostly Judy, and what she did is entirely second, in my untarnished picture, to what she was. Still I do not think I can dissuade myself from putting it down.

They would, of course, inevitably have found each other sooner or later, Mrs Harbottle and Mrs Chichele, but it was I who actually introduced them; my palmy veranda in Rawul Pindi; where the tea-cups used to assemble, was the scene of it. I presided behind my samovar over the early formalities that were almost at once to drop from their friendship, like the sheath of some bursting flower. I deliberately brought them together, so the birth was not accidental, and my interest in it quite legitimately maternal. We always had tea in the veranda in Rawul Pindi, the drawing-room was painted blue, blue for thirty feet up to the whitewashed cotton ceiling; nothing of any value in the way of a human relation, I am sure, could have originated there. The veranda was spacious and open, their mutual observation had room and freedom; I watched it to and fro. I had not long to wait for my reward; the beautiful candour I expected between them was not ten minutes in coming. For the sake of it I had taken some trouble, but when I perceived it reveal-ing I went and sat down beside Judy's husband, Robert Harbottle, and talked about Pharaoh's split hoof. It was only fair; and when next day I got their impressions of one another, I felt single-minded and deserving.

I knew it would be a satisfactory sort of thing to do, but perhaps it was rather more for Judy's sake than for Anna's that I did it. Mrs Harbottle was only twenty-seven then and Robert a major, but he had brought her to India out of an episode too colour-flushed to tone with English hedges; their mar-riage had come, in short, of his divorce, and as too natural a consequence.

In India it well known that the eye becomes accustomed to primitive pigments and high lights; the aesthetic consideration, if nothing else, demanded Robert's exchange. He was lucky to get a Piffer regiment, and the Twelfth were lucky to get him; we were all lucky, I thought, to get Judy. It was an opinion, of course, a good deal challenged, even in Rawul Pindi, where it was thought, especially in the beginning, that acquiescence was the most the Harbottles could hope for. That is not enough in India; cordiality is the common right. I could not have Judy preserving her atmosphere at our tea-parties and gymkhanas. Not that there were two minds among us about 'the case'; it was a preposterous case, sentimentally undignified, from some points of view deplorable. I chose to reserve my point of view, from which I saw it, on Judy's behalf, merely quixotic, preferring on Robert's just to close my eyes. There is no doubt that his first wife was odious to a degree which it is simply pleasanter not to recount, but her malignity must almost have amounted to a sense of humour. Her detestation of her cousin Judy Thynne dated much further back than Robert's attachment. That began in Paris, where Judy, a young widow, was developing a real vein at Julian's. I am entirely convinced that there was nothing, as people say, 'in it,' Judy had not a thought at that time that was not based on Chinese white and permeated with good-fellowship; but there was a good deal of it, and no doubt the turgid imagination of the first Mrs Harbottle dealt with it honestly enough. At all events, she saw her opportunity, and the depths of her indifference to Robert bubbled up venomously into the suit. That it was undefended was the senseless mystery; decency ordained that he and Judy should have made a fight, even in the hope that it would be a losing one. The reason it had to be a losing one—the reason so immensely criticized—was that the petitioning lady obstinately refused to bring her action against any other set of circumstances than those to which, I have no doubt, Judy contributed every indiscretion. It is hard to imagine Robert Harbottle refusing her any sort of justification that the law demands short of beating her, but her malice would accept nothing of which the account did not go for final settlement to Judy Thynne. If her husband wanted his liberty, he should have it, she declared, at that price and no other. Major Harbottle did indeed deeply long for his liberty, and his interesting friend, Mrs Thynne, had, one can only say, the most vivid commiseration for his bondage. Whatever chance they had of winning, to win would be, for the end they had at heart, to lose, so they simply abstained, as it were, from comment upon the detestable procedure which terminated in the rule absolute. I have often wondered whether the whole business would not have been more defensible if there had been on Judy's part any emotional spring for the leap they made. I offer my conviction that there was none, that she was only extravagantly affected by the ideals of the Quarter—it is a transporting atmosphere—and held a view of comradeship which permitted the reversal of the modern situation filled by a blameless correspondent. Robert, of course, was tremendously in love with her; but my theory is that she married him as the logical outcome of her sacrifice and by no means the smallest part of it.

It was all quite unimaginable, as so many things are, but the upshot of it brought Judy to Rawul Pindi, as I have said, where I for one thought her mistake insignificant compared with her value. It would have been great, her value, anywhere; in the middle of the Punjab it was incalculable. To explain why would be to explain British India, but I hope it will appear; and I am quite willing, remember, to take the responsibility if it does not.

Somers Chichele, Anna's son, it is absurd to think, must have been about fifteen then, reflecting at Winchester with the other 'men' upon the comparative merits of tinned sardines and jam roll, and whether a packet of real Egyptians was not worth the sacrifice of either. His father was colonel of the Twelfth; his mother was still charming. It was the year before Dick Forsyth came down from the neighbourhood of Sheikhbudin with a brevet and a good deal of personal damage. I mention him because he proved Anna's charm in the only conclusive way before the eyes of us all; and the station, I remember, was edified to observe that if Mrs Chichele came out of the matter 'straight'—one relapses so easily into the simple definitions of those parts—which she undoubtedly did, she owed it in no small degree to Judy Harbottle. This one feels to be hardly a legitimate reference, but it is something tangible to lay hold upon in trying to describe the web of volitions which began to weave itself between the two that afternoon on my veranda and which afterward became so strong a bond. I was delighted with the thing; its simplicity and sincerity stood out among our conventional little compromises at friendship like an ideal. She and Judy had the assurance of one another; they made upon one another the finest and often the most unconscionable demands. One met them walking at odd hours in queer places, of which I imagine they were not much aware. They would turn deliberately off the Maidan and away from the band-stand to be rid of our irrelevant bows; they did their duty by the rest of us, but the most egregious among us, the Deputy-Commissioner for selection, could see that he hardly counted. I thought I understood, but that may have been my fatuity; certainly when their husbands inquired what on earth they had been talking of, it usually transpired that they had found an infinite amount to say about nothing. It was a little worrying to hear Colonel Chichele and Major Harbottle describe their wifes as 'pals,' but the fact could not be denied, and after all we were in the Punjab. They were pals too, but the terms were different.

People discussed it according to their lights, and girls said in pretty wonderment that Mrs Harbottle and Mrs Chichele were like men, they never kissed each other. I think Judy prescribed these conditions. Anna was far more a person who did as the world told her. But it was a poor negation to describe all that they never did; there was no common little convention of attachment that did not seem to be tacitly omitted between them. I hope one did not too cynically observe that they offered these to their husbands instead; the redeeming observation was their husbands' complete satisfaction. This they maintained to the end. In the natural order of things Robert Harbottle should have paid heavily for interfering as he did in Paris between a woman and what she was entitled to live for. As a matter of fact he never paid anything at all; I doubt whether he ever knew himself a debtor. Judy kept her temperament under like a current and swam with the tides of the surface, taking refreshing dips only now and then which one traced in her eyes and her hair when she and Robert came back from leave. That sort of thing is lost in the sands of India, but it makes an oasis as it travels, and it sometimes seemed to me a curious pity that she and Anna should sit in the shade of it together, while Robert and Peter Chichele, their titular companions, blundered on in the desert. But after all, if you are born blind—and the men were both immensely liked, and the shooting was good.

Ten years later Somers joined. The Twelfth were at Peshawur. Robert Harbottle was Lieutenant-Colonel by that time and had the regiment. Distinction had incrusted, in the Indian way, upon Peter Chichele, its former colonel; he was General Commanding the District and KCB So we were all still together in Peshawur. It was great luck for the Chicheles, Sir Peter's having the district, though his father's old regiment would have made it pleasant enough for the boy in any case. He came to us, I mean, of course, to two or three of us, with the interest that hangs about a victim of circumstances; we understood that he wasn't a 'born soldier'. Anna had told me on the contrary that he was a sacrifice to family tradition made inevitable by the General's unfortunate investments. Bellona's bridegroom was not a role he fancied, though he would make a kind of compromise as best man; he would agree, she said, to be a war correspondent and write picturesque specials for the London halfpenny press. There was the humour of the poor boy's despair in it, but she conveyed it, I remember, in exactly the same tone with which she had said to me years before that he wanted to drive a milk-cart. She carried quite her half of the family tradition, though she could talk of sacrifice and make her eyes wistful, contemplating for Somers the limitations of the drill-book and the camp of exercise, proclaiming and insisting upon what she would have done if she could only have chosen for him. Anna Chichele saw things that way. With more than a passable sense of all that was involved, if she could have made her son an artist in life or a commander-in-chief, if she could have given him the seeing eye or the Order of the Star of India, she would not have hesitated for an instant. Judy, with her single mind, cried out, almost at sight of him, upon them both, I mean both Anna and Sir Peter. Not that the boy carried his condemnation badly, or even obviously; I venture that no one noticed it in the mess; but it was naturally plain to those of us who were under the same. He had put in his two years with a British regiment at Meerut—they nurse subalterns that way for the Indian army—and his eyes no longer played with the tinsel vision of India; they looked instead into the arid stretch beyond. This pre-occupation conveyed to the Surgeon-Major's wife the suggestion that Mr Chichele was the victim of a hopeless attachment. Mrs Harbottle made no such mistake; she saw simply, I imagine, the beginnings of her own hunger and thirst in him, looking back as she told us across a decade of dusty sun-sets to remember them. The decade was there, close to the memory of all of us; we put, from Judy herself downward, an absurd amount of confidence in it.

She looked so well the night she met him. It was English mail day; she depended a great deal upon her letters, and I suppose somebody had writ-ten her a word that brought her that happy, still excitement that is the inner mystery of words. He went straight to her with some speech about his mother having given him leave, and for twenty minutes she patronized him on a sofa as his mother would not have dreamed of doing.

Anna Chichele, from the other side of the room, smiled on the pair.

'I depend on you and Judy to be good to him while we are away,' she said. She and Sir Peter were going on leave at the end of the week to Scotland, as usual, for the shooting.

Following her glance I felt incapable of the proportion she assigned me. 'I will see after his socks with pleasure,' I said. 'I think, don't you, we may leave the rest to Judy?'

Her eyes remained upon the boy, and I saw the passion rise in them, at which I turned mine elsewhere. Who can look unperturbed upon such a privacy of nature as that?

'Poor old Judy!' she went on. 'She never would be bothered with him in all his dear hobble-dehoy time; she resented his claims, the unreasonable creature, used to limit me to three anecdotes a week; and now she has him on her hands, if you like. See the pretty air of deference in the way he lis-tens to her! He has nice manners, the villain, if he is a Chichele!'

'Oh, you have improved Sir Peter's,' I said kindly.

'I do hope Judy will think him worth while. I can't quite expect that he will be up to her, bless him, she is so much cleverer, isn't she, than any of us? But if she will just be herself with him it will make such a difference.'

The other two crossed the room to us at that, and Judy gaily made Somers over to his mother, trailing off to find Robert in the billiard-room.

'Well, what has Mrs Harbottle been telling you?' Anna asked him.

The young man's eye followed Judy, his hand went musingly to his moustache.

'She was telling me,' he said, 'that people in India were sepulchres of themselves, but that now and then one came who could roll away another's stone.'

'It sounds promising,' said Lady Chichele to me.

'It sounds cryptic,' I laughed to Somers, but I saw that he had the key.

I can not say that I attended diligently to Mr Chichele's socks, but the part corresponding was freely assigned me. After his people went I saw him often. He pretended to find qualities in my tea, implied that he found them in my talk. As a matter of fact it was my inquiring attitude that he loved, the knowledge that there was no detail that he could give me about himself, his impressions and experiences, that was unlikely to interest me. I would not for the world imply that he was egotistical or complacent, absolutely the reverse, but he possessed an articulate soul which found its happiness in expression, and I liked to listen. I feel that these are complicated words to explain a very simple relation, and I pause to wonder what is left to me if I wished to describe his commerce with Mrs Harbottle. Luckily there is an alternative; one needn't do it. I wish I had somewhere on paper Judy's own account of it at this period, however. It is a thing she would have enjoyed writing and more enjoyed communicating, at this period.

There was a grave reticence in his talk about her which amused me in the beginning. Mrs Harbottle had been for ten years important enough to us all, but her serious significance, the light and the beauty in her, had plainly been reserved for the discovery of this sensitive and intelligent person not very long from Sandhurst and exactly twenty-six. I was barely allowed a familiar reference, and anything approaching a flippancy was met with penetrating silence. I was almost rebuked for lightly suggesting that she must occasionally find herself bored in Peshawur.

'I think not anywhere,' said Mr Chichele; 'Mrs Harbottle is one of the few people who sound the privilege of living.'

This to me, who had counted Mrs Harbottle's yawns on so many occasions! It became presently necessary to be careful, tactful, in one's implications about Mrs Harbottle, and to recognize a certain distinction in the fact that one was the only person with whom Mr Chichele discussed her at all.

The day came when we talked of Robert; it was bound to come in the progress of any understanding and affectionate colloquy which had his wife for inspiration. I was familiar, of course, with Somer's opinion that the Colonel was an awfully good sort; that had been among the preliminaries and become understood as the base of all references. And I liked Robert Harbottle very well myself. When his adjutant called him a born leader of men, however, I felt compelled to look at the statement consideringly.

'In a tight place,' I said—dear me, what expressions had the freedom of our little frontier drawing-rooms!—'I would as soon depend on him as anybody. But as for leadership—'

'He is such a good fellow that nobody here does justice to his soldierly qualities,' said Mr Chichele, 'except Mrs Harbottle.'

'Has she been telling you about them?' I inquired.

'Well,' he hesitated, 'she told me about the Mulla Nulla affair. She is rather proud of that. Any woman would be.'

'Poor dear Judy!' I mused.

Somers said nothing, but looked at me, removing his cigarette, as if my words would be the better of explanation.

'She has taken refuge in them—in Bob Harbottle's soldierly qualities—ever since she married him,' I continued.

'Taken refuge,' he repeated, coldly, but at my uncompromising glance his eyes fell.

'Well?' I said.

'You mean—'

'Oh, I mean what I say,' I laughed. 'Your cigarette has gone out—have another.'

'I think her devotion to him splendid.'

'Quite splendid. Have you seen the things he brought her from the Simla Art Exhibition? He said they were nice bits of colour, and she has hung them in the drawing-room, where she will have to look at them every day. Let us admire her—dear Judy.'

'Oh,' he said, with a fine air of detachment, 'do you think they are so necessary, those agreements?'

'Well,' I replied, 'we see that they are not indispensable. More sugar? I have only given you one lump. And we know, at all events,' I added, unguardedly, 'that she could never have had an illusion about him.'

The young man looked up quickly. 'Is that story true?' he asked.

'There was a story, but most of us have forgotten it. Who told you?'

'The doctor.'

'The Surgeon-Major,' I said, 'has an accurate memory and a sense of proportion. As I suppose you were bound to get it from somebody, I am glad you got it from him.'

I was not prepared to go on, and saw with some relief that Somers was not either. His silence, as he smoked, seemed to me deliberate; and I had oddly enough at this moment for the first time the impression that he was a man and not a boy. Then the Harbottles themselves joined us, very cheery after a gallop from the Wazir-Bagh. We talked of old times, old friendships, good swords that were broken, names that had carried far, and Somers effaced himself in the perfect manner of the British subaltern. It was a long, pleasant gossip, and I thought Judy seemed rather glad to let her husband dictate its level, which, of course, he did. I noticed when the three rode away together that the Colonel was beginning to sit down rather solidly on his big New Zealander; and I watched the dusk come over from the foot-hills for a long time thinking more kindly than I had spoken of Robert Harbottle.

I have often wondered how far happiness is contributed to a temperament like Judy Harbottle's, and how far it creates its own; but I doubt whether, on either count, she found as much in any other winter of her life except perhaps the remote ones by the Seine. Those ardent hours of hers, when everything she said was touched with the flame of her individuality, came oftener; she suddenly cleaned up her palate and began to translate in one study after another the language of the frontier country, that spoke only in stones and in shadows under the stones and in sunlight over them. There is nothing in the Academy of this year, at all events, that I would exchange for the one she gave me. She lived her physical life at a pace which carried us all along with her; she hunted and drove and danced and dined with such sincere intention as convinced us all that in hunting and driving and dancing and dining there were satisfactions that had been somehow overlooked. The Surgeon-Major's wife said it was delightful to meet Mrs Harbottle, she seemed to enjoy everything so thoroughly; the Surgeon-Major looked at her critically and asked her if she were quite sure she hadn't a night temperature. He was a Scotchman. One night Colonel Harbottle, hearing her give away the last extra, charged her with renewing her youth.

'No, Bob,' she said, 'only imitating it.'

Ah, that question of her youth. It was so near her—still, she told me once, she heard the beat of its flying, and the pulse in her veins answered the false signal. That was afterward, when she told the truth. She was not so happy when she indulged herself otherwise. As when she asked one to remember that she was a middle-aged woman, with middle-aged thoughts and satisfactions.

'I am now really happiest,' she declared, 'when the Commissioner takes me in to dinner, when the General Commanding leads me to the dance.'

She did her best to make it an honest conviction. I offered her a recent success not crowned by the Academy, and she put it down on the table. 'By and by,' she said. 'At present I am reading Pascal and Bossuet.' Well, she was reading Pascal and Bossuet. She grieved aloud that most of our activities in India were so indomitably youthful, owing to the accident that most of us were always so young. 'There is no dignified distraction in this country,' she complained, 'for respectable ladies nearing forty.' She seemed to like to make these declarations in the presence of Somers Chichele, who would look at her with a little queer smile—a bad translation, I imagine, of what he felt.

She gave herself so generously to her seniors that somebody said Mrs Harbottle's girdle was hung with brass hats. It seems flippant to add that her complexion was as honest as the day, but the fact is that the year before Judy had felt compelled, like the rest of us, to repair just a little the ravages of the climate. If she had never done it one would not have looked twice at the absurdity when she said of the powder-puff in the dressing-room, 'I have raised that thing to the level of an immorality,' and sailed in to dance with an uncompromising expression and a face uncompromised. I have not spoken of her beauty; for one thing it was not always there, and there were people who would deny it altogether, or whose considered comment was, 'I wouldn't call her plain.' They, of course, were people in whom she declined to be interested, but even for those of us who could evoke some demonstration of her vivid self her face would not always light in correspondence. When it did there was none that I liked better to look at; and I envied Somers Chichele his way to make it the pale, shining thing that would hold him lifted, in return, for hours together, with I know not what mystic power of a moon upon the tide. And he? Oh, he was dark and delicate, by nature simple, sincere, delightfully intelligent. His common title to charm was the rather sweet seriousness that rested on his upper lip, and a certain winning gratification in his attention; but he had a subtler one in his eyes, which must be always seeking and smiling over what they found; those eyes of perpetual inquiry for the exquisite which ask so little help to create it. A personality to button up in a uniform, good heavens!

As I begin to think of them together I remember how the maternal note appeared in her talk about him.

'His youth is pathetic,' she told me, 'but there is nothing that he does not understand.'

'Don't apologize, Judy,' I said. We were so brusque on the frontier. Besides, the matter still suffered a jocular presentment. Mrs Harbottle and Mr Chichele were still 'great friends'; we could still put them next each other at our dinner-parties without the feeling that it would be 'marked'. There was still nothing unusual in the fact that when Mrs Harbottle was there Mr Chichele might be taken for granted. We were so broad-minded also, on the frontier.

It grew more obvious, the maternal note. I began positively to dread it, almost as much, I imagine, as Somers did. She took her privileges all in Anna's name, she exercised her authority quite as Lady Chichele's proxy. She went to the very limit. 'Anna Chichele,' she said actually in his presence, 'is a fortunate woman. She has all kinds of cleverness, and she has her tall son. I have only one little talent, and I have no tall son.' Now it was not in nature that she could have had a son as tall as Somers, nor was that desire in her eyes. All civilization implies a good deal of farce, but this was a poor refuge, a cheap device; I was glad when it fell away from her sincerity, when the day came on which she looked into my fire and said simply, 'An attachment like ours has no terms.'

'I wonder,' I said.

'For what comes and goes,' she went on dreamily, 'how could there be a formula?'

'Look here, Judy,' I said, 'you know me very well. What if the flesh leaps with the spirit?'

She looked at me, very white. 'Oh no,' she said, 'no.'

I waited, but there seemed nothing more that she could say; and in the silence the futile negative seemed to wander round the room repeating itself like an echo, 'Oh no, no.' I poked the fire presently to drown the sound of it. Judy sat still, with her feet crossed and her hands thrust into the pockets of her coat, staring into the coals.

'Can you live independently, satisfied with your interests and occupations?' she demanded at last. 'Yes, I know you can. I can't. I must exist more than half in other people. It is what they think and feel that matters to me, just as much as what I think and feel. The best of life is in that communication.'

'It has always been a passion with you, Judy,' I replied. 'I can imagine how much you must miss—'

'Whom?'

'Anna Chichele,' I said softly.

She got up and walked about the room, fixing here and there an intent regard upon things which she did not see. 'Oh, I do,' she said at one point, with the effect of pulling herself together. She took another turn or two, and then finding herself near the door she went out. I felt as profoundly humiliated for her as if she had staggered.

The next night was one of those that stand out so vividly, for no reason that one can identify, in one's memory. We were dining with the Harbottles, a small party, for a tourist they had with them. Judy and I and Somers and the traveller had drifted out into the veranda, where the scent of Japanese lilies came and went on the spring wind to trouble the souls of any taken unawares. There was a brightness beyond the foot-hills where the moon was coming, and I remember how one tall clump swayed out against it, and seemed in passionate perfume to lay a burden on the breast. Judy moved away from it and sat clasping her knees on the edge of the veranda. Somers, when his eyes were not upon her, looked always at the lily.

Even the spirit of the globe-trotter was stirred, and he said, 'I think you Anglo-Indians live in a kind of little paradise.'

There was an instant's silence, and then Judy turned her face into the lamp-light from the drawing-room. 'With everything but the essentials,' she said.

We stayed late; Mr Chichele and ourselves were the last to go. Judy walked with us along the moonlit drive to the gate, which is so unnecessary a luxury in India that the servants always leave it open. She swung the stiff halves together.

'Now,' she said, 'it is shut.'

'And I,' said Somers Chichele, softly and quickly, 'am on the other side.'

Even over that depth she could flash him a smile. 'It is the business of my life,' she gave him in return, 'to keep this gate shut.' I felt as if they had forgotten us. Somers mounted and rode off without a word; we were walking in a different direction. Looking back, I saw Judy leaning immoveable on the gate, while Somers turned in his saddle, apparently to repeat the form of lifting his hat. And all about them stretched the stones of Kabul valley, vague and formless in the tide of the moonlight . . .

Next day a note from Mrs Harbottle informed me that she had gone to Bombay for a fortnight. In a postscript she wrote, 'I shall wait for the Chicheles there, and come back with them.' I remember reflecting that if she could not induce herself to take a passage to England in the ship that brought them, it seemed the right thing to do.

She did come back with them. I met the party at the station. I knew Somers would meet them, and it seemed to me, so imminent did disaster loom, that someone else should be there, someone to offer a covering movement or a flank support wherever it might be most needed. And among all our smiling faces disaster did come, or the cold premonition of it. We were all perfect, but Somers's lip trembled. Deprived for a fortnight he was eager for the draft, and he was only twenty-six. His lip trembled, and there, under the flickering station-lamps, suddenly stood that of which there never could be again any denial, for those of us who saw.

Did we make, I wonder, even a pretense of disguising the consternation that sprang up among us, like an armed thing, ready to kill any further suggestion of the truth? I don't know. Anna Chichele's unfinished sentence dropped as if someone had given her a blow upon the mouth. Coolies were piling the luggage into a hired carriage at the edge of the platform. She walked mechanically after them, and would have stepped in with it but for the sight of her own gleaming landau drawn up within a yard or two, and the General waiting. We all got home somehow, taking it with us, and I gave Lady Chichele twenty-four hours to come to me with her face all one question and her heart all one fear. She came in twelve.

'Have you seen it–long?' Prepared as I was her directness was demoralizing.

'It isn't a mortal disease.'

'Oh, for Heaven's sake–'

'Well, not with certainty, for more than a month.'

She made a little spasmodic movement with her hands, then dropped them pitifully. 'Couldn't you do *any*thing?'

I looked at her, and she said at once, 'No, of course you couldn't.'

For a moment or two I took my share of the heavy sense of it, my trivial share, which yet was an experience sufficiently exciting. 'I am afraid it will have to be faced,' I said.

'What will happen?' Anna cried. 'Oh, what will happen?'

'Why not the usual thing?' Lady Chichele looked up quickly as if at a reminder. 'The ambiguous attachment of the country,' I went on, limping but courageous, 'half declared, half admitted, that leads vaguely nowhere, and finally perishes as the man's life enriches itself–the thing we have seen so often.'

'Whatever Judy is capable of it won't be the usual thing. You know that.'

I had to confess in silence that I did.

'It flashed at me–the difference in her–in Bombay.' She pressed her lips together and then went on unsteadily. 'In her eyes, her voice. She was mannered, extravagant, elaborate. With me! All the way up I wondered and worried. But I never thought–' She stopped; her voice simply shook itself into silence. I called a servant.

'I am going to give you a good stiff peg,' I said. I apologize for the 'peg,' but not for the whisky and soda. It is a beverage on the frontier, of which the vulgarity is lost in the value. While it was coming I tried to talk of other things, but she would only nod absently in the pauses.

'Last night we dined with him, it was guest night at the mess, and she was there. I watched her, and she knew it. I don't know whether she tried, but anyway, she failed. The covenant between them was written on her forehead whenever she looked at him, though that was seldom. She dared not look at him. And the little conversation that they had–you would have laughed–it was a comedy of stutters. The facile Mrs Harbottle!'

'You do well to be angry, naturally,' I said; 'but it would be fatal to let yourself go, Anna.'

'Angry? Oh, I am *sick*. The misery of it! The terror of it! If it were anybody but Judy! Can't you imagine the passion of a temperament like that in a woman who has all these years been feeding on herself? I tell you she will take him from my very arms. And he will go—to I dare not imagine what catastrophe! Who can prevent it? Who can prevent it?'

'There is you,' I said.

Lady Chichele laughed hysterically. 'I think you ought to say, "There are you." I—what can I do? Do you realize that it's *Judy*? My friend—my other self? Do you think we can drag all that out of it? Do you think a tie like that can be broken by an accident—by a misfortune? With it all I *adore* Judy Harbottle. I love her, as I have always loved her, and—it's damnable, but I don't know whether, whatever happened, I wouldn't go on loving her.'

'Finish your peg,' I said. She was sobbing.

'Where I blame myself most,' she went on, 'is for not seeing in him all that makes him mature to her—that makes her forget the absurd difference between them, and take him simply and sincerely as I know she does, as the contemporary of her soul if not of her body. I saw none of that. Could I, as his mother? Would he show it to me? I thought him just a charming boy, clever, too, of course, with nice instincts and well plucked; we were always proud of that, with his delicate physique. Just a boy! I haven't yet stopped thinking how different he looks without his curls. And I thought she would be just kind and gracious and delightful to him because he was my son.'

'There, of course,' I said, 'is the only chance.'

'Where—what?'

'He is your son.'

'Would you have me appeal to her? Do you know I don't think I could?'

'Dear me, no. Your case must present itself. It must spring upon her and grow before her out of your silence, and if you can manage it, your confidence. There is a great deal, after all, remember, to hold her in that. I can't somehow imagine her failing you. Otherwise—'

Lady Chichele and I exchanged a glance of candid admission.

'Otherwise she would be capable of sacrificing everything—everything. Of gathering her life into an hour. I know. And do you know if the thing were less impossible, less grotesque, I should not be so much afraid? I mean that the *absolute* indefensibility of it might bring her a recklessness and a momentum which might—'

'Send her over the verge,' I said. 'Well, go home and ask her to dinner.'

There was a good deal more to say, of course, than I have thought proper to put down here, but before Anna went I saw that she was keyed up to the heroic part. This was none the less to her credit because it was the only part, the dictation of a sense of expediency that despaired while it dictated. The noble thing was her capacity to take it, and, amid all that warred in her, to carry it out on the brave high lines of her inspiration. It seemed a literal inspiration, so perfectly calculated that it was hard not to think some-times, when one saw them together, that Anna had been lulled into a sim-ple resumption of the old relation. Then from the least thing possible—the lift of an eyelid—it flashed upon one that between these two every moment was dramatic, and one took up the word with a curious sense of detachment and futility, but with one's heart beating like a trip-hammer with the mad excitement of it. The acute thing was the splendid sincerity of Judy Harbottle's response. For days she was profoundly on her guard, then sud-denly she seemed to become practically, vividly aware of what I must go on calling the great chance, and passionately to fling herself upon it. It was the strangest co-operation without a word or a sign to show it conscious—a play-ing together for stakes that could not be admitted, a thing to hang upon breathless. It was there between them—the tenable ground of what they were to each other: they occupied it with almost an equal eye upon the tide that threatened, while I from my mainland tower also made an anguished calculation of the chances. I think in spite of the menace, they found real beatitudes; so keenly did they set about the business that it brought them moments finer than any they could count in the years that were behind them, the flat and colourless years that were gone. Once or twice the wild idea even visited me that it was, after all, the projection of his mother in Somers that had so seized Judy Harbottle, and that the original was all that was needed to help the happy process of detachment. Somers himself at the time was a good deal away on escort duty: they had a clear field.

I can not tell exactly when—between Mrs Harbottle and myself—it be-came a matter for reference more or less overt, I mean her defined problem, the thing that went about between her and the sun. It will be imagined that it did not come up like the weather; indeed, it was hardly ever to be envis-aged and never to be held; but it was always there, and out of our joint con-sciousness it would sometimes leap and pass, without shape or face. It might slip between two sentences, or it might remain, a dogging shadow, for an hour. Or a week would go by while, with a strong hand, she held it out of sight altogether and talked of Anna—always of Anna. Her eyes shone with the things she told me then: she seemed to keep herself under the influence of them as if they had the power of narcotics. At the end of a time like this she turned to me in the door as she was going and stood silent, as if she could neither go nor stay. I had been able to make nothing of her that after-noon: she had seemed preoccupied with the pattern of the carpet which she traced continually with her riding crop, and finally I, too, had relapsed. She sat haggard, with the fight forever in her eyes, and the day seemed to sombre about her in her corner. When she turned in the door, I looked up with sud-den prescience of a crisis.

'Don't jump,' she said, 'it was only to tell you that I have persuaded Robert to apply for furlough. Eighteen months. From the first of April. Don't touch me.' I suppose I made a movement towards her. Certainly I wanted to throw my arms about her; with the instinct, I suppose, to steady her in her great resolution.

'At the end of that time, as you know, he will be retired. I had some trouble, he is so keen on the regiment, but I think—I have succeeded. You might mention it to Anna.'

'Haven't you?' sprang past my lips.

'I can't. It would be like taking an oath to tell her, and—I can't take an oath to go. But I mean to.'

'There is nothing to be said,' I brought out, feeling indeed that there was not. 'But I congratulate you, Judy.'

'No, there is nothing to be said. And you congratulate me, no doubt!'

She stood for a moment quivering in the isolation she made for herself; and I felt a primitive angry revolt against the delicate trafficking of souls that could end in such ravage and disaster. The price was too heavy; I would have denuded her, at the moment, of all that had led her into this, and turned her out a clod with fine shoulders like fifty other women in Peshawur. Then, perhaps, because I held myself silent and remote and she had no emotion of fear from me, she did not immediately go.

'It will beat itself away, I suppose, like the rest of the unreasonable pain of the world,' she said at last; and that, of course, brought me to her side. 'Things will go back to their proportions. This,' she touched an open rose, 'will claim its beauty again. And life will become—perhaps—what it was before.' Still I found nothing to say, I could only put my arm in hers and walk with her to the edge of the veranda where the syce was holding her horse. She stroked the animal's neck. 'Everything in me answered him,' she informed me, with the grave intelligence of a patient who relates a symptom past. As she took the reins she turned to me again. 'His spirit came to mine like a homing bird,' she said, and in her smile even the pale reflection of happiness was sweet and stirring. It left me hanging in imagination over the source and the stream, a little blessed in the mere understanding.

Too much blessed for confidence, or any safe feeling that the source was bound. Rather I saw it leaping over every obstacle, flashing to its destiny. As I drove to the Club the next day I decided that I would not tell Anna Chichele of Colonel Harbottle's projected furlough. If to Judy telling her would be like taking an oath that they would go, to me it would at least be like assuming sponsorship for their intention. That would be heavy indeed. From the first of April—we were then in March. Anna would hear it soon enough from the General, would see it soon enough, almost, in the *Gazette*, when it would have passed into irrecoverable fact. So I went by her with locked lips, kept out of the way of those eyes of the mother that asked and asked, and would have seen clear to any depth, any hiding-place of knowledge like that. As I pulled up at the Club I saw Colonel Harbottle talking concernedly to the wife of our Second-in-Command, and was reminded that I had not heard for some days how Major Watkins was going on. So I, too, approached Mrs Watkins in her victoria to ask. Robert Harbottle kindly forestalled her reply. 'Hard luck, isn't it? Watkins has been ordered home at once. Just settled into their new house, too—last of the kit came up from Calcutta yesterday, didn't it, Mrs Watkins? But it's sound to go—Peshawur is the worst hole in Asia to shake off dysentery in.'

We agreed upon this and discussed the sale-list of her new furniture that Mrs Watkins would have to send round the station, and considered the chances of a trooper—to the Watkinses with two children and not a penny but his pay it did make it easier not to have to go by a liner—and Colonel Harbottle and I were half-way to the reading-room before the significance of Major Watkins' sick-leave flashed upon me.

'But this,' I cried, 'will make a difference to your plans. You won't—'

'Be able to ask for that furlough Judy wants. Rather not. I'm afraid she's disappointed—she was tremendously set on going—but it doesn't matter tuppence to me.'

I sought out Mrs Harbottle, at the end of the room. She looked radiant; she sat on the edge of the table and swung a light-hearted heel. She was talking to people who in themselves were a witness to high spirits, Captain the Hon. Freddy Gisborne, Mrs Flamboys.

At sight of me her face clouded, fell suddenly into the old weary lines. It made me feel somehow a little sick; I went back to my cart and drove home.

For more than a week I did not see her except when I met her riding with Somers Chichele along the peach-bordered road that leads to the Wazir-Bagh. The trees were all in blossom and made a picture that might well catch dreaming hearts into a beatitude that would correspond. The air was full of spring and the scent of violets, those wonderful Peshawur violets that grow in great clumps, tall and double. Gracious clouds came and trailed across the frontier barrier; blue as an idyll it rose about us; the city smiled in her gardens.

She had it all in her face, poor Judy, all the spring softness and more, the morning she came, intensely controlled, to announce her defeat. I was in the drawing-room doing the flowers; I put them down to look at her. The wonderful telegram from Simla arrived—that was the wonderful part—at the same time; I remembered how the red, white, and blue turban of the telegraph peon bobbed up behind her shoulder in the veranda. I signed and laid it on the table; I suppose it seemed hardly likely that anything could be important enough to interfere at the moment with my impression of what love, unbound and victorious, could do with a face I thought I knew. Love sat there careless of the issue, full of delight. Love proclaimed that between him and Judith Harbottle it was all over—she had met him, alas, in too narrow a place—and I marvelled at the paradox with which he softened every curve and underlined every vivid note of personality in token that it had just begun. He sat there in great serenity, and though I knew that somewhere behind lurked a vanquished woman, I saw her through such a radiance that I could not be sure of seeing her at all . . .

She went back to the very first of it; she seemed herself intensely interested in the facts; and there is no use in pretending that, while she talked, the moral consideration was at all present with me either; it wasn't. Her extremity was the thing that absorbed us; she even, in tender thoughtfulness, diagnosed it from its definite beautiful beginning.

'It was there, in my heart, when I woke one morning, exquisite and strange, the assurance of a gift. How had it come there, while I slept? I assure you when I closed my eyes it did not exist for me. . . . Yes, of course, I had seen him, but only somewhere at dinner . . . As the day went on it changed—it turned into a clear pool, into a flower. And I—think of my not understanding! I was pleased with it! For a long time, for days, I never dreamed that it could be anything but a little secret joy. Then, suddenly— oh, I had not been perceiving enough!—it was in all my veins, a tide, an efflorescence, a thing of my very life.

'Then—it was a little late—I understood, and since—

'I began by hating it—being furious, furious—and afraid, too. Sometimes it was like a low cloud, hovering and travelling always with me, sometimes like a beast of prey that went a little way off and sat looking at me . . .

'I have—done my best. But there is nothing to do, to kill, to abolish. How can I say, "I will not let you in," when it is already there? How can I assume indifference when this thing is imposed upon every moment of my day? And it has grown so sweet—the longing—that—isn't it strange?—I could more willingly give him up than the desire of him. That seems as impossible to part with as life itself.'

She sat reflective for a moment, and I saw her eyes slowly fill.

'Don't—don't *cry*, Judy,' I faltered, wanting to horribly, myself.

She smiled them dry.

'Not now. But I am giving myself, I suppose, to many tears.'

'God help you,' I said. What else was there to say?

'There is no such person,' she replied, gaily. 'There is only a blessed devil.'

'Then you go all the way—to the logical conclusion?'

She hardly hesitated. 'To the logical conclusion. What poor words!'

'May I ask—when?'

'I should like to tell you that quite definitely, and I think I can. The English mail leaves tonight.'

'And you have arranged to take it?'

'We have arranged nothing. Do you know'—she smiled as if at the fresh colours of an idyll— 'we have not even come to the admission? There has been between us no word, no vision. Ah, we have gone in bonds, and dumb! Hours we have had, exquisite hours of the spirit, but never a moment of the heart, a moment confessed. It was mine to give—that moment, and he has waited—I know—wondering whether perhaps it would ever come. And today—we are going for a ride today, and I do not think we shall come back.'

'O Judy,' I cried, catching at her sleeve, 'he is only a boy!'

'There were times when I thought that conclusive. Now the misery of it has gone to sleep; don't waken it. It pleases me to believe that the years are a convention. I never had any dignity, you know, and I seem to have missed the moral deliverance. I only want—oh, you know what I want. Why don't you open your telegram?'

I had been folding and fingering the brown envelope as if it had been a scrap of waste-paper.

'It is probably from Mrs Watkins about the victoria,' I said, feeling its profound irrelevance. 'I wired an offer to her in Bombay. However'—and I read the telegram, the little solving telegram from Army Headquarters. I turned my back on her to read it again, and then I replaced it very carefully and put it in my pocket. It was a moment to take hold of with both hands, crying on all one's gods for steadiness.

'How white you look!' said Mrs Harbottle, with concern. 'Not bad news?'

'On the contrary, excellent news. Judy, will you stay to lunch?'

She looked at me, hesitating. 'Won't it seem rather a compromise on your part? When you ought to be rousing the city—'

'I don't intend to rouse the city,' I said.

'I have given you the chance.'

'Thank you,' I said, grimly, 'but the only real favour you can do me is to stay and lunch.' It was then just on one.

'I'll stay,' she said, 'if you will promise not to make any sort of effort. I shouldn't mind, but it would distress you.'

'I promise absolutely,' I said, and ironical joy rose up in me, and the telegram burned in my pocket.

She would talk of it, though I found it hard to let her go on, knowing and knowing and knowing as I did that for that day at least it could not be. There was very little about herself that she wanted to tell me; she was there confessed a woman whom joy had overcome; it was understood that we both accepted that situation. But in the details which she asked me to take charge of it was plain that she also kept a watchful eye upon fate—matters of business.

We were in the drawing-room. The little round clock in its Armritsar case marked half-past three. Judy put down her coffee-cup and rose to go. As she glanced at the clock the light deepened in her eyes, and I, with her hand in mine, felt like an agent of the Destroyer—for it was half-past three—consumed myself with fear lest the blow had miscarried. Then as we stood, suddenly, the sound of hoofs at a gallop on the drive, and my husband threw himself off at the door and tore through the hall to his room; and in the certainty that overwhelmed me even Judy, for an instant, stood dim and remote.

'Major Jim seems to be in a hurry,' said Mrs Harbottle, lightly, 'I have always liked your husband. I wonder whether he will say tomorrow that he always liked me.'

'Dear Judy, I don't think he will be occupied with you tomorrow.'

'Oh, surely, just a little, if I go tonight.'

'You won't go tonight.'

She looked at me helplessly. I felt as if I were insisting upon her abasement instead of her salvation. 'I wish—'

'You're not going—you're not! You can't! Look!'

I pulled it out of my pocket and thrust it at her—the telegram. It came, against every regulation, from my good friend the Deputy Adjutant-General, in Simla, and it read, '*Row Khurram 12th probably ordered front three hours' time.*'

Her face changed—how my heart leaped to see it change!—and that took command there which will command trampling, even in the women of the camp, at news like this.

'What luck that Bob couldn't take his furlough!' she exclaimed, single-thoughted. 'But you have known this for hours'—there was even something of the Colonel's wife, authority, incisiveness. 'Why didn't you tell me? Ah—I see.'

I stood before her abashed, and that was ridiculous, while she measured me as if I presented in myself the woman I took her to be. 'It wasn't like that,' she said. I had to defend myself. 'Judy,' I said, 'if you weren't in honour bound to Anna, how could I know that you would be in honour bound to the regiment? There was a train at three.'

'I beg to assure you that you have overcalculated,' said Mrs Harbottle. Her eyes were hard and proud. 'And I am not sure'—a deep red swept over her face, a man's blush—'in the light of this I am not sure that I am not honour bound to Anna.'

We had reached the veranda, and at her signal her coachman drove quickly up. 'You have kept me here three hours when there was the whole of Bob's kit to see to,' she said, as she flung herself in; 'you might have thought of that.'

It was a more than usually tedious campaign, and Colonel Robert Harbottle was ambushed and shot in a place where one must believe pure boredom induced him to take his men. The incident was relieved, the newspapers said—and they are seldom so clever in finding relief for such incidents—by the dash and courage shown by Lieutenant Chichele, who, in one of those feats which it has been lately been the fashion to criticize, carried the mortally wounded body of his Colonel out of range at conspicuous risk of depriving the Queen of another officer. I helped Judy with her silent packing; she had forgiven me long before that; and she settled almost at once into the flat in Chelsea which has since been credited with so delightful an atmosphere, went back straight into her own world. I have always kept her first letters about it, always shall. For months after, while the expedition still raged after snipers and rifle-thieves, I discussed with Lady Chichele the probable outcome of it all. I have sometimes felt ashamed of leaping as straight as I did with Anna to what we thought the inevitable. I based no calculation on all Mrs Harbottle had gone back to, just as I had based no calculation on her ten years' companionship in arms when I kept her from the three o'clock train. This last was a retrospection in which Anna naturally could not join me; she never knew, poor dear, how fortunate as to its moment was the campaign she deplored, and nothing to this day can have disturbed her conviction that the bond she was at such magnificent pains to strengthen, held against the strain, as long, happily, as the supreme need existed. 'How right you were!' she often said. 'She did, after all, love me best, dear, wonderful Judy!' Her distress about poor Robert Harbottle was genuine enough, but one could not be surprised at a certain ambiguity; one tear for Robert, so to speak, and two for her boy. It could hardly be, for him, a marriage after his mother's heart. And she laid down with some emphasis that Somers was brilliantly entitled to all he was likely to get—which was natural, too . . .

I had been from the beginning so much 'in it' that Anna showed me, a year later, though I don't believe she liked doing it, the letter in part of which Mrs Harbottle shall finally excuse herself.

'Somers will give you this,' I read, 'and with it take back your son. You will not find, I know, anything grotesque in the charming enthusiasm with which he has offered his life to me; you understand too well, you are too kind. And if you wonder that I can so render up a dear thing which I might keep and would once have taken, think how sweet in the desert is the pool, and how barren was the prospect from Balclutha.'

It was like her to abandon in pride a happiness that asked so much less humiliation; I don't know why, but it was like her. And of course, when one thought of it, she had consulted all sorts of high expediencies. But I sat silent with remembrance, quieting a pang in my heart, trying not to calculate how much it had cost Judy Harbottle to take her second chance.

ᴥ

THE QUARANTINE AT
ALEXANDER ABRAHAM'S

I refused to take that class in Sunday School the first time I was asked. It was not that I objected to teaching in the Sunday School. On the contrary, I rather liked the idea; but it was the Rev. Mr Allan who asked me, and it had always been a matter of principle with me never to do anything a man asked me to do if I could help it. I was noted for that. It saves a great deal of trouble and it simplifies everything beautifully. I had always disliked men. It must have been born in me, because, as far back as I can remember, an antipathy to men and dogs was one of my strongest characteristics. I was noted for that. My experiences through life only served to deepen it. The more I saw of men, the more I liked cats.

So, of course, when the Rev. Allan asked me if I would consent to take a class in Sunday School I said no in a fashion calculated to chasten him wholesomely. If he had sent his wife the first time, as he did the second, it would have been wiser. People generally do what Mrs Allan asks them to do because they know it saves time.

Mrs Allan talked smoothly for half an hour before she mentioned the Sunday School, and paid me several compliments. Mrs Allan is famous for her tact. Tact is a faculty for meandering around to a given point instead of making a bee-line. I have no tact. I am noted for that. As soon as Mrs Allan's conversation came in sight of the Sunday School, I, who knew all along whither it was tending, said, straight out,

'What class do you want me to teach?'

Mrs Allan was so surprised that she forgot to be tactful, and answered plainly for once in her life,

'There are two classes—one of boys and one of girls—needing a teacher. I have been teaching the girls' class, but I shall have to give it up for a little time on account of the baby's health. You may have your choice, Miss MacPherson.'

'Then I shall take the boys,' I said decidedly. I am noted for my decision. 'Since they have to grow up to be men it's well to train them properly betimes. Nuisances they are bound to become under any circumstances; but if they are taken in hand young enough they may not grow up to be such nuisances as they otherwise would and that will be some unfortunate woman's gain.'

Mrs Allan looked dubious. I knew she had expected me to choose the girls. 'They are a very wild set of boys,' she said.

'I never knew boys who weren't,' I retorted.

'I–I–think perhaps you would like the girls best,' said Mrs Allan hesitatingly. If it had not been for one thing–which I would never in this world have admitted to Mrs Allan–I might have liked the girls' class best myself. But the truth was, Anne Shirley was in that class; and Anne Shirley was the one living human being that I was afraid of. Not that I disliked her. But she had such a habit of asking weird, unexpected questions, which a Philadelphia lawyer couldn't answer. Miss Rogerson had that class once and Anne routed her, horse, foot and artillery. *I* wasn't going to undertake a class with a walking interrogation point in it like that. Besides, I thought Mrs Allan required a slight snub. Ministers' wives are rather apt to think they can run everything and everybody, if they are not wholesomely corrected now and again.

'It is not what *I* like best that must be considered, Mrs Allan,' I said rebukingly. 'It is what is best for those boys. I feel that *I* shall be best for *them*.'

'Oh, I've no doubt of that, Miss MacPherson,' said Mrs Allan amiably. It was a fib for her, minister's wife though she was. She *had* doubt. She thought I would be a dismal failure as teacher of a boys' class.

But I was not. I am not often a dismal failure when I make up my mind to do a thing. I am noted for that.

'It is wonderful what a reformation you have worked in that class, Miss MacPherson–wonderful,' said the Rev. Mr Allan some weeks later. He didn't mean to show how amazing a thing he thought it that an old maid noted for being a man hater should have managed it, but his face betrayed him.

'Where does Jimmy Spencer live?' I asked him crisply. 'He came one Sunday three weeks ago and hasn't been back since. I mean to find out why.'

Mr Allan coughed.

'I believe he is hired as handy boy with Alexander Abraham Bennett, out on the White Sands road,' he said.

'Then I am going out to Alexander Abraham Bennett's on the White Sands road to see why Jimmy Spencer doesn't come to Sunday School,' I said firmly.

Mr Allan's eye twinkled ever so slightly. I have always insisted that if that man were not a minister he would have a sense of humour.

'Possibly Mr Bennett will not appreciate your kind interest! He has–ah–a singular aversion to your sex, I understand. No woman has ever been known to get inside of Mr Bennett's house since his sister died twenty years ago.'

'Oh, he is the one, is he?' I said, remembering. 'He is the woman hater who threatens that if a woman comes into his yard he'll chase her out with a pitchfork. Well, he will not chase *me* out!'

Mr Allan gave a chuckle—a ministerial chuckle, but still a chuckle. It irritated me slightly, because it seemed to imply that he thought Alexander Abraham Bennett would be one too many for me. But I did not show Mr Allan that he annoyed me. It is always a great mistake to let a man see that he can vex you.

The next afternoon I harnessed my sorrel pony to the buggy and drove down to Alexander Abraham Bennett's. As usual, I took William Adolphus with me for company. William Adolphus is my favourite among my six cats. He is black, with a white dicky and beautiful white paws. He sat up on the seat beside me and looked far more like a gentleman than many a man I've seen in a similar position.

Alexander Abraham's place was about three miles along the White Sands road. I knew the house as soon as I came to it by its neglected appearance. It needed paint badly; the blinds were crooked and torn; weeds grew up to the very door. Plainly, there was no woman about *that* place. Still, it was a nice house, and the barns were splendid. My father always said that when a man's barns were bigger than his house it was a sign that his income exceeded his expenditure. So it was all right that they should be bigger; but it was all wrong that they should be trimmer and better painted. Still, thought I, what else could you expect of a woman hater?

'But Alexander Abraham evidently knows how to run a farm, even if he is a woman hater,' I remarked to William Adolphus as I got out and tied the pony to the railing.

I had driven up to the house from the back way and now I was opposite a side door opening on the veranda. I thought I might as well go to it, so I tucked William Adolphus under my arm and marched up the path. Just as I was half way up a dog swooped around the front corner and made straight for me. He was the ugliest dog I had ever seen; and he didn't even bark—just came silently and speedily on, with a business-like eye.

I never stop to argue matters with a dog that doesn't bark. I know when discretion is the better part of valour. Firmly clasping William Adolphus, I ran—not to the door, because the dog was between me and it, but to a big, low-branching cherry tree at the back corner of the house. I reached it in time and no more. First thrusting William Adolphus on to a limb above my head, I scrambled up into that blessed tree without stopping to think how it might look to Alexander Abraham if he happened to be watching.

My time for reflection came when I found myself perched half way up the tree with William Adolphus beside me. William Adolphus was quite calm and unruffled. I can hardly say with truthfulness that I was. On the contrary, I admit that I felt considerably upset.

The dog was sitting on his haunches on the ground below, watching us, and it was quite plain to be seen, from his leisurely manner, that it was not his busy day. He bared his teeth and growled when he caught my eye.

'You *look* like a woman hater's dog,' I told him. I meant it for an insult; but the beast took it for a compliment.

Then I set myself to solving the question, 'How am I to get out of this predicament?'

It did not seem easy to solve it.

'Shall I scream, William Adolphus?' I demanded of that intelligent animal. William Adolphus shook his head. This is a fact. And I agreed with him.

'No, I shall not scream, William Adolphus,' I said. 'There is probably no one to hear me except Alexander Abraham, and I have my painful doubts about his tender mercies. Now, it is impossible to go down. Is it, then, William Adolphus, possible to go up?'

I looked up. Just above my head was an open window with a tolerably stout branch extending right across it.

'Shall we try that way, William Adolphus?' I asked.

William Adolphus, wasting no words, began to climb the tree. I followed his example. The dog ran in circles about the tree and looked things not lawful to be uttered. It probably would have been a relief to him to bark if it hadn't been so against his principles.

I got in by the window easily enough, and found myself in a bedroom the like of which for disorder and dust and general awfulness I had never seen in all my life. But I did not pause to take in details. With William Adolphus under my arm I marched downstairs, fervently hoping I should meet no one on the way.

I did not. The hall below was empty and dusty. I opened the first door I came to and walked boldly in. A man was sitting by the window, looking moodily out. I should have known him for Alexander Abraham anywhere. He had just the same uncared-for, ragged appearance that the house had; and yet, like the house, it seemed that he would not be bad looking if he were trimmed up a little. His hair looked as if it had never been combed, and his whiskers were wild in the extreme.

He looked at me with blank amazement in his countenance.

'Where is Jimmy Spencer?' I demanded. 'I have come to see him.'

'How did he ever let you in?' asked the man, staring at me.

'He didn't let me in,' I retorted. 'He chased me all over the lawn, and I only saved myself from being torn piecemeal by scrambling up a tree. You ought to be prosecuted for keeping such a dog! Where is Jimmy?'

Instead of answering Alexander Abraham began to laugh in a most unpleasant fashion.

'Trust a woman for getting into a man's house if she had made up her mind to,' he said disagreeably.

Seeing that it was his intention to vex me I remained cool and collected.

'Oh, I wasn't particular about getting into your house, Mr Bennett,' I said calmly. 'I had but little choice in the matter. It was get in lest a worse fate befall me. It was not you or your house I wanted to see—although I admit that it is worth seeing if a person is anxious to find out how dirty a place *can* be. It was Jimmy. For the third and last time—where is Jimmy?'

'Jimmy is not here,' said Mr Bennett gruffly—but not quite so assuredly. 'He left last week and hired with a man over at Newbridge.'

'In that case,' I said, picking up William Adolphus, who had been exploring the room with a disdainful air, 'I won't disturb you any longer. I shall go.'

'Yes, I think it would be the wisest thing,' said Alexander Abraham—not disagreeably this time, but reflectively, as if there was some doubt about the matter. 'I'll let you out by the back door. Then the—ahem!—the dog will not interfere with you. Please go away quietly and quickly.'

I wondered if Alexander Abraham thought I would go away with a whoop. But I said nothing, thinking this the most dignified course of conduct, and I followed him out to the kitchen as quickly and quietly as he could have wished. Such a kitchen!

Alexander Abraham opened the door—which was locked—just as a buggy containing two men drove into the yard.

'Too late!' he exclaimed in a tragic tone. I understood that something dreadful must have happened, but I did not care, since, as I fondly supposed, it did not concern me. I pushed out past Alexander Abraham—who was looking as guilty as if he had been caught burglarizing—and came face to face with the man who had sprung from the buggy. It was old Dr Blair, from Carmody, and he was looking at me as if he had found me shoplifting.

'My dear Peter,' he said gravely, 'I am *very* sorry to see you here—very sorry indeed.'

I admit that this exasperated me. Besides, no man on earth, not even my old family doctor, has any right to 'My dear Peter' me!

'There is no loud call for sorrow, doctor,' I said loftily. 'If a woman, forty-eight years of age, a member of the Presbyterian church in good and regular standing, cannot call upon one of her Sunday School scholars without wrecking all the proprieties, how old must she be before she can?'

The doctor did not answer my question. Instead, he looked reproachfully at Alexander Abraham.

'Is this how you keep your word, Mr Bennett?' he said. 'I thought that you promised me that you would not let anyone into the house.'

'I didn't let her in,' growled Mr Bennett. 'Good heavens, man, she climbed in at an upstairs window, despite the presence on my grounds of a policeman and a dog! What is to be done with a woman like that?'

'I do not understand what all this means,' I said, addressing myself to the doctor and ignoring Alexander Abraham entirely, 'but if my presence here is so extremely inconvenient to all concerned you can soon be relieved of it. I am going at once.'

'I am very sorry, my dear Peter,' said the doctor impressively, 'but that is just what I cannot allow you to do. This house is under quarantine for smallpox. You will have to stay here.'

Smallpox! For the first and last time in my life I openly lost my temper with a man. I wheeled furiously upon Alexander Abraham.

'Why didn't you tell me?' I cried.

'Tell you!' he said, glaring at me. 'When I first saw you it was too late to tell you. I thought the kindest thing I could do was to hold my tongue and let you get away in happy ignorance. This will teach you to take a man's house by storm, madam!'

'Now, now, don't quarrel, my good people,' interposed the doctor seriously—but I saw a twinkle in his eye. 'You'll have to spend some time together under the same roof and you won't improve the situation by disagreeing. You see, Peter, it was this way. Mr Bennett was in town yesterday—where, as you are aware, there is a bad outbreak of smallpox—and took dinner in a boarding-house where one of the maids was ill. Last night she developed unmistakable symptoms of smallpox. The Board of Health at once got after all the people who were in the house yesterday, so far as they could locate them, and put them under quarantine. I came down here this morning and explained the matter to Mr Bennett. I brought Jeremiah Jeffries to guard the front of the house and Mr Bennett gave me his word of honour that he would not let anyone in by the back way while I went to get another policeman and make all the necessary arrangements. I have brought Thomas Wright and have secured the services of another man to attend to Mr Bennett's barn work and bring provisions to the house. Jacob Green and Cleophas Lee will watch at night. I don't think there is much danger of Mr Bennett's taking the smallpox, but until we are sure you must remain here, Peter.'

While listening to the doctor I had been thinking. It was the most distressing predicament I had ever got into in my life, but there was no sense in making it worse.

'Very well, doctor,' I said calmly. 'Yes, I was vaccinated a month ago, when the news of the smallpox first came. When you go back through

Avonlea kindly go to Sarah Pye and ask her to live in my house during my absence and look after things, especially the cats. Tell her to give them new milk twice a day and a square inch of butter apiece once a week. Get her to put my two dark print wrappers, some aprons, and some changes of under-clothing in my third best valise and have it sent down to me. My pony is tied out there to the fence. Please take him home. That is all, I think.'

'No, it isn't all,' said Alexander Abraham grumpily. 'Send that cat home, too. I won't have a cat around the place—I'd rather have the smallpox.'

I looked Alexander Abraham over gradually, in a way I have, beginning at his feet and travelling up to his head. I took my time over it; and then I said, very quietly,

'You may have both. Anyway, you'll have to have William Adolphus. He is under quarantine as well as you and I. Do you suppose I am going to have my cat ranging at large through Avonlea, scattering smallpox germs among innocent people? I'll have to put up with that dog of yours. You will have to endure William Adolphus.'

Alexander Abraham groaned, but I could see that the way I had looked him over had chastened him considerably.

The doctor drove away, and I went into the house, not choosing to linger outside and be grinned at by Thomas Wright. I hung my coat up in the hall and laid my bonnet carefully on the sitting-room table, having first dusted a clean place for it with my handkerchief. I longed to fall upon that house at once and clean it up, but I had to wait until the doctor came back with my wrapper. I could not clean house in my new suit and a silk shirtwaist.

Alexander Abraham was sitting on a chair looking at me. Presently he said,

'I am *not* curious—but will you kindly tell me why the doctor called you Peter?'

'Because that is my name, I suppose,' I answered, shaking up a cushion for William Adolphus and thereby disturbing the dust of years.

Alexander Abraham coughed gently.

'Isn't that—ahem!—rather a peculiar name for a woman?'

'It is,' I said, wondering how much soap, if any, there was in the house.

'I am *not* curious,' said Alexander Abraham, 'but would you mind telling me how you came to be called Peter?'

'If I had been a boy my parents intended to call me Peter in honour of a rich uncle. When I—fortunately—turned out to be a girl my mother insist-ed that I should be called Angelina. They gave me both names and called me Angelina, but as soon as I grew old enough I decided to be called Peter. It was bad enough, but not so bad as Angelina.'

'I should say it was more appropriate,' said Alexander Abraham, intend-ing, as I perceived, to be disagreeable.

'Precisely,' I agreed calmly. 'My last name is MacPherson, and I live in Avonlea. As you are *not* curious, that will be all the information you will need about me.'

'Oh!' Alexander Abraham looked as if a light had broken in on him. 'I've heard of you. You—ah—pretend to dislike men.'

Pretend! Goodness only knows what would have happened to Alexander Abraham just then if a diversion had not taken place. But the door opened and a dog came in—*the* dog. I suppose he had got tired waiting under the cherry tree for William Adolphus and me to come down. He was even uglier indoors than out.

'Oh, Mr Riley, Mr Riley, see what you have let me in for,' said Alexander Abraham reproachfully.

But Mr Riley—since that was the brute's name—paid no attention to Alexander Abraham. He had caught sight of William Adolphus curled up on the cushion, and he started across the room to investigate him. William Adolphus sat up and began to take notice.

'Call off that dog,' I said warningly to Alexander Abraham.

'Call him off yourself,' he retorted. 'Since you've brought that cat here you can protect him.'

'Oh, it wasn't for William Adolphus' sake I spoke,' I said pleasantly. 'William Adolphus can protect himself.'

William Adolphus could and did. He humped his back, flattened his ears, swore once, and then made a flying leap for Mr Riley. William Adolphus landed squarely on Mr Riley's brindled back and promptly took fast hold, spitting and clawing and caterwauling.

You never saw a more astonished dog than Mr Riley. With a yell of terror he bolted out to the kitchen, out of the kitchen into the hall, through the hall into the room, and so into the kitchen and round again. With each circuit he went faster and faster, until he looked like a brindled streak with a dash of black and white on top. Such a racket and commotion I never heard, and I laughed until the tears came into my eyes. Mr Riley flew around and around, and William Adolphus held on grimly and clawed. Alexander Abraham turned purple with rage.

'Woman, call off that infernal cat before he kills my dog,' he shouted above the din of yelps and yowls.

'Oh, he won't kill him,' I said reassuringly, 'and he's going too fast to hear me if I did call him. If you can stop the dog, Mr Bennett, I'll guarantee to make William Adolphus listen to reason, but there's no use trying to argue with a lightning flash.'

Alexander Abraham made a frantic lunge at the brindled streak as it whirled past him, with the result that he overbalanced himself and went sprawling on the floor with a crash. I ran to help him up, which only seemed to enrage him further.

'Woman,' he spluttered viciously, 'I wish you and your fiend of a cat were in—in—'

'In Avonlea,' I finished quickly, to save Alexander Abraham from committing profanity. 'So do I, Mr Bennett, with all my heart. But since we are not, let us make the best of it like sensible people. And in future you will kindly remember that my name is Miss MacPherson, *not* Woman!'

With this the end came and I was thankful, for the noise those two animals made was so terrific that I expected the policeman would be rushing in, smallpox or no smallpox, to see if Alexander Abraham and I were trying to murder each other. Mr Riley suddenly veered in his mad career and bolted into a dark corner between the stove and the wood-box. William Adolphus let go just in time.

There never was any more trouble with Mr Riley after that. A meeker, more thoroughly chastened dog you could not find. William Adolphus had the best of it and he kept it.

Seeing that things had calmed down and that it was five o'clock I decided to get tea. I told Alexander Abraham that I would prepare it, if he would show me where the eatables were.

'You needn't mind,' said Alexander Abraham. 'I've been in the habit of getting my own tea for twenty years.'

'I daresay. But you haven't been in the habit of getting mine,' I said firmly. 'I wouldn't eat anything you cooked if I starved to death. If you want some occupation you'd better get some salve and anoint the scratches on that poor dog's back.'

Alexander Abraham said something that I prudently did not hear. Seeing that he had no information to hand out I went on an exploring expedition into the pantry. The place was awful beyond description, and for the first time a vague sentiment of pity for Alexander Abraham glimmered in my breast. When a man had to live in such surroundings the wonder was, not that he hated women, but that he didn't hate the whole human race.

But I got up a supper somehow. I am noted for getting up suppers. The bread was from the Carmody bakery and I made good tea and excellent toast; besides, I found a can of peaches in the pantry which, as they were bought, I wasn't afraid to eat.

That tea and toast mellowed Alexander Abraham in spite of himself. He ate the last crust, and didn't growl when I gave William Adolphus all the cream that was left. Mr Riley did not seem to want anything. He had no appetite.

By this time the doctor's boy had arrived with my valise. Alexander

Abraham gave me quite civilly to understand that there was a spare room across the hall and that I might take possession of it. I went to it and put on a wrapper. There was a set of fine furniture in the room, and a comfortable bed. But the dust! William Adolphus had followed me in and his paws left marks everywhere he walked.

'Now,' I said briskly, returning to the kitchen, 'I'm going to clean up and I shall begin with this kitchen. You'd better betake yourself to the sitting-room, Mr Bennett, so as to be out of the way.'

Alexander Abraham glared at me.

'I'm not going to have my house meddled with,' he snapped. 'It suits me. If you don't like it you can leave it.'

'No, I can't. That is just the trouble,' I said pleasantly. 'If I could leave it I shouldn't be here for a minute. Since I can't, it simply has to be cleaned. I can tolerate men and dogs when I am compelled to, but I cannot and will not tolerate dirt and disorder. Go into the sitting-room.'

Alexander Abraham went. As he closed the door, I heard him say, in capitals, 'WHAT AN AWFUL WOMAN!'

I cleaned that kitchen and the pantry adjoining. It was ten o'clock when I got through, and Alexander Abraham had gone to bed without deigning further speech. I locked Mr Riley in one room and William Adolphus in another and went to bed, too. I had never felt so dead tired in my life before. It had been a hard day.

But I got up bright and early the next morning and got a tiptop breakfast, which Alexander Abraham condescended to eat. When the provision man came into the yard I called to him from the window to bring me a box of soap in the afternoon, and then I tackled the sitting-room.

It took me the best part of a week to get that house in order, but I did it thoroughly. I am noted for doing things thoroughly. At the end of the time it was clean from garret to cellar. Alexander Abraham made no comments on my operations, though he groaned loud and often, and said caustic things to poor Mr Riley, who hadn't the spirit to answer back after his drubbing by William Adolphus. I made allowances for Alexander Abraham because his vaccination had taken and his arm was real sore; and I cooked elegant meals, not having much else to do, once I had got things scoured up. The house was full of provisions—Alexander Abraham wasn't mean about such things, I will say that for him. Altogether, I was more comfortable than I had expected to be. When Alexander Abraham wouldn't talk I let him alone; and when he would I just said as sarcastic things as he did, only I said them smiling and pleasant. I could see he had a wholesome awe of me. But now and then he seemed to forget his disposition and talked like a human being. We had one or two real interesting conversations. Alexander Abraham was an intelligent man, though he had got terribly warped. I told him once I thought he must have been nice when he was a boy.

One day he astonished me by appearing at the dinner table with his hair brushed and a white collar on. We had a tiptop dinner that day, and I had made a pudding that was far too good for a woman hater. When Alexander Abraham had disposed of two large platefuls of it, he sighed and said,

'You can certainly cook. It's a pity you are such a detestable crank in other respects.'

'It's kind of convenient being a crank,' I said. 'People are careful how they meddle with you. Haven't you found that out in your own experience?'

'I am *not* a crank,' growled Alexander Abraham resentfully. 'All I ask is to be let alone.'

'That's the very crankiest kind of a crank,' I said. 'A person who wants to be let alone flies in the face of Providence, who decreed that folks for their own good were not to be let alone. But cheer up, Mr Bennett. The quarantine will be up on Tuesday and then you'll certainly be let alone for the rest of your natural life, as far as William Adolphus and I are concerned. You may then return to your wallowing in the mire and be as dirty and comfortable as of yore.'

Alexander Abraham growled again. The prospect didn't seem to cheer him up as much as I should have expected. Then he did an amazing thing. He poured some cream into a saucer and set it down before William Adolphus. William Adolphus lapped it up, keeping one eye on Alexander Abraham lest the latter should change his mind. Not to be outdone, I handed Mr Riley a bone.

Neither Alexander Abraham nor I had worried much about the smallpox. We didn't believe he would take it, for he hadn't even seen the girl who was sick. But the very next morning I heard him calling me from the upstairs landing.

'Miss MacPherson,' he said in a voice so uncommonly mild that it gave me an uncanny feeling, 'what are the symptoms of smallpox?'

'Chills and flushes, pain in the limbs and back, nausea and vomiting,' I answered promptly, for I had been reading them up in a patent medicine almanac.

'I've got them all,' said Alexander Abraham hollowly.

I didn't feel as much scared as I should have expected. After enduring a woman hater and a brindled dog and the early disorder of that house—and coming off best with all three—smallpox seemed rather insignificant. I went to the window and called to Thomas Wright to send for the doctor.

The doctor came down from Alexander Abraham's room looking grave.

'It's impossible to pronounce on the disease yet,' he said. 'There is no certainty until the eruption appears. But, of course, there is every likelihood that it is the smallpox. It is very unfortunate. I am afraid that it will be difficult to get a nurse. All the nurses in town who will take smallpox cases are overbusy now, for the epidemic is still raging there. However, I'll go into town to-night and do my best. Meanwhile, as Mr Bennett does not require any attendance at present, you must not go near him, Peter.'

I wasn't going to take orders from any man, and as soon as the doctor had gone I marched straight up to Alexander Abraham's room with some dinner for him on a tray. There was a lemon cream I thought he could eat even if he had the smallpox.

'You shouldn't come near me,' he growled. 'You are risking your life.'

'I am not going to see a fellow creature starve to death, even if he is a man,' I retorted.

'The worst of it all,' groaned Alexander Abraham, between mouthfuls of lemon cream, 'is that the doctor says I've got to have a nurse. I've got so kind of used to you being in the house that I don't mind you, but the thought of another woman coming here is too much. Did you give my poor dog anything to eat?'

'He has had a better dinner than many a Christian,' I said severely.

Alexander Abraham need not have worried about another woman coming in. The doctor came back that night with care on his brow.

'I don't know what is to be done,' he said. 'I can't get a soul to come here.'

'*I* shall nurse Mr Bennett,' I said with dignity. 'It is my duty and I never shirk my duty. I am noted for that. He is a man, and he has smallpox, and he keeps a vile dog; but I am not going to see him die for lack of care for all that.'

'You're a good soul, Peter,' said the doctor, looking relieved, manlike, as soon as he found a woman to shoulder the responsibility.

I nursed Alexander Abraham through the smallpox, and I didn't mind it much. He was much more amiable sick than well, and he had the disease in a very mild form. Below stairs I reigned supreme and Mr Riley and William Adolphus lay down together like the lion and the lamb. I fed Mr Riley regularly, and once, seeing him looking lonesome, I patted him gingerly. It was nicer than I thought it would be. Mr Riley lifted his head and looked at me with an expression in his eyes which cured me of wondering why on earth Alexander Abraham was so fond of the beast.

When Alexander Abraham was able to sit up he began to make up for the time he'd lost being pleasant. Anything more sarcastic than that man in his convalescence you couldn't imagine. I just laughed at him, having found out that that could be depended on to irritate him. To irritate him still further I cleaned the house all over again. But what vexed him most of all was that Mr Riley took to following me about and wagging what he had of a tail at me.

'It wasn't enough that you should come into my peaceful home and turn it upside down, but you have to alienate the affections of my dog,' complained Alexander Abraham.

'He'll get fond of you again when I go home,' I said comfortingly. 'Dogs aren't very particular that way. What they want is bones. Cats now, they love disinterestedly. William Adolphus has never swerved in his allegiance to me, although you do give him cream in the pantry on the sly.'

Alexander Abraham looked foolish. He hadn't thought I knew that.

I didn't take the smallpox and in another week the doctor came out and sent the policeman home. I was disinfected and William Adolphus was fumigated, and then we were free to go.

'Good-bye, Mr Bennett,' I said, offering to shake hands in a forgiving spirit. 'I've no doubt that you are glad to be rid of me, but you are no gladder than I am to go. I suppose this house will be dirtier than ever in a month's time, and Mr Riley will have discarded the little polish his manners have taken on. Reformation with men and dogs never goes very deep.'

With this Parthian shaft I walked out of the house, supposing that I had seen the last of it and Alexander Abraham.

I was glad to get back home, of course; but it did seem queer and lonesome. The cats hardly knew me, and William Adolphus roamed about forlornly and appeared to feel like an exile. I didn't take as much pleasure in cooking as usual, for it seemed kind of foolish to be fussing over oneself. The sight of a bone made me think of poor Mr Riley. The neighbours avoided me pointedly, for they couldn't get rid of the fear that I might erupt into smallpox at any moment. My Sunday School class had been given to another woman, and altogether I felt as if I didn't belong anywhere.

I had existed like this for a fortnight when Alexander Abraham suddenly appeared. He walked in one evening at dusk, but at first sight I didn't know him he was so spruced and barbered up. But William Adolphus knew him. Will you believe it, William Adolphus, my own William Adolphus, rubbed up against that man's trouser leg with an undisguised purr of satisfaction.

'I had to come, Angelina,' said Alexander Abraham. 'I couldn't stand it any longer.'

'My name is Peter,' I said coldly, although I was feeling ridiculously glad about something.

'It isn't,' said Alexander Abraham stubbornly. 'It is Angelina for me, and always will be. I shall never call you Peter. Angelina just suits you exactly; and Angelina Bennett would suit you still better. You must come back, Angelina. Mr Riley is moping for you, and I can't get along without somebody to appreciate my sarcasms, now that you have accustomed me to the luxury.'

'What about the other five cats?' I demanded.

Alexander Abraham sighed.

'I suppose they'll have to come too,' he sighed, 'though no doubt they'll chase poor Mr Riley clean off the premises. But I can live without him, and I can't without you. How soon can you be ready to marry me?'

'I haven't said that I was going to marry you at all, have I?' I said tartly, just to be consistent. For I wasn't feeling tart.

'No, but you will, won't you?' said Alexander Abraham anxiously. 'Because if you won't, I wish you'd let me die of the smallpox. Do, dear Angelina.'

To think that a man should dare to call me his 'dear Angelina!' And to think that I shouldn't mind!

'Where I go, William Adolphus goes,' I said, 'but I shall give away the other five cats for—for the sake of Mr Riley.'

☙

WE HAVE TO SIT OPPOSITE

Even in the confusion of entering the carriage at Salzburg, Mrs Montrose and her cousin Mrs Forrester noticed the man with the blue tooth. He occupied a corner beside the window. His wife sat next to him. Next to her sat their daughter of perhaps seventeen. People poured into the train. A look passed between Mrs Montrose and Mrs Forrester. The look said, 'These people seem to have filled up the carriage pretty well, but we'd better take these seats while we can as the train is so full. At least we can have seats together.' The porter, in his porter's tyrannical way, piled their suitcases onto the empty rack above the heads of the man with the blue tooth, and his wife, and his daughter, and departed. The opposite rack was full of baskets, bags and miscellaneous parcels. The train started. Here they were. Mrs Montrose and Mrs Forrester smiled at each other as they settled down below the rack which was filled with miscellaneous articles. Clinging vines that they were, they felt adventurous and successful. They had travelled alone from Vienna to Salzburg, leaving in Vienna their doctor husbands to continue attending the clinics of Dr Bauer and Dr Hirsch. And now, after a week in Salzburg, they were happily on their way to rejoin their husbands, who had flown to Munich.

Both Mrs Montrose and Mrs Forrester were tall, slight and fair. They were dressed with dark elegance. They knew that their small hats were smart, suitable and becoming, and they rejoiced in the simplicity and distinction of their new costumes. The selection of these and other costumes, and of these and other hats in Vienna had, they regretted, taken from the study of art, music, and history a great deal of valuable time. Mrs Montrose and Mrs Forrester were sincerely fond of art, music, and history and longed almost passionately to spend their days in the Albertina Gallery and the Kunsthistorische Museum. But the modest shops and shop windows of the craftsmen of Vienna had rather diverted the two young women from the study of art and history, and it was easy to lay the blame for this on the museums and art galleries which, in truth, closed their doors at very odd times. After each day's enchanting pursuits and disappointments, Mrs Montrose and Mrs Forrester hastened in a fatigued state to the café where they had arranged to meet their husbands who by this time had finished their daily sessions with Dr Bauer and Dr Hirsch.

This was perhaps the best part of the day, to sit together happily in the sunshine, toying with the good Viennese coffee or a glass of wine, gazing and being gazed upon, and giving up their senses to the music that flowed under the chestnut trees. (Ah Vienna, they thought, Vienna, Vienna.)

No, perhaps the evenings had been the best time when after their frugal pension dinner they hastened out to hear opera or symphony or wild atavistic gypsy music. All was past now. They had been very happy. They were fortunate. Were they too fortunate?

Mrs Montrose and Mrs Forrester were in benevolent good spirits as they looked round the railway carriage and prepared to take their seats and settle down for the journey to Munich to meet their husbands. In their window corner, opposite the man with the blue tooth, was a large hamper. '*Do* you mind?' asked Mrs Montrose, smiling sweetly at the man, his wife, and his daughter. She prepared to lift the hamper on which the charming view from the carriage window was of course wasted, intending to move it along the seat, and take its place. The man, his wife, and his daughter had never taken their eyes off Mrs Montrose and Mrs Forrester since they had entered the carriage.

'*If* you please,' said the man loudly and slowly in German English, '*if* you please, that place belongs to my wife or to my daughter. For the moment they sit beside me, but I keep that place for my wife or my daughter. That seat is therefore reserved. It is our seat. You may of course use the two remaining seats.'

'I'm sorry,' said Mrs Montrose, feeling snubbed, and she and Mrs Forrester sat down side by side on the two remaining seats opposite the German family. Beside them the hamper looked out of the window at the charming view. Their gaiety and self-esteem evaporated. The train rocked along.

The three continued to stare at the two young women. Suddenly the mother leaned toward her daughter. She put up her hand to her mouth and whispered behind her hand, her eyes remaining fixed on Mrs Montrose. The daughter nodded. She also stared at Mrs Montrose. Mrs Montrose flushed. The mother sat upright again, still looking at Mrs Montrose, who felt very uncomfortable, and very much annoyed at blushing.

The man ceased staring at the two young women. He looked up at the rack above him, which contained their suitcases.

'Those are your suitcases,' he asked, or rather announced.

'Yes,' said Mrs Montrose and Mrs Forrester without smiles.

'They are large,' said the man in a didactic manner, 'they are too large. They are too large to be put on racks. A little motion, a very little motion, and they might fall. If they fall they will injure myself, my wife, or my daughter. It is better,' he continued instructively, 'that if they fall, they should fall upon your heads, not upon our heads. That is logical. They are not my suitcases. They are your suitcases. You admit it. Please to move your suitcases to the opposite rack, where, if they fall, they will fall upon your own heads.' And he continued to sit there motionless. So did his wife. So did his daughter.

Mrs Montrose and Mrs Forrester looked at the suitcases in dismay. 'Oh,' said Mrs Forrester, 'they are so heavy to move. If you feel like that, please won't you sit on this side of the carriage, and we will move across, under our own suitcases, though I can assure you they will not fall. Or perhaps you would help us?'

'We prefer this side of the carriage,' said the man with the blue tooth. 'We have sat here because we prefer this side of the carriage. It is logical that you should move your suitcases. It is not logical that my wife, my daughter, and I should give up our seats in this carriage, or remove your suitcases.'

Mrs Montrose and Mrs Forrester looked at each other with rage in their hearts. All their self-satisfaction was gone. They got up and tugged and tugged as the train rocked along. They leaned resentfully across the erectly sitting man, and his wife and his daughter. They experienced with exasperation the realization that they had better make the best of it. The train, they knew, was crowded. They had to remain in this carriage with this disagreeable family. With much pulling and straining they hauled down the heavy suitcases. Violently they removed the parcels of the German family and lifted their own suitcases onto the rack above their heads, disposing them clumsily on the rack. Panting a little (they disliked panting), they settled down again side by side with high colour and loosened wisps of hair. They controlled their features so as to appear serene and unaware of the existence of anyone else in the railway carriage, but their hearts were full of black hate.

The family exchanged whispered remarks, and then resumed their scrutiny of the two young women, whose elegance had by this time a sort of tipsy quality. The girl leaned toward her mother. She whispered behind her hand to her mother, who nodded. Both of them stared at Mrs Forrester. Then they laughed.

'Heavens!' thought the affronted Mrs Forrester, 'this is outrageous! Why can't Alice and I whisper behind our hands to each other about these people and make them feel simply awful! But they wouldn't feel awful. Well, we can't, just because we've been properly brought up, and it would be too childish. And perhaps they don't even know they're rude. They're just being natural.' She breathed hard in frustration, and composed herself again.

Suddenly the man with the blue tooth spoke. 'Are you English?' he said loudly.

'Yes—well—no,' said Mrs Forrester.

'No—well—yes,' said Mrs Montrose, simultaneously.

A derisive look came over the man's face. 'You must know what you are,' he said, 'either you are English or you are not English. Are you, or are you not?'

'No,' said Mrs Montrose and Mrs Forrester, speaking primly. Their chins were high, their eyes flashed, and they were ready for discreet battle.

'Then are you Americans?' said the man in the same bullying manner.

'No,' said Mrs Montrose and Mrs Forrester.

'You can't deceive *me*, you know,' said the man with the blue tooth, 'I know well the English language. You *say* you are not English. You *say* you are not American. What, then, may I ask, are you? You must be something.'

'We are Canadians,' said Mrs Forrester, furious at this catechism.

'*Canadians*,' said the man.

'Yes, Canadians,' said Mrs Montrose.

'This,' murmured Mrs Forrester to Mrs Montrose, 'is more than I can bear!'

'What did you say?' said the man, leaning forward quickly, his hands on his knees.

'I spoke to my friend,' said Mrs Forrester coldly, 'I spoke about my bear.'

'Yes,' said Mrs Montrose, 'she spoke about her bear.'

'Your bear? Have you a bear? But you cannot have a bear!' said the man with some surprise.

'In Canada I have a bear. I have two bears,' said Mrs Forrester conceitedly.

'That is true,' said Mrs Montrose nodding, 'she has two bears. I myself have five bears. My father has seven bears. That is nothing. It is the custom.'

'What do you do with your bears?' asked the man.

'We eat them,' said Mrs Forrester.

'Yes,' said Mrs Montrose, 'we eat them. It is the custom.'

The man turned and spoke briefly to his wife and daughter, whose eyes opened wider than ever.

Mrs Montrose and Mrs Forrester felt pleased. This was better.

The man with the blue tooth became really interested. 'Are you married?' he asked Mrs Forrester.

'Yes,' she replied. (We'll see what he'll say next, then we'll see what we can do.)

'And you?' he enquired of Mrs Montrose. Mrs Montrose seemed uncertain. 'Well, yes, in a way, I suppose,' she said.

The man with the blue tooth scrutinized Mrs Montrose for a moment.

'*Then*,' he said, as though he had at last found her out, 'if you are married, where is your husband?'

Mrs Montrose took out her pocket handkerchief. She buried her face in her hands, covering her eyes with her handkerchief. Evidently she sobbed.

'Now you see what you've done!' said Mrs Forrester. 'You shouldn't ask questions like that. Just look at what you've done.'

The three gazed fascinated on Mrs Montrose. 'Is he dead or what is he?' asked the man of Mrs Forrester, making the words almost quietly with his mouth.

'Sh!!' said Mrs Forrester very loudly indeed. The three jumped a little. So did Mrs Montrose.

There was silence while Mrs Montrose wiped her eyes. She looked over the heads opposite. The wife leaned toward her husband and addressed him timidly behind her hand. He nodded, and spoke to Mrs Forrester.

'Well,' he said, 'at least you admit that *you* have a husband. If you have a husband then, where is he?'

'Oh, I don't know,' said Mrs Forrester lightly.

'No, she doesn't know,' said Mrs Montrose.

The three on the opposite seat went into a conference. Mrs Montrose and Mrs Forrester did not dare to look at each other. They were enjoying themselves. Their self-esteem had returned. They had impressed. Unfavourably, it is true. But still they had impressed.

The man with the blue tooth pulled himself together. He reasserted himself. Across his waistcoat hung a watch chain. He took his watch out of his pocket and looked at the time. Then to the surprise of Mrs Montrose and Mrs Forrester he took another watch out of the pocket at the other end of the chain. 'You see,' he said proudly, 'I have two watches.'

Mrs Montrose and Mrs Forrester were surprised, but they had themselves well in hand.

Mrs Montrose looked at the watches disparagingly. 'My husband has six watches,' she said.

'Yes, that is true,' nodded Mrs Forrester, 'her husband *has* got six watches, but my husband, like you, unfortunately has only two watches.'

The man put his watches back. Decidedly the battle was going in favour of the two young women. How horrid of us, he was so pleased with his watches, thought Mrs Montrose. Isn't it true that horridness just breeds horridness. We're getting horrider every minute. She regarded the man, his wife and his daughter with distaste but with pity.

'You *say*,' said the man, who always spoke as though their statements were open to doubt, which of course they were, 'that you come from Canada. Do you come from Winnipeg? I know about Winnipeg.'

'No,' said Mrs Montrose, and she spoke this time quite truthfully. 'I come from Vancouver.' Mrs Forrester remained silent.

'And you, where do you come from?' persisted the man in a hectoring tone, addressing Mrs Forrester. Mrs Forrester remained silent, she had almost decided to answer no more questions.

'Oh, do not tell, please do not tell,' begged Mrs Montrose in an anguished way.

'No,' said Mrs Forrester importantly, 'I shall not tell. Rest assured. I shall not tell.'

'Why will she not tell?' demanded the man. He was tortured by curiosity. So was his wife. So was his daughter.

'Sh!!' said Mrs Montrose very loudly.

The man seemed ill at ease. By this time nothing existed in the world for him, or for his wife, or for his daughter but these two Canadian women who ate bears.

'How is it,' asked the man, 'that you no longer buy my trousers?'

'I beg your pardon?' faltered Mrs Montrose. For a moment she lost ground.

'I said,' replied the man, 'why is it that you no longer buy my trousers?'

The ladies did not answer. They could not think of a good answer to that one.

'I,' said the man, 'am a manufacturer of trousers. I make the most beautiful trousers in Germany. Indeed in the world.' (You do not so, thought Mrs Forrester, picturing her husband's good London legs.) 'For three years I receive orders from Winnipeg for my trousers. And now, since two years, yes, since 1929, I receive no more orders for my trousers. Why is that?' he asked, like a belligerent.

'Shall we tell him?' asked Mrs Forrester, looking at Mrs Montrose. Neither of them knew why he had received no more orders for his trousers, but they did not wish to say so. 'Shall we tell him?' asked Mrs Forrester.

'You tell him,' said Mrs Montrose.

'No, *you* tell him,' said Mrs Forrester.

'I do not like to tell him,' said Mrs Montrose, 'I'd rather you told him.' The man with the blue tooth looked from one to the other.

'Very well. I shall tell him,' said Mrs Forrester. 'The fact is,' she said, looking downward, 'that in Canada men no longer wear trousers.'

'What are you saying? That is not true, never can that be true!' said the man in some confusion.

'Yes,' said Mrs Montrose, corroborating sombrely. 'Yes, indeed it is true. When they go abroad they wear trousers, but in Canada, no. It is a new custom.'

'It is the climate,' said Mrs Forrester.

'Yes, that is the reason, it is the climate,' agreed Mrs Montrose.

'But in Canada,' argued the man with the blue tooth, 'your climate is cold. Everyone knows your climate is cold.'

'In the Arctic regions, yes, it is really intensely cold, we all find it so. But not in Winnipeg. Winnipeg is very salubrious.' (That's a good one, thought Mrs Montrose.)

The man turned and spoke rapidly to his wife. She also turned, and looked askance at her daughter. The expressions of the man, his wife, and his daughter were a blend of pleasure and shock. The two liars were delighted.

At last the man could not help asking, 'But they *must* wear something! It is not logical.'

'Oh, it's logical, all right!' said Mrs Forrester.

'But what *do* they wear?' persisted the man.

'I never looked to see,' said Mrs Montrose. '*I* did, I looked,' said Mrs Forrester.

'Well?' asked the man.

'Oh, they just wear kilts,' said Mrs Forrester.

'Kilts? What are kilts? I do not know kilts,' said the man.

'I would rather not tell you,' said Mrs Forrester primly.

'Oh,' said the man.

Mrs Montrose took out her vanity case, and inspected herself, powder puff in hand.

'I do not allow my wife and daughter to paint their faces so,' said the man with the blue tooth.

'No?' said Mrs Montrose.

'It is not good that women should paint their faces so. Good women do not do that. It is a pity.'

(Oh, Alice, thought Mrs Forrester in a fury, he shall not dare!) 'It is a pity,' she hissed, 'that in your country there are no good dentists!'

'Be careful, be careful,' whispered Mrs Montrose.

'What do you mean?' demanded the man with the blue tooth.

(She will go too far, I know she will, thought Mrs Montrose, alarmed, putting out her hand.)

'In our country,' said the rash Mrs Forrester, 'anyone needing attention is taken straight to the State Dentist by the Police. This is done for aesthetic reasons. It is logical.'

'I am going to sleep,' said Mrs Montrose very loudly, and she shut her eyes tight.

'So am I,' said Mrs Forrester, in a great hurry, and she shut her eyes too. This had been hard work but good fun for Mrs Montrose and Mrs

Forrester. They felt, though, that they had gone a little bit too far. It might be as well if they slept, or pretended to sleep, until they reached Munich. They felt that outside their closed eyes was something frightening. The voice of the man with the blue tooth was saying, 'I wish to tell you, I wish to tell you . . .' but Mrs Montrose was in a deep sleep, and so was Mrs Forrester. They sat with their eyes tightly closed, beside the hamper which still occupied the seat with the view by the darkening window. Mrs Montrose had the inside corner, and so by reason of nestling down in the corner, and by reason of having an even and sensible temperament, she really and truly fell asleep at last.

Not so Mrs Forrester. Her eyes were tightly closed, but her mind was greatly disturbed. Why had they permitted themselves to be baited? She pondered on the collective mentality that occupied the seat near to them (knees almost touching), and its results which now filled the atmosphere of the carriage so unpleasantly. She had met this mentality before, but had not been closely confined with it, as now. What of a world in which this mentality might ever become dominant? Then one would be confined with it without appeal or relief. The thought was shocking. She felt unreasonably agitated. She felt rather a fool, too, with her eyes shut tightly. But, if she opened them, she would have to look somewhere, presumably at the family, so it seemed safer to keep them closed. The train sped on. After what seemed to her a very long time, she peeped. The wife and daughter were busy. The husband sat back, hands on knees, chin raised, expectant, eyes closed. His wife respectfully undid his tie, his collar, and his top shirt button. By this time the daughter had opened the hamper, and had taken from it a bottle and a clean napkin. These she handed to her mother. The wife moistened the napkin from the bottle and proceeded to wash her husband, his face, his ears, round the back of his neck, and inside his shirt collar, with great care. 'Like a cat,' thought Mrs Forrester, who had forgotten to shut her eyes.

The man with the blue tooth lowered his raised chin and caught her. 'You see,' he said loudly, 'you see, wives should look properly after their husbands, instead of travelling alone and . . .' But Mrs Forrester was fast asleep again. The whole absurd encounter had begun to hold an element of terror. They had been tempted into folly. She knew—as she screwed up her closed eyes—that they were implicated in fear and folly.

The two young women took care to sleep until the train reached Munich. Then they both woke up.

Many people slept until they reached Munich. Then they all began to wake up.

๛

ANTIGONE

My father ruled a kingdom on the right bank of the river. He ruled it with a firm hand and a stout heart though he was often more troubled than Moses, who was simply trying to bring a stubborn and moody people under God's yoke. My father ruled men who thought they were gods or the instruments of gods or, at very least, god-afflicted and god-pursued. He ruled Atlas who held up the sky, and Hermes who went on endless messages, and Helen who'd been hatched from an egg, and Pan the gardener, and Kallisto the bear, and too many others to mention by name. Yet my father had no thunderbolt, no trident, no helmet of darkness. His subjects were delivered bound into his hands. He merely watched over them as the hundred-handed ones watched over the dethroned Titans so that they wouldn't bother Hellas again.

Despite the care which my father took to maintain an atmosphere of sober common sense in his whole establishment, there were occasional outbursts of self-indulgence which he could not control. For instance, I have seen Helen walking naked down the narrow cement path under the chestnut trees for no better reason, I suppose, than that the day was hot and the white flowers themselves lay naked and expectant in the sunlight. And I have seen Atlas forget the sky while he sat eating the dirt which held him up. These were things which I was not supposed to see.

If my father had been as sensible through and through as he was thought to be, he would have packed me off to boarding school when I was old enough to be disciplined by men. Instead he kept me at home with my two cousins who, except for the accident of birth, might as well have been my sisters. Today I imagine people concerned with our welfare would take such an environment into account. At the time I speak of most people thought us fortunate—especially the girls whose father's affairs had come to an unhappy issue. I don't like to revive old scandal and I wouldn't except to deny it; but it takes only a few impertinent newcomers in any community to force open cupboards which have been decently sealed by time. However, my father was so busy setting his kingdom to rights that he let weeds grow up in his own garden.

As I said, if my father had had all his wits about him he would have sent me to boarding school—and Antigone and Ismene too. I might have fallen in love with the headmaster's daughter and Antigone might have learned that no human being can be right always. She might have found out besides that from the seeds of eternal justice grow madder flowers than any which Pan grew in the gardens of my father's kingdom.

Between the kingdom which my father ruled and the wilderness flows a river. It is this river which I am crossing now. Antigone is with me.

How often can we cross the same river, Antigone asks.

Her persistence annoys me. Besides, Heraklitos made nonsense of her question years ago. He saw a river too—the Inachos, the Kephissos, the Lethaios. The name doesn't matter. He said: See how quickly the water flows. However agile a man is, however nimbly he swims, or runs, or flies, the water slips away before him. See, even as he sets down his foot the water is displaced by the stream which crowds along in the shadow of its flight.

But after all, Antigone says, one must admit that it is the same kind of water. The oolichans run in it as they ran last year and the year before. The gulls cry above the same bank. Boats drift towards the Delta and circle back against the current to gather up the catch.

At any rate, I tell her, we're standing on a new bridge. We are standing so high that the smell of mud and river weeds passes under us out to the straits. The unbroken curve of the bridge protects the eye from details of river life. The bridge is foolproof as a clinic's passport to happiness.

The old bridge still spans the river, but the cat-walk with its cracks and knot-holes, with its gap between planking and handrail has been torn down. The centre arch still grinds open to let boats up and down the river, but a child can no longer be walked on it or swung out on it beyond the water-gauge at the very centre of the flood.

I've known men who scorned any kind of bridge, Antigone says. Men have walked into the water, she says, or, impatient, have jumped from the bridge into the river below.

But these, I say, didn't really want to cross the river. They went Persephone's way, cradled in the current's arms, down the long halls under the pink feet of the gulls, under the booms and towlines, under the soft bellies of the fish.

Antigone looks at me.

There's no coming back, she says, if one goes far enough.

I know she's going to speak of her own misery and I won't listen. Only a god has the right to say: Look what I suffer. Only a god should say: What more ought I to have done for you that I have not done?

Once in winter, she says, a man walked over the river.

Taking advantage of nature, I remind her, since the river had never frozen before.

Yet he escaped from the penitentiary, she says. He escaped from the guards walking round the walls or standing with their guns in the sentry-boxes at the four corners of the enclosure. He escaped.

Not without risk, I say. He had to test the strength of the ice himself. Yet safer perhaps than if he had crossed by the old bridge where he might have slipped through a knot-hole or tumbled out through the railing.

He did escape, she persists, and lived forever on the far side of the river in the Alaska tea and bulrushes. For where, she asks, can a man go farther than to the outermost edge of the world?

The habitable world, as I've said, is on the right bank of the river. Here is the market with its market stalls—the coops of hens, the long-tongued geese, the haltered calf, the bearded goat, the shoving pigs, and the empty bodies of cows and sheep and rabbits hanging on iron hooks. My father's kingdom provides asylum in the suburbs. Near it are the convent, the churches, and the penitentiary. Above these on the hill the cemetery looks down on the people and on the river itself.

It is a world spread flat, tipped up into the sky so that men and women bend forward, walking as men walk when they board a ship at high tide. This is the world I feel with my feet. It is the world I see with my eyes.

I remember standing once with Antigone and Ismene in the square just outside the gates of my father's kingdom. Here from a bust set high on a cairn the stone eyes of Simon Fraser look from his stone face over the river that he found.

It is the head that counts, Ismene said.

It's no better than an urn, Antigone said, one of the urns we see when we climb to the cemetery above.

And all I could think was that I didn't want an urn, only a flat green grave with a chain about it.

A chain won't keep out the dogs, Antigone said.

But his soul could swing on it, Ismene said, like a bird blown on a branch in the wind.

And I remember Antigone's saying: The cat drags its belly on the ground and the rat sharpens its tooth in the ivy.

I should have loved Ismene, but I didn't. It was Antigone I loved. I should have loved Ismene because, although she walked the flat world with us, she managed somehow to see it round.

The earth is an oblate spheroid, she'd say. And I knew that she saw it there before her comprehensible and whole like a tangerine spiked through and held in place while it rotated on the axis of one of Nurse's steel sock needles. The earth was a tangerine and she saw the skin peeled off and the world parcelled out into neat segments, each segment sweet and fragrant in its own skin.

It's the head that counts, she said.

In her own head she made diagrams to live by, cut and fashioned after the eternal patterns spied out by Plato as he rummaged about in the sewing basket of the gods.

I should have loved Ismene. She would live now in some pre-fabricated and perfect chrysolite by some paradigm which made love round and whole. She would simply live and leave destruction in the purgatorial ditches outside her own walled paradise.

Antigone is different. She sees the world flat as I do and feels it tip beneath her feet. She has walked in the market and seen the living animals penned and the dead hanging stiff on their hooks. Yet she defies what she sees with a defiance which is almost denial. Like Atlas she tries to keep the vaulted sky from crushing the flat earth. Like Hermes she brings a message that there is life if one can escape to it in the brush and bulrushes in some dim Hades beyond the river. It is defiance not belief and I tell her that this time we walk the bridge to a walled cave where we can deny death no longer.

Yet she asks her question still. And standing there I tell her that Heraklitos has made nonsense of her question. I should have loved Ismene for she would have taught me what Plato meant when he said in all earnest that the union of the soul with the body is in no way better than dissolution. I expect that she understood things which Antigone is too proud to see.

I turn away from her and flatten my elbows on the high wall of the bridge. I look back at my father's kingdom. I see the terraces rolling down from the red-brick buildings with their barred windows. I remember hands shaking the bars and hear fingers tearing up paper and stuffing it through the meshes. Diktynna, mother of nets and high leaping fear. O Artemis, mistress of wild beasts and wild men.

The inmates are beginning to come out on the screened verandas. They pace up and down in straight lines or stand silent like figures which appear at the same time each day from some depths inside a clock.

On the upper terrace Pan the gardener is shifting sprinklers with a hooked stick. His face is shadowed by the brim of his hat. He moves as economically as an animal between the beds of lobelia and geranium. It is high noon.

Antigone has cut out a piece of sod and has scooped out a grave. The body lies in a coffin in the shade of the magnolia tree. Antigone and I are standing. Ismene is sitting between two low angled branches of the monkey puzzle tree. Her lap is filled with daisies. She slits the stem of one daisy and pulls the stem of another through it. She is making a chain for her neck and a crown for her hair.

Antigone reaches for a branch of the magnolia. It is almost beyond her grip. The buds flame above her. She stands on a small fire of daisies which smoulder in the roots of the grass.

I see the magnolia buds. They brood above me, whiteness feathered on whiteness. I see Antigone's face turned to the light. I hear the living birds call to the sun. I speak private poetry to myself: Between four trumpeting angels at the four corners of the earth a bride stands before the altar in a gown as white as snow.

Yet I must have been speaking aloud because Antigone challenges me: You're mistaken. It's the winds the angels hold, the four winds of the earth. After the just are taken to paradise the winds will destroy the earth. It's a funeral, she says, not a wedding.

She looks towards the building.

Someone is coming down the path from the matron's house, she says.

I notice that she has pulled one of the magnolia blossoms from the branch. I take it from her. It is streaked with brown where her hands have bruised it. The sparrow which she has decided to bury lies on its back. Its feet are clenched tight against the feathers of its breast. I put the flower in the box with it.

Someone is coming down the path. She is wearing a blue cotton dress. Her cropped head is bent. She walks slowly carrying something in a napkin.

It's Kallisto the bear, I say. Let's hurry. What will my father say if he sees us talking to one of his patients?

If we live here with him, Antigone says, what can he expect? If he spends his life trying to tame people he can't complain if you behave as if they were tame. What would your father think, she says, if he saw us digging in the Institution lawn?

Pan comes closer. I glower at him. There's no use speaking to him. He's deaf and dumb.

Listen, I say to Antigone, my father's not unreasonable. Kallisto thinks she's a bear and he thinks he's a bear tamer, that's all. As for the lawn, I say quoting my father without conviction, a man must have order among his own if he is to keep order in the state.

Kallisto has come up to us. She is smiling and laughing to herself. She gives me her bundle.

Fish, she says.

I open the napkin.

Pink fish sandwiches, I say.

For the party, she says.

But it isn't a party, Antigone says. It's a funeral.

For the funeral breakfast, I say.

Ismene is twisting two chains of daisies into a rope. Pan has stopped pulling the sprinkler about. He is standing beside Ismene resting himself on his hooked stick. Kallisto squats down beside her. Ismene turns away, preoccupied, but she can't turn far because of Pan's legs.

> *Father said we never should*
> *Play with madmen in the wood.*

I look at Antigone.

It's my funeral, she says.

I go over to Ismene and gather up a handful of loose daisies from her lap. The sun reaches through the shadow of the magnolia tree.

It's my funeral, Antigone says. She moves possessively toward the body.

An ant is crawling into the bundle of sandwiches which I've put on the ground. A file of ants is marching on the sparrow's box.

I go over and drop daisies on the bird's stiff body. My voice speaks ritual words: Deliver me, O Lord, from everlasting death on this dreadful day. I tremble and am afraid.

The voice of a people comforts me. I look at Antigone. I look her in the eye.

It had better be a proper funeral then, I say.

Kallisto is crouched forward on her hands. Tears are running down her cheeks and she is licking them away with her tongue.

My voice rises again: I said in the midst of my days, I shall not see—

Antigone just stands there. She looks frightened, but her eyes defy me with their assertion.

It's my funeral, she says. It's my bird. I was the one who wanted to bury it.

She is looking for a reason. She will say something which sounds eternally right.

Things have to be buried, she says. They can't be left lying around anyhow for people to see.

Birds shouldn't die, I tell her. They have wings. Cats and rats haven't wings.

Stop crying, she says to Kallisto. It's only a bird.

It has a bride's flower in its hand, Kallisto says.

We shall rise again, I mutter, but we shall not all be changed.

Antigone does not seem to hear me.

Behold, I say in a voice she must hear, in a moment, in the twinkling of an eye, the trumpet shall sound.

Ismene turns to Kallisto and throws the daisy chain about her neck.

Shall a virgin forget her adorning or a bride the ornament of her breast?

Kallisto is lifting her arms towards the tree.

The bridegroom has come, she says, white as a fall of snow. He stands above me in a great ring of fire.

Antigone looks at me now.

Let's cover the bird up, she says. Your father will punish us all for making a disturbance.

He has on his garment, Kallisto says, and on his thigh is written King of Kings.

I look at the tree. If I could see with Kallisto's eyes I wouldn't be afraid of death, or punishment, or the penitentiary guards. I wouldn't be afraid of my father's belt or his honing strap or his bedroom slipper. I wouldn't be afraid of falling into the river through a knot-hole in the bridge.

But, as I look, I see the buds falling like burning lamps and I hear the sparrow twittering in its box: Woe, woe, woe because of the three trumpets which are yet to sound.

Kallisto is on her knees. She is growling like a bear. She lumbers over to the sandwiches and mauls them with her paw.

Ismene stands alone for Pan the gardener has gone.

Antigone is fitting a turf in place above the coffin. I go over and press the edge of the turf with my feet. Ismene has caught me by the hand.

Go away, Antigone says.

I see my father coming down the path. He has an attendant with him. In front of them walks Pan holding the sprinkler hook like a spear.

What are you doing here? my father asks.

Burying a bird, Antigone says.

Here? my father asks again.

Where else could I bury it? Antigone says.

My father looks at her.

This ground is public property, he says. No single person has any right to an inch of it.

I've taken six inches, Antigone says. Will you dig up the bird again?

Some of his subjects my father restrained since they were moved to throw themselves from high places or to tear one another to bits from jealousy or rage. Others who disturbed the public peace he taught to walk in the airing courts or to work in the kitchen or in the garden.

If men live at all, my father said, it is because discipline saves their life for them.

From Antigone he simply turned away.

HELEN WEINZWEIG

❧

CAUSATION

The woman hesitated at first to let him in. 'Piano tuner,' Gyorgi Szigeti said, then waited, leaning against the door frame. He waited for her to decide whether he was a musician and therefore eligible to come in the front door, or whether he was a tradesman to be directed to the rear entrance. What she could not have known was that Gyorgi had no intention of using the servants' entrance. He stood before her, proud in his black bowler hat, his long white silk scarf knotted loosely and flowing down over his shiny black leather jacket. 'Piano tuner,' he repeated to the woman, who had not moved. She was transfixed. 'Oh my God,' she said, 'not you, not you!' He did not question her words: by habit he took no notice of the eccentricities of the rich. Slowly, slowly, she widened the doorway.

No one ever had to show him where the piano was. He found it the way a dog searches out a bone. Traversing miles, it seemed, of Oriental carpets to reach the ebony grand piano at the other end of a vast room, he experienced a numbness, a detachment, as if asleep and dreaming: he had a sense of having once before covered the distance. And the short, sturdy woman in a flowered housecoat (he had noticed) who was following him— he knew her, too. But then, he knew a lot of women, some also short and sturdy, and maybe that's all it was: so many women.

'It's my own piano,' she was saying. Her heavy hand clumped across the keys. 'This B keeps getting out of tune,' striking the note five times to let him hear how bad it was.

Gyorgi Szigeti almost fell to his knees. He was in the presence of a Bechstein grand piano.

She was still talking. 'Everything you see in here, all the furniture in the house, was chosen by my ex-husband. He lets me keep my piano only because he is a music lover.'

Gyorgi removed his black leather jacket, draping it on the back of a gilded chair with curved legs. The bowler hat and silk scarf he arranged carefully on the seat. He ran his fingers over the piano keys. The sound was as brilliant as he remembered a Bechstein to be; the bass was resonant and the top notes vibrant. This was unexpected: in these wealthy homes the pianos were regarded as furniture and tuned only when an anticipated house guest was some sort of performer.

'I'm a singer. A concert artist. An opera star,' she announced. 'That is, I used to be an opera star.'

While Gyorgi worked, she sat on the piano bench, which he had moved aside. She hummed each note in unison with his repeated plunking as he tightened strings. She had perfect pitch. It spurred him on, this breathless attention of hers; then the two of them listening, listening together, both now intent on the climactic moments when he brought each white whole note and each black half note to perfection. He felt like the Creator of All Sound. When he tightened a string, he had a way of tightening his mouth, twisting the left corner upward into his cheek, which resulted in a threatening grimace. Once the ideal sound was achieved, his mouth loosened.

She rose to leave. 'Would you like some coffee?'

Gyorgi looks around, then re-enters the room in his mind, retraces his steps in imagination; but this time, instead of seeing her figure stride out the doorway, as it is doing at this very moment, he sees her laid out in a satin-lined coffin, in the same flowered housecoat; and instead of her sluttish make-up, the face in death is delicately tinted as if in the blush of youth. The mortician's skill has fixed the happiness he, Gyorgi, gave her. After the funeral he stays on in the old house, sleeping in one of the spare rooms, surprised at his delicacy, even in fantasy, in not using the bedroom where he had made her ecstatic. The letter from the lawyers comes, addressed to Gyorgi Szigeti, to this house. She has left him everything. Everything, including the beloved Bechstein, is his. Just in time, before her return interrupts his fateful vision, he recalls with a sudden clarity the source of his images: an account in this morning's newspaper: rich elderly widow . . . a young man of thirty-three . . . they married . . . she died . . . left him everything she owned . . . great wealth . . . her daughters suing . . . old mother was crazy . . . 'They're crazy,' the new heir had protested to the judge, 'she was more fascinating, more of a woman, than those two dried-up broads will ever be if they live to be a hundred.'

Over coffee, perhaps because he had already lived out the scene in his mind, Gyorgi leaned forward and said in a voice deep with sincerity:

'You are still a beautiful woman. You have so much to give . . .'

She eyed him silently. She was about fifty-five, but in her clear, light eyes, raised to meet his directly, age had been postponed. It was a matter of pride with him that in his persuasions Gyorgi rarely lied. In every woman he found qualities he could honestly admire. He went on, emboldened:

'Your eyes—they are the eyes of a girl.'

She denied nothing: that was all that mattered.

'These Bechsteins,' he ventured, 'do not take kindly to the extreme cold

and intense heat of our climate. The wood . . . changes of temperature . . .'
He brought out a small notebook from his back pocket. He could come
back next week. To see if the tuning held.

Uppermost in her mind is the fact that his wide, curved mouth is at odds
with his small, deep-set, dark eyes, suggesting to her an easygoing cruelty.

At his ring the following week she flung open the door. Her face was heavier
than before with rouge and lipstick, her brows blacker, her lids greener. Gyorgi
believed that if he ate enough of the stuff women put on their faces he would
get cancer. In such cases he would put his lips to the bare hollows of her throat.

Today she ignored his pretence of tuning the perfectly tuned instrument. She didn't listen; she chattered.

'Once I was Violetta with the San Francisco Opera Company. Oswald,
my former husband, loved *Traviata*. He loved me. He offered me the world
if I would give up the stage and sing for him alone: wealth, babies, a fire in
the hearth on Sunday nights. Oh, he knows his operas . . . I worked hard,
practised every day. In the evening, with the two babies asleep in the nursery, I sang for him. I dressed for the part. The costumes accumulated: Cio-
Cio San, Carmen, Tosca, Mignon.

'The idyll lasted almost five years. One morning I awoke to find him
standing at the foot of the bed. The room was still dark so that I could not
quite see his face, just the outline of his figure, fully dressed. He had been
waiting, I sensed, for me to awaken. I sat up and then he spoke, slowly and
distinctly:

' "You are not the great artist I thought you were. You cannot place your
voice, and when it comes out from behind your big nose, the glorious music
falls to the floor like a bag of cement. You are ridiculous in the clothes of
the great heroines: you have the passion of a disposable lighter. You have
deceived me." With that he left and never returned.'

'Did he leave you for another woman?' Gyorgi asked, for that is what
he knew of the way of the world.

'No, no, he wouldn't do that. He is a very respectable man.'

'Did he marry again?'

'Ha! The only woman he'd consider would have to be a virgin who
chose marriage to Oswald instead of entering a nunnery.' She gave him a
sly smile. 'You know what? I think Oswald was jealous of my music. When
I played the role of Mimi or Aïda or Desdemona, I became the woman I
was portraying. I didn't mean to, but I escaped him each time—*that's* what
he couldn't stand.'

Gyorgi tilted his head in a pretence of interest. He had no idea what she was talking about, but he realized that she was determined to reveal herself to him. It was as if women had to expose themselves—their defeats, their triumphs, their hopes and beliefs—before they undressed. In his opinion, a nude man in a raincoat was more honest. Gyorgi listened to women for their 'tone' quality, the same way he listened when he was tuning a piano. He noticed that her forehead glistened with perspiration.

'I can't pay you today,' she said. 'Oswald has gone to India to see his guru. He left me without a cent. Again.'

'It's all right,' he said gently, 'you can pay me any time.'

Even after she had paid him, Gyorgi took to dropping in, making his visits sporadic, so that they would seem compulsive, as if he couldn't resist seeing her. She was always unprepared, and would run to comb her hair and put on fresh lipstick. Once he stopped her, saying he liked her the way she was. Above all, he would want her to be perfectly natural with him. She was so moved by these sentiments, she wanted to do something for him in return.

'Would you like to hear Cio-Cio San's farewell aria? No? I see. But you obviously know everything about pianos.'

'I was an apprentice for five years in the Bechstein factory in Berlin.'

'What else can you do?'

'I can build a bomb shelter.'

'Good. Then you can take care of this house. What do you say—live here and look after things. Oh, you will go out to your work as you always have, but instead of a small room in a smelly boardinghouse—ah, I thought so!—you can stay here. Pick any of the five spare rooms. What do you say?'

Gyorgi couldn't speak. He put his hands on his lap lest she see how they shook. A mansion, a Bechstein—all within the space of a few weeks. He hung his head and assumed the obsequious manner of his youth.

Then he went through the house, taking the stairs two at a time. The rooms were full of the kind of masterpieces he had seen only behind thick silken cords in museums. Everything was old and massive or old and fragile; everything was forceful with value. She ran after him, unable to keep up, observing that he moved with an animal grace, as if he had lived all his life out of doors.

'I can't understand why a man would want to leave you. It's a wonderful house,' he said.

'Oswald doesn't care about material things—furniture, cars, clothes—he has no interest in them. He wants to touch the infinite, discover the ineffable; he is on a journey of the spirit, he is concerned only with his immortal soul.'

'So?' said Gyorgi. 'So?' he repeated. 'He has never had to work hard in order to eat.'

'You must know that I still love him.'

Suddenly she was crying, crying for no reason that he could see.

He waved an arm into the air, around and around. 'You have everything; you have it all!'

'Nothing! Nothing, I tell you. There is only the music, notes on a page, enduring, eternal, nothing else exists.' Then, in afterthought, her voice distant, she added, 'You are the exception.'

He chose the sixth bedroom. Hers. Awaiting her in the wide bed, he called out, 'And wash that damned crap off your face.'

When she came back into the room, she grasped the post at the foot of the huge bed, weaving slightly as if drunk, and intoned:

'I adore you, you are low-born, you have no character, you are inevitable. Ours will be an affair of terrible limits. Your insults are without principle. Whatever grief you will cause will come naturally and I shall recover as one does after slipping on ice. Most important, though, Oswald will no longer be able to draw blood with his blunt knives. I shall continue to go to him every week for money. But it will be for you. That will make it easy. No. More than that. I shall *enjoy* the humiliation. I will answer his interrogation: "Why is the butcher's bill so high?" "Because I have a tall, strong man to feed." I will sit in the leather chair in his office while he counts out the ten-dollar bills, slowly, sliding them halfway across the desk. I will lean forward and scoop them up and thank him. Oswald will unbutton his vest and look across at me like a judge with a three-time loser and condemn me, as he always does, with good advice. But I won't care. He has lost his power: tonight I hand it over to you.'

During the prolonged love-making that follows, she opens her eyes a few times. Once she sees his mouth tighten and a corner go up into his cheek into an ugly grimace.

Gyorgi moved in. It was then that he was faced with what he had missed that first time because his head had been bursting with the delirium of his good fortune. There was everywhere a fury of disorder, as if a bomb had gone off in each room separately. The halls had boxes and overshoes strewn about. There was dirt on every surface; old dust that had hardened; mouse droppings in the kitchen and cockroaches in the sinks. She shrugged off his dismay. 'Oswald won't pay for a cleaning woman.'

Gyorgi loved control and completeness. He set about to restore order, spending every weekend sweeping, scrubbing, repairing, room by room, starting with the bedroom. The kitchen alone took a month. The cellar, he figured, could occupy him as long as she lived.

There was no design to her life. Asleep when he left, off in a world of song when he got home; she could not remember what, if anything, she had accomplished, nor what had transpired during the day. 'Some phone calls. Nothing much. How was *your* day?' And showered him with kisses. One of the phone calls, he surmised, was for the frozen chicken pie and canned pea soup that he was eating for dinner. And he, who required a daily pattern to blanket his years, felt a chill of apprehension.

'Now, my handsome Magyar,' she crooned, 'I'll sing for you and you alone. I learned some Hungarian folk songs set by Kodály.'

'I told you a dozen times, I hate Hungarian anything. Maybe there's a soccer game on TV.'

'Don't you ever tire of watching grown men kick a ball?'

'You have the memory of an imbecile: I told you: I was a professional soccer player. I toured Germany.'

Each day Gyorgi went out on his calls. He had given up his black leather jacket and now wore a navy blue blazer with a crest embroidered in red and white on the upper left pocket. He refused to part with his bowler hat and long white scarf. He no longer said, 'Piano tuner' at the front door. Instead, he presented, wordlessly, his business card with his name and elegant new address and *Pianos Tuned to Perfection* embossed in shiny black script. As the days got shorter, he came home earlier and earlier. Some cold days he did not go out at all. He would float about the house, content to hammer, force windows open, stop taps from dripping. She would follow him around like the small daughter he once had. While he worked, she would sit on the floor, always in the flowered housecoat, telling him stories about people she knew.

'You're making it up,' he sometimes accused her. 'No, no,' she protested, 'that's what he really did.' Or, 'She was desperate. A woman in that state will say anything.' His disbelief at times bordered on wonder: did people of wealth and substance really carry on crazy like that? Keeping his eyes on his work, never turning his head, pretending a lofty indifference, he would probe with ruttish questions: what had taken place with her and Oswald in bed; what had she done with other men; how many lovers; in what combinations. And she, without a second thought, would lay open intimacies as one spreads open an umbrella in the rain. And always she hugged her knees and chortled deep in her throat, 'But you, my darling, are the best, you are the champ.' On those days a camaraderie was struck between them and he felt himself to be her equal in the sense that she was no better than he. More than that: he felt himself elevated, and ceased to regret, once and for all, that he was so unschooled that she had to read to him the instructions on a can of varnish.

Every night he made love to her. He treated the whole business as his part of the bargain. In bed his movements were as easy and graceful as when he painted a wall or repaired a broken drainpipe. He was precise; he was unhurried. Afterwards, Gyorgi would turn over as if fatigued, although his exultation was boundless. He did this rather than listen to her. 'You talk too much,' he would say, 'people screw up by talking too much.'

Once she frightened him in the middle of the night by shaking him awake. The bedside lamp was on. She was sitting bolt upright.

'Quickly,' she said in an urgent voice, 'don't think, tell me, quickly, what is life?'

'Life,' he said obediently, 'is. Life is. That's all. You're either alive or dead.'

'Wrong!' she said sharply. 'Life is an imposition. Oswald refuses to admit it. He wants life to be raw, with the bones showing. Today he presented me with a new account book, with more spaces for more entries. He threatened me again: unless I am more exact about the money I spend, he will cut off my alimony. He *imposes* himself on my life.'

Gyorgi condescended. 'What are you complaining about? A short ride in the Mercedes and you're living fat for another week. Perfect octaves don't buy houses like this.'

'You comprehend nothing.' She turned from him. 'You know nothing of the malice that masquerades as virtue. You are young: you still make plans.'

He stared at the long, heavy drapes.

'After the war we were thrown out of Hungary and shipped in boxcars to Germany. We lived behind barbed wire, then in barracks, then in a shack somewhere outside Frankfurt. All night long we heard the screams of the tortured. My brothers and sisters and I jumped out of bed when we heard the cries. We took turns standing on a chair at the small, high window. We could see nothing. Our parents never woke up.'

She studied him: there was no humility in him. She laid her head on his chest and a hand on his shoulder. Gyorgi yawned and lay back with his hands under his head.

'Fate,' she whispered, 'weaves its mysteries in the dark; that is why we do not know our destiny in the light of day.'

'That's true,' he agreed, understanding nothing. He had no sense of the abstract, but he recognized, if not destiny, certainly an opportunity. 'You have a beautiful house. I'm surprised you never married again.'

'Oswald wouldn't like it. Besides, if I married I wouldn't have this beautiful house.'

Gyorgi, startled, heard only the first part: 'Oswald wouldn't like it.' What did Oswald have to do with her desire to marry again? His own life had been a series of divorcements so immutable that he never again saw his parents, his brothers and sisters, two wives, countless lovers, as well as a number of unreasonable employers. If his decision to part, made simply and honestly, was challenged, he used his soccer-field fists, elbows, knees, or boots to make his meaning clear.

'We are lovers now,' he pursued, 'let us be as if married. I will care for you as my father did for my mother; you will care for me as my mother did my father.'

'But you are already here, in my house, in my bed . . .'

Lack of sleep made Gyorgi irritable. She was missing the point.

'From now on,' he rasped, 'you will do a woman's work.'

'Oh, oh,' she moaned, 'more impositions . . .'

'We must speak of necessities,' he went on inexorably. 'Food is a necessity. Respect is a necessity. It is necessary to respect the place you eat and sleep in. The way you live now, you turn roses into shit. Starting tomorrow, you will keep the house clean, wash the clothes, cook the meals. I will take out the garbage, attend the mousetraps, spray the roach powder.'

'My music . . .'

'*Deine Stimme ist zum Kotzen,*' he said as day dawned, 'you have the voice of a crow.'

'Yes, yes,' she said, falling in with his thought, 'I will buy a loom and learn to weave.'

'Don't be stupid. You're too clumsy.'

She flung her faith into the new day. Laughing now and clapping her hands she exclaimed:

'You noticed! Oh, how I do love you!'

She no longer rouges her lips and cheeks nor colours her eyelids. Gyorgi has convinced her of his preference for an unadorned face. This he has done by holding her head down in the bathroom sink filled with water. Her giggles spluttered, she choked, she lost consciousness. She has learned that he means what he says. She thinks he has helped her begin a new life. She telephones everyone she knows to tell them that she gets up in the morning and that she bakes bread.

Just before Christmas there was a party. Gyorgi was surprised, considering her indolence, that she had so many friends. Well, maybe he could understand: she was guileless; she harboured no ill will. He was sent to the convenience store on Summerhill Avenue for peanuts and chips and mixes. 'Not to worry,' she assured him, 'everyone brings a bottle. All we need are enough clean glasses.' He went back and bought five dozen plastic glasses.

Gyorgi dressed for the evening. He wore a white shirt and a patterned silk tie and real gold cuff links—gifts of grateful women. He looked distinguished, almost, in a suit. The synthetic brown cloth hung on his frame like an admiral's uniform. She introduced him: 'Isn't he gorgeous!' He walked behind her and watched gravely while she went about kissing men and 'adoring' them. In his turn he was careful not to flirt with women. He could take no chances: women mistook his compliments for confessions.

He assumed the dignity of the foreman he remembered in the Bechstein factory, hands behind his back, observing everyone, recording, alert to what might be expected of him. He mixed drinks, removed coats, and carried them upstairs; clipped pairs of galoshes and boots together with clothespins. After a while he realized that the guests made no distinction between him and themselves. An envoy from India invited him to a cricket match in Edwards Gardens next summer; Gyorgi invited him in return to a soccer match next summer, also in Edwards Gardens. A pretty psychiatrist wept on his breast in revealing an unhappy marriage; he told her of his own two divorces. A stockbroker took him aside, confided that metals were going to be big, and gave him a business card. Gyorgi went upstairs and got his business card, which he gave to the stockbroker. Gyorgi was overcome by a sophistication he had never known before. In his new expansiveness he slid into discussions.

'Hitler never wanted war,' he said with the authority of one who also has an inside track to matters of importance. 'He waited outside Poland for word from Chamberlain, who double-crossed him and declared war on Germany. The Allies have falsified history. Hitler could have invaded Britain but ordered the generals to hold off, always hoping for peace. The Holocaust was a lie, spread by Jewish international bankers.'

She, meanwhile, had been circling. In the silence that followed his revelations she linked her arm through his and pulled him away just when he was about to heap fact upon startling fact. Tomorrow (he intends) he will tell her: 'It is not respectful for a woman to interrupt a man when he is speaking. You must never do that again.'

Instead, it was she who faced him when everyone had gone. She was calm; there was a hardness about her as she stood looking up at him without a flicker or a twinge. 'You must never, never again reveal your fascism. I will not permit racist talk in my house.'

When the spring sun began to stream through the shiny windows and the lawn gave off a yielding odour, Gyorgi, too, softened. He permitted her to sing for him in the evening, to wear costumes and a little make-up. She accompanied herself at the Bechstein, the rings on both hands flashing under the crystal lights. He listened to her stories of the operas, stories of terror and love and irony and death. He listened and planned. There would be the garden to attend to, storms to be taken down, screens to be installed, dining-room chairs to be repaired. Days of work; music and parties; nights of love. The picture of an old woman dying and leaving him her big house faded, then disappeared altogether.

This night she was dressed as Mimi, looking quite appealing, he thought, in a pink bonnet tied with satin ribbons under her chin. She looked girlish and demure. He even recognized the song in which Mimi asks for a muff to warm her poor, cold hands. Suddenly she broke off, rose abruptly from the piano, turned off the lights, lit a candle, and waving it high overhead, announced:

'I want to die slowly like Mimi.' She placed the candle on the table at the side of his chair and sank at his feet. 'Do you still want to marry me?'

'Marry me . . .?' Gyorgi repeated, and his voice broke. He saw himself answering the ring at the front door, raising his eyebrows, and, if necessary, directing the caller to the servants' entrance. Forgiveness flowed over him. In his mind he sent money to his mother and father to come for a visit to see what he had made of himself. Then would come his brothers and sisters, each in turn. He drew her up on his lap. He removed Mimi's bonnet and stroked her head.

She, dreaming: 'I feel like Gretel,' cradling into him, 'we will be like Hansel and Gretel, alone in the forest. We will learn to live in innocence, like peasants, gathering nuts and berries, protected from evil by our happiness.'

'You people,' he said, shaking his head, 'I love the way you people want to play poor, with your budgets and your diets, with your gurus and your torn jeans.' Suddenly he became angry. 'It is all one big lie: you people couldn't survive a day's hunger.'

'I'm not pretending. When I marry, Oswald cuts off my alimony. This is his house, lock, stock, and four-poster. We will not be allowed to stay here.' Her teeth were clamped together. 'Oswald would never let us live in his house.'

Gyorgi felt evicted, dislodged from a place in his head. Somehow he did not find it odd that he should be striking out at her. But she was off his lap and out of range with a swiftness that surprised him: she must have expected something like this.

'You tricked me!' he shouted. 'The work . . . the hours . . . I cleaned up your bloody mess . . . it was to have been for me, for me, damn you . . . all this time I was busting my ass for him . . . for *his* house . . .'

In his fury he lunged at her. She ran from him and he after her with his fists extended. His anger also brought confusion: images of her friends, lawyers and judges and others in high places before whom he was powerless: he could smell the acid of a jail cell. He heard a crash. He stopped in his tracks as if shot and he heard her laugh. She was standing with her back to the Bechstein, her rump on the keys, her arms flung out and back in the posture of protection. He was astounded that she knew so little about him after all these days and nights that she could think him capable of harming a Bechstein. He banged his knuckles against each other and did not touch her. He opened his fingers and let his arms hang.

'What will become of you?' she taunted. 'You have been spoiled, spoiled by mahogany and fine linen and oil paintings on the walls. You are unfit now for rented rooms and tired waitresses and the hopes of check-out girls.'

So. They had come to the end of the game. It made him sad: he had liked her: he could have been satisfied. Then, doglike, shaking the discovery off himself, he withdrew, walking backwards. Gyorgi kept going, backwards, stepping over the thick carpets for the last time.

Where she is standing, in her shabby Mimi gown, arms still extended against her beloved piano, dry-eyed, ears strained toward the sounds of Gyorgi's departure, she knows already she will soon sit across the desk from fair, florid Oswald. She hears already his instructions: no calls. Hears Oswald's voice without a rise in it saying: 'What happened this time? Hmm. You got off easy. Give me the account.' She knows, too, that Oswald will lace his pale fingers across his chest and quote for the hundredth time: ' "Even among galley slaves there were ten percent volunteers." For God's sake, when will you stop inviting your own destruction.' She sees already her hungry hand as it moves across the desk. She will take the money to keep her safe for yet another little while.

P.K. PAGE

❧

UNLESS THE EYE CATCH FIRE . . .

Unless the eye catch fire
    The God will not be seen . . .
        Where the Wasteland Ends, Theodore Roszak

Wednesday, September 17. The day began normally enough. The quails, cock-aded as antique foot soldiers, arrived while I was having my breakfast. The males black-faced, white-necklaced, cinnamon-crowned, with short, sharp, dark plumes. Square bibs, Payne's grey; belly and sides with a pattern of small stitches. Reassuring, the flock of them. They tell me the macadamiza-tion of the world is not complete.

A sudden alarm, and as if they had one brain among them, they were gone in a rush—a sideways ascending Niagara—shutting out the light, obscur-ing the sky and exposing a rectangle of lawn, unexpectedly emerald. How bright the berries on the cotoneaster. Random leaves on the cherry twirled like gold spinners. The garden was high-keyed, vivid, locked in aspic.

Without warning, and as if I were looking down the tube of a kaleido-scope, the merest shake occurred—moiréed the garden—rectified itself. Or, more precisely, as if a range-finder through which I had been sighting found of itself a more accurate focus. Sharpened, in fact, to an excoriating exactness.

And then the colours changed. Shifted to a higher octave—a *bright spec-trum*. Each colour with its own *light*, its own *shape*. The leaves of the trees, the berries, the grasses—as if shedding successive films—disclosed layer after layer of hidden perfections. And upon these rapidly changing surfaces the 'range-finder'—to really play hob with metaphor!—sharpened its small invis-ible blades.

I don't know how to describe the intensity and speed of focus of this gratuitous zoom lens through which I stared, or the swift and dizzying adjustments within me. I became a 'sleeping top,' perfectly centred, perfect-ly sighted. The colours vibrated beyond the visible range of the spectrum. Yet I saw them. With some matching eye. Whole galaxies of them, blazing and glowing, flowing in rivulets, gushing in fountains—volatile, mercurial, and making lacklustre and off-key the colours of the rainbow.

I had no time or inclination to wonder, intellectualize. My mind seemed astonishingly clear and quite still. Like a crystal. A burning glass.

And then the range-finder sharpened once again. To alter space.

The lawn, the bushes, the trees—still super-brilliant—were no longer *there*. *There*, in fact, had ceased to exist. They were now, of all places in the world, *here*. Right in the centre of my being. Occupying an immense inner space. Part of me. Mine. Except the whole idea of ownership was beside the point. As true to say I was theirs as they mine. I and they were here; they and I, there. (*There, here* . . . odd . . . but for an irrelevant, inconsequential 't' which comes and goes, the words are the same.)

As suddenly as the world had altered, it returned to normal. I looked at my watch. A ridiculous mechanical habit. As I had no idea when the experience began it was impossible to know how long it had lasted. What had seemed eternity couldn't have been more than a minute or so. My coffee was still steaming in its mug.

The garden, through the window, was as it had always been. Yet not as it had always been. Less. Like listening to mono after hearing stereo. But with a far greater loss of dimension. A grievous loss.

I rubbed my eyes. Wondered, not without alarm, if this was the onset of some disease of the retina—glaucoma or some cellular change in the eye itself—superlatively packaged, fatally sweet as the marzipan cherry I ate as a child and *knew* was poison.

If it *is* a disease, the symptoms will recur. It will happen again.

Tuesday, September 23. It *has* happened again.

Tonight, taking Dexter for his late walk, I looked up at the crocheted tangle of boughs against the sky. Dark silhouettes against the lesser dark, but beating now with an extraordinary black brilliance. The golden glints in obsidian or the lurking embers in black opals are the nearest I can come to describing them. But it's a false description, emphasizing as it does the wrong end of the scale. This was a *dark spectrum*. As if the starry heavens were translated into densities of black—black Mars, black Saturn, black Jupiter; or a master jeweller had crossed his jewels with jet and set them to burn and wink in the branches and twigs of oaks whose leaves shone luminous—a leafy Milky Way—fired by black chlorophyll.

Dexter stopped as dead as I. Transfixed. His thick honey-coloured coat and amber eyes, glowing with their own intense brightness, suggested yet another spectrum. A *spectrum of light*. He was a constellated dog, shining, supra-real, against the foothills and mountain ranges of midnight.

I am reminded now, as I write, of a collection of lepidoptera in Brazil—one entire wall covered with butterflies, creatures of daylight—enormous or tiny—blue, orange, black. Strong-coloured. And on the opposite wall their anti-selves—pale night flyers spanning such a range of silver and white and lightest snuff-colour that once one entered their spectral scale there was no end to the subtleties and delicate nuances. But I didn't think like this then. All thought, all comparisons were prevented by the startling infinities of darkness and light.

Then, as before, the additional shake occurred and the two spectrums moved swiftly from without to within. As if two equal and complementary circles centred inside me—or I in them. How explain that I not only *saw* but actually *was* the two spectrums? (I underline a simple, but in this case exactly appropriate, anagram.)

Then the range-finder lost its focus and the world, once again, was back to normal. Dexter, a pale, blurred blob, bounded about within the field of my peripheral vision, going on with his doggy interests just as if a moment before he had not been frozen in his tracks, a dog entranced.

I am no longer concerned about my eyesight. Wonder only if we are both mad, Dexter and I? Angelically mad, sharing hallucinations of epiphany. *Folie à deux?*

Friday, October 3. It's hard to account for my secrecy, for I *have* been secretive. As if the cat had my tongue. It's not that I don't long to talk about the colours but I can't risk the wrong response—(as Gaby once said of a companion after a faultless performance of *Giselle*: 'If she had criticized the least detail of it, I'd have hit her!').

Once or twice I've gone so far as to say, 'I had the most extraordinary experience the other day . . .' hoping to find some look or phrase, some answering, 'So did I.' None has been forthcoming.

I can't forget the beauty. Can't get it out of my head. Startling, unearthly, indescribable. Infuriatingly indescribable. A glimpse of—somewhere else. Somewhere alive, miraculous, newly made yet timeless. And more important still—significant, luminous, with a meaning of which I was part. Except that I—the I who is writing this—did not exist: was flooded out, dissolved in that immensity where subject and object are one.

I have to make a deliberate effort now not to live my life in terms of it; not to sit, immobilized, awaiting the shake that heralds a new world. Awaiting the transfiguration.

Luckily the necessities of life keep me busy. But upstream of my actions, behind a kind of plate glass, some part of me waits, listens, maintains a total attention.

Tuesday, October 7. Things are moving very fast.

Some nights ago my eye was caught by a news item. 'Trucker Blames Colours,' went the headline. Reading on: 'R.T. Ballantyne, driver for Island

Trucks, failed to stop on a red light at the intersection of Fernhill and Spender. Questioned by traffic police, Ballantyne replied: "I didn't see it, that's all. There was this shake, then all these colours suddenly in the trees. Real bright ones I'd never seen before. I guess they must have blinded me." A breathalyzer test proved negative.' Full stop.

I had an overpowering desire to talk to R.T. Ballantyne. Even looked him up in the telephone book. Not listed. I debated reaching him through Island Trucks in the morning.

Hoping for some mention of the story, I switched on the local radio station, caught the announcer mid-sentence:

'. . . to come to the studio and talk to us. So far no one has been able to describe just what the "new" colours are, but perhaps Ruby Howard can. Ruby, you say you actually *saw* "new" colours?'

What might have been a flat, rather ordinary female voice was sharpened by wonder. 'I was out in the garden, putting it to bed, you might say, getting it ready for the winter. The hydrangeas are dried out—you know the way they go. Soft beiges and greys. And I was thinking maybe I should cut them back, when there was this—shake, like—and there they were shining. Pink. And blue. But not like they are in life. Different. Brighter. With little lights, like . . .'

The announcer's voice cut in, 'You say "not like they are in life". D'you think this wasn't life? I mean, do you think maybe you were dreaming?'

'Oh, no,' answered my good Mrs Howard, positive, clear, totally unrattled. 'Oh, no, I wasn't *dreaming*. Not *dreaming*–. . . Why–*this* is more like dreaming.' She was quiet a moment and then, in a matter-of-fact voice, 'I can't expect you to believe it,' she said. 'Why should you? I wouldn't believe it myself if I hadn't seen it.' Her voice expressed a kind of compassion as if she was really sorry for the announcer.

I picked up the telephone book for the second time, looked up the number of the station. I had decided to tell Mrs Howard what I had seen. I dialled, got a busy signal, depressed the bar and waited, cradle in hand. I dialled again. And again.

Later. J. Just phoned. Curious how she and I play the same game over and over.

J: Were you watching Channel 8?

ME: No, I . . .

J: An interview. With a lunatic. One who sees colours and flashing lights.

ME: Tell me about it.

J.: He was a logger—a high-rigger—not that that has anything to do with it. He's retired now and lives in an apartment and has a window-box with geraniums. This morning the flowers were like neon, he said, flashing and shining . . . *Honestly!*

ME: Perhaps he saw something you can't . . .

J: (*Amused*) I might have known you'd take his side. Seriously, what *could* he have seen?

ME: Flashing and shining—as he said.

J: But they couldn't. Not geraniums. And you know it as well as I do. *Honestly*, Babe . . . (She is the only person left who calls me the name my mother called me.) Why are you always so perverse?

I felt faithless. I put down the receiver, as if I had not borne witness to my God.

October 22. Floods of letters to the paper. Endless interviews on radio and TV. Pros, cons, inevitable spoofs.

One develops an eye for authenticity. It's as easy to spot as sunlight. However they may vary in detail, true accounts of the colours have an unmistakable common factor—a common factor as difficult to convey as sweetness to those who know only salt. True accounts are inarticulate, diffuse, unlikely—impossible.

It's recently crossed my mind that there may be some relationship between having seen the colours and their actual manifestation—something as improbable as *the more one sees them the more they are able to be seen*. Perhaps they are always there in some normally invisible part of the electro-magnetic spectrum and only become visible to certain people at certain times. A combination of circumstances or some subtle refinement in the organ of sight. And then—from quantity to quality perhaps, like water to ice—a whole community changes, is able to see, catches fire.

For example, it was seven days between the first time I saw the colours and the second. During that time there were no reports to the media. But once the reports began, the time between lessened appreciably *for me*. Not proof, of course, but worth noting. And I can't help wondering why some people see the colours and others don't. Do some of us have extra vision? Are some so conditioned that they're virtually blind to what's there before their very noses? Is it a question of more, or less?

Reports come in from farther and farther afield; from all walks of life. I think now there is no portion of the inhabited globe without 'shake freaks' and no acceptable reason for the sightings. Often, only one member of a family will testify to the heightened vision. In my own small circle, I am the only witness—or so I think. I feel curiously hypocritical as I listen to my friends denouncing the 'shakers'. Drugs, they say. Irrational—possibly dangerous. Although no sinister incidents have occurred yet—just some mild shake-baiting here and there—one is uneasily reminded of Salem.

Scientists pronounce us hallucinated or mistaken, pointing out that so far there is no hard evidence, no objective proof. That means, I suppose, no photographs, no spectroscopic measurement—if such is possible. Interestingly, seismographs show very minor earthquake tremors—showers of them, like shooting stars in August. Pundits claim 'shake fever'—as it has come to be called—is a variant on flying saucer fever and that it will subside in its own time. Beneficent physiologists suggest we are suffering (why is it *always* suffering, never enjoying?) a distorted form of *ocular spectrum* or after-image. (An after-image of what?) Psychologists disagree among themselves. All in all, it is not surprising that some of us prefer to keep our experiences to ourselves.

January 9. Something new has occurred. Something impossible. Disturbing. So disturbing, in fact, that according to rumour it is already being taken with the utmost seriousness at the highest levels. TV, press and radio—with good reason—talk of little else.

What seemingly began as a mild winter has assumed sinister overtones. Farmers in southern Alberta are claiming the earth is unnaturally hot to the touch. Golfers at Harrison complain that the soles of their feet burn. Here on the coast, we notice it less. Benign winters are our specialty.

Already we don't lack for explanations as to why the earth could not be hotter than usual, nor why it is naturally 'un-naturally' hot. Vague notes of reassurance creep into the speeches of public men. They may be unable to explain the issue, but they can no longer ignore it.

To confuse matters further, reports on temperatures seem curiously inconsistent. What information we get comes mainly from self-appointed 'earth touchers'. And now that the least thing can fire an argument, their conflicting readings lead often enough to inflammatory debate.

For myself, I can detect no change at all in my own garden.

Thursday . . .? There is no longer any doubt. The temperature of the earth's surface *is* increasing.

It is unnerving, horrible, to go out and feel the ground like some great beast, warm, beneath one's feet. As if another presence—vast, invisible—attends one. Dexter, too, is perplexed. He barks at the earth with the same indignation and, I suppose, fear, with which he barks at the first rumblings of earthquake.

Air temperatures, curiously, don't increase proportionately—or so we're told. It doesn't make sense, but at the moment nothing makes sense. Countless explanations have been offered. Elaborate explanations. None adequate. The fact that the air temperature remains temperate despite the higher ground heat must, I think, be helping to keep panic down. Even so, these are times of great tension.

Hard to understand these two unexplained—unrelated?—phenomena: the first capable of dividing families; the second menacing us all. We are like animals trapped in a burning building.

Later. J. just phoned. Terrified. Why don't I move in with her, she urges. After all she has the space and we have known each other forty years. (Hard to believe when I don't feel even forty!) She can't bear it—the loneliness.

Poor J. Always so protected, insulated by her money. And her charm. What one didn't provide, the other did . . . diversions, services, attention.

What do I think is responsible for the heat, she asks. But it turns out she means who. Her personal theory is that the 'shake freaks' are causing it—involuntarily, perhaps, but the two are surely linked.

'How could they possibly cause it?' I enquire. 'By what reach of the imagination . . .?'

'Search *me*!' she protests. 'How on earth should *I* know?' And the sound of the dated slang makes me really laugh.

But suddenly she is close to tears. 'How can you *laugh*?' she calls. 'This is nightmare. Nightmare!'

Dear J. I wish I could help but the only comfort I could offer would terrify her still more.

September. Summer calmed us down. If the earth was hot, well, summers *are* hot. And we were simply having an abnormally hot one.

Now that it is fall—the season of cool nights, light frosts—and the earth like a feverish child remains worryingly hot, won't cool down, apprehension mounts.

At last we are given official readings. For months the authorities have assured us with irrefutable logic that the temperature of the earth could not be increasing. Now, without any apparent period of indecision or confusion, they are warning us with equal conviction and accurate statistical documentation that it has, in fact, increased. Something anyone with a pocket-handkerchief of lawn has known for some time.

Weather stations, science faculties, astronomical observatories all over the world are measuring and reporting. Intricate computerized tables are quoted. Special departments of Government have been set up. We speak now of a new Triassic Age—the Neo-Triassic—and of the accelerated melting of the ice caps. But we are elaborately assured that this could not, repeat not, occur in our lifetime.

Interpreters and analysts flourish. The media are filled with theories and explanations. The increased temperature has been attributed to impersonal agencies such as bacteria from outer space; a thinning of the earth's atmosphere; a build-up of carbon-dioxide in the air; some axial irregularity; a change in the earth's core (geologists are reported to have begun test borings). No theory is too far-fetched to have its supporters. And because man likes a scapegoat, blame has been laid upon NASA, atomic physicists, politicians, the occupants of flying saucers and finally upon mankind at large—improvident, greedy mankind—whose polluted, strike-ridden world is endangered now by the fabled flames of hell.

Yet, astonishingly, life goes on. The Pollack baby was born last week. I received the news as if it were a death. Nothing has brought the irony of our situation home to me more poignantly. And when I saw the perfect little creature in its mother's arms, the look of adoration on her face, I found myself saying the things one always says to a new mother—exactly as if the world had not changed. Exactly as if our radio was not informing us that Nostradamus, the Bible, and Jeane Dixon have all foreseen our plight. A new paperback, *Let Edgar Cayce Tell You Why* sold out in a matter of days. Attendance at churches has doubled. Cults proliferate. Yet even in this atmosphere, we, the 'shake freaks', are considered lunatic fringe. Odd men out. In certain quarters I believe we are seriously held responsible for the escalating heat, so J. is not alone. There have now been one or two nasty incidents. It is not surprising that even the most vocal among us have grown less willing to talk. I am glad to have kept silent. As a woman living alone, the less I draw attention to myself the better.

But, at the same time, we have suddenly all become neighbours. Total strangers greet each other on the street. And the almost invisible couple behind the high hedge appears every time I pass with Dexter—wanting to talk. Desperately wanting to talk.

For our lives are greatly altered by this overhanging sense of doom. It is already hard to buy certain commodities. Dairy products are in very short supply. On the other hand, the market is flooded with citrus fruits. We are threatened with severe shortages for the future. The authorities are resisting rationing but it will have to come, if only to prevent artificial shortages resulting from hoarding.

Luckily the colours are an almost daily event. I see them now, as it were, with my entire being. It is as if all my cells respond to their brilliance and become light too. At such times I feel I might shine in the dark.

No idea of the date. It is evening and I am tired but I am so far behind in my notes I want to get something down. Events have moved too fast for me.

Gardens, parks—every tillable inch of soil—have been appropriated for

food crops. As an able, if aging body, with an acre of land and some knowledge of gardening, I have been made responsible for soybeans—small trifo-
liate plants rich with the promise of protein. Neat rows of them cover what
were once my vegetable garden, flower beds, lawn.

Young men from the Department of Agriculture came last month, bull-
dozed, cultivated, planted. Efficient, noisy desecrators of my twenty years
of landscaping. Dexter barked at them from the moment they appeared and
I admit I would have shared his indignation had the water shortage not
already created its own desolation.

As a Government gardener I'm a member of a new privileged class. I
have watering and driving permits and coupons for gasoline and boots—an
indication of what is to come. So far there has been no clothes rationing.

Daily instructions—when to water and how much, details of mulching,
spraying—reach me from the Government radio station to which I tune first
thing in the morning. It also provides temperature readings, weather fore-
casts and the latest news releases on emergency measures, curfews,
rationing, insulation. From the way things are going I think it will soon be
our only station. I doubt that newspapers will be able to print much longer.
In any event, I have already given them up. At first it was interesting to see
how quickly drugs, pollution, education, women's lib., all became bygone
issues; and, initially, I was fascinated to see how we rationalized. Then I
became bored. Then disheartened. Now I am too busy.

Evening. A call came from J. Will I come for Christmas?

Christmas! Extraordinary thought. Like a word from another language
learned in my youth, now forgotten.

'I've still got some Heidseck. We can get tight.'

The word takes me back to my teens. 'Like old times . . .'

'Yes.' She is eager. I hate to let her down. 'J., I can't. How could I get to
you?'

'In your *car*, silly. *You* still have gas. You're the only one of us who has.'
Do I detect a slight hint of accusation, as if I had acquired it illegally?

'But J., it's only for emergencies.'

'My God, Babe, d'you think *this* isn't an emergency?'

'J., dear . . .'

'*Please*, Babe,' she pleads. 'I'm so afraid. Of the looters. The eeriness.
You must be afraid too. *Please!*'

I should have said, yes, that of course I was afraid. It's only natural to
be afraid. Or, unable to say that, I should have made the soothing noises a
mother makes to her child. Instead, 'There's no reason to be afraid, J.,' I
said. It must have sounded insufferably pompous.

'No reason!' She was exasperated with me. 'I'd have thought there was every reason.'

She will phone again. In the night perhaps when she can't sleep. Poor J. She feels so alone. She *is* so alone. And so idle. I don't suppose it's occurred to her yet that telephones will soon go. That a whole way of life is vanishing completely.

It's different for me. I have the soybeans which keep me busy all the daylight hours. And Dexter. And above all I have the colours and with them the knowledge that there are others, other people, whose sensibilities I share. We are as invisibly, inviolably related to one another as the components of a molecule. I say 'we'. Perhaps I should speak only for myself, yet I feel as sure of these others as if they had spoken. Like the quails, we share one brain—no, I think it is one heart—between us. How do I know this? How *do* I know? I know by knowing. We are less alarmed by the increasing heat than those who have not seen the colours. I can't explain why. But seeing the colours seems to change one—just as certain diagnostic procedures cure the complaint they are attempting to diagnose.

In all honesty I admit to having had moments when this sense of community was not enough, when I have had a great longing for my own kind—for so have I come to think of these others—in the way one has a great longing for someone one loves. Their presence in the world is not enough. One must see them. Touch them. Speak with them.

But lately that longing has lessened. All longing, in fact. And fear. Even my once great dread that I might cease to see the colours has vanished. It is as if through seeing them I have learned to see them. Have learned to be ready to see—passive; not striving to see—active. It keeps me very wide awake. Transparent even. Still.

The colours come daily now. Dizzying. Transforming. Life-giving. My sometimes back-breaking toil in the garden is lightened, made full of wonder, by the incredible colours shooting in the manner of children's sparklers from the plants themselves and from my own work-worn hands. I hadn't realized that I too am part of this vibrating luminescence.

Later. I have no idea how long it is since I abandoned these notes. Without seasons to measure its passing, without normal activities—preparations for festivals, occasional outings—time feels longer, shorter or—more curious still—simultaneous, undifferentiated. Future and past fused in the present. Linearity broken.

I had intended to write regularly, but the soybeans keep me busy pretty well all day and by evening I'm usually ready for bed. I'm sorry however to have missed recording the day-by-day changes. They were more or less minor at first. But once the heat began its deadly escalation, the world as we have known it—'our world'—had you been able to put it alongside 'this world'—would have seemed almost entirely different.

No one, I think, could have foreseen the speed with which everything has broken down. For instance, the elaborate plans made to maintain transportation became useless in a matter of months. Private traffic was first curtailed, then forbidden. If a man from another planet had looked in on us, he would have been astonished to see us trapped who were apparently free.

The big changes only really began after the first panic evacuations from the cities. Insulated by concrete, sewer pipes and underground parkades, high density areas responded slowly to the increasing temperatures. But once the heat penetrated their insulations, Gehennas were created overnight and whole populations fled in hysterical exodus, jamming highways in their futile attempts to escape.

Prior to this the Government had not publicly acknowledged a crisis situation. They had taken certain precautions, brought in temporary measures to ease shortages and dealt with new developments on an *ad hoc* basis. Endeavoured to play it cool. Or so it seemed. Now they levelled with us. It was obvious that they must have been planning for months, only awaiting the right psychological moment to take everything over. That moment had clearly come. What we had previously thought of as a free world ended. We could no longer eat, drink, move without permits or coupons. This was full-scale emergency.

Yet nothing proceeds logically. Plans are made only to be remade to accommodate new and totally unexpected developments. The heat, unpatterned as disseminated sclerosis, attacks first here, then there. Areas of high temperature suddenly and inexplicably cool off—or vice versa. Agronomists are doing everything possible to keep crops coming—taking advantage of hot-house conditions to force two crops where one had grown before—frantically playing a kind of agricultural roulette, gambling on the length of time a specific region might continue to grow temperate-zone produce.

Mails have long since stopped. And newspapers. And telephones. As a member of a new privileged class, I have been equipped with a two-way radio and a permit to drive on Government business. Schools have of course closed. An attempt was made for a time to provide lessons over TV. Thankfully the looting and rioting seem over. Those desperate gangs of angry citizens who for some time made life additionally difficult, have now disappeared. We seem at last to understand that we are all in this together.

Life is very simple without electricity. I get up with the light and go to bed as darkness falls. My food supply is still substantial and because of the soybean crop I am all right for water. Dexter has adapted well to his new life. He is outdoors less than he used to be and has switched to a mainly vegetable diet without too much difficulty.

Evening. This morning a new order over the radio. All of us with special driving privileges were asked to report to our zone garage to have our tires treated with heat-resistant plastic.

I had not been into town for months. I felt rather as one does on returning home from hospital–that the world is unexpectedly large, with voluminous airy spaces. This was exaggerated perhaps by the fact that our whole zone had been given over to soybeans. Everywhere the same rows of green plants–small pods already formed–march across gardens and boulevards. I was glad to see the climate prove so favourable. But there was little else to make me rejoice as I drove through ominously deserted streets, paint blistering and peeling on fences and houses, while overhead a haze of dust, now always with us, created a green sun.

The prolonged heat has made bleak the little park opposite the garage. A rocky little park, once all mosses and rhododendrons, it is bare now, and brown. I was seeing the day as everyone saw it. Untransmuted.

As I stepped out of my car to speak to the attendant I cursed that I had not brought my insulators. The burning tarmac made me shift rapidly from foot to foot. Anyone from another planet would have wondered at this extraordinary quirk of earthlings. But my feet were forgotten as my eyes alighted a second time on the park across the way. I had never before seen so dazzling and variegated a display of colours. How could there be such prismed brilliance in the range of greys and browns? It was as if the perceiving organ–wherever it is–sensitized by earlier experience, was now correctly tuned for this further perception.

The process was as before: the merest shake and the whole park was 'rainbow, rainbow, rainbow'. A further shake brought the park from *there* to *here.* Interior. But this time the interior space had increased. Doubled. By a kind of instant knowledge that rid me of all doubt, I knew that the garage attendant was seeing it too. *We saw the colours.*

Then, with that slight shift of focus, as if a gelatinous film had moved briefly across my sight, everything slipped back.

I really looked at the attendant for the first time. He was a skinny young man standing up naked inside a pair of loose striped overalls cut off at the knee, *sidney* embroidered in red over his left breast pocket. He was blond, small-boned, with nothing about him to stick in the memory except his clear eyes which at that moment bore an expression of total comprehension.

'You . . .' we began together and laughed.

'Have you seen them before?' I asked. But it was rather as one would say 'how do you do?'—not so much a question as a salutation.

We looked at each other for a long time, as if committing each other to memory.

'Do you know anyone else?' I said.

'One or two. Three, actually. Do you?'

I shook my head. 'You are the first. Is it . . . is it . . . always like that?'

'You mean . . .?' he gestured towards his heart.

I nodded.

'Yes,' he said. 'Yes, it is.'

There didn't seem anything more to talk about. Your right hand hasn't much to say to your left, or one eye to the other. There was comfort in the experience, if comfort is the word, which it isn't. More as if an old faculty had been extended. Or a new one activated.

Sidney put my car on the hoist and sprayed its tires.

Some time later. I have not seen Sidney again. Two weeks ago when I went back he was not there and as of yesterday, cars have become obsolete. Not that we will use that word publicly. The official word is *suspended.*

Strange to be idle after months of hard labour. A lull only before the boys from the Department of Agriculture come back to prepare the land again. I am pleased that the soybeans are harvested, that I was able to nurse them along to maturity despite the scorching sun, the intermittent plagues and the problems with water. Often the pressure was too low to turn the sprinklers and I would stand, hour after hour, hose in hand, trying to get the most use from the tiny trickle spilling from the nozzle.

Sometimes my heart turns over as I look through the kitchen window and see the plants shrivelled and grotesque, the baked earth scored by a web of fine cracks like the glaze on a plate subjected to too high an oven. Then it comes to me in a flash that of course, the beans are gone, the harvest is over.

The world is uncannily quiet. I don't think anyone had any idea of how much noise even distant traffic made until we were without it. It is rare indeed for vehicles other than Government mini-cars to be seen on the streets. And there are fewer and fewer pedestrians. Those who do venture out move on their thick insulators with the slow gait of rocking-horses. Surreal and alien, they heighten rather than lessen one's sense of isolation. For one *is* isolated. We have grown used to the sight of helicopters like large dragon-flies hovering overhead—addressing us through their P.A. systems, dropping supplies—welcome but impersonal.

Dexter is my only physical contact. He is delighted to have me inside again. The heat is too great for him in the garden and as, officially, he no longer exists, we only go out under cover of dark.

The order to destroy pets, when it came, indicated more clearly than anything that had gone before, that the Government had abandoned hope. In an animal-loving culture, only direct necessity could validate such an order. It fell upon us like a heavy pall.

When the Government truck stopped by for Dexter, I reported him dead. Now that the welfare of so many depends upon our cooperation with authority, law-breaking is a serious offence. But I am not uneasy about breaking this law. As long as he remains healthy and happy, Dexter and I will share our dwindling provisions.

No need to be an ecologist or dependent on non-existent media to know all life is dying and the very atmosphere of our planet is changing radically. Already no birds sing in the hideous hot dawns as the sun, rising through a haze of dust, sheds its curious bronze-green light on a brown world. The trees that once gave us shade stand leafless now in an infernal winter. Yet as if in the masts and riggings of ships, St Elmo's fire flickers and shines in their high branches, and bioplasmic pyrotechnics light the dying soybeans. I am reminded of how the ghostly form of a limb remains attached to the body from which it has been amputated. And I can't help thinking of all the people who don't see the colours, the practical earth-touchers with only their blunt senses to inform them. I wonder about J. and if, since we last talked, she has perhaps been able to see the colours too. But I think not. After so many years of friendship, surely I would be able to sense her, had she broken through.

Evening . . .? The heat has increased greatly in the last few weeks—in a quantum leap. This has resulted immediately in two things: a steady rising of the sea level throughout the world—with panic reactions and mild flooding in coastal areas; and, at last, a noticeably higher air temperature. It is causing great physical discomfort.

It was against this probability that the authorities provided us with insulator spray. Like giant cans of pressurized shaving cream. I have shut all rooms but the kitchen and by concentrating my insulating zeal on this one small area, we have managed to keep fairly cool. The word is relative, of course. The radio has stopped giving temperature readings and I have no thermometer. I have filled all cracks and crannies with the foaming plastic, even applied a layer to the exterior wall. There are no baths, of course, and no cold drinks. On the other hand I've abandoned clothes and given Dexter a shave and a haircut. Myself as well. We are a fine pair. Hairless and naked.

When the world state of emergency was declared we didn't need to be told that science had given up. The official line had been that the process would reverse itself as inexplicably as it had begun. The official policy—to hold out as long as possible. With this in mind, task forces worked day and night on survival strategy. On the municipal level, which is all I really knew about, everything that could be centralized was. Telephone exchanges, hydro plants, radio stations became centres around which vital activities took place. Research teams investigated the effects of heat on water mains, sewer pipes, electrical wiring; work crews were employed to prevent, protect, or even destroy incipient causes of fire, flood and asphyxiation.

For some time now the city has been zoned. In each zone a large building has been selected, stocked with food, medical supplies and insulating materials. We have been provided with zone maps and an instruction sheet telling us to stay where we are until ordered to move to what is euphemistically called our 'home'. When ordered, we are to load our cars with whatever we still have of provisions and medicines and drive off *at once*. Helicopters have already dropped kits with enough gasoline for the trip and a small packet, somewhat surprisingly labelled 'emergency rations' which contains one cyanide capsule—grim reminder that all may not go as the planners plan. We have been asked to mark our maps, in advance, with the shortest route from our house to our 'home', so that in a crisis we will know what we are doing. These instructions are repeated *ad nauseam* over the radio, along with hearty assurances that everything is under control and that there is no cause for alarm. The Government station is now all that remains of our multi-media. When it is not broadcasting instructions, its mainly pre-recorded tapes sound inanely complacent and repetitive. Evacuation Day, as we have been told again and again, will be announced by whistle blast. Anyone who runs out of food before that or who is in need of medical aid is to use the special gas ration and go 'home' at once.

As a long-time preserver of fruits and vegetables, I hope to hold out until E. Day. When that time comes it will be a sign that broadcasts are no longer possible, that contact can no longer be maintained between the various areas of the community, that the process will not reverse itself in time and that, in fact, our world is well on the way to becoming—oh, wonder of the modern kitchen—a self-cleaning oven.

Spring, Summer, Winter, Fall. What season is it after all? I sense the hours by some inner clock. I have applied so many layers of insulating spray that almost no heat comes through from outside. But we have to have air and the small window I have left exposed acts like a furnace. Yet through it I see the dazzling colours; sense my fellow-men.

Noon. The sun is hidden directly overhead. The world is topaz. I see it through the minute eye of my window. I, the perceiving organ that peers through the house's only aperture. We are one, the house and I—parts of some vibrating sensitive organism in which Dexter plays his differentiated but integral role. The light enters us, dissolves us. We are the golden motes in the jewel.

Midnight. The sun is directly below. Beneath the burning soles of my arching feet it shines, a globe on fire. Its rays penetrate the earth. Upward beaming, they support and sustain us. We are held aloft, a perfectly balanced ball in the jet of a golden fountain. Light, dancing, infinitely upheld.

Who knows how much later. I have just 'buried' Dexter.

This morning I realized this hot little cell was no longer a possible place for a dog. I had saved one can of dog food against this day. As I opened it Dexter's eyes swivelled in the direction of so unexpected and delicious a smell. He struggled to his feet, joyous, animated. The old Dexter. I was almost persuaded to delay, to wait and see if the heat subsided. What if tomorrow we awakened to rain? But something in me, stronger than this wavering self, carried on with its purpose.

He sat up, begging, expectant.

I slipped the meat out of the can.

'You're going to have a really good dinner,' I said, but as my voice was unsteady, I stopped.

I scooped a generous portion of the meat into his dish and placed it on the floor. He was excited, and as always when excited about food, he was curiously ceremonial, unhurried—approaching his dish and backing away from it, only to approach it again at a slightly different angle. As if the exact position was of the greatest importance. It was one of his most amusing and endearing characteristics. I let him eat his meal in his own leisurely and appreciative manner and then, as I have done so many times before, I fed him his final *bonne bouche* by hand. The cyanide pill, provided by a beneficent Government for me, went down in a gulp.

I hadn't expected it to be so sudden. Life and death so close. His small frame convulsed violently, then collapsed. Simultaneously, as if synchronized, the familiar 'shake' occurred in my vision. Dexter glowed brightly, whitely, like phosphorus. In that dazzling, light-filled moment he was no longer a small dead dog lying there. I could have thought him a lion, my sense of scale had so altered. His beautiful body blinded me with its fires.

With the second 'shake' his consciousness must have entered mine for I felt a surge in my heart as if his loyalty and love had flooded it. And like a kind of ground bass, I was aware of scents and sounds I had not known before. Then a great peace filled me—an immense space, light and sweet—and I realized that this was death. Dexter's death.

But how describe what is beyond description?

As the fires emanating from his slight frame died down, glowed weakly, residually, I put on my insulators and carried his body into the now fever-hot garden. I laid him on what had been at one time an azalea bed. I was unable to dig a grave in the baked earth or to cover him with leaves. But there are no predators now to pick the flesh from his bones. Only the heat which will, in time, desiccate it.

I returned to the house, opening the door as little as possible to prevent the barbs and briars of burning air from entering with me. I sealed the door from inside with foam sealer.

The smell of the canned dog food permeated the kitchen. It rang in my nostrils. Olfactory chimes, lingering, delicious. I was intensely aware of Dexter. Dexter immanent. I contained him as simply as a dish contains water. But the simile is not exact. For I missed his physical presence. One relies on the physical more than I had known. My hands sought palpable contact. The flesh forgets slowly.

Idly, abstractedly, I turned on the radio. I seldom do now as the batteries are low and they are my last. Also, there is little incentive. Broadcasts are intermittent and I've heard the old tapes over and over.

But the Government station was on the air. I tuned with extreme care and placed my ear close to the speaker. A voice, faint, broken by static, sounded like that of the Prime Minister.

'. . . all human beings can do, your Government has done for you.' (Surely not a political speech *now*?) 'But we have failed. Failed to hold back the heat. Failed to protect ourselves against it; to protect you against it. It is with profound grief that I send this farewell message to you all.' I realized that this, too, had been pre-recorded, reserved for the final broadcast. 'Even now, let us not give up hope . . .'

And then, blasting through the speech, monstrously loud in the stone-silent world, the screech of the whistle summoning us 'home'. I could no longer hear the P.M.'s words.

I began automatically, obediently, to collect my few remaining foodstuffs, reaching for a can of raspberries, the last of the crop to have grown in my garden when the dawns were dewy and cool and noon sun fell upon us like golden pollen. My hand stopped in mid-air.

I would not go 'home'.

The whistle shrilled for a very long time. A curious great steam-driven cry—man's last. Weird that our final utterance should be this anguished inhuman wail.

The end. Now that it is virtually too late, I regret not having kept a daily record. Now that the part of me that writes has become nearly absorbed, I feel obliged to do the best I can.

I am down to the last of my food and water. Have lived on little for some days—weeks, perhaps. How can one measure passing time? Eternal time grows like a tree, its roots in my heart. If I lie on my back I see winds moving in its high branches and a chorus of birds is singing in its leaves. The song is sweeter than any music I have ever heard.

My kitchen is as strange as I am myself. Its walls bulge with many layers of spray. It is without geometry. Like the inside of an eccentric Styrofoam coconut. Yet, with some inner eye, I see its intricate mathematical structure. It is as ordered and no more random than an atom.

My face is unrecognizable in the mirror. Wisps of short damp hair. Enormous eyes. I swim in their irises. Could I drown in the pits of their pupils?

Through my tiny window when I raise the blind, a dead world shines. Sometimes dust storms fill the air with myriad particles burning bright and white as the lion body of Dexter. Sometimes great clouds swirl, like those from which saints receive revelations.

The colours are almost constant now. There are times when, light-headed, I dance a dizzying dance, feel part of that whirling incandescent matter— what I might once have called inorganic matter!

On still days the blameless air, bright as a glistening wing, hangs over us, hangs its extraordinary beneficence over us.

We are together now, united, indissoluble. Bonded.

Because there is no expectation, there is no frustration.

Because there is nothing we can have, there is nothing we can want.

We are hungry of course. Have cramps and weakness. But they are as if in *another body*. Our body is inviolate. Inviolable.

We share one heart.

We are one with the starry heavens and our bodies are stars.

Inner and outer are the same. A continuum. The water in the locks is level. We move to a higher water. A high sea.

A ship could pass through.

ELIZABETH SPENCER

❧

I, MAUREEN

On the sunny fall afternoon, I (Maureen) saw the girl sitting in the oval-shaped park near the St Lawrence River. She was sitting on green grass, bent lovingly, as though eternally, over her guitar. They are always like that, absorbed, hair falling past their faces, whether boys or girls: there seems little difference between them: they share the tender absorption of mother with child. The whole outside world regards them, forms a hushed circle about them.

I, Maureen, perceived this while driving by on an errand for Mr Massimo.

I used to live out there, on what in Montreal we call the Lakeshore. I did nothing right then, so returning to that scene is painful. I sought relief from the memories of five years ago by letting the girl with the guitar—bending to it, framed in grass, the blue river flowing by—redeem my memories, redeem me, I could only hope, also. Me, Maureen, stung with the identity of bad memories.

Everything any woman in her right mind could want—that was my life. Denis Partham's wife, and not even very pretty or classy: I never had anything resembling looks or background. I was a bit run-down looking, all my life. From the age of two, I looked run-down. People used to say right out to me: 'You've just had luck, that's all.' But Denis said the luck was his. He really thought that, for years and years. Until the day I thought he was dead. After that he had to face it that luck can run out, even for a Partham.

We had a house on the river and it was beautiful, right on the water. It was in Baie d'Urfé, one of the old townships, and you can describe it for yourself, if you so desire. There can be rugs of any texture, draperies of any fabric, paneling both painted and stained, shelves to put books in, cupboards to fill with china and linen. The choice of every upholstery sample or kitchen tile was a top-level decision; the struggle for perfection had a life-and-death quality about it. If my interest was not wholly taken up in all this, if I was play-acting, I did not know it. Are people when measuring and weighing and pondering names for a crown prince, serious? I was expecting the prince; that was why the Parthams gave us the house. Sure enough, the baby was a boy. Two years and another one arrived, a girl. (Isn't Nature great? She belongs to the Parthams.)

In the winter we had cocktails before dinner in a spacious room over-looking the frozen lake, watching the snow drift slowly down, seeing the skaters stroking outward. We had sherry between church services and Sunday lunch. Then the ice boats raced past, silent, fast as dreams.

Our children were beautiful, like children drawn with a pencil over and again in many attitudes, all pure, among many Canadian settings. Denis was handsome, a well-built man, younger than I, with dark hair and a strong, genuine smile. In his world, I was the only dowdy creature. Yet he loved me, heart and soul. And why? I used to sit in a big chair in a corner of the library hunched up like a crow, and wonder this. In summer I sat on the terraces, and there, too, I wondered.

All I knew was that aged twenty-five, a plain, single girl, I had come to the Parthams' big stone house high in Westmount with some friends. It was late, a gathering after a local play. A woman who worked at the library with me had a younger sister in the play and had asked me to come. One of the Parthams was in it, too, so we all got invited up for drinks. Somebody gra-ciously learned that I was living way out in NDG, that area of the unnum-bered middle class, and Denis, who had been talking to me about the library, offered to drive me home. When we reached the house, he turned off the motor, then the lights, and turning to me began to kiss me hungrily. He had fallen silent along the way, and I had felt he was going to do some-thing like this. I simply judged that he was rich boy out for more sexual experience, seeking it outside his own class, the way privileged people often do. Yet he was moved and excited way beyond the average: so I put him down as a boy with problems, and squirmed my way out of his arms and his Oldsmobile as best I could. Next day he telephoned me at the library, longing to see me again. He was that way from then on. He said he could never change. Through all our dates, then through season after season, year after year, I saw how his voice would take on a different note when he saw me, how his eyes would light up. I knew his touch, his sexual currents, his eager kisses, his talk, his thoughts, his tastes. At some point, we got mar-ried. But the marriage, I helplessly realized, had taken place already, in the moment he had seen me in the corner of one of the many Partham living rooms in their great stone house, me (Maureen), completely out of place. Before I knew it, he had enveloped me all over, encased me like a strong vine. My family could believe my good fortune no more than I could. It was too good to last, but it did; too good to be true, but it was. We had, in addi-tion to the Lakeshore house at Baie d'Urfé, an apartment on Drummond Street in Montreal, servants, two cars, wonderful friends, a marvelous life.

Then, one summer day, it happened. It could never unhappen.

Denis was out sailing and in passing under a bridge, the metal mast of the boat struck a live wire. His hand was on the mast and the voltage knocked him down. When they brought him in they had rolled him onto the sail and were carrying him by four improvised corners, like somebody asleep in a hammock. His head was turned to one side. Everyone on our lawn and dock seemed to know from the minute the boat appeared, unexpectedly returned, that something terrible had happened. We crowded forward together, all the family and friends not sailing, left behind on the lawns to swim, sun, play, or talk, and though I was among the first, I felt just as one of them, not special. I saw his face turned to one side, looking (the eyes shut and the skin discoloured blue and red) like a face drowned through a rift in ice. I thought he was dead, and so did we all, even, I later learned, those who were carrying him. They laid him on the lawn and someone said: 'Stay back,' while another, running from the moment the boat touched the dock, was already at the telephone. But by that time there were arms around me, to hold me back from rushing to him. They encountered no forward force. I was in retreat already, running backward from the moment, into another world which had been waiting for me for some time. All they did was hasten me into it. My fierce sprinting backward plus the force of their normal human attention—that of trying to keep a wife from hurling herself with all the velocity of human passion toward her husband, so unexpectedly served up before her as (so it seemed) a corpse—outdid possibility. But we leave the earth with difficulty, and I wasn't up to that. I fell backward sprawling awkwardly; I lay observing the bluest of July skies in which white clouds had filled in giant areas at good distances from the sun. Sky, cloud, and sun completed me, while ambulances wailed and bore away whomever they would.

Denis did not die; he recovered nicely. All life resumed as before.

A month later I made my first attempt at suicide.

It was finally to one of the psychiatrists I saw that I recounted how all of this had started, from a minor event, meaningless *to all but me*. (To me alone the world had spoken.)

I had been sunbathing on the pier a week or so before Denis's accident when two of the children whose parents owned a neighbouring property began to throw things into the water. I could see them—two skinny boys on the neighbouring pier—and know that while they pretended to be hurling rocks and bottles straight out into the lake, they were in reality curving them closer into land, striking near our docking area. I was thinking of getting up to shout at them when it happened. A bit of blue-green glass arching into the sun's rays, caught and trapped an angle of that light, refracting it to me. It struck, a match for lightning. My vision simply for a moment was by this brilliance extinguished; and in the plunge of darkness that ensued I could only see the glass rock reverse its course and speed toward me. It entered my truest self, my consciousness, reverberating with silent brilliance. From that point I date my new beginning. It was a nothing point, an illusion, but an illusion that had happened to me, if there is such a thing. . . .

'If there is such a thing,' the doctor repeated.

'If there is such a thing,' I said again, sounding, I knew, totally mad.

Doctors wait for something to be said that fits a pattern they have learned to be true, just as teachers wait for you to write English or French. If you wrote a new and unknown language they wouldn't know what to do with you—you would fail.

'It explains to me,' I went on, realizing I was taking the risk of being consigned to the asylum at Verdun for an indefinite period, 'why I ran backward instead of forward when I thought Denis was dead. I want my own world. I have been there once. I want to return. If I can't, I might as well be dead.'

'Your attempts to take your own life might be thought of as efforts to join your husband, whom you believed to have reached death,' the doctor suggested. He had a thick European accent, and an odd name, Miracorte. God knows where he was from.

I said nothing.

One day I left home. I had done this before but they had always come for me, tranquilized me, hospitalized me, removed things from me that might be handy ways of self-destruction, talked to me, loved me, nurtured me back to being what they wanted me to be—somebody, in other words, like themselves. This time they didn't come. A doctor came, a new one, younger than the first. He asked from the intercom system in the apartment building in East Montreal which I had fled to, taking the first furnished place I could find, whether he could see me. I let him in.

He was plain English-Canadian from Regina, named Johnson.

'Everyone is a little schizoid,' he said. They had told me that, told me and told me that. 'You choose the other side of the coin, the other side of yourself. You have to have it. If you don't have it, you will die. Don't you know that some people drink themselves into it, others hit drugs, some run off to the bush, some kill or steal or turn into religious freaks? You're a mild case, comparatively speaking. All you want is to be with it, calmly, like a lover.'

I was crying before I knew it, tears of relief. He was the first to consent to my line of feeling. Why had it been so hard, why were they all reluctant to do so? We allow people to mouth platitudes to us one after another, and agree to them blandly, knowing they aren't true, just because there's no bite to them, no danger. The truth is always dangerous, so in agreeing to what I felt, he was letting me in for danger. But it was all that was left to try.

'There's a bank account for you at this address.' He gave me the chequebook and the deposit slip. 'If you need more, call me. Your husband has agreed to this plan.'

I took the chequebook silently, but was vowing already that I would never use it. I was going to get a job.

The young doctor sat frowning, eyes on the floor.

'Denis feels awful,' I said, reading his thoughts aloud. 'This has made him suffer.'

'I didn't say that,' Dr Johnson said. 'It makes you suffer to stay with him. Maybe—well, maybe he can get through better without you than you can with him.'

From then on I was on my own, escaping into the mystery that is East Montreal, a fish thrown barely alive back into the water. Not that I had ever lived there. But to Westmount families who own houses in Baie d'Urfé, East Montreal presents even more of an opaque surface than NDG It is thought to be French, and this is so, but it is also Greek, Italian, Oriental, and immigrant Jewish. I was poor, unattractive as ever; I ached for my children and the sound of Denis's voice, his love, everything I had known. I went through an agony of missing what I could have, all back, and whole as ever, just by picking up the phone, just by taking a taxi and saying, 'Take me home.'

But when I gave in (and I did give in every time the world clicked over and I saw things right side up instead of upside down), odd consequences resulted. I would call a number but strange voices out of unknown business-es or residences would answer, or someone among the Partham friends would say hello, and I would begin to talk about myself—me, *me*, ME—relating imag-ined insults, or telling stories that were only partly true, and though I knew I was doing this, though my mind stood by like a chance pedestrian at the scene of an accident, interested, but a little sickened, with other things to do, still my voice, never lacking for a word, went on. Once I took a taxi home with all my possessions loaded inside, but directed the driver to the wrong turning, overshot the mark and wound up at the wrong driveway. The peo-ple who came out the door knew me; oh, this was horrible; I crouched down out of sight and shouted, 'Go back, go back! Take me home!' (The meaning of home had shifted, the world had flipped once more.)

Again I came on the bus in the middle of a fine afternoon, calm and right within myself, to 'talk things over', sanely to prepare for my return to the family. I found no one there, the house open, the living room empty. I sat down to wait. At a still centre, waiting for loved ones' faces to appear through a radiance of outer sunlight, I stared too hard at nothing, closed my eyes and heard it from the beginning: a silent scream, waxing unbearably. I had come to put out my arms, to say, I have failed to love, but now I know this. I love you, I love you all. What was there in this to make the world shrink back, flee, recede, rock with agony to its fair horizons? I could bear it no longer, and so fled. I ran past one of them, one of the Partham women (my mother-in-law, sister-in-law, aunt-in-law, a cousin?—they look alike, all of them) coming in from the garden in her white work gloves with shears in hand, a flat of cut flowers on her arm. *She* must have screamed also, I saw her mouth make the picture of a scream, but that is unimportant except to her. For if she was Denis's mother she must have wanted to scream ever since I had first walked into her presence, hand in hand with Denis, and then there I was back again, crazy and fleeing with a bruised forehead all purple and gold (in my haste to reach them I had slammed into a door).

My journey back on one rattling bus after another, threading streets under an overcast sky, seemed longer than I could have imagined. I wondered then and since if I had dreamed that journey, if I would not presently wake up in the dark room where my resolution had taken place at 3 a.m. (the hour of weakness and resolve), if the whole matter of getting up, dressing, taking the taxi, were not all a dream of the soul's motion upon deciding, while I myself, like a chained dog, lay still held to sleep and darkness. On the other hand, I wondered whether I had made that same decision and that same trip not once or twice but twenty or thirty times, as though the split side of myself were carrying on a life it would not tell me about. Denis had a brother who was a physicist and used to talk about a 'black hole in space', where matter collapses of its own gravity, ceases to exist in any form that we know of as existence. Yet some existence must continue. Was this myself, turned inside-out like a sleeve, whirled counterclockwise to a vacuum point, when I disappeared would I (Maureen) know it? Confusion thickened in my head.

I thought I saw Denis at the end of a snowy street in East Montreal near Dorchester Boulevard, a child holding to either hand, and so sprang up my fantasy that they often came to watch silently from somewhere just to see me pass, but often as I thought I glimpsed them, I never hastened to close the distance and find the answer.

'You prefer the fantasy to the reality,' Dr Johnson said.

'What made me the way I am? Why have I caused all this?'

'Becoming is difficult.'

'Becoming what?'

'Your alter ego. Your other self.'

'You've said it a hundred times.'

'So what?'

'It makes no sense, my other self. None whatever.'

'You feel it's irrational?'

We both fell silent and looked down as if this self had fallen like an object between us on the floor.

'No one is wholly rational,' Dr Johnson said.

I still sat looking. Rational or not, could it live, poor thing? If I nudged it with my toe, would it move?

'Basically, you are happier now,' he told me.

'I am lonely,' I said. The words fell out, without my knowing it. Perhaps the self on the floor had spoken.

'You like it, or you wouldn't be,' he said at once.

I was surprised by this last remark and returned home with something like an inner smile. For the first time in months I thought of buying something new and pretty and I looked in shop windows along the way. I stopped in a drugstore and got a lipstick. That night I washed my hair. Sitting out on my balcony, watching the people drift by, smoking, the way I always like to do, I put a blanket over my still damp head, for it was only March, and the world was still iced, crusted in decaying snow. I sat like a squaw woman, but inside I felt a little stir of green feeling. I would be happy in this world I'd come to, not just an exile, a maverick that had jumped the fence. I would feel like a woman again.

A woman invisible, floating softly through a June day, I went to church when my daughter was confirmed. I sat far in the back in the dim church, St James on Bishop Street. Seeing her so beautiful, I felt exalted, meaning all the hymns, all the words. But as I was leaving I heard a murmuring behind me and my name spoken. Then a curate was chasing me, calling out my name. I knew him from the old days, didn't I? Wasn't he the one I'd asked to dinner and sherry and tea? He meant everything that was good; he wanted to grasp my hand and speak to me, about forgiveness, love, peace, the whole catalogue. But who stood back of him? Not the kingdom, the power, and the glory, but Parthams, Parthams, and Parthams. I ran like the wind. The air blew white in my face, white as my daughter's communion dress, white as a bridal veil. I stopped at last to gasp it down. No footsteps sounded from behind. I was safe once more. Running backward, I had broken records: forward, I'm unbeatable. This was the grim joke I told myself, skulking home.

'It was a big risk,' Dr Johnson warned me. 'How did you even know about the service?'

'A maid I used to have. She told me.'

'The trouble I've gone to. . . . Don't you realize they want to commit you? If they succeed, you may never get out again.'

'Nobody could keep me from seeing her,' I said. 'Not on that day.'

'To them you're a demon in the sacred place.' He was smiling, but I heard it solemnly. Maybe they were right.

Such, anyway, were my forays into enemy land.

But some were also made to me, in my new country. For I saw them, at times, and at others I thought I saw them, shadows at twilight on the edge of their forest, or real creatures venturing out and toward me; it was often impossible to tell which.

Carole Partham really came, graceful and hesitant, deerlike, and I let her come, perceiving that it was not curiosity or prying that brought her over, but an inner need to break away, to copy me, in some measure.

There she was one twilight, waiting in the pizza restaurant near my entrance. Carole was born a Partham, but her husband was Jim O'Brien, a broker. He was away in Europe, she said. Now's your big chance, she had doubtless told herself.

A smart-looking girl, up to the latest in clothes, a luxury woman, wearing suede with a lynx collar, tall brown rain boots, brushed brown hair.

'Come in,' I urged her, getting her out of that place where, dressed like that, she was making them nervous. 'I'm safe to be with. You can see my place.'

Then she was sitting, smoking, loosening her coat, eyes coasting about here and there, from floor to wall to ceiling. My apartment wasn't much to see. I would have set the dogs on her—dogs of my inner rages—if I hadn't seen her realness. Instead I saw it well: she was frightened. Happy or not? She didn't know. What does life mean? There was panic in the question, if you asked it often enough. She had no answer and her husband was away for quite some time.

'Come work here for a month,' I advised. 'You can get a job, or loaf, or think, or see what happens.'

But her eyes were restless; they stopped at closed drawers, probed at closet doors. Sex! Oh, certainly, I thought. Oh, naturally. I remember Jim O'Brien with his ready talk and his toothy grin flashing over an ever-present, ever-tilted tumbler of martini on the rocks, and the glitter and swagger in his stroll from guest to guest, his intimate flattering talk, and now I knew what I had thought all along: who would marry Jim O'Brien but a woman with a childhood terror still behind the door? And now she'd done it, how could she escape?

'Don't tell them where you are,' I advised. 'I can find a room for you maybe. Somewhere near if you want me to. You can see I've no space here.'

'Oh, I didn't want—'

'Just tell them you've gone away. What about Florida? You can say that.'

Helpless, the eyes roved.

'I've no one here,' I told her. 'No lover, no friend. I work in a photographer's studio. That's all there is to know. You'll see it at the corner. My boss is Mr Massimo. He owns it. There's nothing to know.'

After a long silence, she said, looking down at herself, 'These clothes are wrong.'

'Who cares? Just face it that nobody cares.'

'Nobody cares? Nobody *cares*?' She kept repeating this. It was what she couldn't swallow, had got hung up on, I guess, all by herself. I had hit it by accident.

'I mean,' I said, 'nobody over *here* cares. Over there . . . I don't know about that.'

'Nobody . . . nobody. . . .' Her voice now had gone flat. She got up to go, headed for the terrace window rather than the door, fell through the glass, stumbled over the terrace railing, her fashionable boots flailing the air, skirts sliding up to her neck. . . . But, no, this didn't happen. That wasn't the end of Carole. She went out the door, like anybody else.

She did move to the street for a time; I forget for how long. She brought plain old clothes and tied her head in a scarf. She worked some afternoons for a kind, arthritic Frenchman with white hair who ran a magazine shop. There was also the dark young man who stared down daily from a window four floors up; he descended to trail her home, offering to carry her grocery sack. How nice this tableau looked and how charming it would have been if only his I.Q. had been half-way average. He was once a doorman, I understood, but had kept falling asleep on his feet, like a horse.

She got drunk on resin-tasting wine one night in a Greek restaurant and lured eleven Greek waiters into a cheap hotel room. How sweet and eager and passionate they had seemed! They milled around—or so I was told—not knowing what to do. A humiliation to end all mental nymphomania: Carole escaped unmolested.

She had found a room with a woman whose mother had died and who baby-sat for pin money. On long evenings when she didn't baby-sit she told Carole the story of her life. Otherwise, Carole read, and drank, and told herself the story of her own life. She was happy in the butcher shop once and sat madonna-like with the butcher's cat purring in her lap, but the butcher's Spanish wife did not like her and kicked the cat to say so. Mr Massimo pondered about her. 'How did you know her?' he asked. 'She once knew my sister,' is all I answered.

Old clothes or not, Carole did one thing she didn't intend: she gave out the indefinable air of class. Surely, the street began to say, she was the forerunner of an 'in' group which would soon discover us and then we would all make money and turn into background to be glanced at. So some thought. But when I saw her, knowing better, I saw a host of other women—pretty, cared-for women—walking silently with her, rank on rank, women for whom nothing will ever quite add up. Every day, I guess, she wrote down her same old problems, in different combinations, and every day she got the same sum.

Suddenly, one day, she was before me. 'My month is up. It's been a wonderful experience.'

'I'm glad you thought so.'

We both sat smoking thoughtfully, occasionally glancing at each other. I knew her room had been rifled twice by thieves and that she could not sleep at night when the baby-sitter baby-sat. The faces of those Greek waiters would, I imagine, press on her memory forever. If the world is one, what was the great secret to make those faces accessible to her own self? The answer had escaped her.

'It's been a great experience,' she repeated, smiling brightly, her mouth like painted wood, like a wound.

A voice, another voice, in that same room is talking . . . Vinnie Partham and her husband Charles? It can't be.

'. . . I knew it was safe to see you again when Carole confessed that she had and you were all right. Carole's gone into social work, she got over her crisis whatever it was, and now we're thinking it's time you got through with yours, for you may not be able even to imagine how desolate Denis still is, Maureen. Can you, can you?

'We thought for a long time the problem was sexual but then we decided you were out to destroy us and then we thought your mental condition would make you incapable of anything at all by way of job or friends. But all our theories are wrong, I guess.'

On she goes, with Charles dozing in his chair after the manner of British detectives in the movies, who look dumb but are actually intelligent and wide awake, solving the perfect crime, the difference being that Charles really is both half-asleep and stupid and has never been known to solve anything at all. Vinnie knows it. The phrases have started looping out of her mouth like a backward spaghetti-eating process. Luminous cords reach up and twine with others, grow into patterns of thought. The patterns are dollar signs. I see them forming.

'With Denis having no heart for the estate affairs, what chance have

Charles and I for the consideration he's always extended us? And if you think who, out of a perfect grab bag of women now getting interested, he might actually take it in his head to marry–'

Something dawns on me. Vinnie Partham is never going to stop talking!

I stare at her and stare, feeling cross-eyed with wonder and helpless and hypnotized, like someone watching a force in nature take its course. What can I do? She'll be there forever.

'I'm tired, Vinnie,' I tell her. 'I'm terribly tired.'

They melt away, her mouth is moving still. . . . Did I dream them? Do women still wear long beads? Can it really be they wanted me back for nothing but money? No, money is their name for something else. That chill place, that flaw in the world fabric, that rift in the Partham world about the size of Grand Canyon–they keep trying to fill it, trying to fill it, on and on, throwing everything in to fill it up. It was why Denis wanted me.

Oh, my poor children! Could they ever grow up to look like Aunt Vinnie and Uncle Charles?

At the thought of them, so impossibly beautiful, so possibly doomed, noises like cymbals crash in my ears, my eyes blur and stream. If my visitors were there I could not see them.

But they must be gone, I think, squinting around the room, if they were there at all. If they were ever alive at all . . . if they were ever anywhere.

Through all this, night was coming on; and summer–that, too, was coming on. Vinnie and Charles were dreams. But love is real.

I first saw Michel when he came to the photographer's shop for some application-size pictures. He was thin and ravaged, frowning, worried, *pressé*. I had learned to do routine requests as Mr Massimo was often away taking wedding pictures or attending occasions such as christenings and retirements. Mr Massimo thrived on the events, which included fancy food and lots to drink and dressed-up women. It was when Michel and I got in the semi-dark of the photographing room together that I received his full impact. I stirred about among the electrical cords, the lamp stands; I wielded the heavy-headed camera into focus; I directed his chin to lift, then found him in the lenses, dark and straight. Indian blood? I snapped the shutter.

He said he was new in the neighbourhood, lived up the street, and would come back next day to see the proofs.

But I passed him again, not an hour later, on my way home. He was sitting outdoors at the pizza parlour talking volubly to the street cleaner who had stopped there for a beer. He saw me pass, go in my building, and I felt his regard in my senses.

Who was he? What would he do?

Something revolutionary was what I felt to be in his bones. Political? Then he would be making contacts and arguing for the liberation of the province.

I was wrong. No passion for Quebec but the rent of an empty barber-shop was what had brought him there, one on the lower floor of a small building with a tree in front. He was going to put in one of those shops that sold hippie costumes, Indian shirts, long skirts, built-up shoes, some papier-mâché decorators' items, and some artwork. This would incidentally give him a chance to show some of his own artwork, which had failed to interest the uptown galleries. He was going to leave the barber chairs and mirrors, using them all as decor, props, for the things he sold.

He told me all this when he came to see the photographs. Mr Massimo had gone to a reunion of retired hockey players. Michel looked over the proofs and selected one. He wanted it enlarged, a glossy finish he could reproduce to make ads for his shop. He was telling me how in some detail and I thought that a little more would find him back in Mr Massimo's dark-room, doing it for himself.

'I hope your business works,' I said.

The day before, skirting about among the photographic equipment, we had entangled face to face among some electrical cords, which we had methodically to unplug and unwind to find release from a near embrace. Now, he turned from a scrutiny of his own face to a minute examination of my own.

'If you hope so, then you think it could. *Vous le croyez*, eh?'

'*Moi? J'en sais pas, moi*. What does it matter?'

His elbow skidded on the desk. His face beetled into my own. It was his eyes that were compelling, better than good, making an importance out of themselves, out of my opinions, out of me.

'Your thinking so . . . why, that's strong. You have power. *Vous êtes formidable*. That's it, madame. *C'est ça.*'

A tilt of the head, an inch or two more, and our mouths, once more, might have closed together. My own was dry and thirsty, it woke to tell me so.

He straightened, gathered up his pictures, and neatly withdrew. His step left the doorway empty. I filled the order blank carefully.

It had turned much warmer and after work now I sat on the balcony with the windows open behind me and what I had to call curtains even stirred a bit, a dreamy lift of white in a dusk-softened room. I was moved to put a Mozart record on. I remembered that Mozart had died a pauper and been carried by cart to the outskirts of Vienna in winter and dumped in a hole. To me, that made the music tenderer still. Michel! From the day I'd seen him a private tower had begun to rise about me; its walls were high and strong. I might gnaw toast and jam and gulp coffee standing in my closet-sized kitchen, wriggle into the same old skirt, blouse, sweater, and leather coat (now put away), and walk to work, a drab, square-set, middle-aged woman going past at an accustomed time, but, within myself, a princess came to life and she leaned from high-set window sills. Did Michel know, she kept on asking, as she studied the horizon and admired the blue sky.

He passed the shop twice, once for his enlargement, once to talk; he went by daily on the street. A stir went up about his footsteps. He would change us all. At the very least, I reasoned, he kept my mind off the divorce papers.

One night there was a shouting in the street and a clang of fire engines. I rushed to the balcony and saw where it was: Michel's, up on the corner. A moment later I heard his voice from the shadows, down in the street below, and I hurried to let him in, climbed back with him unseen, opened my door to him for the first time.

He had caught my hands, holding them together in his own, in a grasp warm with life. His explanations blundered out . . . coming back from somewhere, tired, smoking in bed, fell asleep, the stuff collected for the shop catching fire. 'But if they know I'm back, that I set the fire, then the shop will never open. Nobody saw me. Nobody. Will you let me stay? Will you?'

'Smoking in bed, that's crazy.'

'Correct.' He leaned wearily toward me, smiling, sallow cheekbone sharp against my cheek, then holding closer, his mouth searching, and mine searching, too, finding and holding. The will to have him there was present already: it was he who'd set the tower up, and furnished it, for this very thing, for his refuge. But for such enfoldment as we found, the binding of my thought was needed, the total silent agreement that a man and woman make, a matched pattern for love. The heart of his gamble was there. He won it.

Left alone while I worked, Michel sat in the corner and read all day.

'What do you do when you're not reading?' I would ask, coming in from work.

'*Je pense.*'

'*A quoi?*'

'*A toi.*'

'*Tu pense à toi. Et tu le sais bien, toi.*' I was putting down my bag, I was emptying my grocery sack, but always I was turning to him. And I was moving to him. And he to me.

There was talk on the street of the fire, how the whole house had almost caught, and about the strange absence of Michel, whose inflammable junk had caused it all, but for whom nobody had an address or a telephone number.

One day I came from work and the tower stood empty. I knew it before I opened the door; Michel was gone. Through empty space I moved at last to the balcony and there up the street a taxi was pulling up before the rooming house. Out stepped Michel, as though home from a long journey, even carrying a suitcase! For the first time, it seemed, he was discovering his charred quarters, calling out the building superintendent, raising a commotion on the steps for all to hear. Quarreling, shouting, and multiple stories—they went on till nightfall.

Michel tried, at least, to collect the insurance on damages to his property. I never knew for certain if it worked. He said that it did, but he seldom told the truth. It was not his nature. If the fire was accidental, he escaped without a damage suit. But if he did it on purpose, hoping for insurance money to buy a better class of junk, and counting in advance on me to shelter him, then he was a fool to take so much risk. But why begin to care? Liar, cheat, thief, and lover—he stays unchanged and unexplaining. We have never had it out, or made it up, or parted. The tower is dissolving as his presence fades from it, leaves as water drying from a fabric, thread by thread. It floats invisible, but at least undestroyed. I felt this even after his shop opened—even after a dark young girl with long hair and painted eyes came to work there.

He comes and goes. Summer is over. *C'est ça.*

To think the Parthams ever let go is a serious mistake.

I recall a winter night now, lost in driving snow. There is a madness of snow, snow everywhere, teeming, shifting, lofty as curtains in the dream of a mad opera composer, cosmic, yet intimate as a white thread caught in an eyelash. The buses stall on Côte des Neiges: there is a moaning impotence among them, clouds of exhaust and a dimming of their interior lights as they strain to ascend the long hill, but some already have given up and stand dull and bulky, like great animals in herd awaiting some imminent extinction. The passengers file from them. I toil upward from Sherbrooke through a deepening tunnel, going toward the hospital. My son's name has become the sound of my heart. The receptionist directs me to a certain floor.

I think of everyone inside as infinitely small because of the loftiness of the night outside, its mad whiteness, chaotic motion, insatiable teeming. The hospital is a toy with lights, set on the mountain, a bump like a sty. The night will go on forever, it seems to be saying; it will if it wants to and it wants to and it will. So I (human) am small beneath this lofty whim. Perhaps I think like this to minimize the dull yet painful edge of guilt. My son may die; I abandoned him years ago. Yet he wants to see me, and they have thought that he should be permitted to. And I have thought, Why think it is good of them, nobody is that bad? and Why think it is good of me either, no mother is that cold? (But they might have been, and so might I.) Under realms of snow I progress at snail pace, at bug size, proving that great emotion lives in tiny hearts. On the floor, a passing aide, little as a sparrow, indicates the way. At the desk, a nurse, a white rabbit, peers at a note that has been left. Snow at the window, furious, boils. 'Mr Partham regrets he cannot be here. . . . You wish to see the boy? It's number ten.' Swollen feelings lift me down the corridor. I crack the door. 'Mother, is that you?' 'Yes.' 'I knew you'd come.' 'Of course, I came.' His hand, at last, is mine. It is the world.

Night after night I come, through blizzard, through ice and sleet, once in a silenced snow-bound city walking more than half the way into a wind with a -40° wind chill against my face, ant-sized under the glitter of infinite distances, at home with the derision of stars. So I push my stubborn nightly way. 'You are sleepy,' says Mr Massimo at work. 'Why are you so sleepy lately?' I tell him nothing. I can't for yawning.

Bundled in my dark coat, in the shadowy corridor, I sometimes, when Parthams are present, doze. They walk around me, speak to one another, are aware of my presence but do not address it. Denis, once, appearing, stands directly before me; when I lift my head our eyes meet, and they speak and we know it, yes we do. But there is a wall clear as glass between us and if we should fling ourselves through it, it would smash and let us through. Still, we would hurtle past each other. For the glass has a trick in it, a layer at the centre seems to place us face to face but really angles us apart. He knows it, I know it. We have been shown the diagram. He nods and turns away.

Several times I see his wife. I recognize her by the newspaper photographs. She is quietly, expensively dressed, with soft shining hair, the one he should have married in the first place. I do not need the coat. Sitting there in the warm room, why do I wear it? The minute the Parthams leave, I shed it. Its dropping from me is real but a symbol also. I am in the room in the same moment.

We hardly talk at all, my son and I. We know everything there is to know already. I sense the hour, almost the minute, when his health begins to flow back again.

We are sitting together on a Saturday morning. Dawn has come to a clear spotless frozen sky. Smoke from the glittering city beneath us, laid out below the windows, turns white. It plumes upward in windless purity. I have been here through the night. We are talking. It is the last time; I know that, too. The needles have been withdrawn from his arms. Soon the morning routine of the hospital will begin to crackle along the hallway and some

of it will enter here. I look around me and see what things the Parthams
have filled the room with—elegant little transistor radios, sports books and
magazines, a lovely tropical aquarium where brilliant fish laze fin and tail
among the shells and water plants. Nothing has been spared. He is smiling.
His nightmare with the long name—peritonitis—is over. His gaze is weak no
longer, but has entered sunlight, is penetrating and can judge.

So much drops away from a sick person; ideas, personality, ambition,
interests—all the important Partham baggage. When the pressures of the
body turn eccentric and everything is wrong, then they find their secret
selves. But once the Partham body returns, it's a sign of laziness not to look
around, discriminate, find life 'interesting', activities 'meaningful'; it would
be silly not to be a Partham since a Partham is what one so fortunately is.
'Can I come to find you when I get out of here?' my son begs. 'Can I,
Mother?' 'Of course, of course, you can.' 'I promise to.' I am on my way,
before the nurse comes with her thermometers or the elephantine gray
wagon of trays lumbers in. I am into my coat again, retreating from the
Partham gaze. But my insect heart in the unlikely shape of me, almost permanently bent, like a wind-blasted tree, by the awful humours of that phenomenal winter, is incandescent with inextinguishable joy. He will live, he
will live. Nothing, nobody, can take that away. I stumble, slip, list, slide
down frozen pavements, squeaking over surfaces of impacted snow. In the
crystal truth of the day world, the night is done. He will live.

(His name? My son's name? I won't tell you.)

I wing, creep, crawl, hop—what you will—back into my world.

Denis, eventually, seeks me. He comes to find me. A third Partham. I see
him at a street end.

He is grey; the winter has made everybody's skin too pale, except, I suppose, the habitual skiers who go up on peaks where the sun strikes. Denis
used to ski, but not this year. There he is, grey at the street's end. All has
been blown bare and lean by the awful winter. He is himself lean, clean, with
grey overcoat and Persian lamb hat, darker gray trousers, brown, fur-lined
gloves. 'Maureen? Can we go somewhere? Just have a coffee . . . talk a little?' We go to the 'bar-b-q' place. It's impersonal there, being on a busy corner; at the pizza restaurant they would want to know who Denis was, and
why he'd come, and do I have a new boyfriend. Also Michel might pass by.

'He thinks you saved him,' Denis tells me. 'For all I know, it's true. But
he thinks more than that. He's obsessed with you . . . can't talk of anything
else at times. I don't know what to do, Maureen. He thinks you're a saint,
something more than human. Your visits were only half-real to him. They
were like—appearances, apparitions.' He stops, hesitant. It is the appealing,

unsure Denis, absent, I imagine, for most of the time, that I see again as I saw him when we first met, seeking out my eyes, begging for something.

'It must be easy to disillusion him,' I say. 'You, of all people, could best do that.'

'Oh, he's heard all the facts. Not so much from me, mind you . . .'

From his grandmother, I think, and his grandfather and his aunts. Heard all those things he 'ought to know'.

'I didn't know you went there so often, sat for whole nights at a time, it seems.' He is speaking out of a deepening despair, floundering.

'But you saw me there.'

'I know, but I—'

'Didn't you know I loved him, too?'

'You loved—' At the mention of love, his face seems about to shatter into a number of different planes, a face in an abstract painting, torn against itself. 'To me your love was always defective. You—Maureen, when we were first married, I would think over and over, Now is forever; forever is now. Why did you destroy it all? It frightens me to think of you sitting, in the dark hours, with that boy. You could have pinched his life out like a match.'

'I wouldn't do that, Denis. I couldn't hurt what's hurt already.' I could have told him what light is like, as I had seen its illusion that day before his accident, how the jagged force tore into my smoothly surfaced vision. I had tried to tell him once; he thought I was raving. Later I smashed a set of his mother's china, and tore up a beautifully tiled wall with my nails, until they split and the blood ran down.

'I thought I had some force that would help him. That's not why I went but it's why I stayed.'

'It might not have worked,' Denis reflected. 'He might have died anyway.'

'Then you could have blamed me,' I pointed out. 'Then I could have been a witch, an evil spirit.'

'I don't know why you ever had to turn into a spirit at all! Just a woman, a wife, a mother, a human being—! That's all I ever wanted!'

'Believe me, Denis,' I said. '*I don't know either.*'

We'd had it out that way, about a million times. Making no real progress, returning to our old familiar dead end, our hovel, which, in a way, was the only home we had.

I was then inspired to say: 'It just may be, Denis, that if I'd never left, I could never have returned, and if I never had returned, it just may be that he would never have lived, he would have died, Denis, think of that, he would be dead.'

For a moment, I guess he did consider it. His face turned to mine, mouth parted. He slipped little by little into the idea, let himself submerge within it. I will say for Denis: at least, he did that. 'The doctors,' he said at last, 'they were terribly good, you know. The major credit,' he said, finishing his coffee, 'goes to them.'

'Undoubtedly,' I said. He had come to the surface, and turned back into a Partham again.

It had been a clear, still, frozen afternoon when we met, but holding just that soft touch of violet which said that winter would at last give over. Its grip was terrible, but a death grip no longer.

I tried to recall my old routine, to show my Partham side myself. 'I imagine he will find new interests, once he gets more active. He won't think so much about me. But, Denis, if he does want to hold on to something about me, can't you let him?'

'I wouldn't dream of stopping him. It's a matter of proportion, that's all.' He was pulling on his beautiful gloves. 'He's practically made a religion of you.'

As we were going out, I saw it all more clearly and began to laugh. 'Then that's your answer, Denis.'

'What is?'

'If I'm to be a "religion", then there are ways of handling me. Confine me to one hour a week, on Sunday morning . . . I need never get out of bounds. Don't worry about him, Denis. He's a Partham, after all.'

'Maureen? You're bitter, aren't you? People *have* to live, even Parthams. Life *has* to go on.'

We were standing outside by then, at the intersection with my street. He wouldn't enter there, I thought; it was not in accord with his instincts to do so.

'I'm not bitter,' I said. 'I'm helpless.'

'It didn't have to be that way.'

It was like a final exchange; it had a certain ring. He leaned to touch my face, then drew back, moving quickly away, not looking behind.

And now I am waiting for the fourth visitor, my son. I think I will see him, at some street corner, seeking me, find him waiting for me in the pizza shop, hear a voice say, 'Mother? I promised you. . . .' And before I know it, I will have said his name. . . .

I am waiting still.

Mr Massimo, one day, leans at me over his portrait camera. 'I hear you were married to a wealthy man in Westmount,' he says.

'I am a princess in a silver tower,' I reply. 'Golden birds sing to me. I drift around in a long silk gown. What about you?'

'My father was Al Capone's brother. We rode around when young in a secondhand Rolls-Royce with a crest of the House of Savoia painted on the door. Then we got run out of Italy. The family took another name.' He is smiling at me. It is not the story that reaches me, true or false, but the outpouring sun of Italy.

'You'll get me fired,' I tell Michel.

'Come work for me,' he says. 'You can tell fortunes in the back. I'll make you rich.'

He's using me again, working in collage—photography plus painting—he needs Mr Massimo's darkroom. I telephone him when Mr Massimo is gone and he comes to run a print through, or make an enlargement. When this phase passes, he will go again.

But he creates a picture before that, half-photo, half-drawing. He photographs my hands over a blood-red glass globe, lighted from within. I think the fortune-telling idea has given him the image. He makes the light strong; the veins of my hands stand out in great detail; the bones are almost X-ray visible. 'Let me wash my hands,' I say, because dirt shows under the nail tips. 'No, I like it that way, leave it.' So it stays. Watching Michel, I forget to feel anything else, and he is busy timing, setting, focusing. So the hands stay in place as my feelings rock with the sense of the light, and when he shuts it off, finished, we lock the shop up and go home together. Only the next day do I notice that my palm is burned so badly I have to bandage it and go for days in pain. Is the pain for Michel? Damn Michel! The pain is mine, active and virulent. It is mine alone.

The picture, with its background drawing of a woman in evening dress turned from a doorway, and its foreground of hands across a glowing glass, catches on. Michel has others in his package, but none is so popular as this one. He makes enlargements, sells them, makes others, sells those. They go out by the hundreds.

'What is it you carry? *Qu'est-ce que tu as*, Maureen?' Now he is after me, time and again, intense, vulpine, impossible, begging from doorways, brushing my shoulder as he passes in the dark. '*Qu'est-ce que tu as?*'

'I don't know. *Que t'importe, toi?*'

Among his pictures, a US distributor chooses this one, one of three. If I go to certain shops in New York where cheap exotic dress is sold, incense, and apartment decorations of the lowlier sort, bought for their grass-scented pads by homosexual pairs, or by students or young lovers, or by adventurous young people with little taste for permanence, I will see that picture somewhere among them, speaking its silent language. I will look at my hands, see the splash of red that lingers. The world over, copies of it will eventually stick up out of garbage cans, or will be left in vacated apartments. Held to the wall by one thumb tack, it will hang above junk not thought to be worth moving. It celebrates life as fleeting as a dance.

Yet it was created, it happened, and that, in its smallness must pass for everything—must, in this instance, stand for all.

❧

THE MOSLEM WIFE

In the south of France, in the business room of a hotel quite near to the house where Katherine Mansfield (whom no one in this hotel had ever heard of) was writing 'The Daughters of the Late Colonel', Netta Asher's father announced that there would never be a man-made catastrophe in Europe again. The dead of that recent war, the doomed nonsense of the Russian Bolsheviks had finally knocked sense into European heads. What people wanted now was to get on with life. When he said 'life', he meant its commercial business.

Who would have contradicted Mr Asher? Certainly not Netta. She did not understand what he meant quite so well as his French solicitor seemed to, but she did listen with interest and respect, and then watched him signing papers that, she knew, concerned her for life. He was renewing the long lease her family held on the Hotel Prince Albert and Albion. Netta was then eleven. One hundred years should at least see her through the prime of life, said Mr Asher, only half jokingly, for of course he thought his seed was immortal.

Netta supposed she might easily live to be more than a hundred—at any rate, for years and years. She knew that her father did not want her to marry until she was twenty-six and that she was then supposed to have a pair of children, the elder a boy. Netta and her father and the French lawyer shook hands on the lease, and she was given her first glass of champagne. The date on the bottle was 1909, for the year of her birth. Netta bravely pronounced the wine delicious, but her father said she would know much better vintages before she was through.

Netta remembered the handshake but perhaps not the terms. When the lease had eighty-eight years to run, she married her first cousin, Jack Ross, which was not at all what her father had had in mind. Nor would there be the useful pair of children—Jack couldn't abide them. Like Netta he came from a hotelkeeping family where the young were like blight. Netta had up to now never shown a scrap of maternal feeling over anything, but Mr Asher thought Jack might have made an amiable parent—a kind one, at least. She consoled Mr Asher on one count, by taking the hotel over in his lifetime. The hotel was, to Netta, a natural life; and so when Mr Asher, dying, said, 'She behaves as I wanted her to,' he was right as far as the drift of Netta's behaviour was concerned but wrong about its course.

The Ashers' hotel was not down on the seafront, though boats and sea could be had from the south-facing rooms.

Across a road nearly empty of traffic were handsome villas, and behind and to either side stood healthy olive trees and a large lemon grove. The hotel was painted a deep ochre with white trim. It had white awnings and green shutters and black iron balconies as lacquered and shiny as Chinese boxes. It possessed two tennis courts, a lily pond, a sheltered winter garden, a formal rose garden, and trees full of nightingales. In the summer dark, *belles-de-nuit* glowed pink, lemon, white, and after their evening watering they gave off a perfume that varied from plant to plant and seemed to match the petals' colouration. In May the nights were dense with stars and fireflies. From the rose garden one might have seen the twin pulse of cigarettes on a balcony, where Jack and Netta sat drinking a last brandy-and-soda before turning in. Most of the rooms were shuttered by then, for no traveller would have dreamed of being south except in winter. Jack and Netta and a few servants had the whole place to themselves. Netta would hire workmen and have the rooms that needed it repainted—the blue card-room, and the red-walled bar, and the white dining room, where Victorian mirrors gave back glossy walls and blown curtains and nineteenth-century views of the Ligurian coast, the work of an Asher great-uncle. Everything upstairs and down was soaked and wiped and polished, and even the pictures were relentlessly washed with soft cloths and ordinary laundry soap. Netta also had the boiler overhauled and the linen mended and new monograms embroidered and the looking glasses resilvered and the shutters taken off their hinges and scraped and made spruce green again for next year's sun to fade, while Jack talked about decorators and expert gardeners and even wrote to some, and banged tennis balls against the large new garage. He also read books and translated poetry for its own sake and practiced playing the clarinet. He had studied music once, and still thought that an important life, a musical life, was there in the middle distance. One summer, just to see if he could, he translated pages of St John Perse, which were as blank as the garage wall to Netta, in any tongue.

Netta adored every minute of her life, and she thought Jack had a good life too, with nearly half the year for the pleasures that suited him. As soon as the grounds and rooms and cellar and roof had been put to rights, she and Jack packed and went travelling somewhere. Jack made the plans. He was never so cheerful as when buying Baedekers and dragging out their stickered trunks. But Netta was nothing of a traveller. She would have been glad to see the same sun rising out of the same sea from the window every day until she died. She loved Jack, and what she liked best after him was the hotel. It was a place where, once, people had come to die of tuberculosis, yet it held no trace or feeling of danger. When Netta walked with her workmen through sheeted summer rooms, hearing the cicadas and hearing Jack start, stop, start some deeply alien music (alien even when her memory automatically gave her a composer's name), she was reminded that here the dead had never been allowed to corrupt the living; the dead had been dressed for an outing and removed as soon as their first muscular stiffness relaxed. Some were wheeled out in chairs, sitting, and some reclined on portable cots, as if merely resting.

That is why there is no bad atmosphere here, she would say to herself. Death has been swept away, discarded. When the shutters are closed on a room, it is for sleep or for love. Netta could think this easily because neither she nor Jack was ever sick. They knew nothing about insomnia, and they made love every day of their lives—they had married in order to be able to.

Spring had been the season for dying in the old days. Invalids who had struggled through the dark comfort of winter took fright as the night receded. They felt without protection. Netta knew about this, and about the difference between darkness and brightness, but neither affected her. She was not afraid of death or of the dead—they were nothing but cold, heavy furniture. She could have tied jaws shut and weighted eyelids with native instinctiveness, as other women were born knowing the temperature for an infant's milk.

'There are no ghosts,' she could say, entering the room where her mother, then her father had died. 'If there were, I would know.'

Netta took it for granted, now she was married, that Jack felt as she did about light, dark, death, and love. They were as alike in some ways (none of them physical) as a couple of twins, spoke much the same language in the same accents, had the same jokes—mostly about other people—and had been together as much as their families would let them for most of their lives. Other men seemed dull to Netta—slower, perhaps, lacking the spoken shorthand she had with Jack. She never mentioned this. For one thing, both of them had the idea that, being English, one must not say too much. Born abroad, they worked hard at an Englishness that was innocently inaccurate, rooted mostly in attitudes. Their families had been innkeepers along this coast for a century, even before Dr James Henry Bennet had discovered 'the Genoese Rivieras'. In one of his guides to the region, a 'Mr Ross' is mentioned as a hotel owner who will accept English bank cheques, and there is a 'Mr Asher', reliable purveyor of English groceries. The most trustworthy shipping agents in 1860 are the Montale brothers, converts to the Anglican Church, possessors of a British *laissez-passer* to Malta and Egypt. These families, by now plaited like hair, were connections of Netta's and Jack's and still in business from beyond Marseilles to Genoa. No wonder that other men bored her, and that each thought the other both familiar and unique. But of course they were unalike too. When once someone asked them, 'Are you related to Montale, the poet?' Netta answered, 'What poet?' and Jack said, 'I wish we were.'

There were no poets in the family. Apart from the great-uncle who had painted landscapes, the only person to try anything peculiar had been Jack, with his music. He had been allowed to study, up to a point; his father had been no good with hotels—had been a failure, in fact, bailed out four times by his cousins, and it had been thought, for a time, that Jack Ross might be a dunderhead too. Music might do him; he might not be fit for anything else.

Information of this kind about the meaning of failure had been gleaned by Netta years before, when she first became aware of her little cousin. Jack's father and mother—the commercial blunderers—had come to the Prince Albert and Albion to ride out a crisis. They were somewhere between undischarged bankruptcy and annihilation, but one was polite: Netta curtsied to her aunt and uncle. Her eyes were on Jack. She could not read yet, though she could sift and classify attitudes. She drew near him, sucking her lower lip, her hands behind her back. For the first time she was conscious of the beauty of another child. He was younger than Netta, imprisoned in a portable-fence arrangement in which he moved tirelessly, crabwise, hanging on a barrier he could easily have climbed. He was as fair as his Irish mother and sunburned a deep brown. His blue gaze was not a baby's—it was too challenging. He was naked except for shorts that were large and seemed about to fall down. The sunburn, the undress were because his mother was reckless and rather odd. Netta—whose mother was perfect—wore boots, stockings, a longsleeved frock, and a white sun hat. She heard the adults laugh and say that Jack looked like a prizefighter. She walked around his prison, staring, and the blue-eyed fighter stared back.

The Rosses stayed for a long time, while the family sent telegrams and tried to raise money for them. No one looked after Jack much. He would lie on a marble step of the staircase watching the hotel guests going into the cardroom or the dining room. One night, for a reason that remorse was to wipe out in a minute, Netta gave him such a savage kick (though he was not really in her way) that one of his legs remained paralysed for a long time.

'*Why* did you do it?' her father asked her—this is the room where she was shut up on bread and water. Netta didn't know. She loved Jack, but who would believe it now? Jack learned to walk, then to run, and in time to ski and play tennis; but her lifelong gift to him was a loss of balance, a sudden lopsided bend of a knee. Jack's parents had meantime been given a small hotel to run at Bandol. Mr Asher, responsible for a bank loan, kept an eye on the place. He went often, in a hotel car with a chauffeur, Netta perched beside him. When, years later, the families found out that the devoted young cousins had become lovers, they separated them without saying much. Netta was too independent to be dealt with. Besides, her father did not want a rift; his wife had died, and he needed Netta. Jack, whose claim on music had been the subject of teasing until now, was suddenly sent to study in England. Netta saw that he was secretly dismayed. He wanted to be almost anything as long as it was impossible, and then only as an act of grace. Netta's father did think it was his duty to tell her that marriage was, at its best, a parched arrangement, intolerable without a flow of golden guineas and fresh blood. As cousins, Jack and Netta could not bring each other anything except stale money. Nothing stopped them: they were married four months after Jack became twenty-one. Netta heard someone remark at her wedding, 'She doesn't need a husband,' meaning perhaps the practical, matter-of-fact person she now seemed to be. She did have the dry, burned-out look of someone turned inward. Her dark eyes glowed out of a thin face. She had the shape of a girl of fourteen. Jack, who was large, and fair, and who might be stout at forty if he wasn't careful, looked exactly his age, and seemed quite ready to be married.

Netta could not understand why, loving Jack as she did, she did not look more like him. It had troubled her in the past when they did not think exactly the same thing at almost the same time. During the secret meetings of their long engagement she had noticed how even before a parting they were nearly apart—they had begun to 'unmesh', as she called it. Drinking a last drink, usually in the buffet of a railway station, she would see that Jack was somewhere else, thinking about the next-best thing to Netta. The next-best thing might only be a book he wanted to finish reading, but it was enough to make her feel exiled. He often told Netta, 'I'm not holding on to you. You're free,' because he thought it needed saying, and of course he wanted freedom for himself. But to Netta 'freedom' had a cold sound. Is that what I do want, she would wonder. Is that what I think he should offer? Their partings were often on the edge of parting forever, not just because Jack had said or done or thought the wrong thing but because between them they generated the high sexual tension that leads to quarrels. Barely ten minutes after agreeing that no one in the world could possibly know what they knew, one of them, either one, could curse the other out over something trivial. Yet they were, and remained, much in love, and when they were apart Netta sent him letters that were almost despairing with enchantment.

Jack answered, of course, but his letters were cautious. Her exploration

of feeling was part of an unlimited capacity she seemed to have for passionate behaviour, so at odds with her appearance, which had been dry and
sardonic even in childhood. Save for an erotic sentence or two near the end
(which Netta read first) Jack's messages might have been meant for any girl
cousin he particularly liked. Love was memory, and he was no good at the
memory game; he needed Netta there. The instant he saw her he knew all
he had missed. But Netta, by then, felt forgotten, and she came to each new
meeting aggressive and hurt, afflicted with the physical signs of her doubts
and injuries—cold sores, rashes, erratic periods, mysterious temperatures. If
she tried to discuss it he would say, 'We aren't going over all that again, are
we?' Where Netta was concerned he had settled for the established faith,
but Netta, who had a wilder, more secret God, wanted a prayer a minute,
not to speak of unending miracles and revelations.

When they finally married, both were relieved that the strain of partings and of tense disputes in railway stations would come to a stop. Each
privately blamed the other for past violence, and both believed that once
they could live openly, without interference, they would never have a dis-
agreement again. Netta did not want Jack to regret the cold freedom he had
vainly tried to offer her. He must have his liberty, and his music, and other
people, and, oh, anything he wanted—whatever would stop him from saying he was ready to let her go free. The first thing Netta did was to make
certain they had the best room in the hotel. She had never actually owned
a room until now. The private apartments of her family had always been
surrendered in a crisis: everyone had packed up and moved as beds were
required. She and Jack were hopelessly untidy, because both had spent their
early years moving down hotel corridors, trailing belts and raincoats, with
tennis shoes hanging from knotted strings over their shoulders, their arms
around books and sweaters and gray flannel bundles. Both had done
lessons in the corners of lounges, with cups and glasses rattling, and other
children running, and English voices louder than anything. Jack, who had
been vaguely educated, remembered his boarding schools as places where
one had a permanent bed. Netta chose for her marriage a south-facing room
with a large balcony and an awning of dazzling white. It was furnished with
lemonwood that had been brought to the Riviera by Russians for their own
villas long before. To the lemonwood Netta's mother had added English
chintzes; the result, in Netta's eyes, was not bizarre but charming. The
room was deeply mirrored; when the shutters were closed on hot afternoons a play of light became as green as a forest on the walls, and as blue
as seawater in the glass. A quality of suspension, of disbelief in gravity, now
belonged to Netta. She became tidy, silent, less introspective, as watchful
and as reflective as her bedroom mirrors. Jack stayed as he was, luckily; any

alteration would have worried her, just as a change in an often-read story will trouble a small child. She was intensely, almost unnaturally happy.

One day she overheard an English doctor, whose wife played bridge every afternoon at the hotel, refer to her, to Netta, as 'the little Moslem wife'. It was said affectionately, for the doctor liked her. She wondered if he had seen through walls and had watched her picking up the clothing and the wet towels Jack left strewn like clues to his presence. The phrase was collected and passed from mouth to mouth in the idle English colony. Netta, the last person in the world deliberately to eavesdrop (she lacked that sort of interest in other people), was sharp of hearing where her marriage was concerned. She had a special antenna for Jack, for his shades of meaning, secret intentions, for his innocent contradictions. Perhaps 'Moslem wife' meant several things, and possibly it was plain to anyone with eyes that Jack, without meaning a bit of harm by it, had a way with women. Those he attracted were a puzzling lot, to Netta. She had already catalogued them—elegant elderly parties with tongues like carving knives; gentle, clever girls who flourished on the unattainable; untouchable-daughter types, canny about their virginity, wondering if Jack would be father enough to justify the sacrifice. There was still another kind—tough, sunburned, clad in dark colours—who made Netta think in the vocabulary of horoscopes. Her gem—diamonds. Her colour—black. Her language—worse than Netta's. She noticed that even when Jack had no real use for a woman he never made it apparent; he adopted anyone who took a liking to him. He assumed—Netta thought—a tribal, paternal air that was curious in so young a man. The plot of attraction interested him, no matter how it turned out. He was like someone reading several novels at once, or like someone playing simultaneous chess.

Netta did not want her marriage to become a world of stone. She said nothing except, 'Listen, Jack, I've been at this hotel business longer than you have. It's wiser not to be too pally with the guests.' At Christmas the older women gave him boxes of expensive soap. 'They must think someone around here wants a good wash,' Netta remarked. Outside their fenced area of private jokes and private love was a landscape too open, too light-drenched, for serious talk. And then, when? Jack woke up quickly and early in the morning and smiled as naturally as children do. He knew where he was and the day of the week and the hour. The best moment of the day was the first cigarette. When something bloody happened, it was never before six in the evening. At night he had a dark look that went with a dark mood, sometimes. Netta would tell him that she could see a cruise ship floating on the black horizon like a piece of the Milky Way, and she would get that look for an answer. But it never lasted. His memory was too short to let him sulk, no matter what fragment of night had crossed his mind. She knew, having heard other couples all her life, that at least she and Jack never made the conjugal sounds that passed for conversation and that might as well have been bow-wow and quack quack.

If, by chance, Jack found himself drawn to another woman, if the tide of attraction suddenly ran the other way, then he would discover in himself a great need to talk to his wife. They sat out on their balcony for much of one long night and he told her about his Irish mother. His mother's eccentricity—'Vera's dottiness', where the family was concerned—had kept Jack from taking anything seriously. He had been afraid of pulling her mad attention in his direction. Countless times she had faked tuberculosis and cancer and announced her own imminent death. A telephone call from a hospital had once declared her lost in a car crash. 'It's a new life, a new life,' her husband had babbled, coming away from the phone. Jack saw his father then as beautiful. Women are beautiful when they fall in love, said Jack; sometimes the glow will last a few hours, sometimes even a day or two.

'You know,' said Jack, as if Netta knew, 'the look of amazement on a girl's face . . .'

Well, that same incandescence had suffused Jack's father when he thought his wife had died, and it continued to shine until a taxi deposited dotty Vera with her cheerful announcement that she had certainly brought off a successful April Fool. After Jack's father died she became violent. 'Getting away from her was a form of violence in me,' Jack said. 'But I did it.' That was why he was secretive; that was why he was independent. He had never wanted any woman to get her hands on his life.

Netta heard this out calmly. Where his own feelings were concerned she thought he was making them up as he went along. The garden smelled coolly of jasmine and mimosa. She wondered who his new girl was, and if he was likely to blurt out a name. But all he had been working up to was that his mother—mad, spoiled, devilish, whatever she was—would need to live with Jack and Netta, unless Netta agreed to giving her an income. An income would let her remain where she was—at the moment, in a Rudolf Steiner community in Switzerland, devoted to medieval gardening and to getting the best out of Goethe. Netta's father's training prevented even the thought of spending the money in such a matter.

'You won't regret all you've told me, will you?' she asked. She saw that the new situation would be her burden, her chain, her mean little joke sometimes. Jack scarcely hesitated before saying that where Netta mattered he could never regret anything. But what really interested him now was his mother.

'Lifts give her claustrophobia,' he said. 'She mustn't be higher than the second floor.' He sounded like a man bringing a legal concubine into his household, scrupulously anxious to give all his women equal rights. 'And I hope she will make friends,' he said. 'It won't be easy, at her age. One can't live without them.' He probably meant that he had none. Netta had been raised not to expect to have friends: you could not run a hotel and have scores of personal ties. She expected people to be polite and punctual and to mean what they said, and that was the end of it. Jack gave his friendship easily, but he expected considerable diversion in return.

Netta said dryly, 'If she plays bridge, she can play with Mrs Blackley.' This was the wife of the doctor who had first said 'Moslem wife.' He had come down here to the Riviera for his wife's health; the two belonged to a subcolony of flat-dwelling expatriates. His medical practice was limited to hypochondriacs and rheumatic patients. He had time on his hands: Netta often saw him in the hotel reading room, standing, leafing—he took pleasure in handling books. Netta, no reader, did not like touching a book unless it was new. The doctor had a trick of speech Jack loved to imitate: he would break up his words with an extra syllable, some words only, and at that not every time. 'It is all a matter of stu-hyle,' he said, for 'style', or, Jack's favourite, 'Oh, well, in the end it all comes down to su-hex.' 'Uh-hebb and flo-ho of hormones' was the way he once described the behaviour of saints— Netta had looked twice at him over that. He was a firm agnostic and the first person from whom Netta heard there existed a magical Dr Freud. When Netta's father had died of pneumonia, the doctor's 'I'm su-horry, Netta' had been so heartfelt she could not have wished it said another way.

His wife, Georgina, could lower her blood pressure or stop her heart-beat nearly at will. Netta sometimes wondered why Dr Blackley had brought her to a soft climate rather than to the man at Vienna he so admired. Georgina was well enough to play fierce bridge, with Jack and anyone good enough. Her husband usually came to fetch her at the end of the afternoon when the players stopped for tea. Once, because he was oblig-ed to return at once to a patient who needed him, she said, 'Can't you be competent about anything?' Netta thought she understood, then, his resigned repetition of 'It's all su-hex.' 'Oh, don't explain. You bore me,' said his wife, turning her back.

Netta followed him out to his car. She wore an India shawl that had been her mother's. The wind blew her hair; she had to hold it back. She said, 'Why don't you kill her?'

'I am not a desperate person,' he said. He looked at Netta, she looking up at him because she had to look up to nearly everyone except children, and he said, 'I've wondered why we haven't been to bed.'

'Who?' said Netta. 'You and your wife? Oh. You mean me.' She was not offended, she just gave the shawl a brusque tug and said, 'Not a hope.

Never with a guest,' though of course that was not the reason.

'You might have to, if the guest were a maharaja,' he said, to make it all harmless. 'I am told it is pu-hart of the courtesy they expect.'

'We don't get their trade,' said Netta. This had not stopped her liking the doctor. She pitied him, rather, because of his wife, and because he wasn't Jack and could not have Netta.

'I do love you,' said the doctor, deciding finally to sit down in his car. 'Ee-nee-ormously.' She watched him drive away as if she loved him too, and might never see him again. It never crossed her mind to mention any of this conversation to Jack.

That very spring, perhaps because of the doctor's words, the hotel did get some maharaja trade—three little sisters with ebony curls, men's eyebrows, large heads, and delicate hands and feet. They had four rooms, one for their governess. A chauffeur on permanent call lodged elsewhere. The governess, who was Dutch, had a perfect triangle of a nose and said 'whom' for 'who', pronouncing it 'whum'. The girls were to learn French, tennis, and swimming. The chauffeur arrived with a hairdresser, who cut their long hair; it lay on the governess's carpet, enough to fill a large pillow. Their toe-and fingernails were filed to points and looked like kitten's teeth. They came smiling down the marble staircase, carrying new tennis rackets, wearing blue linen skirts and navy blazers. Mrs Blackley glanced up from the bridge game as they went by the cardroom. She had been one of those opposed to their having lessons at the English Lawn Tennis Club, for reasons that were, to her, perfectly evident.

She said, loudly, 'They'll have to be in white.'

'End whay, pray?' cried the governess, pointing her triangle nose.

'They can't go on the courts except in white. It is a private club. Entirely white.'

'Whum do they all think they are?' the governess asked, prepared to stalk on. But the girls, with their newly cropped heads, and their vulnerable necks showing, caught the drift and refused to go.

'Whom indeed,' said Georgina Blackley, fiddling with her bridge hand and looking happy.

'My wife's seamstress could run up white frocks for them in a minute,' said Jack. Perhaps he did not dislike children all that much.

'Whom could,' muttered Georgina.

But it turned out that the governess was not allowed to choose their clothes, and so Jack gave the children lessons at the hotel. For six weeks they trotted around the courts looking angelic in blue, or hopelessly foreign, depending upon who saw them. Of course they fell in love with Jack, offering him a passionate loyalty they had nowhere else to place. Netta watched the transfer of this gentle, anxious gift. After they departed, Jack was bad-tempered for several evenings and then never spoke of them again; they, needless to say, had been dragged from him weeping.

When this happened the Rosses had been married nearly five years. Being childless but still very loving, they had trouble deciding which of the two would be the child. Netta overheard 'He's a darling, but she's a sergeant major and no mistake. And so *mean*.' She also heard 'He's a lazy bastard. He bullies her. She's a fool.' She searched her heart again about children. Was it Jack or had it been Netta who had first said no? The only child she had ever admired was Jack, and not as a child but as a fighter, defying her. She and Jack were not the sort to have animal children, and Jack's dotty mother would probably soon be child enough for any couple to handle. Jack still seemed to adopt, in a tribal sense of his, half the women who fell in love with him. The only woman who resisted adoption was Netta—still burned-out, still ardent, in a manner of speaking still fourteen. His mother had turned up meanwhile, getting down from a train wearing a sly air of enjoying her own jokes, just as she must have looked on the day of the April Fool. At first she was no great trouble, though she did complain about an ulcerated leg. After years of pretending, she at last had something real. Netta's policy of silence made Jack's mother confident. She began to make a mockery of his music: 'All that money gone for nothing!' Or else, 'The amount we wasted on schools! The hours he's thrown away with his nose in a book. All that reading—if at least it had got him somewhere.' Netta noticed that he spent more time playing bridge and chatting to cronies in the bar now. She thought hard, and decided not to make it her business. His mother had once been pretty; perhaps he still saw her that way. She came of a ramshackle family with a usable past; she spoke of the Ashers and the Rosses as if she had known them when they were tinkers. English residents who had a low but solid barrier with Jack and Netta were fences-down with his mad mother: they seemed to take her at her own word when it was about herself. She began then to behave like a superior sort of guest, inviting large parties to her table for meals, ordering special wines and dishes at inconvenient hours, standing endless rounds of drinks in the bar.

Netta told herself, Jack wants it this way. It is his home too. She began to live a life apart, leaving Jack to his mother. She sat wearing her own mother's shawl, hunched over a new, modern adding machine, punching out accounts. 'Funny couple,' she heard now. She frowned, smiling in her mind; none of these people knew what bound them, or how tied they were. She had the habit of dodging out of her mother-in-law's parties by saying, 'I've got such an awful lot to do.' It made them laugh, because they thought this was Netta's term for slave-driving the servants. They thought the staff did the work, and that Netta counted the profits and was too busy with bookkeeping to keep an eye on Jack—who now, at twenty-six, was as attractive as he ever would be.

A woman named Iris Cordier was one of Jack's mother's new friends. Tall, loud, in winter dully pale, she reminded Netta of a blond penguin. Her voice moved between a squeak and a moo, and was a mark of the distinguished literary family to which her father belonged. Her mother, a Frenchwoman, had been in and out of nursing homes for years. The Cordiers haunted the Riviera, with Iris looking after her parents and watching their diets. Now she lived in a flat somewhere in Roquebrune with the survivor of the pair—the mother, Netta believed. Iris paused and glanced in the business room where Mr Asher had signed the hundred-year lease. She was on her way to lunch—Jack's mother's guest, of course.

'I say, aren't you Miss Asher?'

'I was.' Iris, like Dr Blackley, was probably younger than she looked. Out of her own childhood Netta recalled a desperate adolescent Iris with middle-aged parents clamped like handcuffs on her life. 'How is your mother?' Netta had been about to say 'How is Mrs Cordier?' but it sounded servile.

'I didn't know you knew her.'

'I remember her well. Your father too. He was a nice person.'

'And still is,' said Iris, sharply. 'He lives with me, and he always will. French daughters don't abandon their parents.' No one had ever sounded more English to Netta. 'And your father and mother?'

'Both dead now. I'm married to Jack Ross.'

'Nobody told me,' said Iris, in a way that made Netta think, Good Lord, Iris too? Jack could not possibly seem like a patriarchal figure where she was concerned; perhaps this time the game was reversed and Iris played at being tribal and maternal. The idea of Jack, or of any man, flinging himself on that iron bosom made Netta smile. As if startled, Iris covered her mouth. She seemed to be frightened of smiling back.

Oh, well, and what of it, Iris too, said Netta to herself, suddenly turning back to her accounts. As it happened, Netta was mistaken (as she never would have been with a bill). That day Jack was meeting Iris for the first time.

The upshot of these errors and encounters was an invitation to Roquebrune to visit Iris's father. Jack's mother was ruthlessly excluded, even though Iris probably owed her a return engagement because of the lunch. Netta supposed that Iris had decided one had to get past Netta to reach Jack—an inexactness if ever there was one. Or perhaps it was Netta Iris

wanted. In that case the error became a farce. Netta had almost no knowledge of private houses. She looked around at something that did not much
interest her, for she hated to leave her own home, and saw Iris's father,
apparently too old and shaky to get out of his armchair. He smiled and he
nodded, meanwhile stroking an aging cat. He said to Netta, 'You resemble
your mother. A sweet woman. Obliging and quiet. I used to tell her that I
longed to live in her hotel and be looked after.'

Not by me, thought Netta.

Iris's amber bracelets rattled as she pushed and pulled everyone
through introductions. Jack and Netta had been asked to meet a young
American Netta had often seen in her own bar, and a couple named Sandy
and Sandra Braunsweg, who turned out to be Anglo-Swiss and twins. Iris's
long arms were around them as she cried to Netta, 'Don't you know these
babies?' They were, like the Rosses, somewhere in their twenties. Jack
looked on, blue-eyed, interested, smiling at everything new. Netta supposed
that she was now seeing some of the rather hard-up snobbish—snobbish
what? 'Intelligumhen-sia,' she imagined Dr Blackley supplying. Having
arrived at a word, Netta was ready to go home; but they had only just
arrived. The American turned to Netta. He looked bored, and astonished
by it. He needs the word for 'bored', she decided. Then he can go home,
too. The Riviera was no place for Americans. They could not sit all day
waiting for mail and the daily papers and for the clock to show a respectable
drinking time. They made the best of things when they were caught with a
house they'd been rash enough to rent unseen. Netta often had them then
en pension for meals: a hotel dining room was one way of meeting people.
They paid a fee to use the tennis courts, and they liked the bar. Netta would
notice then how Jack picked up any accent within hearing.

Jack was now being attentive to the old man, Iris's father. Though this
was none of Mr Cordier's business, Jack said, 'My wife and I are first
cousins, as well as second cousins twice over.'

'You don't look it.'

Everyone began to speak at once, and it was a minute or two before
Netta heard Jack again. This time he said, 'We are from a family of great. . . .'
It was lost. What now? Great innkeepers? Worriers? Skinflints? Whatever it
was, old Mr Cordier kept nodding to show he approved.

'We don't see nearly enough of young men like you,' he said.

'True!' said Iris loudly. 'We live in a dreary world of ill women down
here.' Netta thought this hard on the American, on Mr Cordier, and on the
male Braunsweg twin, but none of them looked offended. 'I've got no time
for women,' said Iris. She slapped down a glass of whiskey so that it
splashed, and rapped on a table with her knuckles. 'Shall I tell you why?'

Because women don't tick over. They just simply don't tick over.' No one disputed this. Iris went on: women were underinformed. One could have virile conversations only with men. Women were attached to the past through fear, whereas men had a fearless sense of history. 'Men tick,' she said, glaring at Jack.

'I am not attached to a past,' said Netta, slowly. 'The past holds no attractions.' She was not used to general conversation. She thought that every word called for consideration and for an answer. 'Nothing could be worse than the way we children were dressed. And our mothers—the hard waves of their hair, the white lips. I think of those pale profiles and I wonder if these women were ever young.'

Poor Netta, who saw herself as profoundly English, spread consternation by being suddenly foreign and gassy. She talked the English of expatriate children, as if reading aloud. The twins looked shocked. But she had appealed to the American. He sat beside her on a scuffed velvet sofa. He was so large that she slid an inch or so in his direction when he sat down. He was Sandra Braunsweg's special friend: they had been in London together. He was trying to write.

'What do you mean?' said Netta. 'Write what?'

'Well—a novel, to start,' he said. His father had staked him to one year, then another. He mentioned all that Sandra had borne with, how she had actually kicked and punched him to keep him from being too American. He had embarrassed her to death in London by asking a waitress, 'Miss, where's the toilet?'

Netta said, 'Didn't you mind being corrected?'

'Oh, no, it was just friendly.'

Jack meanwhile was listening to Sandra telling about her English forebears and her English education. 'I had many years of undeniably excellent schooling,' she said. 'Mitten Todd.'

'What's that?' said Jack.

'It's near Bristol. I met excellent girls from Italy, Spain. I took *him* there to visit,' she said, generously including the American. 'I said, "Get a yellow necktie." He went straight out and bought one. I wore a little Schiaparelli. Bought in Geneva but still a real . . . A yellow jacket over a gray . . . Well, we arrived at my excellent old school, and even though the day was drizzly I said, "Put the top of the car back." He did so at once, and then he understood. The interior of the car harmonized perfectly with the yellow and gray.' The twins were orphaned. Iris was like a mother.

'When Mummy died we didn't know where to put all the Chippendale,' said Sandra, 'Iris took a lot of it.'

Netta thought, She is so silly. How can he respond? The girl's dimples and freckles and soft little hands were nothing Netta could have ever described: she had never in her life thought a word like 'pretty'. People were beautiful or they were not. Her happiness had always been great enough to allow for despair. She knew that some people thought Jack was happy and she was not.

'And what made you marry your young cousin?' the old man boomed at Netta. Perhaps his background allowed him to ask impertinent questions; he must have been doing so nearly forever. He stroked his cat; he was confident. He was spokesman for a roomful of wondering people.

'Jack was a moody child and I promised his mother I would look after him,' said Netta. In her hopelessly un-English way she believed she had said something funny.

At eleven o'clock the hotel car expected to fetch the Rosses was nowhere. They trudged home by moonlight. For the last hour of the evening Jack had been skewered on virile conversations, first with Iris, then with Sandra, to whom Netta had already given 'Chippendale' as a private name. It proved that Iris was right about concentrating on men and their ticking—Jack even thought Sandra rather pretty.

'Prettier than me?' said Netta, without the faintest idea what she meant, but aware she had said something stupid.

'Not so attractive,' said Jack. His slight limp returned straight out of childhood. *She* had caused his accident.

'But she's not always clear,' said Netta. 'Mitten Todd, for example.'

'Who're you talking about?'

'Who are *you?*'

'Iris, of course.'

As if they had suddenly quarrelled they fell silent. In silence they entered their room and prepared for bed. Jack poured a whiskey, walked on the clothes he had dropped, carried his drink to the bathroom. Through the half-shut door he called suddenly, 'Why did you say that asinine thing about promising to look after me?'

'It seemed so unlikely, I thought they'd laugh.' She had a glimpse of herself in the mirrors picking up his shed clothes.

He said, 'Well, is it true?'

She was quiet for such a long time that he came to see if she was still in the room. She said, 'No, your mother never said that or anything like it.'

'We shouldn't have gone to Roquebrune,' said Jack. 'I think those bloody people are going to be a nuisance. Iris wants her father to stay here, with the cat, while she goes to England for a month. How do we get out of that?'

'By saying no.'

'I'm rotten at no.'

'I told you not to be too pally with women,' she said, as a joke again, but jokes were her way of having floods of tears.

Before this had a chance to heal, Iris's father moved in, bringing his cat in a basket. He looked at his room and said, 'Medium large.' He looked at his bed and said, 'Reasonably long.' He was, in short, daft about measurements. When he took books out of the reading room, he was apt to return them with 'This volume contains about 70,000 words' written inside the back cover.

Netta had not wanted Iris's father, but Jack had said yes to it. She had not wanted the sick cat, but Jack had said yes to that too. The old man, who was lost without Iris, lived for his meals. He would appear at the shut doors of the dining room an hour too early, waiting for the menu to be typed and posted. In a voice that matched Iris's for carrying power, he read aloud, alone: 'Consommé. Good Lord, again? Is there a choice between the fish and the cutlet? I can't possibly eat all of that. A bit of salad and a boiled egg. That's all I could possibly want.' That was rubbish, because Mr Cordier ate the menu and more, and if there were two puddings, or a pudding and ice cream, he ate both and asked for pastry, fruit, and cheese to follow. One day, after Dr Blackley had attended him for faintness, Netta passed a message on to Iris, who had been back from England for a fortnight now but seemed in no hurry to take her father away.

'Keith Blackley thinks your father should go on a diet.'

'He can't,' said Iris. 'Our other doctor says dieting causes cancer.'

'You can't have heard that properly,' Netta said.

'It is like those silly people who smoke to keep their figures,' said Iris. 'Dieting.'

'Blackley hasn't said he should smoke, just that he should eat less of everything.'

'My father has never smoked in his life,' Iris cried. 'As for his diet, I weighed his food out for years. He's not here forever. I'll take him back as soon as he's had enough of hotels.'

He stayed for a long time, and the cat did too, and a nuisance they both were to the servants. When the cat was too ailing to walk, the old man carried it to a path behind the tennis courts and put it down on the gravel to die. Netta came out with the old man's tea on a tray (not done for everyone, but having him out of the way was a relief) and she saw the cat lying on its side, eyes wide, as if profoundly thinking. She saw unlicked dirt on its coat and ants exploring its paws. The old man sat in a garden chair, wearing a panama hat, his hands clasped on a stick. He called, 'Oh, Netta, take her away. I am too old to watch anything die. I know what she'll do,' he said, indifferently, his voice falling as she came near. 'Oh, I know that. Turn on her back and give a shriek. I've heard it often.'

Netta disburdened her tray onto a garden table and pulled the tray cloth under the cat. She was angered at the haste and indecency of the ants. 'It would be polite to leave her,' she said. 'She doesn't want to be watched.'

'I always sit here,' said the old man.

Jack, making for the courts with Chippendale, looked as if the sight of the two conversing amused him. Then he understood and scooped up the cat and tray cloth and went away with the cat over his shoulder. He laid it in the shade of a Judas tree, and within an hour it was dead. Iris's father said, 'I've got no one to talk to here. That's my trouble. That shroud was too small for my poor Polly. Ask my daughter to fetch me.'

Jack's mother said that night, 'I'm sure you wish that I had a devoted daughter to take me away too.' Because of the attention given the cat she seemed to feel she had not been nuisance enough. She had taken to saying, 'My leg is dying before I am,' and imploring Jack to preserve her leg, should it be amputated, and make certain it was buried with her. She wanted Jack to be close by at nearly any hour now, so that she could lean on him. After sitting for hours at bridge she had trouble climbing two flights of stairs; nothing would induce her to use the lift.

'Nothing ever came of your music,' she would say, leaning on him. 'Of course, you have a wife to distract you now. I needed a daughter. Every woman does.' Netta managed to trap her alone, and forced her to sit while she stood over her. Netta said, 'Look, Aunt Vera, I forbid you, I absolutely forbid you, do you hear, to make a nurse of Jack, and I shall strangle you with my own hands if you go on saying nothing came of his music. You are not to say it in my hearing or out of it. Is that plain?'

Jack's mother got up to her room without assistance. About an hour later the gardener found her on a soft bed of wallflowers. 'An inch to the left and she'd have landed on a rake,' he said to Netta. She was still alive when Netta knelt down. In her fall she had crushed the plants, the yellow minted *giroflées de Nice*. Netta thought that she was now, at last, for the first time, inhaling one of the smells of death. Her aunt's arms and legs were turned and twisted; her skirt was pulled so that her swollen leg showed. It seemed that she had jumped carrying her walking stick—it lay across the path. She often slept in an armchair, afternoons, with one eye slightly open. She opened that eye now and, seeing she had Netta, said, 'My son.' Netta was thinking, I have never known her. And if I knew her, then it was Jack or myself I could not understand. Netta was afraid of giving orders, and of telling people not to touch her aunt before Dr Blackley could be summoned, because she knew that she had always been mistaken. Now Jack was there, propping his mother up, brushing leaves and earth out of her hair. Her head dropped on his shoulder. Netta thought from the sudden heaviness that her aunt had died, but she sighed and opened that one eye again, saying this time, 'Doctor?' Netta left everyone doing the wrong things to her dying–no, her murdered–aunt. She said quite calmly into a telephone, 'I'm afraid that my aunt must have jumped or fallen from the second floor.'

Jack found a letter on his mother's night table that began, 'Why blame Netta? I forgive.' At dawn he and Netta sat at a card table with yesterday's cigarettes still not cleaned out of the ashtray, and he did not ask what Netta had said or done that called for forgiveness. They kept pushing the letter back and forth. He would read it and then Netta would. It seemed natural for them to be silent. Jack had sat beside his mother for much of the night. Each of them then went to sleep for an hour, apart, in one of the empty rooms, just as they had done in the old days when their parents were juggling beds and guests and double and single quarters. By the time the doctor returned for his second visit Jack was neatly dressed and seemed wide awake. He sat in the bar drinking black coffee and reading a travel book of Evelyn Waugh's called *Labels*. Netta, who looked far more untidy and underslept, wondered if Jack wished he might leave now, and sail from Monte Carlo on the Stella Polaris.

Dr Blackley said, 'Well, you are a dim pair. She is not in pu-hain, you know.' Netta supposed this was the roundabout way doctors have of announcing death, very like 'Her sufferings have ended.' But Jack, looking hard at the doctor, had heard another meaning. 'Jumped or fell,' said Dr Blackley. 'She neither fell nor jumped. She is up there enjoying a damned good thu-hing.'

Netta went out and through the lounge and up the marble steps. She sat down in the shaded room on the chair where Jack had spent most of the night. Her aunt did not look like anyone Netta knew, not even like Jack. She stared at the alien face and said, 'Aunt Vera, Keith Blackley says there is nothing really the matter. You must have made a mistake. Perhaps you fainted on the path, overcome by the scent of wallflowers. What would you like me to tell Jack?'

Jack's mother turned on her side and slowly, tenderly, raised herself on an elbow. 'Well, Netta,' she said, 'I daresay the fool is right. But as I've been given quite a lot of sleeping stuff, I'd as soon stay here for now.'

Netta said, 'Are you hungry?'

'I should very much like a ham sandwich on English bread, and about that much gin with a lump of ice.'

She began coming down for meals a few days later. They knew she had crept down the stairs and flung her walking stick over the path and let herself fall hard on a bed of wallflowers—had even plucked her skirt up for a bit of accuracy; but she was also someone returned from beyond the limits, from the other side of the wall. Once she said, 'It was like diving and suddenly realizing there was no water in the sea.' Again, 'It is not true that your life rushes before your eyes. You can see the flowers floating up to you. Even a short fall takes a long time.'

Everyone was deeply changed by this incident. The effect on the victim herself was that she got religion hard.

'We are all hopeless nonbelievers!' shouted Iris, drinking in the bar one afternoon. 'At least, I hope we are. But when I see you, Vera, I feel there might be something in religion. You look positively temperate.'

'I am allowed to love God, I hope,' said Jack's mother.

Jack never saw or heard his mother anymore. He leaned against the bar, reading. It was his favourite place. Even on the sunniest of afternoons he read by the red-shaded light. Netta was present only because she had supplies to check. Knowing she ought to keep out of this, she still said, 'Religion is more than love. It is supposed to tell you why you exist and what you are expected to do about it.'

'You have no religious feelings at all?' This was the only serious and almost the only friendly question Iris was ever to ask Netta.

'None,' said Netta. 'I'm running a business.'

'I love God as Jack used to love music,' said his mother. 'At least he said he did when we were paying for lessons.'

'Adam and Eve had God,' said Netta. 'They had nobody *but* God. A fat lot of good that did them.' This was as far as their dialectic went. Jack had not moved once except to turn pages. He read steadily but cautiously now, as if every author had a design on him. That was one effect of his mother's incident. The other was that he gave up bridge and went back to playing the clarinet. Iris hammered out an accompaniment on the upright piano in the old music room, mostly used for listening to radio broadcasts. She was the only person Netta had ever heard who could make Mozart sound like an Irish jig. Presently Iris began to say that it was time Jack gave a concert. Before this could turn into a crisis Iris changed her mind and said what he wanted was a holiday. Netta thought he needed something: he seemed to be exhausted by love, friendship, by being a husband, someone's son, by trying to make a world out of reading and sense out of life. A visit to England to meet some stimulating people, said Iris. To help Iris with her tiresome father during the journey. To visit art galleries and bookshops and go to concerts. To meet people. To talk.

This was a hot, troubled season, and many persons were planning journeys—not to meet other people but for fear of a war. The hotel had emptied out by the end of March. Netta, whose father had known there would never be another catastrophe, had her workmen come in, as usual. She could hear the radiators being drained and got ready for painting as she packed Jack's clothes. They had never been separated before. They kept telling each other that it was only for a short holiday—for three or four weeks. She was surprised at how neat marriage was, at how many years and feelings could be folded and put under a lid. Once, she went to the window so that he would not see her tears and think she was trying to blackmail him. Looking out, she noticed the American, Chippendale's lover, idly knocking a tennis ball against the garage, as Jack had done in the early summers of their life; he had come round to the hotel looking for a partner, but that season there were none. She suddenly knew to a certainty that if Jack were to die she would search the crowd of mourners for a man she could live with. She would not return from the funeral alone.

Grief and memory, yes, she said to herself, but what about three o'clock in the morning?

By June nearly everyone Netta knew had vanished, or, like the Blackleys, had started to pack. Netta had new tablecloths made, and ordered new white awnings, and two dozen rosebushes from the nursery at Cap Ferrat. The American came over every day and followed her from room to room, talking. He had nothing better to do. The Swiss twins were in England. His father, who had been backing his writing career until now, had suddenly changed his mind about it—now, when he needed money to get out of Europe. He had projects for living on his own, but they required a dose of funds. He wanted to open a restaurant on the Riviera where nothing but chicken pie would be served. Or else a vast and expensive café where people would pay to make their own sandwiches. He said that the was seeing the food of the future, but all that Netta could see was customers asking for their money back. He trapped her behind the bar and said he loved her; Netta made other women look like stuffed dolls. He could still remember the shock of meeting her, the attraction, the brilliant answer she had made to Iris about attachments to the past.

Netta let him rave until he asked for a loan. She laughed and wondered if it was for the chicken-pie restaurant. No—he wanted to get on a boat sailing from Cannes. She said, quite cheerfully, 'I can't be Venus and Barclays Bank. You have to choose.'

He said, 'Can't Venus ever turn up with a letter of credit?'

She shook her head. 'Not a hope.'

But when it was July and Jack hadn't come back, he cornered her again. Money wasn't in it now: his father had not only relented but had virtually ordered him home. He was about twenty-two, she guessed. He could still plead successfully for parental help and for indulgence from women. She said, no more than affectionately, 'I'm going to show you a very pretty room.'

A few days later Dr Blackley came alone to say goodbye.

'Are you really staying?' he asked.

'I am responsible for the last eighty-one years of this lease,' said Netta. 'I'm going to be thirty. It's a long tenure. Besides, I've got Jack's mother and she won't leave. Jack has a chance now to visit America. It doesn't sound sensible to me, but she writes encouraging him. She imagines him suddenly very rich and sending for her. I've discovered the limit of what you can feel about people. I've discovered something else,' she said abruptly. 'It is that sex and love have nothing in common. Only a coincidence, sometimes. You think the coincidence will go on and so you get married. I suppose that is what men are born knowing and women learn by accident.'

'I'm su-horry.'

'For God's sake, don't be. It's a relief.'

She had no feeling of guilt, only of amazement. Jack, as a memory, was in a restricted area—the tennis courts, the cardroom, the bar. She saw him at bridge with Mrs Blackley and pouring drinks for temporary friends. He crossed the lounge jauntily with a cluster of little dark-haired girls wearing blue. In the mirrored bedroom there was only Netta. Her dreams were cleansed of him. The looking glasses still held their blue-and-silver-water shadows, but they lost the habit of giving back the moods and gestures of a Moslem wife.

About five years after this, Netta wrote to Jack. The war had caught him in America, during the voyage his mother had so wanted him to have. His limp had kept him out of the Army. As his mother (now dead) might have put it, all that reading had finally got him somewhere: he had spent the last years putting out a two-pager on aspects of European culture—part of a scrupulous effort Britain was making for the West. That was nearly all Netta knew. A Belgian Red Cross official had arrived, apparently in Jack's name, to see if she was still alive. She sat in her father's business room, wearing a coat and a shawl because there was no way of heating any part of the hotel now, and she tried to get on with the letter she had been writing in her head, on and off, for many years.

'In June, 1940, we were evacuated,' she started, for the tenth or eleventh time. 'I was back by October. Italians had taken over the hotel. They used the mirror behind the bar for target practice. Oddly enough it was not smashed. It is covered with spiderwebs, and the bullet hole is the spider. I had great trouble over Aunt Vera, who disappeared and was found finally in one of the attic rooms.

'The Italians made a pet of her. Took her picture. She enjoyed that. Everyone who became thin had a desire to be photographed, as if knowing they would use this intimidating evidence against those loved ones who had missed being starved. Guilt for life. After an initial period of hardship, during which she often had her picture taken at her request, the Italians brought food and looked after her, more than anyone. She was their mama. We were annexed territory and in time we had the same food as the Italians. The thin pictures of your mother are here on my desk.

'She buried her British passport and would never say where. Perhaps under the Judas tree with Mr Cordier's cat, Polly. She remained just as mad and just as spoiled, and that became dangerous when life stopped being ordinary. She complained about me to the Italians. At that time a complaint was a matter of prison and of death if it was made to the wrong person. Luckily for me, there was also the right person to take the message.

'A couple of years after that, the Germans and certain French took over and the Italians were shut up in another hotel without food or water, and some people risked their well-being to take water to them (for not everyone preferred the new situation, you can believe me). When she was dying I asked her if she had a message for one Italian officer who had made such a pet of her and she said, 'No, why?' She died without a word for anybody. She was buried as "Rossini", because the Italians had changed people's names. She had said she was French, a Frenchwoman named Ross, and so some peculiar civil status was created for us—the two Mrs Rossinis.

'The records were topsy-turvy; it would have meant going to the Germans and explaining my dead aunt was British, and of course I thought I would not. The death certificate and permission to bury are for a Vera Rossini. I have them here on my desk for you with her pictures.

'You are probably wondering where I have found all this writing paper. The Germans left it behind. When we were being shelled I took what few books were left in the reading room down to what used to be the wine cellar and read by candlelight. You are probably wondering where the candles came from. A long story. I even have paint for the radiators, large buckets that have never been opened.

'I live in one room, my mother's old sitting room. The business room can be used but the files have gone. When the Italians were here your mother was their mother, but I was not their Moslem wife, although I still had respect for men. One yelled, "*Luce, luce*", because your mother was showing a light. She said, "Bugger you, you little toad." He said, "Granny, I said '*luce*' not '*Duce*'."

'Not long ago we crept out of our shelled homes, looking like cave dwellers. When you see the hotel again, it will be functioning. I shall have painted the radiators. Long shoots of bramble come in through the card-room windows. There are drifts of leaves in the old music room and I saw scorpions and heard their rustling like the rustle of death. Everything that could have been looted has gone. Sheets, bedding, mattresses. The neighbours did quite a lot of that. At the risk of their lives. When the Italians were here we had rice and oil. Your mother, who was crazy, used to put out grains to feed the mice.

'When the Germans came we had to live under Vichy law, which meant each region lived on what it could produce. As ours produces nothing, we got quite thin again. Aunt Vera died plump. Do you know what it means when I say she used to complain about me?

'Send me some books. As long as they are in English. I am quite sick of the three other languages in which I've heard so many threats, such boasting, such a lot of lying.

'For a time I thought people would like to know how the Italians left and the Germans came in. It was like this: They came in with the first car moving slowly, flying the French flag. The highest-ranking French official in the region. Not a German. No, just a chap getting his job back. The Belgian Red Cross people were completely uninterested and warned me that no one would ever want to hear.

'I suppose that you already have the fiction of all this. The fiction must be different, oh very different, from Italians sobbing with homesickness in the night. The Germans were not real, they were specially got up for the events of the time. Sat in the white dining room, eating with whatever plates and spoons were not broken or looted, ate soups that were mostly water, were forbidden to complain. Only in retreat did they develop faces and I noticed then that some were terrified and many were old. A radio broadcast from some untouched area advised the local population not to attack them as they retreated, it would make wild animals of them. But they were attacked by some young boys shooting out of a window and eight hostages were taken, including the son of the man who cut the maharaja's daughters' black hair, and they were shot and left along the wall of a café on the more or less Italian side of the border. And the man who owned the café was killed too, but later, by civilians—he had given names to the Gestapo once, or perhaps it was something else. He got on the wrong side of the right side at the wrong time, and he was thrown down the deep gorge between the two frontiers.

'Up in one of the hill villages Germans stayed till no one was alive. I was at that time in the former wine cellar, reading books by candlelight.

'The Belgian Red Cross team found the skeleton of a German deserter in a cave and took back the helmet and skull to Knokkele-Zoute as souvenirs.

'My war has ended. Our family held together almost from the Napoleonic adventures. It is shattered now. Sentiment does not keep families whole—only mutual pride and mutual money.'

This true story sounded so implausible that she decided never to send it. She wrote a sensible letter asking for sugar and rice and for new books; nothing must be older than 1940.

Jack answered at once: there were no new authors (he had been asking people). Sugar was unobtainable, and there were queues for rice. Shoes had been rationed. There were no women's stockings but lisle, and the famous American legs looked terrible. You could not find butter or meat or tinned pineapple. In restaurants, instead of butter you were given miniature golf balls of cream cheese. He supposed that all this must sound like small beer to Netta.

A notice arrived that a CARE package awaited her at the post office. It meant that Jack had added his name and his money to a mailing list. She refused to sign for it; then she changed her mind and discovered it was not from Jack but from the American she had once taken to such a pretty room. Jack did send rice and sugar and delicious coffee but he forgot about books. His letters followed; sometimes three arrived in a morning. She left them sealed for days. When she sat down to answer, all she could remember were implausible things.

Iris came back. She was the first. She had grown puffy in England—the result of drinking whatever alcohol she could get her hands on and grimly eating her sweets allowance: there would be that much less gin and choco-late for the Germans if ever they landed. She put her now wide bottom on a comfortable armchair—one of the few chairs the first wave of Italians had not burned with cigarettes or idly hacked at with daggers—and said Jack had been living with a woman in America and to spare the gossip had let her be known as his wife. Another Mrs Ross? When Netta discovered it was dim-pled Chippendale, she laughed aloud.

'I've seen them,' said Iris. 'I mean I saw them together. King Charles and a spaniel. Jack wiped his feet on her.'

Netta's feelings were of lightness, relief. She would not have to tell Jack about the partisans hanging by the neck in the arches of the Place Masséna at Nice. When Iris had finished talking, Netta said, 'What about his music?'

'I don't know.'

'How can you not know something so important?'

'Jack had a good chance at things, but he made a mess of everything,' said Iris. 'My father is still living. Life really is too incredible for some of us.'

A dark girl of about twenty turned up soon after. Her costume, a grey dress buttoned to the neck, gave her the appearance of being in uniform. She unzipped a military-looking bag and cried, in an unplaceable accent, '*Ha*llo, *ha*llo, Mrs Ross? A few small gifts for you,' and unpacked a bottle of Haig, four tins of corned beef, a jar of honey, and six pairs of American nylon stockings, which Netta had never seen before, and were as good to have under a mattress as gold. Netta looked up at the tall girl.

'Remember? I was the middle sister. With,' she said gravely, 'the typical middle-sister problems.' She scarcely recalled Jack, her beloved. The memory of Netta had grown up with her. 'I remember you laughing,' she said, without loving that memory. She was a severe, tragic girl. 'You were the first adult I ever heard laughing. At night in bed I could hear it from your balcony. You sat smoking with, I suppose, your handsome husband. I used to laugh just to hear you.'

She had married an Iranian journalist. He had discovered that political prisoners in the United States were working under lamentable conditions in tin mines. President Truman had sent them there. People from all over the world planned to unite to get them out. The girl said she had been to Germany and to Austria, she had visited camps, they were all alike, and that was already the past, and the future was the prisoners in the tin mines.

Netta said, 'In what part of the country are these mines?'

The middle sister looked at her sadly and said, 'Is there more than one part?'

For the first time in years, Netta could see Jack clearly. They were silently sharing a joke; he had caught it too. She and the girl lunched in a corner of the battered dining room. The tables were scarred with initials. There were no tablecloths. One of the great-uncle's paintings still hung on a wall. It showed the Quai Laurenti, a country road alongside the sea. Netta, who had no use for the past, was discovering a past she could regret. Out of a dark, gentle silence—silence imposed by the impossibility of telling anything real—she counted the cracks in the walls. When silence failed she heard power saws ripping into olive trees and a lemon grove. With a sense of deliverance she understood that soon there would be nothing left to spoil. Her great-uncle's picture, which ought to have changed out of sympathetic magic, remained faithful. She regretted everything now, even the three anxious little girls in blue linen. Every calamitous season between then and now seemed to descend directly from Georgina Blackley's having said 'white' just to keep three children in their place. Clad in buttoned-up grey, the middle sister now picked at corned beef and said she had hated her father, her mother, her sisters, and most of all the Dutch governess.

'Where is she now?' said Netta.

'Dead, I hope.' This was from someone who had visited camps. Netta sat listening, her cheek on her hand. Death made death casual: she had always known. Neither the vanquished in their flight nor the victors returning to pick over rubble seemed half so vindictive as a tragic girl who had disliked her governess.

Dr Blackley came back looking positively cheerful. In those days men still liked soldiering. It made them feel young, if they needed to feel it, and it got them away from home. War made the break few men could make on their own. The doctor looked years younger, too, and very fit. His wife was not with him. She had survived everything, and the hardships she had undergone had completely restored her to health—which had made it easy for her husband to leave her. Actually, he had never gone back, except to wind up the matter.

'There are things about Georgina I respect and admire,' he said, as husbands will say from a distance. His war had been in Malta. He had come here, as soon as he could, to the shelled, gnawed, tarnished coast (as if he had not seen enough at Malta) to ask Netta to divorce Jack and to marry him, or live with him—anything she wanted, on any terms.

But she wanted nothing—at least, not from him.

'Well, one can't defeat a memory,' he said. 'I always thought it was mostly su-hex between the two of you.'

'So it was,' said Netta. 'So far as I remember.'

'Everyone noticed. You would vanish at odd hours. Dis-hup-pear.'

'Yes, we did.'

'You can't live on memories,' he objected. 'Though I respect you for being faithful, of course.'

'What you are talking about is something of which one has no specific memory,' said Netta. 'Only of seasons. Places. Rooms. It is as abstract to remember as to read about. That is why it is boring in talk except as a joke, and boring in books except for poetry.'

'You never read poetry.'

'I do now.'

'I guessed that,' he said.

'That lack of memory is why people are unfaithful, as it is so curiously called. When I see closed shutters I know there are lovers behind them. That is how the memory works. The rest is just convention and small talk.'

'Why lovers? Why not someone sleeping off the wine he had for lunch?'

'No. Lovers.'

'A middle-aged man cutting his toenails in the bathtub,' he said with unexpected feeling. 'Wearing bifocal lenses so that he can see his own feet.'

'No, lovers. Always.'

He said, 'Have you missed him?'

'Missed who?'

'Who the bloody hell are we talking about?'

'The Italian commander billeted here. He was not a guest. He was here by force. I was not breaking a rule. Without him I'd have perished in every way. He may be home with his wife now. Or in that fortress near Turin where he sent other men. Or dead.' She looked at the doctor and said, 'Well, what would you like me to do? Sit here and cry?'

'I can't imagine you with a brute.'

'I never said that.'

'Do you miss him still?'

'The absence of Jack was like a cancer which I am sure has taken root, and of which I am bound to die,' said Netta.

'You'll bu-hury us all,' he said, as doctors tell the condemned.

'I haven't said I won't.' She rose suddenly and straightened her skirt, as she used to do when hotel guests became pally. 'Conversation over,' it meant.

'Don't be too hard on Jack,' he said.

'I am hard on myself,' she replied.

After he had gone he sent her a parcel of books, printed on greyish paper, in warped wartime covers. All of the titles were, to Netta, unknown. There was *Fireman Flower* and *The Horse's Mouth* and *Four Quartets* and *The Stuff to Give the Troops* and *Better Than a Kick in the Pants* and *Put Out More Flags*. A note added that the next package would contain Henry Green and Dylan Thomas. She guessed he would not want to be thanked, but she did so anyway. At the end of her letter was 'Please remember, if you mind too much, that I said no to you once before.' Leaning on the bar, exactly as Jack used to, with a glass of the middle sister's drink at hand, she opened *Better Than a Kick in the Pants* and read, '. . . two Fascists came in, one of them tall and thin and tough looking; the other smaller, with only one arm and an empty sleeve pinned up to his shoulder. Both of them were quite young and wore black shirts.'

Oh, thought Netta. I am the only one who knows all this. No one will ever realize how much I know of the truth, the truth, the truth, and she put her head on her hands, her elbows on the scarred bar, and let the first tears of her after-war run down her wrists.

The last to return was the one who should have been first. Jack wrote that he was coming down from the north as far as Nice by bus. It was a common way of travelling and much cheaper than by train. Netta guessed that he was mildly hard up and that he had saved nothing from his war job. The bus came in at six, at the foot of the Place Masséna. There was a deep-blue late-afternoon sky and pale sunlight. She could hear birds from the public gardens nearby. The Place was as she had always seen it, like an elegant drawing room with a blue ceiling. It was nearly empty. Jack looked out on this sunlighted, handsome space and said, 'Well, I'll just leave my stuff at the bus office, for the moment'—perhaps noticing that Netta had not invited him anywhere. He placed his ticket on the counter, and she saw that he had not come from far away: he must have been moving south by stages. He carried an aura of London pub life; he had been in London for weeks.

A frowning man hurrying to wind things up so he could have his first drink of the evening said, 'The office is closing and we don't keep baggage here.'

'People used to be nice,' Jack said.

'Bus people?'

'Just people.'

She was hit by the sharp change in his accent. As for the way of speaking, which is something else again, he was like the heir to great estates back home after a Grand Tour. Perhaps the estates had run down in his absence. She slipped the frowning man a thousand francs, a new pastel-tinted bill, on which the face of a calm girl glowed like an opal. She said, 'We shan't be long.'

She set off over the Place, walking diagonally—Jack beside her, of course. He did not ask where they were headed, though he did make her smile by saying, 'Did you bring a car?', expecting one of the hotel cars to be parked nearby, perhaps with a driver to open the door; perhaps with cold chicken and wine in a hamper, too. He said, 'I'd forgotten about having to tip for every little thing.' He did not question his destination, which was no farther than a café at the far end of the square. What she felt at that instant was intense revulsion. She thought, I don't want him, and pushed away some invisible flying thing—a bat or a blown paper. He looked at her with surprise. He must have been wondering if hardship had taught Netta to talk in her mind.

This is it, the freedom he was always offering me, she said to herself, smiling up at the beautiful sky.

They moved slowly along the nearly empty square, pausing only when some worn-out Peugeot or an old bicycle, finding no other target, made a swing in their direction. Safely on the pavement, they walked under the arches where partisans had been hanged. It seemed to Netta the bodies had been taken down only a day or so before. Jack, who knew about this way of dying from hearsay, chose a café table nearly under a poor lad's bound, dangling feet.

'I had a woman next to me on the bus who kept a hedgehog all winter in a basketful of shavings,' he said. 'He can drink milk out of a wineglass.' He hesitated. 'I'm sorry about the books you asked for. I was sick of books by then. I was sick of rhetoric and culture and patriotic crap.'

'I suppose it is all very different over there,' said Netta.

'God, yes.'

He seemed to expect her to ask questions, so she said, 'What kind of clothes do they wear?'

'They wear quite a lot of plaids and tartans. They eat at peculiar hours. You'll see them eating strawberries and cream just when you're thinking of having a drink.'

She said, 'Did you visit the tin mines, where Truman sends his political prisoners?'

'*Tin* mines?' said Jack. 'No.'

'Remember the three little girls from the maharaja trade?'

Neither could quite hear what the other had to say. They were partially deaf to each other.

Netta continued softly, 'Now, as I understand it, she first brought an American to London, and then she took an Englishman to America.'

He had too much the habit of women, he was playing too close a game, to waste points saying, 'Who? What?'

'It was over as fast as it started,' he said. 'But then the war came and we were stuck. She became a friend,' he said. 'I'm quite fond of her'—which Netta translated as, 'It is a subterranean river that may yet come to light.' 'You wouldn't know her,' he said. 'She's very different now. I talked so much about the south, down here, she finally found some land going dirt cheap at Bandol. The mayor arranged for her to have an orchard next to her property, so she won't have neighbours. It hardly cost her anything. He said to her, "You're very pretty."'

'No one ever had a bargain in property because of a pretty face,' said Netta.

'Wasn't it lucky,' said Jack. He could no longer hear himself, let alone Netta. 'The war was unsettling, being in America. She minded not being active. Actually she was using the Swiss passport, which made it worse. Her brother was killed over Bremen. She needs security now. In a way it was sorcerer and apprentice between us, and she suddenly grew up. She'll be better off with a roof over her head. She writes a little now. Her poetry isn't bad,' he said, as if Netta had challenged its quality.

'Is she at Bandol now, writing poetry?'

'Well, no.' He laughed suddenly. 'There isn't a roof yet. And, you know, people don't sit writing that way. They just think they're going to.'

'Who has replaced you?' said Netta. 'Another sorcerer?'

'Oh, *he* . . . he looks like George II in a strong light. Or like Queen Anne. Queen Anne and Lady Mary, somebody called them.' Iris, that must have been. Queen Anne and Lady Mary wasn't bad—better than King Charles and his spaniel. She was beginning to enjoy his story. He saw it, and said lightly, 'I was too preoccupied with you to manage another life. I couldn't see myself going on and on away from you. I didn't want to grow middle-aged at odds with myself.'

But he had lost her; she was enjoying a reverie about Jack now, wearing one of those purple sunburns people acquire at golf. She saw him driving an open car, with large soft freckles on his purple skull. She saw his mistress's dog on the front seat and the dog's ears flying like pennants. The revulsion she felt did not lend distance but brought a dreamy reality closer still. He must be thirty-four now, she said to herself. A terrible age for a man who has never imagined thirty-four.

'Well, perhaps you have made a mess of it,' she said, quoting Iris.

'What mess? I'm here. *He*—'

'Queen Anne?'

'Yes, well, actually Gerald is his name; he wears nothing but brown. Brown suit, brown tie, brown shoes. I said, "*He* can't go to Mitten Todd. He won't match."'

'Harmonize,' she said.

'That's it. Harmonize with the—'

'What about Gerald's wife? I'm sure he has one.'

'Lucretia.'

'No, really?'

'On my honour. When I last saw them they were all together, talking.'

Netta was remembering what the middle sister had said about laughter on the balcony. She couldn't look at him. The merest crossing of glances made her start laughing rather wildly into her hands. The hysterical quality of her own laughter caught her in midair. What were they talking about? He hitched his chair nearer and dared to take her wrist.

'Tell me, now,' he said, as if they were to be two old confidence men getting their stories straight. 'What about you? Was there ever . . .' The glaze of laughter had not left his face and voice. She saw that he would make her his business, if she let him. Pulling back, she felt another clasp, through a wall of fog. She groped for this other, invisible hand, but it dissolved. It was a lost, indifferent hand; it no longer recognized her warmth. She understood: He is dead . . . Jack, closed to ghosts, deaf to their voices, was spared this. He would be spared everything, she saw. She envied him his imperviousness, his true unhysterical laughter.

Perhaps that's why I kicked him, she said. I was always jealous. Not of women. Of his short memory, his comfortable imagination. And I am going to be thirty-seven and I have a dark, an accurate, a deadly memory.

He still held her wrist and turned it another way, saying, 'Look, there's paint on it.'

'Oh, God, where is the waiter?' she cried, as if that were the one important thing. Jack looked his age, exactly. She looked like a burned-out child who had been told a ghost story. Desperately seeking the waiter, she turned to the café behind them and saw the last light of the long afternoon strike the mirror above the bar—a flash in a tunnel; hands juggling with fire. That unexpected play, at a remove, borne indoors, displayed to anyone who could stare without blinking, was a complete story. It was the brightness on the looking glass, the only part of a life, or a love, or a promise, that could never be concealed, changed, or corrupted.

Not a hope, she was trying to tell him. He could read her face now. She reminded herself, If I say it, I am free. I can finish painting the radiators in peace. I can read every book in the world. If I had relied on my memory for guidance, I would never have crept out of the wine cellar. Memory is what ought to prevent you from buying a dog after the first dog dies, but it never does. It should at least keep you from saying yes twice to the same person.

'I've always loved you,' he chose to announce—it really was an announcement, in a new voice that stated nothing except facts.

The dark, the ghosts, the candlelight, her tears on the scarred bar—*they* were real. And still, whether she wanted to see it or not, the light of imagination danced all over the square. She did not dare to turn again to the mirror, lest she confuse the two and forget which light was real. A pure white awning on a cross street seemed to her to be of indestructible beauty. The window it sheltered was hollowed with sadness and shadow. She said with the same deep sadness, 'I believe you.' The wave of revulsion receded, sucked back under another wave—a powerful adolescent craving for something simple, such as true love.

Her face did not show this. It was set in adolescent stubbornness, and this was one of their old, secret meetings when, sullen and hurt, she had to be coaxed into life as Jack wanted it lived. It was the same voyage, at the same rate of speed. The Place seemed to her to be full of invisible traffic—first a whisper of tires, then a faint, high screeching, then a steady roar. If Jack heard anything, it could be only the blood in the veins and his loud, happy thought. To a practical romantic like Jack, dying to get Netta to bed right away, what she was hearing was only the uh-hebb and flo-ho of hormones, as Dr Blackley said. She caught a look of amazement on his face:

Now he knew what he had been deprived of. *Now* he remembered. It had been Netta, all along.

Their evening shadows accompanied them over the long square. 'I still have a car,' she remarked. 'But no petrol. There's a train.' She did keep on hearing a noise, as of heavy traffic rushing near and tearing away. Her own quiet voice carried across it, saying, 'Not a hope.' He must have heard that. Why, it was as loud as a shout. He held her arm lightly. He was as buoyant as morning. This *was* his morning—the first light on the mirror, the first cigarette. He pulled her into an archway where no one could see. What could I do, she asked her ghosts, but let my arm be held, my steps be guided?

Later, Jack said that the walk with Netta back across the Place Masséna was the happiest event of his life. Having no reliable counter-event to put in its place, she let the memory stand.

MARGARET LAURENCE

❧

THE RAIN CHILD

I recall the sky that day—overcast, the flat undistinguished grey nearly forgotten by us here during the months of azure which we come to regard as rights rather than privileges. As always when the rain hovers, the air was like syrup, thick and heavily still, over-sweet with flowering vines and the occasional ripe paw-paw that had fallen and now lay yellow and fermented, a winery for ants.

I was annoyed at having to stay in my office so late. Annoyed, too, that I found the oppressive humidity just before the rains a little more trying each year. I have always believed myself particularly well-suited to this climate. Miss Povey, of course, when I was idiotic enough to complain one day about the heat, hinted that the change of life might be more to blame than the weather.

'Of course, I remember how bothersome you found the heat one season,' I parried. 'Some years ago, as I recollect.'

We work well together and even respect one another. Why must we make such petty stabs? Sitting depressed at my desk, I was at least thankful that when a breeze quickened we would receive it here. Blessings upon the founders of half a century ago who built Eburaso Girls' School at the top of the hill, for at the bottom the villagers would be steaming like crabs in a soup pot.

My leg hurt more than it had in a long time, and I badly wanted a cup of tea. Typical of Miss Povey, I thought, that she should leave yet another parental interview to me. Twenty-seven years here, to my twenty-two, and she still felt acutely uncomfortable with African parents, all of whom in her eyes were equally unenlightened. The fact that one father might be an illiterate cocoa farmer, while the next would possibly be a barrister from the city—such distinctions made no earthly difference to Hilda Povey. She was positive that parents would fail to comprehend the importance of sending their little girls to school with the proper clothing, and she harped upon this subject in a thoroughly tedious manner, as though the essence of education lay in the possession of six pairs of cotton knickers. Malice refreshed me for a moment. Then, as always, it began to chill. Were we still women, in actuality, who could bear only grudges, make venom for milk? I exaggerated for a while in this lamentably oratorical style, dramatizing the trivial for lack of anything great. Hilda, in point of fact, was an excellent headmistress. Like a budgerigar she darted and fussed through her days, but underneath the twittering there was a strong disciplined mind and a heart more pious than mine. Even in giving credit to her, however, I chose words churlishly—why had I not thought 'devout' instead of 'pious', with its undertones of self-righteousness? What could she possibly have said in my favour if she had been asked? That I taught English competently, even sometimes with love? That my irascibility was mainly reserved for my colleagues? The young ones in Primary did not find me terrifying, once they grew used to the sight of the lady in stout white drill skirt and drab lilac smock faded from purple, her greying hair arranged in what others might call a *chignon* but for me could only be termed a 'bun', a lady of somewhat uncertain gait, clumping heavily into the classroom with her ebony cane. They felt free to laugh, my forest children, reticent and stiff in unaccustomed dresses, as we began the alien speech. 'What are we doing, class?' And, as I sat down clumsily on the straight chair, to show them, they made their murmured and mirthful response—'We ah siddeen.' The older girls in Middle School also seemed to accept me readily enough. Since Miss Harvey left us to marry that fool of a government geologist, I have had the senior girls for English literature and composition. Once when we were taking *Daffodils*, Kwaale came to class with her arms full of wild orchids for me. How absurd Wordsworth seemed here then. I spoke instead about Akan poetry, and read them the drum prelude *Anyaneanyane* in their own tongue as well as the translation. Miss Povey, hearing of it, took decided umbrage. Well. Perhaps she would not have found much to say in my favour after all.

I fidgeted and perspired, beginning to wonder if Dr Quansah would show up that day at all. Then, without my having heard his car or footsteps, he stood there at my office door, his daughter Ruth beside him.

'Miss—' He consulted a letter which he held in his hand. 'Miss Violet Nedden?'

'Yes.' I limped over to meet him. I was, stupidly, embarrassed that he had spoken my full name. Violet, applied to me, is of course quite ludicrous and I detest it. I felt as well the old need to explain my infirmity, but I refrained for the usual reasons. I do not know why it should matter to me to have people realize I was not always like this, but it does. In the pre-sulpha days when I first came here, I developed a tropical sore which festered badly; this is the result. But if I mention it to Africans, they tend to become faintly apologetic, as though it were somehow their fault that I bear the mark of Africa upon myself in much the same way as any ulcerated beggar of the streets.

Dr Quansah, perhaps to my relief, did not seem much at ease either. Awkwardly, he transferred Miss Povey's typewritten instructions to his left hand in order to shake hands with me. A man in his middle fifties, I judged him to be. Thickly built, with hands which seemed too immense to be a doctor's. He was well dressed, in a beige linen suit of good cut, and there was about his eyes a certain calm which his voice and gestures lacked.

His daughter resembled him, the same strong coarse features, the same skin shade, rather a lighter brown than is usual here. At fifteen she was more plump and childish in figure than most of our girls her age. Her frock was pretty and expensive, a blue cotton with white daisies on it, but as she was so stocky it looked too old for her.

'I don't know if Miss Povey told you,' Dr Quansah began, 'but Ruth has never before attended school in this—in her own country.'

I must have shown my surprise, for he hastened on. 'She was born in England and has lived all her life there. I went there as a young man, you see, to study medicine, and when I graduated I had the opportunity to stay on and do malaria research. Ultimately my wife joined me in London. She—she died in England. Ruth has been in boarding schools since she was six. I have always meant to return here, of course. I had not really intended to stay away so long, but I was very interested in malaria research, and it was an opportunity that comes only once. Perhaps I have even been able to accomplish a certain amount. Now the government here is financing a research station, and I am to be in charge of it. You may have heard of it—it is only twenty miles from here.'

I could see that he had had to tell me so I should not think it odd for an African to live away from his own country for so many years. Like my impulse to explain my leg. We are all so anxious that people should not think us different. See, we say, I am not peculiar—wait until I tell you how it was with me.

'Well,' I said slowly, 'I do hope Ruth will like it here at Eburaso.'

My feeling of apprehension was so marked, I remember, that I attempted exorcism by finding sensible reasons. It was only the season, I thought, the inevitable tension before the rains, and perhaps the season of regrets in myself as well. But I was not convinced.

'I, too, hope very much she will like it here,' Dr Quansah said. He did not sound overly confident.

'I'm sure I shall,' Ruth said suddenly, excitedly, her round face beaming. 'I think it's great fun, Miss Nedden, coming to Africa like this.'

Her father and I exchanged quick and almost fearful glances. She had spoken, of course, as any English schoolgirl might speak, going abroad.

I do not know how long Ruth Quansah kept her sense of adventure. Possibly it lasted the first day, certainly not longer. I watched her as carefully as

I could, but there was not much I could do.

I had no difficulty in picking her out from a group of girls, although she wore the same light green uniform. She walked differently, carried herself differently. She had none of their easy languor. She strode along with brisk intensity, and in consequence perspired a great deal. At meals she ate virtually nothing. I asked her if she had no appetite, and she looked at me reproachfully.

'I'm starving,' she said flatly. 'But I can't eat this food, Miss Nedden. I'm sorry, but I just can't. That awful mashed stuff, sort of greyish yellow, like some funny kind of potatoes—it makes me sick.'

'I'm afraid you'll have to get used to cassava,' I said, restraining a smile, for she looked so serious and so offended. 'African food is served to the girls here, naturally. Personally I'm very fond of it, groundnut stew and such. Soon you won't find it strange.'

She gave me such a hostile glance that I wondered uneasily what we would do if she really determined to starve herself. Thank heaven she could afford to lose a few pounds.

Our girls fetched their own washing water in buckets from our wells. The evening trek for water was a time of singing, of shouted gossip, of laughter, just as it was each morning for their mothers in the villages, taking the water vessels to the river. The walk was not an easy one for me, but one evening I stumbled rather irritably and unwillingly down the stony path to the wells.

Ruth was there, standing apart from the others. Each of the girls in turn filled a bucket, hoisted it up onto her head and sauntered off, still chattering and waving, without spilling a drop. Ruth was left alone to fill her bucket. Then, carrying it with both her hands clutched around the handle, she began to struggle back along the path. Perhaps foolishly, I smiled. It was done only in encouragement, but she mistook my meaning.

'I expect it looks very funny,' she burst out. 'I expect they all think so, too.'

Before I could speak she had swung the full bucket and thrown it from her as hard as she could. The water struck at the ground, turning the dust to ochre mud, and the bucket rattled and rolled, dislodging pebbles along its way. The laughter among the feathery *niim* trees further up the path suddenly stopped, as a dozen pairs of hidden eyes peered. Looking bewildered, as though she were surprised and shocked by what she had done, Ruth sat down, her sturdy legs rigid in front of her, her child's soft face creased in tears.

'I didn't know it would be like this, here,' she said at last. 'I didn't know at all.'

In the evenings the senior girls were allowed to change from their school uniforms to African cloth, and they usually did so, for they were very concerned with their appearances and they rightly believed that the dark-printed lengths of mammy-cloth were more becoming to them than their short school frocks. Twice a week it was my responsibility to hobble over and make the evenings rounds of the residence. Ruth, I noticed, changed into one of her English frocks, a different one each time, it appeared. Tact had never been my greatest strength, but I tried to suggest that it might be better if she would wear cloth like the rest.

'Your father would be glad to buy one for you, I'm sure.'

'I've got one—it was my mother's,' Ruth replied. She frowned. 'I don't know how to put it on properly. They—they'd only laugh if I asked them. And anyway—'

Her face took on that defiance which is really a betrayal of uncertainty.

'I don't like those cloths,' she said clearly. 'They look like fancy-dress costumes to me. I'd feel frightfully silly in one. I suppose the people here haven't got anything better to wear.'

In class she had no restraint. She was clever, and she knew more about English literature and composition than the other girls, for she had been taught always in English, whereas for the first six years of their schooling they had received most of their instruction in their own language.

But she would talk interminably, if allowed, and she rushed to answer my questions before anyone else had a chance. Abenaa, Mary Ansah, Yaa, Kwaale and all the rest would regard her with eyes which she possibly took to be full of awe for her erudition. I knew something of those bland brown eyes, however, and I believed them to contain only scorn for one who would so blatantly show off. But I was wrong. The afternoon Kwaale came to see me, I learned that in those first few weeks the other girls had believed, quite simply, that Ruth was insane.

The junior teachers live in residence in the main building, but Miss Povey and I have our own bungalows, hers on one side of the grounds, mine on the other. A small grove of bamboo partially shields my house, and although Yindo the garden boy deplores my taste, I keep the great spiny clumps of prickly pear that grow beside my door. Hilda Povey grows zinnia and nasturtiums, and spends hours trying to coax an exiled rosebush into bloom, but I will have no English flowers. My garden burns magnificently with jungle lily and poinsettia, which Yindo gently uproots from the forest and puts in here.

The rains had broken and the air was cool and lightened. The downpour began predictably each evening around dusk, so I was still able to have my tea outside. I was exceedingly fond of my garden chair. I discovered it years ago at Jillaram's Silk Palace, a tatty little Indian shop in the side streets of the city which I seldom visited. The chair was rattan with a high fan-shaped back like a throne or a peacock's tail, enamelled in Chinese red and decorated extravagantly with gilt. I had never seen anything so splendidly garish, so I bought it. The red had since been subdued by sun and the gilt was flaking, but I still sat enthroned in it each afternoon, my ebony sceptre by my side.

I did not hear Kwaale until she greeted me. She was wearing her good cloth, an orange one patterned with small black stars that wavered in their firmament as she moved. Kwaale had never been unaware of her woman-hood. Even as a child she walked with that same slow grace. We did not need to hope that she would go on and take teacher training or anything of that sort. She would marry when she left school, and I believed that would be the right thing for her to do. But sometimes it saddened me to think of what life would probably be for her, bearing too many children in too short a span of years, mourning the inevitable deaths of some of them, working bent double at the planting and hoeing until her slim straightness was warped. All at once I felt ashamed in the presence of this young queen, who had only an inheritance of poverty to return to, ashamed of my comfort and my heaviness, ashamed of my decrepit scarlet throne and trivial game.

'Did you want to see me, Kwaale?' I spoke brusquely.

'Yes.' She sat down on the stool at my feet. At first they had thought Ruth demented, she said, but now they had changed their minds. They had seen how well she did on her test papers. She was sane, they had decided, but this was so much the worse for her, for now she could be held respon-sible for what she did.

'What does she do, Kwaale?'

'She will not speak with us, nor eat with us. She pretends not to eat at all. But we have seen her. She has money, you know, from her father. The big palm grove—she goes there, and eats chocolate and biscuits. By herself. Not one to anyone else. Such a thing.'

Kwaale was genuinely shocked. Where these girls came from, sharing was not done as a matter of moral principle, but as a necessary condition of life.

'If one alone eats the honey,' Kwaale said primly in Twi, 'it plagues his stomach.'

It was, of course, a proverb. Kwaale was full of them. Her father was a village elder in Eburaso, and although he did precious little work, he was a highly respected man. He spoke continuously in proverbs and dispensed his wisdom freely. He was a charming person, but it was his wife, with the cas-sava and peppers and medicinal herbs she sold in the market, who had made it possible for some of their children to obtain an education.

'That is not all,' Kwaale went on. 'There is much worse. She becomes angry, even at the young ones. Yesterday Ayesha spoke to her, and she hit the child on the face. Ayesha–if it had been one of the others, even–'

Ayesha, my youngest one, who had had to bear so much. Tears of rage must have come to my eyes, for Kwaale glanced at me, then lowered her head with that courtesy of the heart which forbids the observing of another's pain. I struggled with myself to be fair to Ruth. I called to mind the bleakness of her face as she trudged up the path with the water bucket.

'She is lonely, Kwaale, and does not quite know what to do. Try to be patient with her.'

Kwaale sighed. 'It is not easy–'

Then her resentment gained command. 'The stranger is like passing water in the drain,' she said fiercely.

Another of her father's proverbs. I looked at her in dismay.

'There is a different saying on that subject,' I said dryly, at last. 'We had it in chapel not so long ago–don't you remember? From Exodus. "Thou shalt not oppress a stranger, for ye know the heart of a stranger, seeing ye were strangers in the land of Egypt".'

But Kwaale's eyes remained implacable. She had never been a stranger in the land of Egypt.

When Kwaale had gone, I sat unmoving for a while in my ridiculous rattan throne. Then I saw Ayesha walking along the path, so I called to her. We spoke together in Twi, Ayesha and I. She had begun to learn English, but she found it difficult and I tried not to press her beyond her present limits. She did not even speak her own language very well, if it was actually her own language–no one knew for certain. She was tiny for her age, approximately six. In her school dress she looked like one of those stick figures I used to draw as a child–billowing garments, straight lines for limbs, and the same disproportionately large eyes.

'Come here, Ayesha.'

Obediently she came. Then, after the first moment of watchful survey which she still found necessary to observe, she scrambled onto my lap. I was careful–we were all careful here–not to establish bonds of too-great affection. As Miss Povey was fond of reminding us, these were not our children. But with Ayesha, the rule was sometimes hard to remember. I touched her face lightly with my hand.

'Did an older girl strike you, little one?'

She nodded wordlessly. She did not look angry or upset. She made no bid for sympathy because she had no sense of having been unfairly treated. A slap was not a very great injury to Ayesha.

'Why?' I asked gently. 'Do you know why she did that thing?'

She shook her head. Then she lifted her eyes to mine.

'Where is the monkey today?'

She wanted to ignore the slap, to forget it. Forgetfulness is her protection. Sometimes I wondered, though, how much could be truly forgotten and what happened to it when it was entombed.

'The monkey is in my house,' I said. 'Do you want to see her?'

'Yes.' So we walked inside and brought her out into the garden, my small and regal Ankyeo who was named, perhaps frivolously, after a great queen mother of this country. I did not know what species of monkey Ankyeo was. She was delicate-boned as a bird, and her fur was silver. She picked with her doll fingers at a pink hibiscus blossom, and Ayesha laughed. I wanted to make Ankyeo perform all her tricks, in order to hear again that rare laughter. But I knew I must not try to go too fast. After a while Ayesha tired of watching the monkey and sat cross-legged beside my chair, the old look of passivity on her face. We would have to move indoors before the rain started, but for the moment I left her as she was.

Ruth did not approach silently, as Kwaale and Ayesha had done, but with a loud crunching of shoes on the gravel path. When she saw Ayesha she stopped.

'I suppose you know.'

'Yes. But it was not Ayesha who told me.'

'Who, then?'

Of course I would not tell her. Her face grew sullen.

'Whoever it was, I think it was rotten of her to tell—'

'It did not appear that way to the girl in question. She was protecting the others from you, and that is a higher good in her eyes than any individual honour in not tattling.'

'Protecting—from me?' There was desolation in her voice, and I relented.

'They will change, Ruth, once they see they can trust you. Why did you hit Ayesha?'

'It was a stupid thing to do,' Ruth said in a voice almost inaudible with shame, 'and I felt awful about it, and I'm terribly sorry. But she—she kept asking me something, you see, over and over again, in a sort of whining voice, and I—I just couldn't stand it anymore.'

'What did she ask you?'

'How should I know?' Ruth said. 'I don't speak Twi.'

I stared at her. 'Not—any? I thought you might be a little rusty, but I never imagined—my dear child, it's your own language, after all.'

'My father has always spoken English to me,' she said. 'My mother spoke in Twi, I suppose, but she died when I was under a year old.'

'Why on earth didn't you tell the girls?'

'I don't know. I don't know why I didn't—'

I noticed then how much thinner she had grown and how her expression had altered. She no longer looked like a child. Her eyes were implacable as Kwaale's.

'They don't know anything outside this place,' she said. 'I don't care if I can't understand what they're saying to each other. I'm not interested, anyway.'

Then her glance went to Ayesha once more.

'But why were they so angry—about her? I know it was mean, and I said I was sorry. But the way they all looked—'

'Ayesha was found by the police in Lagos,' I said reluctantly. 'She was sent back to this country because one of the constables recognized her speech as Twi. We heard about her and offered to have her here. There are many like her, I'm afraid, who are not found or heard about. She must have been stolen, you see, or sold when she was very young. She has not been able to tell us much. But the Nigerian police traced her back to several slave-dealers. When they discovered her she was being used as a child prostitute. She was very injured when she came to us here.'

Ruth put her head down on her hands. She sat without speaking. Then her shoulders, hunched and still, began to tremble.

'You didn't know,' I said. 'There's no point in reproaching yourself now.'

She looked up at me with a kind of naive horror, the look of someone who recognizes for the first time the existence of cruelty.

'Things like that really happen here?'

I sighed. 'Not just here. Evil does not select one place for its province.'

But I could see that she did not believe me. The wind was beginning to rise, so we went indoors. Ayesha carried the stool, Ruth lifted my red throne, and I limped after them, feeling exhausted and not at all convinced just then that God was in His heaven. What a mercy for me that the church in whose mission school I had spent much of my adult life did not possess the means of scrutinizing too precisely the souls of its faithful servants.

We had barely got inside the bungalow when Ayesha missed the monkey. She flew outside to look for it, but no amount of searching revealed Ankyeo. Certain the monkey was gone forever, Ayesha threw herself down on the damp ground. While the wind moaned and screeched, the child, who never wept for herself, wept for a lost monkey and would not be comforted. I did not dare kneel beside her. My leg was too unreliable, and I knew I would not be able to get up again. I stood there, lumpish and helpless, while Ruth in the doorway shivered in her thin and daisied dress.

Then, like a veritable angel of the Lord, Yindo appeared, carrying

Ankyeo. Immediately I experienced a resurrection of faith, while at the same time thinking how frail and fickle my belief must be, to be so influenced by a child and a silver-furred monkey.

Yindo grinned and knelt beside Ayesha. He was no more than sixteen, a tall thin-wristed boy, a Dagomba from the northern desert. He had come here when he was twelve, one of the scores of young who were herded down each year to work the cocoa farms because their own arid land had no place for them. He was one of our best garden boys, but he could not speak to anyone around here except in hesitant pidgin English, for no one here knew his language. His speech lack never bothered him with Ayesha. The two communicated in some fashion without words. He put the monkey in her arms and she held Ankyeo closely. Then she made a slight and courtly bow to Yindo. He laughed and shook his head. Drawing from his pocket a small charm, he showed it to her. It was the dried head of a chameleon, with blue glass beads and a puff of unwholesome-looking fur tied around it. Ayesha understood at once that it was this object which had enabled Yindo to find the monkey. She made another and deeper obeisance and from her own pocket drew the only thing she had to offer, a toffee wrapped in silver foil which I had given her at least two weeks ago. Yindo took it, touched it to his talisman, and put both carefully away.

Ruth had not missed the significance of the ritual. Her eyes were dilated with curiosity and contempt.

'He believes in it, doesn't he?' she said. 'He actually believes in it.'

'Don't be so quick to condemn the things you don't comprehend,' I said sharply.

'I think it's horrible.' She sounded frightened. 'He's just a savage, isn't he, just a—'

'Stop it, Ruth. That's quite enough.'

'I hate it here!' she cried. 'I wish I were back at home.'

'Child,' I said, 'this is your home.'

She did not reply, but the denial in her face made me marvel at my own hypocrisy.

Each Friday Dr Quansah drove over to see Ruth, and usually on these afternoons he would call in at my bungalow for a few minutes to discuss her progress. At first our conversations were completely false, each of us politely telling the other that Ruth was getting on reasonably well. Then one day he dropped the pretence.

'She is very unhappy, isn't she? Please—don't think I am blaming you, Miss Nedden. Myself, rather. It is too different. What should I have done, all those years ago?'

'Don't be offended, Dr Quansah, but why wasn't she taught her own language?'

He waited a long moment before replying. He studied the clear amber tea in his cup.

'I was brought up in a small village,' he said at last. 'English came hard to me. When I went to Secondary School I experienced great difficulty at first in understanding even the gist of the lectures. I was determined that the same thing would not happen to Ruth. I suppose I imagined she would pick up her own language easily, once she returned here, as though the knowledge of one's family tongue was inherited. Of course, if her mother had lived—'

He set down the teacup and knotted his huge hands together in an unexpressed anguish that was painful to see.

'Both of them uprooted,' he said. 'It was my fault, I guess, and yet—'

He fell silent. Finally, his need to speak was greater than his reluctance to reveal himself.

'You see, my wife hated England, always. I knew, although she never spoke of it. Such women don't. She was a quiet woman, gentle and—obedient. My parents had chosen her and I had married her when I was a very young man, before I first left this country. Our differences were not so great, then, but later in those years in London—she was like a plant, expected to grow where the soil is not suitable for it. My friends and associates—the places I went for dinner—she did not accompany me. I never asked her to entertain those people in our house. I could not—you see that?'

I nodded and he continued in the same low voice with its burden of self-reproach.

'She was illiterate,' he said. 'She did not know anything of my life, as it became. She did not want to know. She refused to learn. I was—impatient with her. I know that. But—'

He turned away so I would not see his face.

'Have you any idea what it is like,' he cried, 'to need someone to talk to, and not to have even one person?'

'Yes,' I said. 'I have a thorough knowledge of that.'

He looked at me in surprise, and when he saw that I did know, he seemed oddly relieved, as though, having exchanged vulnerabilities, we were neither of us endangered. My ebony cane slipped to the ground just then, and Dr Quansah stooped and picked it up, automatically and casually, hardly noticing it, and I was startled at myself, for I had felt no awkwardness in the moment either.

'When she became ill,' he went on, 'I do not think she really cared whether she lived or not. And now, Ruth—you know, when she was born, my wife called her by an African name which means "child of the rain". My wife missed the sun so very much. The rain, too, may have stood for her own tears. She had not wanted to bear her child so far from home.'

Unexpectedly, he smiled, the dark features of his face relaxing, becoming less blunt and plain.

'Why did you leave your country and come here, Miss Nedden? For the church? Or for the sake of Africans?'

I leaned back in my mock throne and re-arranged, a shade ironically, the folds of my lilac smock.

'I thought so, once,' I replied. 'But now I don't know. I think I may have come here mainly for myself, after all, hoping to find a place where my light could shine forth. Not a very palatable admission, perhaps.'

'At least you did not take others along on your pilgrimage.'

'No. I took no one. No one at all.'

We sat without speaking, then, until the tea grew cold and the dusk gathered.

It was through me that Ruth met David Mackie. He was an intent, lemon-haired boy of fifteen. He had been ill and was therefore out from England, staying with his mother while he recuperated. Mrs Mackie was a widow. Her husband had managed an oil palm plantation for an African owner, and when he died Clare Mackie had stayed on and managed the place herself. I am sure she made a better job of it than her husband had, for she was one of those frighteningly efficient women, under whose piercing eye, one felt, even the oil palms would not dare to slacken their efforts. She was slender and quick, and she contrived to look dashing and yet not unfeminine in her corded jodhpurs and open-necked shirt, which she wore with a silk paisley scarf at the throat. David was more like his father, thoughtful and rather withdrawn, and maybe that is why I had agreed to help him occasionally with his studies, which he was then taking by correspondence.

The Mackies' big whitewashed bungalow, perched on its cement pillars and fringed around with languid casuarina trees, was only a short distance from the school, on the opposite side of the hill to the village. Ruth came to my bungalow one Sunday afternoon, when I had promised to go to the Mackies', and as she appeared bored and despondent, I suggested she come along with me.

After I had finished the lesson, Ruth and David talked together amicably enough while Mrs Mackie complained about the inadequacies of local labour and I sat fanning myself with a palm leaf and feeling grateful that fate had not made me one of Clare Mackie's employees.

'Would you like to see my animals?' I heard David ask Ruth, his voice still rather formal and yet pleased, too, to have a potential admirer for his treasures.

'Oh yes.' She was eager; she understood people who collected animals. 'What have you got?'

'A baby crocodile,' he said proudly, 'and a cutting-grass—that's a bush rat, you know, and several snakes, non-poisonous ones, and a lot of assorted toads. I shan't be able to keep the croc long, of course. They're too tricky to deal with. I had a duiker, too, but it died.'

Off they went, and Mrs Mackie shrugged.

'He's mad about animals. I think they're disgusting. But he's got to have something to occupy his time, poor dear.'

When the two returned from their inspection of David's private zoo, we drove back to the school in the Mackies' bone-shaking jeep. I thought no more about the visit until late the next week, when I realized that I had not seen Ruth after classes for some days. I asked her, and she looked at me guilelessly, certain I would be as pleased as she was herself.

'I've been helping David with his animals,' she explained enthusiastically. 'You know, Miss Nedden, he wants to be an animal collector when he's through school. Not a hobby—he wants to work at it always. To collect live specimens, you see, for places like Whipsnade and Regent's Park Zoo. He's lent me a whole lot of books about it. It's awfully interesting, really it is.'

I did not know what to say. I could not summon up the sternness to deny her the first friendship she had made here. But of course it was not 'here', really. She was drawn to David because he spoke in the ways she knew, and of things which made sense to her. So she continued to see him. She borrowed several of my books to lend to him. They were both fond of poetry. I worried, of course, but not for what might be thought the obvious reasons. Both Ruth and David needed companionship, but neither was ready for anything more. I did not have the fears Miss Povey would have harboured if she had known. I was anxious for another reason. Ruth's friendship with David isolated her more than ever from the other girls. She made even less effort to get along with them now, for David was sufficient company.

Only once was I alarmed about her actual safety, the time when Ruth told me she and David had found an old fishing pirogue and had gone on the river in it.

'The river—' I was appalled. 'Ruth, don't you know there are crocodiles there?'

'Of course.' She had no awareness of having done anything dangerous. 'That's why we went. We hoped to catch another baby croc, you see. But we had no luck.'

'You had phenomenal luck,' I snapped. 'Don't you ever do that again. Not ever.'

'Well, all right,' she said regretfully. 'But it was great fun.'

The sense of adventure had returned to her, and all at once I realized why. David was showing Africa to her as she wanted to be shown it—from the outside.

I felt I should tell Dr Quansah, but when I finally did he was so upset that I was sorry I had mentioned it.

'It is not a good thing,' he kept saying. 'The fact that this is a boy does not concern me half so much, to be frank with you, as the fact that he is a European.'

'I would not have expected such illogicalities from you, Dr Quansah.' I was annoyed, and perhaps guilty as well, for I had permitted the situation.

Dr Quansah looked thoughtfully at me.

'I do not think it is that. Yes—maybe you are right. I don't know. But I do not want my daughter to be hurt by any—stupidity. I know that.'

'David's mother is employed as manager by an African owner.'

'Yes,' Dr Quansah said, and his voice contained a bitterness I had not heard in it before, 'but what does she say about him, in private?'

I had no reply to that, for what he implied was perfectly true. He saw from my face that he had not been mistaken.

'I have been away a long time, Miss Nedden,' he said, 'but not long enough to forget some of the things that were said to me by Europeans when I was young.'

I should not have blurted out my immediate thought, but I did.

'You have been able to talk to me—'

'Yes.' He smiled self-mockingly. 'I wonder if you know how much that has surprised me?'

Why should I have found it difficult then, to look at him, at the face whose composure I knew concealed such aloneness? I took refuge, as so often, in the adoption of an abrupt tone.

'Why should it be surprising? You liked people in England. You had friends there.'

'I am not consistent, I know. But the English at home are not the same as the English abroad—you must have realized that. You are not typical, Miss Nedden. I still find most Europeans here as difficult to deal with as I ever did. And yet—I seem to have lost touch with my own people, too. The young laboratory technicians at the station—they do not trust me, and I find myself getting so very impatient with them, losing my temper because they have not comprehended what I wanted them to do, and—'

He broke off. 'I really should not bother you with all this.'

'Oh, but you're not.' The words came out with an unthinking swiftness which mortified me later when I recalled it. 'I haven't so many people I can talk with, either, you know.'

'You told me as much, once,' Dr Quansah said gently. 'I had not forgotten.'

Pride has so often been my demon, the tempting conviction that one is able to see the straight path and to point it out to others. I was proud of my cleverness when I persuaded Kwaale to begin teaching Ruth Quansah the language of her people. Each afternoon they had lessons, and I assisted only when necessary to clarify some point of grammar. Ruth, once she started, became quite interested. Despite what she had said, she was curious to know what the other girls talked about together. As for Kwaale, it soothed her rancour to be asked to instruct, and it gave her an opportunity to learn something about Ruth, to see her as she was and not as Kwaale's imagination had distorted her. Gradually the two became, if not friends, at least reasonably peaceful acquaintances. Ruth continued to see David, but as her afternoons were absorbed by the language lessons, she no longer went to the Mackies' house quite so often.

Then came the Odwira. Ruth asked if she might go down to the village with Kwaale, and as most of the girls would be going, I agreed. Miss Povey would have liked to keep the girls away from the local festivals, which she regarded as dangerously heathen, but this quarantine had never proved practicable. At the time of the Odwira the girls simply disappeared, permission or not, like migrating birds.

Late that afternoon I saw the school lorry setting off for Eburaso, so I decided to go along. We swerved perilously down the mountain road, and reached the village just in time to see the end of the procession, as the chief, carried in palanquin under his saffron umbrella, returned from the river after the rituals there. The palm-wine libations had been poured, the souls of the populace cleansed. Now the Eburasahene would offer the new yams to the ancestors, and then the celebrations would begin. Drumming and dancing would go on all night, and the next morning Miss Povey, if she were wise, would not ask too many questions.

The mud and thatch shanties of the village were empty of inhabitants and the one street was full. Shouting, singing, wildly excited, they sweated and thronged. Everyone who owned a good cloth was wearing it, and the women fortunate enough to possess gold earrings or bangles were flaunting them before the covetous eyes of those whose bracelets and beads were only coloured glass. For safety I remained in the parked lorry, fearing my unsteady leg in such a mob.

I spotted Kwaale and Ruth. Kwaale's usual air of tranquillity had vanished. She was all sun-coloured cloth and whirling brown arms. I had never seen anyone with such a violence of beauty as she possessed, like surf or volcano, a spendthrift splendour. Then, out of the street's turbulence of voices I heard the low shout of a young man near her.

'Fire a gun at me.'

I knew what was about to happen, for the custom was a very old one. Kwaale threw back her head and laughed. Her hands flicked at her cloth and for an instant she stood there naked except for the white beads around her hips, and her *amoanse*, the red cloth between her legs. Still laughing, she knotted her cloth back on again, and the young man put an arm around her shoulders and drew her close to him.

Ruth, tidy and separate in her frock with its pastel flowers, stared as though unable to believe what she had seen. Slowly she turned and it was then that she saw me. She began to force her way through the crowd of villagers. Instantly Kwaale dropped the young man's hand and went after her. Ruth stood beside the lorry, her eyes appealing to me.

'You saw—you saw what she—'

Kwaale's hand was clawing at her shoulder then, spinning her around roughly.

'What are you telling her? It is not for you to say!'

Kwaale thought I would be bound to disapprove. I could have explained the custom to Ruth, as it had been explained to me many years ago by Kwaale's father. I could have told her it used to be 'Shoot an arrow', for Mother Nyame created the sun with fire, and arrows of the same fire were shot into the veins of mankind and became lifeblood. I could have said that the custom was a reminder that women are the source of life. But I did not, for I was by no means sure that either Kwaale or the young man knew the roots of the tradition or that they cared. Something was permitted at festival time—why should they care about anything other than the beat of their own blood?

'Wait, Ruth, you don't understand—'

'I understand what she is,' Ruth said distinctly. 'She's nothing but a—'

Kwaale turned upon her viciously.

'Talk, you! Talk and talk. What else could you do? No man here would want you as his wife—you're too ugly.'

Ruth drew away, shocked and uncertain. But Kwaale had not finished.

'Why don't you go? Take all your money and go! Why don't you?'

I should have spoken then, tried to explain one to the other. I think I did, after a paralysed moment, but it was too late. Ruth, twisting away, struggled around the clusters of people and disappeared among the trees on the path that led back to the mountain top.

The driver had trouble in moving the lorry through the jammed streets. By the time we got onto the hill road Ruth was not there. When we reached the school I got out and limped over to the Primary girls who were playing outside the main building. I asked if they had seen her, and they twirled and fluttered around me like green and brown leaves, each trying to outdo the others in impressing me with their display of English.

'Miss Neddeen, I seein' she. Wit' my eye I seein' she. She going deah—'

The way they pointed was the road to the Mackies' house.

I did not especially want the lorry to go roaring into the Mackies' compound as though the errand were urgent or critical, so when we sighted the casuarina trees I had the driver stop. I walked slowly past David's menagerie, where the cutting-grass scratched in its cage and the snakes lay in bright apathetic coils. Some sense of propriety made me hesitate before I had quite reached the house. Ruth and David were on the verandah, and I could hear their voices. I suppose it was shameful of me to listen, but it would have been worse to appear at that moment.

'If it was up to me—' David's voice was strained and tight with embarrassment. 'But you know what she's like.'

'What did she say, David? What did she say?' Ruth's voice, desperate with her need to know, her fear of knowing.

'Oh, well—nothing much.'

'Tell me!'

Then David, faltering, ashamed, tactless.

'Only that African girls mature awfully young, and she somehow got the daft notion that—look here, Ruth, I'm sorry, but when she gets an idea there's nothing anyone can do. I know it's a lot of rot. I know you're not the ordinary kind of African. You're almost—almost like a—like us.'

It was his best, I suppose. It was not his fault that it was not good enough. She cried out, then, and although the casuarina boughs hid the two from my sight, I could imagine their faces well enough, and David's astounded look at the hurt in her eyes.

'Almost—' she said. Then with a fury I would not have believed possible, 'No, I'm not! I'm not like you at all. I won't be!'

'Listen, Ruth—'

But she had thrust off his hand and had gone. She passed close to the place where I stood but she did not see me. Once again I watched her running. Running and running, into the forest where I could not follow.

I was frantic lest Miss Povey should find out and notify Dr Quansah before we could find Ruth. I had Ayesha go all through the school and grounds, for she could move more rapidly and unobtrusively than I. I waited, stumping up and down my garden, finally forcing myself to sit down and assume at least the appearance of calm. At last Ayesha returned. Only tiredness showed in her face, and my heart contracted.

'You did not find her, little one?'

She shook her head. 'She is not here. She is gone.'

Gone. Had she remained in the forest, then, with its thorns and strangular vines, its ferned depths that could hide death, its green silences? Or had she run as far as the river, dark and smooth as oil, deceptively smooth, with its saurian kings who fed of whatever flesh they could find? I dared not think.

I did something then that I had never before permitted myself to do. I picked up Ayesha and held the child tightly, not for her consoling but for my own. She reached out and touched a finger to my face.

'You are crying. For her?'

Then Ayesha sighed a little, resignedly.

'Come then,' she said. 'I will show you where she is.'

Had I known her so slightly all along, my small Ayesha whose childhood lay beaten and lost somewhere in the shanties and brothels of Takoradi or Kumasi, the airless upper rooms of palm-wine bars in Lagos or Kaduna? Without a word I rose and followed her.

We did not have far to go. The gardeners' quarters were at the back of the school grounds, surrounded by *niim* trees and a few banana palms. In the last hut of the row, Yindo sat cross-legged on the packed-earth floor. Beside him on a dirty and torn grass mat Ruth Quansah lay, face down, her head buried in her arms.

Ayesha pointed. Why had she wanted to conceal it? To this day I do not really know, nor what the hut recalled to her, nor what she felt, for her face bore no more expression than a pencilled stick-child's, and her eyes were as dull as they had been when she first came to us here.

Ruth heard my cane and my dragged foot. I know she did. But she did not stir.

'Madam—' Yindo's voice was nearly incoherent with terror. 'I beg you. You no give me sack. I Dagomba man, madam. No got bruddah dis place. I beg you, mek I no go lose dis job—'

I tried to calm him with meaningless sounds of reassurance. Then I asked him to tell me. He spoke in a harsh whisper, his face averted.

'She come dis place like she crez'. She say—do so.' He gestured unmistakably. 'I—I try, but I can no do so for she. I too fear.'

He held out his hands then in an appeal both desperate and hopeless. He was a desert man. He expected no mercy here, far from the dwellings of his tribe.

Ruth still had not moved. I do not think she had even heard Yindo's words. At last she lifted her head, but she did not speak. She scanned slowly the mud walls, the tin basin for washing, the upturned box that served as table, the old hurricane lamp, and in a niche the grey and grinning head of the dead chameleon, around it the blue beads like naive eyes shining and beside it the offering of a toffee wrapped in grimy silver paper.

I stood there in the hut doorway, leaning on my ebony cane to support my cumbersome body, looking at the three of them but finding nothing simple enough to say. What words, after all, could possibly have been given to the outcast children?

I told Dr Quansah. I did not spare him anything, nor myself either. I imagined he would be angry at my negligence, my blundering, but he was not.

'You should not blame yourself in this way,' he said. 'I do not want that. It is—really, I think it is a question of time, after all.'

'Undoubtedly. But in the meantime?'

'I don't know.' He passed a hand across his forehead. 'I seem to become tired so much more than I used to. Solutions do not come readily any more. Even for a father like myself, who relies so much on schools, it is still not such an easy thing, to bring up a child without a mother.'

I leaned back in my scarlet chair. The old rattan received my head, and my absurdly jagged breath eased.

'No,' I said. 'I'm sure it can't be easy.'

We were silent for a moment. Then with some effort Dr Quansah began to speak, almost apologetically.

'Coming back to this country after so long away—you know, I think that is the last new thing I shall be able to do in my life. Does that seem wrong? When one grows older, one is aware of so many difficulties. Often they appear to outweigh all else.'

My hands fumbled for my cane, the ebony that was grown and carved here. I found and held it, and it both reassured and mocked me.

'Perhaps,' I said deliberately. 'But Ruth—'

'I am taking her away. She wants to go. What else can I do? There is a school in the town where a cousin of mine lives.'

'Yes. I see. You cannot do anything else, of course.'

He rose. 'Goodbye,' he said, 'and—'

But he did not finish the sentence. We shook hands, and he left.

At Eburaso School we go on as before. Miss Povey and I still snipe back and forth, knowing in our hearts that we rely upon our differences and would miss them if they were not there. I still teach my alien speech to the young ones, who continue to impart to it a kind of garbled charm. I grow heavier and I fancy my lameness is more pronounced, although Kwaale assures me this is not the case. In few enough years I will have reached retirement age.

Sitting in my garden and looking at the sun on the prickly pear and the poinsettia, I think of that island of grey rain where I must go as a stranger, when the time comes, while others must remain as strangers here.

Rachel Wyatt

❧

The Day Marlene Dietrich Died

On the day Marlene Dietrich died, Richard Mawson left the cottage near Grenoble and set out to visit his mother in Sussex. He locked the white front door and trailed his hand over the flowers by the wall, inhaling a mixture of herbs and young roses. His work could wait. And so could the new waitress in the bistro. She had slim legs and vermilion hair and the other day he had said to her, 'That park over there is the place for lovers. It inspired a great writer to write his masterpiece.'

You are out of your mind! Words of his first wife, she of the limited vocabulary. Years ago, standing in the Louvre, she had said that to him. People had stared. She had said it loud and often, about his work, his life, his choice of music, the clothes he wore.

You're crazy! The voice of Ellen, his second. Fewer words. But she had preferred Bob Dylan.

In chorus they would have told him it was madness to set off on this trip now with four weeks of steady work still to be done on his book just because a woman he had supposed immortal was dead.

The car that came with the cottage was an old Peugeot and it ran like a dream. *Use it, use it*, the Duvaliers had said, thinking of local errands only. He had decided to drive to Paris and fly from there. He could visit the Louvre on his way back and treat himself to the violent colours of the nineteenth century before plunging into the cold stone and marble of antiquity. And the journey would give him time to think about a new title for his manuscript. *The Effects of Wartime Song Lyrics on Current Gender Politics* was five words too long.

His mother's name was Frances but for years she had called herself Francine. She was seventy-one-and-a-half and could well be cracking up from the arthritis she had been mentioning intermittently for twenty years. As for her heart, the gesture of hand on chest as if to show him that yes, indeed, she had a heart and all the pain in it was caused by him, came to his mind with awful clarity. That heart might even now be beating slowly and more slowly day by day, threatening to stop. Her eyes too were getting weaker. *I have an appointment with the optometrist. Just stronger lenses, darling.*

Blindly she was moving into the area of easy accidents. Stairwells, lift shafts, heavy traffic; deathtraps all. The phone call would come. *Your mother is asking for you.* Summoned by proxy.

He hadn't seen her since the last quarrel three years ago. He had phoned now and then, a cool and dutiful son. The sound of duty in his voice brought out reproach in hers. She wasn't going to start now apologising for her lovers, for the times in his childhood she had said, 'Go out to play, Richard, sweetheart,' and locked the door behind him. And that argument had ended like all the others with her telling him to buy a decent suit and grow up and him shouting back, 'I'm thirty-seven, Mother!'

He stopped in a little place near Lyon for lunch, steak à cheval and a bottle of red, and then drove on with Marlene singing for him, *I'm warm again, in love again.* She sat there on a barrel showing her suspenders and sang, *Ich bin die fesche Lola.*

He sang along with her and didn't notice the curve till he was in it and the stone wall loomed up in front of him, and then he screamed out in fear. 'Marlene! Mother!! Mummy!'

Blackness. Awakening. And then as he struggled out of the car and examined its dented front, its battered side, he kicked it, felt fury rise up; touched his head, saw blood on his hand, wanted to scream again.

The gendarmes were for once sympathetic. So monsieur was really used to the roads? Just a little wine for lunch? Regular two-month stay in their lovely country to do research and to write? Interesting! They advised him, after keeping him in a steamy office for three hours, to get a taxi back to Lyon and from there take the TGV. No doubt the insurance company would pay for the damage to the car. The problem could be settled on his return. A man on his way to see his sick and aging mother. Eh bien. The train would be leaving at eight p.m.

The younger policeman smiled at him with the smile of a ruler who had charge over all his comings and goings and who knew that his mother was a young woman of twenty-nine who had long legs and who would welcome him at the door, naked, a maenad.

Richard wanted to lash out, to bash the young confident face, mark it with his knuckles, draw blood. He stood outside the gendarmerie, his back against the wall till his breath returned to normal and his fists unclenched.

I could have died.

At the station in Lyon they told him that there was no seat on a train to Paris till midnight. Summer crowds, monsieur. Already here in May. Les touristes! Other more hostile invasions had been less unpopular.

He tried to change his plans and fly from Lyon but the planes too were fully booked. You have a plane ticket from Paris, monsieur! He looked up at the hazy sky for a sign that would tell him to stay with the Duvaliers'

Peugeot, wait till it was repaired, to turn round and go back to his cottage and the new waitress and forget England.

The woman who came up to him and offered him her body was not slim, did not have good legs nor a fine complexion. She had a slight lisp and was wearing a sweater too tight and a skirt too short. And she was hungry. After dinner he took her to his room and made love to her unkindly. Later on, she agreed to go with him for a gentle walk beside the river. She talked about her life as it had been once and mentioned that she had a son aged five whom she saw off to school every morning.

'See his picture. I call him René. But I wish I'd called him something better, a solid name like Richard. Perhaps when he grows up, he'll be a writer like you.'

The trees bent over the river, branches sweeping the surface. When he put his hands on her shoulders she turned to him and smiled. He had not thought to fill the pockets of her coat with stones. The branches swished to and fro brushing the water violently. And her face as she looked back at him was wet.

On the train his fellow passenger turned to talk to him. 'You're from where?'

'Manchester.'

'What do you do?'

They always asked because his French was not perfect and he was too young to have given up another life to spend declining years in one place.

'I'm a singer,' he told her, tired for once of truth.

'Marlene Dietrich died yesterday,' she said.

He wanted to say, *What's it to you! What does it matter to you? Who are you that you can use her name in that familiar way?*

But she went on, 'We're using the same currency now. That has to count for something.'

He bit into the white hard baguette and crumbs spilled down from his mouth. Everybody was an expert. Everybody knew everything. Information technology. Universal access. At the university, other lecturers blamed the telly for slack work, for poor perceptions when it was their own lack of imagination that made students into zombies.

He laughed at the others in his department. He knew they laughed at him. They tittered and muttered about his research. If he had been scouring graveyards, battlefields, searching for wounds and old bones, they would have taken him seriously. When they heard sounds of singing coming from his office, voices of Vera and Frank and Bing, the jokes of Bob Hope, they shook their heads and went back to their boring searches into the current political soul. They saw his work as a poor excuse for scholarship, his clothes as affectation, and his desire for solitude as a symptom of madness.

When he had mentioned Grenoble to the new lecturer in Economics, she, smiling, had turned her neat face to him in academic complicity and said, 'Ah Stendhal!' and waited for a loving response. When he replied, 'George Formby!' she had moved away to join the others.

He went to the St Jacques near the Jardin des Plantes where he usually stayed in Paris and took a room for the night.

In the hotel lobby a woman sat crying. Her name was Carla.

'You can't understand,' she said. 'You can't know what I feel.'

'I'm on my way to have breakfast.'

'Do you think I want to eat.' She turned on him, angry, full of horror at his lack of understanding. 'Coffee perhaps. Give me time to change.'

He phoned to let his mother know that he was approaching and would be there the next day late or, at any rate, the day after.

His mother, in a quavery voice, said, 'Did you know Marlene Dietrich died yesterday? I remember her saying in that documentary somebody made, "I've been photographed to death."'

It wasn't the camera that killed her, Mother! She was old, like you.

Carla, when she returned, had dried her tears, was wearing purple, a scarf tied round her neck in that neat foreign way, colours of green and blue and black and turquoise.

'How do you tie your scarf?'

'Like a man's tie.'

She fingered the knot as she sat there talking.

'They said she couldn't walk, never went out. But she did, she went out every day. Every day about this time, she went by the boulangerie on the corner, the one over there. About this time. She bought three croissants which made me think she was not alone. No one could eat three croissants for breakfast, and theirs are particularly large. See. See. There she is. Buying her croissants. She is not dead.'

She pointed and he looked and saw an old bent woman with a scarf on her head and her raincoat collar turned up, wearing boots and carrying a plastic bag. Not a single feature could be seen. Not a glimmer of fame or riches and no retinue of wishful men to walk behind her. This old lady had not danced and sung her way through his life. Had not made movies that were old when he was young.

'Let's go for a walk,' he said to Carla.

'What about—you know.'

'Later if there's time.'

He took her to the cemetery to see where the grave might have been had Marlene wished to be buried there. And he said, 'She is dead. Dead.

And will be taken back to Germany.'

'Why there?'

'She wanted to be near her mother.'

'What about her lovers?'

He saw a long grave, suffocated in flowers, a grave stretching half across Paris, a grave in which the bodies of her old lovers lay. Exhumed and sent from Hollywood, from London, from Berlin, from Sicily, and laid beside her, facing her. *I'm warm again. In love again.*

'Why have you brought me here?'

'Why do people go anywhere?'

He put his hands on the scarf, on her chest. She thought it must be time and said, 'Not here.'

But he replied, 'No better place,' and pulled and pulled on the knot of the scarf she had tied for him in advance and afterwards left her there while she was still faintly gasping.

He picked up his bag from the hotel and took the bus to Charles de Gaulle and paid the fee to take an earlier flight.

Even three years ago, his mother had begun to stoop; her hair was by now thin on top and her face probably like a parchment, dried and full of wrinkles. 'I will love you. I will be your only love,' he murmured to himself and sang 'Lili Marlene' under his breath and wished for lamplight and the soft glow of gas mantles. Everywhere nowadays light was harsh. Neon made much of life into a B-movie.

They were slow in the car rental office at Gatwick. He wanted to bang on the desk and shout, This is my home. I'm on my way to see my mother. She is old, maybe dying. Minutes count. GIVE ME A CAR! Finally the young man handed him a set of keys and released him.

He drove slowly south into the rolling countryside. The trees were heavy with leaves, the grass lush, the sun soft and unthreatening.

I'm on my way, Mother.

He could stay in his old room for the rest of the summer, live with her, take care of her, do his research in the library, ask her to sing the songs she had sung then, as she went from camp to camp with ENSA in the war. *The best time of my life, sweetheart. Before you were born.*

The house was still there. He felt a sense of relief as if it might have disappeared and left a gap in the road, as if the shrubs, dull evergreens planted by his father years before—*your father came to like darkness in the war*—might have grown over the place. But it was there, the house. It reached out to him. The windows glowed clean; the outside light was on as if she had left it on all these years to await his return. It was daylight and the outside light was on! Inside him the anger softened. *Save electricity! Do you think I'm made of money?* had been one of his father's cries. And now his mother had left the light on overnight perhaps and maybe for days, just for him, for his return.

He walked up the path—the hedge needed cutting, well, he would cut the hedge—and saw himself:

Walking down that path behind his father's coffin.

Walking down that path, bride on his arm.

Walking down that path with his new bicycle.

Walking down that path with his new bride.

Walking down that path alone with his suitcase.

You do not need to go to Manchester, his mother had called after him as if there were jobs available everywhere and he had taken that one for spite.

She was there inside.

He looked through the window and watched his mother. She was setting out two places on the table. She had put a starched place mat at either end, lacy heirlooms from a time when people knew how to starch lightly, how to iron without ripping lacework to shreds. In the centre of the table, more highly polished than he had remembered it, was a single red rose in a light vase, its stem showing through the glass. She was in the act of laying down a silver knife when she looked up and saw him. And he was staring at her and thinking this is my home, this is my mother and I forgive her. This is my home, this is my mother and.

His mother came to the door and said, 'Oh dear, did I leave that light on again. I'm getting very forgetful.'

She came to him smiling and put her hands on his cheeks, just in the way he remembered. And she said, 'How lovely to see you, sweetheart. You're looking well. Over there agrees with you. What a surprise. Why didn't you let me know the exact time?'

She looked slimmer, was wearing a brown skirt, a blouse in shades of pink, high-heeled shoes that set off her slim legs, and her hair was tinted a rosy beige.

Still she was his mother and he could forgive her.

'What a nice surprise,' she said.

He beheld her. She looked very, very well. She smelt lightly of *Carnation*. He had made this journey assuming she would be tottering, perhaps close to death. And now here she was, looking as if she was on the very verge of life. For several moments, he had no words to say. He would stay on and take her to London every day to theatres, to galleries. Make up for time and love lost. Hand in hand, they would go and have great times and he would listen again to her wartime stories and the old tale of her lost lover. And she would sing to him, sing the old sad songs to him of soldiers gone to war and of the women waiting at home for them in vain.

She said, 'Darling. Put your bag in your old room. You don't want to be spending your time with dreary old me. I'm sure you want to see your friends. There's a train to Victoria at one. You've got a car? Just come and go as you like.'

He said, 'I've come all this way to see you.'

'Angel, how sweet.'

And then she said, 'The pub serves a very good smoked trout.'

She smiled at him slyly just in the way he remembered.

'But you and me,' she went on, 'we'll have a lovely, cosy dinner tonight or maybe tomorrow.'

'Yes, Mother.'

He carried his bag back outside. She, uncorking a bottle of wine, did not notice. He thought he heard her singing the song she had often sung to him. *Ich bin von Kopf bis Fuss auf Liebe eingestellt.* And he remembered how she would tap his head and then his feet and repeat the line again. Liebchen, she would say. My little love.

Richard had liked it better when she sang fast and loud, *I am the naughty Lola,* and turned on the piano stool and swung her legs at him and laughed. And they had both laughed.

I can't help it. It's my nature.

He put his case in the car and walked to the Green. There was no one about. It was lunchtime. Everybody was at home or in the pub.

He sat down by the pond to watch the swans, and when a young woman, blue suit, nice eyes, thick ankles, sat down on the same bench to feed the birds and offered him a crust, he accepted it gratefully.

Soon he would say to her, *Robert Louis Stevenson lived near here, and if we walk up on the Downs just a little way we can see the place that inspired him to write his third novel.*

And she would follow him, the literary man, and discover too late that his true interest was in the songs of the Second World War.

ALICE MUNRO

THE ALBANIAN VIRGIN

In the mountains, in Maltsia e madhe, she must have tried to tell them her name, and 'Lottar' was what they made of it. She had a wound in her leg, from a fall on sharp rocks when her guide was shot. She had a fever. How long it took them to carry her through the mountains, bound up in a rug and strapped to a horse's back, she had no idea. They gave her water to drink now and then, and sometimes *raki*, which was a kind of brandy, very strong. She could smell pines. At one time they were on a boat and she woke up and saw the stars, brightening and fading and changing places— unstable clusters that made her sick. Later she understood that they must have been on the lake. Lake Scutari, or Sckhoder, or Skodra. They pulled up among the reeds. The rug was full of vermin, which got under the rag tied around her leg.

At the end of her journey, though she did not know it was the end, she was lying in a small stone hut that was an outbuilding of the big house, called the *kula*. It was the hut of the sick and dying. Not of giving birth, which these women did in the cornfields, or beside the path when they were carrying a load to market.

She was lying, perhaps for weeks, on a heaped-up bed of ferns. It was comfortable, and had the advantage of being easily changed when fouled or bloodied. The old woman named Tima looked after her. She plugged up the wound with a paste made of beeswax and olive oil and pine resin. Several times a day the dressing was removed, the wound washed out with *raki*. Lottar could see black lace curtains hanging from the rafters, and she thought she was in her room at home, with her mother (who was dead) looking after her. 'Why have you hung up those curtains?' she said. 'They look horrible.'

She was really seeing cobwebs, all thick and furry with smoke—ancient cobwebs, never disturbed from year to year.

Also, in her delirium, she had the sensation of some wide board being pushed against her face—something like a coffin plank. But when she came to her senses she learned that it was nothing but a crucifix, a wooden cru- cifix that a man was trying to get her to kiss. The man was a priest, a Franciscan. He was a tall, fierce-looking man with black eyebrows and moustache and a rank smell, and he carried, besides the crucifix, a gun that she learned later was a Browning revolver. He knew by the look of her that she was a giaour—not a Muslim—but he did not understand that she might be a heretic. He knew a little English but pronounced it in a way that she could not make out. And she did not then know any of the language of the Ghegs. But after her fever subsided, when he tried a few words of Italian on her, they were able to talk, because she had learned Italian at school and had been travelling for six months in Italy. He understood so much more than anyone else around her that she expected him, at first, to understand everything. What is the nearest city? she asked him, and he said, Skodra. So go there, please, she said—go and find the British Consulate, if there is one. I belong to the British Empire. Tell them I am here. Or if there is no British Consul, go to the police.

She did not understand that under no circumstances would anybody go to the police. She didn't know that she belonged now to this tribe, this *kula*, even though taking her prisoner had not been their intention and was an embarrassing mistake.

It is shameful beyond belief to attack a woman. When they had shot and killed her guide, they had thought that she would turn her horse around and fly back down the mountain road, back to Bar. But her horse took fright at the shot and stumbled among the boulders and she fell, and her leg was injured. Then they had no choice but to carry her with them, back across the border between the Crna Gora (which means Black Rock, or Montenegro) and Maltsia e madhe.

'But why rob the guide and not me?' she said, naturally thinking robbery to be the motive. She thought of how starved they looked, the man and his horse, and of the fluttering white rags of his headdress.

'Oh, they are not robbers!' said the Franciscan, shocked. 'They are honest men. They shot him because they were in blood with him. With his house. It is their law.'

He told her that the man who had been shot, her guide, had killed a man of this *kula*. He had done that because the man he had killed had killed a man of his *kula*. This would go on, it had been going on for a long time now, there were always more sons being born. They think they have more sons than other people in the world, and it is to serve this necessity.

'Well, it is terrible,' the Franciscan concluded, 'But it is for their honour, the honour of their family. They are always ready to die for their honour.'

She said that her guide did not seem to be so ready, if he had fled to Crna Gora.

'But it did not make any difference, did it?' said the Franciscan. 'Even if he had gone to America, it would not have made any difference.'

At Trieste she had boarded a steamer, to travel down the Dalmatian Coast. She was with her friends Mr and Mrs Cozzens, whom she had met in Italy, and their friend Dr Lamb, who had joined them from England. They put in at the little port of Bar, which the Italians call Antivari, and stayed the night at the European Hotel. After dinner they walked on the terrace, but Mrs Cozzens was afraid of a chill, so they went indoors and played cards. There was rain in the night. She woke up and listened to the rain and was full of disappointment, which gave rise to a loathing for these middle-aged people, particularly for Dr Lamb, whom she believed the Cozzenses had summoned from England to meet her. They probably thought she was rich. A transatlantic heiress whose accent they could almost forgive. These people ate too much and then they had to take pills. And they worried about being in strange places—what had they come for? In the morning she would have to get back on the boat with them or they would make a fuss. She would never take the road over the mountains to Cetinge, Montenegro's capital city—they had been told that it was not wise. She would never see the bell tower where the heads of Turks used to hang, or the plane tree under which the Poet-Prince held audience with the people. She could not get back to sleep, so she decided to go downstairs with the first light, and, even if it was still raining, to go a little way up the road behind the town, just to see the ruins that she knew were there, among the olive trees, and the Austrian fortress on its rock and the dark face of Mount Lovchen.

The weather obliged her, and so did the man at the hotel desk, producing almost at once a tattered but cheerful guide and his underfed horse. They set out—she on the horse, the man walking ahead. The road was steep and twisting and full of boulders, the sun increasingly hot and the intervening shade cold and black. She became hungry and thought she must turn back soon. She would have breakfast with her companions, who got up late.

No doubt there was some sort of search for her, after the guide's body was found. The authorities must have been notified—whoever the authorities were. The boat must have sailed on time, her friends must have gone with it. The hotel had not taken their passports. Nobody back in Canada would think of investigating. She was not writing regularly to anyone, she had had a falling-out with her brother, her parents were dead. You won't come home till all your inheritance is spent, her brother had said, and then who will look after you?

When she was being carried through the pine forest, she awoke and found herself suspended, lulled—in spite of the pain and perhaps because of the *raki*—into a disbelieving surrender. She fastened her eyes on the bundle that was hanging from the saddle of the man ahead of her and knocking against the horse's back. It was something about the size of a cabbage, wrapped in a stiff and rusty-looking cloth.

I heard this story in the old St Joseph's Hospital in Victoria from Charlotte, who was the sort of friend I had in my early days there. My friendships then seemed both intimate and uncertain. I never knew why people told me things, or what they meant me to believe.

I had come to the hospital with flowers and chocolates. Charlotte lifted her head, with its clipped and feathery white hair, toward the roses. 'Bah!' she said. 'They have no smell! Not to me, anyway. They are beautiful, of course.

'You must eat the chocolates yourself,' she said. 'Everything tastes like tar to me. I don't know how I know what tar tastes like, but this is what I think.'

She was feverish. Her hand, when I held it, felt hot and puffy. Her hair had all been cut off, and this made her look as if she had actually lost flesh around her face and neck. The part of her under the hospital covers seemed as extensive and lumpy as ever.

'But you must not think I am ungrateful,' she said. 'Sit down. Bring that chair from over there—she doesn't need it.'

There were two other women in the room. One was just a thatch of yellow-grey hair on the pillow, and the other was tied into a chair, wriggling and grunting.

'This is a terrible place,' said Charlotte. 'But we must just try our best to put up with it. I am so glad to see you. That one over there yells all night long,' she said, nodding toward the window bed. 'We must thank Christ she's asleep now. I don't get a wink of sleep, but I have been putting the time to very good use. What do you think I've been doing? I've been making up a story, for a movie! I have it all in my head and I want you to hear it. You will be able to judge if it will make a good movie. I think it will. I would like Jennifer Jones to act in it. I don't know, though. She does not seem to have the same spirit anymore. She married that mogul.

'Listen,' she said. '(Oh, could you haul that pillow up more, behind my head?) It takes place in Albania, in northern Albania, which is called Maltsia e madhe, in the nineteen-twenties, when things were very primitive. It is about a young woman travelling alone. Lottar is her name in the story.'

I sat and listened. Charlotte would lean forward, even rock a little on her hard bed, stressing some point for me. Her puffy hands flew up and down, her blue eyes widened commandingly, and then from time to time she sank back onto the pillows, and she shut her eyes to get the story in focus again. Ah, yes, she said. Yes, yes. And she continued.

'Yes, yes,' she said at last. 'I know how it goes on, but that is enough for now. You will have to come back. Tomorrow. Will you come back?'

I said, yes, tomorrow, and she appeared to have fallen asleep without hearing me.

The *kula* was a great, rough stone house with a stable below and the living quarters above. A veranda ran all the way around, and there would always be an old woman sitting there, with a bobbin contraption that flew like a bird from one hand to the other and left a trail of shiny black braid, mile after mile of black braid, which was the adornment of all the men's trousers. Other women worked at the looms or sewed together the leather sandals. Nobody sat there knitting, because nobody would think to sit down to knit. Knitting was what they did while they trotted back and forth to the spring with their water barrels strapped to their backs, or took the path to the fields or to the beech wood, where they collected the fallen branches. They knitted stockings—black and white, red and white, with zigzag patterns like lightning strokes. Women's hands must never be idle. Before dawn they pounded the bread dough in its blackened wooden trough, shaped it into loaves on the backs of shovels, and baked it on the hearth. (It was corn bread, unleavened and eaten hot, which would swell up like a puffball in your stomach.) Then they had to sweep out the *kula* and dump the dirty ferns and pile up armloads of fresh ferns for the next night's sleep. This was often one of Lottar's jobs, since she was so unskilled at everything else. Little girls stirred the yogurt so that lumps would not form as it soured. Older girls might butcher a kid and sew up its stomach, which they had stuffed with wild garlic and sage and apples. Or they would go together, girls and women, all ages, to wash the men's white head scarves in the cold little river nearby, whose waters were clear as glass. They tended the tobacco crop and hung the ripe leaves to dry in the darkened shed. They hoed the corn and cucumbers, milked the ewes.

The women looked stern but they were not so, really. They were only preoccupied, and proud of themselves, and eager for competition. Who could carry the heaviest load of wood, knit the fastest, hoe the most rows of cornstalks? Tima, who had looked after Lottar when she was sick, was the most spectacular worker of all. She would run up the slope to the *kula* with a load of wood bound to her back that looked ten times as big as herself. She would leap from rock to rock in the river and pound the scarves as if they were the bodies of enemies. 'Oh, Tima, Tima!' the other women cried out in ironic admiration, and 'Oh, Lottar, Lottar!' in nearly the same tones, when Lottar, at the other end of a scale of usefulness, let the clothes drift away downstream. Sometimes they whacked Lottar with a stick, as they would a donkey, but this had more exasperation in it than cruelty. Sometimes the young ones would say, 'Talk your talk!' and for their entertainment she would speak English. They wrinkled up their faces and spat, at such peculiar sounds. She tried to teach them words—*hand, nose,* and so on. But these seemed to them jokes, and they would repeat them to each other and fall about laughing.

Women were with women and men were with men, except at times in the night (women teased about such times were full of shame and denial, and sometimes there would be a slapping) and at meals, when the women served the men their food. What the men did all day was none of the women's business. Men made their ammunition, and gave a lot of care to their guns, which were in some cases very beautiful, decorated with engraved silver. They also dynamited rocks to clear the road, and were responsible for the horses. Wherever they were, there was a lot of laughing, and sometimes singing and firing off of blanks. While they were at home they seemed to be on holiday, and then some of them would have to ride off on an expedition of punishment, or to attend a council called to put an end to some particular bout of killing. None of the women believed it would work—they laughed and said that it would only mean twenty more shot. When a young man was going off on his first killing, the women made a great fuss over his clothes and his haircut, to encourage him. If he didn't succeed, no woman would marry him—a woman of any worth would be ashamed to marry a man who had not killed—and everyone was anxious to have new brides in the house, to help with the work.

One night, when Lottar served one man his food—a guest; there were always guests invited for meals around the low table, the *sofra*—she noticed what small hands he had, and hairless wrists. Yet he was not young, he was not a boy. A wrinkled, leathery face, without a moustache. She listened for his voice in the talk, and it seemed to her hoarse but womanish. But he smoked, he ate with the men, he carried a gun.

'Is that a man?' Lottar said to the woman serving with her. The woman shook her head, not willing to speak where the men might hear them. But the young girls who overheard the question were not so careful. 'Is that a man? Is that a man?' they mimicked Lottar. 'Oh, Lottar, you are so stupid! Don't you know when you see a Virgin?'

So she did not ask them anything else. But the next time she saw the Franciscan, she ran after him to ask him her question. What is a Virgin? She had to run after him, because he did not stop and talk to her now as he had when she was sick in the little hut. She was always working when he came to the *kula*, and he could not spend much time with the women anyway—he sat with the men. She ran after him when she saw him leaving, striding down the path among the sumac trees, heading for the bare wooden church and the lean-to church house, where he lived.

He said it was a woman, but a woman who had become like a man. She did not want to marry, and she took an oath in front of witnesses that she never would, and then she put on men's clothes and had her own gun, and her horse if she could afford one, and she lived as she liked. Usually she was poor, she had no woman to work for her. But nobody troubled her, and she could eat at the *sofra* with the men.

Lottar no longer spoke to the priest about going to Skodra. She understood now that it must be a long way away. Sometimes she asked if he had heard anything, if anybody was looking for her, and he would say, sternly, no one. When she thought of how she had been during those first weeks—giving orders, speaking English without embarrassment, sure that her special case merited attention—she was ashamed at how little she had understood. And the longer she stayed at the *kula*, the better she spoke the language and became accustomed to the work, the stranger was the thought of leaving. Someday she must go, but how could it be now? How could she leave in the middle of the tobacco-picking or the sumac harvest, or during the preparations for the feast of the Translation of St Nicholas?

In the tobacco fields they took off their jerkins and blouses and worked half naked in the sun, hidden between the rows of tall plants. The tobacco juice was black and sticky, like molasses, and it ran down their arms and was smeared over their breasts. At dusk they went down to the river and scrubbed themselves clean. They splashed in the cold water, girls and big, broad women together. They tried to push each other off balance, and Lottar heard her name cried then, in warning and triumph, without contempt, like any other name: 'Lottar, watch out! Lottar!'

They told her things. They told her that children died here because of the *Striga*. Even grown-up people shrivel and die sometimes, when the *Striga* has put her spell on them. The *Striga* looks like a normal woman, so you do not know who she is. She sucks blood. To catch her, you must lay a cross on the threshold of the church on Easter Sunday when everybody is inside. Then the woman who is the *Striga* cannot come out. Or you can follow the woman you suspect, and you may see her vomit up the blood. If you can manage to scrape up some of this blood on a silver coin, and carry that coin with you, no *Striga* can touch you, ever.

Hair cut at the time of the full moon will turn white.

If you have pains in your limbs, cut some hair from your head and your armpits and burn it—then the pains will go away.

The *oras* are the devils that come out at night and flash false lights to bewilder travellers. You must crouch down and cover your head, else they will lead you over a cliff. Also they will catch the horses and ride them to death.

The tobacco had been harvested, the sheep brought down from the slopes, animals and humans shut up in the *kula* through the weeks of snow and cold rain, and one day, in the early warmth of the spring sun, the women brought Lottar to a chair on the veranda. There, with great ceremony and delight, they shaved off the hair above her forehead. Then they combed some black, bubbling dye through the hair that remained. The dye was greasy—the hair became so stiff that they could shape it into wings and buns as firm as blood puddings. Everybody thronged about, criticizing and admiring. They put flour on her face and dressed her up in clothes they had pulled out of one of the great carved chests. What for, she asked, as she found herself disappearing into a white blouse with gold embroidery, a red bodice with fringed epaulets, a sash of striped silk a yard wide and a dozen yards long, a black-and-red wool skirt, with chain after chain of false gold being thrown over her hair and around her neck. For beauty, they said. And they said when they had finished, 'See! She is beautiful!' Those who said it seemed triumphant, challenging others who must have doubted that the transformation could be made. They squeezed the muscles in her arms, which she had got from hoeing and wood-carrying, and patted her broad, floured forehead. Then they shrieked, because they had forgotten a very important thing—the black paint that joins the eye-brows in a single line over the nose.

'The priest is coming!' shouted one of the girls, who must have been placed as a lookout, and the woman who was painting the black line said, 'Ha, he will not stop it!' But the others drew aside.

The Franciscan shot off a couple of blanks, as he always did to announce his arrival, and the men of the house fired off blanks also, to welcome him. But he did not stay with the men this time. He climbed at once to the veranda, calling, 'Shame! Shame! Shame on you all! Shame!

'I know what you have dyed her hair for,' he said to the women. 'I know why you have put bride's clothes on her. All for a pig of a Muslim!

'You! You sitting there in your paint,' he said to Lottar. 'Don't you know what it is for? Don't you know they have sold you to a Muslim? He is coming from Vuthaj. He will be here by dark!'

'So what of it?' said one of the women boldly. 'All they could get for her was three napoleons. She has to marry somebody.'

The Franciscan told her to hold her tongue. 'Is this what you want?' he said to Lottar. 'To marry and infidel and go to live with him in Vuthaj?'

Lottar said no. She felt as if she could hardly move or open her mouth, under the weight of her greased hair and her finery. Under this weight she struggled as you do to rouse yourself to a danger, out of sleep. The idea of marrying the Muslim was still too distant to be the danger—what she understood was that she would be separated from the priest, and would never be able to claim an explanation from him again.

'Did you know you were being married?' he asked her. 'Is it something you want, to be married?'

No, she said. No. And the Franciscan clapped his hands. 'Take off that gold trash!' he said. 'Take those clothes off her! I am going to make her a Virgin!'

'If you become a Virgin, it will be all right,' he said to her. 'The Muslim will not have to shoot anybody. But you must swear you will never go with a man. You must swear in front of witnesses. *Per quri e per kruch.* By the stone and by the Cross. Do you understand that? I am not going to let them marry you to a Muslim, but I do not want more shooting to start on this land.'

It was one of the things the Franciscan tried so hard to prevent—the selling of women to Muslim men. It put him into a frenzy, that their religion could be so easily set aside. They sold girls like Lottar, who would bring no price anywhere else, and widows who had borne only girls.

Slowly and sulkily the women removed all the rich clothes. They brought out men's trousers worn and with no braid, and a shirt and head scarf. Lottar put them on. One woman with an ugly pair of shears chopped off most of what remained of Lottar's hair, which was difficult to cut because of the dressing.

'Tomorrow you would have been a bride,' they said to her. Some of them seemed mournful, some contemptuous. 'Now you will never have a son.'

The little girls snatched up the hair that had been cut off and stuck it on their heads, arranging various knots and fringes.

Lottar swore her oath in front of twelve witnesses. They were, of course, all men, and looked as sullen as the women about the turn things had taken. She never saw the Muslim. The Franciscan berated the men and said that if this sort of thing did not stop he would close up the churchyard and make them bury their dead in unholy ground. Lottar sat at a distance from them all, in her unaccustomed clothes. It was strange and unpleasant to be idle. When the Franciscan had finished his harangue, he came over and stood looking down at her. He was breathing hard because of his rage, or the exertions of the lecture.

'Well, then,' he said. 'Well.' He reached into some inner fold of his clothing and brought out a cigarette and gave it to her. It smelled of his skin.

A nurse brought in Charlotte's supper, a light meal of soup and canned peaches. Charlotte took the cover off the soup, smelled it, and turned her head away. 'Go away, don't look at this slop,' she said, 'Come back tomorrow—you know it's not finished yet.'

The nurse walked with me to the door, and once we were in the corridor she said, 'It's always the ones with the least at home who turn the most critical. She's not the easiest in the world, but you can't help kind of admiring her. You're not related, are you?'

Oh, no, I said. No.

'When she came in it was amazing. We were taking her things off and somebody said, oh, what lovely bracelets, and right away she wanted to sell them! Her *husband* is something else. Do you know him? They are really quite the characters.'

Charlotte's husband, Gjurdhi, had come to my bookstore by himself one cold morning less than a week earlier. He was pulling a wagon full of books, which he had wrapped up in a blanket. He had tried to sell me some books once before, in their apartment, and I thought perhaps these were the same ones. I had been confused then, but now that I was on my own ground I was able to be more forceful. I said no, I did not handle secondhand books, I was not interested. Gjurdhi nodded brusquely, as if I had not needed to tell him this and it was of no importance to our conversation. He continued to pick up the books one by one, urging me to run my hands over the bindings, insisting that I note the beauty of the illustrations and be impressed by the dates of publication. I had to repeat my refusal over and over again, and I heard myself begin to attach some apologies to it, quite against my own will. He chose to understand each rejection as applying to an individual book and would simply fetch out another, saying vehemently, 'This too! This is very beautiful. You will notice. And it is very old. Look what a beautiful old book!'

They were travel books, some of them, from the turn of the century. Not so very old, and not so beautiful, either, with their dim, grainy photographs. *A Trek Through the Black Peaks. High Albania. Secret Lands of Southern Europe.*

'You will have to go to the Antiquarian Bookstore,' I said. 'The one on Fort Street. It isn't far to take them.'

He made a sound of disgust, maybe indicating that he knew well enough where it was, or that he had already made an unsuccessful trip there, or that most of these books had come from there, one way or another, in the first place.

'How is Charlotte?' I said warmly. I had not seen her for a while, although she used to visit the store quite often. She would bring me little presents—coffee beans coated with chocolate to give me energy; a bar of pure glycerine soap to counteract the drying effects, on the skin, of having to handle so much paper. A paperweight embedded with samples of rocks found in British Columbia, a pencil that lit up in the dark (so that I could see to write up bills if the lights should go out). She drank coffee with me, talked, and strolled about the store, discreetly occupied, when I was busy. Through the dark, blustery days of fall she wore the velvet cloak that I had first seen her in, and kept the rain off with an oversized, ancient black umbrella. She called it her tent. If she saw that I had become too involved with a customer, she would tap me on the shoulder and say, 'I'll just silently steal away with my tent now. We'll talk another day.'

Once, a customer said to me bluntly, 'Who is that woman? I've seen her around town with her husband. I guess he's her husband. I thought they were peddlers.'

Could Charlotte have heard that, I wondered. Could she have detected a coolness in the attitude of my new clerk? (Charlotte was certainly cool to her.) There might have been just too many times when I was busy. I did not actually think that the visits had stopped. I preferred to think that an interval had grown longer, for a reason that might have nothing to do with me. I was busy and tired, anyway, as Christmas loomed. The number of books I was selling was a pleasant surprise.

'I don't want to be any kind of character assassin,' the clerk had said to me. 'But I think you should know that that woman and her husband have been banned from a lot of stores in town. They're suspected of lifting things. I don't know. He wears that rubber coat with the big sleeves and she's got her cloak. I do know for sure that they used to go around at Christmastime and snip off holly that was growing in people's gardens. Then they took it round and tried to sell it in apartment buildings.'

On that cold morning, after I had refused all the books in his wagon, I asked Gjurdhi again how Charlotte was. He said that she was sick. He spoke sullenly, as if it were none of my business.

'Take her a book,' I said. I picked out a Penguin light verse. 'Take her this—tell her I hope she enjoys it. Tell her I hope she'll be better very soon. Perhaps I can get around to see her.'

He put the book into his bundle in the wagon. I thought that he would probably try to sell it immediately.

'Not at home,' he said. 'In the hospital.'

I had noticed, each time he bent over the wagon, a large, wooden crucifix that swung down outside his coat and had to be tucked back inside. Now this happened again, and I said, thoughtlessly, in my confusion and contrition, 'Isn't that beautiful! What beautiful dark wood! It looks medieval.'

He pulled it over his head, saying, 'Very old. Very beautiful. Oak wood. Yes.'

He pushed it into my hand, and as soon as I realized what was happening I pushed it back.

'*Wonderful* wood,' I said. As he put it away I felt rescued, though full of irritable remorse.

'Oh, I hope Charlotte is not very sick!' I said.

He smiled disdainfully, tapping himself on the chest—perhaps to show me the source of Charlotte's trouble, perhaps only to feel for himself the skin that was newly bared there.

Then he took himself, the crucifix, the books, and the wagon out of my store. I felt that insults had been offered, humiliations suffered, on both sides.

Up past the tobacco field was a beech wood, where Lottar had often gone to get sticks for the fire. Beyond that was a grassy slope—a high meadow— and at the top of the meadow, about half an hour's climb from the *kula*, was a small stone shelter, a primitive place with no window, a low doorway and no door, a corner hearth without a chimney. Sheep took cover there; the floor was littered with their droppings.

That was where she went to live after she became a Virgin. The incident of the Muslim bridegroom had taken place in the spring, just about a year after she first came to Maltsia e madhe, and it was time for the sheep to be driven to their higher pastures. Lottar was to keep count of the flock and see that they did not fall into ravines or wander too far away. And she was to milk the ewes every evening. She was expected to shoot wolves, if any came near. But none did; no one alive now at the *kula* had ever seen a wolf. The only wild animals Lottar saw were a red fox, once, by the stream, and the rabbits, which were plentiful and unwary. She learned to shoot and skin and cook them, cleaning them out as she had seen the butcher girls do at the *kula* and stewing the meatier parts in her pot over the fire, with some bulbs of wild garlic.

She did not want to sleep inside the shelter, so she fixed up a roof of branches outside, against the wall, this roof an extension of the roof of the building. She had her heap of ferns underneath, and a felt rug she had been given, to spread on the ferns when she slept. She no longer took any notice of the bugs. There were some spikes pushed into the wall between the dry stones. She did not know why they were there, but they served her well for hanging up the milk pails and the few pots she had been provided with. She brought her water from the stream, in which she washed her own head scarf, and herself sometimes, more for relief from the heat than out of concern about her dirtiness.

Everything was changed. She no longer saw the women. She lost her habits of constant work. The little girls came up in the evenings to get the milk. This far away from the *kula* and their mothers, they became quite wild. They climbed up on the roof, often smashing through the arrangement of branches which Lottar had contrived. They jumped into the ferns and sometimes snatched an armful of them to bind into a crude ball, which they threw at one another until it fell apart. They enjoyed themselves so much that Lottar had to chase them away at dusk, reminding them of how frightened they got in the beech wood after dark. She believed that they ran all the way through it and spilled half the milk on their way.

Now and then they brought her corn flour, which she mixed with water and baked on her shovel by the fire. Once they had a treat, a sheep's head—she wondered if they had stolen it—for her to boil in her pot. She was allowed to keep some of the milk, and instead of drinking it fresh she usually let it go sour, and stirred it to make yogurt to dip her bread in. That was how she preferred it now.

The men often came up through the wood shortly after the little girls had run through it on their way down. It seemed that this was a custom of theirs, in the summer. They liked to sit on the banks of the stream and fire off blanks and drink *raki* and sing, or sometimes just smoke and talk. They were not making this expedition to see how she was getting on. But since they were coming anyway, they brought her presents of coffee and tobacco and were full of competing advice on how to fix up the roof of her shelter so it wouldn't fall down, how to keep her fire going all night, how to use her gun.

Her gun was an old Italian Martini, which had been given to her when she left the *kula*. Some of the men said that gun was unlucky, since it had belonged to a boy who had been killed before he himself had even shot anybody. Others said that Martinis in general were unlucky, hardly any use at all.

Mausers were what you needed, for accuracy and repeating power.

But Mauser bullets were too small to do enough damage. There were men walking around full of Mauser holes—you could hear them whistle as they passed by.

Nothing can really compare with a heavy flintlock that has a good packing of powder, a bullet, and nails.

When they weren't talking about guns, the men spoke of recent killings, and told jokes. One of them told a joke about a wizard. There was a wizard held in prison by a Pasha. The Pasha brought him out to do tricks in front of guests. Bring a bowl of water, said the wizard. Now, this water is the sea. And what port shall I show you on the sea? Show a port on the

island of Malta, they said. And there it was. Houses and churches and a
steamer ready to sail. Now would you like to see me step on board that
steamer? And the Pasha laughed. Go ahead! So the wizard put his foot in
the bowl of water and stepped on board the steamer and went to America!
What do you think of that!

'There are no wizards, anyway,' said the Franciscan, who had climbed
up with the men on this evening, as he often did. 'If you had said a saint,
you might have made some sense.' He spoke severely, but Lottar thought he
was happy, as they all were, as she too was permitted to be, in their presence
and in his, though he paid no attention to her. The strong tobacco that they
gave her to smoke made her dizzy and she had to lie down on the grass.

The time came when Lottar had to think about moving inside her house.
The mornings were cold, the ferns were soaked with dew, and the grape
leaves were turning yellow. She took the shovel and cleaned the sheep droppings off the floor, in preparation for making up her bed inside. She began
to stuff grass and leaves and mud into the chinks between the stones.

When the men came they asked her what she was doing that for. For
the winter, she said, and they laughed.

'Nobody can stay here in the winter,' they said. They showed her how
deep the snow was, putting hands against their breastbones. Besides, all the
sheep would have been taken down.

'There will be no work for you—and what will you eat?' they said. 'Do
you think the women will let you have bread and yogurt for nothing?'

'How can I go back to the *kula*?' Lottar said. 'I am a Virgin, where
would I sleep? What kind of work would I do?'

'That is right,' they said kindly, speaking to her and then to each other.
'When a Virgin belongs to the *kula* she gets a bit of land, usually, where she
can live on her own. But this one doesn't really belong to the *kula*, she has
no father to give her anything. What will she do?'

Shortly after this—and in the middle of the day, when visitors never
came—the Franciscan climbed the meadow, all alone.

'I don't trust them,' he said. 'I think they will try again to sell you to a
Muslim. Even though you have been sworn. They will try to make some
money out of you. If they could find you a Christian, it might not be so
bad, but I am sure it will be an infidel.'

They sat on the grass and drank coffee. The Franciscan said, 'Do you
have any belongings to take with you? No. Soon we will start.'

'Who will milk the ewes?' said Lottar. Some of the ewes were already
working their way down the slope; they would stand and wait for her.

'Leave them,' said the Franciscan.

In this way she left not only the sheep but her shelter, the meadow, the wild grape and the sumac and mountain ash and juniper bushes and scrub oak she had looked at all summer, the rabbit pelt she had used as a pillow and the pan she had boiled her coffee in, the heap of wood she had gathered only that morning, the stones around her fire—each one of them known to her by its particular shape and colour. She understood that she was leaving, because the Franciscan was so stern, but she did not understand it in a way that would make her look around, to see everything for the last time. That was not necessary, anyway. She would never forget any of it.

As they entered the beech wood the Franciscan said, 'Now we must be very quiet. I am going to take another path, which does not go so near the *kula*. If we hear anybody on the path, we will hide.'

Hours, then, of silent walking, between the beech trees with their smooth elephant bark, and the black-limbed oaks and the dry pines. Up and down, crossing the ridges, choosing paths that Lottar had not known existed. The Franciscan never hesitated and never spoke of a rest. When they came out of the trees at last, Lottar was very surprised to see that there was still so much light in the sky.

The Franciscan pulled a loaf of bread and a knife from some pocket in his garment, and they ate as they walked.

They came to a dry riverbed, paved with stones that were not flat and easily walkable but a torrent, a still torrent of stones between fields of corn and tobacco. They could hear dogs barking, and sometimes people's voices. The corn and tobacco plants, still unharvested, were higher than their heads, and they walked along the dry river in this shelter, while the daylight entirely faded. When they could not walk anymore and the darkness would conceal them, they sat down on the white stones of the riverbed.

'Where are you taking me?' Lottar finally asked. At the start she had thought they must be going in the direction of the church and the priest's house, but now she saw that this could not be so. They had come much too far.

'I am taking you to the Bishop's house,' said the Franciscan. 'He will know what to do with you.'

'Why not to your house?' said Lottar. 'I could be a servant in your house.'

'It isn't allowed—to have a woman servant in my house. Or in any priest's house. This Bishop now will not allow even an old woman. And he is right, trouble comes from having a woman in the house.'

After the moon rose they went on. They walked and rested, walked and rested, but never fell asleep, or even looked for a comfortable place to lie down. Their feet were tough and their sandals well worn, and they did not get blisters. Both of them were used to walking long distances—the Franciscan in his far-flung parish and Lottar when she was following the sheep.

The Franciscan became less stern—perhaps less worried—after a while and talked to her almost as he had done in the first days of their acquaintance. He spoke Italian, though she was now fairly proficient in the language of the Ghegs.

'I was born in Italy,' he said. 'My parents were Ghegs, but I lived in Italy when I was young, and that was where I became a priest. Once I went back for a visit, years ago, and I shaved off my moustache, I do not know why. Oh, yes, I do know—it was because they laughed at me in the village. Then when I got back I did not dare show my face in the *madhe*. A hairless man there is a disgrace. I sat in a room in Skodra until it grew again.'

'Is it Skodra we are going to?' said Lottar.

'Yes, that is where the Bishop is. He will send a message that it was right to take you away, even if it is an act of stealing. They are barbarians, in the *madhe*. They will come up and pull on your sleeve in the middle of Mass and ask you to write a letter for them. Have you seen what they put up on the graves? The crosses? They make the cross into a very thin man with a rifle across his arms. Haven't you seen that?' He laughed and shook his head and said, 'I don't know what to do with them. But they are good people all the same—they will never betray you.'

'But you thought they might sell me in spite of my oath.'

'Oh, yes. But to sell a woman is a way to get some money. And they are so poor.'

Lottar now realized that in Skodra she would be in an unfamiliar position—she would not be powerless. When they got there, she could run away from him. She could find someone who spoke English, she could find the British Consulate. Or, if not that, the French.

The grass was soaking wet before dawn and the night got very cold. But when the sun came up Lottar stopped shivering and within an hour she was hot. They walked on all day. They ate the rest of the bread and drank from any stream they found that had water in it. They had left the dry river and the mountains far behind. Lottar looked back and saw a wall of jagged rocks with a little green clinging around their bases. That green was the woods and meadows which she had thought so high. They followed paths through the hot fields and were never out of the sound of barking dogs. They met people on the paths.

At first the Franciscan said, 'Do not speak to anybody—they will wonder who you are.' But he had to answer when greetings were spoken.

'Is this the way to Skodra? We are going to Skodra to the Bishop's house. This is my servant with me, who has come from the mountains.'

'It is all right, you look like a servant in these clothes,' he said to Lottar. 'But do not speak—they will wonder, if you speak.'

I had painted the walls of my bookstore a clear, light yellow. Yellow stands for intellectual curiosity. Somebody must have told me that. I opened the store in March of 1964. This was in Victoria, in British Columbia.

I sat there at the desk, with my offerings spread out behind me. The publishers' representatives had advised me to stock books about dogs and horses, sailing and gardening, bird books and flower books—they said that was all anybody in Victoria would buy. I flew against their advice and brought in novels and poetry and books that explained about Sufism and relativity and Linear B. And I had set out these books, when they came, so that Political Science could shade into Philosophy and Philosophy into Religion without a harsh break, so that compatible poets could nestle together, the arrangement of the shelves of books—I believed—reflecting a more or less natural ambling of the mind, in which treasures new and forgotten might be continually surfacing. I had taken all this care, and now what? Now I waited, and I felt like somebody who had got dramatically dressed up for a party, maybe even fetching jewels from the pawnshop or the family vault, only to discover that it was just a few neighbours playing cards. It was just meat loaf and mashed potatoes in the kitchen, and a glass of fizzy pink wine.

The store was often empty for a couple of hours at a time, and then when somebody did come in, it would be to ask about a book remembered from the Sunday-school library or a grandmother's bookcase or left behind twenty years ago in a foreign hotel. The title was usually forgotten, but the person would tell me the story. It is about this little girl who goes out to Australia with her father to mine the gold claims they have inherited. It is about the woman who had a baby all alone in Alaska. It is about a race between one of the old clipper ships and the first steamer, way back in the 1840s.

Oh, well. I just thought I'd ask.

They would leave without a glance at the riches around them.

A few people did exclaim in gratitude, said what a glorious addition to the town. They would browse for half an hour, an hour, before spending seventy-five cents.

It takes time.

I had found a one-room apartment with a kitchenette in an old building at a corner called the Dardanelles. The bed folded up into the wall. But

I did not usually bother to fold it up, because I never had any company. And the hook seemed unsafe to me. I was afraid that the bed might leap out of the wall sometime when I was eating my tinned soup or baked-potato supper. It might kill me. Also, I kept the window open all the time, because I believed I could smell a whiff of escaping gas, even when the two burners and the oven were shut off. With the window open at home and the door open at the store, to entice the customers, it was necessary for me to be always bundled up in my black woolly sweater or my red corduroy dressing gown (a garment that had once left its pink tinge on all my forsaken husband's handkerchiefs and underwear). I had difficulty separating myself from these comforting articles of clothing so that they might be washed. I was sleepy much of the time, underfed and shivering.

But I was not despondent. I had made a desperate change in my life, and in spite of the regrets I suffered every day, I was proud of that. I felt as if I had finally come out into the world in a new, true skin. Sitting at the desk, I made a cup of coffee or of thin red soup last an hour, clasping my hands around the cup while there was still any warmth to be got from it. I read, but without purpose or involvement. I read stray sentences from the books that I had always meant to read. Often these sentences seemed so satisfying to me, or so elusive and lovely, that I could not help abandoning all the surrounding words and giving myself up to a peculiar state. I was alert and dreamy, closed off from all particular people but conscious all the time of the city itself—which seemed a strange place.

A small city, here at the western edge of the country. Pockets of fakery for tourists. The Tudor shop fronts and double-decker buses and flowerpots and horse-drawn rides: almost insulting. But the sea light in the street, the spare and healthy old people leaning into the wind as they took their daily walks along the broom-topped cliffs, the shabby, slightly bizarre bungalows with their monkey-puzzle trees and ornate shrubs in the gardens. Chestnut trees blossom as spring comes on, hawthorn trees along the streets bear red-and-white flowers, oily-leaved bushes put out lush pink and rosered blooms such as you would never see in the hinterlands. Like a town in a story, I thought—like the transplanted seaside town of the story set in New Zealand, in Tasmania. But something North American persists. So many people, after all, have come here from Winnipeg or Saskatchewan. At noon a smell of dinners cooking drifts out of poor, plain apartment buildings. Frying meat, boiling vegetables—farm dinners being cooked, in the middle of the day, in cramped kitchenettes.

How could I tell what I liked so much? Certainly it was not what a new merchant might be looking for—bustle and energy to raise the hope of commercial success. *Not much doing* was the message the town got across to me.

And when a person who is opening a store doesn't mind hearing the message *Not much doing* you could ask, What's going on? People open shops in order to sell things, they hope to become busy so that they will have to enlarge the shop, then to sell more things, and grow rich, and eventually not have to come into the shop at all. Isn't that true? But are there other people who open a shop with the hope of being sheltered there, among such things as they most value—the yarn or the teacups or the books—and with the idea only of making a comfortable assertion? They will become a part of the block, a part of the street, part of everybody's map of the town, and eventually of everybody's memories. They will sit and drink coffee in the middle of the morning, they will get out the familiar bits of tinsel at Christmas, they will wash the windows in spring before spreading out the new stock. Shops, to these people, are what a cabin in the woods might be to somebody else—a refuge and a justification.

Some customers are necessary, of course. The rent comes due and the stock will not pay for itself. I had inherited a little money—that was what had made it possible for me to come out here and get the shop going—but unless business picked up to some extent I could not last beyond the summer. I understood that. I was glad that more people started coming in as the weather warmed up. More books were sold, survival began to seem possible. Book prizes were due to be awarded in the schools at the end of term, and that brought the schoolteachers with their lists and their praise and their unfortunate expectation of discounts. The people who came to browse were buying regularly, and some of them began to turn into friends—or the sort of friends I had here, where it seemed I would be happy to talk to people day after day and never learn their names.

When Lottar and the priest first saw the town of Skodra, it seemed to float above the mud flats, its domes and steeples shining as if they were made of mist. But when they entered it in the early evening all this tranquillity vanished. The streets were paved with big, rough stones and were full of people and donkey carts, roving dogs, pigs being driven somewhere, and smells of fires and cooking and dung and something terrible—like rotten hides. A man came along with a parrot on his shoulder. The bird seemed to be shrieking curses in an unknown language. Several times the Franciscan stopped people and asked the way to the Bishop's house, but they pushed by him without answering or laughed at him or said some words he didn't understand. A boy said that he would show the way, for money.

'We have no money,' the Franciscan said. He pulled Lottar into a doorway and there they sat down to rest. 'In Maltsia e madhe,' he said, 'many of these who think so well of themselves would soon sing a different tune.'

Lottar's notion of running away and leaving him had vanished. For one thing, she could not manage to ask directions any better than he could. For another, she felt that they were allies who could not survive in this place out of sight of each other. She had not understood how much she depended on the smell of his skin, the aggrieved determination of his long strides, the flourish of his black moustache.

The Franciscan jumped up and said he had remembered—he had remembered now the way to the Bishop's house. He hurried ahead of her through narrow, high-walled back streets where nothing of houses or courtyards could be seen—just walls and gates. The paving stones were thrust up so that walking here was as difficult as in the dry riverbed. But he was right, he gave a shout of triumph, they had come to the gate of the Bishop's house.

A servant opened the gate and let them in, but only after some high-pitched argument. Lottar was told to sit on the ground just inside the gate, and the Franciscan was led into the house to see the Bishop. Soon someone was sent through the streets to the British Consulate (Lottar was not told this), and he came back with the Consul's manservant. It was dark by then, and the Consul's servant carried a lantern. And Lottar was led away again. She followed the servant and his lantern to the consulate.

A tub of hot water for her to bathe in, in the courtyard. Her clothes taken away. Probably burned. Her greasy black, vermin-infested hair cut off. Kerosene poured on her scalp. She had to tell her story—the story of how she came to Maltsia e madhe—and this was difficult, because she was not used to speaking English, also because that time seemed so far away and unimportant. She had to learn to sleep on a mattress, to sit on a chair, to eat with a knife and fork.

As soon as possible they put her on a boat.

Charlotte stopped. She said, 'That part is not of interest.'

I had come to Victoria because it was the farthest place I could get to from London, Ontario, without going out of the country. In London, my husband, Donald, and I had rented a basement apartment in our house to a couple named Nelson and Sylvia. Nelson was an English major at the university and Sylvia was a nurse. Donald was a dermatologist, and I was doing a thesis on Mary Shelley—not very quickly. I had met Donald when I went to see him about a rash on my neck. He was eight years older than I was—a tall, freckled, blushing man, cleverer than he looked. A dermatologist sees grief and despair, though the problems that bring people to him may not be in the same class as tumours and blocked arteries. He sees sabotage from within, and truly unlucky fate. He sees how matters like love and happiness can be governed by a patch of riled-up cells. Experience of this sort had made Donald kind, in a cautious, impersonal way. He said that my rash was probably due to stress, and that he could see that I was going to be a wonderful woman, once I got a few problems under control.

We invited Sylvia and Nelson upstairs for dinner, and Sylvia told us about the tiny town they both came from, in Northern Ontario. She said that Nelson had always been the smartest person in their class and in their school and possibly in the whole town. When she said this, Nelson looked at her with a perfectly flat and devastating expression, an expression that seemed to be waiting with infinite patience and the mildest curiosity for some explanation, and Sylvia laughed and said, 'Just kidding, of course.'

When Sylvia was working late shifts at the hospital, I sometimes asked Nelson to share a meal with us in a more informal way. We got used to his silences and his indifferent table manners and to the fact that he did not eat rice or noodles, eggplant, olives, shrimp, peppers, or avocados, and no doubt a lot of other things, because those had not been familiar foods in the town in Northern Ontario.

Nelson looked older than he was. He was short and sturdily built, sallow-skinned, unsmiling, with a suggestion of mature scorn and handy pugnaciousness laid over his features, so that it seemed he might be a hockey coach, or an intelligent, uneducated, fair-minded, and foul-mouthed foreman of a construction gang, rather than a shy, twenty-two-year-old student.

He was not shy in love. I found him resourceful and determined. The seduction was mutual, and it was a first affair for both of us. I had once heard somebody say, at a party, that one of the nice things about marriage was that you could have real affairs—an affair before marriage could always turn out to be nothing but courtship. I was disgusted by this speech, and frightened to think that life could be so bleak and trivial. But once my own affair with Nelson started, I was amazed all the time. There was no bleakness or triviality about it, only ruthlessness and clarity of desire, and sparkling deception.

Nelson was the one who first faced up to things. One afternoon he turned on his back and said hoarsely and defiantly, 'We are going to have to leave.'

I thought he meant that he and Sylvia would have to leave, they could not go on living in this house. But he meant himself and me. 'We' meant himself and me. Of course he and I had said 'we' of our arrangements, of our transgression. Now he had made it the 'we' of our decision—perhaps of a life together.

My thesis was supposed to be on Mary Shelley's later novels, the ones nobody knows about. *Lodore, Perkin Warbeck, The Last Man.* But I was really more interested in Mary's life before she learned her sad lessons and buckled down to raising her son to be a baronet. I loved to read about the other women who had hated or envied or traipsed along: Harriet, Shelley's first wife, and Fanny Imlay, who was Mary's half sister and may have been in love with Shelley herself, and Mary's stepsister, Mary Jane Clairmont, who took my own name—Claire—and joined Mary and Shelley on their unwed honeymoon so that she could keep on chasing Byron. I had often talked to Donald about impetuous Mary and married Shelley and their meetings at Mary's mother's grave, about the suicides of Harriet and Fanny and the persistence of Claire, who had a baby by Byron. But I never mentioned any of this to Nelson, partly because we had little time for talk and partly because I did not want him to think that I drew some sort of comfort or inspiration from this mishmash of love and despair and treachery and self-dramatizing. I did not want to think so myself. And Nelson was not a fan of the nineteenth century or the Romantics. He said so. He said that he wanted to do something on the Muckrakers. Perhaps he meant that as a joke.

Sylvia did not behave like Harriet. Her mind was not influenced or impeded by literature, and when she found out what had been going on, she went into a wholesome rage.

'You blithering idiot,' she said to Nelson.

'You two-faced twit,' she said to me.

The four of us were in our living room. Donald went on cleaning and filling his pipe, tapped it and lit it, nursed and inspected it, drew on it, lit it again—all so much the way someone would do in a movie that I was embarrassed for him. Then he put some books and the latest copy of *Macleans* into his briefcase, went to the bathroom to get his razor and to the bedroom to get his pajamas, and walked out.

He went straight to the apartment of a young widow who worked as a secretary at his clinic. In a letter he wrote to me later, he said that he had never thought of this woman except as a friend until that night, when it suddenly dawned on him what a pleasure it would be to love a kind and sensible, *unwracked-up* sort of person.

Sylvia had to be at work at eleven o'clock. Nelson usually walked her over to the hospital—they did not have a car. On this night she told him that she would rather be escorted by a skunk.

That left Nelson and me alone together. The scene had lasted a much shorter time than I had expected. Nelson seemed gloomy but relieved, and if I felt that short shrift had been given to the notion of love as a capturing tide, a glorious and harrowing event, I knew better than to show it.

We lay down on the bed to talk about our plans and ended up making love, because that was what we were used to doing. Sometime during the night Nelson woke up and thought it best to go downstairs to his own bed.

I got up in the dark, dressed, packed a suitcase, wrote a note, and walked to the phone at the corner, where I called a taxi. I took the six-o'clock train to Toronto, connecting with the train to Vancouver. It was cheaper to take the train, if you were willing to sit up for three nights, which I was.

So there I sat, in the sad, shambling morning in the day coach, coming down the steep-walled Fraser Canyon into the sodden Fraser Valley, where smoke hung over the small, dripping houses, the brown vines, the thorny bushes and huddled sheep. It was in December that this earthquake in my life had arrived. Christmas was cancelled for me. Winter with its snowdrifts and icicles and invigorating blizzards was cancelled by this blurred season of muck and rain. I was constipated, I knew that I had bad breath, my limbs were cramped, and my spirits utterly bleak. And did I not think then, What nonsense is it to suppose one man so different from another when all that life really boils down to is getting a decent cup of coffee and room to stretch out in? Did I not think that even if Nelson were sitting here beside me, he would have turned into a grey-faced stranger whose desolation and unease merely extended my own?

No. No. Nelson would still be Nelson to me. I had not changed, with regard to his skin and his smell and his forbidding eyes. It seemed to be the outside of Nelson which came most readily to my mind, and in the case of Donald it was his inner quakes and sympathies, the laboured-at kindness and those private misgivings that I had got knowledge of by wheedling and conniving. If I could have my love of these two men together, and settle it on one man, I would be a happy woman. If I could care for everybody in the world as minutely as I did for Nelson, and as calmly, as uncarnally as I did now for Donald, I would be a saint. Instead, I had dealt a twofold, a wanton-seeming, blow.

The regular customers who had changed into something like friends were: a middle-aged woman who was a chartered accountant but preferred such reading as *Six Existentialist Thinkers*, and *The Meaning of Meaning*; a provincial civil servant who ordered splendid, expensive works of pornography such as I had not known existed (their elaborate Oriental, Etruscan connections seemed to me grotesque and uninteresting, compared to the simple, effective, longed-for rituals of myself and Nelson); a Notary Public who lived behind his office at the foot of Johnson Street ('I live in the slums,' he told me. 'Some night I expect a big bruiser of a fellow to lurch around the corner hollering "*Ste-el-la*"') and the woman I knew later as Charlotte—the Notary Public called her the Duchess. None of these people cared much for one another, and an early attempt that I made to bring the accountant and the Notary Public into conversation was a fizzle.

'Spare me the females with the withered, painted faces,' the Notary Public said, the next time he came in. 'I hope you haven't got her lurking around anywhere tonight.'

It was true that the accountant painted her thin, intelligent, fifty-year-old face with a heavy hand, and drew on eyebrows that were like two strokes of India ink. But who was the Notary Public to talk, with his stumpy, nicotined teeth and pocked cheeks?

'I got the impression of a rather superficial fellow,' the accountant said, as if she had guessed and bravely discounted the remarks made about herself.

So much for trying to corral people into couples, I wrote to Donald. *And who am I to try?* I wrote to Donald regularly, describing the store, and the city, and even, as well as I could, my own unaccountable feelings. He was living with Helen, the secretary. I wrote also to Nelson, who might or might not be living alone, might or might not be reunited with Sylvia. I didn't think he was. I thought she would believe in inexcusable behaviour and definite endings. He had a new address. I had looked it up in the London phone book at the public library. Donald, after a grudging start, was writing back. He wrote impersonal, mildly interesting letters about people we both knew, events at the clinic. Nelson did not write at all. I started sending registered letters. Now I knew at least that he picked them up.

Charlotte and Gjurdhi must have come into the store together, but I did not understand that they were a couple until it was time for them to leave. Charlotte was a heavy, shapeless, but quick-moving woman, with a pink face, bright blue eyes, and a lot of glistening white hair, worn like a girl's, waving down over her shoulders. Though the weather was fairly warm, she was wearing a cape of dark grey velvet with a scanty grey fur trim—a garment that looked as if it belonged, or had once belonged, on the stage. A loose shirt and a pair of plaid wool slacks showed underneath, and there were open sandals on her broad, bare, dusty feet. She clanked as if she wore hidden armour. An arm reaching up to get a book showed what caused the clanking. Bracelets—any number of them, heavy or slender, tarnished or bright. Some were set with large, square stones, the colour of toffee or blood.

'Imagine this old fraud being still on the go,' she said to me, as if continuing some desultory and enjoyable conversation.

She had picked up a book by Anaïs Nin.

'Don't pay any attention,' she said. 'I say terrible things. I'm quite fond of the woman, really. It's him I can't stand.'

'Henry Miller?' I said, beginning to follow this.

'That's right.' She went on talking about Henry Miller, Paris, California, in a scoffing, energetic, half-affectionate way. She seemed to have been neighbours, at least, with the people she was talking about. Finally, naively, I asked her if this was the case.

'No, no. I just feel I know them all. Not personally. Well—personally. Yes, personally. What other way is there to know them? I mean, I haven't met them, face-to-face. But in their books? Surely that's what they intend? I know them. I know them to the point where they bore me. Just like anybody you know. Don't you find that?'

She drifted over to the table where I had laid out the New Directions paperbacks.

'Here's the new bunch, then,' she said. 'Oh, my,' she said, widening her eyes at the photographs of Ginsberg and Corso and Ferlinghetti. She began reading, so attentively that I thought the next thing she said must be part of some poem.

'I've gone by and I've seen you here,' she said. She put the book down and I realized she meant me. 'I've seen you sitting in here, and I've thought a young woman would probably like to be outside some of the time. In the sun. I don't suppose you'd consider hiring me to sit there, so you could get out?'

'Well, I would like to—' I said.

'I'm not so dumb. I'm fairly knowledgeable, really. Ask me who wrote Ovid's *Metamorphoses*. It's all right, you don't have to laugh.'

'I would like to, but I really can't afford to.'

'Oh, well. You're probably right. I'm not very chic. And I would probably foul things up. I would argue with people if they were buying books I thought were dreadful.' She did not seem disappointed. She picked up a copy of *The Dud Avocado* and said, 'There! I have to buy this, for the title.'

She gave a little whistle, and the man it seemed to be meant for looked up from the table of books he had been staring at, near the back of the store. I had known he was there but had not connected him with her. I thought he was just one of those men who wander in off the street, alone, and stand looking about, as if trying to figure out what sort of place this is or what the books are for. Not a drunk or a panhandler, and certainly not anybody to be worried about—just one of a number of shabby, utterly uncommunicative old men who belong to the city somewhat as the pigeons do, moving restlessly all day within a limited area, never looking at people's faces. He was wearing a coat that came down to his ankles, made of some shiny, rubberized, liver-coloured material, and a brown velvet cap with a tassel. The sort of cap a doddery old scholar or a clergyman might wear in an English movie. There was, then, a similarity between them—they were both wearing things that might have been discards from a costume box. But close up he looked years older than she. A long, yellowish face, drooping tobacco-brown eyes, an unsavoury, straggling moustache. Some faint remains of handsomeness, or potency. A quenched ferocity. He came at her whistle—which seemed half serious, half a joke—and stood by, mute and self-respecting as a dog or a donkey, while the woman prepared to pay.

At that time, the government of British Columbia applied a sales tax to books. In this case it was four cents.

'I can't pay that,' she said. 'A tax on books. I think it is immoral. I would rather go to jail. Don't you agree?'

I agreed. I did not point out—as I would have done with anybody else—that the store would not be let off the hook on that account.

'Don't I sound appalling?' she said. 'See what this government can do to people? It makes them into *orators*.'

She put the book in her bag without paying the four cents, and never paid the tax on any future occasion.

I described the two of them to the Notary Public. He knew at once who I meant.

'I call them the Duchess and the Algerian,' he said. 'I don't know what the background is. I think maybe he's a retired terrorist. They go around the town with a wagon, like scavengers.'

I got a note asking me to supper on a Sunday evening. It was signed *Charlotte*, without a surname, but the wording and handwriting were quite formal.

My husband Gjurdhi and I would be delighted—

Up until then I had not wished for any invitations of this sort and would have been embarrassed and disturbed to get one. So the pleasure I felt surprised me. Charlotte held out a decided promise; she was unlike the others whom I wanted to see only in the store.

The building where they lived was on Pandora Street. It was covered with mustard stucco and had a tiny, tiled vestibule that reminded me of a public toilet. It did not smell, though, and the apartment was not really dirty, just horrendously untidy. Books were stacked against the walls, and pieces of patterned cloth were hung up droopily to hide the wallpaper. There were bamboo blinds on the window, sheets of coloured paper—surely flammable—pinned over the light bulbs.

'What a darling you are to come,' cried Charlotte. 'We were afraid you would have tons more interesting things to do than visiting ancient old us. Where can you sit down? What about here?' She took a pile of magazines off a wicker chair. 'Is that comfortable? It makes such interesting noises, wicker. Sometimes I'll be sitting here alone and that chair will start creaking and cracking exactly as if someone were shifting around in it. I could say it was a presence, but I'm no good at believing in that rubbish. I've tried.'

Gjurdhi poured out a sweet yellow wine. For me a long-stemmed glass that had not been dusted, for Charlotte a glass tumbler, for himself a plastic cup. It seemed impossible that any dinner could come out of the little kitchen alcove, where foodstuffs and pots and dishes were piled helter-skelter, but there was a good smell of roasting chicken, and in a little while Gjurdhi brought out the first course—platters of sliced cucumber, dishes of yogurt. I sat in the wicker chair and Charlotte in the single armchair. Gjurdhi sat on the floor. Charlotte was wearing her slacks, and a rose-coloured T-shirt which clung to her unsupported breast. She had painted her toenails to match the T-shirt. Her bracelets clanked against the plate as she picked up the slices of cucumber. (We were eating with our fingers.) Gjurdhi wore his cap and a dark-red silky dressing gown over his trousers. Stains had mingled with its pattern.

After the cucumber, we ate chicken cooked with raisins in golden spices, and sour bread, and rice. Charlotte and I were provided with forks, but Gjurdhi scooped the rice up with the bread. I would often think of this meal in the years that followed, when this kind of food, this informal way of sitting and eating, and even some version of the style and the untidiness of the room, would become familiar and fashionable. The people I knew, and I myself, would give up—for a while—on dining-room tables, matching wineglasses, to some extent on cutlery or chairs. When I was being entertained, or making a stab at entertaining people, in this way, I would think of Charlotte and Gjurdhi and the edge of true privation, the risky authenticity that marked them off from all these later imitations. At the time, it was all new to me, and I was both uneasy and delighted. I hoped to worthy of such exoticism but not to be tried too far.

Mary Shelley came to light shortly. I recited the titles of the later novels, and Charlotte said dreamily, 'Per-kin War-beck. Wasn't he the one—wasn't he the one who pretended to be a little Prince who was murdered in the Tower?'

She was the only person I had ever met—not a historian, not a *Tudor* historian—who had known this.

'That would make a movie,' she said. 'Don't you think? The question I always think about Pretenders like that is who do *they* think they are? Do they believe it's true, or what? But Mary Shelley's own life is the movie, isn't it? I wonder there hasn't been one made. Who would play Mary, do you think? No. No, first of all, start with Harriet. Who would play Harriet?'

'Someone who would look well drowned,' she said, ripping off a golden chunk of chicken. 'Elizabeth Taylor? Not a big enough part. Susannah York?'

'Who was the father?' she wondered, referring to Harriet's unborn baby. 'I don't think it was Shelley. I've never thought so. Do you?'

This was all very well, very enjoyable, but I had hoped we would get to explanations—personal revelations, if not exactly confidences. You did expect some of that, on occasions like this. Hadn't Sylvia, at my own table, told about the town in Northern Ontario and about Nelson's being the smartest person in the school? I was surprised at how eager I found myself, at last, to tell my story. Donald and Nelson—I was looking forward to telling the truth, or some of it, in all its wounding complexity, to a person who would not be surprised or outraged by it. I would have liked to puzzle over my behaviour, in good company. Had I taken on Donald as a father figure— or as a parent figure, since both my parents were dead? Had I deserted him because I was angry at *them* for deserting *me*? What did Nelson's silence mean, and was it now permanent? (But I did not think, after all, that I would tell anybody about the letter that had been returned to me last week, marked 'Not Known at This Address.')

This was not what Charlotte had in mind. There was no opportunity, no exchange. After the chicken, the wineglass and the tumbler and cup were taken away and filled with an extremely sweet pink sherbet that was easier to drink than to eat with a spoon. Then came small cups of desperately strong coffee. Gjurdhi lit two candles as the room grew darker, and I was given one of these to carry to the bathroom, which turned out to be a toilet with a shower. Charlotte said the lights were not working.

'Some repairs going on,' she said. 'Or else they have taken a whim. I really think they take whims. But fortunately we have our gas stove. As long as we have a gas stove we can laugh at their whims. My only regret is that we cannot play any music. I was going to play some old political songs—"I dreamed I saw Joe Hill last night,"' she sang in a mocking baritone. 'Do you know that one?'

I did know it. Donald used to sing it when he was a little drunk. Usually the people who sang 'Joe Hill' had certain vague but discernible political sympathies, but with Charlotte I did not think this would be so. She would not operate from sympathies, from principles. She would be playful about what other people took seriously. I was not certain what I felt about her. It was not simple liking or respect. It was more like a wish to move in her element, unsurprised. To be buoyant, self-mocking, gently malicious, unquenchable.

Gjurdhi, meanwhile, was showing me some of the books. How had this started? Probably from a comment I made—how many of them there were, something of that sort—when I stumbled over some on my way back from the toilet. He was bringing forward books with bindings of leather or imitation leather—how could I know the difference?—with marbled endpapers, watercolour frontispieces, steel engravings. At first, I believed admiration might be all that was required, and I admired everything. But close to my ear I heard the mention of money—was that the first distinct thing I had ever heard Gjurdhi say?

'I only handle new books,' I said. 'These are marvellous, but I don't really know anything about them. It's a completely different business, books like these.'

Gjurdhi shook his head as if I had not understood and he would now try, firmly, to explain again. He repeated the price in a more insistent voice. Did he think I was trying to haggle with him? Or perhaps he was telling me what he had paid for the book? We might be having a speculative conversation about the price it might be sold for—not about whether I should buy it.

I kept saying no, and yes, trying to juggle these responses appropriately. *No*, I cannot take them for my store. *Yes*, they are very fine. *No*, truly, I'm sorry, I am not the one to judge.

'If we had been living in another country, Gjurdhi and I might have done something,' Charlotte was saying. 'Or even if the movies in this country had ever got off the ground. That's what I would love to have done. Got work in the movies. As extras. Or maybe we are not bland enough types to be extras, maybe they would have found bit parts for us. I believe extras have to be the sort that don't stand out in a crowd, so you can use them over and over again. Gjurdhi and I are more memorable than that. Gjurdhi in particular—you could *use* that face.'

She paid no attention to the second conversation that had developed, but continued talking to me, shaking her head indulgently at Gjurdhi now and then, to suggest that he was behaving in a way she found engaging, though perhaps importunate. I had to talk to him softly, sideways, nodding all the while in response to her.

'Really you should take them to the Antiquarian Bookstore,' I said. 'Yes, they are quite beautiful. Books like these are out of my range.'

Gjurdhi did not whine, his manner was not ingratiating. Peremptory, rather. It seemed as if he would give me orders, and would be most disgusted if I did not capitulate. In my confusion I helped myself to more of the yellow wine, pouring it into my unwashed sherbet glass. This was probably a dire offense. Gjurdhi looked horridly displeased.

'Can you imagine illustrations in modern novels?' said Charlotte, finally consenting to tie the two conversations together. 'For instance, in Norman Mailer? They would have to be abstracts. Don't you think? Sort of barbed wire and blotches?'

I went home with a headache and a feeling of jangled inadequacy. I was a prude, that was all, when it came to mixing up buying and selling with hospitality. I had perhaps behaved clumsily, I had disappointed them. And they had disappointed me. Making me wonder why I had been asked.

I was homesick for Donald, because of 'Joe Hill.'

I also had a longing for Nelson, because of an expression on Charlotte's face as I was leaving. A savouring and contented look that I knew had to do with Gjurdhi, though I hardly wanted to believe that. It made me think that after I walked downstairs and left the building and went into the street, some hot and skinny, slithery, yellowish, indecent old beast, some mangy but urgent old tiger, was going to pounce among the books and the dirty dishes and conduct a familiar rampage.

A day or so later I got a letter from Donald. He wanted a divorce, so that he could marry Helen.

I hired a clerk, a college girl, to come in for a couple of hours in the afternoon, so I could get to the bank, and do some office work. The first time Charlotte saw her she went up to the desk and patted a stack of books sitting there, ready for quick sale.

'Is this what the office managers are telling their minions to buy?' she said. The girl smiled cautiously and didn't answer.

Charlotte was right. It was a book called *Psycho-Cybernetics*, about having a positive self-image.

'You were smart to hire her instead of me,' Charlotte said. 'She is much niftier-looking, and she won't shoot her mouth off and scare the customers away. She won't have *opinions*.'

'There's something I ought to tell you about that woman,' the clerk said, after Charlotte left.

That part is not of interest.

'What do you mean?' I said. But my mind had been wandering, that third afternoon in the hospital. Just at the last part of Charlotte's story I had thought of a special-order book that hadn't come in, on Mediterranean cruises. Also I had been thinking about the Notary Public, who had been beaten about the head the night before, in his office on Johnson Street. He was not dead but he might be blinded. Robbery? Or an act of revenge, outrage, connected with a layer of his life that I hadn't guessed at?

Melodrama and confusion made this place seem more ordinary to me, but less within my grasp.

'Of course it is of interest,' I said. 'All of it. It's a fascinating story.'

'Fascinating,' repeated Charlotte in a mincing way. She made a face, so she looked like a baby vomiting out a spoonful of pap. Her eyes, still fixed on me, seemed to be losing colour, losing their childish, bright, and self-important blue. Fretfulness was changing into disgust. An expression of vicious disgust, she showed, of unspeakable weariness—such as people might show to the mirror but hardly ever to one another. Perhaps because of the thoughts that were already in my head, it occurred to me that Charlotte might die. She might die at any moment. At this moment. Now.

She motioned at the water glass, with its crooked plastic straw. I held the glass so that she could drink and supported her head. I could feel the heat of her scalp, a throbbing at the base of her skull. She drank thirstily, and the terrible look left her face.

She said, 'Stale.'

'I think it would make an excellent movie,' I said, easing her back onto the pillows. She grabbed my wrist, then let it go.

'Where did you get the idea?' I said.

'From life,' said Charlotte indistinctly. 'Wait a moment.' She turned her head away, on the pillow, as if she had to arrange something in private. Then she recovered, and she told a little more.

Charlotte did not die. At least she did not die in the hospital. When I came in rather late, the next afternoon, her bed was empty and freshly made up. The nurse who had talked to me before was trying to take the temperature of the woman tied in the chair. She laughed at the look on my face.

'Oh, no!' she said. 'Not that. She checked out of here this morning. Her husband came and got her. We were transferring her to a long-term place out in Saanich, and he was supposed to be taking her there. He said he had the taxi outside. Then we get this phone call that they never showed up! They were in great spirits when they left. He brought her a pile of money, and she was throwing it up in the air. I don't know—maybe it was only dollar bills. But we haven't a clue where they've got to.'

I walked around to the apartment building on Pandora Street. I thought they might simply have gone home. They might have lost the instructions about how to get to the nursing home and not wanted to ask. They might have decided to stay together in their apartment no matter what. They might have turned on the gas.

At first I could not find the building and thought that I must be in the wrong block. But I remembered the corner store and some of the houses. The building had been changed—that was what had happened. The stucco had been painted pink; large, new windows and French doors had been put in; little balconies with wrought-iron railings had been attached. The fancy balconies had been painted white, the whole place had the air of an ice-cream parlour. No doubt it had been renovated inside as well, and the rents increased, so that people like Charlotte and Gjurdhi could have no hope of living there. I checked the names by the door, and of course theirs were gone. They must have moved out some time ago.

The change in the apartment building seemed to have some message for me. It was about vanishing. I knew that Charlotte and Gjurdhi had not actually vanished—they were somewhere, living or dead. But for me they had vanished. And because of this fact—not really because of any loss of them—I was tipped into dismay more menacing than any of the little eddies of regret that had caught me in the past year. I had lost my bearings. I had to get back to the store so my clerk could go home, but I felt as if I could as easily walk another way, just any way at all. My connection was in danger—that was all. Sometimes our connection is frayed, it is in danger, it seems almost lost. Views and streets deny knowledge of us, the air grows thin. Wouldn't we rather have a destiny to submit to, then, something that claims us, anything, instead of such flimsy choices, arbitrary days?

I let myself slip, then, into imagining a life with Nelson. If I had done so accurately, this is how it would have gone.

He comes to Victoria. But he does not like the idea of working in the store, serving the public. He gets a job teaching at a boys' school, a posh place where his look of lower-class toughness, his bruising manners, soon make him a favourite.

We move from the apartment at the Dardanelles to a roomy bungalow a few blocks from the sea. We marry.

But this is the beginning of a period of estrangement. I become pregnant. Nelson falls in love with the mother of a student. I fall in love with an intern I meet in the hospital during labour.

We get all over all this—Nelson and I do. We have another child. We acquire friends, furniture, rituals. We go to too many parties at certain seasons of the year, and talk regularly about starting a new life, somewhere far away, where we don't know anybody.

We become distant, close—distant, close—over and over again.

As I entered the store, I was aware of a man standing near the door, half looking in the window, half looking up the street, then looking at me. He was a short man dressed in a trench-coat and a fedora. I had the impression of someone disguised. Jokingly disguised. He moved toward me and bumped my shoulder, and I cried out as if I had received the shock of my life, and indeed it was true that I had. For this really was Nelson, come to claim me. Or at least to accost me, and see what would happen.

We have been very happy.
I have often felt completely alone.

There is always in this life something to discover.
The days and the years have gone by in some sort of blur.
On the whole, I am satisfied.

When Lottar was leaving the Bishop's courtyard, she was wrapped in a long cloak they had given her, perhaps to conceal her ragged clothing, or to contain her smell. The Consul's servant spoke to her in English, telling her where they were going. She could understand him but could not reply. It was not quite dark. She could still see the pale shapes of roses and oranges in the Bishop's garden.

The Bishop's man was holding the gate open.

She had never seen the Bishop at all. And she had not seen the Franciscan since he had followed the Bishop's man into the house. She called out for him now, as she was leaving. She had no name to call, so she called, '*Xoti! Xoti! Xoti*,' which means 'leader' or 'master' in the language of the Ghegs. But no answer came, and the Consul's servant swung his lantern impatiently, showing her the way to go. Its light fell by accident on the Franciscan standing half concealed by a tree. It was a little orange tree he stood behind. His face, pale as the oranges were in that light, looked out of the branches, all its swarthiness drained away. It was a wan face hanging in the tree, its melancholy expression quite impersonal and undemanding, like the expression you might see on the face of a devout but proud apostle in a church window. Then it was gone, taking the breath out of her body, as she knew too late.

She called him and called him, and when the boat came into the harbour at Trieste he was waiting on the dock.

ᐤ

Lilian

Like the pages of a pop-up book, the scenes of love remain, three-dimensional, the furniture asking more attention than the flat doll who is more like wallpaper, a bedspread, a detail rather than the focus of memory. It might have been a way of dealing with pain but instead is the source of it, flat loss in so many really remembered rooms. Like a book, too, it can be shut and stored on a shelf with only the spine exposed, *Lilian*, without author or publishing house, but there is a prominent date, 1952. The twinge of pain is like the ache of a bone broken twenty-five years ago; you tend to think of the present weather rather than the old accident. Until someone asks, 'How did it happen? Why does it still hurt?' A lover's question. Then there is the furniture again and the flat figure, and you, like a huge, old child, poke a finger as large as your old self once was into the flimsy trap of a very old beginning.

'There,' you say, 'are the twin beds pushed together. That's my desk at the foot of them. You can see the photographs I kept under the glass, the list of letters owing, a pair of gloves with the tips cut out of the fingers. It was very cold. That little gas fire didn't work very well, and it was expensive. We hadn't any money. That's the door to the kitchen, and that one went into the hall.'

'But where is she?'

'Out, probably . . . no, she's in the kitchen. She's just come in from work and is putting on a kettle for tea.'

'I want to see her.'

There she is, simply a woman standing by a small gas stove, her back turned.

'Her face!' she insists.

But none of her faces is properly filled in. One has only the trace of a cheekbone, another simply a pair of glasses, and the hair's not real, put on carelessly by a crayon the wrong colour. Her clothes, like those of a paper doll, are more important: a suede jacket, a grey skirt with two pleats down the front nearly to the ankles. She has a purple and grey scarf, a pale lavender twin set. She can be undressed. How long has it been since anyone wore that sort of bra? You'd forgotten about the peach-coloured underwear. The body itself is an exaggeration of breasts and pubic hair, done in black and white.

'She looks very . . . English,' she says, charmingly daunted.

You laugh, touch the very real red-gold hair, turn a face to you which you don't have to struggle to remember or forget, never sure which it is, and kiss a mouth which will never taste of tea. Her breasts are freely available to you under the pale green shirt. Trousers the same colour are on an elastic waistband. You have made love with her often enough to know that she likes to come first, quickly, in disarray, one exposed breast at your mouth, your hand beneath trousers pulled down only low enough to reveal the mound of curly red-gold hair. To feel compromised excites her aggression, and you have learned not to be surprised at the swiftness of her retaliation, fake-coming to her assault so that you can both finally lie naked in a long feasting pleasure, where she can make no comparisons because her husband never does that, because you and Lilian had never even heard of it. When you came upon it in a novel written by a man, she was long since gone, but your need to taste her was as sharp as your simpler desire had been on those dark, English afternoons when she came in, her hair smelling of the tube, her face and hands cold, wanting a bath first to get warm, wanting her tea, before the ten minutes of touching which was all it ever occurred to either of you to do.

'Was she very good?' her voice asks, breath against your thigh.

Your tongue lies into her what is not a lie. The first woman is perfect, being a woman, even if everyone after that is far, far better, as has certainly been the case. Nearly without exception.

'Look at me.'

You do. She is the age Lilian was, thirty. Nearly all of them have been, though you've grown twenty-five years older, will be forty-five in a few days' time. Her mouth from so much lovemaking is dark and swollen, her chin chafed, as if by winter weather. You are glad it is very cold outside, an excuse for her if she needs one.

'She's the only one you ever lived with?'

You nod.

'Why?'

'She was free.'

She begins to cry, tears of a sort you had not seen until after Lilian. You wonder if that's one of the ways you've set Lilian apart, being able to remember that she never cried like that for herself or you. They are tears you have watched on a dozen faces since. You don't really want her to begin to talk about her children, but you don't stop her as you do if she mentions her husband, even to abuse him. You have not asked her to leave any of them. It is she, not you, who is unhappy about spending only a rare night in your bed. Most meetings have to be timed as if they were evenings at the PTA. She tries not to share her guilt about how she is neglecting her children's teachers. The guilt she feels about neglecting you is confused by the fact that you are never neglected in her thoughts. You are her private obsession. She leaves behind a toothbrush, a comb, a shirt to encourage the same state of mind in you.

'I must go. It's time to go,' she is saying, wiping her eyes on the clothes she is gathering up.

You admire her fully realized body as she walks across the room. She pauses and turns to you.

'Why did she leave you?'

'Because I am not a man,' you answer, as you have answered the same question a dozen times before.

'She married then?'

'No. Eventually she found a woman to live with.'

She turns away again, puzzled. You would not have tried to explain further even if she'd stayed to ask. Once you did try. The anger that had obliterated Lilian's face and left her body grossly exposed in black and white, like a cheap polaroid picture, obliterated and stripped the questioner, who should have known then she was being raped and did not, flattered by the force of it.

The water is running in the shower now. She must go home, smelling as if she'd been to the PTA. On a better night, you would shower with her, mark her with quick pleasures. You might even joke about putting a little chalk dust in her hair. Tonight you put on a kimono, tidy your own clothes away, open the door to your study and turn the light on over your desk. You are sorting papers when she comes to the doorway, dressed and ready to leave.

'Are you angry with me?'

'Of course not.'

You are never angry now. You go to her, kiss her throat, smile.

'God, she must regret it. Every time she reads about you . . .'

You shake your head, wearing your expression of tolerant indulgence for her admiration of your work, your success. The fantasy she is calling up is one you've tried to nourish for years but even the most outlandish fantasy needs some shred of evidence to feed on. You have none. Lilian always believed in your work. Success wouldn't increase or diminish that, and it would never bring her back.

'Don't shake your head. You're too modest . . . well, you are, about your work.' But you have made her laugh now at the immodesties she enjoys. 'You're so beautifully unlike a man.'

Usually you help her to leave, but now you cannot because you so much want her to go.

'I want to be with you on your birthday. Why does it have to be on a Sunday night?'

'It isn't. It's on any night you can get away.'

'You don't let yourself mind about anything, do you? I wish I could be like that. I'll be horrible to the children and to him all evening, knowing you're alone, wanting to be with you. Will you be alone?'

'Actually, I like to be alone on my birthday. It's my one antisocial day of the year. Well, that and New Year's Eve.'

'Just the same, miss me a little.'

You agree to. You know you will miss her . . . a little. Inflicting a little pain is necessary to her as a way of sharing it. When she can't, she won't come back; and you are slower now to encourage the break, though you know that to extend the strain on her for too long is a matter of diminishing returns. It's not that you'd have any difficulty replacing her. There is an understudy in the wings right now, who is free on your birthday, but you won't see her. She seems young, though she's thirty. Lilian at that age had none of the vestiges of childishness you notice increasingly now. She had not been raising children, of course, and was not absorbed, as all the others have been, with the ways of children and therefore inclined to tip into baby talk or take delight in small surprises. She had been as absorbed in her work as you were in yours.

'You're tired,' she says.

'I'm getting old.'

Again she laughs, as you intend her to, and now you must help her leave even though you want her to go. It takes only a gesture, a quick fingering into her still wet centre.

'Oh, don't love, don't. I've got to go.'

'Then go . . . quickly.'

So beautifully unlike a man? So unbeautifully like one, and you've got so good at it that you manage this sort of thing very well by now. Then, as your turn back from seeing her out, there before you again, instead of your carefully tidied living room, is that pop-up book interior, the desk with its comic gloves at the foot of the shoved-together twin beds. You try to stay as large as the years have made you, as invulnerable to that anger and pain, suffered by a person twenty-five years ago, no bigger than your fucking finger, but your hand is on the desk chair. You pull it out and sit down. The gloves fit. The notes you are taking are for a book written so long ago you have almost forgotten it. The kitchen door opens, and there in it is Lilian, not a cardboard caricature, but Lilian herself. You keep on working. You do not want her to speak.

'Look at me,' she says, and you do, surprised by the clarity of her face, afraid.

'You don't want a lover and a friend; you want a wife or a mistress.'

'What's the difference?' you ask.

'You're not a man. You have to grow up to be a woman, caring as much about my work as I care about yours.'

'I can't.'

As she begins to change, fade, flattens to the cardboard figure you are now so familiar with, you grow into that huge, old child again, alone again as you have been at every beginning since, whether birthday, New Year's Eve, or love affair, closing the cover of the one book you will never write, *Lilian*.

❧

Anita's Dance

It was a morning fit to convert any pessimist, and a Sunday to boot. Anita spent part of it in the garden virtuously weeding; then she poured enough coffee to float an army into her special mug and brought it out into the garden. Instead of reading, she sat stretching her neck to the sun and thinking how lucky she was; nothing to do but please herself all day. From time to time friends lectured her about being selfish and set in her ways, an old maid. And it was true she was sometimes lonely. She had, however, no reason to feel sorry for herself when she compared her life to theirs. She had a house, a garden, a car, a piano. A good job. A greedy, bad-tempered cat. Two eyes, a nose, and ten fingers, all in good working order. What did she have to feel sorry about? And was happiness selfish?

She mused over her library book. She had never really wanted to get married, except for a brief and embarrassing episode when she was at university. A boy she was very fond of had wanted her to drop her scholarship, marry him and put him through law school. Her fondness had ceased abruptly when he argued that, being male, he had more right to an education than she had. Winning the argument had hurt a lot.

Those days were over, she thought, and if she was wrong, she had no daughter to tell her so in exemplary form. I have my house, she thought, my garden with delphiniums and daisies and poppies. My piano, on which I have taught myself to play the simplest and saddest waltzes of Chopin. I have company in the form of a bad-tempered cat. What is more, I have a date with Clive this afternoon. I feel good with Clive. The something that is between us is nothing; there is no self-consciousness. We swim towards each other as if the water were our element. All's right with the world.

She had wanted to study literature but on practical grounds had chosen economics instead. She still, however, attempted to keep up with good books and now she was reading a novel by a man in England called Berger, who was supposed to be both good and avant garde. She opened it now, and put on her sunglasses.

It was good: his main characters were small souls, which showed a sort of left-wing point of view, but she liked the way he got into both their heads at once and managed to stay there, so she could feel both the room they were in and the beating of their rather constricted hearts.

It took place in a small employment agency; both characters, the owner and his clerk, were weighing large changes in their private lives while appearing to deal with clients. The owner, a fiftyish man who had always lived with his sister, was considering independence: marriage even.

She looked up and smiled at the sun. That was funny. She read on.

A woman came into the agency to look for a housekeeping job. A largish, comfortable, middle-aged woman. The proprietor had an instant vision of the comfort she could provide for him: a well-kept house—not too well-kept, Canadian and mowed in the lawn departments, just a sort of comfy English house, fish and chips for tea, a kettle on the hob.

'I could live with that,' Anita said to herself. 'What I couldn't live with, not ever, is a set-up like this plus a job, plus three children and entertaining for a junior executive now portly and senior. No wonder I'm the way I am.'

She frowned at the book, closed it, and put it down. It had revealed to her a seam of domesticity she had been avoiding recognizing: it was cosy, and it was basically English working class, and basically (except for a mob of children) what she had come from.

She had never wanted her mother's life, one of flying elbows and fits of bad temper and aspirations that were a muddle of impulses. Her mother had never seemed to be able to think anything through, she was always anaemic from childbearing and exhausted from scrubbing; crying out 'You girls . . .' Get this, fetch that, turn off the soup, scrub the sink, do the dishes, iron that. When she was an old woman they had bought her an automatic washing machine with a window in the door and found her sitting on the basement steps watching it like television. 'I was remembering the day Lanie got her hair caught in the wringer,' she said.

Anita shuddered: that dream of cosy domesticity was a male dream; she'd been living in a man's world too long. The real thing she'd lived through and it was what had made her so happy to get a scholarship to university. Never mind that she'd had to char and work in a grocery store to put herself through.

She stretched lazily. The cat was scowling at her through the kitchen window; he didn't like her to be happy. Too bad for him. She was going to enjoy this day. Clive and she weren't meeting until two and she didn't even have to change.

She heard scuffling footsteps on the gravel, the footsteps of her brother Jack. 'Oh damn,' she thought. 'He's found me.'

'Hi Nita, how's tricks?'

'Where did you come from, Jack?'

He was big and he was stupid, something of a bad dream: the one who hadn't succeeded. 'Oh well, you know,' he said, plunking himself down on the chaise longue so it clicked and shivered. 'I was wondering if you had any jobs for me, like.'

'Broke again, eh? Want some coffee?'

'Sure.'

She slammed the kitchen door as she went in. The cat gave her a satisfied look, pleased that her moment of glory was over. She poured Jack a coffee, creamed and sugared it, and stumbled as she went out, staining her white summer pants. 'Here,' she thrust it at him.

He sat up like a patient in bed and began not so much to drink as to inhale it. He looked badly hung over. 'What have you been doing lately?' she asked.

'I been doing . . . well, littla this, littla that. Delivering leaflets. You know.'

She knew. He was no good, Jack, and that was that.

'I keep up with the work around here myself,' she said. 'I don't really have anything for you to do.'

'There must be something, the way you lie around reading all the time.'

She refused to rise to the bait.

'Lanie's poorly,' he said. 'I was there yesterday.'

He must be making the rounds again, she thought, borrowing from all of us.

'She's got cancer,' he said, almost with satisfaction: the voice of the child at school announcing family bad news for current events class. 'She looks awful, and she can hardly move.'

'She's doing all right,' Anita said.

'Gotta get worse before you get better, eh? I don't think she'll get better. Ross is scared out of his wits. You should take the kids.'

'I can't. I go out to work, remember?'

'I remember,' he said and continued to stare at her, trying to put her in the wrong before he asked her for money.

'I wrote to Rosie but she's just had an operation. Kit's on the sick list too. Bill won't open the door to me. In the old days, a family stuck together.'

'Maybe we still do,' she said evenly, furious with him. 'Look, I have to go out and see a man about a dog. If ten dollars would do you, I could see you on your way.'

'Drop me off somewhere?'

It wasn't the clothes he was wearing, it was the condition he was in: tousled and dirty. 'Ten bucks and a subway ticket. That's it, Jack.'

'You always were a tight old broad.'

She went inside again, slamming the door, and pounded to the front of the house so hard that the petals shivered off the poppies she had set in a bowl in the front hall. She dashed upstairs and changed into another pair of trousers. As she went down again she made sure the front door was locked, then the back. 'Here,' she said, handing him ten dollars and a ticket. 'You can stay and finish your coffee. I have to be off.' She put her library book in her purse and strode off without looking behind her.

She was meeting Clive at the end of the subway line and they were going out in the country to browse through antique shops. That way he wouldn't have to drive downtown to her place first. That way, she thought grimly, he avoided Jack, thank God.

She had known him for only a few months and hadn't taken him seriously at first. An ordinary man with an ordinary job, he had seemed: indeed there was nothing special about him except the fact that they got on together, very well indeed. There were still in the wonderful time stage, however, and she wondered vaguely if that would change. He was divorced, and he had made it plain he wanted to set up housekeeping with someone again. She didn't know whether she wanted to live with anyone else: it had been so long since she hadn't had the morning paper and the morning clock and the morning coffee to herself that she was afraid she would resent an intruder.

She saw him swing into the parking lot and smiled to herself. An intruder! He got out of the car and came towards her, a smile on his face. He had a wide, rather shy smile, a funny walk. 'Hi,' she said, and ran towards him. 'Marvellous day.'

'Wonderful.' He put her into the car like the gentleman he was, said, 'Belt up, now,' and headed north.

Ordinarily, this act of merely strapping herself in beside him made her happy, but today it was different. Jack niggled and danced in her mind. Being mean to Jack made her feel like the mean, ignorant child she no doubt had been, that Jack still was.

'What's the matter?' Clive said. 'You're twitchy.'

'I'm mean-tempered today,' she said. 'As bad as Martha the cat. My brother Jack turned up. The no-good one.'

'You have one of those, have you? Most people do. I always used to wonder why they felt sorry for me being an only child. How much did you give him?'

So that was on her face too. He read her well. 'I was having such a good time,' she said, 'reading in the garden. Then in stomped Jack, and I still feel shattered.'

'Whom were you reading?'

'John Berger.'

'I'm always amazed at your taste: hardly anyone's heard of him. Look, about your brother, you'd better tell me about him and get it off your mind. No use having a day in the country if we're not in good spirits. Was he mother's blue-eyed boy?'

Suddenly she heard her mother yell, 'You girls, Nita, Rosie, look after that Jackie and make sure he don't fall in the well.' She hunched herself and said, 'First, you have to understand we were small-town people and not what you'd call well off.' She had used the genteel phrase for so long it didn't surprise her any more.

'Born with a plastic spoon?'

'Tin. My father was a sergeant in the army.'

'Powerful influence?'

'When he was there. There were four girls, then Jackie and Bill. Jackie tore the wings off flies and drowned our kitten in the rain barrel: we hated him. I'm sure he was disturbed or something, but I don't bleed for him; he was an awful kid and he's an awful man.'

'I was a social worker in my first incarnation,' he said, profile to the wind against a blue and scudding sky. 'No good at it, but I met a lot of them, awful boys who never grew up. I suppose they radicalized a lot of big sisters in their day. How often has he been inside?'

'I suppose three or four times: petty theft, drunkenness, nothing big or skilful. We were no help to him, you know. He needed a lot of attention from adults, not sisters who'd rather be doing something else.'

'Don't flog yourself, for heaven's sake. There are bad apples, and handing them the barrel doesn't help. Where is he now?'

'In my backyard on the chaise, I suppose. I gave him ten bucks and a subway ticket. But there's no real hope he's gone yet.'

Clive looked down at her and slowed the car down. 'I think,' he said, 'that we'd better go back . . .'

'Clive, I don't want to spoil your day in the country.'

'You're more important than a day in the country and you're miserable. And that oaf is probably inside drinking the liquor cabinet: you can't win with those guys, Nita.'

'I locked the doors.'

'He's probably got Martha to open up for him by now; come on.'

He turned the car and drove very fast down the half-empty Sunday highway into town. They were home in twenty minutes.

They went in the front door and found Jack reclining with his work boots on the white corduroy sofa. He was drinking Nita's precious duty-free French cognac from her last trip to Europe from a kitchen glass.

'Jack!' she roared.

'Snob,' he said with an impish smile. 'So you caught me, you and your fine feller here. Nice coat he's got on. You're coming up and up and up in the world, aren't you, girl? Ma would be proud of you.' But he swung his boots off the chesterfield.

'I think you'd better go,' Clive said. 'You're bothering Anita.'

'Do you think so, Mr Pretty-boy? What are you doing hanging around our Nita? Don't you know she's our Educated Woman, too good for a man? Why, all she cares about is white velvet and books and doilies. She don't even go to visit the sick and the dying, she . . .' He spoke in a stage Irishman's accent. Anita's blood began to rise and she could hear children in the background chanting, 'Nita's a nitwit, Nita's a nobody . . .'

'Jack,' she said. 'Get out.'

'And why would I want to get out, with a fine house to come to and a fine sister to look after me?'

'You should go,' said Clive, being reasonable, trying, being also, Anita thought, very sweet and middle class, 'because you sister has asked you to go.'

'Oh, I never did nothing Nita told me. It was Rosie had the good left hook. Nita was nothing, all skin and bone and no bust. No wonder she never got married or nothing. But then you wouldn't be so foolish, mister, would you, as not to open a package before you put it on the shelf?' His mouth turned down and he leered at Clive. He stood up and prepared to raise the bottle to his lips.

On the one hand, Anita wanted to laugh because he was being a self-defeating grotesque, asking for punishment, exile, anything: he had always been like that. But she was also very, very angry. She could hear all the fourteen-year-old boys in the world whispering, 'Nita Nobody, got no tits . . .' and the rest of it, which was worse. The rest of us reclaimed ourselves, she thought, as Mother wanted us to. We got out of misery and brutality. We stopped swearing, read books, got at least a smattering of education: cleaned up the family act.

Jack took a swig from the bottle. Clive balled his fists. Nita looked at the two of them and sized them: Clive was taller, but Clive was nervous. Clive had never had to punch anyone out.

Jack put the bottle down. Nita took his measure and lashed out, one two, one two, and bang bang bang on his falling head with her fists. Jack went down like a lamb.

Nita sat down on the sofa and started to cry. Clive sat down beside her and put his arm around her. Jack came to.

'Nita, you shouldn't have ought to have done that. Nita, you damn well broke me false teeth.'

'Get out, Jack,' she said. 'Get flaming well out of this house and don't come back. If you don't or if you ever come back, I'll flaming well . . . I'll call your probation officer.'

Jack stood up, holding his head, trying again. 'Nita, you're a hard woman. You should know,' he said to Clive, 'this is the kind of woman you're after: she's got no heart, she's all hollow.'

'Shut up, Jack, and go and tell your government psychiatrist you're persecuted by your sister,' Nita said. 'Get out. Get on with you. Go home and tell your mother she wants you.'

He went.

Anita sat trying to pull herself together. In the scuffle she had lost more than a lamp: the brandy bottle oozed on the carpet, the glass was broken. She sat up and sighed. She looked at Clive.

'Well,' she said. 'Now you know.'

Clive got up and reappeared with a cloth. He began sponging the brandy out of the carpet. 'Look,' he said, 'there's something I should tell you, but I want to know first how you did that?'

'What?'

'That wonderful kayo; I've never seen anything like it.'

'I wasn't born a lady and a scholar,' she said. 'I was born on the outskirts of Camp Borden, a longer time ago than you were, I have to come clean and tell you that. I was one of six children. Circumstances were not good. But in addition to being a sergeant, my father was a fighter, and when he got a beer or two into him he'd spar with anyone he could find. We saved my mother a lot.'

Clive disappeared for a moment again. She picked up the fallen glass, looked at herself in the mirror, smoothed down her hair. Thought desperately: now he knows. It's over.

Clive reappeared with a tray and glasses. 'It's our turn for a drink. There's something I said I would tell you, and I will. The real reason my wife and I got divorced was boredom. We never got quite so low as Graham Greene, who had a tooth out once when he couldn't stand it anymore. But we got bored in a terrible way; we got so bored we felt we needed some kind of violence; we knew it wasn't for us, but we started to pick fights because we drove each other crazy. All our friends celebrated when they heard we were getting a divorce. Perfection drives everybody up the wall.'

She managed to look up at him and smile.

'So drink up, love. I don't care what happens between us; I know it won't bore me. But if we ever do take up living together and things get all sedate and cosy, would you . . .'

'I'd do anything for you,' she heard herself say, not believing she had said it, but hearing it anyway.

'Well, I'm not really that way, but . . . well, hell, Nita: you're magnificent in the boxing ring.'

Much later he said, after tangling with her, 'It wasn't that I wanted violence: I wanted a feeling that I was alive, that you were alive, that even our hair was growing.'

She smiled at her professor again and rubbed her bruised hands together.

JOAN CLARK

❧

THE TRAIN FAMILY

Years ago, after I moved from the East to the West Coast, I started dreaming about railway tracks. I didn't have this dream while I was on the tracks, travelling, but only after I had been here a while, after I had bought a townhouse and my children and I had settled ourselves in Victoria. In other words, the dream began when I had reached the end of the line and was looking back from where I'd come.

In my dream I'm in the middle of the country, on the prairies, sleeping in the lower berth with my daughters. While I'm asleep, I'm dreaming the tracks are being taken up as soon as we pass over them. There are workmen in heavy jackets and peaked caps outside in the dark. They're picking up the railway ties, carrying them off to build houses, barns, fences. I see iron rails, loose and disjointed as dinosaur bones, sliding into gullies and ditches. The earth closes over, grows miles of rough prairie grass. You understand I was dreaming about dreaming, that the panic came when I wanted to wake up and couldn't, when I wanted to get off the train to stop the workmen but was immobilized in my berth.

Stan and I have talked about this dream. He says it shows my contrariness, that just when I finally get myself going forward, I want to turn around and go back. He says this jokingly, fondly. It's meant to tease me about being a homebody, of not wanting to spend half my life on the road with him. I tell him the dream has to do with what I left behind. Ever since I drifted out of childhood, one way and another I've been trying to get back. I see childhood as the wellspring of pure being, a source of unbridled self-centredness and joy.

It's true men have been taking up the tracks in places like Catalina, Port Mouton, Blissfield, you can pick them off across the country. I sometimes wonder what the railway has done with the defunct passenger cars: the dining cars, the club cars, the cabooses. I like to imagine them as being regrouped in a place of their own. Caboosetown. No Petro-Canada or Midas Muffler here. It's strictly residential and pedestrian, the paths named after places where the train no longer goes. I see window boxes, picket fences, shutters. Even when they are on the end of the train, cabooses look as if they were meant to be cottages. In Caboosetown, wheels are out of sight, hidden behind latticework, hollyhocks, shrubbery. Maybe this is a retirement colony, one of those busily humming communities with an active Golden Age club. There are a lot of pastel colours, hearts and flowers, angels stencilled on the walls. One of the passenger cars is a movie theatre. The dining car is, of course, a restaurant. The mayor and the minister use the club car for ceremonies, weddings, burials. Though no one is travelling anywhere that you can see, they are unwilling to give up their rites of passage.

When I was thirteen and living in Sydney Mines, Cape Breton, I had a train family. This was during the time when my father was trying to make a go of his rope-making business and there was a lot of uncertainty about money. There were four children in my imaginary family, a boy and a girl, a boy and a girl, in that order. There was a mother and a father. They lived in a caboose. I wasn't in the family. I was their manager. These people were faceless. They had no personalities. They were cardboard figures. Age and sex were important only because of the clothes they wore. I ordered their clothes. I can't remember ordering food; apparently this family never ate. I ordered clothes for two seasons, spring/summer, winter/fall. Sometimes I gave in and allowed a small indulgence: an Easter hat, a corduroy weskit in forest green, a magenta shorty coat. Mostly I was strict with my purchases and stuck to the basics, underwear and pyjamas for everyone, skirts and blouses for the girls, pants and shirts for the boys. The mother wore a cotton-print housedress, the father a windbreaker and trousers in cotton drill. I didn't have a job picked out for the father. He wasn't a coal miner, I knew that much. I wanted to keep his clothes clean. He wasn't a doctor or a dentist. They made more money than I had to spend. Probably I saw him as a telegraph operator, a ticket agent, some job connected with the railway.

At first I parked the caboose in a vacant lot next to the graveyard, above Greener's Cliff. When winter came, I worried about the wind sweeping off the ice in the Gulf of St Lawrence. I moved the caboose out of town and into the woods, where the family would have enough fuel for their stove and there was shelter from the weather. I had never been inside a caboose and imagined it larger than it was. I saw space for two bedrooms curtained off, girls on one side, boys on the other. The mother and father slept in the living room on a dropback davenport. Each bedroom had a double bed and a chest of drawers: one drawer each for inner wear; one drawer for outer wear. The clothing and furniture were ordered from Eaton's catalogue. I spent a lot of time making lists. When a new catalogue came out, I abandoned my old lists and made up new ones. I was bewitched by newness, by yards of unsullied paper stamped with patches of gaudy colour. The hypnotic instructions drew me in: *move softly in supple rayons, weather the winter in style, spot a winner.* I mooned over the captions in the girls' wear section: *top honours, lively twosome, chipper checks.* I was wooed by matching outfits: a cherry red tam and red mitts, a velveteen hood and velveteen muff, twin sweater sets.

I wanted a matching living-room set. It wasn't as friendly as odds and ends of furniture, but it was more hopeful. A living-room set invited people to sit down together and have serious conversation. It put order and decorum into their lives. I wanted my family to have a wine velour chesterfield with two matching chairs, a walnut coffee table and walnut end tables, all of which I could buy for $183.55. If I bought this set, I would have to get rid of the davenport to make room for the chesterfield. There was something indecent about expecting parents to share a narrow chesterfield. There was no other place inside the caboose for them to sleep. They would have to go. I orphaned the children and revised the budget. The children didn't miss their parents, but I did. They thrived on adversity, but the responsibility of supporting the family on my own put too big a strain on me. I needed a father to bring home the bacon, to balance the budget. There was no question of the mother going out to work. She had to put the wash through the wringer on Mondays. She had to darn socks and scrub the floor.

I took away the matching set and reinstated the parents along with the davenport. Now the family had to make do with leatherette hassocks and an unfinished drop-leaf table with the legs sawn off. In struggling with these decisions, it never occurred to me to shop in the town stores. The management of my family had to be carried out in secrecy, in the privacy of my bedroom. Besides, even in a poor town like Sydney Mines, stores provided more choices than I could handle. As my train family became older and the children outgrew their clothes, more money was required to keep them dressed. I had to have more than a cretonne curtain separating the girls from the boys. I worried how I would manage these changes. I picked at my food, bit my fingernails, lost sleep. I thought about moving my family into a house I passed on my way to school, but it didn't suit. The house was too grand, too prosperous-looking. I was afraid that, if I moved my family into so large a house, my budget would get out of hand. I looked around town for something more modest, a bungalow, a four-room cottage. There were plenty of those in town, but I rejected them all. The truth was I couldn't imagine my family living anywhere but inside the caboose.

My father wasn't at all like the father in the train family. My father didn't like working for anyone else. He ran his own show. He started his rope-making business, his spice-bottling plant, got into real estate, kept a second-hand store, whatever he could do to keep himself employed and support a family. I don't think my father was suited to supporting a family. It put too big a strain on him. He wanted too much for us. I don't think he was suited to business. He had been brought up in a business family in Cape Breton, entrepreneurial Scots stock, people who talked about figures in two colours, red and black, who linked pride with being self-employed, being beholden to no one, marching to your own tune.

My father kept a ledger for his accounts. It was a heavy book with a grey cloth cover, steel rivets on the spine. Inside were alphabetized dividers with green leather tabs embossed in gold. My father carried this ledger with him wherever he went. He kept it in a brown, zippered briefcase my mother gave him one Christmas. When business wasn't going well, my father would sit at the dining-room table with the ledger and overhaul his accounting system. He would make new categories, label more pages, move figures from one column to another, so that what had once been a debit would now become a credit. After working for hours at the table, he would stand up and pace the floor, chain-smoking, gesturing with his hands as he explained the new system to my mother, who sat on the chesterfield listening, nodding occasionally. He used words like depreciation, promissory note, accounts receivable. I didn't know what most of these words meant. I wasn't interested in them, but I understood that once again my father had managed to move money from one place to another and, in so doing, had created more than he had before. I knew that he was feeling pleased in the same way my mother did after she rearranged the furniture in the living room. I understood the power of this, that by transforming the room, she had transformed herself. She had made a fresh start, given herself another chance.

Somewhere along the line my mother had chosen to sit on the chesterfield and listen to my father. She could do this because she could see her life stretching ahead of her on the tracks in a way my father couldn't. My mother could have left my father, left all that anxiety and worry about money, gone back to being employed as a nurse, lived on real money. She didn't mind working for someone else. Maybe she was waiting until my sister and I left home. Maybe she left it too long. Maybe she decided leaving would require too much physical and emotional strain, that it would take more energy than she had, that it wasn't worth the effort. My mother wasn't ambitious. She didn't make sweeping gestures. She didn't have a grand design for herself, not like my father, who often spoke of becoming a millionaire. My mother reached a point where she sat back and took my father as he was. This humbled my father, made him grateful. If she thought he was foolhardy or mistaken, she never let on. I think my father had an oversupply of ambition, more than was good for him. His ambition hyped him up, made him uneasy and fretful, difficult to live with.

Stan says he gave up ambition when he resigned from the nine-to-five rat race. Stan lives with me, though it's probably more accurate to say he camps here when he's not somewhere else. Stan is a nomad. A onetime computer man, he speaks of himself as programmed to go forward. He got into computers early, when he owned an advertising agency in the States. Like me, Stan married young. He spent twenty-five years working ten hours a day to support a wife and five kids. He made hundreds of thousands of dollars, which went out faster than they came in. He says that, when he moved to Canada, he cut up his credit cards, cashed in his stocks, and left the money market for good. Now he does carpentry and key-cutting to support himself.

Recently Stan remodelled a house in Nanaimo, extending the dining room into the garage to make an atrium. Now that he has enough money to keep him going for three months, he's gone back on the road, this time to Alaska. Stan says he doesn't need a home base. Not me. I need some place to come back to. I've been on two long trips with Stan: one driving to Arkansas and on to Mexico, the other across Canada as far as Newfoundland. Stan is the perfect traveller. He'll eat anything, stop anywhere, go down any road. When we're travelling, I depend on him to make arrangements, solve problems. He knows how to repair tires, make a fire from damp wood, cook bannock over a primus stove. He enjoys luxury, small indulgences. For the Alaskan trip he installed a skylight in the van roof, added a detachable screened porch with a folding table and chairs, built in a compact-disc player. I watched him do all this knowing he was assuming I would come along.

Three weeks ago, I was invited to give a one-woman show in Halifax, in the gallery at The Mount. This is something I've been waiting for. I've been in a dozen group shows, but I've never had a show of my own. The lead time is a scant five months, which means I'm probably a substitute for someone else. I told Stan I wouldn't be going to Alaska, I would be staying home to work. 'Bring your buckets of papier-mâché and your paints with you,' Stan said. 'You can work in the porch while I cook supper and poke around.' I told him he'd missed the point, that I didn't want to work on the road. I wanted to be left alone. I wanted to give my full attention to my work, not what was left over. Stan offered to cut the trip from three months to two. I refused the offer. Stan told me I'd been unfair, leading him along, saying I might go. He said I should have told him earlier that I wouldn't be coming so he could have made other arrangements. He packed his clothes, both summer and winter, carried his wood-carving tools, and his CDs out to the van. Before he closed the door behind him, he said he might not be back. I didn't watch him go. I didn't wave from the window. I kept my head down, feet rooted to the floor. Stan drove away. I unplugged the phone, went downstairs to the basement, and got to work.

Some critics call me a sculptural primitive, others a primitive sculpturalist. They don't know what to do with my work, where to put me. There has been some argument as to whether I'm an artist at all, whether what I do is closer to being craft than an art form. I think of my work as theatre, entertainment. I compose stage sets, think in scenes. I call these scenes set pieces. Some of my set pieces are open. My park-bench series was like that. Grass trailed off at the edges; there were no walls or fences. In the series I'm making for the Halifax show, the set pieces are closed. The scenes take place inside rooms, boxes, cars. *Cow Pad* is a scatological set, an apartment for cows. Everything in the pad is round and brown: rugs, stools, tables, pictures, plates. The wallpaper design looks like Danish pastry. *Loony bin* is a large box filled with pairs of loons. Some are singing duets, some are in straitjackets, some are in bizarre sexual positions. There is something less serious about an artist who recycles newspaper, perhaps because the materials are cheap. As an art form, papier-mâché is labour intensive. It doesn't require expensive equipment, doesn't need firing, it simply dries out. It takes paint well, is easily turned to caricature and decoration.

I work on a table made from a discarded door, one window over from the washer and dryer. My tools are often kitchen utensils: paring knife, spoon, fork, skewer, basting brush. Most of these tools are used to make patterns, which I paint over in bold colours so they look like fabric designs. This gives my work the kind of folksiness associated with Grandma Moses, or a sampler stitched with Home Sweet Home.

For the past week I've been working on a set piece entitled *The Train Family*. This is a circus family of animals who live in a caboose, open at the top. I have already made the figures, painted a caboose a fire-engine red, and printed Barnum & Bailey on both sides in canary yellow. There are four children in this family. The eldest boy is a brown monkey with a hula hoop, the eldest girl a seal balancing a ball on the end of her nose. The other boy and girl are a poker-playing rhinoceros and a hippo. It takes most of a day to paint these figures. Each article of clothing has its own design. Afterwards there will be the walls and floor to paint, and a matching set of furniture.

I am contented doing this. It is all I want. It is all I need, for the time being. The days pass, a week, then two. When I'm not working in the basement, I drive out to Kost's orchard to check my beehives or I go for a long walk in Beacon Hill Park. In the evenings I bake bread. I read. I visit Em, talk to my children on the phone.

The father in my train family is an elephant. Like Stan, his torso is heavy and thick, his legs short. I have chosen an elephant because he looks bulky and comfortable, the same as Stan. I paint on blue-striped overalls, a railwayman's cap, put the elephant in the caboose window, reading a map.

I try not to think what Stan had in mind when he said he would have made other arrangements for the trip. Did he mean asking one of his children along, another woman?

I'm tall for a woman, taller than Stan. The mother in this family is a giraffe, a somnambulant, slow-moving animal who towers over the others in the caboose as she stands on tripod legs, staring backwards, looking down the tracks. As a final touch, I give her a telescope.

At last *The Train Family* is finished and I give it two coats of varathane. Before I cover it with plastic and store it on a shelf, I spin it around on a lazy Susan, eyeing it critically, checking the view from all directions. I'm pleased and not pleased. It will sell, I know that much, but it's too literal to suit me. There is something conventional and plodding about it. Perhaps there's too much of myself in it. Uneasiness sets in, as it always does after I've finished something and haven't begun another. This has to do with energy draining away, being transferred to an inert lump of paper and paint. It has to do with seeing the result of my efforts in front of me, diminished, circumscribed. I liked *The Train Family* better when it was inside my head.

Stan could be anywhere between here and Fairbanks. He could have decided to go somewhere else, gone in another direction. There have been no postcards or letters. I know he will eventually return, if only to pick up his wine-making equipment, his Elvis records, his carpentry tools. Now, when I go downstairs to work, I plug in the phone, as a concession.

I think about the last time I was in Toronto visiting my sister. I think about a man and a woman I saw come out of a large brick building and walk along Maitland Street. They were wearing plastic raincoats, belts loose at the back. He was on the outside with his arm around her waist. The other hand held an umbrella over their heads. She had her arm crooked on his shoulder which was a natural way to embrace, given the difference in their heights. She was a good six inches taller than he and had her head tilted sideways to accommodate the umbrella. They looked about the same age, in their mid thirties. They may have been no more than good friends, but I saw them as lovers. They had that relaxed companionableness and gratitude of people who have recently made love. I saw an aura around them, a soft, intimate light they carried with them outside. I saw a room in a first-floor apartment, a painted radiator, a hide-a-bed folded out, blankets on the floor. I saw a man and a woman walking around the room naked, in no hurry to put on their clothes, free from vanity and regret. These are the moments I would miss.

In our years together I have pushed Stan and myself into four or five of these separations, not all of them having to do with travel. I can't remember the details of Stan's other departures, but I could probably have made adjustments, been less perverse. This time I could have gone with Stan as far as Fairbanks or Anchorage and flown back, or done it the other way around. Instead I dug in my heels, proclaimed independence, was careless with my lover and friend. After years of managing a family, I covet aloneness. What some people might call loneliness, I call solitude. I think of my enforced solitude as an air-raid drill, an emergency plan. From time to time I am compelled to go underground and test my survival equipment for what lies ahead. I am always surprised to find it still works. There is something exhilarating about this discovery. I emerge from my bunker rejoicing, grateful for my aliveness, my sense of well-being. Which is why, given the chance, I will probably risk love and do it again.

CAROL SHIELDS

❧

THE ORANGE FISH

Like others of my generation I am devoted to food, money, and sex; but I have an ulcer and have been unhappily married to Lois-Ann, a lawyer, for twelve years. As you might guess, we are both fearful of aging. Recently Lois-Ann showed me an article she had clipped from the newspaper, a profile of a well-known television actress who was described as being 'deep in her thirties.'

'That's what we are,' Lois-Ann said sadly, 'deep in our thirties.' She looked at me from behind a lens of tears.

Despite our incompatibility, the two of us understand each other, and I knew more or less what it was she was thinking: that some years ago, when she was twenty-five, she made up her mind to go to Vancouver Island and raise dahlias, but on the very day she bought her air ticket, she got a letter in the mail saying she'd been accepted at law school. 'None of us writes our own script,' she said to me once, and of course she's right. I still toy—I confess this to you freely—with my old fantasy of running a dude ranch, with the thought of well-rubbed saddles and harnesses and the whole sweet leathery tip of possibility, even though I know the dude market's been depressed for a decade, dead in fact.

Not long ago, on a Saturday morning, Lois-Ann and I had one of our long talks about values, about goals. The mood as we sat over breakfast was sternly analytical.

'Maybe we've become trapped in the cult of consumerism and youth worship,' I suggested.

'Trapped by our *zeitgeist*,' said Lois-Ann, who has a way of capping a point, especially my point.

A long silence followed, twenty seconds, thirty seconds. I glanced up from an emptied coffee cup, remembered that my fortieth birthday was only weeks away, and felt a flare of panic in my upper colon. The pain was hideous and familiar. I took a deep breath as I'd been told to do. Breathe in, then out. Repeat. The trick is to visualize the pain, its substance and colour, and then transfer it to a point outside the body. I concentrated on a small spot above our breakfast table, a random patch on the white wall. Often this does the trick, but this morning the blank space, the smooth drywall expanse of it, seemed distinctly accusing.

At one time Lois-Ann and I had talked about wallpapering the kitchen or at least putting up an electric clock shaped like a sunflower. We also considered a ceramic bas-relief of cauliflowers and carrots, and after that a little heart-shaped mirror bordered with rattan, and, more recently, a primitive map of the world with a practical acrylic surface. We have never been able to agree, never been able to arrive at a decision.

I felt Lois-Ann watching me, her eyes as neat and neutral as birds' eggs. 'What we need,' I said, gesturing at the void, 'is a picture.'

'Or possibly a print,' said Lois-Ann, and immediately went to get her coat.

Three hours later we were the owners of a cheerful lithograph titled *The Orange Fish*. It was unframed, but enclosed in a sandwich of twinkling glass, its corners secured by a set of neat metal clips. The mat surrounding the picture was a generous three inches in width—we liked that—and the background was a shimmer of green; within this space the orange fish was suspended.

I wish somehow you might see this fish. He is boldly drawn, and just as boldly coloured. He occupies approximately eighty per cent of the surface and has about him a wet, dense look of health. To me, at least, he appears to have stopped moving, to be resting against the wall of green water. A stream of bubbles, each one separate and tear-shaped, floats above him, binding him to his element. Of course he is seen in side profile, as fish always are, and this classic posture underlines the tranquillity of the whole. He possesses, too, a Buddha-like sense of being in the *right* place, the only place. His centre, that is, where you might imagine his heart to be, is sweetly orange in colour, and this colour diminishes slightly as it flows toward the semi-transparency of fins and the round, ridged, non-appraising mouth. But it was his eye I most appreciated, the kind of wide, ungreedy eye I would like to be able to turn onto the world.

We made up our minds quickly; he would fit nicely over the breakfast table. Lois-Ann mentioned that the orange tones would pick up the colours of the seat covers. We were in a state of rare agreement. And the price was right.

Forgive me if I seem condescending, but you should know that, strictly speaking, a lithograph is not an original work of art, but rather a print from an original plate; the number of prints is limited to ten or twenty or fifty or more, and this number is always indicated on the piece itself. A tiny inked set of numbers in the corner, just beneath the artist's signature, will tell you, for example, that our particular fish is number eight out of an existing ten copies, and I think it pleased me from the start to think of those other copies, the nine brother fish scattered elsewhere, suspended in identical seas of green water, each pointed soberly in the same leftward direction. I found myself in a fanciful mood, humming, installing a hook on the kitchen wall, and hanging our new acquisition. We stepped backward to admire it, and later Lois-Ann made a Spanish omelet with fresh fennel, which we ate beneath the austere eye of our beautiful fish.

As you well know, there are certain necessary tasks that coarsen the quality of everyday life, and while Lois-Ann and I went about ours, we felt calmed by the heft of our solemn, gleaming fish. My health improved from the first day, and before long Lois-Ann and I were on better terms, often sharing workaday anecdotes or pointing out curious items to each other in the newspaper. I rediscovered the girlish angularity of her arms and shoulders as she wriggled in and out of her little nylon nightgowns, smoothing down the skirts with a sly, sweet glance in my direction. For the first time in years she left the lamp burning on the bedside table and, as in our early days, she covered me with kisses, a long nibbling trail up and down the ridge of my vertebrae. In the morning, drinking our coffee at the breakfast table, we looked up, regarded our orange fish, smiled at each other, but were ritualistically careful to say nothing.

We didn't ask ourselves, for instance, what kind of fish this was, whether it was a carp or a flounder or a monstrously out-of-scale goldfish. Its biological classification, its authenticity, seemed splendidly irrelevant. Details, just details; we swept them aside. What mattered was the prismatic disjection of green light that surrounded it. What mattered was that it existed. That it had no age, no history. It simply *was*. You can understand that to speculate, to analyse overmuch, interferes with that narrow gap between symbol and reality, and it was precisely in the folds of that little gap that Lois-Ann and I found our temporary refuge.

Soon an envelope arrived in the mail, an official notice. We were advised that the ten owners of *The Orange Fish* met on the third Thursday evening of each month. The announcement was photocopied, but on decent paper with an appropriate logo. Eight-thirty was the regular time, and there was a good-natured reminder at the bottom of the page about the importance of getting things going punctually.

Nevertheless we were late. At the last minute Lois-Ann discovered a run in her pantyhose and had to change. I had difficulty getting the car started, and of course traffic was heavy. Furthermore, the meeting was in a part of the city that was unfamiliar to us. Lois-Ann, although a clever lawyer, has a poor sense of spatial orientation and told me to turn left when I should have turned right. And then there was the usual problem with parking, for which she seemed to hold me responsible. We arrived at eight-forty-five, rather agitated and out of breath from climbing the stairs.

Seeing that roomful of faces, I at first experienced a shriek in the region of my upper colon. Lois-Ann had a similar shock of alarm, what she afterwards described to me as a jolt to her imagination, as though an axle in her left brain had suddenly seized.

Someone was speaking as we entered the room. I recognized the monotone of the born chairman. 'It is always a pleasure,' the voice intoned, 'to come together, to express our concerns and compare experiences.'

At that moment the only experience I cared about was the sinuous river of kisses down my shoulders and backbone, but I managed to sit straight on my folding chair and to look alert and responsible. Lois-Ann, in lawyer-like fashion, inspected the agenda, running a little gold pencil down the list of items, her tongue tight between her teeth.

The voice rumbled on. Minutes from the previous meeting were read and approved. There was no old business. Nor any new business. 'Well, then,' the chairman said, 'who would like to speak first?'

Someone at the front of the room rose and gave his name, a name that conveyed the double-pillared boom of money and power. I craned my neck, but could see only a bush of fine white hair. The voice was feeble yet dignified, a persisting quaver from a soft old silvery throat, and I realized after a minute or two that we were listening to a testimonial. A mystical experience was described. Something, too, about the 'search for definitions' and about 'wandering in the wilderness' and about the historic symbol of the fish in the Western Tradition, a secret sign, an icon expressing providence. 'My life has been altered,' the voice concluded, 'and given direction.'

The next speaker was young, not more than twenty I would say. Lois-Ann and I took in the flare of dyed hair, curiously angled and distinctively punk in style. You can imagine our surprise: here of all places to find a spiked bracelet, black nails, cheeks outlined in blue paint, and a forehead tattooed with the world's most familiar expletive. *The Orange Fish* had been a graduation gift from his parents. The framing alone cost two hundred dollars. He had stared at it for weeks, or possibly months, trying to understand what it meant; then revelation rushed in. 'Fishness' was a viable alternative. The orange fins and sneering mouth said no to 'all that garbage that gets shovelled on your head by society. So keep swimming and don't take any junk,' he wound up, then sat down to loud applause.

A woman in a neatly tailored mauve suit spoke for a quarter of an hour about her investment difficulties. She'd tried stocks. She'd tried the bond market. She'd tried treasury bills and mutual funds. In every instance she found herself buying at the peak and selling just as the market bottomed out. Until she found out about investing in art. Until she found *The Orange Fish*. She was sure, now, that she was on an upward curve. That success was just ahead. Recently she had started to be happy, she said.

A man rose to his feet. He was in his mid-fifties, we guessed, with good teeth and an aura of culture lightly worn. 'Let me begin at the beginning,' he said. He had been through a period of professional burn-out, arriving every day at his office exhausted. 'Try to find some way to brighten up the place,' he told his secretary, handing her a blank cheque. *The Orange Fish* appeared the next day. Its effect had been instantaneous: on himself, his staff, and also on his clients. It was as though a bright banner had been raised. Orange, after all, was the colour of celebration, and it is the act of celebration which has been crowded out of contemporary life.

The next speaker was cheered the moment he stood. He had, we discovered, travelled all the way from Japan, from the city of Kobe—making our little journey across the city seem trivial. As you can imagine, his accent was somewhat harsh and halting, but I believe we understood something of what he said. In the small house where he lives, he has hung *The Orange Fish* in the traditional tokonoma alcove, just above the black lacquered slab of wood on which rests a bowl of white flowers. The contrast between the sharp orange of the fish's scales and the unearthly whiteness of the flowers' petals reminds him daily of the contradictions that abound in the industrialized world. At this no one clapped louder than myself.

A fish is devoid of irony, someone else contributed in a brisk, cozy voice, and is therefore a reminder of our lost innocence, of the era which predated double meanings and trial balloons. But, at the same time, a fish is more and also less than its bodily weight.

A slim, dark-haired woman, hardly more than a girl, spoke for several minutes about the universality of fish. How three-quarters of the earth's surface is covered with water, and in this water leap fish by the millions. There are people in this world, she said, who have never seen a sheep or a cow, but there is no one who is not acquainted with the organic shape of the fish.

'We begin our life in water,' came a hoarse and boozy squawk from the back row, 'and we yearn all our days to return to our natural element. In water we are free to move without effort, to be most truly ourselves.'

'The interior life of the fish is unknowable,' said the next speaker, who was Lois-Ann. 'She swims continuously, and is as mute, as voiceless as a dahlia. She speaks at the level of gesture, in circling patterns revived and repeated. The purpose of her eye is to decode and rearrange the wordless world.'

'The orange fish,' said a voice which turned out to be my own, 'will never grow old.'

I sat down. Later my hand was most warmly shaken. During the refreshment hour I was greeted with feeling and asked to sign the membership book. Lois-Ann put her arms around me, publicly, her face shining, and I knew that when we got home she would offer me a cup of cocoa. She would leave the bedside lamp burning and bejewel me with a stream of kisses. You can understand my feeling. Enchantment. Ecstasy. But waking up in the morning we would not be the same people.

I believe we all felt it, standing in that brightly lit room with our coffee cups and cookies: the woman in the tailored mauve suit, the fiftyish man with the good teeth, even the young boy with his crown of purple hair. We were, each of us, speeding along a trajectory, away from each other, and away from that one fixed point in time, the orange fish.

But how helplessly distorted our perspective turned out to be. What none of us could have known that night was that *we* were the ones who were left behind, sheltered and reprieved by a rare congeniality and by the pleasure that each of us feels when our deepest concerns have been given form.

That very evening, in another part of the city, ten thousand posters of the orange fish were rolling off a press. These posters—which would sell first for $10, then $8.49, and later $1.95—would decorate the rumpled bedrooms of teenagers and the public washrooms of filling stations and beer halls. Within a year a postage stamp would be issued, engraved with the image of the orange fish, but a fish whose eye, miniaturized, would hold a look of mild bewilderment. And sooner than any of us would believe possible, the orange fish would be slapped across the front of a Sears flyer, given a set of demeaning eyebrows, and cruelly bisected with an invitation to stock up early on back-to-school supplies.

There can be no turning back at this point, as you surely know. Winking off lapel buttons and earrings, stamped onto sweatshirts and neckties, doodled on notepads and in the margin of love letters, the orange fish, without a backward glance, will begin to die.

Audrey Thomas

ʕ

Local Customs

Years from now will he say to himself, 'the breasts of that American girl had a bloom on them, like grapes.' A combination of sun oil and the blowing sand, of course, but magic then, magic and terrifying to the twelve-year-old boy who was trying to look and not to look, both at the same time. Years from now will he perhaps rub his thumb and two fingers together and smile? As though he had actually touched them instead of merely staring across at her from his usual observation post under the dusty tamarisk tree. She and her friend are talking to the blind man, who lies propped on one elbow, on his suncot, not looking at either girl but somewhere off to one side. This has nothing to do with modesty; the blind man never looks at the people to whom he is talking. The wind and the fifteen yards between them keep Edward from hearing the conversation, but every so often he hears the blind man laugh and say 'We Churmans, ha ha ha, we Churmans.' His second day on the beach, Edward chased a newspaper which was blowing away in the wind. He brought the runaway pages to a middle-aged man, very tanned, who was sitting under one of the beach umbrellas. The paper was in German but Edward knew that most Germans spoke English. 'Is this your paper?' he said, embarrassed by his high, thin, schoolboy voice. The man frowned in his direction.

'*Bitte?*'

'Your paper.' Edward thrust it at the man.

'Ah, the newspaper. My wife's newspaper, I am afraid. I am blind.'

Edward could just make out the shape of the man's eyes behind the thick dark glasses.

That day at lunch Anna said, 'I wonder what's the matter with that man? It looks as though there's something wrong with his legs.' Edward's father was reading a book, reaching absently for a forkful of salad from time to time. Edward took after his father; they were both long and thin and had the kind of skin that did not tan. Anna was his father's girlfriend.

'Who?' said Edward's father, not looking up.

'The German man over there, with the wife who is always smiling. She holds onto him—or rather, he holds onto her—wherever they go. She pretty well has to stand him up and sit him down.'

'He's blind,' Edward said. 'He told me so this morning.'

'Ah, so.' Anna nodded her head at him and smiled. She had big white even teeth and was very pretty. Edward liked her in spite of himself. She was almost always willing to play cards or backgammon with him and she never called him Teddy, the way his mother did. ('Teddy's being so difficult lately,' he heard her say, talking on the telephone to one of her friends. And then, 'like father, like son.') And he knew Anna had nightmares. The walls between the rooms were thin and he had heard her crying out and moaning in the night. Edward knew a lot about bad dreams.

'His wife is Greek,' Edward said, 'but they've lived in Germany for years and years. She inherited a house in one of the villages, so they come here in the summer. They also have a house in Munich and a chalet in the Austrian alps.'

'You are very good at finding things out,' Anna said.

'Not really. He likes to talk.'

And it was true—the blind man liked to talk. In English, in German, in bad Greek. From the time they arrived in the morning, his wife driving the white Mercedes, until they left in the late afternoon, the blind man lay on his suncot and talked to anyone who would listen. His wife, in a black bathing suit, her dark hair pulled into a low knot at the back of her neck, made trips across the beach and up to the café-bar for bottles of cold water and glasses of iced coffee. It was hard to tell how old she was, with her smooth brown skin and calm, untroubled face. She seemed to smile at everyone and had a special smile and greeting for Edward ever since he had rescued her newspaper. Twice a day she took her husband's hand and led him into the blue water, where they stood side by side up to their necks, facing the open sea for perhaps ten minutes. Then they turned and walked slowly back to their place under the beach umbrella. She handed him his towel and got him settled and went back for a swim on her own. She was a very strong swimmer and one day Edward had a strange thought. What if she got fed up looking after her husband and simply swam away?

In the last few days the wind had gotten worse. The umbrella man has stopped renting out umbrellas because the wind just knocks them out of their stands. '*Oxi,*' he said, 'no,' shaking his head this morning at Edward, who likes to help with the umbrellas and cots, lining them up very early and then collecting the money from the people who want to rent them. One hundred drachmas for an umbrella, fifty drachmas each for a cot.

'*Kaputt,*' the umbrella man says, '*verstehen?*'

'I'm *not German,*' Edward insists, but the umbrella man ignores this and always addresses him as though he were. Although Edward knows perfectly well that there were good Germans and bad Germans during the Second World War it upsets him to actually be mistaken for one. Anna said once that she couldn't understand how the Greeks could bear to see a German without wanting to put a bullet through his head.

For three days now the wind has howled all night, rattling the louvred doors and windows in the hotel bedrooms, blowing sand into all the corners. A forest fire is raging in the north. All the young men from the northern villages have been conscripted to fight the fire. Big-bellied water bombers fly back and forth all day. Dmitri, Edward's friend who owns the hotel and café-bar, tells him that some of the islanders are saying it was the tourists who caused the fire but that this isn't true. Last year's fire was started by an old man burning brush in his field and this year's was probably caused by lightning.

'Or maybe the government starts it, who knows?'

Edward does not understand. Dmitri likes him because he collects all the empty bottles from the beach and generally makes himself useful. Dmitri doesn't mind Edward asking him questions.

'Why would the government start a fire?'

'Take people's mind from politics, from troubles.'

Edward still doesn't understand. It is a small island; sometimes, in the evenings, you can smell the forests burning in the north. The sunsets are spectacular.

Empty containers for Manhattan Ice-Cream, Tartuffo Gelato Italiano, Coke bottles, Sprite bottles, Pizz lemonade, beer, water bottles, Marlboro packets: during the night the wind sweeps all the rubbish into heaps against the low stone wall which separates the beach from the café and the parking lot in front of the small hotel. By 7:00 a.m. Edward has had his first swim of the day and is sorting through the rubbish. If he finds bits of broken glass, or bottle caps, he places them carefully in a plastic bag.

'You good boy,' Dmitri says, 'maybe you no go back to England. You stay here with me.'

Dmitri isn't married. Everybody thinks, at first, that his sister Fotula is his wife. It is really Fotula who owns the place; property here is passed on to the daughters, not the sons. Dmmi, as his friends and family call him, spent five years working in restaurants in New Jersey and Montreal, living in cheap boarding houses and sending money back so that Fotula could build the thirteen-room hotel. In return she sent him photographs of how the work was coming on. Anna has the pink card which advertises the hotel pasted in her diary:

NEAR BEACH RESTAURANT
PERA AMMOS
IF YOU ENJOY SWIMMING AND PINETREES
SURROUNDING IS NO BETTER PLACE

Dmmi and Fotula wear T-shirts made for them by a satisfied client. PERA AMMOS they say, GOLDEN SANDS BEACH RESORT. On the glass case in front of the bar are a lot of pictures of Dmmi in his T-shirt, with his arm around various pretty girls. He says to Edward, 'You think I should make new T-shirt? "Fotula is no my wife"?' He is a handsome dark-haired man of about forty-five. At least Anna says he is handsome; Edward notices he is getting a fat belly.

The whole family works at one job or another about the place. No matter how early Edward arrives with his sack of bottles, the old granny, the *yia yia*, is already sitting on a straight chair on one side of the door to the kitchen, stuffing tomatoes or green peppers, stringing beans. The old grandpa sits on the other side peeling an enormous pan of potatoes. Dmitri and Fotula's older brother, who is a bit simple, sweeps up and waits on tables. A handsome nephew runs the gift shop and even the umbrella man is some sort of relation. The older brother and his wife, who is the chambermaid, have two naughty children who are alternately kissed and slapped. They hold up the wet sheets for their mother to hang on the line, and fall asleep, in the evenings, on their granny's lap.

Edward is an only child. Since the divorce, his parents never speak to one another except over the telephone, and his grandparents live in distant cities. He has already been a boarder at school for three years.

'You think I should get a wife?' Dmitri says to Edward one day. 'Maybe nice English womans?' They are busy setting out chairs and wiping down tables. Edward smiles but doesn't answer. If he had thought Dmitri was Fotula's husband, Dmitri had thought Anna was Edward's older sister. He had shown them to the same room. Anna had thought this was very funny.

On the beach an Englishman walks by; he is big and boisterous and wears a black T-shirt with CATS printed on one side, two green cat's eyes on the other. 'I say,' he calls to no one in particular, certainly not to the boy, for Edward has seen this man has no time for children, 'crossing the beach in this wind is like crossing the Gobi Desert!' He is a stupid man with a stupid wife and two stupid daughters. The girls parade around in just their bikini bottoms and are dreadful show-offs. Their breasts have just begun to swell. One has nipples the colour of field mushrooms; the other's are dusty pink, like pencil rubbers. They play frisbee and a game involving two large plastic bats and a tennis ball; they stand at the water's edge each afternoon, squealing and hoping everybody is looking at them, flinging their arms around and missing perfectly easy throws. Edward watches them from the shade of the tamarisk tree. One day they asked him to play and when he shook his head and hurried away they laughed.

'We Churmans,' the blind man says, 'ha ha ha.' He is passing around photographs of his houses.

It is hard to know where to look. Although there is a sign in Greek, English, German and Italian which says NUDITY IS FORBIDDEN, many women are bare-breasted. And some of the Greek women are very fat. They look terrible in their two-piece suits, their stomachs spilling over in yellowish rolls. Some have dreadful scars and he doesn't see how they can expose themselves like that, talking away to one another, shouting at their children, passing out food. The little Greek boys fill empty Pizz bottles with sea-water and run along the shore, pouring out the water in long streams, shouting 'Pizz, pizz' and laughing.

But the other beach is much worse. On the other beach, the beach where Anna and Edward's father go, everyone is stark naked—man, woman, and child. Anna knew about the other beach before they came; she has been to this island once before. On their first day, after the business about the rooms had been sorted out and they had unpacked, Anna said, 'Come with me and I will show you the most beautiful beach in the world.' She led them up a path along the steep cliffs beyond the bay. They walked for about ten minutes and then she started down towards the water. They followed, slipping and sliding behind her, not always sure where to put their feet, until they came out on a small beach covered in smooth grey pebbles, as though they had stumbled upon a gigantic nest of stone eggs. A hundred yards from shore two men, completely naked, were diving from a large rock. 'And now,' Anna said, spreading her towel over the smooth, round pebbles, 'now we take off our clothes and let the sun shine all over us.' She was unbuttoning her skirt as she spoke. Soon she and his father had shed all their clothes, their bodies very pale compared to the few other people lying on the beach or swimming in the blue-green water.

'Come on Teddy,' his father said, 'it's all right. Anna says we're allowed to swim nude over here. Off with your clothes. You look as though you could do with a bit of sunshine.'

Nude. It rhymed with rude. What an ugly word.

Anna stood smiling at him. 'It feels so nice; why don't you give it a try?'

'In a minute,' he said. He spread out his towel and carefully anchored it at the corners with large grey stones.

Anna and his father lay down side by side, faces to the sun, holding hands.

'Aren't you glad we came?' she asked. She leaned over and kissed his father on the belly. His father's cock stirred and thickened. Edward went quickly to the water's edge, pulled off his shorts and ran into the water. The rocks were slippery here and he fell once or twice but was quickly over his head.

When Anna had stood there smiling at him she was wearing only the necklace of blue beads his father had bought her in Athens. For their 'anniversary' he had said. The man in the shop swore they were genuine mummy beads and now Edward, swimming, remembered the Mummy Room at the British Museum and one mummy in particular. The brownish bandages covering the body were covered in turn by a broken net of blue beads. Where did the jeweller in Athens get his? From men who robbed tombs? It seemed strange to him, as he floated on his back in the cool water, the sun so hot against his closed eyes, that Anna would want to wear something like that, something that had been shut up in a tomb for hundreds and hundreds of years, maybe something that had a curse on it.

Edward had been on a school tour of the museum and the guide had told them all about curses connected with the tombs. When they were going through from one hall to another there had been a marble statue of a girl, a goddess maybe, lying on her stomach, asleep. One of the boys pretended to stick his finger up her bum when the guard wasn't looking.

When Edward came out of the water he quickly wrapped himself in his towel and moved away from Anna and his father.

He went one more time to the pebble beach and sat in the shade of the cliff. A French couple came to share the shade and the woman showed him an angry red circle on her arm. '*La méduse*,' she said, '*attention!*' Edward was surprised that anyone would think he was French. Her husband was wearing only the top of his wetsuit and had been spearing fish. When Edward looked puzzled (What was a *méduse*?) he said, 'jelayfish' then turned his back and began talking to his wife in rapid French.

After that Edward said he preferred the sandy beach by the hotel. For a moment he thought his father was angry. Then he shrugged. 'It's up to you. We can join you at lunchtime. If you need anything, just put it on the bill.' And so their routine was quickly established. Edward stayed on the sandy beach; he helped Dmitri and the umbrella man; he swam; he watched. Sometimes he ate lunch with his father and Anna. Sometimes he helped Dmitri and his brother wait on tables. Lunch was their busiest time, for the buses had arrived from the town by then, and the people in cars and young men riding motor scooters or hanging on behind the driver. The beach filled up and everybody wanted beer or Sprite or Pizz, salad, moussaka, fish and chips, ice-cream, and iced coffee. One day Dmitri asked him to take an order to the family with the English girls and he refused. Dmitri laughed.

'What's the matter? They your girlfriends?'

Edward shook his head, furious. He went back to his room and lay on his bed until lunchtime was almost over. Anna, worried that he'd had too much sun, brought him a big plate of watermelon and played Snap with him until the sun was lower in the sky. His father sat on the adjoining balcony reading a book and when he suggested they all go to the other taverna, about ten minutes away and in the opposite direction to the pebble beach, Edward, who had always refused before out of loyalty to Dmitri, agreed at once. Anna and his father liked the other taverna better in the evenings. It was lively and cooler and often had local musicians. The evening was pleasant and they stayed late, walking back along the cliffs. A girl had fallen from the path and onto the rocks a few weeks before. She had been drunk and there was no moon. A German girl. Edward thought of her lying there in the darkness, her head split open like a watermelon, and watched very carefully where he put his feet.

And the next day Dmitri offered to show him some card tricks so they were friends again.

'So how you like this ice-land,' Dmitri said, shuffling the cards. Edward shook his head, puzzled. 'Karpathos, how you like it?'

'Eye-land,' Edward corrected him, 'this eye-land.'

On the beach Greek-American women changed from one language to another in the middle of a sentence. 'Okay, *pethi mou*, now you're really going to get it!' Switching the backs of their children's legs with narrow bamboo fishing poles. Edward was learning, slowly, but the air was full of words he didn't understand. He tried to imagine Dmitri learning English in Elizabeth, New Jersey.

One morning when Edward went down to arrange his things in his favourite spot under the tamarisk tree, a young man was there, curled up in a cotton sleeping bag. Edward wasn't sure what to do. He felt that this was his spot, although he knew that it wasn't, not really. He also knew that if he didn't arrange his things now, before he had breakfast, somebody else would come along and claim it. The tree provided shade all day and you didn't have to pay for an umbrella. And the whole beach was there in front of him, like a continuous film. As he stood there, undecided, the young man turned over and opened his eyes.

'Good morning,' he said. He was German. 'I am taking your place?'

Edward shrugged. 'Not really. But I like it here under the tree. I don't tan very well,' he confessed.

The young man sat up and the sleeping bag fell back around his waist. He laughed.

'I also. I do not tan very well.' He showed Edward his back. 'Yesterday

I fall asleep in the sun. Now I am all burned up.' When he stepped out of the sleeping bag, the backs of his legs were bright red.

'You could get sunstroke,' Edward said. 'You should be careful.'

The man nodded. 'Yah. I drank some beer and I fall asleep. Very dumb.'

'Where were you?'

'On the other beach, mit the rocks.'

'Where are you staying?'

'I have a little tent,' he said. 'I am staying on the beaches mostly. But the wind is too strong and pulls it down, my tent. And the sun is very hot.'

'You should stay out of the sun today,' Edward said, 'or you will get sick.' He offered him one side of the shade from the tree.

The man went to shave and wash up in the public washroom and Edward went for his breakfast. Anna and his father were still asleep. The only people in the café were Dmitri and the old granny and grandpa and the couple Anna called 'the newly-weds,' although the girl didn't wear a wedding ring. She was taking a picture of her boyfriend eating yoghurt and honey. She was always taking pictures of her boyfriend or he of her. 'James Hooper,' he said to her now, posing, 'this is your life.'

The young German asked if he could join Edward for breakfast. Edward said yes, but added he had to hurry and help the umbrella man set out the cots and umbrellas. The man nodded and smiled. Edward liked the way he looked right at you.

'*Kalli-mara*,' Dmitri said to Edward, '*Tee-kanees?*'

'*Kalla*,' Edward replied.

'You speak Greek?' the young man said to Edward.

'A little.'

They spent the day together, under the tamarisk tree. The young man's name was Karl. He was tall and thin, with reddish hair and pale blue eyes. He seemed always to be wearing a slight frown but he had a nice smile. He had a degree in psychology, he said, but couldn't get a job, so he was selling potatoes in a shop in Berlin.

'I am very bad. Some ladies come in and they want very cheap potatoes, not much money, and some are wanting very expensive potatoes, high class, and I always forget what lady wants what potatoes. I am not a very good potato-seller.'

Edward told him a little about his school and where he lived in Sussex and a little about his father and Anna, although he said 'my father and stepmother' which was what she was, really, and it sounded nicer.

'Are you married?' he said.

'Me? I am too shy. Someday maybe.'

The German was travelling alone. He was very well organized and had only his small rucksack and tent and cotton sleeping bag. Edward's father and Anna made fun of the Americans with their enormous packs. 'Life-support systems,' they called them. They would approve of the way this man travelled so lightly.

'I bring only—what you call them—necessaries,' he said. 'But a book of course. One book. However, even with one book I am not very far.' It was a very fat paperback, *Gravity's Rainbow*.

'What's it about?' Edward asked.

'The wars,' the young man said.

Edward thought he said 'divorce.'

'But I am not in the mood for reading. I like to watch. For example,' he said, smiling, 'you notice how the women lie when they lie on the beach. Always with one leg up, only one, like so,' and he bent his right leg into a triangle. 'And the mothers, they are always calling so loudly to their children, do this, don't do that. And the young girls are always rubbing each other with oil.' He showed Edward a small black notebook in which he wrote down what he saw. Edward told him about the 'newly-weds' who were always taking pictures and about all the Greeks from New Jersey.

'Yah. On this island most all the men go away to make money. They send money back. They come back to visit, to die. They fix up the villages.'

They were going to a village that night, Edward said, to a festival. They were being picked up by a taxi. He wanted to invite his new friend to come with them but wasn't sure how Anna and his father would feel about that. Dmitri's handsome nephew was supposed to be minding the gift shop but instead was showing off with a friend of his, a young man in a white panama hat, for some Greek-American girls. They had a tape-recorder going full blast.

'"Beat it", ' the young German said, laughing. '"Beat it". You like Michael Jackson? You like to dance?'

Edward shrugged. The blind man's wife came across the beach in her black bathing suit. She smiled her special smile.

'And how are you today?' she said.

'Everybody knows you,' his new friend said, admiringly. It made Edward feel good to hear him say it.

That evening they arrived early at the mountain village because Anna wanted to be up there when the sun set. Edward had sat in front with the taxi driver, whose name was Adonis. He had a horn that played 'My Old Kentucky Home.' The air was very cool and they sat on a stone wall, outside the church, waiting for the procession to begin. Anna wore an embroidered shawl over her sundress and looked very beautiful. But Edward's father became impatient when he discovered the procession wouldn't start for some time and suggested they go for a walk. So they walked away from the village, past grape-vines and terraces of olive trees, past a house where two small children were being coached in the dancing by a mama and a proud grandpa. And further along a very new, very black baby goat showed off for them while its mother calmly ate her dinner. Anna and Edward's father walked with their arms around one another; Edward dropped a little behind. The sunset turned the stone terraces, the fields, their faces, the whole sky golden, then rose, then a deep orangey-red. Somewhere a group of musicians were playing the strange, mournful, repetitive music they had heard before at the other taverna on the beach. Edward said it reminded him of bees and his father smiled at him. 'That's a very interesting perception.'

Walking back to the main village they came upon the musicians entering a house. 'They will go from house to house tonight and make up songs to honour the people,' Anna said. She had been reading the guidebook. A little further on, through an open doorway, Edward saw a man in a brown suit, humming to himself, select a gaudy tie from an open chest of drawers.

The taverna, which was famous for its home-made sausages, was jammed with people. The proprietor's son, not much older than Edward, was very busy laying plastic tablecloths, bringing baskets of bread, bottles of retsina and beer, plates of the famous sausages. The blind man and his wife were sitting with a large group. When she saw Edward, the blind man's wife, in a full red skirt and red blouse, her hair braided into a crown on top of her head, got up from the table and came across the room. She gave Edward and his father and Anna each a sprig of wild thyme.

'It is the custom here,' she said, 'on feast days.'

'If there were some instrument to measure happiness,' Anna said, 'I'm sure that mine, tonight, would break it.'

'Anna,' Edward's father said, 'will you do me the honour of marrying me?'

Edward saw his friend, the young German, over in a corner reading his book. They smiled and waved.

'Another new friend?' Edward's father said.

'He has a degree in clinical psychology,' Edward said, 'but has to sell potatoes in Berlin.'

'Isn't he wonderful?' Anna said. 'Edward, would you do me the honour of marrying me?'

One morning very early Edward and Karl walked over the cliffs and all the way into the town. Karl showed him how to find the path even when it didn't look as though there was one and how there were small heaps of stone every so often, 'little stone men' Karl called them, when the path made a sudden turn, and splashes of red paint. Karl needed to find out when boats were leaving for Crete. He had to be in Athens on a certain day to get his flight back to Berlin. He really wanted to take an old boat that went all the way to Piraeus but nobody knew exactly when it would arrive and nobody knew where he could get a ticket. 'Dmmi says it is a very funny boat,' Karl told Edward, 'but when I say how funny he just laughs.' Instead of his usual singlet of khaki shirt Karl was wearing a blue shirt covered in bright flowers. It made him look quite different. 'You like it?' Karl said. 'I wear it for the very first time.'

Edward imagined himself, in a few years, travelling from place to place with his rucksack on his back.

The walk along the cliffs took just over an hour and they watched the sun rise as they walked along. The air smelled of wild thyme and oregano. They passed a field of oats, golden in the morning light.

'So sometimes I am thinking we are in the Bible,' Karl said.

In town they had a Nescafé at the port and then visited the bank, the travel agent, the post office, a vegetable shop where they bought round yellow melons and grapes, a shop that sold yoghurt, one that sold nuts and spirits. Everything fit neatly into Karl's rucksack.

Anna had asked Edward to try and match some embroidery silk. They found a shop with hundreds of boxes of silks and cottons, and with the aid of the proprietor, a very old man, they were able to match the sample exactly. The shop had a painted fish on a sign outside the door and it also sold fishing equipment—fishing line and sinkers, fishnet, flippers, masks. Karl, who had a snorkelling outfit, offered to buy one for Edward. That afternoon they took their gear to the pebble beach and went snorkelling in the deep water. Edward was amazed to find that he could see right through the bodies of some of the fish. Sometimes they brushed against his mask; sometimes they brushed against his body or swam between his legs. Karl, who was swimming alongside him, warned him away from a group of what looked like pale purple bubbles. Back on the beach, drying off, he told Edward they were jellyfish. Edward remembered the French woman and her warning about the *méduse*.

Anna came over to where they were sitting and asked to borrow the mask and snorkel. Edward's flippers were too small; Karl's were too big. She stood there, smiling, swinging the mask and talking to the young man. She was a soft brown all over and wore nothing but the blue and silver necklace.

Edward noticed how, when the water ran over the shingle as it flowed back into the sea, it made a hissing sound.

The blind man lies on his suncot and laughs—'Ha ha ha, we Churmans, ha ha ha.' Edward, tired of sitting still, wishing Anna were there so he could show her his latest card trick, gets up, picks up his snorkelling equipment and goes down to the water.

Edward sees the octopus first. As the crowd gathers, he keeps repeating it: 'I'm the one that found it!' He wishes Anna and his father would come back.

He had been snorkelling for about an hour and as he came in towards the beach he kept his face down in the water until the last minute, until he was almost lying on the sand. That was when a clump of something swam between his mask and the edge of the shore. Whatever it was had brushed against his cheek and he stood up in a panic. It was a small octopus, flesh-coloured, and now it lay quite quietly, the tips of its tentacles curling and uncurling, just under the surface of the water. Perhaps it had hurt itself when it collided with his mask. Edward knelt down in the water to have a better look. The young man in the panama hat was walking by. His green-and-white striped swimming trunks were much too tight and now he stood above Edward, smiling.

'What you got?'

Edward didn't like the young man but he was too excited to keep quiet and ignore him.

'It's an octopus! It crashed right into my mask! Do you think it's hurt?'

'*Otopothi*,' the young man said, squatting down. 'Very nice to eat.' He gave it a poke with his finger and the tentacles curled in upon themselves like strange warty fingers, like the tips of young ferns. Its eyes were shut tight. The young man laughed. He wore a large gold cross on a gold chain. His chest, his belly, his legs were covered in whorls of coarse black hair.

'Very nice to eat. I show you.' He reached down quickly and picked up the creature. Now the tentacles twisted around the young man's hand. He offered the octopus to Edward.

'You like? I show you how to fix. Dmmi cook it for you.' The tentacles curled, uncurled (*'la méduse, attention!'*). Edward put his hands behind his back.

The man in the panama hat laughed, showing glints of gold among his strong white teeth.

'You no like?'

Edward hesitated. A small crowd had gathered. The young man laughed again and called to two of his friends. He said something in Greek and they laughed and came forward. Edward wondered what it would be like to grab the octopus and run with it, drop it in the blind man's lap. Would the blind man's wife stop smiling, then?

The three young men moved out a bit into the water, forming a loose triangle. The man in the hat let the octopus go and they began to play with it, scooting it through the water towards one another, standing up to their knees in water, laughing. Edward stood near but not too near, watching. The octopus was frantic now; it turned an ugly red and squirted its ink at the young men. Their legs were covered in it and this made them laugh even harder. The man in the panama hat called something to two pretty Greek girls and rubbed the black stuff into the skin of his thighs. The girls giggled.

As more and more people joined the crowd Edward called out, 'I'm the one that found it! It crashed right into my mask!' But still he stood at the edge of the game, in his flippers, holding the mask and snorkel. He wanted to touch the octopus, to hold it, maybe get somebody to take a photograph. He could see the 'newly-weds' in the crowd; the girl, as usual, had her camera on a cord around her wrist. He could see the English girls, who had left off making an elaborate sand castle and stood there, shameless, their little titties sticking out for everybody to see. But the idea of really holding the thing made him feel sick. The way it would twist and turn, curl and uncurl against his hand. It was horrible to think about, horrible to look at, boneless, like a wrinkled purse made of skin. Big ones could kill a man. What if there were big ones out there, under the cliffs where he'd been swimming? The afternoon sun beat down on the back of his neck.

The man in the panama hat was tired of the game. He scooped up the octopus and looked around for Edward.

'You sure you no like? Very nice to eat.' (Surprising his father and Anna at dinner that night. 'Dmmi cooked something special. I caught it.') He shook his head.

'Okay. Thank you for my supper.' The man in the hat began to walk to the far side of the beach, where the rocks were. The crowd broke up. Edward took his flippers off and followed at a distance, walking just at the edge of the water.

When the man got to the rocks he began slapping the octopus against the rocks, very hard. The first blow must have killed it. Slap, slap—it sounded like wet wash against a rock, like wet towels. In the showers at school, sometimes the prefects would slap the younger boys with towels. Slap. Slap. It was horrible, beastly. Why hadn't he swum back out with it and let it go? Edward knew what he was doing; he'd seen the fishermen sometimes, early in the morning, slapping octopus against the rocks and his German friend had explained why they did this. 'We are pounding the veal,' he said, 'they are pounding the octopus.' He had given Edward his address in Berlin. 'Maybe someday you will come and see me.' Edward wished Karl was there right now. He'd know what to do.

The man in the panama hat walked back along the beach, the dead octopus draped over his arm, the tentacles hanging down, not twisting now, limp, harmless.

One of the pretty Greek girls called to him and he stopped. While Edward watched the young man tore off a tentacle and threw it to the girl. She caught it, ('bravo, bravo' called the man in the panama hat), wound it around her wrist like some horrible bracelet, smiled and went on talking to her friend.

The two stupid English girls had gone up to the café for ice-cream or drinks. Their mother and father were asleep in their suncots farther along the beach. Edward, who was now very familiar with the kitchen of Dmitri and Fotula, thought that the mother's skin was turning the colour of a cockroach. He put on his flippers and glancing around to make sure no one was looking, he quickly stamped the sandcastle into the ground. Served them right. Then he turned and walking backwards, went into the sea. He wet his mask, spit on it, rubbed the spit around. He put the mask on, bit the mouthpiece of the snorkel, turned away from the beach and began to swim. He tried not to think about the dead octopus, about the tentacle torn off and draped over the girl's arm or the possibility of others out there somewhere, waiting.

And that night he had a strange dream. He is on one of the turquoise and cream buses, going into the port. There is a young man on the bus and perhaps an older man who isn't feeling very well. He turns around in his seat and in the seat behind Edward sees a Greek girl holding an octopus in her lap. He thinks, 'now I will get to see the colour of its eyes.' He suggests to the girl that she tickle it so that its eyes will open. She does this and it looks right at him—its eyes are a bright, bright blue. Then it begins to turn into a baby, quite a pretty round-faced baby, and it smiles. But as it opens its mouth wider Edward can see that as well as having a mouth and lips it has a hole, like a large siphon, at the back of its throat. It is very round, this hole, and fleshy, and the edges are moving slightly in and out.

Edward wakes up to the sound of Anna crying out in the other room.

ELISABETH HARVOR

❧

THERE GOES THE GROOM

Cold rainy spring with tulips in tight bud late into May—all of their tulip parts the same streamlined lizard green. It wasn't until the middle of June that the days at last turned so bizarrely southern that in the ravine at the end of the long park an army of parasites began to spin a haze of what looked like white fur on all the catkins. So that by the first day of summer whole groves of leafy trees were bridal with poison blossoms.

But then summer hurried by, as summer will, was over in no time, and one evening in the early fall I was standing dreaming at the kitchen sink while I was rinsing teacups and saucers under very hot water. Thinking of nothing. But then nothing was ever nothing, whenever I thought I was thinking of nothing I was always thinking of love, and after I'd finished shaking the drops from the cups and was drying them I discovered that there was something about the teacups' delicate warmth beaming through the tea-towel cloth that was making me imagine touching a man's face after I'd turned to him in bed in the dark. I had sexual thoughts often enough to make me feel lonely too, but there was nothing that could make me feel lonelier than this craving to touch a man's face. There were times when it could make me forget the world even more absolutely than thoughts of touching a man's body could. Or having a man crazy to touch my body. Sometimes when I was alone in the house and was carrying a basket of laundry up from the basement I'd even kiss and nuzzle the warm heap of pillowslips and shirts while at the same time I'd be feeling quite caressed myself, would feel as if a dry but warm hand had tucked a lock of my hair behind one of my ears while the hand's owner was looking into my eyes as if he could find the true answers to questions about tenderness there: Are you a serious person? Are you as serious about being with me like this as I need you to be?

But out in the real world, school was starting again and at the beginning of the second week of September there was a call from Mr Dunphy, Tom's French teacher, wanting to let me know that Tom was skipping French class.

It was a windy wet afternoon and so before I went up to Tom's room I drew my cardigan out of the hall closet. It felt damp, as if it had a haze of dew on it from the rain, but I pulled it on anyway as I made my way up the stairs, and even buttoned it up primly before I knocked on Tom's door.

Then six quick little knocks, fierce and parental.

'What,' said the trapped voice, sullen and wary.

'I need to talk to you for a minute.'

'So?'

'So could I come in?'

'So you could come in.'

I opened his door and went into his room and carefully sat on the end of his bed. But once I'd told him what Dunphy had said, he called me a failure.

'In what way?' I asked him. I spoke in a high warning voice. A precise voice. (Precise but frightened.) 'At least be explicit,' I said. 'You can't call a person a failure and then not come up with even one single way in which that person *is* a failure. . . .'

He gazed at me. A long careful look that made me think of Norman—Norman arranging his objections in an orderly row so that he could begin one of his bracing and accusatory pep talks. It always surprised me when either of our children resembled their parents. Most of their childhood they had seemed to be so free of the taint of heredity. This made it all the more shocking to encounter, in a hitherto innocent arrangement of nose and eyes and mouth, a smile that could rise to a pair of eyes that had decided to turn against me. 'Okay,' he said. 'You want me to be explicit, I'll be explicit—I consider you a total failure as a human being, is that explicit enough for you?'

My throat was all at once in so much pain that I had to leave him and go into my own room and sit down on my bed. I was in despair, not only about this moment, but about the future, the future as endless present, exactly like this present I was living through now. I looked at my untidy bedroom and saw it as an untidy bedroom in a too tiny (and too untidy) rented house. I looked at the wet window and was glad it wasn't sunny because sun always seemed, if I was feeling sad, infinitely sadder than rain. I gazed in a dull way down at the scatter of pencils and spilled pennies and bus tickets and a jar of Tiger Balm and a stump of pink lipstick rolled to a stop at the heel of a shoe, and I thought: And things won't get better.

But the next morning already there was a reprieve, and we lived through the following three weeks calmly enough, no reproaches, meeting mainly for meals, all of us busy out in the world. At least until the afternoon I came home to hear Tom out in the kitchen banging the cast-iron frying pan onto the stove. Before I'd even hung up my jacket, he was wailing at me, 'Where's the mustard, for fuck's sake? And don't you think we should at least *try* to get some organization in this crummy hell-hole? We're out of butter too, Mum! And there's this bowl of really mouldy guck at the back of the fridge. . . .'

Bruno, sitting at the dining-room table and cutting out a pink cardboard lion for a project at school, seemed to hate both of us. He dropped his scissors onto the floor and then scooped them up and in a rage pelted them at the sofa. 'Why is everybody always yelling in this house?' he yelled. 'Why can't a person ever get any peace?' And he stamped up the stairs in a fury and slammed his bedroom door.

Much later that night, when the house was quiet and Tom and Bruno were up in their beds and (I hoped) sound asleep, I dragged a garbage bag over to the fridge and scooped wilted things into it, feeling ashamed. I found bewildering items in clouded but once-clear plastic bags: a zucchini squash, its insides gone liquidly soft; a mildewed onion. Also two plastic containers of yogurt, never opened until now and growing grey fur. And iceberg lettuce in a forgotten brown paper bag and of such ancient vintage that it was leaking a fetid caramel-coloured sauce. I remembered that there was no system to my housework, no rules to keep down the dirt. Take the way I'd let anyone at all clomp into the main part of the house in big winter boots, the broken-off segments of slush-tread turning the kitchen floor muddy and repellent.

Hills of oranges backed hills of tomatoes, the tomatoes almost translucent in the hot fall sunshine. Beyond the fruit stalls, boxed-in small fields of red tulips. And beyond the tulips, sorting efficiently through a basket of apples, a sharp-faced but pretty grey-haired woman in mannish black slacks and a short-sleeved silk shirt the same red as the flowers. Bruno and Tom came to stand with quiet urgency beside me—they all at once seemed tall, quiet and tall—and then Tom whispered that the woman in the red shirt was a former girlfriend of Norman's. A woman named Dorie. He said in a low voice, 'We'll go get the salami and meet you out at the deli.'

I pretended to assess the tomatoes while I studied the woman picking out apples. She finally chose three and was then ready to walk fatly and briskly away. The leather strap of her handbag (bumping on her left hip) and the leather strap of her camera case (bumping on her right hip) gave her a dark leather X across her silky and competent back.

The lawyer, Douglas Walcott, was only in his late twenties, but above his pebbled red necktie he had adultly sorrowful eyes. Older man's eyes and an older man's tie. His fingers played on the raised silk pebbles as if they were the buttons on an unhappy accordion, and while I was telling him that I didn't personally want anything from my husband, all I wanted was fair child support for as long as my children were living at home, he watched me shrewdly, doubtfully.

Outside the tall windows, Ottawa stretched far below us, tiny and shining city. I told Walcott that when I'd told my husband I was going to begin divorce proceedings against him, he had surprised me by asking, 'Why can't things just stay as they are?'

'Are you sure your husband is not still hoping for a reconciliation?'

'Oh, no—I am sure he is not.'

'But if he won't give you the house and you don't get any money, what's to become of you?'

'I do have a job,' I primly reminded him.

'But you've already told me it doesn't pay very well. And isn't it only a part-time job? Didn't you say so yourself?'

'Yes.'

'And so why won't you take whatever help you can get?'

'Because I want to be free of him.'

'And if he sells the house?'

'Then I'll get a share of the profits—'

'Half, surely. That's what you're entitled to.'

'Yes. But not quite half. More like a third, I think.'

'Why is that?'

'Because he put some of his own money into it. He used his own money to build an apartment down in the basement and then we rented it out—'

'His own money?' he asked me sharply. 'In what way?'

'Money he had to borrow. From his mother.'

I could see him turning this over in his mind and feeling contempt for my husband—even more contempt than the contempt he must have felt he was required to feel as my legal adviser. But then he rallied, frowned down at my file. 'And you've worked where else? In a library. But not as a librarian, I gather. And in an art gallery out west, but that was years ago. And as a receptionist for a dentist, but that was only for a little over a year. And besides, none of these jobs could be called a trade or a profession. And so my advice to you is to go for the house. Failing that, you should most certainly get some kind of help. . . .'

'You don't think I'll be able to manage on my own?' I asked him, and I was shocked to hear how flirty my voice sounded. I was even smiling a little as I decided to ask him an even more dangerous question, I even held my right hand pressed to my heart to ask it: 'Do I look to *you* like a person who will *fail* ? '

He blushed, and so I had my terrible answer.

I could feel myself blushing too. But I was also all at once determined to show him—to show everyone—what a grand success I could be.

But at that same moment he stood. 'I want you to get something, some kind of protection. In case things don't always go well for you. . . .' Then he asked me to step out into the hall for a minute or two. 'I'd like to introduce you to my senior partner.'

I followed him out into the hallway and then waited while he went into an office with C. Miller MacLeod painted on its door. I could hear their lowered voices, part of a phrase now and then. From the older lawyer, not Walcott. I heard the older voice say '. . . talk some sense into her . . .' and as a sort of depressing background music to the older lawyer's voice I kept hearing Walcott's voice saying over and over: in case things don't always go well for you, in case things don't always go well for you, in case things don't always go well for you. . . . But then the older voice came closer and a door opened and C. Miller MacLeod stepped out into the hall, his eyes bright with inquiry as he said in a Scots voice, 'Good day, Mrs Gradzik.'

We shook hands. But I found myself feeling ill at ease under the clinical brutality of his gaze. He said, 'I suppose you might marry again.' But his eyes seemed to say he doubted it. And then he asked me how old I was, if I didn't mind his asking.

'Thirty-nine.'

'That old!' He gazed at me with a mournful candour. 'Statistically, the chances are against it then.'

My face burned as I boarded the elevator and then sank to the street. And when I described my feelings to my friend Deedee the next day at work I told her I'd walked away from that place wanting to enact the whole scene all over again, told her I'd wanted to speak to C. Miller MacLeod in a cold entertained voice, told her I'd wanted to tell him that I considered myself to be above and beyond statistics. 'I wanted to yell at him, "What in the name of God have statistics got to do with *me*?" '

Deedee was stapling piles of notes together, but she looked up at me to say, '"Everything!" God yelled back at Kristina Gradzik.'

When Tom and Bruno came home after seeing a movie with Norman the following Sunday night, the first thing Bruno said to me was, 'Dad has a new girlfriend.'

I asked him what she was like.

'She wears big earrings and she laughs a lot.'

Tom glanced at Bruno, then turned to me. His gaze was both cynical and imploring. 'Yeah,' he said. 'She's really nervous too. You get so you want to tell her to stuff a sock in her mouth or something.'

But Bruno seemed to be lost in some infatuated dream. He said, 'Her earrings are *immense*.' He looked feverish, exhausted. He said, 'What are those things that little kids are always running behind with a stick? You know—in nursery rhymes. . . .'

'Oh yeah,' said Tom. 'Hoops.'

I had a question, too. 'Did Dad tell you her name?'

Tom said he did. 'But now I can't remember it.'

Bruno looked up from the book he was reading. Or was pretending to read. 'I remember it,' he whispered. 'Her name is Elaine.'

My divorce hearing was set for early November. Norman would not need to put in an appearance, Walcott said. But I should bring along a friend for moral support. I asked Deedee if she could come with me, and she said she could. But she made it clear that she was in total agreement with Walcott: Please don't be a masochist, please try to get yourself something, please don't be a fool.

Walcott called me the night before I was to go to the courthouse. 'I have just one last request. One last thing I want you to do for yourself. I want you to ask your husband to give you a dollar a year. It's vital that you get it, especially in circumstances such as yours. Because what it'll mean is we can haul him into court if ever you should have the misfortune to find yourself ill or destitute. We'll have some claim on him. And if he won't willingly help you, we can garnishee his wages. So give him a call tonight and ask him to meet you at court tomorrow morning so he can tell the judge he'll pay you the annual dollar.'

I said I would. I was all at once beginning to suspect that Walcott had been right all along and that my future was quicksand. I pictured a dollar with the pale-green queen on it and I felt afraid.

I called Norman first thing after supper. But he wouldn't commit himself on the phone. 'I'll meet you tomorrow morning at the courthouse. On my way to work.' And it seemed to me that he said the word 'work' as if only he—in all of the work-addicted Western world—truly knew what real work was. But then he had something else to tell me. He'd had a letter from my mother, a response to his news that we were getting divorced. 'A letter of support' was how he described it, a letter from Loo—because that's what he called her—telling him that I was a hard person and that she sent him her love.

I said, 'What a bitch.'

Yes, he said in a sober but contented voice—he, too, had been somewhat taken aback by it. 'It was fairly savage,' he said. 'About you, my darling. Not that I didn't agree with ninety per cent of it.'

'What I want to know is, did it make you think less of Loo?'

'To tell you the truth, my darling, I never thought all that much of Loo in the first place.'

Winter was already on its way the next morning, the darkish early November morning of my divorce, and the upstairs hallway was cold but steamy from everyone's shower. I stared out at the dim day as I pulled on my most narrow black skirt, my black nylons. The blouse I buttoned myself into was a pink silk with weakened pleats in its sleeves. I fitted my feet into my old gold party pumps—the ones that looked as if they'd had Celtic designs tattooed on their toes. They were utterly wrong, anyone could see that, but I did not have the energy to kick them off and work my feet into more appropriate footgear. My head hurt me, and while I was brushing my hair my eyes started to fill. I didn't feel sad, only a bit sick and dizzy. I felt I must concentrate very hard in order not to disgrace myself in some unprecedented way in the courtroom.

Deedee was waiting for me in the downstairs corridor of the courthouse on a long churchy oak pew—the only calm one in a long row of quietly desperate strangers. Her lips were chapped, lipstickless. She had pulled on one of her husband's old parkas and was wearing her hair loose and her Navajo earrings. She didn't seem to be entirely awake yet. I was so grateful to her for getting up early to come to be with me that I whispered, 'I don't know how I'll ever be able to thank you for everything.'

Out of the side of her mouth she said, 'Don't go getting all emotional now—Norman'll see you. He's here already, he just went to get himself a coffee.'

Norman came along the hallway at that very moment, looking as if he'd had to stop and lean his head against a tree on his way to the courthouse and throw up. He spoke coldly to Deedee, as if he despised her for being his wife's loyal friend. Then he turned his cold attention to me. 'You're the one who wanted the clean break,' he told me. 'And so there won't be any dollar.' He stood for a moment, holding the empty paper cup in his hand. His tiepin was stuck into an expensive silk tie the dull pink of a snout. It made him look elegant, adenoidal. He looked like a man who would always be dapper. He crushed his paper cup in one hand, poked it into a pocket. 'It's better for you this way, believe me.'

Then he fled down the hallway.

The atmosphere in the courtroom seemed to me to be the atmosphere of a solemn nightmare—the air charged with a kind of well-bred, nervous shame. And even though the court clerk read out a document that proclaimed that my husband had said I was a good mother and would be the one to be getting the custody of the children, I bowed my head as if he had read out the opposite.

Once I had got my decree nisi, I could tell that Deedee was in a fury about the dollar all over again, because after we'd closed the courtroom's heavy door behind us, she yanked her parka hood rebukingly up.

In an attempt to appease her, I tried a little joke. 'Decree nisi. Sounds Japanese.'

She stared straight ahead.

'This corridor smells exactly like the corridors in my old high school. Marble halls and Dustbane.'

No response. Only the sound of our footsteps, walking fast.

'Don't worry about Norman not helping me out. If ever I'm in any kind of real trouble, he'll help me out, I know he will. . . .'

'You can say it, friend, I don't have to believe it.'

'He'll give me a lecture, but he'll also give me the money. . . .'

Her not answering was like footsteps:

no answer

no answer

no answer

no answer

We opened another heavy door and stepped out into the city's arctic air and the wind tore at us. Even inside my heavy winter coat I could feel it nosing its way up my bloated silk sleeves. But now Deedee was talking again, now she was saying that what was really dumber than dumb was for lawyers to ask ex-husbands to give their ex-wives a dollar a year. What man wouldn't smell a rat, she said, when all he had to pay his ex-wife was one pathetic little dollar? Why not make it a sum that didn't sound like a scam? But then she seemed to tire of the subject because what she said next was, 'Let's go to one of the little cafés down by the market, get ourselves some hot soup,' and so we left her car where it was and walked fast toward Rideau Street, into the tearful wind.

Summer sounds tinkled in the clear winter air—wind chimes knocking against one another in the polar breeze of the entrance to the café we settled on—and after the waitress had brought us our soup, Deedee tore open a croissant and mashed butter into it, shoved half of it into her mouth, then painfully swallowed it to say, 'You know what you should be doing? You should be thinking of ways to keep the wolf from the door. . . .' And then she told me that I reminded her of a parable. 'Or is it a fable? You know the one. The one about the grasshopper and the cricket. Isn't it the cricket who only wants to have a good time? And then ends up dying of starvation in the middle of a blizzard?'

'I don't only want to have a good time,' I said. I hardly even want to have a good time at *all*, I thought. I spread my cold fingers out over the steam from my soup. But I knew that I also loved money, or at least loved the things that money could buy. Loved money—not to hoard, but to squander. Knew that if I had money I'd become an out-of-control spendthrift.

Knew that I loved embroidered batiste blouses and exquisite underthings in plum silk and peach silk, knew that I loved rare scents and creams. I pictured a tall-windowed room furnished with rugs that were expensively threadbare, historic, a room equipped with a low fire and flowers, a lovely red room with low-hung and small gloomy landscapes that would announce my unassuming and perfect good taste. And yet at the same time that I was longing for the glamour of money, I was also longing for the glamour of poverty. I longed for poverty the way I longed for pain at the dentist's. I wanted it to happen, and to happen quickly, because once it happened it would be over and done with, and then I wouldn't be in pain any more. And yet I knew that this was flawed thinking; dental pain was brief pain, and poverty pain was long pain—poverty pain just kept compounding itself, like a bank certificate's interest. 'I do worry,' I said. 'I worry all the time.' But then I only found myself thinking of how happy I was to make my escape from my marriage and of the way that Norman, at family gatherings, used to too easily be persuaded to get up to make a little speech. Not quite an endless little speech, but quite endless enough. How smug he used to look then, his eyes closed as he basked in the sound of his own platitudes, feeding on them. And then I remembered the way, when he had to get up at night to go to the bathroom, he would pull on his socks and then tuck his pyjama legs into them. How diabolically methodical that had seemed to me to be. I was jealous, I suppose, because I was too impulsive to bother to kick my feet into my slippers and so would invariably choose to run over the chilly floors barefoot and come down with a cold.

I told Deedee about the letter my mother had sent to Norman, and about the way Norman called my mother Loo. 'But then she's always adored him, he's her kind of guy. And do you know what else? The whole time he was telling me about her letter he kept calling me "my darling."'

'Bet he'll keep in touch with her after the divorce,' said Deedee, narrowing her eyes to look out at the bright windy street. 'Send her little presents, little love notes, he's the type. Anything to make *you* look bad, my darling—'

I smiled at her. I was feeling expansive. 'And what do you think these little love notes will say?'

'Oh, they'll be profound,' she said airily. '"Dearest Loo, how are *you*?"'

We laughed, and I found myself thinking how really enjoyable it was, getting divorced. It was pleasant. This whole lunch was pleasant. It seemed to me that Deedee and I had never before had such a pleasant conversation.

But now Deedee was quoting someone, some futurologist she'd heard on her car radio on her way to the courthouse. 'And according to him, things will only get worse and worse: war, famine, pestilence.'

The pleasant day blew away.

'Don't be a fool,' said Deedee. 'And please don't sit there looking so phoney and noble—it doesn't become you. . . .'

But she was wrong about me. I believed in the worst, always, and always believed it would happen to me. Or did I? Didn't I also believe just the opposite? Whenever I tried to answer a magazine quiz about personality types I always scored high for opposing qualities. I was an optimist, but also a pessimist. I had a great need for solitude, but I was also an extrovert. I was poorly organized, but also a compulsive. 'Don't worry so much,' I said, and as I said it I was struck by how much I sounded like Tom and Bruno when they were about to do some ill-advised thing. I even went so far as to say what they always said: 'Everything will be fine.'

After we'd closed ourselves into the stale cold of Deedee's car she asked me if Norman had a girl.

'The boys say he does—a hyperactive woman whose name is Elaine.'

Snow started to fall heavily just before noon on New Year's Eve, and by four-thirty the storm had been upgraded to a blizzard. While Tom was over at the stove making himself cocoa, I stood at the kitchen window feeding myself pretzels and looking out at the big wind in the trees. I remembered making cocoa for myself when I was a child—the pleasure of lifting the wrinkled disk of grey cocoa skin up from the top of the steaming hot cocoa with a fork.

Then it was time to bring the leftover goose and cold cooked apples and prunes out to the round table in the living room. Tom and I served everything onto the heavy blue-leafed pottery plates and then I called Bruno.

He came to the table with a riddle for us. 'What did Napoleon keep up his sleevies?'

We tried to guess, but we couldn't.

'His armies!'

'Moaning and gnashing of teeth,' said Tom. But I suspected he'd be brooding about it all through the meal. And, sure enough, while I was serving the apple cake with one of the silver spatulas I'd been given as a bride, he tilted back in his chair to say to Bruno, 'Okay, Herr Gradzik. Okay, mein Herr, vhat did Napoleon keep opp his sleevies?'

'Apart from his armies?'

'*Ja.*'

Bruno looked over at me. But I had to tell him that I was no good at these things.

'Do you give up?'

We gave up.

'His Elbas.'

'That's extremely clever, Tom.'

Bruno said, 'I don't get it.'

Tom told him the story of Napoleon's years of exile. 'For a while he was on the island of Elba, but then he was exiled to the island of Ste Hélène. And that's where he died, isn't it, Mum? On the island of Ste Hélène?'

'One of the two, but I'm not sure which one.'

Tom wanted to know if it was just old age that he died from.

'I think they think now that he may have been poisoned. It seems to me that I read somewhere that they dug up his body and the whole corpse was green. . . .' And again I thought of the green queen on the dollar.

The next day, just before lunch, Norman came to pick the boys up for New Year's brunch and a movie, and I spent the afternoon washing my hair and going to the living-room window every twenty minutes or so. What was I looking for? I didn't know. The house seemed tauntingly empty, but ordinarily this emptiness wouldn't have bothered me at all; ordinarily I'd be overjoyed to have the place all to myself—ordinarily there would be so many things I'd want to do, left to my own devices: narcissistic, self-indulgent private things. I could make love to myself or read from the book I kept hidden under the sweaters up in my sweater drawer—a wine paperback with raised silver letters that looked quilted, bloated, and on its back cover two bold silver questions: A DARK PERVERSION? OR IMAGINATIVE LOVE PLAY? I could even wander around the house in the nude if I felt so inclined—something I could never do when the boys were at home—or turn the radio up loud and dance to it. But I didn't seem to want to do any of these things, I seemed to expect myself to be incredibly ladylike, to set a good example to myself for the new year.

Tom and Bruno came back just after dark. They clomped into the house, pushing and poking at one another, buoyed up by some joke they had just told or been told, and as they lunged past me, Tom said in a low voice, 'All systems on alert, Madam Mother—the Father is coming in to have a brief word with you. . . .' And then I could hear the two of them tramping up the stairs and snickering to each other, as if the words 'the Father' and 'brief word' could not possibly belong in the same conversation. But their warning made me scuttle up the stairs right behind them to fix myself up—not for Norman, but just so he wouldn't be able to tell himself I looked drab. I could already hear him neatly kicking the snow off his boots—six precise little taps against the outside lower doorstep. I breathlessly peered at myself in the tall mirror in the upper hallway and saw that my blouse was lopsided. I tucked it back into my trousers and brushed my hair fast but then took my time going back down the stairs.

Norman was already standing in the centre of the living room and was sheepishly smiling up at me as I came walking down. He had grown his beard again and it was now so curly and black it made him look darkly cherubic. Night snow sparkled in it. He heeled off his overshoes. 'Kris, I wanted to speak to you privately for a moment.'

'Fine,' I said in a cool voice. 'Go right ahead.'

He took off his coat, then went to hang it up in the vestibule, and as he came back into the living room again I couldn't help thinking: How handsome he looks! In his pale-lilac shirt! And his tie. He had always had such an instinct for picking the really stunning ones. This one was in muted army and mud colours, a new variation on one of the old hand-blocked designs.

'Kris—I'm getting married again.'

I was amazed, and to hide my amazement I quickly said, 'Is her name Elaine?'

But the question seemed to make him uneasy. He said, 'Her name is Dorie.'

'Oh,' I said. And then: 'I think Tom and Bruno pointed her out to me at the market once. She was buying apples—'

His left eye seemed to flinch at this, seemed to say: Naturally you would want to be ironical. Out of bitterness—or out of envy perhaps—but I'm the one who's getting married again, I'm the one life will get better for.

I asked him when the actual ceremony was to be.

'On the sixteenth of June. Then we'll be going to Europe for three weeks. Dorie has relatives over in Scotland, and one of her Scottish uncles owns a place down in Spain. . . .'

I wondered if he was at all remembering our own time in Spain, two weeks in a little town called Palamos. On the Costa Brava.

'He barely even uses the damn thing and so she's free to borrow it any time she wants to. A hacienda, I suppose you could call it. On the Costa Brava. . . .'

I wanted to ask him more questions. Which was odd, because ordinarily I couldn't wait for him to go. Ordinarily his going would fill me with the most wonderful euphoria. And ordinarily Norman, seeing how much I really wanted him to go, would inflict his presence on me just a little bit longer. He would pull on his coat, but then think of some other quick thing he needed to tell me. He would hesitate in the vestibule, then come back into the living room again and take off his coat. And yet he would look very serious as he opened up a whole new area for discussion, as if the last thing in the world he wanted to do was thwart me. But this time, sensing how much my curiosity was aroused—how much I wanted him to stay, for once—he seemed eager to be off.

I stood at the window and watched the military swing of the squared shoulders of his black coat as he walked down the snow-packed path to the corral where his car was parked.

There goes the groom.

(I was trying to get my euphoria back.)

But footsteps were coming down the dark stairs behind me. It was Tom. As he passed by me, he said in a low voice, 'Maybe it's better for you not to stand at the window right now, Mum—Dorie might see you. She came in the car with him.'

'Oh,' I said, startled. And I stepped fast to one side, hid myself behind the protective weave of the curtain. But from my new vantage point I could still watch Norman's headlights backing bumpily away in the clear winter night.

I could hear Tom out in the kitchen too, making himself toast, the rasp of the knife over the dry toasted bread.

I walked down to the kitchen, stood for a moment in the doorway. 'Thanks for telling me not to stand at the window.'

He said sure, no problem.

'Did Dad tell you his news? That he's planning to marry Dorie?'

'So *that's* it. All afternoon I could tell he had some big thing up his sleeve.'

'Opp his sleevies?'

But neither of us laughed.

'Apparently Dorie has an uncle who owns a place over in Spain, on the Costa Brava, half the time he doesn't even bother to use it, so maybe you and Bruno'll get a chance to stay there some time when Dad and Dorie are over there on vacation.'

'Big deal,' Tom, with dark loyalty, answered.

But in the end he would want to go, it would be only human to want to go to Spain, Bruno would want to go too, and I pictured my two sons stretched out on a long and spectacular beach on the Costa Brava, two young men by the ocean, growing away from me even as they were sunbathing, and possibly even sunbathing on the same beach Norman and I had christened our own little beach, half an hour from Palamos and so long ago, one of the instructive little tricks irony would play with time and geography. Or at the very least they would lie on that same Spanish coast and under that same Spanish sun.

But then I saw the ocean as a darker ocean, more Swedish than Spanish, and a plump-thighed Dorie was awkwardly dispensing food from a basket, and the conversation she was trying to keep alive with Tom and Bruno was overly polite, trivial, and Norman was making strained and obvious little jokes, and the boys didn't even want to be in Spain in the first place, they only wanted to be back at home with their friends.

But I wondered if Deedee had really meant it when she'd called me a masochist, and after a few moments I went up to my room and slid open the drawer where I kept the book on sado-masochism hidden. I had underlined something in it, months ago, a line or two in an excerpt from a book called *Eros, The Meaning of My Life*, and now I wanted to see what it was that I had found so thrilling. I found the underlined lines almost at once, and although it seemed to me now that they weren't all that shocking, or at least not all that shocking when compared with so much of the rest of the book (I realized that I'd been expecting and even dreading words that would convey some brutal pleasure anticipated), a quick glance told me that they still had the power to make me feel shame: 'I felt the stimulus powerfully in my private parts. I felt the pulse beat of my raging blood hammering in my vulva. I felt close to fainting and almost threatened to sink to the floor, overpowered by the excitement. . . .' And as I stood reading them again it occurred to me that they must have evoked feelings from deepest childhood—the almost unbearable sexual excitement of a game I had played with my brothers when we had all been so young that we hadn't called the game Husband and Wife but Father and Mother.

But I had no sooner fitted the book back into its drawer than I was imagining these particular words being lifted out of context—someone was reading them aloud to someone—and I was all at once afraid of how laughable they (and therefore I) would seem, and at this same moment I made myself imagine myself old—perhaps ill, perhaps destitute; I might even be dying or was even possibly already (newly) dead, and Tom and Bruno were going through my 'effects.' Because wasn't that what people's possessions were called, after they were dead? Their effects? The effects that would, one way or another, affect others? I saw one son, then the other son, pick up my clandestine book. I saw them reading the damning words—*raging, hammering, vulva*—I saw them exchange a bewildered look. But is this possible? Our little mother?

Of course I could see to it that this didn't happen, could carry the book down to the garbage can this very minute, could shove it deep down under four or five hats of grapefruit, the toppled earthy damp mounds of coffee grounds, crushed eggshells. And if even that didn't feel like protection enough, I could do worse: tear off the cover, tear the quilted silver letters into bloated silver bits, rip out all the pages, pour coffee down on them, smear them with jam.

But I couldn't do it, I didn't want to throw the book away, I was attached to it, I planned to read it again.

I instead went into the bathroom to look at myself in the mirror. I wanted to see what my face would have to tell me. I thought: So it's really over then, something final has happened. But I knew I shouldn't lie to myself. From now on, there would be complications. From now on, whenever Norman brought the boys home after dinner and a movie there would always be the possibility of another face there, and Norman walking that tightrope between the two faces. The face in the house. The face in the car window. I saw it as lost and white, watching me from the other side.

MARGARET ATWOOD

❧

BLUEBEARD'S EGG

Sally stands at the kitchen window, waiting for the sauce she's reducing to come to a simmer, looking out. Past the garage the lot sweeps downwards, into the ravine; it's a wilderness there, of bushes and branches and what Sally thinks of as vines. It was her idea to have a kind of terrace, built of old railroad ties, with wild flowers growing between them, but Edward says he likes it the way it is. There's a playhouse down at the bottom, near the fence; from here she can just see the roof. It has nothing to do with Edward's kids, in their earlier incarnations, before Sally's time; it's more ancient than that, and falling apart. Sally would like it cleared away. She thinks drunks sleep in it, the men who live under the bridges down there, who occasionally wander over the fence (which is broken down, from where they step on it) and up the hill, to emerge squinting like moles into the light of Sally's well-kept back lawn.

Off to the left is Ed, in his windbreaker; it's officially spring, Sally's blue scylla is in flower, but it's chilly for this time of year. Ed's windbreaker is an old one he won't throw out; it still says WILDCATS, relic of some team he was on in high school, an era so prehistoric Sally can barely imagine it; though picturing Ed at high school is not all that difficult. Girls would have had crushes on him, he would have been unconscious of it; things like that don't change. He's puttering around the rock garden now; some of the rocks stick out too far and are in danger of grazing the side of Sally's Peugeot, on its way to the garage, and he's moving them around. He likes doing things like that, puttering, humming to himself. He won't wear work gloves, though she keeps telling him he could squash his fingers.

Watching his bent back with its frayed, poignant lettering, Sally dissolves; which is not infrequent with her. *My darling Edward*, she thinks. *Edward Bear, of little brain. How I love you.* At times like this she feels very protective of him.

Sally knows for a fact that dumb blondes were loved, not because they were blondes, but because they were dumb. It was their helplessness and confusion that were so sexually attractive, once; not their hair. It wasn't false, the rush of tenderness men must have felt for such women. Sally understands it.

For it must be admitted: Sally is in love with Ed because of his stupidity, his monumental and almost energetic stupidity: energetic, because Ed's stupidity is not passive. He's no mere blockhead; you'd have to be working at it to be that stupid. Does it make Sally feel smug, or smarter than he is, or even smarter than she really is herself? No; on the contrary, it makes her humble. It fills her with wonder that the world can contain such marvels as Ed's colossal and endearing thickness. He is just so *stupid.* Every time he gives her another piece of evidence, another tile that she can glue into place in the vast mosaic of his stupidity she's continually piecing together, she wants to hug him, and often does; and he is so stupid he can never figure out what for.

Because Ed is so stupid he doesn't even know he's stupid. He's a child of luck, a third son who, armed with nothing but a certain feeble-minded amiability, manages to make it through the forest with all its witches and traps and pitfalls and end up with the princess, who is Sally, of course. It helps that he's handsome.

On good days she sees his stupidity as innocence, lamb-like, shining with the light of (for instance) green daisied meadows in the sun. (When Sally starts thinking this way about Ed, in terms of the calendar art from the service-station washrooms of her childhood, dredging up images of a boy with curly golden hair, his arm thrown around the neck of an Irish setter— a notorious brainless beast, she reminds herself—she knows she is sliding over the edge, into a ghastly kind of sentimentality, and that she must stop at once, or Ed will vanish, to be replaced by a stuffed facsimile, useful for little else but an umbrella stand. Ed is a real person, with a lot more to him than these simplistic renditions allow for; which sometimes worries her.) On bad days though, she sees his stupidity as wilfulness, a stubborn determination to shut things out. His obtuseness is a wall, within which he can go about his business, humming to himself, while Sally, locked outside, must hack her way through the brambles with hardly so much as a transparent raincoat between them and her skin.

Why did she choose him (or, to be precise, as she tries to be with herself and sometimes is even out loud, *hunt him down*), when it's clear to everyone she had other options? To Marylynn, who is her best though most recent friend, she's explained it by saying she was spoiled when young by reading too many Agatha Christie murder mysteries, of the kind in which the clever and witty heroine passes over the equally clever and witty first-lead male, who's helped solve the crime, in order to marry the second-lead male, the stupid one, the one who would have been arrested and condemned and executed if it hadn't been for her cleverness. Maybe this is how she sees Ed: if it weren't for her, his blundering too-many-thumbs kindness would get him into all sorts of quagmires, all sorts of sink-holes he'd never be able to get himself out of, and then he'd be done for.

'Sink-hole' and 'quagmire' are not flattering ways of speaking about other women, but this is what is at the back of Sally's mind; specifically, Ed's two previous wives. Sally didn't exactly extricate him from their clutches. She's never even met the first one, who moved to the west coast fourteen years ago and sends Christmas cards, and the second one was middle-aged and already in the act of severing herself from Ed before Sally came along. (For Sally, 'middle-aged' means anyone five years older than she is. It has always meant this. She applies it only to women, however. She doesn't think of Ed as middle-aged, although the gap between them is considerably more than five years.)

Ed doesn't know what happened with these marriages, what went wrong. His protestations of ignorance, his refusal to discuss the finer points, is frustrating to Sally, because she would like to hear the whole story. But it's also cause for anxiety: if he doesn't know what happened with the other two, maybe the same thing could be happening with her and he doesn't know about that, either. Stupidity like Ed's can be a health hazard, for other people. What if he wakes up one day and decides that she isn't the true bride after all, but the false one? Then she will be put into a barrel stuck full of nails and rolled downhill, endlessly, while he is sitting in yet another bridal bed, drinking champagne. She remembers the brand name, because she bought it herself. Champagne isn't the sort of finishing touch that would occur to Ed, though he enjoyed it enough at the time.

But outwardly Sally makes a joke of all this. 'He doesn't *know*,' she says to Marylynn, laughing a little, and they shake their heads. If it were them, they'd know, all right. Marylynn is in fact divorced, and she can list every single thing that went wrong, item by item. After doing this, she adds that her divorce was one of the best things that ever happened to her. 'I was just a nothing before,' she says. 'It made me pull myself together.'

Sally, looking across the kitchen table at Marylynn, has to agree that she is far from being a nothing now. She started out re-doing people's closets, and has worked that up into her own interior-design firm. She does the houses of the newly rich, those who lack ancestral furniture and the confidence to be shabby, and who wish their interiors to reflect a personal taste they do not in reality possess.

'What they want are mausoleums,' Marylynn says, 'or hotels,' and she cheerfully supplies them. 'Right down to the ash-trays. Imagine having someone else pick out your ash-trays for you.'

By saying this, Marylynn lets Sally know that she's not including her in that category, though Sally did in fact hire her, at the very first, to help with a few details around the house. It was Marylynn who redesigned the wall of closets in the master bedroom and who found Sally's massive Chinese mahogany table, which cost her another seven hundred dollars to have stripped. But it turned out to be perfect, as Marylynn said it would. Now she's dug up a nineteenth-century keyhole desk, which both she and Sally know will be exactly right for the bay-windowed alcove off the living room. 'Why do you need it?' Ed said in his puzzled way. 'I thought you worked in your study.' Sally admitted this, but said they could keep the telephone bills in it, which appeared to satisfy him. She knows exactly what she needs it for: she needs it to sit at, in something flowing, backlit by the morning sunlight, gracefully dashing off notes. She saw a 1940s advertisement for coffee like this once, and the husband was standing behind the chair, leaning over, with a worshipful expression on his face.

Marylynn is the kind of friend Sally does not have to explain any of this to, because it's assumed between them. Her intelligence is the kind Sally respects.

Marylynn is tall and elegant, and makes anything she is wearing seem fashionable. Her hair is prematurely grey and she leaves it that way. She goes in for loose blouses in cream-coloured silk, and eccentric scarves gathered from interesting shops and odd corners of the world, thrown carelessly around her neck and over one shoulder. (Sally has tried this toss in the mirror, but it doesn't work.) Marylynn has a large collection of unusual shoes; she says they're unusual because her feet are so big, but Sally knows better. Sally, who used to think of herself as pretty enough and now thinks of herself as doing quite well for her age, envies Marylynn her bone structure, which will serve her well when the inevitable happens.

Whenever Marylynn is coming to dinner, as she is today—she's bringing the desk, too—Sally takes especial care with her clothes and makeup. Marylynn, she knows, is her real audience for such things, since no changes she effects in herself seem to affect Ed one way or the other, or even to register with him. 'You look fine to me,' is all he says, no matter how she really looks. (But does she want him to see her more clearly, or not? Most likely not. If he did he would notice the incipient wrinkles, the small pouches of flesh that are not quite there yet, the network forming beneath her eyes. It's better as it is.)

Sally has repeated this remark of Ed's to Marylynn, adding that he said it the day the Jacuzzi overflowed because the smoke alarm went off, because an English muffin she was heating to eat in the bathtub got stuck in the toaster, and she had to spend an hour putting down newspaper and mopping up, and only had half an hour to dress for a dinner they were going to. 'Really I looked like the wrath of God,' said Sally. These days she finds herself repeating to Marylynn many of the things Ed says: the stupid things. Marylynn is the only one of Sally's friends she has confided in to this extent.

'Ed is cute as a button,' Marylynn said. 'In fact, he's just like a button: he's so bright and shiny. If he were mine, I'd get him bronzed and keep him on the mantelpiece.'

Marylynn is even better than Sally at concocting formulations for Ed's particular brand of stupidity, which can irritate Sally: coming from herself, this sort of comment appears to her indulgent and loving, but from Marylynn it borders on the patronizing. So then she sticks up for Ed, who is by no means stupid about everything. When you narrow it down, there's only one area of life he's hopeless about. The rest of the time he's intelligent enough, some even say brilliant: otherwise, how could he be so successful?

Ed is a heart man, one of the best, and the irony of this is not lost on Sally: who could possibly know less about the workings of hearts, real hearts, the kind symbolized by red satin surrounded by lace and topped by pink bows, than Ed? Hearts with arrows in them. At the same time, the fact that he's a heart man is a large part of his allure. Women corner him on sofas, trap him in bay-windows at cocktail parties, mutter to him in confidential voices at dinner parties. They behave this way right in front of Sally, under her very nose, as if she's invisible, and Ed lets them do it. This would never happen if he were in banking or construction.

As it is, everywhere he goes he is beset by sirens. They want him to fix their hearts. Each of them seems to have a little something wrong—a murmur, a whisper. Or they faint a lot and want him to tell them why. This is always what the conversations are about, according to Ed, and Sally believes it. Once she'd wanted it herself, that mirage. What had she invented for him, in the beginning? A heavy heart, that beat too hard after meals. And he'd been so sweet, looking at her with those stunned brown eyes of his, as if her heart were the genuine topic, listening to her gravely as if he'd never heard any of this twaddle before, advising her to drink less coffee. And she'd felt such triumph, to have carried off her imposture, pried out of him that minuscule token of concern.

Thinking back on this incident makes her uneasy, now that she's seen her own performance repeated so many times, including the hand placed lightly on the heart, to call attention of course to the breasts. Some of these women have been within inches of getting Ed to put his head down on their chests, right there in Sally's living room. Watching all this out of the corners of her eyes while serving the liqueurs, Sally feels the Aztec rise within her. *Trouble with your heart? Get it removed,* she thinks. *Then you'll have no more problems.*

Sometimes Sally worries that she's a nothing, the way Marylynn was before she got a divorce and a job. But Sally isn't a nothing; therefore, she doesn't need a divorce to stop being one. And she's always had a job of some sort; in fact she has one now. Luckily Ed has no objection; he doesn't have much of an objection to anything she does.

Her job is supposed to be full-time, but in effect it's part-time, because Sally can take a lot of the work away and do it at home, and, as she says, with one arm tied behind her back. When Sally is being ornery, when she's playing the dull wife of a fascinating heart man—she does this with people she can't be bothered with—she says she works in a bank, nothing important. Then she watches their eyes dismiss her. When, on the other hand, she's trying to impress, she says she's in PR In reality she runs the in-house organ for a trust company, a medium-sized one. This is a thin magazine, nicely printed, which is supposed to make the employees feel that some of the boys are doing worthwhile things out there and are human beings as well. It's still the boys, though the few women in anything resembling key positions are wheeled out regularly, bloused and suited and smiling brightly, with what they hope will come across as confidence rather than aggression.

This is the latest in a string of such jobs Sally has held over the years: comfortable enough jobs that engage only half of her cogs and wheels, and that end up leading nowhere. Technically she's second-in-command: over her is a man who wasn't working out in management, but who couldn't be fired because his wife was related to the chairman of the board. He goes out for long alcoholic lunches and plays a lot of golf, and Sally runs the show. This man gets the official credit for everything Sally does right, but the senior executives in the company take Sally aside when no one is looking and tell her what a great gal she is and what a whiz she is at holding up her end.

The real pay-off for Sally, though, is that her boss provides her with an endless supply of anecdotes. She dines out on stories about his dim-wittedness and pomposity, his lobotomized suggestions about what the two of them should cook up for the magazine; *the organ*, as she says he always calls it. 'He says we need some fresh blood to perk up the organ,' Sally says, and the heart men grin at her. 'He actually said that?' Talking like this about her boss would be reckless—you never know what might get back to him, with the world as small as it is—if Sally were afraid of losing her job, but she isn't. There's an unspoken agreement between her and this man: they both know that if she goes, he goes, because who else would put up with him? Sally might angle for his job, if she were stupid enough to disregard his family connections, if she coveted the trappings of power. But she's just fine where she is. Jokingly, she says she's reached her level of incompetence. She says she suffers from fear of success.

Her boss is white-haired, slender, and tanned, and looks like an English gin ad. Despite his vapidity he's outwardly distinguished, she allows him that. In truth she pampers him outrageously, indulges him, covers up for him at every turn, though she stops short of behaving like a secretary: she doesn't bring him coffee. They both have a secretary who does that anyway. The one time he made a pass at her, when he came in from lunch visibly reeling, Sally was kind about it.

Occasionally, though not often, Sally has to travel in connection with her job. She's sent off to places like Edmonton, where they have a branch. She interviews the boys at the middle and senior levels; they have lunch, and the boys talk about ups and downs in oil or the slump in the real-estate market. Then she gets taken on tours of shopping plazas under construction. It's always windy, and grit blows into her face. She comes back to home base and writes a piece on the youthfulness and vitality of the West.

She teases Ed, while she packs, saying she's going off for a rendezvous with a dashing financier or two. Ed isn't threatened; he tells her to enjoy herself, and she hugs him and tells him how much she will miss him. He's so dumb it doesn't occur to him she might not be joking. In point of fact, it would have been quite possible for Sally to have had an affair, or at least a one- or two-night stand, on several of these occasions: she knows when those chalk lines are being drawn, when she's being dared to step over them. But she isn't interested in having an affair with anyone but Ed.

She doesn't eat much on the planes; she doesn't like the food. But on the return trip, she invariably saves the pre-packaged parts of the meal, the cheese in its plastic wrap, the miniature chocolate bar, the bag of pretzels. She ferrets them away in her purse. She thinks of them as supplies, that she may need if she gets stuck in a strange airport, if they have to change course because of snow or fog, for instance. All kinds of things could happen, although they never have. When she gets home she takes the things from her purse and throws them out.

Outside the window Ed straightens up and wipes his earth-smeared hands down the sides of his pants. He begins to turn, and Sally moves back from the window so he won't see that she's watching. She doesn't like it to be too obvious. She shifts her attention to the sauce: it's in the second stage of a *sauce suprême*, which will make all the difference to the chicken. When Sally was learning this sauce, her cooking instructor quoted one of the great chefs, to the effect that the chicken was merely a canvas. He meant as in painting, but Sally, in an undertone to the woman next to her, turned it around. 'Mine's canvas anyway, sauce or no sauce,' or words to that effect.

Gourmet cooking was the third night course Sally has taken. At the moment she's on her fifth, which is called *Forms of Narrative Fiction*. It's half reading and half writing assignments—the instructor doesn't believe you can understand an art form without at least trying it yourself—and Sally purports to be enjoying it. She tells her friends she takes night courses to keep her brain from atrophying, and her friends find this amusing: whatever else may become of Sally's brain, they say, they don't see atrophying as an option. Sally knows better, but in any case there's always room for improvement. She may have begun taking the courses in the belief that this would make her more interesting to Ed, but she soon gave up on that idea: she appears to be neither more nor less interesting to Ed now than she was before.

Most of the food for tonight is already made. Sally tries to be well organized: the overflowing Jacuzzi was an aberration. The cold watercress soup with walnuts is chilling in the refrigerator, the chocolate mousse ditto. Ed, being Ed, prefers meatloaf to sweetbreads with pine nuts, butterscotch pudding made from a package to chestnut purée topped with whipped cream. (Sally burnt her fingers peeling the chestnuts. She couldn't do it the easy way and buy it tinned.) Sally says Ed's preference for this type of food comes from being pre-programmed by hospital cafeterias when he was younger: show him a burned sausage and a scoop of instant mashed potatoes and he salivates. So it's only for company that she can unfurl her *boeuf en daube* and her salmon *en papillote*, spread them forth to be savoured and praised.

What she likes best about these dinners though is setting the table, deciding who will sit where and, when she's feeling mischievous, even what they are likely to say. Then she can sit and listen to them say it. Occasionally she prompts a little.

Tonight will not be very challenging, since it's only the heart men and their wives, and Marylynn, whom Sally hopes will dilute them. The heart men are forbidden to talk shop at Sally's dinner table, but they do it anyway. 'Not what you really want to listen to while you're eating,' says Sally. 'All those tubes and valves.' Privately she thinks they're a conceited lot, all except Ed. She can't resist needling them from time to time.

'I mean,' she said to one of the leading surgeons, 'basically it's just an exalted form of dress-making, don't you think?'

'Come again?' said the surgeon, smiling. The heart men think Sally is one hell of a tease.

'It's really just cutting and sewing, isn't it?' Sally murmured. The surgeon laughed.

'There's more to it than that,' Ed said, unexpectedly, solemnly.

'What more, Ed?' said the surgeon. 'You could say there's a lot of embroidery, but that's in the billing.' He chuckled at himself.

Sally held her breath. She could hear Ed's verbal thought processes lurching into gear. He was delectable.

'Good judgement,' Ed said. His earnestness hit the table like a wet fish. The surgeon hastily downed his wine.

Sally smiled. This was supposed to be a reprimand to her, she knew, for not taking things seriously enough. *Oh, come on, Ed*, she could say. But she knows also, most of the time, when to keep her trap shut. She should have a light-up JOKE sign on her forehead, so Ed would be able to tell the difference.

The heart men do well. Most of them appear to be doing better than Ed, but that's only because they have, on the whole, more expensive tastes and fewer wives. Sally can calculate these things and she figures Ed is about par.

These days there's much talk about advanced technologies, which Sally tries to keep up on, since they interest Ed. A few years ago the heart men got themselves a new facility. Ed was so revved up that he told Sally about it, which was unusual for him. A week later Sally said she would drop by the hospital at the end of the day and pick Ed up and take him out for dinner; she didn't feel like cooking, she said. Really she wanted to check out the facility; she likes to check out anything that causes the line on Ed's excitement chart to move above level.

At first Ed said he was tired, that when the day came to an end he didn't want to prolong it. But Sally wheedled and was respectful, and finally Ed took her to see his new gizmo. It was in a cramped, darkened room with an examining table in it. The thing itself looked like a television screen hooked up to some complicated hardware. Ed said that they could wire a patient up and bounce sound waves off the heart and pick up the echoes, and they would get a picture on the screen, an actual picture, of the heart in motion. It was a thousand times better than an electrocardiogram, he said: they could see the faults, the thickenings and cloggings, much more clearly.

'Colour?' said Sally.

'Black and white,' said Ed.

Then Sally was possessed by a desire to see her own heart, in motion, in black and white, on the screen. At the dentist's she always wants to see the X-rays of her teeth, too, solid and glittering in her cloudy head. 'Do it,' she said, 'I want to see how it works,' and though this was the kind of thing Ed would ordinarily evade or tell her she was being silly about, he didn't need much persuading. He was fascinated by the thing himself, and he wanted to show it off.

He checked to make sure there was nobody real booked for the room. Then he told Sally to slip out of her clothes, the top half, brassière and all.

He gave her a paper gown and turned his back modestly while she slipped it on, as if he didn't see her body every night of the week. He attached electrodes to her, the ankles and one wrist, and turned a switch and fiddled with the dials. Really a technician was supposed to do this, he told her, but he knew how to run the machine himself. He was good with small appliances.

Sally lay prone on the table, feeling strangely naked. 'What do I do?' she said.

'Just lie there,' said Ed. He came over to her and tore a hole in the paper gown, above her left breast. Then he started running a probe over her skin. It was wet and slippery and cold, and felt like the roller on a roll-on deodorant.

'There,' he said, and Sally turned her head. On the screen was a large grey object, like a giant fig, paler in the middle, a dark line running down the centre. The sides moved in and out; two wings fluttered in it, like an uncertain moth's.

'That's it?' said Sally dubiously. Her heart looked so insubstantial, like a bag of gelatin, something that would melt, fade, disintegrate, if you squeezed it even a little.

Ed moved the probe, and they looked at the heart from the bottom, then the top. Then he stopped the frame, then changed it from a positive to a negative image. Sally began to shiver.

'That's wonderful,' she said. He seemed so distant, absorbed in his machine, taking the measure of her heart, which was beating over there all by itself, detached from her, exposed and under his control.

Ed unwired her and she put on her clothes again, neutrally, as if he were actually a doctor. Nevertheless this transaction, this whole room, was sexual in a way she didn't quite understand; it was clearly a dangerous place. It was like a massage parlour, only for women. Put a batch of women in there with Ed and they would never want to come out. They'd want to stay in there while he ran his probe over their wet skins and pointed out to them the defects of their beating hearts.

'Thank you,' said Sally.

Sally hears the back door open and close. She feels Ed approaching, coming through the passages of the house towards her, like a small wind or a ball of static electricity. The hair stands up on her arms. Sometimes he makes her so happy she thinks she's about to burst; other times she thinks she's about to burst anyway.

He comes into the kitchen, and she pretends not to notice. He puts his arms around her from behind, kisses her on the neck. She leans back, pressing herself into him. What they should do now is go into the bedroom (or even the living room, even the den) and make love, but it wouldn't occur to Ed to make love in the middle of the day. Sally often comes across articles in magazines about how to improve your sex life, which leave her feeling disappointed, or reminiscent: Ed is not Sally's first and only man. But she knows she shouldn't expect too much of Ed. If Ed were more experimental, more interested in variety, he would be a different kind of man altogether: slyer, more devious, more observant, harder to deal with.

As it is, Ed makes love in the same way, time after time, each movement following the others in an exact order. But it seems to satisfy him. Of course it satisfies him: you can always tell when men are satisfied. It's Sally who lies awake, afterwards, watching the pictures unroll across her closed eyes.

Sally steps away from Ed, smiles at him. 'How did you make out with the women today?' she says.

'What women?' says Ed absently, going towards the sink. He knows what women.

'The ones out there, hiding in the forsythia,' says Sally. 'I counted at least ten. They were just waiting for a chance.'

She teases him frequently about these troops of women, which follow him around everywhere, which are invisible to Ed but which she can see as plain as day.

'I bet they hang around outside the front door of the hospital,' she will say, 'just waiting till you come out. I bet they hide in the linen closets and jump out at you from behind, and then pretend to be lost so you'll take them by the short cut. It's the white coat that does it. None of those women can resist the white coats. They've been conditioned by Young Doctor Kildare.'

'Don't be silly,' says Ed today, with equanimity. Is he blushing, is he embarrassed? Sally examines his face closely, like a geologist with an aerial photograph, looking for telltale signs of mineral treasure: markings, bumps, hollows. Everything about Ed means something, though its difficult at times to say what.

Now he's washing his hands at the sink, to get the earth off. In a minute he'll wipe them on the dish towel instead of using the hand towel the way he's supposed to. Is that complacency, in the back turned to her? Maybe there really are these hordes of women, even though she's made them up. Maybe they really do behave that way. His shoulders are slightly drawn up: is he shutting her out?

'I know what they want,' she goes on. 'They want to get into that little dark room of yours and climb up onto your table. They think you're delicious. They'll gobble you up. They'll chew you into tiny pieces. There won't be anything left of you at all, only a stethoscope and a couple of shoelaces.'

Once Ed would have laughed at this, but today he doesn't. Maybe she's said it, or something like it, a few times too often. He smiles though, wipes his hands on the dish towel, peers into the fridge. He likes to snack.

'There's some cold roast beef,' Sally says, baffled.

Sally takes the sauce off the stove and sets it aside for later: she'll do the last steps just before serving. It's only two-thirty. Ed has disappeared into the cellar, where Sally knows he will be safe for a while. She goes into her study, which used to be one of the kids' bedrooms, and sits down at her desk. The room has never been completely redecorated: there's still a bed in it, and a dressing table with a blue flowered flounce Sally helped pick out, long before the kids went off to university: 'flew the coop,' as Ed puts it.

Sally doesn't comment on the expression, though she would like to say that it wasn't the first coop they flew. Her house isn't even the real coop, since neither of the kids is hers. She'd hoped for a baby of her own when she married Ed, but she didn't want to force the issue. Ed didn't object to the idea, exactly, but he was neutral about it, and Sally got the feeling he'd had enough babies already. Anyway, the other two wives had babies, and look what happened to them. Since their actual fates have always been vague to Sally, she's free to imagine all kinds of things, from drug addiction to madness. Whatever it was resulted in Sally having to bring up their kids, at least from puberty onwards. The way it was presented by the first wife was that it was Ed's turn now. The second wife was more oblique: she said that the child wanted to spend some time with her father. Sally was left out of both these equations, as if the house wasn't a place she lived in, not really, so she couldn't be expected to have any opinion.

Considering everything, she hasn't done badly. She likes the kids and tries to be a friend to them, since she can hardly pretend to be a mother. She describes the three of them as having an easy relationship. Ed wasn't around much for the kids, but it's him they want approval from, not Sally; it's him they respect. Sally is more like a confederate, helping them get what they want from Ed.

When the kids were younger, Sally used to play Monopoly with them, up at the summer place in Muskoka Ed owned then but has since sold. Ed would play too, on his vacations and on the weekends when he could make it up. These games would all proceed along the same lines. Sally would have an initial run of luck and would buy up everything she had a chance at. She didn't care whether it was classy real estate, like Boardwalk or Park Place, or those dingy little houses on the other side of the tracks; she would even buy train stations, which the kids would pass over, preferring to save their cash reserves for better investments. Ed, on the other hand, would plod along, getting a little here, a little there. Then, when Sally was feeling flush, she would blow her money on next-to-useless luxuries such as the electric light company; and when the kids started to lose, as they invariably did, Sally would lend them money at cheap rates or trade them things of her own, at a loss. Why not? She could afford it.

Ed meanwhile would be hedging his bets, building up blocks of property, sticking houses and hotels on them. He preferred the middle range, respectable streets but not flashy. Sally would land on his spaces and have to shell out hard cash. Ed never offered deals, and never accepted them. He played a lone game, and won more often than not. Then Sally would feel thwarted. She would say she guessed she lacked the killer instinct; or she would say that for herself she didn't care, because after all it was only a game, but he ought to allow the kids to win, once in a while. Ed couldn't grasp the concept of allowing other people to win. He said it would be condescending towards the children, and anyway you couldn't arrange to have a dice game turn out the way you wanted it to, since it was partly a matter of chance. If it was chance, Sally would think, why were the games so similar to one another? At the end, there would be Ed, counting up his paper cash, sorting it out into piles of bills of varying denominations, and Sally, her vast holdings dwindled to a few shoddy blocks on Baltic Avenue, doomed to foreclosure: extravagant, generous, bankrupt.

On these nights, after the kids were asleep, Sally would have two or three more rye-and-gingers than were good for her. Ed would go to bed early—winning made him satisfied and drowsy—and Sally would ramble about the house or read the endings of murder mysteries she had already read once before, and finally she would slip into bed and wake Ed up and stroke him into arousal, seeking comfort.

Sally has almost forgotten these games. Right now the kids are receding, fading like old ink; Ed on the contrary looms larger and larger, the outlines around him darkening. He's constantly developing, like a Polaroid print, new colours emerging, but the result remains the same: Ed is a surface, one she has trouble getting beneath.

'Explore your inner world,' said Sally's instructor in *Forms of Narrative Fiction*, a middle-aged woman of scant fame who goes in for astrology and the Tarot pack and writes short stories, which are not published in any of the magazines Sally reads. 'Then there's your outer one,' Sally said afterwards, to her friends. 'For instance, she should really get something done about her hair.' She made this trivial and mean remark because she's fed up with her inner world; she doesn't need to explore it. In her inner world is Ed, like a doll within a Russian wooden doll, and in Ed is Ed's inner world, which she can't get at.

She takes a crack at it anyway: Ed's inner world is a forest, which looks something like the bottom part of their ravine lot, but without the fence. He wanders around in there, among the trees, not heading in any special direction. Every once in a while he comes upon a strange-looking plant, a sickly plant choked with weeds and briars. Ed kneels, clears a space around it, does some pruning, a little skilful snipping and cutting, props it up. The plant revives, flushes with health, sends out a grateful red blossom. Ed continues on his way. Or it may be a conked-out squirrel, which he restores with a drop from his flask of magic elixir. At set intervals an angel appears, bringing him food. It's always meatloaf. That's fine with Ed, who hardly notices what he eats, but the angel is getting tired of being an angel. Now Sally begins thinking about the angel: why are its wings frayed and dingy grey around the edges, why is it looking so withered and frantic? This is where all Sally's attempts to explore Ed's inner world end up.

She knows she thinks about Ed too much. She knows she should stop. She knows she shouldn't ask, 'Do you still love me?' in the plaintive tone that sets even her own teeth on edge. All it achieves is that Ed shakes his head, as if not understanding why she would ask this, and pats her hand. 'Sally, Sally,' he says, and everything proceeds as usual; except for the dread that seeps into things, the most ordinary things, such as rearranging the chairs and changing the burnt-out lightbulbs. But what is it she's afraid of? She has what they call everything: Ed, their wonderful house on a ravine lot, something she's always wanted. (But the hill is jungly, and the house is made of ice. It's held together only by Sally, who sits in the middle of it, working on a puzzle. The puzzle is Ed. If she should ever solve it, if she should ever fit the last cold splinter into place, the house will melt and flow away down the hill, and then. . . .) It's a bad habit, fooling around with her head this way. It does no good. She knows that if she could quit she'd be happier. She ought to be able to: she's given up smoking.

She needs to concentrate her attention on other things. This is the real reason for the night courses, which she picks almost at random to coincide with the evenings Ed isn't in. He has meetings, he's on the boards of charities, he has trouble saying no. She runs the courses past herself, mediaeval history, cooking, anthropology, hoping her mind will snag on something; she's even taken a course in geology, which was fascinating, she told her friends, all that magma. That's just it: everything is fascinating, but nothing enters her. She's always a star pupil, she does well on the exams and impresses the teachers, for which she despises them. She is familiar with her brightness, her techniques; she's surprised other people are still taken in by them.

Forms of Narrative Fiction started out the same way. Sally was full of good ideas, brimming with helpful suggestions. The workshop part of it was anyway just like a committee meeting, and Sally knew how to run those, from behind, without seeming to run them: she'd done it lots of times at work. Bertha, the instructor, told Sally she had a vivid imagination and a lot of untapped creative energy. 'No wonder she never gets anywhere, with a name like Bertha,' Sally said, while having coffee afterwards with two of the other night-coursers. 'It goes with her outfits, though.' (Bertha sports the macramé look, with health-food sandals and bulky-knit sweaters and hand-weave skirts that don't do a thing for her square figure, and too many Mexican rings on her hands, which she doesn't wash often enough.) Bertha goes in for assignments, which she calls learning by doing. Sally likes assignments: she likes things that can be completed and then discarded, and for which she gets marks.

The first thing Bertha assigned was The Epic. They read *The Odyssey* (selected passages, in translation, with a plot summary of the rest); then they poked around in James Joyce's *Ulysses*, to see how Joyce had adapted the epic form to the modern-day novel. Bertha had them keep a Toronto notebook, in which they had to pick out various spots around town as the ports of call in *The Odyssey*, and say why they had chosen them. The note-books were read out loud in class, and it was a scream to see who had chosen what for Hades. (The Mount Pleasant Cemetery, McDonald's, where, if you eat the forbidden food, you never get back to the land of the living, the University Club with its dead ancestral souls, and so forth.) Sally's was the hospital, of course; she had no difficulty with the trench filled with blood, and she put the ghosts in wheelchairs.

After that they did The Ballad, and read gruesome accounts of murders and betrayed love. Bertha played them tapes of wheezy old men singing tra-ditionally, in the Doric mode, and assigned a newspaper scrapbook, in which you had to clip and paste up-to-the-minute equivalents. The *Sun* was the best newspaper for these. The fiction that turned out to go with this kind of plot was the kind Sally liked anyway, and she had no difficulty con-cocting a five-page murder mystery, complete with revenge.

But now they are on Folk Tales and the Oral Tradition, and Sally is hav-ing trouble. This time, Bertha wouldn't let them read anything. Instead she read to them, in a voice, Sally said, that was like a gravel truck and was not conducive to reverie. Since it was the Oral Tradition, they weren't even allowed to take notes; Bertha said the original hearers of these stories couldn't read, so the stories were memorized. 'To recreate the atmosphere,' said Bertha, 'I should turn out the lights. These stories were always told at night.' 'To make them creepier?' someone offered. 'No,' said Bertha. 'In the days, they worked.' She didn't do that, though she did make them sit in a circle.

'You should have seen us,' Sally said afterwards to Ed, 'sitting in a circle, listening to fairy stories. It was just like kindergarten. Some of them even had their mouths open. I kept expecting her to say, "If you need to go, put up your hand." ' She was meaning to be funny, to amuse Ed with this account of Bertha's eccentricity and the foolish appearance of the students, most of them middle-aged, sitting in a circle as if they had never grown up at all. She was also intending to belittle the course, just slightly. She always did this with her night courses, so Ed wouldn't get the idea there was anything in her life that was even remotely as important as he was. But Ed didn't seem to need this amusement or this belittlement. He took her information earnestly, gravely, as if Bertha's behaviour was, after all, only the procedure of a specialist. No one knew better than he did that the procedures of specialists often looked bizarre or incomprehensible to onlookers. 'She probably has her reasons,' was all he would say.

The first stories Bertha read them, for warm-ups ('No memorizing for *her,*' said Sally), were about princes who got amnesia and forgot about their true loves and married girls their mothers had picked out for them. Then they had to be rescued, with the aid of magic. The stories didn't say what happened to the women the princes had already married, though Sally wondered about it. Then Bertha read them another story, and this time they were supposed to remember the features that stood out for them and write a five-page transposition, set in the present and cast in the realistic mode. ('In other words,' said Bertha, 'no real magic.') They couldn't use the Universal Narrator, however: they had done that in their Ballad assignment. This time they had to choose a point of view. It could be the point of view of anyone or anything in the story, but they were limited to one only. The story she was about to read, she said, was a variant of the Bluebeard motif, much earlier than Perrault's sentimental rewriting of it. In Perrault, said Bertha, the girl has to be rescued by her brothers; but in the earlier version things were quite otherwise.

This is what Bertha read, as far as Sally can remember:

There were once three young sisters. One day a beggar with a large basket on his back came to the door and asked for some bread. The eldest sister brought him some, but no sooner had she touched him than she was compelled to jump into his basket, for the beggar was really a wizard in disguise. ('So much for United Appeal,' Sally murmured. 'She should have said, "I gave at the office." ') The wizard carried her away to his house in the forest, which was large and richly furnished. 'Here you will be happy with me, my darling,' said the wizard, 'for you will have everything your heart could desire.'

This lasted for a few days. Then the wizard gave the girl an egg and a bunch of keys. 'I must go away on a journey,' he said, 'and I am leaving the house in your charge. Preserve this egg for me, and carry it about with you everywhere; for a great misfortune will follow from its loss. The keys open every room in the house. You may go into each of them and enjoy what you find there, but do not go into the small room at the top of the house, on pain of death.' The girl promised, and the wizard disappeared.

At first the girl contented herself with exploring the rooms, which contained many treasures. But finally her curiosity would not let her alone. She sought out the smallest key, and, with beating heart, opened the little door at the top of the house. Inside it was a large basin full of blood, within which were the bodies of many women, which had been cut to pieces; nearby were a chopping block and an axe. In her horror, she let go of the egg, which fell into the basin of blood. In vain did she try to wipe away the stain: every time she succeeded in removing it, back it would come.

The wizard returned, and in a stern voice asked for the egg and the keys. When he saw the egg, he knew at once she had disobeyed him and gone into the forbidden room. 'Since you have gone into the room against my will,' he said, 'you shall go back into it against your own.' Despite her pleas he threw her down, dragged her by the hair into the little room, hacked her into pieces, and threw her body into the basin with the others.

Then he went for the second girl, who fared no better than her sister. But the third was clever and wily. As soon as the wizard had gone, she set the egg on a shelf, out of harm's way, and then went immediately and opened the forbidden door. Imagine her distress when she saw the cut-up bodies of her two beloved sisters; but she set the parts in order, and they joined together and her sisters stood up and moved, and were living and well. They embraced each other, and the third sister hid the other two in a cupboard.

When the wizard returned he at once asked for the egg. This time it was spotless. 'You have passed the test,' he said to the third sister. 'You shall be my bride,' ('And second prize,' said Sally, to herself this time, 'is *two* weeks in Niagara Falls.') The wizard no longer had any power over her, and had to do whatever she asked. There was more, about how the wizard met his comeuppance and was burned to death, but Sally already knew which features stood out for her.

At first she thought the most important thing in the story was the forbidden room. What would she put in the forbidden room, in her present-day realistic version? Certainly not chopped-up women. It wasn't that they were too unrealistic, but they were certainly too sick, as well as being too obvious. She wanted to do something more clever. She thought it might be a good idea to have the curious woman open the door and find nothing there at all, but after mulling it over she set this notion aside. It would leave her with the problem of why the wizard would have a forbidden room in which he kept nothing.

That was the way she was thinking right after she got the assignment, which was a full two weeks ago. So far she's written nothing. The great temptation is to cast herself in the role of the cunning heroine, but again it's too predictable. And Ed certainly isn't the wizard; he's nowhere near sinister enough. If Ed were the wizard, the room would contain a forest, some ailing plants and feeble squirrels, and Ed himself, fixing them up; but then, if it were Ed the room wouldn't even be locked, and there would be no story.

Now, as she sits at her desk, fiddling with her felt-tip pen, it comes to Sally that the intriguing thing about the story, the thing she should fasten on, is the egg. Why an egg? From the night course in Comparative Folklore she took four years ago, she remembers that the egg can be a fertility symbol, or a necessary object in African spells, or something the world hatched out of. Maybe in this story it's a symbol of virginity, and that is why the wizard requires it unbloodied. Women with dirty eggs get murdered, those with clean ones get married.

But this isn't useful either. The concept is so outmoded. Sally doesn't see how she can transpose it into real life without making it ridiculous, unless she sets the story in, for instance, an immigrant Portuguese family, and what would she know about that?

Sally opens the drawer of her desk and hunts around in it for her nail file. As she's doing this, she gets the brilliant idea of writing the story from the point of view of the egg. Other people will do the other things: the clever girl, the wizard, the two blundering sisters, who weren't smart enough to lie, and who will have problems afterwards, because of the thin red lines running all over their bodies, from where their parts joined together. But no one will think of the egg. How does it feel, to be the innocent and passive cause of so much misfortune?

(Ed isn't the Bluebeard: Ed is the egg. Ed Egg, blank and pristine and lovely. Stupid, too. Boiled, probably. Sally smiles fondly.)

But how can there be a story from the egg's point of view, if the egg is so closed and unaware? Sally ponders this, doodling on her pad of lined paper. Then she resumes the search for her nail file. Already it's time to begin getting ready for her dinner party. She can sleep on the problem of the egg and finish the assignment tomorrow, which is Sunday. It's due on Monday, but Sally's mother used to say she was a whiz at getting things done at the last minute.

After painting her nails with *Nuit Magique*, Sally takes a bath, eating her habitual toasted English muffin while she lies in the tub. She begins to dress, dawdling; she has plenty of time. She hears Ed coming up out of the cellar; then she hears him in the bathroom, which he has entered from the hall door. Sally goes in through the other door, still in her slip. Ed is standing at the sink with his shirt off, shaving. On the weekends he leaves it until necessary, or until Sally tells him he's too scratchy.

Sally slides her hands around his waist, nuzzling against his naked back. He has very smooth skin, for a man. Sally smiles to herself: she can't stop thinking of him as an egg.

'Mmm,' says Ed. It could be appreciation, or the answer to a question Sally hasn't asked and he hasn't heard, or just an acknowledgement that she's there.

'Don't you ever wonder what I think about?' Sally says. She's said this more than once, in bed or at the dinner table, after dessert. She stands behind him, watching the swaths the razor cuts in the white of his face, looking at her own face reflected in the mirror, just the eyes visible above his naked shoulder. Ed, lathered, is Assyrian, sterner than usual; or a frost-covered Arctic explorer; or demi-human, a white-bearded forest mutant. He scrapes away at himself, methodically destroying the illusion.

'But I already know what you think about,' says Ed.

'How?' Sally says, taken aback.

'You're always telling me,' Ed says, with what might be resignation or sadness; or maybe this is only a simple statement of fact.

Sally is relieved. If that's all he's going on, she's safe.

Marylynn arrives half an hour early, her pearl-coloured Porsche leading two men in a delivery truck up the driveway. The men install the keyhole desk, while Marylynn supervises: it looks, in the alcove, exactly as Marylynn has said it would, and Sally is delighted. She sits at it to write the cheque. Then she and Marylynn go into the kitchen, where Sally is finishing up her sauce, and Sally pours them each a Kir. She's glad Marylynn is here: it will keep her from dithering, as she tends to do just before people arrive. Though it's only the heart men, she's still a bit nervous. Ed is more likely to notice when things are wrong than when they're exactly right.

Marylynn sits at the kitchen table, one arm draped over the chairback, her chin on the other hand; she's in soft grey, which makes her hair look silver, and Sally feels once again how banal it is to have ordinary dark hair like her own, however well-cut, however shiny. It's the confidence she envies, the negligence. Marylynn doesn't seem to be trying at all, ever.

'Guess what Ed said today?' Sally says.

Marylynn leans further forward. 'What?' she says, with the eagerness of one joining in a familiar game.

'He said, "Some of these feminists go too far," ' Sally reports. '"*Feminists*." Isn't that sweet?'

Marylynn holds the pause too long, and Sally has a sudden awful thought: maybe Marylynn thinks she's showing off, about Ed. Marylynn has always said she's not ready for another marriage yet; still, Sally should watch herself, not rub her nose in it. But then Marylynn laughs indulgently, and Sally, relieved, joins in.

'Ed is unbelievable,' says Marylynn. 'You should pin his mittens to his sleeves when he goes out in the morning.'

'He shouldn't be let out alone,' says Sally.

'You should get him a seeing-eye dog,' says Marylynn, 'to bark at women.'

'Why?' says Sally, still laughing but alert now, the cold beginning at the ends of her fingers. Maybe Marylynn knows something she doesn't; maybe the house is beginning to crumble, after all.

'Because he can't see them coming,' says Marylynn. 'That's what you're always telling me.'

She sips her Kir; Sally stirs the sauce. 'I bet he thinks I'm a feminist,' says Marylynn.

'You?' says Sally. 'Never.' She would like to add that Ed has given no indication of thinking anything at all about Marylynn, but she doesn't. She doesn't want to take the risk of hurting her feelings.

The wives of the heart men admire Sally's sauce; the heart men talk shop, all except Walter Morly, who is good at by-passes. He's sitting beside Marylynn, and paying far too much attention to her for Sally's comfort. Mrs Morly is at the other end of the table, not saying much of anything, which Marylynn appears not to notice. She keeps on talking to Walter about St Lucia, where they've both been.

So after dinner, when Sally has herded them all into the living room for coffee and liqueurs, she takes Marylynn by the elbow. 'Ed hasn't seen our desk yet,' she says, 'not up close. Take him away and give him your lecture on nineteenth-century antiques. Show him all the pigeon-holes. Ed loves pigeon-holes.' Ed appears not to get this.

Marylynn knows exactly what Sally is up to. 'Don't worry,' she says, 'I won't rape Dr Morly; the poor creature would never survive the shock,' but she allows herself to be shunted off to the side with Ed.

Sally moves from guest to guest, smiling, making sure everything is in order. Although she never looks directly, she's always conscious of Ed's presence in the room, any room; she perceives him as a shadow, a shape seen dimly at the edge of her field of vision, recognizable by the outline. She likes to know where he is, that's all. Some people are on their second cup of coffee. She walks towards the alcove: they must have finished with the desk by now.

But they haven't, they're still in there. Marylynn is bending forward, one hand on the veneer. Ed is standing too close to her, and as Sally comes up behind them she sees his left arm, held close to his side, the back of it pressed against Marylynn, her shimmering upper thigh, her ass to be exact. Marylynn does not move away.

It's a split second, and then Ed sees Sally and the hand is gone; there it is, on top of the desk, reaching for a liqueur glass.

'Marylynn needs more Tia Maria,' he says. 'I just told her that people who drink a little now and again live longer.' His voice is even, his face is as level as ever, a flat plain with no signposts.

Marylynn laughs. 'I once had a dentist who I swear drilled tiny holes in my teeth, so he could fix them later,' she says.

Sally see Ed's hand outstretched towards her, holding the empty glass. She takes it, smiling, and turns away. There's a roaring sound at the back of her head; blackness appears around the edges of the picture she is seeing, like a television screen going dead. She walks into the kitchen and puts her cheek against the refrigerator and her arms around it; as far as they will go. She remains that way, hugging it; it hums steadily, with a sound like comfort. After a while she lets go of it and touches her hair, and walks back into the living room with the filled glass.

Marylynn is over by the french doors, talking with Walter Morly. Ed is standing by himself, in front of the fireplace, one arm on the mantelpiece, his left hand out of sight in his pocket.

Sally goes to Marylynn, hands her the glass. 'Is that enough?' she says.

Marylynn is unchanged. 'Thanks, Sally,' she says, and goes on listening to Walter, who has dragged out his usual piece of mischief: some day, when they've perfected it, he says, all hearts will be plastic, and this will be a vast improvement on the current model. It's an obscure form of flirtation. Marylynn winks at Sally, to show that she knows he's tedious. Sally, after a pause, winks back.

She looks over at Ed, who is staring off into space, like a robot which has been parked and switched off. Now she isn't sure whether she really saw what she thought she saw. Even if she did, what does it mean? Maybe it's just that Ed, in a wayward intoxicated moment, put his hand on the nearest buttock, and Marylynn refrained from a shriek or a flinch out of good breeding or the desire not to offend him. Things like this have happened to Sally.

Or it could mean something more sinister: a familiarity between them, an understanding. If this is it, Sally has been wrong about Ed, for years, forever. Her version of Ed is not something she's perceived but something that's been perpetrated on her, by Ed himself, for reasons of his own. Possibly Ed is not stupid. Possibly he's enormously clever. She thinks of moment after moment when this cleverness, this cunning, would have shown itself if it were there, but didn't. She has watched him so carefully. She remembers playing Pick Up Sticks, with the kids, Ed's kids, years ago: how if you moved one stick in the tangle, even slightly, everything else moved also.

She won't say anything to him. She can't say anything: she can't afford to be wrong, or to be right either. She goes back into the kitchen and begins to scrape the plates. This is unlike her—usually she sticks right with the party until it's over—and after a while Ed wanders out. He stands silently, watching her. Sally concentrates on the scraping: dollops of *sauce suprême* slide into the plastic bag, shreds of lettuce, rice, congealed and lumpy. What is left of her afternoon.

'What are you doing out here?' Ed asks at last.

'Scraping the plates,' Sally says, cheerful, neutral. 'I just thought I'd get a head start on tidying up.'

'Leave it,' says Ed. 'The woman can do that in the morning.' That's how he refers to Mrs Rudge, although she's been with them for three years now; *the woman*. And Mrs Bird before her, as though they are interchangeable. This has never bothered Sally before. 'Go on out there and have a good time.'

Sally puts down the spatula, wipes her hands on the hand towel, puts her arms around him, holds on tighter than she should. Ed pats her shoulder. 'What's up?' he says; then, 'Sally, Sally.' If she looks up, she will see him shaking his head a little, as if he doesn't know what to do about her. She doesn't look up.

Ed has gone to bed. Sally roams the house, fidgeting with the debris left by the party. She collects empty glasses, picks up peanuts from the rug. After a while she realizes that she's down on her knees, looking under a chair, and she's forgotten what for. She goes upstairs, creams off her make-up, does her teeth, undresses in the darkened bedroom and slides into bed beside Ed, who is breathing deeply as if asleep. *As if.*

Sally lies in bed with her eyes closed. What she sees is her own heart, in black and white, beating with that insubstantial moth-like flutter, a ghostly heart, torn out of her and floating in space, an animated valentine with no colour. It will go on and on forever; she has no control over it. But now she's seeing the egg, which is not small and cold and white and inert but larger than a real egg and golden pink, resting in a nest of brambles, glowing softly as though there's something red and hot inside it. It's almost pulsing; Sally is afraid of it. As she looks it darkens: rose-red, crimson. This is something the story left out, Sally thinks: the egg is alive, and one day it will hatch. But what will come out of it?

SHARON BUTALA

❧

FEVER

Cecilia had slept well the first part of the night, but later she was dimly aware of a restlessness on Colin's part that kept pulling her up from the dreamless depths of her heavy sleep to a pale awareness of something being not right. She remembered feeling hot and must have thrown off all her covers, an act unusual for her since she was almost always too cold, and often resorted to a flannel nightgown even in summer. About two-thirty she came fully awake, shivering because she was uncovered, and in her gropings for blankets, found that Colin was hugging all the bedcovers tightly to himself.

She woke him, pushing against his shoulder, then touching his cheek and forehead with her palm, puzzled and then alarmed by the hotness of his skin and the dry heat radiating from his body.

'I'm sick,' he mumbled, with a mixture of fear and irritation in his voice that woke her further.

'What's the matter?' she asked.

'I'm sick,' he repeated, a whisper this time, and gave a little moan, involuntarily it seemed, as though he had been stricken suddenly with pain.

She fumbled for the bedside lamp, its location forgotten from the evening before when they had checked in, exhausted from their long flight and the delay when they had changed planes in Winnipeg. The lamp on, she blinked, staring down at him, trying to tell if his pallor was real or just the consequence of poor light or her grogginess.

'I'll need a doctor,' he said, his eyes closed, and he clenched his jaw as if against the chattering of his teeth, or pain.

Cecilia was confused, vague pictures passed through her mind, vanishing before she could catch them. She sat up in bed, put both hands over her face, and tried to make sense of things. They had arrived in Calgary, Colin was sick, he said he needed a doctor. She put her hands down and was disconcerted to find him staring at her with an expression that was—surely not—beseeching. But yes, that's what it was. He was beseeching her to do something, and his eyes were the eyes of someone in extremity such as she sometimes caught a glimpse of on the news on television, frighteningly dark, holding depths she had never guessed at before.

She wanted to close her eyes again, to sink back into sleep, to wake in the morning to find him well, or gone.

Colin grunted once, softly, and she got out of bed, went to the desk, and opened the phone book.

'It's my stomach,' he said, and his voice was strained now and pitched too high. She looked back at him, saw he had raised his head off the pillow and that his black hair, always neatly trimmed and short, was pushed by his restlessness into spikes like a punker's. She wanted to laugh. 'Call the desk,' he said, straining to say it loudly enough for her to hear, then his head fell back on the pillow. But the way his head dropped like a stone as if he had fallen that suddenly into unconsciousness made her dial zero.

They drove the short distance to the hospital in an ambulance, down deserted, icy streets, the siren senselessly screeching. Almost at once Colin was taken from the emergency ward to a bed in a ward three flights up. It was a small room across from the nursing station, and it was equipped with valves, dials and tubes attached to the wall at the head of his bed that the other rooms Cecilia had glanced into as they went down the hall, didn't have. This, and his proximity to the nursing station, alarmed Cecilia. Or rather, these facts registered, she knew this meant he was seriously ill, and that she should be alarmed. But she found she felt no fear, or at least, she didn't think she did.

It was four a.m. Cecilia stood by his bed looking down on him while a nurse on the other side, for at least the third time since their arrival, took his blood pressure, counted his pulse, and listened to his chest.

Colin's eyelids flickered open. Closing them, he said to Cecilia, 'You came.' She wondered if he had forgotten that she had come with him to Calgary, that he wasn't alone on this business trip as he usually was, and if he thought, in his fever-distorted mind, that she had flown in to be with him when he was taken ill. She drew in a breath to explain, but the paper-like sheen of his eyelids, which looked now as though they had been sealed shut and not merely closed, silenced her. She looked to the nurse but the nurse seemed to be avoiding looking at her.

'He's not likely to be awake much,' she said to Cecilia in a tentative tone, casting a glance at her that Cecilia couldn't interpret. 'The doctor wants to talk to you.' Cecilia went out into the hall where the doctor was leaning on the counter and sleepily making notes in a patient's chart. When he saw her, he stopped writing. Cecilia approached him slowly, and waited for him to speak.

'He's a very sick man,' the doctor said to her, solemnly. For a second Cecilia thought she hadn't heard him correctly. When she didn't reply, he said, 'I know it's a surprise, since he's so healthy and strong looking, but whatever is bothering him has hit him hard. We'll have to watch him close-ly.' He said something further about vital signs and some medical jargon that she didn't listen to. She interrupted him.

'But what's wrong with him?'

'We have to wait till the lab opens in the morning to get the results of the tests and to do more,' he said, 'before we can pinpoint the problem, but we've got a nurse with him full time for now, and if we need to, we can have him in the OR in minutes.' He seemed used to the bewildered silences of rel-atives, because he filled the pauses when she, her mind crowded with not so much questions as dark, empty spaces that refused to form themselves into words, could only look up at him in silence.

'I think you might as well go back to your hotel and get some sleep,' he said, looking vaguely, with red-rimmed eyes, down the empty, polished cor-ridor. 'Mrs Purdy will call you if he should get worse.' He said good night and left her standing there, holding tightly onto the nursing station counter with one hand.

She looked in on Colin once more, the nurse was taking his blood pres-sure again, before she took a taxi back to the hotel. It was when she was in bed that she began to wonder if he would die. Her mind shied at the idea, it wasn't possible. And what could be the matter with him? The doctor had given her no clue, at least she didn't think he had. She wondered if she had done the right thing by coming back to the hotel, or if she should have stayed at the hospital. Did the nurses think badly of her because she had gone? This worried her for a while, but finally, she fell asleep.

When she woke it was only three hours later. Light was streaming in around the curtains and she could hear traffic in the street below. She was at once fully alert and knew she wouldn't be able to go back to sleep. Before her eyes had opened she thought of Colin, remembering what the doctor had said and how Colin seemed to have gone away even from behind his sealed eyelids, and she felt momentarily angry with him for deserting her and then for spoiling their trip.

She phoned the hospital and was told that he was not awake, that his condition was pretty much the same, and that the test results wouldn't be back from the lab for a while yet.

'I'll be there in an hour,' she said, feeling the need to assure them of her interest, and then, because it seemed to be important to do the normal thing, she bathed, dressed, and went downstairs to the hotel restaurant to order breakfast even though she was neither hungry nor thirsty.

The restaurant was almost empty. While she waited for her coffee she noticed a tall, thin man who looked a little like Colin, although he was not so dark, sitting at a table near the window eating breakfast. He glanced up and caught her watching him. She lowered her eyes quickly, but when he passed her table on his way out of the room, he smiled briefly, wryly at her, indicating by this the oddness of them finding themselves the only two people in such a big restaurant. She observed that his eyes were blue, not brown like Colin's. She recalled then that he had checked in just ahead of them the night before.

She drank her coffee and her orange juice and ate a piece of toast politely, carefully, not tasting it, then went back to the hospital.

As she arrived two white-coated women were wheeling Colin, bed and all, out of his room and down the hall in the direction where the labs were. The empty room, with intravenous and oxygen tubes connected to nothing, and the silent dials on the wall, gave her such a peculiar feeling that she went into the TV room to wait for them to bring him back. When he returned he was still drifting in and out of consciousness. Nurses, aides, and lab technicians hurried in and out of the room, speaking in loud voices to Colin and softly to her, as if she were the sick one. They took his pulse, his temperature and blood pressure and poked him with needles, then measured his blood into little glass vials. The doctor came alone and nodded good morning to her, then left. Later he came again, this time with two other doctors. In the hallway they murmured in soft voices to her, speculating about the cause of his illness, enumerating the results of tests, and commenting on what each one might mean.

'But will he be all right?' she asked. The doctors looked at their feet and mumbled some more, while she stood too close to them, lifting her head to hear better, trying to understand what they were saying, or rather, what they were not saying.

In the afternoon Colin spoke to her.

'This will be all right,' he said, in a new, high-pitched voice. Although his eyes were directed to her, she had a feeling that he was actually looking at something beyond or behind her. 'I am frightened.' Having failed to show any sign of fear, he closed his eyes. It was such a contradictory, puzzling message that she discounted it entirely, blaming it on the drugs they were giving him for pain and to control his fever.

Not long after that she began to wonder if the doctors had been trying to tell her that Colin might die. But she could not believe that Colin's death was in the cards for either of them at this moment, and after a pause, she dismissed the thought.

By nine in the evening his illness had still not been identified. Talk had gone from appendicitis or food poisoning to a malfunctioning gall bladder to a kidney ailment or bowel dysfunction to every possible virus from influenza to AIDS. Cecilia went back to the hotel, hesitated for a second in the empty lobby, since she still didn't feel hungry, then went into the restaurant anyway.

There were a few more people scattered around at the tables now, talking quietly, drinks on their tables in front of them, or cups of coffee. The hostess seated Cecilia, then left her. As she was picking up the menu, she realized someone was speaking to her.

For the last few hours she had had a steady, quiet hum in her head that put a distance between her and the voices of other people. She tried to make it stop by shaking her head, by concentrating very hard on anyone speaking to her, and then by reciting to herself her own name, Colin's name, the names of their children, and their street address at home. None of these had helped and eventually she had given in and allowed herself to be lulled into the hum.

She turned her head slowly in the direction of the voice, expecting to find that it wasn't she who was being addressed. But the man she had seen at breakfast was leaning toward her from the next table where he was sitting.

'Pardon?' Cecilia said.

'I said the hostess seems to think we should talk to each other, since she placed us so close together.' Cecilia glanced around. It was true. In a room three-quarters empty, the hostess had placed them at adjacent tables. How had she not noticed him? 'I believe I saw you check in with your husband,' he remarked. 'I suppose he's off doing business.'

'Yes,' she said, 'I mean, no.' It was hard to talk through the hum. 'I'm sorry, I haven't had much sleep. He was taken ill last night. He's in the hospital.'

'I thought there was something wrong,' he said, and leaned toward her again. 'You looked,' he paused, 'sort of in shock. I hope it's not too serious.' She hesitated, not sure what to say. There was a warm intensity in his blue eyes that calmed her.

'Yes,' she said. 'It's very serious. He's unconscious most of the time. I left because,' she felt herself frown, 'I was too tired to do anything else. I wanted to get away,' then was embarrassed at what she had said. She had a quick mental picture of Ingrid Bergman being torn away from the bedside of her dying husband by well-meaning friends–No! No, I don't want to leave! Let me stay!–and managed not to laugh.

He seemed to be absorbing her remark, mulling it over, and now he nodded briskly, a quick acceptance or agreement.

'Yes,' he said. 'You need to get a perspective.'

'I guess that's it,' she said, a little dubiously. He smiled at her quickly, impersonally. They didn't speak again for a while.

'Please don't think I'm being too forward,' he said after several minutes had passed, 'but I'd enjoy it if you'd have your dinner here, at my table. It's lonely, all this eating by yourself.' Cecilia found herself standing, then awkwardly sitting in the chair he held out for her. Some part of her perhaps regretted this action she was taking, but she found no will to resist what seemed to be her inclination.

'It is lonely,' she agreed, in a serious tone.

The waitress came and took their orders. If she was surprised to find them sitting together, she gave no sign.

'I don't want to intrude on your privacy,' he said carefully, not looking at her, 'but do you know anyone in Calgary? Are you alone in this?'

Cecilia told him how Colin was thinking of opening a branch of his sporting goods business in the city if it looked like it would be profitable, how they had talked about maybe moving West if things went well, how she had come with him because she'd never been west of Winnipeg before, and now this had happened. And no, she didn't know a soul in Calgary.

'I've told our children he's sick, but nothing else, and I told his sister not to come . . . yet.'

'Then let me be your friend,' he said. Cecilia was overcome with embarrassment. She took a sip from her glass of water. 'I'm a representative for a chemical company,' he said. 'I make regular rounds through southern Alberta, among other things, selling chemicals to the dealers who sell them to farmers. I have a wife and three kids in Edmonton where our head office is.'

He was touching his cutlery, moving his hands with precision and a certain amount of tension which she couldn't read, but when he finished speaking he lifted his head and smiled at her in a way that was almost embarrassed. 'And I liked you as soon as I saw you standing in the lobby last night with that same puzzled look on your face while your husband checked you in.'

'I saw you too,' she said, finally, and noticed that the hum in her head had lessened and that the room was a pleasant temperature, not too cold as she usually found restaurants. She relaxed a little, then thought of Colin.

'If you're worried, phone the hospital again,' he said. 'There are pay phones in the lobby.'

When he left her at the elevator, he paused, and leaning in the open door, kissed her gently, not quickly, on her mouth. Thinking about it later as she lay in bed, she told herself, I knew he was going to do it and I didn't back away or try to stop him. I wanted him to kiss me. And she felt a burning through her body, even in her arms and the palms of her hands, a burning that she recognized as sexual longing. She who had never been unfaithful, who had never dreamt of such a thing, and Colin so sick.

She passed another restless night and was at the hospital before eight.

Several doctors were standing around Colin's bed gazing silently down on him while the head nurse stood by tensely. She noticed Cecilia in the doorway and spoke in an undertone to one of the doctors.

'Ah,' he said, turning to Cecilia.

'I'll stop in at noon,' the second doctor said. He and the third doctor walked out of the room past Cecilia and down the hall.

'I'm Dr Jameson,' the first doctor said to her. 'Dr Ransom asked me to have a look in.'

Colin lay motionless on the bed, his eyes closed, an unnaturally red spot of colour high on each cheek. His lips too, were more vividly coloured than usual. Dr Jameson took her arm and said, 'Let's just sit down and talk this over.' He guided her into a small office behind the nursing station, held a chair for her and sat down himself.

'Now,' he said, 'your husband is very sick. But you know that.'

She said, 'Have you found out what's wrong with him?' He didn't reply directly, but instead, not looking at her, began to list the different tests they had done and the result of each. He remarked on certain possibilities and dismissed them with a gesture or left them open. Cecilia tried to listen to him, but her mind wandered to Colin's strange colouring, to the fact the head nurse was a different one, and to wondering who Dr Jameson was and what might be his field of specialty.

Gradually it dawned on her that Colin was worse, a good deal worse, and that was why Dr Jameson had brought her into this room and why the nurses and aides at the station or passing down the hall had avoided looking at her as she followed him.

She tried to get a grip on this idea, to admit, to force it to penetrate the shield of her own bewildering indifference. She repeated to herself, Colin is desperately ill, but still no shiver of fear passed down her spine. Dr Jameson stopped talking and went away. Cecilia went back to Colin's bedside.

At noon he opened his eyes and spoke to her.

'They are coming with flowers,' he said. 'They want to speak to us. Be ready.'

'Yes, Colin,' she replied, and bent to kiss him on his hot, dry forehead, but as her lips touched his skin, he turned his head fretfully away from her much as a cranky, feverish child might, and screwed up his face before he lapsed back into unconsciousness. Later he said, 'It is very big and there is an echo like silver.'

They were keeping the door to his room closed now and had hung a 'No Visitors' sign on it. Nurses moved swiftly, silently in and out of the darkened room, staring down at Colin with pursed lips before they went away again.

'I don't understand it,' Dr Jameson muttered to Colin on one of his several brief visits.

At eleven that night the head nurse came, put her arm around Cecilia's shoulders and told her to go back to the hotel and try to sleep.

'I know you want to be here, but you don't want to collapse when he needs you. Is the rest of the family on its way?' Cecilia shook her head numbly, no.

'His parents are dead,' she said, 'and I don't want our children here. If he isn't better by morning, I'll tell his sister to come.'

'Go back to the hotel,' the nurse said in a kindly way, 'if you are carrying this alone. I'll call you at once if I think you should be here.'

Cecilia obeyed and took a taxi back to the hotel. Just as she entered the lobby the doors of the elevator opened and the man she had talked with the night before stepped out as if he had arranged to meet her.

'You look so tired,' he said to her, without any preliminaries or surprise. 'Come and have a drink with me before you go to bed.'

'I don't think I could sleep anyway,' she said. They went together into the bar across from the restaurant and Cecilia had a glass of scotch. She inhaled its fumes, finding them delicious, she let them rush into her brain.

'He's worse,' she said. 'He may not live through the night,' but her own words carried no meaning, she frowned with the effort to feel them, but they seemed to be as on the other side of an impenetrable glass wall. Finally, she abandoned the effort; she was too tired. 'I guess I shouldn't be here,' she said, meaning that she should have stayed at Colin's bedside, not that she shouldn't be in the hotel bar with a strange man.

He was thoughtful for a second, then shook his head.

'No,' he said. 'There comes a moment . . . If it's his fate . . .' She studied him. He had such bright eyes, so blue, and the intensity in them fascinated her. She remembered Colin's eyes the night he had gotten sick, as if, behind their transparent glistening surface, they opened into worlds she hadn't been to, hadn't known existed, didn't want to know about. He took her hand and held it tightly.

'Hold on,' he said. 'You're not alone. I'll stick with you.' At that moment all she could feel was the pressure, almost too hard, and the warmth of his hand around hers. And then he put his other hand on the side of her face. She turned her head into his palm and breathed in the smell of his flesh, she opened her mouth and touched her tongue to his palm, tasting the faint salt taste. They sat that way for a moment, she with her eyes closed, until he loosened his hold on her hand, and slid his other hand down to her shoulder.

'Better?' he asked. Yes, she was better. Surprised, she opened her eyes. He was staring at her with a slight frown, his blue eyes burning with a steady light.

He walked with her to the elevator and this time, instead of letting her get on alone, he got on too, and pushed the button for his floor which came before hers. The elevator stopped, the doors opened, he got off and began to say good night to her in an oddly formal, unsmiling way, when she stepped off the elevator beside him. He stared at her, perplexed, not speaking. She touched his arm in a tentative, supplicating way, holding her eyes on his face.

He hesitated, then took his room key out of his pocket and led her down the hall.

His room was identical to hers except that it was less tidy and he had left a lamp burning. The desk was covered with papers he had evidently been working on, and his pyjamas lay across the foot of his bed. She closed her eyes again and after a pause, he kissed her.

At one moment, finding herself in a posture both undignified and profoundly arousing, she had felt a second's horror at what she was doing. For she had never consented to such behaviour—or even thought of it—before in her life. She was reminded of the ugly grappling of pornography, and for a second she was filled with distaste at where her body had taken her, as though she had wakened now, but only to the flesh, to the room, to the rug on the floor and the bed and the walls and the dusty TV set in the corner, and to his hands and mouth on her, and hers on him; she was filled with amazement.

And my husband, sick, dying, she thought.

She told him what Colin had said, about the big room with the echo like silver.

'Maybe he really is somewhere else,' the man said. 'Maybe he's somewhere in a big place and it has an echo like silver. It sounds beautiful,' he added. 'It doesn't sound like you should be worried about him.'

'I didn't like the sound of it,' she replied. 'So remote, so cold.' She shivered, lying in his arms, and was glad of the warmth of his flesh against hers.

'We thought it might be his pancreas,' Dr Jameson said to her in the morning, 'but now we've ruled that out, too.' She had given him their family doctor's number so that Dr Jameson could consult with him about Colin's medical history. She could have told him there was nothing: flu, colds, a broken bone in his foot.

At noon the head nurse who had been on duty when Colin was admitted came in and read the record of his vital signs and intake and output of fluids that lay on the stand by his bed.

'That's better,' she murmured, then went out without saying anything more. Cecilia meditated on this till the nursing shifts changed at three and the new nursing team came in and clustered around Colin's bed. She was about to ask if he was improving when the new head nurse said to the others, 'A slight improvement here.' Cecilia could see no difference, except perhaps that the unnaturally bright colour in his cheeks had faded.

After they had gone, she stood beside his bed.

'Did you hear that, Colin?' she asked. 'They say you're getting better.' Colin's eyelids flickered and he looked at her with that same well of darkness behind his eyes.

'The blueness of things,' he said, in a voice that might have been awestruck, had it not been so faint.

'The antibiotics are working,' she said. There was no response. She wanted to reach down and shake him. She was his wife, she had been his wife for fifteen years. They had children. What right had he to ignore her in this way? The doctors and nurses whisking in and out of his room barely glanced at her, spoke to her only occasionally, waited politely for her to leave the room before they pulled the curtain around his bed to do some unspeakable thing to him. Was she of no account at all? But Colin had become a stranger, while the man she had gone to bed with the night before was not. She tried to summon some remorse for what she had done, or sympathy for Colin lying so ill and in pain, but all she could feel was anger.

At six the nurse who took his vital signs replied, when Cecilia asked her, that Colin's fever was still elevated, and she smiled at Cecilia in a commiserating way.

'A little change this afternoon,' she said, 'but now he's much the same.'

Around seven Colin said loudly, in a clear voice, 'Let me sleep,' then, more quietly, 'I'm tired and the music lulls me.' Cecilia put her hand on his forehead. It was damply cool now, and beads of cool sweat sat on his upper lip. He didn't respond to her touch and after a moment, she took her hand away.

At nine she went back to the hotel. The man she had slept with wasn't in the lobby or the restaurant. She went directly to the bar, stopped in the doorway and peered from table to table through the smoky gloom. He was seated on a stool at the bar and when he glanced back and saw her standing in the doorway, he stood at once, put some money beside his half-full glass, and came immediately to where she waited for him. They went to the elevator, got on, and went up to his room.

This time their coupling was less dramatic, less violently experimental than it had been the night before. Lying beside him on his rumpled bed before she returned to her room, she said, 'Today when I tried to talk to him, he said, "the blueness of things." What do you suppose he was dreaming about?'

'Or thinking,' he said. 'Or maybe he was somewhere else.'

'Do you think he's trying to tell me something?' Cecilia asked. 'No,' she answered her own question, 'I don't think he is. But what did he mean?'

'Maybe he'll be able to tell you when he wakes up,' the man said. 'You should write down what he says so you can ask him.'

'If he wakes up,' she heard herself say, and refused to amend or qualify what she had said.

'Do you love him?' he asked her. In the same unemotional voice she replied, 'Yes, or I did when I married him and we've been married fifteen years, so if I don't love him anymore, I don't think it makes any difference.'

'Tell me then . . .' he said carefully, and paused. 'Tell me. Do you ever wish that . . .' He paused again. 'Do you ever wish that he would die?'

'No,' she said. 'Why would I wish that?'

He shrugged, was perhaps a bit embarrassed. 'To free you.'

She started to ask him why he thought she wanted to be free, then realized where she was and what she had just done. She got off the bed and gathered her clothing.

'No,' she said. 'I don't wish that.' When she had dressed she left the room without saying good night. He didn't say anything either, although she had glanced at him before she closed the door behind her and saw that he was watching her steadily across the shadowed room.

In the late morning Colin opened his eyes.

'You're here,' he said to her and his expression seemed almost amused.

'Yes,' she said softly and rose from her chair in the corner to stand by his bed.

'I feel like I've been on a long journey,' Colin said, looking up at the ceiling, 'and now I'm so tired.'

His words, his tone of voice were so obviously normal that her stomach turned over. He closed his eyes slowly and seemed to fall asleep. Cecilia went to find a nurse to report this turn of events to and the nurse was so surprised that she came with Cecilia, setting down the tray she was carrying on a trolley as they passed it. She took Colin's blood pressure, his pulse, and then his temperature.

'I think there might be some difference,' she said cautiously.

Colin didn't wake again or speak until Cecilia was preparing to leave for the hotel. His voice was very faint as he asked her about the children and the appointments he had missed. Then he began to shiver so violently that Cecilia rang his bell and got a nurse in at once. The nurse came in, took his temperature, went out of the room and returned with a thick white wool blanket. She covered Colin and in a few moments he had stopped shivering. Cecilia waited a little longer and when it seemed clear that this had passed, she went back to the hotel.

Her friend was waiting in the bar for her and when he saw her coming toward him, he stood quickly and reached in his pocket for money. She crossed the room and sat on the stool beside him.

'I'll have a scotch and ice,' she said to the bartender.

'Bad day?' her friend asked, after a moment.

'Good day, I think,' she replied, and told him that although Colin was still very weak and sick, he was sometimes awake now and lucid.

'Have they figured out what was the matter with him?' the man asked.

'A rare tropical disease picked up off a toilet seat?' she suggested, and began to laugh. She put her hand over her mouth and bent her head, while her torso convulsed with spasms of rolling laughter that she couldn't stop. She couldn't catch her breath, she couldn't see anything for the tears of laughter filling her eyes. Alarmed, she made a great effort and managed to stop. She took a few deep breaths, wiped her eyes, and blew her nose. A giggle burst out and she caught it and stifled it. Her friend sat beside her looking at her in a way that was concerned, yet faintly amused. He didn't touch her.

'Come on,' he said, and Cecilia rose and followed him to the elevators. They went to his room and he began kissing her hungrily, pressing her body roughly against his, holding her so tightly she could barely breathe.

'What?' he said, into her hair, sensing some coolness in her that had been absent before. He began to fondle her with less ferocity and more tenderness. They made love again, and Cecilia dressed and went to her room immediately after.

She found that she couldn't sleep and sat up in bed watching a long, silly movie, then lay in the darkness with her eyes open till very late. She was later than usual going to breakfast, too, and the man she had been spending her nights with wasn't there, had probably already left on his day of driving out to the nearby towns.

Colin was propped up in a half-sitting position when she arrived at the hospital.

'I think I remember getting sick,' he said to her, as if she had been in the room with him all along, 'but I don't remember the hotel room and I can't remember the flight here at all.' After a pause he said, 'Calgary,' as if to remind himself. His voice was still weak and his eyes kept closing, as if he was too exhausted to keep them open. She bent to kiss his lips, but he turned his head away so that she met his cool cheek.

Off and on during the day he woke to tell her something as if he were reconstructing, for his own instruction, as much of the past week as he could.

'I came here in an ambulance, right?' he said, looking out the window to the even blue of the winter sky.

'Yes,' she said. 'I had to convince the doctor who came to the hotel that . . .'

'It must have been late,' he said. She opened her mouth to reply, but he had already moved on. 'One-thirty, I think. I think I remember those numbers in red on the clock.'

It went on like that, a monologue. A soliloquy, she thought, and gave up trying to converse with him.

Dr Jameson came in, and after he had studied Colin's chart and examined him, he took Cecilia out into the hall.

'He seems to be mending,' he told her. 'His fever's down, he's fully conscious, no longer complaining of pain.'

'But what was wrong with him?' Cecilia asked.

'If he keeps improving, I'd think you could take him home in two or three days.'

'But what made him sick?' Cecilia asked again.

'A good question,' he said, and turned his back on her to walk briskly away down the corridor.

That night when she returned to the hotel she slipped quickly past the entrance to the bar, and waited nervously till the elevator came. She thought she had caught a glimpse of her lover sitting in his usual place at the bar, but she went past so quickly, she couldn't be sure.

He was waiting for her at breakfast the next morning.

'Where were you last night?' he asked.

'Nowhere,' she said, embarrassed. 'I was tired.'

He got up from his table, bringing his coffee cup, and sat down at hers.

'I missed you,' he said, and she noticed again how very blue his eyes were, and his manner of fixing them on her so that she seemed to be the sole object in the room. 'Meet me tonight.'

'Colin's getting better,' she said, suddenly, running her words into his. 'He's conscious and clear-headed. I'll be able to take him home in a couple of days.' He set his cup carefully into its saucer.

'To tell the truth,' he said, 'this is my last day in this district. I leave in the morning.' She glanced quickly at him and noticed that the intensity in his eyes had faded, that he was not even looking at her.

'Your wife will be glad to see you,' she said.

He gave her a wry look, then glanced at his watch and said, 'I'd better get going if I want to finish up today.' She said, 'I'm late, too,' although she wasn't particularly.

At the door they stopped and faced each other. Cecilia was stricken with embarrassment, muttered a short, 'See you,' and hurried to the elevator. She didn't think he had said anything. Just before the door shut, blocking her view, she saw him buttoning his overcoat and reaching for his briefcase which he had set on the floor by his feet. He wasn't looking at her. The elevator doors shut.

'We've moved him,' a nurse said gaily to her as she neared the nursing station. She pointed to a door down the hall, almost at the end.

Colin was awake, his intravenous apparatus had been taken away, and this room had no gadgets attached to the walls. It looked like a bedroom.

'They've started me on clear fluids,' he said, and his voice was stronger. 'They're going to get me up this afternoon.'

'Oh?' she said.

'But I can't sleep,' he complained, like a child. 'I try to sleep, but I just lie there.'

'You slept for a week,' she said, cheerfully. 'Maybe you don't need to sleep anymore.'

'Of course I need to sleep,' he said irritably. 'I wasn't asleep before. I was . . .'

'What?' Cecilia broke in sharply. 'What were you doing all week? What?' She went close to the bed, but didn't try to kiss him or touch him. He looked up at her, disconcerted, and she saw that the blackness had gone from his eyes leaving them a translucent, yellowish brown. He blinked several times.

'What are you talking about?' he asked, his peevishness returning.

'All week,' she said, patient now, 'you said things to me. You said you were somewhere. You said . . .' His expression was growing puzzled, was there an edge of panic creeping into his voice?

'What do you mean?' He squirmed away from her, like a small child.

'You said you were somewhere big. You said there was an echo like silver. You said . . .'

'Don't, Cecilia,' he said, and the sound of her own name stopped her, brought the blood rushing to her cheeks. Colin looked away again to the rectangle of pale blue that was all he could see from his window, then turned his head slowly till he was looking at the wall at the foot of his bed.

'I've been sick,' he said, and the distance returned to his voice and his eyes. 'I've been sick,' he repeated, while she waited. 'It's hard . . .' She leaned closer, his voice had grown so faint. 'To come back.' His eyes closed, and gradually his face smoothed.

How thin he had grown. Now his nose was prominent, even hawk-like, and his eyes seemed larger. She found herself wanting to put her hands on each side of his face, gently, to kiss his thin, fever-cracked lips, to lie sleeping beside him, pressed against the warmth of his sickness-wracked body. She stood quietly, looking down on him as he slept.

She wanted to tell him that she too had been gone, that she had been exploring, lost, in a wild, violent country, that she had narrowly escaped, that she had had to tear herself away, lest the swamps and bogs and blackness claim her forever.

She stood looking down at her sleeping husband. His eyelids twitched, his lips moved, he winced as if the pain had returned, and out of the corners of his eyes, a few tears came and crept slowly down his temples to disappear in his hair.

CYNTHIA FLOOD

❧

MY FATHER TOOK
A CAKE TO FRANCE

My father stands before the bakery window. He is going to buy a cake for
my mother.

He is a young man, twenty-six in 1928, and he is tall, bony, of angular
visage. His hair is pale, his glasses extremely clean. Thirty or fifty years
hence he will look, as they say, distinguished; at present the clothes afford-
able by the son of a Canadian Methodist minister simply cover his limbs.

In his left coat pocket is Eliot's *The Waste Land*, of which he has been
mentally reciting the opening lines as he walks the noisy London streets in
search of a bakery. Irony, pastry, flowers, death—my father relishes the con-
trasts and stirs Eliot's metaphors in his mind, sure that no other graduate
of Toronto's Victoria College (motto: The truth shall make you free) thinks
such thoughts.

My father is happy, desperately happy, to be in England. His brain has
brought him here. The happiness soars from his faith that England is better than Canada: older, deeper, stronger, more highly patterned, more richly and complexly flavoured, more romantic—oh, infinitely more romantic.
And here he is, *he* is, in London, en route to Paris from Oxford, to the City
of Light from the City with her dreaming spires. Hogtown is far away.

In Paris is my mother. She is there because a married Oxford student
is so far outside the norm as to be inconceivable to the university authorities. Somehow, from that fact, my parents have moved to a decision that
while my father studies in England my mother will live in France. Soon my
father will see her. He is desperately happy, though from his looks no one
would guess either the desperation or the happiness or their entanglement
within him. Dour, stiff, critical—that is his aspect. (Say the word 'Toronto'
and I see him walking toward me down the cold white street, his hat firm
on his head, his briefcase swinging, above the snow, the long thick tweed
coat swaying as he advances sternly. Because I am a girl, he will take his hat
off to me.)

This aspect now faces the confections displayed within the bakery window.

My father has a tendency to stick his lower lip forward, and thus his
chin; the latter is sharp and long, just like mine. His blue eyes glitter. As he

ages, his eyes will not change, will always be blue like shadows in snow or ice in sunlight; although his infrequent smile smooths the chin's point and softens the steep drop from temple to jaw, the eyes do not change. They look now through the glasses through the bakery window through the glass display shelves to a woman back there in the shop. She glances away. My father's heart contracts.

He opens the shop door, and with delight he hears the little English bell tinkling, pinging—not a harsh North American buzz or ring, not a machine: a bell, attached to its string, silver trembling in the sun, the sounding centre of the fragrance that fills the shop, a warm yeasty floury doughy sugary fragrance with undertones of almond essence and ginger. My father inhales, inhales, and begins to smile. Then he sees the woman behind the counter and is silenced by a rush of shyness. His mouth goes tight, straight, thin. For she is a fair English flower. Oh, she has it all—her eyes are grey, her hair curled light, her complexion apple blossom grafted to cherry, and she is freshness and cleanliness incarnate in a pink shortsleeved dress with a white bibbed apron. On her forearms and the backs of her hands is flour, which also powders her right temple just below a dip of curls.

My father takes off his hat.

'Good morning, sir,' she says, and my father's heart dissolves.

In the spired city my father is the Canadian student. He is intelligent, yes, highly intelligent, a remarkably good writer, really a most distinguished mind—but still he can never be what he feels, he *knows*, he should have been. There will always have been Humberside Collegiate instead of Marlborough or Stowe, always Longbranch summers and the house on Hewitt Avenue in a modest Toronto neighbourhood (of which my grandmother said, departing thence after twenty-five years, 'I never liked the West End'). There will never have been the small English manor house, sparely furnished with good, old pieces, never the youthful rambles in the tender English countryside and the boyish familiarity with spinney and copse, or possibly tor and moor. . . . Instead, my father has canoed on Lake Muskoka. The generations of quiet educated sensibility, of sureness that *This is how we have always done things*—no. The Ontario farm is too near. And on this side of the Atlantic, in Paris, Mme Papillon, my parents' landlady, points frequently to alleged scratches on *her* furniture and says to her Canadian tenants, in tones at once depressed and threatening, '*Voyez comme il s'abîme!*' So, even as my father feasts on the Oxford libraries, exhilarates in recognition, relishes the exercise of his intellectual musculature, some part of him feels he is beaten before he starts. As he would say, will say frequently throughout his life, 'All, all is ashes.'

But not here. Here in the warm quiet bakery the sun is yellow in the

window, he has money in his pocket, and a pretty woman stands before him
to do his bidding, sir. Soon he will take the boat-train for Dover. On board
the ferry, he will stand alone and ecstatic at the bow and recite 'Fair stood
the wind for France' and 'Nobly, nobly to the northwest Cape St Vincent
died away' (both, like 'Dover Beach,' learned by heart at Humberside).

France: hungrily, my father will watch that legendary country rise from
horizon into actual earth where he can set his flat Canadian foot. Soon he
will hear French all about him. Not the crude ugly patois they speak in
Quebec (all his life he will rejoice in the belief that every Quebecois who
travels to France meets incomprehension and contempt), no, *real* French,
France French. My father regrets very much that he cannot pronounce a
rolled French R. His tongue simply will not make that sound. . . . But
France will come later, Paris, the little apartment in Mme Papillon's building, my mother. Right now he must buy his cake.

He looks again at the beautiful young woman behind the counter. His
shyness begins to dissipate, subsumed by another emotion: pleasure, at the
thought that this beauty will soon fade. In my father's other coat pocket is
Arnold Bennett's *The Old Wives' Tale*, a wonderful novel, a masterpiece, no
one writes like that any more. . . . On the train from Oxford that morning
he has read and reread Bennett's introductory description of the book's gen-
esis, is well on the way to memorizing it. Decades later, my father will recite
these paragraphs repeatedly, interminably, as he will also the scene in which
Sophia, sitting by Gerald Scales's frightful corpse, is brought to the door of
her own death by the understanding that 'Youth and vigour had come to
that. Youth and vigour always came to that. Everything came to that.' By
preference, my father will select as audiences for these recitations people
who are near either the beginning or the end of life. He will also take inor-
dinate and lifelong pleasure, laughing helplessly, in Constance's embarrassed description of her sister's exotic pet: 'It's a French dog, one of those
French dogs.'

Now my father looks at the youth and freshness behind the counter
with an aesthetic pleasure that is distanced because for him these are obsta-
cles that stand in the way of the status and respect he knows are his due.
Further, although he readily imagines the speed with which these attributes
will become their hideous opposites in the person now facing him, he does
not refer that process to himself. Too many scholarly achievements, honours, points of recognition lie ahead.

Looking at the young woman in the bakery, what my father feels is nostalgia for the moment, right now while it still is the moment. He may even
feel desire *for* nostalgia, that wrenching union of mournfulness and delight.

'Would you be kind enough, miss,' he says, speaking formally, though aware in helpless annoyance that his accent instantly marks him as non-English, possibly in her ignorant ear even as American, which annoys him still more, 'would you be kind enough to tell me the names of these cakes?'

'Of course, sir.'

Her small plump hands, dusted with flour and springing with gold hair, move pointing along the upper shelf of the display case.

Ratafias, gingerbread nuts, macaroons. Snow cake, sponge cake, Savoy cake.

'I'm sure I don't know why Savoy, sir. There's orange-flower water in it.'

My mother, marrying my father, carries mock-orange. Characteristically impulsive, she breaks the sprigs off a shrub they pass while walking towards their ceremony in the little London church (it will be bombed flat in the Battle of Britain). Because she loves the smell of the mock-orange she overrides my father's objections, his wish to buy her a *real* bouquet. She will plant mock-orange in the garden of every house they rent and in that of the one they finally own, when he retires.

The plump hands and the soft voice go on. Lemon cake, pound cake, seed cake. A Pavini cake.

'Eyetalian, sir. They use a rice flour.'

My father is delighted at the incorrect pronunciation in the gentle voice, for he is developing a nice ability to rank British speakers of English. Her respectful attitude, also, the way she looks repeatedly up at him under her lashes to confirm that she is to continue naming the cakes—most satisfactory. Holiday cake, plum cake, almond ca—

My father holds up his hand and the young woman stops in mid-word. That gesture of his, so powerful, so characteristic, has even stopped Mme Papillon, that stalwart bearer of the arms of the French *petit bourgeoisie*. How? When my father, having heard the *Voyez comme il s'abîme* accusation once too often, says in his solid Ontario French and with his right hand raised, '*Eh bien, nous allons. Nous partons, ma femme et moi,*' the landlady stands speechless before him.

'Is there a queen cake?' Now where has he picked up this name? I cannot imagine.

'Queen cakes here sir? Oh no sir. You must make your little queens at home, sir, and eat them fresh from the oven.'

And she smiles, to soften the response. She is so sweet, so blooming, so feminine, that though there remain several unidentified cakes my father goes right off into a kind of trance. His hand is still upheld and he exudes such an atmosphere of *Do not speak to me* that the young woman remains silent, transfixed—just like Mme Papillon, who finds her apologies and assurances blown to powder before the cold wind of my father's displeasure, and who only finds out that my parents do not intend to leave her apartment through the fact that they stay.

Which cake? Perhaps the one with the small white roses. Or that one, with what seem to be daisies, eyes of the day—some small white flower. A cake for my mother, in Paris. My father thinks of my mother. He extends his fingers before him towards the glass case and moves them back and forth in the air as if composing, or running scales on the piano.

No, resentfully, he does not play the piano, although God knows he has the hands for it, long, broad, agile, because his sister got the childhood lessons purely for being that: a sister. And what did she do with her training? What? Nothing. Nothing. Fifty years later, after my father's funeral, I learn from my aunt how she bowed, and willingly, to those terrible grinding loving pressures of family, and sacrificed—there is no other word—her own hopes (not even plans, so young were they) for travel and the study of music abroad. Abroad, abroad, that radiant word and world abroad: she diverted carefully-saved funds into the channel marked 'post-graduate education of gifted elder brother.' A girl.

My father moves his fingers along the air and the young woman looks at him, bewildered. What is this odd plain bespectacled commanding young man about?

My father is no longer aware of her. He feels only the intense need to find the right cake, the cake that will say what must be said, the cake that will be for my mother.

Now my mother is and always has been a handsome woman, energetic, with snapping hazel eyes and a lively play of expression and a nose as strong as her will; yet all his life my father yearns, or part of him yearns, for her to be fragile, delicate. He yearns himself to be the lover who gives gifts to this being who is other, oh very other, mysterious, unknown, in fact unknowable, as strange and distant as the inner reality of France or England is to a Canadian (this though my mother like my father is Canadian born and raised). A perfect metaphor for this prism of my father's relationship with my mother is his present status as an Oxford student. As such, he has attained an ideal separation between the life of the intellect and that of the heart and flesh, between a world of many men and a world of one woman, for he has literally to journey from one to the other across land and water, to cross national boundaries, to go through customs. And the one world knows the other not at all, not at all (although Mme Papillon probably disapproves of my parents' living arrangements as sharply as any Oxford don). Also, my mother speaks French much more fluently than my father does.

My mother, this other being, if correctly presented according to my father's fantasy, would be adorned, no, would be veiled in lace, silks, embroidery, furs. She would wear jewels. She would recline, beautifully; my father thinks of pictures in the *Illustrated London News*, sees the languid hand trailing over the edge of the cushion-heaped chaise longue, the curled tendrils of hair clustering delicately about the slender throat. . . . As the marriage moves on through the decades to its golden jubilee, my father will develop an entire verbal routine (one of many, on various topics) about my mother, more specifically about his own failure to make her a marchioness. He will elaborate on his failure to provide her with a suitable establishment, a suitably lovely house—in England, of course, not in ratty raw Canada where he has been compelled to eke out his miserable sordid existence and where she too has therefore been immured—no, a suitably lovely Queen Anne house, with flanking pavilions in perfect symmetry and formal gardens sloping to the lake. . . . In my teens I find this routine amusing, in my twenties embarrassing. In my thirties I despise it. Now in my forties I feel a sour pity that slowly sweetens.

The woman in the English bakery keeps thinking that my father is pointing, finally, to his choice, and moves up and down accordingly behind the display case. But my father is still not aware of her. He has dropped her into that enormous wastebasket where he keeps people whom he does not currently need. So he moves, and she moves. Which shall it be: the one with the long sliding curls of chocolate? with the stippling of jam? with the corrugations born of a special pan, and these all glazed and shining? Which? My father's hands, duplicates of mine to the last crease and wrinkle, go up and down along the glass.

My father stops. He points to the lower shelf. The young woman bends down. The fabric of her clothing bends too, with a gentle cracking sound, and seems to exude yet stronger, sweeter wafts of that marvellous baking fragrance with which the shop is suffused. With her two pretty hands she removes the cake that my father is pointing to, and she lays it silently before him on the counter. The clean grained wood, white from scrubbing, might be an altar.

He inspects his choice. This cake, of the sandwich type, is softly round; its sides are innocent of icing; in the crack between its layers lies a streak of golden glossy stickiness; and on its white-iced bosom it bears three beautifully modelled *fleurs-de-lis*.

Then my father smiles. The dour face splits and everything except the blue ice changes so forcefully that the young woman, astonished, taken all unawares, smiles back, dimpling at her customer in the most enchanting way. She answers his question before he even asks it.

'This, sir? It's a French cake, one of those French cakes. Gat*to*,' she finishes.

My father in turn is charmed, taken, completely, and only by continuing to smile can he signal his intention to purchase. He and the young woman, smiling, together contemplate the cake.

Then, as he gazes on the ancient armorial bearings of the kings of France, my father feels three tears rise.

The first is for the pain of exclusion. He does not want to be a king, no—in fact a long way down inside my father is a belief that no one, no one in the world is quite so good as a scholar—but he would dearly love to be a citizen of a nation ruled by kings. He wants real, resident monarchs, not people thousands of miles away across grey cold ocean who turn up in Canada every few years and wave from the rears of trains. He wants to be bound in his own person to all the glittering bloody sonorous history of Europe, where century lies on century like the multiple towers of Troy. And he wants *not* to live in a nation that is at best a blueprint only, laid thinly on hostile earth that scarcely knows the plough.

The next tear is for irony, beloved irony, for here collapsed into a cake is that same heroic, embattled, glorious tale of Europe. And is this not always the fate of human enterprise? Aspiration, promise, struggle, heartbreak—all come down to dust, an evanescent sugariness, an ache in the teeth. An aching sweetness. With that is the third tear, for here is my mother.

'What is in the middle?' my father asks, pointing to the filling.

'Jam, sir. Mirabelle.'

My father sees my mother, right now, in the Paris apartment. She is wearing her favourite dress, cream with broad vertical stripes of indigo. The dropped waistline suits her. He sees her short dark shining hair and her broadlipped smile that comes quickly. Her eyebrows, strong and black, lift up and down as she talks and laughs. Her arms move vigorously—perhaps she is polishing the furniture so that it will not *s'abîme*, although this is unlikely, for all her life my mother lacks interest in housekeeping. She values literature and talk and good food and rose-gardens much more highly. Probably she is telling a story, which she does better than anyone. The gestures enliven the fabric of her dress so that the loose panels of linen move about over her large beautiful breasts. My father makes a terrible face, standing there in the English bakery. This contorted flesh startles the young woman. What is happening to her customer? What happens between my mother and father is not as his senses tell him it could be. If, if, a thousand impossible ifs—impossible as the manor house, the public school, the panelled library, the heat of summer silence on the Devon Lincoln Hampshire Sussex Cheshire hills. Mirabelle: beauty to be wondered at.

Half a century later, my father will be torn with rage at the construction of the new airport in Quebec: Mirabel. Storming, bullying, rasping, erect at the end of his long shining dinner table (polished by his own clean-ing woman to the point where he can see his own face reflected in his own table), he will harangue friends and family into impotent seething submis-sion as he spits out his hatred of the French-Canadians, the damned frogs with their hands in the till, spits it out all over the well-done roast beef he is simultaneously and perfectly carving. Then he will fall silent. He will sit down. He will cover his own meat with horseradish and eat it in large pieces, and ignore the timid resumption of conversation at his table. He will not recognize anyone else's presence, not even my mother's, so deep will he be in the caverns of his rage, his freezing resentment that the world refuses to order itself as it ought. Laying his large knife and fork parallel across his plate, he will grimace terribly. For dessert there will be my mother's trifle: his favourite.

'Have you changed your mind, sir? I'll put it back, shall I?' The pretty hands take hold of the cake plate.

'No,' says my father, his voice angry and low. 'No. I'll take it.' He has taken my mother. He has married her. He will buy the cake, and he will ride the Dover ferry to Calais, repeatedly, for he will love her, love her above all others, all his life long. He will do his best to give her the French kings.

Meanwhile here is this shopgirl who has witnessed him in the act of emotion. He feels the cold rich anger rising.

'How much?' he asks roughly. The young woman is disconcerted. Her answering smile is not full. She names the price.

Now this is calamity. Calamity, indignity, catastrophe, insult, humiliation.

For my father, buying the cake will mean that he cannot have lunch before he boards the ferry. Obviously a missed lunch is no great matter, but that *is* not the matter. A man of his gifts should not have to make a miser-able paltry puny choice like this. Both a gift for his wife and a pleasant lunch for himself should be easily possible. He should not have to give a second thought to their cost. My father stands silent in the bakery, chill with rage, while the mordant juices of resentment eat into his consciousness.

Why is he poor and why are so many unworthy people rich? Stupid vulgar Canadians who could not write a shapely sentence if their lives depended on it, who know nothing of Greek mythology or the French impressionists or Dickens or Macaulay, who say *anyways* and *lay down*, who holiday in Florida (in later life he will reserve a special loathing for these), who are Jews or have funny names from Eastern Europe or both, who do not have university degrees, who wear brown suits. . . .

My father glares down at the young woman in the English bakery. He stands tall, rigid, barely containing explosive movement. His face lengthens.

The prominent cheek and jaw bones elongate.

In the young woman's body, the smallest possible movement occurs: a shrinking.

My father senses it, tells the direction of her feelings, presses in immediately, concentrates his gaze so that it is chilled metal, cold and killing, and sends its force out to nip her warm flesh. He will not let her go. Concentration, intensity, strength. He makes the glare persist. Do that long enough, and the other person will collapse, he knows. I know that. My father grips the counter.

She moves, she takes two little steps back. The fatal shining appears in her eyes.

My father is glad.

Deliberately counting out the money for the cake, my father piles it on the white wood surface between himself and the young woman. As always following anger, he breathes quickly, harshly, but the rage-induced blotches on his face begin to subside.

Trails of warm water move down the young woman's cheeks as she rings the payment into the till. Then, taking a sheet of scored white cardboard, she begins to form it into a box for the cake. She works quickly, neatly, and the tears stop coming, but a damp glossy track runs down each cheek.

My father is charmed. How pretty she looks, how endearing, with those little silver designs on her face! Already the cake is in the box. The string whirls off a ball suspended from the ceiling. She manipulates it deftly so the fibre goes over and under and round and about. Quickly, there is the finished box. She has even provided a pair of carrying loops through which my father can put his fingers; hers leave the loops and so push the cake box across the counter towards him.

'That is very pretty,' my father says admiringly. Surprised that the young woman does not respond, he rephrases his compliment. 'You do that very well.'

To this she does respond, in a manner archetypal among people interacting with my father. She smiles—a little, not fully—and utters a null monotonous answer, not meeting his eyes. 'It is a butterfly knot, sir.'

Then she walks through a doorway behind the counter and closes the door.

My father stands alone in the warm quiet fragrant room.

A few months before my father's death, he sits with my mother in their sunny garden, near the roses blooming by his study door, and reads aloud a letter from an old friend on holiday in France. This friend refers, amid descriptions of landscape and weather and food, to the servants at the country house where he is staying.

My father cries. Beating his thin hand on his thin knee, he asks shrilly why he has been stuck in this hole in Canada, why he has not been the one chosen for the sojourn in the well-staffed French chateau. Why has he been exiled to the Siberia of the scholar's life in this country where no one appreciates him or his abilities? Why did there not exist, when he was young, the plethora of scholarships and fellowships for study abroad available now to every Tom Dick and Harry who manages for God's sake to scrape through a general arts BA?

Around him flowers the radiant garden that my mother has created, loving every hour of the labour involved. The flower beds give way to plain lawn, where crab-apples stand, and this lawn in turn slopes down to a duck-spotted brook overhung with willows. Inside, in the study, the walls and drawers and shelves are thick with honours garnered from every possible Canadian source.

Soon he will have lunch. The delicious Italian chicken soup, with tortellini, is based on a stock that takes my mother a full day to prepare; in these last few months of his cancer, this is one of the few dishes he enjoys. His digestion is much disordered because, after several surgeries, his long body lacks some of its original innards, these having been substituted by a revolting and unsatisfactory American contraption made of plastic and intended to prolong his life. *Il s'abîme.*

Several times my parents' cleaning woman, a constant in their lives for fifteen years, finds my father's beautiful slippers—blue suede, a Christmas gift from my mother—stained with excrement. Surreptitiously, she sponges them clean and sets them in the sun. She tells me sharply not to let the professor know that she knows about his little accidents; my father tells me sharply not to let her know that he has seen her taking his stained slippers away. I watch him standing alone on the sunlit deck, looking down at the slippers drying there, and I can tell that there are tears in his eyes.

At twenty-six, my father stands on the sidewalk—no, the pavement—out in the cood April sun, with the bell's music fading on his ear, breeding lilacs in the dead land and tears in his eyes. . . . He has been humiliated. The day is ruined. The journey is spoiled.

But. In his left pocket is Eliot and Bennett is in his right. He is a student at the greatest university in the English-speaking world, which means the greatest. He is about to take ship to Europe where he will see my mother again, again. And he has the cake. He has it at a sacrifice, true; it has not come as he wanted it; all the context was wrong, awkward, difficult, unseemly. But the plain fact remains that he has got it. Who ever has been such, done such?

In his last illness, when he is if anything even more bad-tempered than

he has habitually been since youth, he mentions this cake to me, apparently en route to another retelling of the *s'abîme* episode. He tells me that he
bought a cake in London and took it all the way to Paris, to my mother, as
a treat for their weekend together. He tells me. 'I took a cake to France,' he
says to me insistently. 'Wasn't that a romantic thing to do? Think of me,
that young man, all his life to come.' And then, contemptuously. 'You've
never done anything like that.' He abandons the story. His face resettles into
its customary bitter folds. He turns away.

And so my father took the cake to France, to Paris, to that small apartment of Mme Papillon's where the furniture did or did not *s'abîme*. There
he presented it to his wife, my mother. She. . . .

Beth Brant
(Degonwadonti)

❧

A Long Story

Dedicated to my Great-Grandmothers Eliza Powless and Catherine Brant

'About 40 Indian children took the train at this depot for the Philadelphia Indian School last Friday. They were accompanied by the government agent, and seemed a bright looking lot.'

The Northern Observer
(Massena, New York, July 20, 1892)

'I am only beginning to understand what it means for a mother to lose a child.'

Anna Demeter, *Legal Kidnapping*
(Beacon Press, Boston, 1977)

1890

It has been two days since they came and took the children away. My body is greatly chilled. All our blankets have been used to bring me warmth. The women keep the fire blazing. The men sit. They talk among themselves. We are frightened by this sudden child-stealing. We signed papers, the agent said. This gave them rights to take our babies. It is good for them, the agent said. It will make them civilized, the agent said. I do not know *civilized*.

I hold myself tight in fear of flying apart in the air. The others try to feed me. Can they feed a dead woman? I have stopped talking. When my mouth opens, only air escapes. I have used up my sound screaming their names—She Sees Deer! He Catches The Leaves! My eyes stare at the room, the walls of scrubbed wood, the floor of dirt. I know there are people here, but I cannot see them. I see a darkness, like the lake at New Moon. Black, unmoving. In the centre, a picture of my son and daughter being lifted onto the train. My daughter wearing the dark blue, heavy dress. All of the girls dress alike. Never have I seen such eyes! They burn into my head even now. My son. His hair cut. Dressed as the white men, his arms and legs covered by cloth that made him sweat. His face, streaked with tears. So many children crying, screaming. The sun on our bodies, our heads. The train screeching like a crow, sounding like laughter. Smoke and dirt pumping out of the insides of the train. So many people. So many children. The women, standing as if in prayer, our hands lifted, reaching. The dust sifting down on our palms. Our palms making motions at the sky. Our fingers closing like the claws of the bear.

I see this now. The hair of my son held in my hands. I rub the strands, the heavy braids coming alive as the fire flares and casts a bright light on the black hair. They slip from my fingers and lie coiled on the ground. I see this. My husband picks up the braids, wraps them in cloth; he takes the pieces of our son away. He walks outside, the eyes of the people on him. I see this. He will find a bottle and drink with the men. Some of the women will join him. They will end the night by singing or crying. It is all the same. I see this. No sounds of children playing games and laughing. Even the dogs have ceased their noise. They lay outside each doorway, waiting. I hear this. The voices of children. They cry. They pray. They call me. *Nisten ha.* I hear this. *Nisten ha.**

1978

I am wakened by the dream. In the dream my daughter is dead. Her father is returning her body to me in pieces. He keeps her heart. I thought I screamed . . . *Patricia!* I sit up in bed, swallowing air as if for nourishment. The dream remains in the air. I rise to go to her room. Ellen tries to lead me back to bed, but I have to see once again. I open her door. She is gone. The room empty, lonely. They said it was in her best interests. How can that be? She is only six, a baby who needs her mothers. She loves us. This has not happened. I will not believe this. Oh god, I think I have died.

Night after night, Ellen holds me as I shake. Our sobs stifling the air in our room. We lie in our bed and try to give comfort. My mind can't think beyond last week when she left. I would have killed him if I'd had the chance! He took her hand and pulled her to the car. The look in his eyes of triumph. It was a contest to him, Patricia the prize. He will teach her to hate us. He will! I see her dear face. That face looking out the back window of his car. Her mouth forming the words *Mommy, Mama.* Her dark braids tied with red yarn. Her front teeth missing. Her overalls with the yellow flower on the pocket, embroidered by Ellen's hands. So lovingly she sewed the yellow wool. Patricia waiting quietly until she was finished. Ellen promised to teach her designs—chain stitch, french knot, split stitch. How Patricia told everyone that Ellen made the flower just for her. So proud of her overalls.

I open the closet door. Almost everything is gone. A few things hang there limp, abandoned. I pull a blue dress from the hanger and take it back to my room. Ellen tries to take it from me, but I hold on, the soft blue cotton

*Mother

smelling of my daughter. How is it possible to feel such pain and live? 'Ellen?!' She croons my name. 'Mary, Mary, I love you.' She sings me to sleep.

1890

The agent was here to deliver a letter. I screamed at him and sent curses his way. I threw dirt in his face as he mounted his horse. He thinks I'm a crazy woman and warns me, 'You better settle down, Annie.' What can they do to me? I am a crazy woman. This letter hurts my hand. It is written in their hateful language. It is evil, but there is a message for me.

I start the walk up the road to my brother. He works for the whites and understands their meanings. I think about my brother as I pull the shawl closer to my body. It is cold now. Soon there will be snow. The corn has been dried and hangs from our cabin, waiting to be used. The corn never changes. My brother is changed. He says that *I* have changed and bring shame to our clan. He says I should accept the fate. But I do not believe in the fate of child-stealing. There is evil here. There is much wrong in our village. My brother says I am a crazy woman because I howl at the sky every evening. He is a fool. I am calling the children. He says the people are becoming afraid of me because I talk to the air and laugh like the raven overhead. But I am talking to the children. They need to hear the sound of me. I laugh to cheer them. They cry for us.

This letter burns my hands. I hurry to my brother. He has taken the sign of the wolf from over the doorway. He pretends to be like those who hate us. He gets more and more like the child-stealers. His eyes move away from mine. He takes the letter from me and begins the reading of it. I am confused. This letter is from two strangers with the names Martha and Daniel. They say they are learning civilized ways. Daniel works in the fields, growing food for the school. Martha cooks and is being taught to sew aprons. She will be going to live with the schoolmaster's wife. She will be a live-in girl. What is a *live-in girl*? I shake my head. The words sound the same to me. I am afraid of Martha and Daniel, these strangers who know my name. My hands and arms are becoming numb.

I tear the letter from my brother's fingers. He stares at me, his eyes traitors in his face. He calls after me, 'Annie! Annie!' That is not my name! I run to the road. That is not my name! There is no Martha! There is no Daniel! This is witch work. The paper burns and burns. At my cabin, I quickly dig a hole in the field. The earth is hard and cold, but I dig with my nails. I dig, my hands feeling weaker. I tear the paper and bury the scraps. As the earth drifts and settles, the names Martha and Daniel are covered. I look to the sky and find nothing but endless blue. My eyes are blinded by the colour. I begin the howling.

1978

When I get home from work, there is a letter from Patricia. I make coffee and wait for Ellen, pacing the rooms of our apartment. My back is sore from the line, bending over and down, screwing the handles on the doors of the flashing cars moving by. My work protects me from questions, the guys making jokes at my expense. But some of them touch my shoulder lightly and briefly as a sign of understanding. The few women, eyes averted or smiling in sympathy. No one talks. There is no time to talk, the noise taking up all space and breath.

I carry the letter with me as I move from room to room. Finally I sit at the kitchen table, turning the paper around in my hands. Patricia's printing is large and uneven. The stamp has been glued on halfheartedly and is coming loose. Each time a letter arrives, I dread it, even as I long to hear from my child. I hear Ellen's key in the door. She walks into the kitchen, bringing the smell of the hospital with her. She comes toward me, her face set in new lines, her uniform crumpled and stained, her brown hair pulled back in an imitation of a french twist. She knows there is a letter. I kiss her and bring mugs of coffee to the table. We look at each other. She reaches for my hand, bringing it to her lips. Her hazel eyes are steady in her round face.

I open the letter. *Dear Mommy. I am fine. Daddy got me a new bike. My big teeth are coming in. We are going to see Grandma for my birthday. Daddy got me new shoes. Love Patricia.* She doesn't ask about Ellen. I imagine her father standing over her, coaxing her, coaching her. The letter becomes ugly. I tear it in bits and scatter them out the window. The wind scoops the pieces into a tight fist before strewing them in the street. A car drives over the paper, shredding it to garbage and mud.

Ellen makes a garbled sound. 'I'll leave. If it will make it better, I'll leave.' I quickly hold her as the dusk moves into the room and covers us. 'Don't leave. Don't leave.' I feel her sturdy back shiver against my hands. She kisses my throat, and her arms tighten as we move closer. 'Ah, Mary. I love you so much.' As the tears threaten our eyes, the taste of salt is on our lips and tongues. We stare into ourselves, touching the place of pain, reaching past the fear, the guilt, the anger, the loneliness.

We go to our room. It is beautiful again. I am seeing it new. The sun is barely there. The colours of cream, brown, green mixing with the wood floor. The rug with its design of wild birds. The black ash basket glowing on the dresser, holding a bouquet of dried flowers bought at a vendor's stand. I remember the old woman, laughing and speaking rapidly in Polish as she wrapped the blossoms in newspaper. Ellen undresses me as I cry. My desire for her breaking through the heartbreak we share. She pulls the covers back, smoothing the white sheets, her hands repeating the gestures done at work. She guides me onto the cool material. I watch her remove the uniform of work. An aide to nurses. A healer of spirit.

She comes to me full in flesh. My hands are taken with the curves and soft roundness of her. She covers me with the beating of her heart. The rhythm steadies me. Heat is centring me. I am grounded by the peace between us. I smile at her face above me, round like a moon, her long hair loose and touching my breasts. I take her breast in my hand, bring it to my mouth, suck her as a woman—in desire, in faith. Our bodies join. Our hair braids together on the pillow. Brown, black, silver, catching the last light of the sun. We kiss, touch, move to our place of power. Her mouth, moving over my body, stopping at curves and swells of skin, kissing, removing pain. Closer, close, together, woven, my legs are heat, the centre of my soul is speaking to her. I am sliding into her, her mouth is medicine, her heart is the earth, we are dancing with flying arms. I shout, I sing, I weep salty liquid, sweet and warm it coats her throat. This is my life. I love you Ellen, I love you Mary, I love, we love.

1891

The moon is full. The air is cold. This cold strikes at my flesh as I remove my clothes and set them on fire in the withered corn field. I cut my hair, the knife sawing through the heavy mass. I bring the sharp blade to my arms, legs, and breasts. The blood trickles like small red rivers down my body. I feel nothing. I throw the tangled webs of my hair into the flames. The smell, like a burning animal, fills my nostrils. As the fire stretches to touch the stars, the people come out to watch me—the crazy woman. The ice in the air touches me.

They caught me as I tried to board the train and search for my babies. The white men tell my husband to watch me. I am dangerous. I laugh and laugh. My husband is good only for tipping bottles and swallowing anger. He looks at me, opening his mouth and making no sound. His eyes are dead. He wanders from the cabin and looks out on the corn. He whispers our names. He calls after the children. He is a dead man.

Where have they taken the children? I ask the question of each one who travels the road past our door. The women come and we talk. We ask and ask. They say there is nothing we can do. The white man is like a ghost. He slips in and out where we cannot see. Even in our dreams he comes to take away our questions. He works magic that resists our medicine. This magic has made us weak. What is the secret about them? Why do they want our children? They sent the Blackrobes many years ago to teach us new magic. It was evil! They lied and tricked us. They spoke of gods who would forgive us if we believed as they do. They brought the rum with the cross. This god is ugly! He killed our masks. He killed our men. He sends the women screaming at the moon in terror. They want our power. They take our children to remove the inside of them. Our power. They steal our food, our sacred rattle, the stories, our names. What is left?

I am a crazy woman. I look to the fire that consumes my hair and see their faces. My daughter. My son. They still cry for me, though the sound grows fainter. The wind picks up their keening and brings it to me. The sound has bored into my brain. I begin howling. At night I dare not sleep. I fear the dreams. It is too terrible, the things that happen there. In my dream there is wind and blood moving as a stream. Red, dark blood in my dream. Rushing for our village. The blood moves faster. There are screams of wounded people. Animals are dead, thrown in the blood stream. There is nothing left. Only the air echoing nothing. Only the earth soaking up blood, spreading it in the four directions, becoming a thing there is no name for. I stand in the field watching the fire. The People watching me. We are waiting, but the answer is not clear yet. A crazy woman. That is what they call me.

1979

After taking a morning off work to see my lawyer, I come home, not caring if I call in. Not caring, for once, at the loss in pay. Not caring. My lawyer says there is nothing more we can do. I must wait. As if there has been something other than waiting. He has custody and calls the shots. We must wait and see how long it takes for him to get tired of being a mommy and a daddy. So, I wait.

I open the door to Patricia's room. Ellen and I keep it dusted and cleaned in case my baby will be allowed to visit us. The yellow and blue walls feel like a mockery. I walk to the windows, begin to systematically tear down the curtains. I slowly start to rip the cloth apart. I enjoy hearing the sounds of destruction. Faster, I tear the material into strips. What won't come apart with my hands, I pull at with my teeth. Looking for more to destroy, I gather the sheets and bedspread in my arms and wildly shred them to pieces. Grunting and sweating, I am pushed by rage and the searing wound in my soul. Like a wolf, caught in a trap, gnawing at her own leg to set herself free, I begin to beat my breasts to deaden the pain inside. A noise gathers in my throat and finds the way out. I begin a scream that turns to howling, then becomes hoarse choking. I want to take my fists, my strong fists, my brown fists, and smash the world until it bleeds. Bleeds! And all the judges in their flapping robes, and the fathers who look for revenge, are ground, ground into dust and disappear with the wind.

The word *lesbian*. Lesbian. The word that makes them panic, makes them afraid, makes them destroy children. The word that dares them. Lesbian. *I am one.* Even for Patricia, even for her, *I will not cease to be!* As I kneel amidst the colourful scraps, Raggedy Anns smiling up at me, my chest gives a sigh. My heart slows to its normal speech. I feel the blood pumping outward to my veins, carrying nourishment and life. I strip the room naked. I close the door.

❧

COMPATRIOTS

Lucy heard the car's motor wind down before it turned off the gravel road a quarter of a mile west of the house. Maybe it was Bunky. She hurried and left the outhouse. She couldn't run if she wanted to. It would be such a relief to have this pregnancy over with. She couldn't see the colour of the vehicle, for the slab fence was between the house and the road. That was just as well. She'd been caught in the outhouse a few times, and it still embarrassed her to have a car approach while she was in there.

She got inside the house just as the car came into view. It was her aunt, Flora. Lucy looked at the clock. It was seven-thirty. She wondered what was going on so early in the morning. Flora and a young white woman approached the house. Bob barked furiously at them. Lucy opened the door and yelled at him. 'I don't know what's wrong with Bob; he never barks at me,' said Flora.

'He's probably barking at her,' explained Lucy. 'Not many whites come here.'

'Oh, this is Hilda Afflerbach. She's from Germany,' began Flora. 'Remember? I told you I met her at the Calgary Stampede? Well, she got off the seven o'clock bus, and I don't have time to drive her all the way down to my house. I took her over to my mother's, but she's getting ready to go to Lethbridge. Can she stay with you till I get off work?'

Lucy smiled. She knew she was boxed in. 'Yeah, but I've got no running water in the house. You have to go outside to use the toilet,' she said, looking at Hilda.

'Oh, that's okay,' her aunt answered. 'She's studying about Indians, anyway. Might as well get the true picture, right? Oh, Hilda, this is my niece, Lucy.' Flora lowered her voice and asked, 'Where's Bunky?'

'He never came home last night. I was hoping it was him coming home. He's not supposed to miss any more work. I've got his lunch fixed in case he shows up.' Lucy poured some water from a blue plastic water jug into a white enamel basin and washed her hands and face. 'I haven't even had time to make coffee. I couldn't sleep waiting for him to come home.' She poured water into a coffeemaker and measured out the coffee into the paper filter.

'I'd have some coffee if it was ready, but I think I'd better get to work.

We have to punch in now; it's a new rule. Can't travel on Indian time anymore,' said Flora. She opened the door and stepped out, then turned to say, 'I think the lost has returned,' and continued down the steps.

The squeak of the dusty truck's brakes signalled Bunky's arrival. He strode toward the door, barely acknowledging Flora's presence. He came in and took the lunch pail Lucy had. 'I stayed at Herbie's,' was all he said before he turned and went out. He started the truck and beeped the horn.

'I'll go see what he wants.' She motioned to Flora to wait.

When Bunky left, she went to Flora. 'Maybe it's a good thing you came here. Bunky didn't want to go to work 'cause he had a hangover. When he found out Hilda was going to be here all day, he decided he'd rather go to work.'

'If I don't have to leave the office this afternoon, I'll bring the car over and you can drive Hilda around to look at the reserve, okay?'

'Sure, that'll be good. I can go and do my laundry in Spitzee.' She surveyed the distant horizon. The Rockies were spectacular, blue and distinct. It would be a nice day for a drive. She hoped it would be a repeat of yesterday, not too hot, but, as she stood there, she noticed tiny heat waves over the wheat fields. Well, maybe it won't be a repeat, she thought. Her baby kicked inside of her, and she said, 'Okay, I'd better go tend to the guest.' She didn't relish having a white visitor, but Flora had done her a lot of favours and Hilda seemed nice.

And she was. Hilda made friends with the kids, Jason and Melissa, answering their many questions about Germany as Lucy cooked. She ate heartily, complimenting Lucy on her cooking even though it was only the usual scrambled eggs and fried potatoes with toast and coffee. After payday, there'd be sausages or ham, but payday was Friday and today was only Tuesday.

'Have you heard of Helmut Walking Eagle?' Hilda wanted to know.

'Yeah, well, I really don't know him to talk to him, but I know what he looks like. He's from Germany, too. I always see him at Indian dances. He dresses up like an Indian.' She had an urge to tell her that most of the Indians wished Helmut would disappear.

'I want to see him,' Hilda said. 'I heard about him and I read a book he wrote. He seems to know a lot about the Indians, and he's been accepted into their religious society. I hope he can tell me things I can take home. People in Germany are really interested in Indians. They even have clubs.'

Lucy's baby kicked, and she held her hand over the spot. 'My baby kicks if I sit too long. I guess he wants to do the dishes.'

Hilda got up quickly and said, 'Let me do the dishes. You can take care of the laundry.'

'No, you're the visitor. I can do them,' Lucy countered. But Hilda was persistent, and Lucy gave in.

Flora showed up just after twelve with the information that there was a sun-dance going on on the north side of the reserve. 'They're already camping. Let's go there after work. Pick me up around four.'

'I can't wait to go to the sun-dance! Do you go to them often?' Hilda asked Lucy.

'No, I never have. I don't know much about them,' Lucy said.

'But why? Don't you believe in it? It's your culture!' Hilda's face showed concern.

'Well, they never had sun-dances here—in my whole life there's never been a sun-dance here.'

'Really, is that true? But I thought you have them every year here.'

'Not here. Over on the Blood Reserve they do and some places in the States, but not here.'

'But don't you want to go to a sun-dance? I think it's so exciting!' Hilda moved forward in her seat and looked hopefully at Lucy.

Lucy smiled at her eagerness. 'No, I don't care to go. It's mostly those mixed-up people who are in it. You see, Indian religion just came back here on the reserve a little while ago, and there are different groups who all quarrel over which way to practise it. Some use Sioux ways, and others use Cree. It's just a big mess,' she said, shaking her head.

Hilda looked at Lucy, and Lucy got the feeling she was telling her things she didn't want to hear.

Lucy had chosen this time of day to do her wash. The Happy Suds Laundromat would be empty. As a rule, the Indians didn't show up till after lunch with their endless garbage bags of laundry.

After they had deposited their laundry in the machines, Lucy, Hilda, and the kids sauntered down the main street to a cafe for lunch. An unkempt Indian man dogged them, talking in Blackfoot.

'Do you know what he's saying?' asked Hilda.

'He wants money. He's related to my husband. Don't pay any attention to him. He always does this,' said Lucy. 'I used to give him money, but he just drinks it up.'

The cafe was a cool respite from the heat outside, and the cushioned seats in the booth felt good. They sat by the window and ordered hamburgers, fries, and lemonade. The waitress brought tall, frosted glasses, and beads of water dripped from them.

'Hello, Lucy,' a man's shaky voice said, just when they were really enjoying their lunch. They turned to look at the Indian standing behind Hilda. He was definitely ill. His eyes held pain, and he looked as though he might collapse from whatever ailed him. His hands shook, perspiration covered his face, and his eyes roamed the room constantly.

Lucy moved over to make room for him, but he kept standing and asked her, 'Could you give me a ride down to Badger? The cops said I have to leave town. I don't want to stay 'cause they might beat me up.'

'Yeah, we're doing laundry. I've got Flora's car. This is her friend, Hilda. She's from Germany.'

The sick man barely nodded at her, then, turning back to Lucy, he asked her, 'Do you have enough to get me some soup. I'm really hungry.'

Lucy nodded and the man said, 'I'll just sit in the next booth.'

'He's my uncle,' Lucy explained to Hilda as she motioned to the waitress. 'His name is Sonny.'

'Order some clear soup or you'll get sick,' Lucy suggested to her uncle.

He nodded, as he pulled some paper napkins out of a chrome container on the table and wiped his face.

The women and children left Sonny with his broth and returned to the laundromat. As they were folding the clothes, he came in. 'Here, I'll take these,' he said, taking the bags from Lucy. His hands shook, and the effort of lifting the bags was clearly too much for him. 'That's okay,' protested Lucy, attempting to take them from him, 'they're not that heavy. Clothes are always lighter after they've been washed.'

'Hey, Lucy, I can manage. You're not supposed to be carrying big things around in your condition.' Lucy let him take the plastic bags, which he dropped several times before he got to the car. The cops had probably tired of putting him in jail and sending him out each morning. She believed the cops did beat up Indians, although none was ever brought to court over it. She'd take Sonny home, and he'd straighten out for a few weeks till he got thirsty again, and he'd disappear as soon as he got money. It was no use to hope he'd stop drinking. Sonny wouldn't quit drinking till he quit living.

As they were pulling out of town, Lucy remembered she had to get some Kool-Aid and turned the car into the Stop-n-Go Mart. Hilda got out with her and noticed the man who had followed them through the streets sitting in the shade of a stack of old tires.

'Hey, tamohpomaat sikaohki,' he told Lucy on her way into the store.

'What did he say? Sikaohki?' queried Hilda.

The Kool-Aid was next to the cash register and she picked up a few packages, and laid them on the counter with the money. When the cashier turned to the register, Lucy poked Hilda with her elbow and nodded her head toward the sign behind the counter. Scrawled unevenly in big, black letters, it said, 'Ask for Lysol, vanilla, and shaving lotion at the counter.'

They ignored the man on the way to the car. 'That's what he wants;

he's not allowed to go into the stores 'cause he steals it. He wanted vanilla. The Indians call it "sikaohki"; it means "black water." '

Although the car didn't have air-conditioning, Lucy hurried toward it to escape the blistering heat. When she got on the highway, she asked her uncle, 'Did you hear anything about a sun-dance?'

At first he grunted a negative 'Huh-uh,' then, 'Oh, yeah, it's across the river, but I don't know where. George Many Robes is camping there. Saw him this morning. Are you going there?'

'Flora and Hilda are. Hilda wants to meet that German guy, Helmut Walking Eagle. You know, that guy who turned Indian?'

'Oh yeah, is he here?' he said indifferently, closing his eyes.

'Probably. He's always in the middle of Indian doings,' said Lucy.

'Shit, that guy's just a phony. How could anybody turn into something else? Huh? I don't think I could turn into a white man if I tried all my life. They wouldn't let me, so how does that German think he can be an Indian. White people think they can do anything—turn into Chinese or Indian— they're crazy!'

Sonny laid his head back on the seat and didn't say another word. Lucy felt embarrassed, but she had to agree with him; it seemed that Indians had come into focus lately. She'd read in the papers how some white woman in Hollywood became a medicine woman. She was selling her book on her life as a medicine woman. Maybe some white person or other person who wasn't Indian would get fooled by that book, but not an Indian. She herself didn't practise Indian religion, but she knew enough about it to know that one didn't just join an Indian religious group if one were not raised with it. That was a lot of the conflict going on among those people who were involved in it. They used sacred practices from other tribes, Navajo and Sioux, or whatever pleased them.

The heat of the day had reached its peak, and trails of dust hung suspended in the air wherever cars or trucks travelled the gravel roads on the reserve. Sonny fashioned a shade behind the house underneath the clothesline in the deep grass, spread a blanket, and filled a gallon jar from the pump. He covered the water with some old coats, lay down, and began to sweat the booze out.

The heat waves from this morning's forecast were accurate. It was just too hot. 'Lordy, it's hot,' exclaimed Lucy to Hilda as they brought the laundry in. 'It must be close to ninety-five or one hundred. Let's go up to Badger to my other aunt's house. She's got a tap by her house and the kids can cool off in her sprinkler. Come on, you kids. Do you want to go run in the sprinkler?'

The women covered the windows on the west side where the sun would shine. 'I'm going to leave all the windows open to let the air in,' said Lucy, as she walked around the house pushing them up.

Lucy's aunt's house sat amongst a clutter of junk. 'Excuse the mess,' she smiled at Hilda, waving her arm over her yard. 'Don't wanna throw it away, it might come in handy.' There were thick grass and weeds crisscrossed with paths to and from the clothesline, the outhouse, the woodstove. Lucy's aunt led them to an arbour shaded with huge spruce branches.

'This is nice,' cooed Hilda, admiring the branches. Lucy's aunt beamed, 'Yes, I told my old man, "Henry, you get me some branches that's not gonna dry up and blow away," and he did. He knows what's good for him. You sit down right here, and I'll get us some drinks.' She disappeared and soon returned with a large thermos and some plastic tumblers.

They spent the afternoon hearing about Henry, as they watched the kids run through the sprinkler that sprayed the water back and forth. Once in a while, a suggestion of a breeze would touch the women, but it was more as if they imagined it.

Before four, they left to pick Flora up and headed back to Lucy's. 'It's so hot after being in that cool cement building all day!' exclaimed Flora, as she settled herself into the car's stifling interior. 'One thing for sure, I'm not going home to cook anything. Lucy, do you think Bunky would mind if you came with us? I'll get us some Kentucky Fried Chicken and stuff in town so you don't have to cook. It's too hot to cook, anyway.' She rolled up a newspaper and fanned her face, which was already beginning to flush.

'No, he won't care. He'll probably want to sleep. We picked Sonny up in town. Both of them can lie around and get better. The kids would bother them if we were there.'

It was a long ride across the Napi River toward the Porcupine Hills. A few miles from the Hills, they veered off until they were almost by the river. 'Let's get off,' said Flora.

Hilda gasped at what she saw before her. There was a circle of tepees and tents with a large open area in the middle. Exactly in the centre of the opening was a circular structure covered with branches around the sides. Next to this was a solitary unpainted tepee. Some of the tepees were painted with lines around the bottom; others had orbs bordering them, and yet others had animal figures painted on them. Smoke rose from stoves outside the tepees as people prepared their evening meals. Groups of horses stood languidly in the waning heat of the day, their heads resting on one another's backs and their tails occasionally flicking insects away. The sound of bantering children and yapping dogs carried to where they stood.

'Let's eat here,' the kids said, poking their head to look in the bags of food. Flora and Lucy spread a blanket on the ground, while Hilda continued to stand where she was, surveying the encampment. Flora pointed out the central leafy structure as the sacred area of prayer and dance.

'The tepee next to it is the sacred tepee. That's where the holy woman who is putting up the sun-dance stays the entire time. That's where they have the ceremonies.'

'How many sun-dances have you been to?' asked Hilda.

'This is my first time, but I know all about this from books,' said Flora. 'Helmut Walking Eagle wrote a book about it, too. I could try to get you one. He sells them cheaper to Indians.'

Hilda didn't eat much and kept looking down at the camp. 'It's really beautiful,' she said, as if to herself.

'Well, you better eat something before you get left out,' advised Lucy. 'These kids don't know when to stop eating chicken.'

'Yeah,' agreed Flora. 'Then we can go down and see who's all there.' Hilda had something to eat, and then they got back into the car and headed down toward the encampment. They drove around the edge of the camp and stopped by Flora's cousin's tent. 'Hi, Delphine,' said Flora, 'I didn't know you were camping here.'

Lucy knew Flora and Delphine were not especially close. Their fathers were half-brothers, which made them half-cousins. Delphine had grown up Mormon and had recently turned to Indian religion, just as Flora had grown up Catholic and was now exploring traditional beliefs. The same could be said about many of the people here. To top things off, there was some bad feeling between the cousins about a man, some guy they both had been involved with in the past.

'Can anybody camp here? I've got a tepee. How about if I camp next to you.'

Delphine bridled. 'You're supposed to camp with your own clan.'

Flora looked around the camp. 'I wonder who's my clan. Say, there's George Many Robes, he's my relation on my dad's side. Maybe I'll ask him if I can camp next to him.'

Delphine didn't say anything but busied herself with splitting kindling from a box of sawn wood she kept hidden underneath a piece of tarp. Jason spied a thermos under the tarp and asked for a drink of water.

'I have to haul water, and nobody pays for my gas,' grumbled Delphine, as she filled a cup halfway with water.

'Oh, say,' inquired Flora, 'do you know if Helmut Walking Eagle is coming here? This girl is from Germany, and she wants to see him.'

'Over there, that big tepee with a Winnebago beside it. That's his camp,' Delphine answered, without looking at them.

'Is she mad at you?' Jason asked Flora.

'Yeah, it must be the heat,' Flora told him with a little laugh.

Elsie Walking Eagle was cooking the evening meal on a camp stove out-side the tepee. She had some folding chairs that Lucy would've like to sit down in, but Elsie didn't ask any of them to sit down though she was friend-ly enough.

'Is your husband here?' asked Flora.

'No, he's over in the sacred tepee,' answered Elsie.

'How long is he going to take?'

'Oh, he should be home pretty soon,' Elsie said, tending her cooking.

'Do you mind if we just wait? I brought this girl to see him. She's from Germany, too,' Flora said.

Lucy had never seen Helmut in anything other than Indian regalia. He was a smallish man with blond hair, a broad face, and a large thin nose. He wore his hair in braids and always wore round, pink shell earrings. Whenever Lucy saw him, she was reminded of the Plains Indian Museum across the line.

Helmut didn't even glance at the company but went directly inside the tepee. Flora asked Elsie, 'Would you tell him we'd like to see him?'

'Just wait here. I'll go talk to him,' Elsie said, and followed her husband inside. Finally, she came out and invited them in. 'He doesn't have much time to talk with you, so . . .' Her voice trailed off.

The inside of the tepee was stunning. It was roomy, and the floor was covered with buffalo hides. Backrests, wall hangings, parfleche bags, and numerous artifacts were magnificently displayed. Helmut Walking Eagle sat resplendent amidst his wealth. The women were dazzled. Lucy felt herself gaping and had to shush her children from asking any questions.

Helmut looked at them intently and rested his gaze on Hilda. Hilda walked toward him, her hand extended in greeting, but Helmut ignored it. Helmut turned to his wife and asked in Blackfoot, 'Who is this?'

'She says she's from Germany,' was all Elsie said, before making a quick move toward the door.

'Wait!' he barked in Blackfoot, and Elsie stopped where she was.

'I only wanted to know if you're familiar with my home town Weisbaden?' said Hilda.

'Do you know what she's talking about?' Helmut asked Elsie in Blackfoot. Elsie shook her head in a shamed manner.

'Why don't you ask *her* questions about Germany?' He hurled the words at Hilda, then, looking meanly at his wife, he added, 'She's been there.' Elsie flinched, and, forcing a smile, waved weakly at the intruders and asked them in a kind voice to come outside. As Lucy waited to leave, she looked at Helmut whose jaw twitched with resentment. His anger seemed to be tangibly reaching out to them.

'Wow!' whispered Hilda in Lucy's ear.

Outside, Flora touched a book on the fold-out table. Its title read *Indian Medicine* and in smaller letters, *A Revival of Ancient Cures and Ceremonies*. There was a picture of Helmut and Elsie on the cover. Flora asked, 'Is this for sale?'

'No, that one's for someone here at camp, but you can get them in the bookstores.'

'How much are they?' Flora asked, turning the book over.

'They're twenty-seven dollars. A lot of work went into it,' Elsie replied.

Helmut, in Blackfoot, called out his wife's name, and Elsie said to her unwelcome callers, 'I don't have time to visit. We have a lot of things to do.' She left them and went in to her husband.

'Do you think she wrote that book?' Lucy asked Flora.

'He's the brains; she's the source,' Flora said. 'Let's go. My kids are probably wondering what happened to me.'

'I'm sorry I upset her husband. I didn't mean to,' said Hilda. 'I thought he would be willing to teach me something, because we're both German.'

'Maybe you could buy his book,' suggested Lucy.

'Look,' said Flora, 'if you're going to be around for a while, I'm going to a sun-dance this next weekend. I'm taking a few days off work. I have a friend up north who can teach you about Indian religion. She's a medicine woman. She's been to Germany. Maybe she even went to your home town.'

'Oh, really!' gushed Hilda. 'Of course, I'll be around. I'd love to go with you and meet your friends.'

'You can come into the sweat with us. First, you'll need to buy four square yards of cotton . . .' began Flora.

But Hilda wasn't really listening to her. She looked as if she were already miles and miles away in the north country. Now, a sweat, she thought, would be real Indian.

HIMANI BANNERJI

❧

ON A COLD DAY

I

The morning Asima jumped from her seventh-storey balcony it was especially cold. The city lay in the grip of a cold wave which made this December an unusually cold one. But the day was not grey or overcast. Instead, a hard white light encased the city in a crystal jar, under which the black bare branches of trees clawed upwards for air, the outlines of houses looked sharply defined and silent, and the smoke from their chimneys, wispy and thin, struggled under a pale blue sky.

The white cold light fell on Asima, as indifferently as on the phone booth, the pizza store and the sequined models in the shop windows. There she lay, sprawled on the sidewalk, quite close to the curb, with red liquid oozing out of the back of her head, and from under her face, which was in profile. This blackish red liquid must have been warm because as it came in contact with cold air, it smoked. The light caught this smoke as well, and Asima's face was visible through its shimmering haze. If she had convulsed a few times immediately after falling, now she was perfectly still, as were all other objects on the sidewalk, for instance the battered coke can that lay very near her outstretched hand, as though she had been sipping it as she fell. The brown hand, with the fingers slightly curled, looked small, helpless and somehow irrelevant, as did her little gold earring in which a strand of hair had got caught.

II

All morning Asima had been restless. She had wandered from room to room aimlessly. She walked through the small two-bedroom apartment as though it contained miles of road within it, and the road went in circles, and nowhere in particular. It could be said that she was trying to tidy the apartment, or pack up things, or both. For objects such as pieces of clothing, bags, and sandals lay here and there, but unfolded and scattered about. She had also pulled out some letters. The contents of a drawer, including some colour photographs, lay spilled on the floor as well. She had emptied out her bathroom cabinet, and also partially the closet next to it, and the pillows on the beds had cases pulled away from them. It seemed that she had been searching for something, as surely as she had been trying to sort or pack.

Her face had a particularly intent look to it, her movements were both precise and aimless. As she walked from room to room, from corner to corner, object to object, she felt, smelled and eyed them searchingly. She was looking for something that she did not find. In her linear, rectangular living room she sat from time to time on her striped foam couch, or at her kitchen table, with its recipe pad, salt and pepper shakers, bright Woolworth coasters and a half-filled teapot. Certainly Asima could not find what she had been looking for. As she lifted up each object for a close inspection, something seemed to be always missing—a part, a function, a meaning perhaps. Because she could not seem to understand either what they were doing there or meant her to do to them. Their meaning, or even command for action to her, remained implacably sealed under their form and exterior. She broke a fingernail trying to go beneath the hard skin of the coffee cup and did not seem to realize that the cold dregs of tea that lay at its bottom signified a sip, a drink.

Her detachment from the objects in the room, the walls and the space enclosed between them, felt oppressive to her, as if the emptiness of the space was actually a heavy, solid object which kept expanding, pushing her against the wall and choking her.

She looked out through the window onto the sunlit city outside. There was still room out there, she felt, and those things outside were houses where people lived, and down below there were roads where there were people, cars, lights, noises, voices, movements. Whatever it was that she was looking for was out there, in the sunlight, on the road, under the sky and in the outline of houses under the sky. It was as though there was a message there for her, a letter from home speaking a familiar language, it called out to her, to get away from this silent, enclosed, solidly empty space that expanded, squeezing tight against her ribcage.

Asima stood near the window looking out for a while. She put down the photograph she had been scrutinizing, holding up to her ear to hear a voice, and a pair of child's bracelets that she had been clutching with the photograph—gently—on the window sill.

Even before her body found the door to the balcony, her eyes had gone out into the world, they had jumped into the road, milled about with people and cars, and jostled past two dogs on a leash and in red coats, past toy stores and the secondhand clothing store. Now she was surefooted, aimed towards a destination. As she went to the edge of the balcony, the world rose up to her, the road was both horizontal and vertical, on the ground and touching her balcony door. She climbed over the low railing that separated her from it and she stepped on the air. For her it was the firmest of grounds.

It moved with the speed of waterfalls, of light, of souls leaving the body on their marvellous flights.

III

Mr Abdul Jalal was taking a sip of the coffee that he had freshly brewed for customer take-out, when he noticed Asima rapidly moving down past his window. The smoking hot coffee missed the aim of his lips and drowned his neatly trimmed butterfly moustache instead, calling forward an exclamation.

'Ya Allah!' said Mr Jalal, checking out with himself. 'We have a woman suiciding here? Or maybe she just fell or even got pushed out?'

At this last, his eyes turned inward, as it were, and he could see a pair of hands, and yes, they were male hands, a husband most likely, pushing a woman towards an open balcony door, pushing and shoving her until he got her over the edge. This thought and vision happened instantaneously, and simultaneously gave Mr Jalal a purposive rather than a speculative thought. Putting aside his coffee cup, which had suddenly lost all meaning and become a pointless appendage, he reached for his phone, which lay black and solid next to the tray where baklavas from last week's delivery lay encrusted with drying honey.

To the voice of the operator he explained. 'I am calling a cop,' he said, 'a woman jump down from above. I see her from my window.' To whatever it was that the operator said on the other side, he pronounced his gratitude. Putting the receiver down in its cradle, Mr Jalal stepped out from behind the counter. Absentmindedly he wiped his fingers on his corduroy pants, and picked up his coat, scarf, and gloves. He dressed himself methodically, as though going out on a visit. He ran his hand across his moustache as he always did on such occasions, opened the glass door of his shop and stepped out onto the sidewalk.

There the woman lay on the sidewalk. He could see her, even though the shocked and curious passersby had partially surrounded her.

To no one in particular he shouted out—'I call the cops already.' No one responded to him. He walked a step further. It was bitterly cold. The woman, he noticed, had nothing warm on. A flower-patterned acrylic housecoat, open at the chest, showing part of a gold chain and the top of her left breast; her feet were bare and stiff; and her face was brown-skinned and young. His countrywoman? Mr Jalal wanted to cover her with a blanket, something to keep her warm and cover her shame. 'But she is dead,' he thought, his hands up in a gesture of prayer. The name of Allah bounced off the cold face of Asima for a few brief seconds, until the howling of the police sirens drowned out Mr Jalal's prayer.

IV

Debbie Barton, or Devika Bardhan, as she was once called in her native Calcutta, was on her way to the office. It was about nine o'clock in the morning, very bitterly cold, and she was a little late. As she stepped out of the warmth of the subway station, Debbie felt the cold hit her in the face like a fist. She was a little breathless from its impact at first, but picked up speed soon enough, drawing the collar of her coat tightly against her throat. Her eyes went instinctively to the huge glass panes of the clothing stores she passed, and there, in one shop window, sprawled between two mannequins, white and blond, their breasts and crotches thrust out, she saw herself in a flowered nightdress sprawled on the sidewalk! This pulled her up short, and she wheeled around, to view the body of Asima on the sidewalk.

Horrified and fascinated at the same time, she slowly walked towards the body. And as she looked at Asima more closely, this uncanny feeling of resemblance gave way to relief as the feeling of seeing herself reflected in a mirror made room for the recognition of difference. A woman from either India or Pakistan, or Bangladesh or Sri Lanka, or for that matter from Trinidad or Guyana, or Africa or Fiji—from just about anywhere in the world, of South Asian origin, as the newspapers said, lay in front of her, dead and cold. Yet in that face neither young nor old, she saw something of herself, and even some of her friends. Standing a few feet away from the body, among a gradually increasing circle of passersby, she searched the fragile face in front of her for clues. What, she wondered, could drive her to do this? To die like this, she thought, in this cold country. Coming all the way here to die! The brown face in front of her, the wisps of hair on the face, the gold earrings glistening in the sun—she looked searchingly at each item. Suddenly she felt the impulse to touch the woman lying on the ground, to sit next to her and cradle her head on her lap, to take a coat from the shop window to cover her from the cold. She felt herself go colder when she noticed the purple tinge settling into Asima's lips and cheeks, the brown of the extended arm taking on a grey and the stiffness of hard wood.

A woman from my own country, she thought. Doesn't she have anyone? Why is no one looking for her? A husband, a child, a relative? What is her name? Who is she? The woman lying before her could give no answer.

But even though she gave no direct answers as to her personal identity, the dead woman sent forth a wave of images to Debbie. Her sheer presence on the sidewalk, her black hair and brown Indian face, her feet lightly calloused at the heels, all riveting and obstructing the traffic as though a mango tree in bloom or a palm tree had suddenly sprung up in the middle of this cold concrete. Busy streets of her own city, its warmth, smells, dust and colours overwhelmed Debbie Barton, who now saw herself as she had been only a few years ago, in a starched sari, a braid down her back, carrying her sister's automatic umbrella, waiting at the end of the road near her parents' house for a cycle rickshaw to show up. It was uncanny how she could see herself, as though in a mirror, someone else, from a long time ago. Devika Bardhan of Jadavpur had no idea about the permed, made-up, perfumed Debbie, who changed her name because a counsellor had advised her to, as one of the stocks-in-trade for finding a job.

'Debbie Barton,' said the counsellor, whose surface was as shiny as new nail polish. 'It's a neat, easy, nice name. Every employer wants to be able to pronounce their employees' names without going to heritage language classes.' Debbie thought that was a good idea too. It certainly saved having to coach people or wince every time they mispronounced her name. She had learned the phrase 'Can't complain.' She said, 'Can't complain.' She had been working at the cash in a nearby clothing store. She was young, attractive and adaptable. There was a future for her here.

Her mind again drifted to the woman in front of her, she lay like a question mark before her. Debbie had a frantic desire to know her history, at least her name, and of course who pushed her out into the street from such a high place, from the safety of her home. A husband, she thought, maybe he pushed her, or maybe he just left her, alone, in this big city, without a penny, without a future or a past. So she was fed up and just jumped. And yet there was this silence, and of course Debbie would never really know, except maybe tomorrow a little news item would appear in the paper.

But in the middle of the silent space that lay in the cold air between Debbie Barton and the dead woman on the stark grey pavement, the police arrived, their lights flashing, their sirens hooting, their neat blue and black outfits matching the cold air in precision and trimness. Backing off many steps to their curtly ejected order, Debbie saw how healthy and pink these officers of law looked, and how like deaf and blind men, neither seeing nor hearing, with pairs of black gloved hands, they moved various props around onto which with the help of the ambulance men, they placed the cold, stiff remains of the brown woman. As they lifted the stretcher, Debbie's hands went up to her forehead, palms joined in a gesture of both homage and prayer.

Mr Abdul Jalal, whose hands were also uplifted, noticed this gesture. Quietly he moved over to her, they were almost at the door of his grocery and take-out coffee and snack store. Fixing Debbie with his grave eyes, he asked, 'You know her? Your countrywoman maybe?'

'No, I don't know her,' said Debbie, 'but yes, she's from my country.' Though the crowd was dispersing now, Debbie stood there, unable to move in any direction. The cold was biting into her bones again, something she had not noticed in the last while. She felt dazed, the idea of right away walking into her workplace quite unnerved her. Where could she go? So, without thinking she turned around and followed Mr Abdul Jalal into his store.

As she sat in a chair at one of two small tables stuck away between two shelves of canned goods, she was still cold and huddled into her coat, her hands and feet tingled as if stimulated by little electric shocks. The big toe of her left foot also hurt somewhat, a symptom she had developed by forcing her feet into closed high-heeled shoes, without which they would not hire her, it seemed.

'A coffee please,' she said to Mr Jalal, who had retreated behind his counter now, and was carefully putting away his outer garments under it. The store was small, it sold dry goods of Middle Eastern variety, odds and ends such as brass bowls and scarves, and coffee and sweets for take-out.

Mr Abdul Jalal brought her a coffee, pulled up a chair near her table, and sat down. It seemed as if they had attended a funeral together, and had now achieved a state of courteous intimacy. 'Why do you think she did it?' he asked her, as if she had been a sister of the deceased.

'I don't know,' said Debbie. 'Perhaps she wasn't happy, perhaps someone pushed her.'

'Who?' asked Mr Jalal. 'Her husband maybe?'

'Maybe,' said Debbie rather absentmindedly. She neither felt obliged to talk, nor felt it necessary to avoid his probing. She was just comfortable, with this talkativeness and curiosity about others' affairs. It made her feel she existed, and that the two of them were real persons together.

How different, she thought . . . and she recalled the morning as it had passed before she saw the dead woman . . . It was past seven when she had got up, made herself tea, ate some cereal with a bowl of milk, stared at a set of clothes which felt not like her own but a set of costumes or disguises. She sat in her kitchen for a while, working herself up to get dressed, to put on her makeup, which made her dark brown skin look rather ashen, and to go to work. She had to develop the right motivation and the right attitudes, she thought as she applied a little Cover Girl rouge to her cheeks. She should probably get a diploma in one of the community colleges. While leaving her apartment, one more time she noticed the peeling wall at the top of the radiator, heard the hiss and sputter, and dreaded the cold she would encounter as she bent down to zip up her boots. On her way down she looked in vain for a letter from home. Once on the street she again had this peculiar feeling of unreality, as though she was somewhere where she had no business being, nor knew exactly how she got there.

At the subway station she waited humbly, deferentially at the end of the line. She was going to ask a question today which she had rehearsed in her mind. She shunned any such exercise normally, since the answers came grudgingly and curtly, without her having the courage to get any detail. She got a feeling that she was not quite there, a feeling of invisibility compounded by the fact that a white woman jumped the queue, banging her with her huge shoulder bag, but did not look back once or say 'sorry.' The same woman, however, bumped into a white young woman and hastily said, 'Sorry, real sorry' in a penitent voice, while the young woman said, 'You just butted into the line.'

A small agitation followed in the line, white people spoke to each other across her head, face, body, as though she were invisible. Slowly, as she stood there struggling to keep herself from completely disappearing, she looked at the white people, they were losing their faces, sex, and details of clothing and becoming one mass of a cold ice colour. This feeling continued with her as she sat in the train, making herself as small as possible, knees straight and together, hands over them, her handbag not exceeding the boundaries of her lap. Two white people sat on either side of her, and they kept expanding, squeezing her out of the very little space that she took. She looked at the passengers across from her seat—a white young male whose legs were aggressively thrust forward with knees jutting out, and a white woman sitting comfortably with a magazine, taking just as much room as she needed. Her purple coat, matching scarf and beautifully groomed hair and shiny skin with a discreet touch of makeup exuded a confidence that Debbie could never have. At the time of leaving the train Debbie inadvertently banged into a white man, and even though she said 'Sorry' instantly, she heard him mutter something about 'fucking pakis' under his breath. Then she had come onto the street and seen herself lying on the pavement, reflected in the shop window. It was a nasty shock, but now in Mr Abdul Jalal's store, faced with his questioning, she felt that she was gaining a body and a voice, that someone actually heard and saw her. He even had questions for her.

'What country do you come from? Are you alone here? How long do you live here? Are you married? Why are you alone, a girl should have a husband if she is alone in this country.' Back in her own country if a shopkeeper asked her these kinds of questions she would not answer him—she would leave the store with some rude or curt reply. But here it was a different matter. Very soon she had told Mr Abdul Jalal about her worries regarding her old parents, her brothers' unemployment and her own ambitions. He in his turn, arranging tins of stuffed grape leaves, tahini and ready-made humus, packets of cardamom and other wares, confided to her his extensive business plans, worries about his relatives in Palestine, his son's misdemeanours. They talked as do refugees who find themselves in the same camp.

Finally she asked him for the time. She was indeed very late for work, but decided to go anyway. She didn't want any pay docked for Christmas, when the girls at the office gave each other presents. Though she was not a Christian, she could not stay away because it brought an air of liveliness to their workplace.

As she made her way to the door she turned around to thank Mr Abdul Jalal. He was still preoccupied with the dead woman. 'I wish I knew what her name was so I could offer a prayer,' he said.

Debbie could never understand what made her lie at this last moment.

'Actually,' she said, 'actually I knew her. Not well, just met her at a party. I just didn't want to talk about it. Her husband had just left her and taken away their kid. She didn't have a job, her English wasn't great and she was really down—depressed.'

Mr Abdul Jalal turned his heavy gaze at her. 'So what was her name?' he asked.

'Oh, Devika. Devika Bardhan,' said Debbie.

'What kind of name is that?'

'From India,' she replied, 'from a city called Calcutta.'

'I heard of Calcutta,' said Mr Abdul Jalal. 'A big Muslim community there too. OK,' he said, 'I'll offer up a prayer for her when I go to the mosque this evening.'

'Thank you,' said Debbie, and stepped out into the street and the cold whiteness of the city.

❧

NIGHT TRAVELLERS

'When a woman has intercourse,' Mika told herself, 'she thinks of what might happen.' She climbed in the night the hill that led away from the river and James. She travelled in a black and white landscape because it was void of details that would have demanded her attention. And the night was also a cover. Above, the starlit summer sky served only to make God seem more remote, withdrawn. As she walked, she took comfort in the sound of the frogs in the moist ditches on either side of the road, the call of an owl hunting in the park below.

Men, she was certain, thinking of both James and Maurice, didn't think of such things as a seed piercing another seed and a baby growing instantly, latching itself fast to the sides of her life. Men were inside themselves when they shot their juices. It was just another trick that God played, to keep the babies coming. Replenish the earth. Well—she was doing her job.

She reached the top of the hill and then she stooped slightly, giving in to the weight of a stone which she cradled close to her breasts. If Maurice should ever think to ask, she would be able to say, 'I was out gathering rocks for my rock garden. It's the only time I can go, when the children are sleeping.' And she would still be telling the truth.

She stopped to catch her breath and turned to look back at the park beside the river. Lot's wife looking back with longing towards a forbidden city. But unlike Lot's wife, she did not become a pillar of salt. From among the trees in the park, light shone out from the tiny window in James's bunkhouse. He had turned on the lantern. Pride made her wish that he would have stood for a few decent moments and watched while she climbed the hill. For this reason she'd kept her back straight until she was certain he couldn't see her anymore. But already, he was stretched out, lost in one of the many books he kept on the floor beside the cot. What did she expect? That had been their agreement, not to look for anything from each other. She had Maurice and the children. He had his dream of voyages in a sailboat.

At the top of the hill, the road stretched broad and straight, one half mile to the centre of town. She could see lights as cars on Main Street headed in and swiftly out of town. She passed by the grove of fruit trees that surrounded her parents' garden. The scent of ripe fruit carried across the road and she thought of the apples her mother had given to her, baskets of them, in the bottom of the cupboard. Her parents' white cottage stood beyond the garden in the darkness. I'm sorry, she said. I forgot about the apples. But with the children my hands are already full. She thought of the children, round cheeked and flushed with their dreams and her step quickened.

Beyond the ditch, there was a sudden rustling sound, like an animal rising up quickly. Mika, startled, stood still and listened. A dark figure stepped from the cover of the fruit trees onto the path that joined the cottage to the road.

'Who's there?' She heard movement, fabric rubbing against fabric. A dry cough. 'Papa, is that you?'

Her father came forward in the darkness. Relief made her knees weak.

'Liebe, Mika. I was hoping, but I knew in my heart it was you.'

Knew it was me, what? What did he know? 'What are you doing up so late?' she asked instead. 'The night air isn't good for your lungs.'

'When one of my children is in trouble, I don't worry about such things.'

'What's this, trouble?' she asked. She felt her heart jump against the stone she clutched tightly to her breast. As he turned towards her, he was illuminated by the moon and she saw that he'd pulled his pants on over his night clothes. His shirt lay open, exposing the onion-like skin on his chest to the cool breeze. She saw concern for her in the deep lines in his face. If only he would use anger, it would be easier to oppose him.

'Nah, you know of what I speak. I've seen your coming and going. I've seen him. I'm ashamed for you.'

'What you've seen is me gathering rocks for a rock garden.' She held up the stone. 'I gather them from beneath the bridge.'

'Mika.' There was sorrow in his voice.

It was the same tone of voice he'd used on her all her life. It made her change her course of action because she didn't want to be responsible for his sorrow. It was the same thing with Maurice. Peace at all costs. Maurice had forced himself on her and she'd forgiven him because of an offer to build a new window in the kitchen. She hated that about herself.

'So, you've seen my coming and going and you're ashamed for me. I'm not.'

He blocked her path. 'Come to the house. We should talk and—'

She pushed around him and began to walk away. Talk? Talk about Maurice and his black night moods? About another baby coming in a house full of babies? No, we will talk about my responsibilities instead.

'Have you travelled that far then,' she heard him call after her, 'that you can now make excuses for your behaviour? What am I to tell the elders at church?'

Before her, silhouetted against the sky, the flutter of wedge-shaped wings, two bats feeding on insects. They would become entangled in her hair. She heard his light step on the road and then he walked beside her. 'Why should you tell them anything?' she asked. 'It's none of their concern. What I do is my own business.'

'We're a community,' he said. 'People united by our belief, like a family. When one member hurts, the whole family suffers.'

'A family. I'm not part of that family,' Mika said. 'I don't belong anywhere.'

'How can you say that? The women welcome you into their homes. They pray for you.'

'Oh, they welcome me, alright. I'm to be pitied, prayed for. It gives them something to do.'

They walked for a few moments without speaking. He pulled at his thick white moustache, the way he did when he was deep in thought. She stopped, turned to him. 'Look, Papa. You know they don't accept Maurice. Even if he wanted to go, they don't invite him into their homes. They don't really accept me, either. So, if you feel it's important to tell the elders, tell them. I don't care.'

The bats—their flight was a dance, a sudden dipping, a flutter, a smooth glide and they swerved back in among the trees. Gone. She walked faster. 'The children are alone,' she said.

'Oh, so you think of the children at least?' he said.

'Of course I think of them. I need something for myself too.'

He put his large cool hand on her arm and drew her to the side of the road. His sun-tinged complexion had paled and there was fear in his eyes. 'But not this,' he said. 'Not this. What are you saying? You need to ask God to forgive you. The wages of sin is death.'

Always, Bible verses, given in love but becoming brick walls, erected swiftly in her path. The hair on her arms and neck prickled. 'Papa,' she said. 'It's my sin and it's my death. Leave me be.' She lifted the stone up and away from her breast and slammed it into the ground. She turned from him quickly and ran with her hands pressed against her stomach.

She undressed quickly, her heart still pounding, and listened to their sounds, the children, breathing all through the house. She'd stood first in one doorway, listening for them, then in another, and finally she'd bent over the baby in the crib at the foot of her bed. She'd felt for him in the dark, found a moist lump beneath the blankets. She'd changed his diaper without awaking him. Maurice was not home. He was still at the hotel. She waited for her heart to be still so that she could sleep. She rubbed her stomach gently. What would it be, she wondered, this one that she carried with her to

James? Would it be touched or bent in any way by her anger? Below, a door opened. She stiffened, then rolled over and faced the wall as Maurice came up the stairs.

'What are you thinking?' James asked.

Mika swung her legs over the side of the cot and sat up. Her feet rested in a trapezoid of moonlight which shone through the small window of the bunkhouse. She'd been half-listening to James telling her about some one person he knew who had never let him down. His voice rose and fell in its strange British accent and she was able to think above it. Through the other small window at the end of the bunkhouse, she could see her parents' cottage, a white sentinel on a hill. It was in darkness once again, but she was certain her father's white face looked out from behind the lace curtains.

'Oh, I'm not thinking about any one thing in particular.' But all day she'd been wondering, how could you be forgiven by God for something you'd done if you weren't sorry you'd done it?

He rose up on his elbow and ran his hand along her arm. The smell of the bunkhouse was his smell, faintly like nutmeg, the warmth of sun trapped in weathered grey planks and it was also the smell of the other men who had slept there; the men who had come to town as James had after the flood to help clean and rebuild it. She put her hand overtop his.

'God, you're beautiful,' he said.

'Don't say that.'

'What, not say you're beautiful?' He laughed and sat up beside her. He reached for his cigarettes on the windowsill. 'You're a strange one.'

He was tired of listening to himself talk and had drawn her in by saying, 'You're beautiful.' In the beginning, he'd pranced around her, so obviously delighted that he'd charmed her into coming away from the riverbank with him, through the park to this bunkhouse. He'd followed her about, picking up the clothing she'd shed, hanging it over a chair so she wouldn't look rumpled when she left. He was a meticulous lovemaker. He began by kissing the bottoms of her feet, the backs of her knees, her belly, causing the swing of the pendulum inside her to pause for several seconds at midpoint, so that she was neither being repelled nor attracted but suspended and still.

'Why don't you want me to tell you that you're beautiful?' James asked.

Because she didn't think she was beautiful. There was nothing beautiful about a person who would come home swollen and moist from lovemaking into the bed of another man. But what Maurice had done was not beautiful either. Two wrongs don't make a right, she'd instruct her own children.

'No, what I meant was, don't say God. Don't bring God into this.'

Their thighs touched as they sat on the edge of the cot and she was amazed at how quickly she had become accustomed to the touch and smell of another man. The flare of his match revealed his exquisitely ugly nose. It was a fleshy hook pitted with blackheads. His chin and the skin around his mouth was deeply scarred by acne. You're so ugly, she'd once told him. She'd watched for evidence of injury, a faltering of his tremendous self-confidence. He'd laughed at her attempt, saw through it. She saw him daily as he walked past the house and he was always in a hurry, loose-jointed and thin, moving towards some vision he had of himself and his future.

He held the lit cigarette up to his watch. 'Shouldn't you think about heading back? It's almost twelve.'

'I've still got time.'

He got up from the cot and his tanned chest moved into the trapezoid of light and then his buttocks, pinched together, muscular as he walked to the table beneath the window. He gathered up her hairpins and dropped them into her lap. He never forgot. He made certain each time that she left exactly as she'd come. She scooped the pins up and put them into the pocket of her dress.

'Don't you think you should fix your hair?'

'It's alright. Maurice is never home before I am.'

He leaned over her, kissed her forehead. He slipped his hand inside her unbuttoned dress and fondled her. 'I love your breasts. I think that's what I'll miss the most about Canada, your beautiful sexy breasts.'

She put her arms about his neck and drew him down on top of her. 'Once I'm gone,' he said into her neck, 'if we ever meet again, it will be chance. You know that, don't you?'

'Yes.' In another month he wouldn't want her anyway. Already she could feel the baby between them. She listened to the sound of his heart pushing against her chest. The wind had fallen and the silence in the park was complete, the river still. The moment passed. She fingered the hairpins in her pocket. She pulled them loose and scattered them into the folds of his blanket. He'd find them tomorrow. When he was making his bed, tight corners, planning his day, his mind leaping forward to the next event, he'd find her pins and he'd think of her for one second. She knew he wouldn't think of her longer than that, or wonder what she might be doing at that moment or try and recall her features as she did his; she even longed for the sight of his lanky body, his brown trousers flapping loosely about his ankles, the funny way he walked, arms swinging, leading with his ugly nose. I thought of you today, he'd said once, and I got this enormous stiff prick. I think of you too. She couldn't say, I love you.

'You'd better go,' he said. 'Before I change my mind and keep you here with me all night.'

She pushed him from her, sat up and buttoned her dress. She used his comb and began combing her hair which was tangled and damp with sweat. The comb seemed to contain some residue of his energy, a reminder of the range of feelings she'd experienced only thirty minutes before. James got up, walked to the door and she followed him. He stood naked on the step. She gave him the comb. He plucked her dark hairs from its teeth and let the breeze catch them away. Above them, the stars were brilliant and clear. 'Will you come tomorrow?' he asked.

'I don't know. If I can, I will.'

'Try.' He took her hand in his. He pressed the hairpins into her hand. 'You've forgotten these.'

Mika walked up the hill away from the park, the river, James. She heard nothing of the sounds of the night, the singing of insects, the owl hunting, nor did she see the phosphorous glow of fireflies among the tall grasses in the ditch. She was listening to the sound of her feet on the road, her heart beating, her breath labouring slightly as she climbed the hill and her thoughts. How could she be forgiven by God and brought to a state of serenity and continue to see James at the same time?

When she reached the top of the hill, her father waited on the path, pacing back and forth, swishing mosquitoes from his arms with a switch of leaves. Mika walked faster so that he would know she had no intention of stopping. He ceased pacing. She lifted her head and strode by him. She felt the sting of leaves on her legs. She stopped suddenly, her breath caught in her throat, and fought back anger. He threw the switch aside.

'Where is the stone you've been searching for tonight?' he asked.

'I have nothing to say. You can't make me argue with you. If you want to argue, then do it with yourself.' Her voice did not betray her anger. She still felt the biting edge of the leaves on her skin. She walked away swiftly, and then faster until she was running from him. Her breath became tight and then a spot of fire burned in her centre. But she wouldn't stop running until she was home, safe, behind the door.

She sat at the kitchen table and pressed her face against the cool arborite. To be alone for once, just to be left alone. She listened to a fly buzzing against a window. The wind in the kitchen curtain swept against the potted plant. Water dripped into the sink. Something sticky against her arms—she sat up and frowned as her hand met toast crumbs and smears of jam left behind by one of the children. Her legs felt weak as she went over to the sink to stop the dripping of water and to get a cloth to wash the table. She reached to turn the light on above the sink and saw through the window her father entering the yard. She stood with her hands pressed to her face and waited. She wouldn't answer the door and he might think that she was upstairs, sleeping.

His light touch on the door, a gentle knock and—silence. Above her, the sound of electricity in the clock. He coughed twice. She could see him fumbling for his pocket, to spit his blood-flecked mucus into a handkerchief.

'Mika, I know you're there. Mika, open the door.'

It wasn't locked, but she knew he wouldn't come in unless she opened it.

'You're causing much sorrow,' he said. 'Your mother has been crying most of the day.'

Crying over children is a waste of time, Mika thought. In the end, they do what they want.

'She says for me to tell you, think of eternity.'

The anger erupted. She stepped towards the closed door. 'Eternity? Eternity? Papa, I've spent all my life preparing for eternity. No one tells me how to live each day. Right here, where I am.'

She heard him sigh. 'But when you think of it, we're here for such a little time when you consider all of eternity,' he said.

'Yes, and it's my little time. Mine. Not yours.'

He didn't speak for a few moments. She held her breath. She waited for him to leave. She sensed his wretched disappointment in her, his fading spirit. I can't help that, she told herself.

'Mika, one thing,' he said. His voice was barely more than a whisper. 'There's something wrong with your thinking. If we could just talk. I'm not well. I need to know before I—' He broke off and began to cough.

Before I die. She finished the sentence for him. She turned her back to the door and pressed her knuckles into her teeth and bit into them. Anger rose and grew until her fists were free and raised up. That he would try to use his illness against her. It's my life, she told herself. It's my life.

'Go away,' she cried. She faced the door once again and stamped her foot. 'Go away.' She would tear the curtains from the windows, upset chairs, bring all the children running to stare at her anger. She would let them see what had been done to her, she would tell them, it's my life. She would— she gasped. A sharp kick in her belly, then a fluttering of a limb against her walls. Another movement, a sliding downward, a memory drawing her inside instantly like a flick of a knuckle against her temple. The baby. Like all the others asleep in the rooms upstairs, it travelled with her.

'Mika, please. I care for you.'

She opened the door and stood before him, head bent and arms hanging by her sides. They faced each other. His shoulders sagged beneath his thin shirt. 'Come in,' she said. 'I'll lend you one of Maurice's sweaters.' She began to cry.

He stepped inside quickly and put his hand on her shoulder. 'Yes, yes,' he said. 'That's it. You must cry over what you've done. It's the beginning of healing. God loves a meek and contrite heart.'

She leaned into him, felt the sharpness of his rib cage beneath her arms. I cry because I can't have what I want. He's going away soon. I am meek and contrite because he doesn't want anything more than just a fleeting small part of what I am. I am filled with sorrow because I know myself too well. If I could have him, I wouldn't want him.

'It's over,' he said. 'You won't go and see that man again.'

She heard the rasping sound of fluids in his chest. She loved him.

'No, I won't see him anymore.'

She turned her face against his chest and stared into the night beyond him. She felt empty, barren, but at peace. In the garden, a bright glow flared suddenly and she thought, it's a cigarette. But the glow rose and fell among the vegetation and then became bead-shaped, blue, brighter, her desire riding the night up and up in a wide arc, soaring across the garden into the branches of thick trees. A firefly, Mika thought. And she watched it until it vanished.

❧

HERE AND NOW

As it happened, Alison was wearing black when the phone call came; black velvet, cut low in front, with a thin silver chain at her throat. Only minutes before, she had been under the shower. Before that, she had been shovelling snow from the driveway. She had got the car out before the surface slicked over again, and before the city ploughs came through to toss a fresh barricade across the top of the drive. She had showered and put on the black dress. Car keys in hand, she was just pulling the front door shut behind her.

Damn, she thought. Will I answer it or not?

Afterwards it seemed to her that she had known from the first microsecond of the first ring. Four o'clock on a winter's Sunday afternoon, Lake Ontario veined with early ice, darkness already closing in: this is when such phone calls come. In Brisbane it was tomorrow already, it was dawn on Monday morning. Such phone calls are made at dawn.

At the Faculty Club, Alison's car slewed a little on the ice, nudged a parked Toyota, hesitated, then slid obediently into the neighbouring space. She sat trembling slightly, her hands on the wheel, the engine still running, and stared through the windshield at the Brisbane River. Here, on the lip of the campus, a membrane of ice already stretched across the water for as far as she could see. The membrane was thinner than a fingernail, milky white.

(High in the mango tree, hidden from the other children, frightened, she sucks comfort from the milk iceblocks her mother makes.)

'Metro Toronto engineers,' the car radio announced, 'are mystified by this morning's explosions in the city's sewer system. Throughout the streets in the downtown core, sewer caps have been popping like champagne corks, an extraordinary sight on a quiet Sunday morning in Toronto.'

It is still Sunday here, Alison thought. It is not Monday yet.

It is still now, she thinks.

She turns off radio and ignition and gets out of the car, stepping with infinite care so as not to fracture the thin membranes of ice and time. The air, several degrees below zero, turns into crystal splinters in her lashes and nostrils. Something hurts. It is important to breathe very carefully.

Inside the Faculty Club, champagne corks are popping like pistol shots; a Christmas party, a retirement celebration for a distinguished colleague, two sabbatical farewells, all rolled into one elegant festive affair. Soon Alison will play her public part, make her speech. Then the small talk that rises like wisps of fog will engulf her and drift up river with her, past Kenmore, past the westernmost suburbs of Brisbane, up into the Great Dividing Range. She will be able to make her escape. She is desperate for solitude and rainforest.

'Wonderfully done,' someone enthuses, handing her another drink. 'A fitting tribute.'

She has skated through it then, on thin ice and champagne. Soon it will be possible to leave. She smiles and talks and laughs and talks and smiles. In her glass, the ice in the champagne punch twists and dwindles. She holds the glass up to the light. The icecubes are as thin as the wafers of capiz shell that wash up on Queensland beaches.

'Alison,' someone says. 'Congratulations. I just heard the news.'

Alison holds herself very still. 'Yes?' she says faintly. She will not be able to speak of it yet. They will have to excuse her.

'Your invitation to Sydney, I mean, for next year. You must be thrilled. When do you go?'

'Ah,' she says. Her voice comes from a long way off. 'Nothing can be done on a Sunday. I'll have to make arrangements in the morning.'

Her colleague raises a quizzical eyebrow as she slides away, nodding, nodding, smiling. Discreetly heading for the cloakroom, head lowered, she collides with Walter who has propped himself against a shadowy window niche. She mumbles an apology and lurches on.

'Alison,' he calls in his frail and elderly voice.

'Walter. Oh, Walter, I'm sorry.' She turns back and hugs him.

'Please join me,' he begs.

'Oh Walter, I'm not fit company.'

'You're my favourite company,' he says. 'These things, these things . . .' He waves vaguely at the room with his knobbed walking stick. 'I find these things difficult. I only come because I'm perverse.' Walter's own retirement party is twenty-five years behind him, though he has just recently published yet another scholarly book. 'I'm the loneliest man in the world,' he says. 'Do you know how old I am?'

She knows of course, everyone knows, that he's ninety. The acuity of his mind and speech is a local wonder. Only time gets muddled for him. He gets the First and Second World Wars confused; he fought in both.

'I'm as old as Methuselah,' he says, 'and as fond of Australians as ever. Have I told you why?'

He has of course. Many times. He has spoken of the Australian and

New Zealand regiments stationed near him in Italy. That was during the Second World War. Or was it the first? In one of those wars, an Australian saved his life, dragging his wounded body through enemy fire.

'That was partly why,' he says. 'That was the beginning. But even more than that it's the whales.'

'The whales?' she asks, politely. She has not heard about the whales.

'Dying on the beaches. All the way from Tasmania to Queensland, a shocking thing.'

'When was this, Walter?'

'Now,' he says, agitated, a little annoyed with her. 'Here and now!' He is tapping on his forehead with his walking stick, a semaphore of distress. 'Beached and gasping and dying by the hundreds.'

'Walter, I hadn't . . .' She is confused. She is guilty of something. 'I've heard nothing. Was this on the news?'

'Yes,' he says. 'And in the National Geographic. Stranded high and dry, out of their element, the loneliest, most awful . . .' There are tears in his eyes. 'But the people of the coast are forming water lines, passing buckets, keeping them wet and alive. One by one, they are being dragged back to the water and towed out to sea. Wonderful people, the Australians. I walk along the beaches, you know, and watch. You hear a lot of rough talk out there, and some people think Australians are crude, but I know what I see.'

He hunches into the window seat and stares out at the freezing lake. 'It was because of the whales that I sent my son out there, after the war. He never came back.'

'I didn't know you had a son in Australia, Walter.'

'School was never the place for him. It happens often, doesn't it, with the children of scholars? And after that trouble, after the penitentiary. I couldn't think of a better place to give him a fresh start. I thought: Australians will make a man of him. Look at the way they fight and the way they are with whales.'

'Walter,' she murmurs, leaning her forehead momentarily against his. She is afraid of this confluence of griefs. She is afraid the sewer caps will not hold.

'What I'm sorry about,' Walter says, 'is that I never told him . . . I mean, I should have said to him: I *am* proud of your racing car driving. There have been all these other things, all these . . . We go on and on, you know, fathers do, about the disappointments. But I should have told him: I do admire your courage and speed behind that wheel!'

In the window seat, he seems to fold himself up into nothing.

'I visited the place. I visit. I go there often, more and more often now. It's a very steep and winding road, you can see how dangerous. From Cairns up to the Atherton Tableland, do you know it?'

She nods, unable to speak. The roads of Queensland, north and south, are imprinted in her veins. She stares at the map of her forearm and sees the hairpin turns on the way from Cairns to Kuranda.

'You can see it was an accident, can't you?' he says. 'He had everything to live for, a young wife and a little boy. We stay in touch. My grandson still sends me Christmas cards from Australia.

'Sometimes,' he says, 'I think I may have told him I was proud of the driving. Sometimes I think I remember saying it.'

'Walter,' she says shakily, embracing him. 'Merry Christmas, dear Walter. Forgive me. I have to go.'

She manages, somehow to get out to her car. She sits in the darkness, holding herself very still. She turns on the car radio in time for the hourly news bulletin. 'Sewer caps popping like corks,' she hears. She turns it off and leans on the wheel and begins to shiver. She shivers violently, her teeth chattering, her body possessed by the shakes. Her bones clatter, even her skin is noisy, the din of her thoughts drowns out the tapping at her window. It is not until Walter leans across the front of her car and signals through the windshield that she can make him out, dimly, through the thin tough cataract of Sunday. She blinks several times. He taps on the window again.

'Walter,' she says shocked, opening the door. 'God, Walter, get in the car. You *mustn't* stand out in this cold, you'll catch your . . .'

'I would like to think so,' he says quietly. 'It's been a terribly long and lonely wait. Alison, you can tell an old man anything. What is it, dear child?'

'My mother,' she begins to say. She puts her head against Walter's weathered shoulder and sobs. Orphaned at fifty: it sounds faintly embarrassing and comic, it's not supposed to be a major shock, it's not even listed in the register of traumas. 'My mother,' she begins again, quietly, 'died in Brisbane at 4:40 a.m. this Monday morning.'

She looks out at the frozen loop of a Queensland river. 'My mother,' she says, frowning a little, 'died in the early hours of tomorrow morning.'

Walter feels the car come plummeting off the Kuranda road, turning cartwheels through ferns and bougainvillea. It twists and twists and goes on falling through the gaping hole that opens somewhere behind his ribs. He hears the explosion that is now and always taking place.

'There is such gentleness,' he says, stroking Alison's cheek, 'in the most unexpected people, the roughest people. The way those men pass the buckets of water from hand to hand, the way they stroke the whales with wet cloths. I have never forgotten it.'

Tomorrow, Alison thinks, I will fly all the way back to the beginning.

ﾑ

CELIA BEHIND ME

There was a little girl with large smooth cheeks and very thick glasses who lived up the street when I was in public school. Her name was Celia. It was far too rare and grown-up a name, so we always laughed at it. And we laughed at her because she was a chubby, diabetic child, made peevish by our teasing.

My mother always said, 'You must be nice to Celia, she won't live forever,' and even as early as seven I could see the unfairness of that position. Everybody died sooner or later, I'd die too, but that didn't mean everybody was nice to me or to each other. I already knew about mortality and was prepared to go to heaven with my two aunts who had died together in a car crash with their heads smashed like overripe melons. I overheard the bit about the melons when my mother was on the telephone, repeating that phrase and sobbing. I used to think about it often, repeating the words to myself as I did other things so that I got a nice rhythm: 'Their heads smashed like melons, like melons, like melons.' I imagined the pulpy insides of muskmelons and watermelons all over the road.

I often thought about the melons when I saw Celia because her head was so round and she seemed so bland and stupid and fruitlike. All rosy and vulnerable at the same time as being the most *awful* pain. She'd follow us home from school, whining if we walked faster than she did. Everybody always walked faster than Celia because her short little legs wouldn't keep up. And she was bundled in long stockings and heavy underwear, summer and winter, so that even her clothes held her back from our sturdy, leaping pace over and under hedges and across backyards and, when it was dry, or when it was frozen, down the stream bed and through the drainage pipe beneath the bridge on Church Street.

Celia, by the year I turned nine in December, had failed once and was behind us in school, which was a relief because at least in class there wasn't someone telling you to be nice to Celia. But she'd always be in the playground at recess, her pleading eyes magnified behind those ugly lenses so that you couldn't look at her when you told her she couldn't play skipping unless she was an ender. 'Because you can't skip worth a fart,' we'd whisper in her ear. 'Fart, fart, fart,' and watch her round pink face crumple as she stood there, turning, turning, turning the rope over and over.

As the fall turned to winter, the five of us who lived on Brubacher Street and went back and forth to school together got meaner and meaner to Celia. And, after the brief diversions of Christmas, we returned with a vengeance to our running and hiding and scaring games that kept Celia in a state of terror all the way home.

My mother said, one day when I'd come into the kitchen and she'd just turned away from the window so I could see she'd been watching us coming down the street, 'You'll be sorry, Elizabeth. I see how you're treating that poor child, and it makes me sick. You wait, young lady. Some day you'll see how it feels yourself. Now you be nice to her, d'you hear?'

'But it's not just me,' I protested. 'I'm nicer to her than anybody else, and I don't see why I have to be. She's nobody special, she's just a pain. She's really dumb and she can't do anything. Why can't I just play with the other kids like everybody else?'

'You just remember I'm watching,' she said, ignoring every word I'd said. 'And if I see one more snowball thrown in her direction, by you or by anybody else, I'm coming right out there and spanking you in front of them all. Now you remember that!'

I knew my mother, and knew this was no idle threat. The awesome responsibility of now making sure the other kids stopped snowballing Celia made me weep with rage and despair, and I was locked in my room after supper to 'think things over.'

I thought things over. I hated Celia with a dreadful and absolute passion. Her round guileless face floated in the air above me as I finally fell asleep, taunting me: 'You have to be nice to me because I'm going to die.'

I did as my mother bid me, out of fear and the thought of the shame that a public spanking would bring. I imagined my mother could see much farther up the street than she really could, and it prevented me from throwing snowballs or teasing Celia for the last four blocks of our homeward journey. And then came the stomach-wrenching task of making the others quit.

'You'd better stop,' I'd say. 'If my mother sees you she's going to thrash us all.'

Terror of terrors that they wouldn't be sufficiently scared of her strap-wielding hand; gut-knotting fear that they'd find out or guess what she'd really said and throw millions of snowballs just for the joy of seeing me whipped, pants down in the snowbank, screaming. I visualized that scene all winter, and felt a shock of relief when March brought such a cold spell that the snow was too crisp for packing. It meant a temporary safety for Celia, and respite for me. For I knew, deep in my wretched heart, that were it not for Celia I was next in line for humiliation. I was kind of chunky and wore glasses too, and had sucked my thumb so openly in kindergarten that 'Sucky' had stuck with me all the way to Grade 3 where I now balanced at a hazardous point, nearly accepted by the amorphous Other Kids and always at the brink of being laughed at, ignored or teased. I cried very easily, and prayed during those years—not to become pretty or smart or popular, all aims too far out of my or God's reach, but simply to be strong enough not to cry when I got called Sucky.

During that cold snap, we were all bundled up by our mothers as much as poor Celia ever was. Our comings and goings were hampered by layers of flannel bloomers and undershirts and ribbed stockings and itchy wool against us no matter which way we turned; mitts, sweaters, scarves and hats, heavy and wet-smelling when the snot from our dripping noses mixed with the melting snow on our collars and we wiped, in frigid resignation, our sore red faces with rough sleeves knobbed over with icy pellets.

Trudging, turgid little beasts we were, making our way along slippery streets, breaking the crusts on those few front yards we'd not yet stepped all over in glee to hear the glorious snapping sound of boot through hard snow. Celia, her glasses steamed up even worse than mine, would scuffle and trip a few yards behind us, and I walked along wishing that some time I'd look back and she wouldn't be there. But she always was, and I was always conscious of the abiding hatred that had built up during the winter, in conflict with other emotions that gave me no peace at all. I felt pity, and a rising urge within me to cry as hard as I could so that Celia would cry too, and somehow realize how bad she made me feel, and ask my forgiveness.

It was the last day before the thaw when the tension broke, like northern lights exploding in the frozen air. We were all a little wingy after days of switching between the extremes of bitter cold outdoors and the heat of our homes and school. Thermostats had been turned up in a desperate attempt to combat the arctic air, so that we children suffered scratchy, tingly torment in our faces, hands and feet as the blood in our bodies roared in confusion, first freezing, then boiling. At school we had to go outside at recess—only an act of God would have ever prevented recess, the teachers had to have their cigarettes and tea—and in bad weather we huddled in a shed where the bicycles and the janitor's outdoor equipment were stored.

During the afternoon recess of the day I'm remembering, at the end of the shed where the girls stood, a sudden commotion broke out when Sandra, a rich big girl from Grade 4, brought forth a huge milk-chocolate bar from her pocket. It was brittle in the icy air, and snapped into little bits in its foil wrapper, to be divided among the chosen. I made my way cautiously to the fringe of her group, where many of my classmates were receiving their smidgens of sweet chocolate, letting it melt on their tongues like dark communion wafers. Behind me hung Celia, who had mistaken my earlier cries of 'Stop throwing snowballs at Celia!' for kindness. She'd been mooning behind me for days, it seemed to me, as I stepped a little farther forward to see that there were only a few pieces left. Happily, though, most mouths were full and the air hummed with the murmuring sound of chocolate being pressed between tongue and palate.

Made bold by cold and desire, I spoke up. 'Could I have a bit, Sandra?' She turned to where Celia and I stood, holding the precious foil in her mittened hand. Wrapping it in a ball, she pushed it over at Celia. Act of kindness, act of spite, vicious bitch or richness seeking expiation? She gave the chocolate to Celia and smiled at her. 'This last bit is for Celia,' she said to me.

'But I can't eat it,' whispered Celia, her round red face aflame with the sensation of being singled out for a gift. 'I've got di-a-beet-is.' The word. Said so carefully. As if it were a talisman, a charm to protect her against our rough healthiness.

I knew it was a trick. I knew she was watching me out of the corner of her eye, that Sandra, but I was driven. 'Then could I have it, eh?' The duress under which I acted prompted my chin to quiver and a tear to start down my cheek before I could wipe it away.

'No, no, no!' jeered Sandra then. 'Suckybabies can't have sweets either. Di-a-beet-ics and Suck-y-ba-bies can't eat chocolate. Give it back, you little fart, Celia! That's the last time I ever give you anything!'

Wild, appreciative laughter from the chocolate-tongued mob, and they turned their backs on us, Celia and me, and waited while Sandra crushed the remaining bits into minuscule slivers. They had to take off their mitts and lick their fingers to pick up the last fragments from the foil. I stood there and prayed: 'Dear God and Jesus, I would please like very much not to cry. Please help me. Amen.' And with that the clanging recess bell clanked through the playground noise, and we all lined up, girls and boys in straight, straight rows, to go inside.

After school there was the usual bunch of us walking home and, of course, Celia trailing behind us. The cold of the past few days had been making us hurry, taking the shortest routes on our way to steaming cups of Ovaltine and cocoa. But this day we were all full of that peculiar energy that swells up before a turn in the weather and, as one body, we turned down the street that meant the long way home. Past the feed store where the Mennonites tied their horses, out the back of the town hall parking-lot and then down a ridge to the ice-covered stream and through the Church Street culvert to come out in the unused field behind the Front Street stores; the forbidden adventure we indulged in as a gesture of defiance against the parental 'come right home.'

We slid down the snowy slope at the mouth of the pipe that seemed immense then but was really only five feet in diameter. Part of its attraction was the tremendous racket you could make by scraping a stick along the corrugated sides as you went through. It was also long enough to echo very nicely if you made good booming noises, and we occasionally titillated each other by saying bad words at one end that grew as they bounced along the pipe and became wonderfully shocking in their magnitude . . . poopy, Poopy, POOpy, POOOOPy, POOOOPPYYY!

I was last because I had dropped my schoolbag in the snow and stopped to brush it off. And when I looked up, down at the far end, where the white plate of daylight lay stark in the darkness, the figures of my four friends were silhouetted as they emerged into the brightness. As I started making great sliding steps to catch up, I heard Celia behind me, and her plaintive, high voice: 'Elizabeth! Wait for me, okay? I'm scared to go through alone. Elizabeth?'

And of course I slid faster and faster, unable to stand the thought of being the only one in the culvert with Celia. Then we would come out together and we'd really be paired up. What if they always ran on ahead and left us to walk together? What would I ever do? And behind me I heard the rising call of Celia, who had ventured as far as a few yards into the pipe, calling my name to come back and walk with her. I got right to the end, when I heard another noise and looked up. There they all were, on the bridge looking down, and as soon as they saw my face began to chant, 'Better wait for Celia, Sucky. Better get Celia, Sucky.'

The sky was very pale and lifeless, and I looked up in the air at my breath curling in spirals and felt, I remember this very well, an exhilarating, clear-headed instant of understanding. And with that, raced back into the tunnel where Celia stood whimpering half-way along.

'You little fart!' I screamed at her, my voice breaking and tearing at the words. 'You little diabetic fart! I hate you! I hate you! Stop it, stop crying, I hate you! I could bash your head in I hate you so much, you fart, you fart! I'll smash your head like a melon! And it'll go in pieces all over and you'll die. You'll die, you diabetic. You're going to die!' Shaking her, shaking her and banging her against the cold, ribbed metal, crying and sobbing for grief and gasping with the exertion of pure hatred. And then there were the others, pulling at me, yanking me away, and in the moral tones of those who don't actually take part, warning me that they were going to tell, that Celia probably was going to die now, that I was really evil, they would tell what I said.

And there, slumped in a little heap was Celia, her round head in its furry bonnet all dirty at the back where it had hit against the pipe, and she was hiccupping with fear. And for a wild, terrible moment I thought I had killed her, that the movements and noises her body made were part of dying.

I ran.

I ran as fast as I could back out the way we had come, and all the way back to the schoolyard. I didn't think about where I was going, it simply seemed the only bulwark to turn to when I knew I couldn't go home. There were a few kids still in the yard but they were older and ignored me as I tried the handle of the side door and found it open. I'd never been in the school after hours, and was stricken with another kind of terror that it might be a strappable offence. But no one saw me, even the janitor was blessedly in another part of the building, so I was able to creep down to the girls' washroom and quickly hide in one of the cubicles. Furtive, criminal, condemned.

I was so filled with horror I couldn't even cry. I just sat on the toilet seat, reading all the things that were written in pencil on the green, wooden walls. *G.R. loves M.H.* and *Y.F. hates W.S. for double double sure. Mr. Becker wears ladies pants.* Thinking that I might die myself, die right there, and then it wouldn't matter if they told on me that I had killed Celia.

But the inevitable footsteps of retribution came down the stone steps before I had been there very long. I heard the janitor's voice explaining he hadn't seen any children come in and then my father's voice saying that the others were sure this is where Elizabeth would be. And they called my name, and then came in, and I guess saw my boots beneath the door because I suddenly thought it was too late to scrunch them up on the seat and my father was looking down at me and grabbed my arm, hurting it, pulling me, saying 'Get in the car, Elizabeth.'

Both my mother and my father spanked me that night. At first I tried not to cry, and tried to defend myself against their diatribe, tried to tell them when they asked, 'But whatever possessed you to do such a terrible thing?' But whatever I said seemed to make them more angry and they became so soured by their own shame that they slapped my stinging buttocks for personal revenge as much as for any rehabilitative purposes.

'I'll never be able to lift my head on this street again!' my mother cried, and it struck me then, as it still does now, as a marvellous turn of phrase. I thought about her head on the street as she hit me, and wondered what Celia's head looked like, and if I had dented it at all.

Celia hadn't died, of course. She'd been half-carried, half-dragged home by the heroic others, and given pills and attention and love, and the doctor had come to look at her head but she didn't have so much as a bruise. She had a dirty hat, and a bad case of hiccups all night, but she survived.

Celia forgave me, all too soon. Within weeks her mother allowed her to walk back and forth to school with me again. But, in all the years before she finally died at seventeen, I was never able to forgive her. She made me discover a darkness far more frightening than the echoing culvert, far more enduring than her smooth, pink face.

❧

No More Denver Sandwiches

It's cold. Dead cold. The middle of winter. They're sitting in Robin's Donuts looking at the Saturday paper. Holidays are discounted. The economy's lousy. Fly to Mazatlán, air and hotel, for less than it costs you to stay at home. Or Hawaii, Cuba, Jamaica, Palm Springs.

'Hey, you've been to Palm Springs,' he says to her. 'How about let's go there. It's cheap. What's it like?'

'It was another life,' she says. 'I'm not going back. Not only can't. Won't. Finished, final, over.'

'Yah, but what's it like?' he persists. 'Every year it's advertised. Bob Hope is there if he's still alive. Dinah Shore and the Dinah Shore Open. All the tennis greats and Elizabeth Taylor and Betty Ford and the drug people. There must be something there.'

So she tells him.

I was young, married. A good idea at the time; finally not such a great idea. His parents went to Palm Springs every winter. All their friends did. Dozens of couples, married for years, well off. The men would pack cardigan sweaters in light colours and their clubs in leather bags. The ladies had florals, pastel knits, and bathing suits with skirts.

My ex-husband was sick with colds off and on all winter. His parents were concerned. They sent us tickets. Come down, we have an extra room. They always took a condo near friends. Why not, I figured. I hadn't travelled much. Palm Springs was where the movie stars went. They told me—sure I'd see some. My father-in-law claimed he'd seen that guy who had a TV series, who owned a baseball team. The one with the pale eyes. Why not? I liked the idea of getting on a plane in winter and getting off in summer.

It was night when we landed and really late. The plane had been held up in Minneapolis and by the time we arrived it was maybe ten, maybe later. They opened the door of the plane and I remember walking through the opening onto the top step of those stairs they wheel up and the air just smacked me in the face. Dark and hot and wet. Soft with flowers and diesel and the smell of earth, rubber on warm asphalt, and the flat sound of cars honking in the heavy air.

People moved around in short-sleeved shirts. The dark men unloading the plane had bare arms. To me, coming from winter, they looked naked. I couldn't breathe and I remember being so excited by all of it that I felt like running and running to say how great it was. Palm trees. I'd never seen palm trees. They were so exotic I couldn't believe they'd grow around an airport. And flowers, fat flowers everywhere. People were wearing sandals. My nylons were hot. My hair was back-combed and sprayed stiff and I could smell the lacquer softening in the humidity.

We had to rent a car and drive through Los Angeles to get to Palm Springs. We had no idea how far. The guy at the car rental said just follow this road to the turn-off and then left onto the highway, we'd see signs. I was hungry. I wanted a burger and fries. I wanted a chocolate milkshake. I wanted to take off my nylons and knit suit. I wanted to trot beside the car in the fluorescent green grass. I wanted to check those palm trees to see if they were real.

Why can't we stop for a burger first before we leave LA, I wanted to know, but he said his parents would be worried, we were already late. We'd find something once we got on the highway.

Of course, neither of us had ever driven on an American freeway. If you have you know there's no getting off, there's nowhere to eat, there's just four lanes of cars each way and that's it.

Then he said we could eat once we got there, at a Denny's or a Sambo's. Can you imagine a restaurant called Sambo's today? I think, if you can believe it, they served pancakes in the Aunt Jemima tradition. But I knew what would happen. We'd go straight to his parents' place because you couldn't worry Mom and Dad and once we got there she'd offer to make us a Denver sandwich. It's gruesome. Scrambled eggs with little pieces of pink salami chopped in and green onion which never got fried, only warm. Warm green onion, wet eggs, pink meat bits. No one young eats that. Or she'd say cereal. A bowl of cereal. No one young eats cereal at night either.

That food did a lot of damage and in fact I figured it killed his dad. Colon cancer. Forty-seven years they were married and he never had roughage in his diet. Nothing fresh or whole. All those years she never let him near uncooked food. He loved fresh corn in the summer. She'd ration it, counting the cobs like he was on an allowance. Maybe she should have let him have all the corn he wanted. I bet she wonders.

Sure enough, 'I'll make you eggs. How about a Denver sandwich?' and he says, 'Okay, Mom.' The trip was like that.

We ate and unpacked and I changed and went outside to the patio. All the shrubs had lights under them and they floated in the dark like little clouds of vegetation. The pool was lit around the edges and the water was turquoise like in the movies. There were crickets or frogs and a TV was on in someone's condo. What I figured was a round kiddies' pool turned out to be a Jacuzzi. The sky was very dark and up in the mountains I could see the lights of houses which I knew belonged to movie stars. I figured this would be okay and I knew what I wanted.

I wanted to go to the restaurant where Frank Sinatra ate. I wanted to have drinks with fruit on plastic swords, a shrimp cocktail, Caesar salad, Chateaubriand, rare, a stuffed baked potato and something flaming for dessert. I wanted to sit in a leather banquette in the corner against the wall, facing out so I could see everyone and they could see me. I would wear my black dress with the low back and my shoulders would be tanned. I would have a pearl bracelet on one wrist. I would wear my hair up in a French twist and a few tendrils would escape at my cheek and neck and they would curl a little from the heat. Sipping cocktails, whoever I was with would lean near my ear and whisper that the man who'd just come in and taken a chair at the table near ours was a known Mafia figure.

'Right here, here in this restaurant right now?' and I wouldn't believe whoever it was telling me that, because even though he might have been wearing too much hair tonic he looked quite nice and handsome in a rough kind of way.

I knew, eating my shrimp cocktail, that this was a man who could order what he wanted in a restaurant and get it. I could tell, when I got up and excused myself and walked right past him to the ladies' room that he didn't have to raise his voice to be heard. I was certain, when I saw him ordering from the wine list, that when he was cruel it hurt him deeply and I couldn't finish my steak after he looked directly at me, smiled, and lifted his glass.

I wanted, at the end of my dinner, to get up and walk past his table again. I wanted him to stand up and be close enough so I could smell his hair tonic. I wanted him to take my wrist, the one without the bracelet, very firmly, but not to hurt me, and insist I sit down with him at his table, stay with him, be with him dark and dangerous, go with him where it was dangerous, quickly, and never be frightened, to a place with horses and fast cars and elegant casinos and maybe yachts, to turn night into day if we wanted, to be so quick and beautiful that New York composers would write songs about us and to never eat Denver sandwiches again.

Every day the men golfed. The ladies played cards which I didn't know how to do and didn't want to learn. I read in the sun by the pool, only me and some kids, somebody's grandchildren and their nanny, and after I'd had enough sun and done I don't know how many laps in the turquoise pool I'd change and walk the few streets over to Palm Canyon Drive, the street with all the shops and I'd prowl the stores looking for movie stars. I didn't see any, not one. I did see a lot of blond people, young and old, even one old woman pulling her own oxygen tank, poor soul, and everyone was really dressed. A lot of big flower prints which I knew I couldn't wear back home and never figured I'd be in Palm Springs again so while I tried on lots of clothes in those stores looking for movie stars, I didn't find anything much to buy.

A couple of times, at night, we went out to restaurants and I kept on the lookout for stars and my Mafia man. There I was, a kid really, anxious for everything. Life in gulps. I wanted the edgy stuff, the gentle stuff. I wanted to spin and never catch my breath, spin until I fell.

Most nights we ate in with his parents. After dinner their friends would come over for coffee, instant decaf and Sara Lee baking. I would sit between two people on the sofa, someone on either side of me, nice enough people, no, actually they weren't nice now that I'm telling it—small, dull, smug people is really what they were, the friends of my ex-husband's parents. I'd sit there with my wonderful tanned body. I'd sit there with my dark hair and my big eyes. I'd turn my head from one to the other to answer their questions. I'd look across the room at the wives and husbands of the friends of my in-laws, and language I'd heard but never uttered would bubble to my lips. I knew if I sat longer I'd shout 'Have you ever fucked someone you're not married to?' and I'd get up and clear dishes. I'd run water and look out at the hot green shrubs and the turquoise water and then I'd excuse myself and go to sleep.

I kept hoping I'd see someone famous. I hadn't given up on that. I wanted to know how tall were they. Did they have good skin or did they wear thick make-up? If I saw them in person I knew I could tell. I was curious about their mates. Did stars attract beautiful mates or could someone handsome be married to someone they just loved who might be plain. Did they drive their own cars when they were on vacation and did they pay cash? Did they in fact have to buy their clothes or did people give them gifts just to have them wear their things?

So late afternoons I'd be on Palm Canyon Drive and like I wanted to know everything and be everywhere, I wanted to be glamorous too. Why not?

I was trying on a pant suit and this one I could see myself wearing at home. It was a dark green linen. The jacket was sleeveless which I liked for my tanned shoulders and it buttoned down the front. The neckline was wide and cut a little low but if I had to I could pull it closed with a pin. I thought, with all the blondes, young and old, showing everything they had, day or night, I could wear a jacket with the neck cut in such a way that the tops of my very young breasts showed too. Why not? I was quite pleased and was close to buying the outfit, thinking I'd maybe come back for it when the saleslady said to me that it looked just as nice on me as it had on what's her name, the movie star from France who was involved with the skier.

She packed it for me and that night I insisted we eat out, alone. It turned out my in-laws were eating out too and had gone early. If you eat early there, there's a discount. All these wealthy people vacationing in an expensive resort lining up to eat almost before dark to save five bucks. My ex-husband was in the living room watching TV.

Here I come. I could see myself from where he sat. Young. Made crazy by the smell of orange blossoms in the air every night. Brown shoulders. Dark hair, big dark eyes. Excited. Wearing something new. Me and a French movie star in the same outfit. The air outside smells good. So do I. I walk into the living room slowly. I'm in high-heeled sandals to go with the outfit and I don't want to trip on the shag carpeting. He's going to be wild for this. The whole time we've been here he's been looking at everyone's cleavage. I'm offering the tops of my young breasts. Just a little showing. I walk in slowly, my heart pounding.

He looks at me. I smile. 'Do yourself up,' he says. 'You look like a tramp.'

I stayed with him for a couple more years.

Bonnie Burnard

❧

Crush

It's Thursday morning and it's hot, hot, hot. The girl is painting the kitchen cupboards. The paint stinks up the room, stinks up the whole house. Her summer-blonde ponytail and her young brown shoulders are hidden in the cupboards, and a stranger coming into the kitchen, seeing only the rounded buttocks in the terrycloth shorts and the long well-formed legs, might think he was looking at part of a woman.

She's tired. She babysat last night. It's not the best job she can get; there are other kids, easier kids. She takes the job because of him, for the chance to ride alone with him in the dark on the way home. She thinks she's in love.

She remembers him at the beach, throwing his kids around in the water, teaching them not to be afraid. She doesn't try to imagine anything other than what she has seen, because it's already more than enough. His back and thighs she will remember when she is seventy and has forgotten others.

Her mother stands over the ironing board just inside the dining room door. Thunk, hiss, thunk, hiss. The kitchen table separates them. It has been piled impossibly high with dishes and cans of soup and corn and tea towels and bags of sugar and flour and pickling salt. Spice jars have been pitched here and there, rest askew in the crevices of the pile. The cupboards are hot and empty. She has nearly finished painting them.

Neither the girl nor her mother has spoken for over an hour. It is too hot. She leans back out of the cupboards, unbuttons her blouse and takes it off, tossing it toward the table. It floats down over the dishes. She wants to take off her bra, but doesn't.

Her mother doesn't lift her head from the ironing. 'You be careful Adam doesn't catch you in that state, young lady. He'll be coming through that door with the bread any minute.' Her sleeveless housedress is stained with sweat. It soaks down toward her thick waist.

Maybe I want him to, the girl thinks.

'Have you picked out the bathing suit you want?' Her mother glances up at her. The bathing suit is to be the reward for the painting. 'It's time you started to think about modesty. It's beginning to matter.'

'No.' The girl watches the fresh blue paint obliterate the old pale green. She's lying. She has picked out her suit. It's the one on the dummy in the window downtown, the one the boys gather around. She knows she won't be allowed to have it. Mrs Stewart in the ladies shop wouldn't even let her try it on, said it wasn't suitable for her. But it is. It's the one she wants.

She hears the scream of the ironing board as her mother folds it up and then she hears again her mother's voice.

'I'm going downtown for meat. You put that blouse on before I leave. Get it on. I'm as hot as you are and you don't see me throwing my clothes off.'

Her mother stands checking the money in her billfold, waiting until the last button is secure before she moves toward the back door. 'I'll bring you some cold pop.' The screen door bangs.

The girl steps down from the paint-splattered chair. She goes to the sink and turns the water on full, letting it run to cold. She opens the freezer door, uses her thumbs to free the tray of ice-cubes. She fills a peanut butter glass with ice and slows the tap, watches the water cover the snapping cubes. She sips slowly, with her jaw locked, the ice bumps cold against her teeth as she drinks. She lifts a cube from the glass and holds it in her hand, feels it begin to soften against the heat of her palm. She raises her hand to her forehead and rubs the ice against her skin, back into her hair, down her cheek, down over her throat. The ice-cube is small now, just a round lump. Her hand is cold and wet.

His hand was wet when he danced with her at the Firemen's dance. Not the same wet though, not the same at all. His buddies stood around and hollered things about him liking the young stuff and everyone laughed, even the wives. She laughed too, pretending she understood how funny it was, his touching her. But she can still feel the pressure of his hand on her back, any time she wants to she can remember how it steadied her, how it moved her the way he wanted her to move. It should have been hard to move together, but it was easy, like dreaming.

She wonders how close he is to their house. She dries her hand on the tea towel hanging from the stove door. She undoes the top button of her blouse, then the next, and the next, and the next. It slips from her shoulders and lands in a heap on the floor. She unfastens her bra, eases it down over her brown arms, drops it.

She climbs back up on the chair and begins to paint again. Although the paint is thick and strong, she can't smell it any more. She works slowly, deliberately, the chair solid under her feet. The stale green paint disappears beneath the blue.

She turns at his sudden, humming entrance, the bang of the screen door no warning at all. He stands on the mat with the tray of fresh baking slung around his neck, shifting his weight from one foot to the other, suddenly quiet. She comes down from the chair, steps over the heap of her clothes and stands in front of him, as still as the surface of a hot summer lake.

'Jesus,' he says.

'I wanted to show you,' she says.

He backs out the door quickly, doesn't leave Thursday's two loaves of white and one whole wheat.

The girl can hear her mother's voice through the open back door. It sounds uneasy and unnaturally loud. She bends down and picks up her bra, although she knows there won't be time. She knows, too, that she will be punished, and in some new way.

He's in the truck and he's wishing he had farther to go than the next block. Lord, he thinks. What the hell was that?

He checks his rearview mirror. Her mother could come roaring out after him any minute. She could be forgiven for thinking there was something going on. He's a sitting duck in this damned truck. Just deliver your bread, he thinks. And then, Shit. A drive. He'll go for a drive. To clear his head.

He goes out past the gas station, past the beer store, out of the town onto a side road bordered by fence-high corn. He drives a few miles with the window down, letting the hot breeze pull the sweat from his face and arms. He eases the truck over to the shoulder.

He knows his only hope is that she tells her mother the truth. Which could be unlikely. Shit. If her mother decided he was in on it, there'll be phone calls, there'll be hell to pay. His wife won't believe it. He doesn't believe it and he was there. Maybe the smart thing to do is just lie low and hope, pray, that her mother is embarrassed enough to keep her mouth shut. If it's going to come up, it'll come up soon and he'll just have to say it was a surprise, a real big surprise, and they can give him a lie detector on it if they want.

The girl has never given him even one small clue that she was thinking in those terms. And he can certainly see a clue coming. When he picks her up and drives her home, she always hides herself behind a pile of school-books hunched up tight against her sweater. She's a good sitter, the kids love her. He likes talking to her and he always makes a point of being nice to her. And she helped him teach the kids to swim because his wife wouldn't, and he didn't even look at her, can't even picture her in a bathing suit.

So damned hot. He leans back in the seat, unbuttons his shirt and lights a Player's. The sight of her drifts back through the smoke that hangs around him. It's been a long time since he's seen fresh, smooth, hard breasts. Not centrefold stuff, not even as nice as his wife before the kids, but nice just the same. Yeah. Nice. He shifts around in his seat. Damn.

It's like she just discovered them. Or maybe she got tired of being the only one who knew. Now he knows and what the hell's he supposed to do about it? Man, this is too complicated for a Thursday morning.

The picture drifts back again and this time he holds it for a while. He's sure they've never been touched. He thinks about dancing with her that once and how easy she was in his arms. Not sexy, just easy. Like she trusted him. He can't remember ever feeling that before. They sure didn't trust him when he was seventeen, had no business trusting him. And what he gets from his wife isn't trust, not exactly.

She could be crazy. She's the age to be crazy. But he remembers her eyes on him and whatever it was they were saying, it had sweet all to do with crazy.

Back the picture comes again, and he closes his eyes and the breasts stay with him, safe behind the lids of his eyes. He can see a narrow waist and squared shoulders. He hears words, just a few, although he doesn't know what they are, and he feels a gentleness come into his hands, he feels his cupped hands lift toward her skin and then he hears a racket near his feet and he opens his eyes to see a wretched crow on the open floor of the truck beside the bread tray; it's already clawed its way through the waxed paper, it's already buried its beak. He kicks hard and waves his arms and yells the bird away and he throws the truck in gear and tells himself out loud, 'You're crazy, man, that's who's crazy.'

The mother stands watching the girl do up the top button of her blouse. She holds the package of meat in one hand, the bottle of pop in the other. The pale brown paper around the meat is dark and soft where blood has seeped through. She walks over to the fridge, puts the meat in the meat keeper and the pop beside the quarts of milk on the top shelf. She closes the fridge door with the same care she would use on the bedroom door of a sleeping child. When she turns the girl has climbed up on the chair in front of the cupboards and is lifting the brush.

'Get down from that chair,' she says.

The girl rests the brush across the top of the paint can and steps down.

'I could slap you,' the mother says, calmly. This is not a conversation she has prepared herself for. This is not a conversation she ever expected to have. She cannot stop herself from looking at the girl's young body, cannot stop the memory of her own body and the sudden remorse she feels knowing it will never come back to her. She longs to feel the sting of a slap on her hand and to imagine the sting on the girl's cheek. But she pushes the anger aside, out of the way. She pulls a chair from the table, away from the mess of cupboard things piled there, and sits down in the middle of the room, unprotected.

'Sit down,' she says.

The girl sits where she is, on the floor, her brown legs tucked under her bum as they were tucked through all the years of listening to fairy tales. The mother can smell her fear.

'How much did you take off?'

The girl does not answer. She looks directly into her mother's eyes and she does not answer.

The mother begins the only way she knows how.

'I had a crush on your father. That's how it started with us, because I had a crush on him. He was only a little older than me but I think it's the same. I don't know why it should happen with you so young, but I'm sure it's the same. The difference is I didn't take my clothes off for him. And he wasn't married. Do you understand? It's wrong to feel that way about someone if he's married and it's wrong to take your clothes off.' She remembers other talks, remembers pulling the girl into her arms and carrying her up to bed.

The girl picks at a crusty scab on her ankle.

'The way you feel has got nothing to do with the way things are. You've embarrassed him. I could tell at the gate that he was embarrassed. You won't be babysitting for them anymore. He'll tell his wife and they'll have a good laugh about it. You've made a fool of yourself.' Oh, she thinks, don't say that.

'You will feel this way from now on. Off and on from now on. You have to learn to live with it. I wish it hadn't happened so soon. Now you just have to live with it longer. Do you understand?'

The girl shrugs her shoulders, lifts the scab from her skin.

'Women have this feeling so they will marry, so they will have children. It's like a grand plan. And you've got to learn to live within that plan. There will be a young man for you, it won't be long. Maybe five years. That's all. You've got to learn to control this thing, this feeling, until that young man is there for you.'

The mother gets up from the chair and goes to the fridge. She takes out the pop and opens it, dividing it between two clean glasses which she takes from a tray on top of the fridge. She hands one to the girl, insisting.

'If you don't control it, you will waste it, bit by bit, and there won't be a young man, not to marry. And they'll take it from you, any of them, because they can't stop themselves from taking it. It's your responsibility not to offer it. You just have to wait, wait for the one young man and you be careful who he is, you think about it good and hard and then you marry him and then you offer it.'

The girl gets up from the floor and puts her glass, still almost full, on the counter by the sink.

'I'd like to go now,' she says.

The mother drains her glass. She feels barren. She is not a mother anymore, not in the same way. It is as if the girl's undressing has wiped them both off the face of the earth.

The girl has run away from the house, out past the gas station and the beer store, onto a grid road that divides the cornfields. She is sitting in a ditch, hidden, surrounded by long grass and thistles.

She knows she's ruined it, knows the babysitting days are over. Not because he was embarrassed. He wasn't embarrassed, he was afraid. It's the first time she's ever made anyone afraid. She will find a way to tell him that she didn't mean to scare him.

She wishes her mother had just slapped her. She hears again the feelings her mother had about her father in some other time, some other century. She covers her ears. She hated having to hear it, it was awful, and that stuff about holding back and then getting married some day, she knows all about that. That's what all the women do, and it's likely what she'll end up doing because there doesn't seem to be any way to do anything else.

Except maybe once in a while. If she can learn not to scare people.

She feels absolutely alone and she likes it. She thinks about his back and his dark thighs and about standing there in the kitchen facing him. It's the best feeling she's ever had. She won't give it up.

She crosses her arms in front of her, puts one hand over each small breast and she knows she isn't wrong about this feeling. It is something she will trust, from now on. She leans back into the grass, throws her arms up over her head and stares, for as long as she can, at the hot July sun.

GAIL SCOTT

❧

TALL COWBOYS AND TRUE

They left Annabelle, the last frontier town, tucked under an outcrop in the Rockies. She locked her sleeping children carefully in the house trailer. She took his hand. They walked along the Main Street. Horses and oil tankers, hitched to the same posts, fitfully pawed the sand, eyeing each other nervously.

They passed a poor cowboy sitting in front of a blind house. His faded knees jerked over the edge of the verandah. It was hot. He waited for the explosion of bullets that would never come. He feared taking refuge in the house. It was damp and dark. The cowboy preferred the risks of riding the rail.

They came to the edge of town. The man squeezed her close. 'Baby, you're beautiful,' he said. 'We'll go places.' The woman's hand hardened. He told her to stop worrying. 'Your sister will take care of your kids.' Back in the trailer camp the women played cards while they waited in silence from the children's screams for the men to come in their loud boots, the beer gushing out of their bottles. She looked at his red sneakers and nodded.

They stuck out their thumbs in the dust by the side of the road. The cars went by oiled black. The metal waves reflected the sun painfully into her eyes. Behind her a crowd of ragged vultures cowered over an old Indian. A woman in sky-blue moccasins waded unevenly through the long grass towards him. After her ran a small girl with grasshopper legs. The young woman licked her dry lips and smiled at the child. The man saw nothing. He lit a cigarette, his thoughts galloping confidently towards the sunset.

Her children were alone in the trailer. They slept soundly. It was hot. She wanted to sit. The pavement was sticky. She raised her head towards the horizon. It was blocked by the carefully ticking crotches of grain elevators. She looked wildly around. Behind her, out of a deep ditch, rose a powerful white charger. A cowboy stepped forth in rich embroidered boots and a cowlick. He motioned them into a bower of plush purple flowers. She took her place in the back between rows of blossoming shirts, her man in the front, and the great white beast retook to the ditch leaping forward between the cool clay walls well below the burning gilt fields.

At last. She leaned back, breathing in the blotting paper perfume. Her man opened a soft volume of Lenin, his sneakers tucked noiselessly beneath him. The clay walls sped by outside. The children's cries receded. Through the rear-view mirror the cowboy watched her. She ignored him and sighed. 'Twas a good ride. His eye fastened on her moist lips slowly smiling at how her father hated hitchhikers. Oh the children. The children alone. She quickly looked up. The eye was fixed on the button on her left breast. DES AILES AUX GRENOUILLES it said over a small blue frog with butterfly wings. 'You French?' asked a well-honed voice tightening like a lasso.

From behind the cool white columns of my verandah I watch Véronique Paquette walk by terriblement décolletée. The priest gives her shit every Sunday but she still does it just the same. Across the street Claude Bédard flirts on the front lawn with his girlfriend Bijou. 'Frogs,' says my father one of three bank managers all brothers. Drunkenly, they flex their flabby lip muscles at Véronique from their rocking chairs on the hot prairie. Then my father looks up at me and screams: 'Stick your nose back in that Bible. It's Sunday.'

'You French?' repeated the well-honed voice honed even higher.

'Non. No. Mais. Ispeakit.' A nervous tickle titillated the pit of her stomach. The cowboy's eye flinted like steel in the mirror. He shifted into pass and the charger rose above the deep ditch into dry fields flaring with the fluorescent yellow of rape. There could be a fire you know. What if the fields caught on fire? The children alone in the trailer. The eye stared steadily. Her man was unaware. He turned the pages of State and Revolution, his sneakers tucked snugly beneath him. She began talking to the eye quite fast. 'It's beautiful here. Blue sky up above. All you need is love . . .' She stopped, guilty, ridiculous.

'Yeah.' The eye watched. The voice grew golden again. 'Big money on the gasline. Bad years back home I come up here to work.' The eye unlatched from her lips and pointed prayerfully towards the horizon still cluttered with wooden crotches. 'Seas of oil,' he said. The car hood shone in the midnight sun. 'You from near here?' she asked in a small voice. He took a picture from his breast pocket and passed it back. 'My mother and I farm in Mackenzie.' The woman had a fair wide forehead like her son. Her lips were drawn back tight in a bun. On the back it was written: 'He who putteth his hand on the plough and looks back is in danger of internal damnation.'

Interlude: A True Cowboy In Love

'Look Ma no hands.' The police car careens sideways across the road and hovers breathlessly over the high precipice. I put my hand on my stomach, staring at the perpendicular cliffs hanging below. 'Don't look back,' says the new hitchhiker (with red sneakers) to me and my children beside me. He winks in a friendly way. A clitoris pounds in a closet. My

*uncle has sold me a trailer to spare the family the shame. I am heading down the valley
to hide my fatherless children. I will push it through the pass to Annabelle. The car tears
away from the temptation and shoots into a curve. 'The thing about police cars,' says the
fat young driver whose pants stink, 'is you can drive no hands to hold onto guns.' Close
behind him on the front seat Ma smiles from under her greasy grey hair. 'I always buy
police cars,' he says to us over his shoulder. 'The way we take off from stopsigns in
curstairs. Boy do the cops get peed off.'*

*Ma puts her hand close to his unsavoury crotch. He grins at her recklessly. We are
descending rapidly as a white balloon towards the town where the trailer is. The cliffs
become sandy like a setting from a cowboy movie sparsely henspecked with sage. But the
cherry blossoms waft up from the valley below where the Ogo Pogo has just surfaced
between the feet of a petrified water-skier. 'Maybe we'll see the Ogo Pogo,' says Ma. Her
hand creeps closer to the crotch. He steps on the gas. We race through the town. There are
cowboy boots on the hotel steps and frightened moustaches on coffee cups in the windows.
On top of the false front façade it reads:* CONFESS AND YE SHALL SAVE.

The charger cowboy's crotch was impeccable. His Adam's apple had tightened into a thoughtful knot. 'You know you French and folks in the east
don't give prairie farmers their due profits for wheat flour.' At last her man
looked up from Lenin. 'Capitalism,' he said. 'Centralized markets. You're
too far from Toronto.'

. The eye in the mirror turned momentarily towards him, but was inter-
cepted en route by a six-inch fuchsia statue on the dashboard. It returned
immediately to fix again on her face.

'Do you know the Lord?'

She looked out the window. The rape fields were still on fire under the
horizontal rays of the midnight sun. It was hot in the trailer. The baby
whimpered weakly while the three-year-old pushed the stool against the
refrigerator door. He always did that to reach the handle and then of course
he couldn't open the door because the stool was in the way. But suddenly
the charger dipped again, not into a ditch but into a long narrow valley
whose walls were cool blue green. The eye filled with a great grey light.

'This is called the Valley of the Peace,' said the voice. 'It was filled with
fornicating good-for-nothings (excuse me miss he tipped his Stetson) with
whom the settlers had to fight and teach how to farm.' They were approaching a long silver river. Aging deep-tanned faces rocked in rocking chairs in
front of dilapidated wooden dwellings crushed by the ranch houses superimposed on their roofs.

'I don't feel so good,' she said to her companion. 'It's only a cat,' he said
absently. His eyes were on the works of Lenin whose picture was strong and
stern on the front cover. The fuchsia Christ smiled from the dashboard.

The baby whimpered. She wished she could put a clothespin on his tongue. Peace. Now I'll have peace. Her father's hand is rummaging through the clothespin box. She feels the pain as he pries open her mouth.

The cowboy handed her a pamphlet. 'I am the way, the truth, and the life,' it said. She smiled sweetly, bravely, lips closed to hide her bleeding tongue. The tickle in her stomach turned into a giggle and rose to gag her. 'I've seen it before,' she said. Back in the trailer camp the boy was pushing a spoon between the baby's dried compressed lips.

'You mean you know Jesus?' asked the cowboy. His well-honed voice took on the timbre of a stained-glass window. 'It's always nice to meet someone else spreading the word of the Lord so that the peoples of the world can learn the errors of their ways.'

'That's racist,' she thought, spreading wide her legs in silent protest.

'That's racist,' said the Leninist, looking up from his book. 'Really,' she said, handing back the pamphlet. The hyenic laughter swelled within her. She squeezed her lips to keep it from hissing out. 'I've seen it . . .'

The cowboy stopped the car. He turned around to look at her. She snapped her knees together. 'You mean you know the Lord and you looked back. He who putteth his hand on the plough and looks back is in danger of internal damnation.'

The charger minced forward, uncertainly. 'I don't feel so good,' she said to her companion, putting her hand on her stomach. 'The children . . .' He didn't seem to hear. He said nothing.

The brilliant quicksilver river approached. 'In his relationship with you,' said the voice, hued higher again, 'did Jesus uh hold up his end of the stick?'

'What d'ya mean?' she said. Like giant feces the laughter moved in to her mouth. The eye saw the fishtails glittering at the corners of her lips.

'Help,' she said to her companion. He didn't hear for he was furiously writing notes on the flyleaf of his book.

'The stick,' said the cowboy more insistently, beginning to squirm in his seat. 'The stick. In his bargain with you did Jesus hold up his end of the stick?' Underneath like an error ran the quicksilver river.

The cowboy squirmed harder on his seat. 'The stick. Whose end of the stick?' he said louder. 'It was you who didn't hold up your end of the stick. It was, wasn't it? Wasn't it, huh? I know it was.'

Interlude: A True Cowboy in Love

The police car is racing down into the valley, past the sagebrush into the beautiful cherry blossoms. 'It smells like cherry Chiclets,' says the son. 'I bet anything we see the Ogo Pogo,' says Ma. The hitchhikers have left. She fondles his pee-stained pants.

'I know Jesus,' cried the cowboy, rocking back and forth. He grabbed the statuette, waving it over his head like a lariat. 'Jesus never lets down his end of the stick. The stick . . .'

The car hit the valley wall with a thud. The red sneakers floated out the window, the laces trailing behind like spurs. The cowboy bled over the steering wheel, pierced by the statuette.

Her strawberry hair rose up the side of the valley. At last it was dark on the prairie. She sped through the cool night in her white shirt and white jeans. The baby was almost dead. She would get there before the headlines. In the first light of dawn she sped past the ticking-crotch silhouettes into Annabelle. The cops were coming towards her trailer with can openers. She sped through the dust past the poor cowboy's house. He slept on the rail, his spurs stuck in the wood. Gently (so as not to waken him) she untangled his legs and shoved his young strong body into the damp dangers of the forbidden house. She reached her trailer two strides before the police. Then she was fleeing, a child in each arm, their skin soft and warm against hers. New sensations were rising along her spine.

SUSAN SWAN

❧

THE MAN DOLL

I made the doll for Elizabeth. I wanted to build a surrogate toy that would satisfy my friend so completely I would never have to listen to her litany of grievances against the male sex again.

I constructed the doll by hand. I am a bio-medical engineer, but at that time I was still an intern. I couldn't afford to buy Elizabeth one of the million-dollar symbiotes called Pleasure Boys which the wealthy women and gay men purchase in our exclusive department stores.

I didn't like these display models anyhow. Their platinum hair and powder-blue eyes (identical to the colouring of Pleasure Girls) looked artificial and their electronic brains had overdeveloped intellects. I wanted something different from the run-of-the-mill life form for Elizabeth. I wanted a deluxe model that would combine the virility component of a human male with the intuitive powers of the female. In short, I wanted a Pleasure Boy whose programming emphasized the ability to give emotional support.

I made my doll in secret, requisitioning extra parts whenever some limbs or organs were needed at the Cosmetic Clinic in human repairs where I worked. So it was easy for me to get the pick of anatomical bargains. I particularly liked the selection of machine extensions offered by the Space Force Bank. After careful consideration, I chose long, sinewy hands, arms and legs, and made sure they were the type that could be willed into action in a twinkling. The Space Force Bank agreed to simulate the doll's computer brain from mine for $1,500. The exterior of the doll was made out of plastic and silicone that was lifelike to the touch. I placed a nuclear reactor the size of a baseball in the chest cavity, just where the heart is in the human body. The reactor warmed the doll by transmitting heat to a labyrinth of coils. The reactor uses a caesium source that yields an 80 per cent efficiency rate with a life expectancy of just over thirty years. The doll was activated by a handheld switch.

I smuggled the materials home from the Clinic and each night in my flat I worked on the doll. I wanted it to be a perfect human likeness, so exact in detail that Elizabeth wouldn't guess it was a symbiote. I applied synthetic hair in transplants (matched with my own hair colour) and shaped its face with the help of liquid silicone. My money had almost run out by the time

I got to the sex organs, but luckily I was able to find a cheap set from a sec-ondhand supplier. For $250 I bought an antique organ that belonged to a 180-year-old Pleasure Boy. I hoped it would work under pressure.

Our laws forbid symbiotes to waste human food. But I gave the doll a silicone esophagus and a crude bladder because I wanted it to have some-thing to do on social occasions. Its body was able to ingest and pass out a water and sugar solution. Of course, the doll didn't defecate. Its nuclear waste products were internally controlled and required changing once every ten years.

At the last moment I realized I had forgotten to add dye to the pupils, so its eyes were almost colourless. But in all other aspects, my doll looked normal.

When I installed its reactor, the doll came to life, lolling contentedly in my apartment, ignoring the discomfort of its mummy case and its helmet of elastic bandages and gauze. The doll called me 'Maker' and, despite its post-operative daze, began to display a talent for understanding and devotion.

It could sense when I was in a blue mood and sighed sympathetically behind its bandages. When I came home, exhausted from catering to the sci-entists at the Clinic, the doll would be waiting for me at the door of my apartment, ready to serve me dinner. Soon, I was unable to keep my hands off it. I decided it wouldn't spoil my present to Elizabeth if I tried it out ahead of time. Playfully I stroked and kissed the symbiote, and showed it how to peel back its groin bandage so we could have sex. To my delight, the doll operated above normal capacity, thanks to its desire to give pleasure.

Like any commercial symbiote, my doll was capable of orgasm but not ejaculation. It is illegal for a doll to create life. The sole function of a sym-biote must be recreational.

At the end of five months I removed its protective case and found myself staring at a symbiote who gazed back with a remarkable calm, lov-ing air. It had red hair and freckles, just like me, and a pair of cute pear-shaped ears.

My desire to give the doll to Elizabeth vanished.

I fell in love with my creation.

I called the doll Manny.

The next year with Manny was happy. I felt confident; I worked at the Clinic with zeal and diligence, knowing that at the end of the day I would be going home to Manny; his cooking and his kisses! (Something about the way I had juxtaposed his two oricularis oris muscles made the touch of his lips sensational.)

Secretly, I worried Manny might harbour resentment about a life built around ministering to my needs. Pleasure Boys have no rights, but Manny was still an organism with a degree of self-interest. If I neglected his pro-grammed needs, he might deteriorate. When I confessed my fear, the doll laughed and hugged me.

'I want to be the slave,' he said. 'I need to be of service.'

Over the next six months I began to see less of my doll. I had graduat-ed to the rank of engineer in facial repairs and was neglecting our home life.

I decided it was time to give Manny some social experiences, so I asked Elizabeth to the flat for a meal.

I felt a thrill of pride when Elizabeth walked in and didn't give Manny a suspicious look. Manny wore an ascot and a tweed sports suit. He beamed at the two of us as he placed a spinach quiche on the table.

'You look familiar,' Elizabeth mused.

'Everybody says I look like Tina', the doll said breezily.

'You do,' Elizabeth said. 'Where did you meet Tina anyhow?'

'I'd rather hear about you,' the doll replied. 'Are you happy?'

Elizabeth started and looked at me for an explanation. I grinned.

'Go on. Tell him about your troubles with men.'

'Tina, my problems would bore Manny,' Elizabeth said nervously.

'No they wouldn't,' Manny said. 'I like to help people with their troubles.'

Elizabeth laughed and threw up her hands.

'I can't find a man who is decent, Manny. Every affair starts off well and then I find the guy has feet of clay.'

I saw Manny glance down at his plastic feet. He was smiling happily.

'I must be too much of a perfectionist,' Elizabeth sighed, 'but there are days when I'd settle for a good machine.'

I nodded and noticed Manny's colourless eyes watching Elizabeth as if he were profoundly moved. I thought he could be a little less sympathetic. If he knew Elizabeth like I did, Manny would realize Elizabeth enjoyed feel-ing dissatisfied.

Suddenly, Manny reached over and patted Elizabeth's hand. Elizabeth burst into tears and Manny continued to hold her hand, interlocking his fingers with hers in a deeply understanding way. In profile, the doll looked serene. Elizabeth was staring at him through her tears with an expression of disbelief. I knew Elizabeth was waiting for the doll to frown and suggest that she pull herself together.

Of course, the doll's programming prohibited uncaring reactions. Manny was unique, not only among male symbiotes, but among men. What man loved as unselfishly as my doll?

During dinner, Elizabeth quizzed Manny about his background and the doll gracefully handled her questions.

'I'm Tina's invention,' he quipped. 'I call her "Maker." It's our private joke.'

Elizabeth giggled and so did Manny. I winced. Why did my doll sound so happy? The understanding look on Manny's face, as Elizabeth whined about her love life, was a bit sickening! I noticed the doll lightly brush against Elizabeth's shoulder when he replenished the wine, and in disgust, I stood up and cleared away the dishes. When I came out of the kitchen, Manny was standing by the door holding hands with Elizabeth.

'Elizabeth needs me now, Tina,' the doll said. He paused to help my friend on with her coat. Then he gave her shoulder a loving squeeze. 'Elizabeth, I feel as if I were made just for you.'

My doll leaned over and offered her his sensational oricularis oris muscles, and suddenly I felt angry.

'You can't leave me, Manny,' I said. 'I own you.'

'Tina. You don't mean what you say,' Manny replied sweetly. 'You know dolls have rights too.'

'Who says?' I cried. 'You can't procreate. You can't eat. And your retinas are colourless.'

'Manny eats,' Elizabeth said. 'I saw him.'

'He just drinks,' I said, starting to shout. 'Elizabeth, Manny is my doll. Don't you dare walk out of my apartment with my possession.'

'Manny is not a doll,' Elizabeth said. 'You're making it up because you're jealous.'

'Manny, I'm warning you. If you leave me, I'll deactivate your program.'

'My Maker is not the sort of human to be petty,' Manny replied. Hand-in-hand, my doll and Elizabeth walked out of the apartment. 'Goodbye, Tina dear,' Manny called in an extremely sincere tone. I threw myself at the closed door, beating my fists against it, screaming my doll's name. Then I sank to my knees. I had made the doll for Elizabeth, but decided to keep him for myself. For the first time, I realized it didn't matter. My programming ensured that Manny would be drawn to whoever had most need of him.

For the next month, I was too depressed to see Elizabeth and Manny. I felt angry with my friend for taking my doll, although I scolded myself for being irrational. Now that Manny was gone, I regretted the way I had neglected him. I daydreamed nostalgically about the activities we might have done together. Why hadn't we gone shopping, or out to the movies? It made me sad to think we had never strolled arm-in-arm in the park like a normal couple.

True to his programming, Manny called me every day to see how I was doing. My pride stopped me from listening to his concerned inquiries and I slammed the phone down. Then one evening my symbiote phoned late and caught me offguard. I'd had an argument with my Clinic supervisor. This time, I was glad to hear my doll's friendly baritone.

'Tina, I'm worried about you,' Manny chided. 'The grapevine says you're working too hard.'

'Hard enough,' I agreed, relieved that someone cared.

'Dinner here this Tuesday. I won't take no for an answer.'

That Tuesday, I changed out of my lab coat and headed for Elizabeth's apartment. At the entrance to the building, three dolls were talking to the doorman. One of the dolls, a Pleasure Girl with shoulder-length platinum hair, asked the doorman to let them in so they could see a friend. The doorman shook his head.

'No dolls allowed in before six,' the doorman said. 'ASTARTE TOWERS is a respectable space block.' He made a slashing motion in the air with his gloved hand. Then he pushed the female doll on its chest. The doll groaned as if it were hurt and tottered backwards. For a second, it looked like it was going to fall. Then it slumped onto the curb and began to weep pitifully. The two male dolls rushed over to comfort it. Except for the unactivated models in store windows, I had never observed dolls in a group before. The sight of the symbiotes acting like humans made me uneasy. I hurried past the sobbing doll and her companions, and ran into the lobby.

In the apartment, I found Elizabeth reading a newspaper. Manny was setting the table. Elizabeth looked relaxed. But Manny! Why, the doll looked beatific! His synthetic curls shone with a copper glow and a suntan had brought out more large brown freckles. Then I remembered hearing that Elizabeth had gone on a Caribbean cruise.

'How wonderful to see you, Tina,' Manny said. 'Are you still mad at your old symbiote?'

I shook my head.

Joyfully, he embraced me. He told me about his holiday and asked about my new job. I immediately began to describe the way I had engineered a dish-face deformity. When I finished, I realized that Elizabeth had been listening intently too; apparently, she had no interest in going into her usual litany of grievances against the male sex.

Suddenly, Elizabeth said, 'Did you see any dolls at the door?'

'One or two,' I admitted. 'What are they doing here?'

'A few come, every day. They sometimes bring a human. If they can get by the doorman, Manny lets them come in and talks to them.' Elizabeth sighed and shrugged. 'I suppose there's nothing wrong with it. Except I worry that they tire Manny.'

'Elizabeth, I am tireless,' Manny laughed, bending over and kissing my friend on the nape of her neck. I remembered just how tireless Manny could be.

Elizabeth grabbed his silicone hand and kissed it hungrily. 'Selfless, you mean.' She looked dreamy. 'Tina, where did you find this paragon?'

'I already told you. I made him for you.' I smiled.

'Do you think I'm going to believe that line of yours?' Elizabeth laughed. 'It's time you forgave me for being with Manny.'

'What are you talking about?' I asked.

'Elizabeth thinks I'm human,' Manny smiled. 'I've tried to show her I'm a doll, but she goes out of the room and refuses to listen.' He paused, bewildered. 'The dolls think I'm human, too.'

'No doll could ever make *me* happy,' Elizabeth giggled.

'Serving your needs fulfils my function,' Manny replied.

'Isn't Manny funny?' Elizabeth said. 'He says the cutest things!'

Before I could answer, the door opened and the symbiotes who had been arguing with the doorman rushed in uttering cries of glee.

'Pleasure Girl #024 found a way in through the back entrance,' one of the male dolls said triumphantly.

The female doll kissed Manny fiercely on both his cheeks.

'Pleasure Boy #025 is the one who suggested we try another door,' she said. 'Aren't we clever for sex toys?' Then she noticed Elizabeth and me, and she blushed guiltily. 'Excuse me. I forgot humans were listening.'

'Don't apologize,' said the other male doll. 'We have the right to breathe like anybody else.'

The dolls murmured agreement and then turned back to Manny, who was holding up a jug of liquid. I guessed it contained a sugar and water solution. Manny poured the liquid into glasses. The dolls lifted the glasses in a toast and pretended to drink Manny's solution.

I stared at the dolls without speaking to them. Once again, I felt uneasy. The symbiotes were claiming human privileges. Not only were they acting as if they had the right to consume precious food resources, but the dolls were also appropriating human metaphors. I wasn't certain about the design type of the other symbiotes, but no air passed through Manny's system. His lungs were a tiny non-functional sac next to the caesium reactor. I had stuck in the sac to designate lung space in case I decided later to give Manny a requirement for oxygen.

Now the dolls began to complain loudly about their lot as pleasure toys. My doll listened solemnly, stroking each of their hands in turn while Elizabeth and I looked on blankly. Then one of the male dolls threw himself at Manny's feet.

'Why are we discriminated against, Manny?' the doll wailed. 'Why can't we procreate like humans do?'

Tears slowly dripped from Manny's clear eyes. He held out his arms and embraced the dolls, who in turn cried and embraced each other. In the midst of the hubbub I slipped out and left Elizabeth with the emotional dolls. Then I hurried back to the Clinic and calmed myself by working until dawn repairing a pair of cauliflower ears.

Three months went by. This time Elizabeth rang up and asked me to meet her at the Earth Minister's television studio. Elizabeth said that Manny had left her to become a spokesman for a political lobby of humans and symbiotes.

Manny's group could be heard in the background of the Earth Minister's daily broadcasts shouting their demands. Elizabeth wanted me to persuade Manny to give up politics. She wanted Manny back so they could start a family. She said that she would do 'something unthinkable' that evening unless she could convince Manny to return.

Gently, I tried to point out that Manny was only a doll, but the more I pleaded with her to forget about my symbiote, the more desperate she sounded. I agreed to meet her at the studio. Just before I left my apartment, I stuck my handheld switch into my pocket. I decided the time had come to deactivate Manny. It was illogical for the symbiotes to think dolls had rights. I felt sympathy for them as organisms, but their aspirations were making pests out of what were once perfectly good recreational objects.

The studio was ten minutes by air, but it took me over half an hour to force my way through the crowd at the studio door. I noticed with a start that there were hundreds of human heads among the masses of synthetic ones.

Finally, I found a seat at the back of the auditorium. At that moment the lights dimmed and then flared brightly as the Earth Minister walked out onto a dais at the front of the room, followed by a television crew pushing cameras. The crowd immediately began to chant, 'Manny for Earth Minister' and 'Symbiotes are humans too.'

I heard a noise at the front of the room and Manny was lifted onto the platform. Then Manny shook hands with the Earth Minister, a stocky human with an anxious smile. Now the crowd cheered more wildly than before, and Manny turned and lifted up his arms as if he wanted to embrace them all. He looked striking in his deep-magenta safari suit.

Just then, Elizabeth appeared by my side, weeping.

'Isn't it awful?' she whispered. 'This swarm of dolls? Oh, Tina, I was just too busy with other things, so Manny went into politics. But I can't live without him.'

'Sure you can,' I sighed and looked over the crowd at Manny's synthetic head. 'You already are.'

Manny spotted me and waved. I hesitated, then smiled and waved back.

'Tina, you're not paying attention,' Elizabeth sniffed. 'I want Manny back. I want to have children with him.'

'Look, Elizabeth,' I said. I felt in my pocket for the switch. 'Manny is a doll—a do-it-yourself model. His brains cost over a thousand dollars and his sex organs were two-fifty.'

Elizabeth blushed. 'Manny has talked about the help you gave him, but no symbiote could do what he does.'

'He's a Pleasure Boy,' I argued. 'I should know. I made him. Haven't you noticed he doesn't eat or defecate? And that's not all. He can't procreate either.'

'Nothing you say will make me believe Manny is a doll,' Elizabeth shouted, and then she slapped my face!

Angrily, I grabbed her and dragged her towards the dais. 'I'll show you his extensions, his hair strips, his silicone mouth . . .!'

'Tina! Please! Don't hurt Manny!' Elizabeth cried, ducking her head as if she expected me to hit her. Even though I am bigger than Elizabeth, I was surprised at how easily cowed she was.

I tightened my grip on my friend's arm. 'I'm going to take you up there,' I yelled, 'and deactivate him in front of everyone. Manny the doll has come to an end.'

'No, Tina! I'll do what you want! I'll forget him!' Elizabeth said and plucked at my arm. 'I know Manny's a doll, but I love him. I've never loved anybody before.'

She bowed her head, and for a second I relaxed my grip. At that moment, a great gust of sighs filled the studio and the oscillating physical mass knocked us apart as it pushed towards the dais where Manny sat. The Earth Minister toppled from his seat and the crowd hoisted Manny into the air.

Suddenly, the doll looked my way. His placid, colourless eyes met mine. I pulled the switch out of my pocket and threw it away. In the next moment, the mass of dolls and humans carried Manny off on a sea of hands. I wasn't surprised—as I strained for a last glimpse—to see a blissful look on my doll's face.

EDNA ALFORD

❧

THE LATE DATE

Some stories should be told straight, Marilyn thought. She knew that now. But at the time, she had spoken of her experience as a late date. In the residence, in the dark, whispered staccato across the tiles between the beds, to Gail, her roommate from Trestle. Since then she had told her tale many times over the years and there was no longer any feeling attached to it other than the concern about the telling itself, the timing, the well-delivered line.

Until today. If it hadn't been for Heather, her hammer and clatter, Marilyn knew she would have been able to perpetuate the lie through middle age and menopause, right into old age. Even now a part of her would have preferred it that way. The altered version had come to feel a lot like truth over the years.

Most of the morning Heather had been on the patio, sawing, of all things, hammering and clattering in a way you would have expected from one of those do-it-yourself women on television who kept trying to persuade Marilyn to identify various basic carpenter tools and put them to use. One of these programs followed 'Keep Fit' which Marilyn never missed because her body, of late, had begun to develop folds, the atrophy of the flesh taken hold, she believed, prematurely, like the grey which she had streaked in such a way that it would turn entirely blond in the sun. Most of the time she spent on the patio these days was for the fresh air and the light, not the tan, which in her case was usually a burn anyway that turned to uneven blotches of brown before nightfall. This process not only disgusted her but gave her something of a fright because of the cancer scare. The push for Vitamin D which was on around the time Heather had been born was gone, replaced with warnings against the danger of taking too much sun. Ultraviolet rays were the culprits, they said. So she had covered up her arms before she took her coffee out to the patio for the ten o'clock break. She didn't have to teach but she had a stack of papers to mark and couldn't really afford to take the whole day off. She had put on her sunglasses, too, before she had come out, carried a wide-brimmed cotton hat, shielded her face from the sun. There were minor side-effects, webs of wrinkles at the corners of the eyes, spawned by the sun, they said now, not by smiles. The sun induced reflexive frowns instead.

She chose a green plastic webbed lawn chair in front of Heather's open-air shop, sat down and put on her hat. She had no trouble reading the letters upside down on the sign her daughter painted, alternately frowning, perplexed, and faintly smiling, lost in some private thought.

> I AM NOT
> A VIRGIN–
> AND I AM *NOT*
> A WHORE–

The letters were painted in chunky black blocks lined on the inner edges with a luminescent red, and, although they were very large, there was room on the sign for more–as if what was already written there were not enough. Shocked, Marilyn dropped the hand with which she shielded her eyes to her lap, leaned over the sign for a reluctant but closer look as if it were a corpse she had been asked to positively identify. It must be for the march, she thought numbly. Heather had said something at breakfast about a march.

Large, unwieldy lilac bushes, purple and French white surrounded the concrete blocks of the patio, leaving only a narrow path to the garden at the back. Their odour was oppressive in the heat, the spears sprung by the sun almost overnight. Early this year. They had never bloomed before until mid-June.

'Where did you get the boards?'

'The bristleboard?'

'No, the lumber.'

'At Beaver on the South Side. They're one by two's,' she said, glancing at them over her shoulder. They were stacked neatly on her right. She had placed Ron's heavy-duty automatic stapler beside them. Marilyn had given it to him last year around this time, for Father's Day. When Heather returned to the sign, her auburn hair fell over her eyes. She had begun to wear it long and the sun accentuated the natural red highlights, like Ron's. She had washed it after breakfast and it was, Marilyn had to concede, lovely, wavy, clean. She flicked it back from her forehead, away from her eyes. It swung perfectly to the side, a good cut. Good and thick and clean.

Marilyn set her cup on the cement beside her chair and stood up. She had been the same age as Heather was now, just over eighteen, had just finished her first year at the university. General Arts, the perfect program for a girl who wanted a liberal education, and lots of time to decide what she really wanted to be. As Marilyn had told Heather more than once, an arts degree in itself didn't qualify you for much. Marilyn had later gone on to the college of education, then to teach.

The summer between her first and second year of university, she had applied for a job as a psychiatric aide. In those days they called the position Summer Relief. Every spring the provincial psychiatric hospitals recruited summer replacement staff in a basement room on campus which one reached by means of a network of brightly lit, subterranean tunnels. The applicants were almost all young women. In fact, not one young man could be found among the recruits assigned to the same hospital as she had been, perhaps because the wages were so low, perhaps for other reasons.

Certainly the competition for summer jobs seemed to Marilyn as fierce then as it appeared now. Two hundred fifty dollars per month minus thirty-two dollars a month for room and board in residence was not lucrative by any means, but it would help pay for tuition and books the following year. They were to take their meals in the staff dining room of the main building which one reached in the early hours of the morning and late at night by means of a subterranean tunnel connecting the main building with the residence.

For those who had no previous employment experience in the real world and no family connections in business, the possibility of getting a regular job—the ones usually reserved for young women such as clerking, cleaning, typing—was remote and Marilyn had been elated to land any job whatsoever, even this one. Elated, although she had been advised against taking it by a very perceptive professor whose mother had worked in a similar institution and who felt that the price exacted by such employment would likely be far greater than any amount of money could offset. Theoretically, he was quite right, of course. She had, in retrospect, agreed with him a thousand times.

Her mother and father delivered her. The highway was flat and straight, the fields flat and green and all around them so that it seemed as if they were the centre of an enormous green circumference and were moving through a tube, half green, half blue, tilted, suspended at that radial line on the central standard clock which marked the end of her childhood and her protected walk with them. They were silent, apprehensive too. She thought they would never get there, that somehow her father had his foot on the gas pedal and the brake at the same time.

Now, with Heather, Marilyn knew what they must have felt then, on the way down that clear spring day. She and Ron had tried to give their daughter shelter and they had, to nurture her and, at the same time, allow her the freedom she needed to learn and think for herself. Marilyn laughed. And so she has, she thought, peering through her fingers at the sign. So she has. Heather looked up. Now Marilyn wished she could have given her a cocoon, camouflage, to keep her safe from what she knew was in the world, what she had begun to learn when she was barely eighteen.

Recently she had read an article which declared that the decade would be marked by images of dismemberment, mutilation, and rare disease. The author of the article was alarmed by the rise of an apparently malignant tendency in the human psyche to derive pleasure from such imagery. Several of Marilyn's friends, women she had met the year of her summer relief, were still in the field and had told her some of the things they had seen over the years, were witness and nurse to the numberless victims rising like wraiths from the pit, men and women and children who preceded the images or followed them—no one seemed to know which.

Certain uncomfortable fragments of that eighteenth summer had resurfaced when Marilyn read the article; but she had put them out of her mind, or rather replaced them very carefully in the deeper recesses on a solid shelf in the hope that they would remain there, not fall off again, reappear behind her eyes. This did not prevent her from hauling out her humorous anecdote about the first 'man', correction, 'men' she ever saw when it seemed to be socially appropriate, that is whenever certain allowable indiscretions were afoot, too many drinks, an intolerable boredom with broadloom and rare bric-a-brac. On such occasions Marilyn would describe the experience as the highlight of her 'liberal education'. How I put myself through an institution of higher learning in a most unusual way. Garnished with her famous one-liners. After all, it was a party, wasn't it. The mandate was entertainment. The story had to be palatable, served, as it were, with dry martinis and fresh paté.

The high sun on the back of her head, like a lamp in a projector, drove the lighted image round inside her dark skull, taste, touch, sight, sound, smell, a better example by far than she had used in her lecture before dismissing her students, before the Friday bell. A spherical film. Dizzy, she stumbled forward, caught her sandal on the corner of a concrete block and almost fell, staggered around and sat down again, alarmed.

'Mom?' Heather said, beginning to rise, reaching up as if to catch her but it would have been impossible, too late. She was too far away. She could never have been there in time.

'I'm all right, Heather. Too much sun. I'll move my chair over to the corner in the shade.' Which she did. But the move had the effect of convincing her that the management had only dimmed the lights. The show was not over at all; in fact, had just begun.

Marilyn took off her hat and shook her head from side to side which loosened the pressed hair and cooled the wet scalp beneath but had no effect whatsoever on the film, brought no measurable relief from the dizziness. She had applied so much pressure to her eyes that now she could hardly see outside her head at all. Inside, the intensity of the light increased. She thought it might help if she spoke.

'Married,' she declared to the back of Heather's head, then laughed.

'Pardon?'

'I said "married". I know what you're going to write next. On the sign. You're going to write "What am I?" It just struck me. "I AM NOT A VIRGIN AND I AM NOT A WHORE—" *What am I?* comes next, right? And I say—a married woman.' Marilyn laughed. 'I'm your mother. That's what I'm supposed to say, isn't it? Do I get a prize?'

'The booby prize maybe. God, Mom, I'm not Bob Hope, you know. I'm not doing this for laughs.'

'I know, Heather, for heaven's sake, I know. Just a little old-fashioned joke. Humour your old mother. If I were you I'd never pass up a good laugh, or any laugh for that matter. *It's a long way to Tipperary, it's a long way to go*—' Marilyn sang.

'If that's your idea of another joke, my face cracks—with pleasure, right? Leacock, if I remember my grade ten English. Something to do with celluloid collars. Besides, it hasn't been all that funny for you, correct?' Heather looked up, directly into her eyes.

'Right,' Marilyn said. An interlude. The shorts. Coming attractions. No relief in sight.

After she had checked in at the administration office in the main building, her mother and father drove her over to the residence across the grounds which were manicured, the fine lawns interrupted at regular intervals by well-ordered flower beds, circles and diamonds of loam containing perfectly linear rows of geraniums, petunias, and marigolds surrounded with alyssum.

And the lilacs. The purple and white garlands of lilacs weaving in and out around the grounds, the suffocating smell of lilacs surrounding the copper-domed shell of the main building. Red. Brick. Red brick. Bricks, thousands and screaming thousands from Medicine Hat. Tons and tons of screaming brick locked in mortar. As if enough of them could keep the madness out—of the rest of the world, that is, Marilyn thought. In, if you looked at it from the point of view of the staff. Nothing was more obvious to her now than the fact that it hadn't worked, the multiplicity of madness being what it is.

In fact, the institution to which she had been assigned was already pioneering in two areas. One, psychopharmacology, including the development of LSD, and two, the dismantling of the enormous reptilian 'institution' to which she had come. In its hey-day, it had sheltered or incarcerated, depending on how you wanted to look at it, more than thirty-five hundred patients, a larger city by far than the host community named on the official map distributed throughout the province, the one followed by her father the day they drove down.

The latter development had attracted a great deal of attention through-out North America and, under a hairdryer in the residence, Marilyn herself had read the accounts of the miraculous transformation, (none of which mentioned the mortared dome, the shell), the transfer of all the patients from this institution to half-way houses and nursing homes, back into the community. She read these articles in major American psychiatric journals, was duly impressed by the awesome progress leviathan madness had made since the days of 999 in Toronto and the concept of asylum as sanctuary.

Diminishing patient count was critical. The entire staff knew yester-day's number by the time they hit the floor for the seven o'clock shift. And Marilyn was dismayed by the aged, bespectacled man in an old felt hat who that first day tapped with his cane on the glass doors of 1 C-D, beseeching her to let him back in, as if summer relief could do any such thing. Some of these old boys, she was told in passing, had been in for thirty years, knew more about the place than senior staff, called it home.

'Go way. Get back, old man,' she heard one of the staff say. 'He wants back in the dorm, the crazy old son-of-a-bitch. Remember the poem he used to say when we put them down to bed. Hit the hay, old man. Hit the hay.

> "Now I lay me down to sleep
> I pray the Lord my soul to keep
> and if I die before I wake
> I pray the Lord my soul to take
> the goddamn stupid effing little bitch."

Gordon, get the switch. Jesus, he's completely incontinent, pissing on the rads at the new place. Making himself right at home, I guess. Get the switch. One thing you can say about this place is it sure as hell must look safe to them compared with what's going on outside.'

He came back to the hospital every day. Eventually he was readmitted to Marilyn's ward. What she remembered most about working with this par-ticular patient, apart from his shorn head, was his boots. Bending over his boots. Tying the laces on his boots. Big, black, leather-soled boots. All of them had the boots. But this man had, on several occasions, used them on other patients. And once on a female staff. She couldn't remember his name.

That first night in residence had not gone well. After the preliminaries, where are you from and what are you taking at university—Gail from Trestle, Physics, Chemistry, and Biology; Marilyn from Saskatoon, English, French, and Philosophy—they unpacked, lined the tops of their vanities with tiny ornamental bottles of perfume, lipsticks, alarm clocks, and various creams, stuffed the drawers with clothes, nylon stockings, hair rollers, notepaper, and envelopes for letters home. Then they went to bed and immediately fell into an uneasy silence, rigid beneath the pristine sheets, abrasive with starch, the silence in the dark broken only once when the housemother entered the room with a flashlight on her rounds, cast a tight shaft of light through the room which ricocheted off the wall. She had come to check if they were there. They were not. In their minds, both she and Gail were on their way north, back home. They slept fitfully. Marilyn had a dream which confirmed all her worst suspicions about the job and the place; and Gail had an asthma attack, the first of many which were to occur with frightening regularity whenever she came off shift. Marilyn listened to her laboured breathing intermittently throughout the night. From their early, tentative talk, Marilyn gathered that Gail had come from a family very much like her own. And that she was just as afraid as Marilyn of the dawn.

The next day they showered, dressed, and descended through the residence stairwell to the basement which contained a recreation room, laundry facilities, and at the far end, a large door, gun-metal grey, the small high window reinforced with wire mesh. They read the rectangular silk-screened sign on the door. A red arrow directed them through: TO SEWING ROOM. TO LOCKSMITH. TO MAINTENANCE. TO MAIN BUILDING. Each with a yellow arrow pointing left or right.

'We'd better get a move on,' Gail said. 'We wouldn't want to miss our fitting, now would we, dear,' she mimicked the housemother, an exaggerated high-pitched whisper. 'You'd think we were on our way to the mezzanine of Mayfair Fashions for godsakes, something for grad or maybe a bridal gown.'

They entered the tunnel which turned out to be surprisingly bright with painted pipes, red and yellow and white, running along the ceiling on either side of the fluorescent lights. There was a continuous mural of large sunflowers along one wall. It looked as if it had been painted by a child or like something you might find in a prehistoric cave. Later Marilyn learned the first year university students had gussied the tunnel up the previous spring during their festival of Van Gogh whom they had crowned the patron saint of madness and of art. Clever, Marilyn thought.

When they reached the sewing room, a Mrs Clements, identified so by a badge, black on white, appeared from behind a partition at the back. Marilyn stared at the badge, a primer on the nature of institutional life. Everything and everybody tagged, from head to toe, Marilyn thought, if you tended toward morbid humour. Mrs Clements called Gail into the fitting room first. She returned transformed. A la Nightingale. All she needed was a lamp. Later, Marilyn would look back on that moment as prophetic. Gail stayed on after the rest of them had fled back to campus in the fall. She was the only one of them who would become a nurse.

There were no uniforms in Marilyn's size, Mrs Clements said, but she would do the best she could. Marilyn told her she liked the tunnel, which she honestly did. Mrs Clements eyed her quizzically through the slits of a narrow half-squint, as if she'd just arrived from another planet. Which, in a way, she had. 'Yes,' Mrs Clements finally said, 'I suppose you would.'

'How long have you been here then?' Marilyn asked.

'Long enough to remember finding the old defectives in the tunnel eating salamanders after they'd wriggled out of their jackets over on 2B and gone AWOL. This was before they brought in the drugs. Oh, I remember the salamander snacks all right. You don't forget a thing like that.'

'Pardon?'

'Away without leave,' she said. 'That's the only part of it you wouldn't understand. The rest is plain English.' Mrs Clements stood back and looked at her. 'You're nothing but a twig, are you, dear. Wear that one and leave these with me. I'll take them up. Bring the one you have on back with you next time you come.'

The uniform Marilyn wore was four sizes too big and four inches from the floor. It was starched as stiff as a board. She looked as if Mrs Clements had dressed her up for Halloween. If she had had a small red nubbled plastic nurse's kit with the tablets of candy hearts, the outfit would have been complete. The uniform was short-sleeved and, within minutes, Marilyn had begun to develop a collar of red rash at her neck and two smaller bands of itchy lumps around her upper arms. She had them all summer long. The hems of the skirt which met at the front of the uniform clacked as she left the room. Mrs Clements laughed softly.

By the time they had found the dining room through the labyrinth of walls and halls, had asked directions twice along the way, they were late for breakfast. They hardly had time for the coffee and lukewarm porridge and toast. There were only a few staff left in the dining room when they arrived, lingering over coffee, assigned to another shift, perhaps, Marilyn thought, afternoons, evenings, maybe nights. She was afraid that sooner or later her name would come up and she would be assigned to nights.

When she finished breakfast, she placed her tray in the aluminum rack near the door. Gail followed. They had been told to report to different wards, Gail, 2B, Marilyn 1C-D Left, which was in another wing. The face of the woman appeared in the doorway before them, out of nowhere it seemed, but she must have been waiting there quietly, perhaps for a long time.

'No and no and no and no,' she bellowed toward the open door through which Marilyn and Gail were about to leave. 'I will not believe that this is so.' Her hair was grey, cut straight across and blunt around the ears— a few years later this would become fashionable but then Marilyn and Gail and most other girls wore their hair bouffant, back-combed with a rat tail comb, shellacked, in veritable hives.

The woman had the wildest eyes Marilyn had ever seen, Hollywood's idea of Jane Eyre's eyes. But this was as far as you could get from the silver screen, Marilyn thought. She wore a faded, sagging shirtwaist, short sleeved, a small floral print which used to be pale blue but now was closer to grey. She looked so clean, Marilyn thought, so fiercely clean, scrubbed the way fastidious mothers keep their children when there is no water. Marilyn stood as if stunned. So did Gail. The woman was blocking their way. Arms outstretched, she began to sing and sway.

'Motherhood and apple pie, motherhood and apple pie, apple pie and other lies—'

'Excuse us,' Gail finally said from behind Marilyn.

The interruption enraged the woman. She grabbed hold of the door frame with one hand and flung the other arm out toward them. 'I will not believe that this is so!' she shrieked and spit into Marilyn's face. 'Such a cacophony and such a howl will ring down, ring down millennia—such a howl as has never been heard before—the angels will bow. The voices of those who nurtured and bled and born and began again, suckled you over all this time. WE WILL CRY. WE WILL CRY.'

All of this rapid fire. Marilyn was, as she had feared she would be, terrified, paralyzed.

'IF THIS IS DONE,' the woman screamed, and then she began to hiss, 'you will not hear your various gods or any one alone or none again. My voice will be in all of you—in all your good goodbyes, obstructing all your high and heavenly ways—forever, yea for all time.'

'Dolorum,' she chanted, 'and Hecuba dragged backward into the gloom with you. The myth of the cloud and the eyes will be *nothing* in the rising tide this time. YOU DO SO KNOW WHAT YOU DO. OH YES YOU DO. Every mother you ever had or dreamt of having, every woman you ever had or dreamt of having, every have you've ever had or dreamt of having, every halving and coming together and halving, halving—'

What had frightened Marilyn most was not the power of the tirade, although she had to confess she had nothing whatsoever in her life with which to compare it and she had been in church nearly every Sunday morning of her life. What petrified her was the fact that the other staff behind them remained inert all that time, engaged in quiet conversation. The incident in memory stopped in time, a jammed projector, and the crazy she raged over the same words again and again while Marilyn and Gail remained passive, silent. For an instant, Marilyn had even felt that she was the one who was out of step, not this woman raving in front of her eyes.

Then the woman began to smile and sing, plaintively this time, like a child, really more of a sigh than a song, the same tuneless song as before, 'Motherhood and apple pie, apple pie, apple pie–'

'Wind her up, Gracie, that's the end of the set. Floor show's over till the next shift.' A tall, blond young man had come up from behind them and extended his hand toward the woman. She reached out for the hand, then curtsied, her head down; after she had risen, he placed his right hand behind his back in a gesture of gallantry and he bowed. Then he cupped his left hand toward Marilyn and Gail and in a stage-whisper said, 'Listen to this.' He turned to the woman. 'What's your name?' he asked.

She smiled and chanted in the same numb song sigh as before, 'Suzie Suzie Rotten-Crotch, Rotten-Crotch, Rotten-Crotch–'

Then to Gail and Marilyn again, 'But we call her Amazing Grace. That's what she usually sings. Besides, Grace is her name.' He turned back to her. 'Right?' he said. She did not respond. 'Move along, Gracie,' he said, 'I gotta go to work.' She stepped aside and he walked through the doorway. Marilyn and Gail were right behind him.

Moving along the corridor, the young man glanced over his shoulder at Marilyn and Gail. 'You summer relief?' he asked.

'Yes,' Gail replied, 'first day on the job.'

'Great,' he said. 'We could use a little fresh blood around here. That was Grace. A woman ahead of her time. She was an English teacher, Master's, I'm told. Figures she's cornered the market on false faith and the big bang. My name's Bill Neilson. What wards you been assigned?'

It happened that his ward was the same as Marilyn's. He directed Gail toward her floor. She had been assigned to the defectives, he said. 'You and me are with the old geezers down on 1 C-D.' They continued down the corridor. For some reason, he did not seem in the least worried about getting there on time. 'What's your name?' he asked as he slipped his key into the lock of a door which divided two wards, the movement easy, automatic, as if he'd opened it a million times before.

'Marilyn,' she replied.

'As in Monroe?'

'No,' she said. Bill Neilson wore bifocals, very thick on one side, almost opaque. She hadn't noticed it right away, but he had practically no vision left in that eye. Later, he told her his vision had never been good and that the one eye had been injured in a schoolyard fight when he was just a kid. Somebody in the eighth grade had hit him with a stick. But the other eye, instead of deteriorating along with it, had progressively improved and would, he hoped, continue to do so.

'Hey, Monroe,' one of the staff called from the main bathroom on the ward, 'c'mere.' They had all begun to call her 'Monroe' after they heard Bill use the name at lunch. Marilyn hesitated outside the door.

'I just have to finish cleaning up the games in the day room,' she called back.

'Hey! Miss Summer Relief!' another voice yelled, Mr Zwicky whom she had just met. 'We've got a job for you to do in here.' Marilyn knew. This was toward the end of the first shift and she knew they were up to something sinister even before they called her. But she couldn't believe it. Initiation of a sort, she thought. She was familiar with the form but not the sport. She folded her arms across the sturdy breast of her new uniform.

'Bet you never saw anything like this,' Mr Zwicky said as she entered the room.

A young, but veteran aide regarded Marilyn with amusement. The aide was leaning against a cupboard on the opposite wall, the frosted gloss of a plum lipstick pressed to her teeth in a ridiculous thin grin, in a let's-see-how-the-varsity-virgin-handles-this, borderline leer. She was humming the tune from the beauty pageants, 'Here she comes, Miss America.'

'No,' Marilyn found herself speaking in a remarkably clear voice, in spite of the flush of embarrassment and resentment on her face. 'No I haven't. Never before.'

There was a row of open showers at the far end of the room. Porcelain. The white bowels of the old institution worn out, pocked and greying in eroded spots. Inserted in each stall was the alabaster flesh of one old man, all sizes represented, mostly stooped and some protecting, even then, most private parts. But mainly they stood with their arms limp at their sides, legs slightly apart, as if they were in a line-up like the ones Marilyn had seen on the silver screen in crime movies. She was jolted by her response which at first she could not articulate, but which eventually came, rose clearly from her open throat. 'At least the bowels of hell are clean.' And to herself, in that still, that quiet part of her where no one ever sees—*They do it to each other too. Of course they do.*

She glared at Bill who was standing beside a trolley of white towels with some of the other staff, some she hadn't even seen before; they must be from the afternoon shift, Marilyn thought. Mr Zwicky and the aide had laughed out loud but Bill did not even smile, had regarded her carefully through his glasses which had slid low on the bridge of his nose.

'We used to use the hoses,' Mr Zwicky said, holding a thick white canvas rope with a chrome nozzle on the end, 'before the pills—I believe they refer to it in admin as the psychopharmacological revolt—but now we just turn on the overhead spray. I remember the day they put them in.'

'Revolution,' Bill said on his way out.

That first shift had almost swallowed her whole. After supper in the staff dining room, they went back to the residence and the girls on summer relief began to gather in the lounge in the basement from their scattered rooms. Everyone eventually spoke—everyone but Marilyn. The stories began to emerge. Perhaps that was where she had learned how to handle her anecdotes. Serena Wainwright had been sent up to the dispensary for fallopian tubes. The worst of it was, she had gone. She was mortified. She was an honours Biology student. She would never live it down, she said. We wouldn't ever tell anyone, would we now. Let's all take a vow—and so the evening went. That bloody vow. There were many such as the summer progressed. They may as well have had their lips sewn shut when they left, they had taken so many vows of silence and discretion. None of them had daughters then—nor had they even thought of them.

Later that week, after the shift had changed, Bill stopped Marilyn in the corridor and asked her to go out with him on the weekend. Saturday night.

All day long the girls in the residence primped and curled their hair, painted their nails, tried on each other's dresses and lipsticks. And, for the first time since she had arrived, Marilyn thought she might make out all right here. She might survive. She was excited, proud, in fact, that she had been asked out so soon, and more than a little eager to get off the hospital grounds.

After supper in the staff dining room, gooey dumplings in string beef stew followed by a bright red cube of India rubber Jello, Marilyn had skipped her way back through the tunnel to the residence and took the stairs two at a time up to her room.

She and Gail giggled in front of their vanity mirrors. They traded eyeshadow. Marilyn was wearing a pale green mohair sweater, popcorn stitch, and Gail had decided to wear a blue seersucker dress. So Marilyn traded her blue shadow for the green. She also backcombed Gail's hair and loaned her a pale blue velvet bow comb. These combs were a particularly popular accessory that spring. Gail posed in front of her mirror with her hand on the back of her neck just as she had seen the starlets do in the pictures in *Screenplay Magazine*. 'If only the guys in Trestle could see me now,' she said.

Marilyn told her she thought her date, who worked in Maintenance, was cute, and Gail said she thought Bill was too, in his own way, even if he couldn't see his hand in front of his face. He had nice hair. 'And ears,' Gail said and snickered, 'also a good physique.' That's what they used to call it then. A good physique.

They agreed they wouldn't be late coming in, at any cost, because if you broke the curfew, you got CB'd, the housemother said, and could you imagine anything worse, they said, than to be confined to barracks in a dump like this, for days, maybe even weeks. On their way down to the lounge, the voices of other girls echoed in the hall, diminished to whispers when Gail and Marilyn passed the open doors. Secrets sifting through the air. An isolated laugh. Someone softly cursing her wet hair.

Gail's date came first. The girls from the residence had begun to gather, regular staff and summer relief together. They sat in the lounge where they waited, those who had dates. Those who did not stayed in their rooms or wafted periodically past the lounge wearing their pink plastic curlers or towels on their heads and old jeans, making it perfectly clear that they weren't waiting for anything or anyone, and couldn't have cared less.

There were three pay phones in booths just off the lounge. They rang constantly that Saturday evening and finally one of the calls was for Marilyn. Bill. He said he would be a little late, would she wait for him. She said yes, she would. No problem. She had been in town all afternoon, since right after shift, and she wasn't really ready anyway.

Marilyn sat on one of the sofas which lined the walls and watched the other girls make or wait for calls. She had only been away from home one week. On Sunday evening she would phone her family as she had promised. The longer she sat thinking about it, the more she wondered what on earth she would tell them. Last night I went out on a late date. At least they had heard of things like that. Providing, of course, she wasn't stood up. More to the point she wanted to ask why. Why didn't you tell me before? The world is not the way you made it out to be.

An old man, Yacob Cain, had died that morning on her ward. He was impacted, they told her, and they laughed when she hadn't known what that was. And yesterday the barbers came to shave the old men. One of the barbers was short and asked the patients if any of them had had any luck in the bushes lately. It took Marilyn a few moments to figure out what on earth that might mean. Until the barber winked at her and smiled. He told gruesome stories about the hanging tree on the front lawn where many a patient had met his end, or hers, over the years, ever since they had opened the doors, the tall barber said.

And the little Charlie who sat in the barber's chair and roared like a lion every time the barber came near him with the long razor. The little Charlie who saw pillars of animals moving up toward heaven and the stars, up through the ceiling of the patients' dining hall where he sat and ate like a bird, he was so enthralled. And Hershel who spent all of his days rubbing off the arrows painted on the floor, thin trails of yellow arrows leading the old men toward the toilets without doors and the sinks, the stink of incontinence everywhere. And James who sometimes ate his own excrement and sometimes painted his chrome glint-armed chair in the day room. Half a

dozen of them, maybe more, pinned to the walls of the corridors on crosses of their own construction, invisible in the air; one of them regular as a
cuckoo clock cried out to the empty air, 'The Itmosphere, O my God, the
Itmosphere.' All her old men, showered and shorn. And now Marilyn knew
exactly what she would say when she phoned, would say if only she could.
Come down and take me home, back to the patio surrounded with honeysuckle and lilac, iris and bleeding heart, back to the small lawn and the lingering of the long summer afternoon with a good novel and a tall cold glass
of pale pink lemonade. And a radio and a song. 'Hot town, summer in the
city,' or 'The morning sun is shining like a red rubber ball,' 'Oh, Sweet Pea,
come on and dance with me,' 'Zorba the Greek'. How could she make it
through one more day let alone the rest of the summer.

On Tuesday afternoon, she had been sent to 3K to pick up some special medication and there she had met a woman who never stopped talking.
As soon as Marilyn set foot on the floor, the woman began to follow her.
'My name is Cheryl. I was raped when I was seventeen. I was walking
across the railroad tracks under the overhead bridge by Early's Seed and
Feed in Saskatoon you know and a man jumped out of the dark and
grabbed my arm and it broke and that was twenty-three years ago and they
brought me here and they didn't know what happened to me I never spoke
since then not a single word and now they give me some new pills and I
spoke they're pink and white and pretty soon I'll be all better don't you
think and then they'll let me go and I'll go home my name is Cheryl I was
raped when I was seventeen I was walking across the railroad tracks under
the overhead bridge by Early's Seed and Feed in Saskatoon you know and
a man jumped out of the dark and grabbed my arm and it broke and that
was twenty-three years ago—'

Which is a far cry, Dad, Marilyn said to him in her head, from the joke
Mr Archibald told you when you were raking the lawn just before we drove
down. The one about the prostitute walking across the overhead bridge
with no underpants on, headed for 20th Street, and an Englishman walking
along underneath at the same time looks up and sees what you know he
sees. 'Pretty airy up there, ain't it sweetie?' he says in his Cockney, and she
hollers down, 'What'd ya expect? Feathers?'

Go away, she told Cheryl, told all the pictures reeling in her head. Just
go away. And don't for God's sake tell me this is real, this place. She began
to understand old Grace, Amazing Grace, and for the first time, she became
aware of the lethal danger here. It was possible that by the time she got
home, Marilyn Marie Dufreysne, whoever she used to be, could have disappeared without a trace.

Mr Amien, the supervisor of her ward, found her on her coffee break sitting beside the billiard table in the day room with a branch of lilac she had picked when they were out for the afternoon walk. She had removed the small purple flowers from a blossom on the stem, one by one, dropped them on the floor in front of her. She was in the process of gathering them all up, cupping her hand to hold the delicate debris when Mr Amien walked in. 'You'd better get the broom, Marilyn, you'll drive yourself round the bend trying to get them all that way.' He sat down beside her, a large man with big hands, a strong thick neck. 'While I'm here,' he added, 'I'm going to give you a little free advice. Let them go. Let some things go. You can't keep them all. It's not up to you to do the accounts. You come from a good home. I could tell that about you right away. You're green. You've had more than your share of love, too many safe nights.' He lit a cigarette. 'You're walking around without a skin. You're packing all of this in and you can't. Toughen up. Let some things fall by the way.

'When you leave this place, just go. The staff here, a lot of us are getting on. We grew old here. We're just like the chronics,' he laughed, 'we've got no place to go.' He stood, walked toward the tall bright windows of the day room, windows wavy with the heat, and looked out. 'No,' he said, 'that's not true.' He stood quietly for a few moments while Marilyn regarded his back, the seam down the centre of his long white coat. 'But you,' he said slowly, 'as long as you leave it where it lies, who knows. You could do anything you want. If you don't it will drag you down with it, so help me God. And no matter where you are, no matter who you're with, it will eat you from the inside out. It will swallow you whole. I know your type.' At coffee that morning, Marilyn remembered Mr Zwicky whispering to the aide that Mrs Amien's divorce papers had finally come through.

Bill appeared at the residence door just as Marilyn was about to go back to her room. Never again, she had made up her mind, I don't care what excuse he comes up with. Hell will freeze over before I go out with him.

'Put your shoes on Nellie, we're a goin' to the city,' he said, smiling.

'Not this time,' Marilyn replied. 'I'm not going. I don't think you're my type.'

'I called,' he said, his smile fading, 'but I guess I didn't actually tell you what was going on. I'm sorry about that. Really.' He paused. She said nothing. 'I was with Wally Salt and Grant McKay. We had to take Grant into the Psyche Centre. He went up the pole, crossed over to the other side. I could tell he was headed in that direction, was well on his way when I met him yesterday morning in the hall over on the garden wing. He wanted us to stay with him awhile. Just sit. Dope and booze. Even a little glue, if you can believe it, the stupid son-of-a-bitch. So we did that and then Wally and I went over to the hotel for a beer.'

'It's already ten o'clock,' Marilyn said. 'The curfew's midnight.'

'I'll get you back all right. Sign out.' She hesitated as if she were thinking it over twice. 'Come on Monroe,' he said, 'we're wasting valuable time.'

'My name is Marilyn Dufreysne. Marilyn Marie Dufreysne. If you
can't say that, don't say anything.' The housemother looked up from her
book and appeared to smirk. While Marilyn signed out, the woman never
spoke, just glanced from Bill to her, then back to Bill. Something told
Marilyn she knew more about him than she should, more than she would
say. On the way down the residence steps, Bill told her the housemother
was his aunt. His whole extended family had worked at the hospital at one
time or another, he said. 'A family tradition, maybe some sort of quirky
genetic trait. Too bad it wasn't law, eh? Anyway, lots of the families in this
town went the same way,' he said.

They walked slowly through the grounds along a paved path which
wound around the side of the hospital to the main parking lot. There was
only half a moon but it shone on the bank of lilacs at the back of the lot
dividing the hospital from the rest of the world. There were two cars parked
near the wall of the building although the lot was usually full during the
day. Bill stopped at a side door lodged in a wall of solid brick. There were
no windows on this side on the ground floor. He pulled a cluster of rattling
keys from his pocket. 'Just a sec,' he said, 'I have to check on something here
before we go. You staying or coming with me?'

Marilyn followed him in through a narrow hall lit dimly with a small
yellow light bulb. Another door. Another key, and the hall opened into a
wider hall, a long hall which looked as if it had no end, just intermittent yellow bulbs and a receding, unreachable point in the dim distance where the
walls appeared to intersect. They passed what seemed like a hundred doors,
some with silk-screened labels, new and faded. Some doors remained
unmarked. All she could hear was the sound of their walking and the
monotonous hum of a large fan, the occasional gurgle in a hidden pipe,
sewage stalking out or fresh water moving in, fluids moving back and forth
from floor to floor in the deep institutional night.

Finally Bill stopped and unlocked a door clearly marked PATHOLOGY/
MORGUE. They hesitated there. The top of Marilyn's head barely reached
his shoulder. He looked over it and she looked up at him.

'Do you come here often?' Marilyn asked in a thin voice, mocking. He
looked away.

'No,' she heard him say softly to the black and white tiles on the
checkerboard floor, 'no,' to the disinfectant air. 'Only when one of my
friends check in. Overnight.'

The passed through an anteroom banked with large, unlabelled drawers and entered a small, cool room. No windows. Only the one door. A single extended tube of soft fluorescent light was suspended beneath a row of cupboards on the wall to the right. Everything was made of stainless steel, the sinks, the cupboards full of narrow drawers labelled in type or fine black ink. In the centre of the room there was a long steel table surrounded by a gradually sloping trough, like a lip, which ran around it and into a small steel sink which Marilyn supposed was at the foot end. The table was very clean, a shaft of dull gleam fell across it through the doorway from the yellow bulb of the anteroom.

Bill flicked a switch and filled the room with a funnel of blue-white light which descended from the stem of a surgical lamp centred directly above the table and, for a moment, obliterated everything. Marilyn felt nothing at first except the fright. Yet the fear moved quickly on, she had no idea why.

And then she was calm, a cool colloidal calm. Now, she realized she hadn't felt that way for years. When Heather was a baby and she nursed her in the night, sometimes then she felt it coming on.

When she looked around the room again, she found Bill standing in front of a shelf which held several large clear jars. All of them marked. Patient: Yacob Cain. Liver, Stomach, Right Lung, Brain. Heart. These organs were preserved in some kind of brine. Marilyn thought of pickled eggs. Then, for a moment, the organs looked like continents to her, mapped, as if someone had taken a globe and carved all of the continents out, then carefully placed them separately in jars and set them, evenly spaced, upon this shelf. But this image, too, was instantly replaced by her old friend, Frankenstein, which, after all, made more sense, she thought. She'd seen the movie at the Broadway Theatre with her brother when she was eight. Dr Frankenstein bottling brains. She had run out through the lobby onto the sidewalk, raced all the way down Broadway to Ruth, up Landsdowne, home, all the way home. She had run all the way away, but it was too late. She knew as soon as she was through the kitchen door. He was there. And over the days and weeks and months, she gradually got used to having him in her head, and by and by came to know that she would always carry him with her, regardless of her age.

They walked out the way they came in, took the same route back to the parking lot, Bill stopping at every door he had to lock, turning his back to Marilyn, rattling keys, then moving toward her once more. Near the end of the corridor, he traced with his hand up the length of her spine, under her sweater, beginning at the small. And she was the first out the door into the lilac air, the first one in the car, the first one on the blanket by the river, the first with her face to the stars.

Marilyn started and began to tremble when she remembered their coming together. She had felt as if she were coming apart, pieces of her flying through the dark, lying on the table, on the floor, on the counter, in the sink, in the corners, clinging to the ceiling, and some part of her tapping on the door, wanting, not out but back in again, in to that other girl she had left back there before the small, cool room and the wet dark, the girl who saw the world as whole, all the blossoms back on the stem, everything and everybody mended.

It couldn't be done, of course. And she knew. But, at the same time, (and this was still a mystery to her), she also knew that it could. That they could make another one, out of the flesh of the past, out of the spent parts. The legacy of all the people on earth who had ever lived, who had cradled the singular universe.

'I know why you took me there,' she said on the way back to the residence. 'I knew it all along. I didn't do it because of that.'

'Really,' he smiled over at her, the fine stubble of a faint beard along his jaw visible in the soft light from the dash. His glasses low and heavy on the bridge of his nose. 'The fact of the matter is I never took you anywhere. I was under the impression that I asked you and that you went down there of your own free will. You could have stayed back at the car.'

'Besides,' she went on, 'you didn't seem all that close to him if you want my opinion. On the ward. As far as I could see.'

'Yacob and I go back a long way.'

'You teased him unmercifully.'

'We had an understanding, Yacob and me. He was the first patient I ever saw. He was planting flowers on the grounds the day my dad first took me up to the hospital on his day off to pick up his check. Yacob and I have been looking after each other off and on now for the past three and a half years, although tonight, I have to admit, it feels like three and a half hundred.'

'I didn't do it for Yacob Cain,' she said. 'I want you to know that. I did it for you and me.' She paused. 'Or maybe both. I don't know. Who knows. Does everybody always have to know? All I can say is they must be a hell of a lot smarter than I am if they always know.'

He smiled again. 'You're all right Marilyn Marie Dufreysne,' he said quietly. 'You got a good head. I think you're going to make out all right in this life.'

'I'm never going to go to bed with you again,' she said, 'if that's what you think. You know that, don't you. You played your ace.'

'We didn't go to bed, if you'll remember right. We did it on the river bank. Unless you're the kind who calls it a river bed. I suppose that'd be more refined. Incorrect—but more refined.'

'Well, the consequences of this evening could very likely be more serious for me than for you, if you know what I mean—and I'm sure you do.'

'Look, I'm not perfect and neither are you. If you don't learn anything else while you're here, you'll learn that. That much at least I can safely guarantee.'

'It doesn't necessarily make things right,' she said. Then quietly, 'It doesn't necessarily mean I'm sorry either.' He looked at her curiously, surprised.

The next night in residence, after lights out, Marilyn told Gail about the showers and the morgue and the various parts of Yacob Cain who had died on her ward the day before yesterday; and she told her about her late date. Bill Neilson was horrible to have taken her down there in the first place, she said. She wouldn't be in the least surprised if the shower trick that first day hadn't been his brain wave. She had been confined to barracks for two weeks because of him. And she had decided she would never ever in this life go out with Bill Neilson again.

Yet here she had spent the whole afternoon with him, she thought now. Four hundred miles away and twenty-seven years later. She wondered what had become of him. Was he married? Did he have kids? Had he moved to Montreal or Winnipeg? Had he stayed?

Heather was finished with the first sign. Marilyn looked at it for a long time. The morning after feeling come again, she thought, the moment gone and no way of knowing when or even if it would come again. Even now, after all these years with Ron, when it was over and the bedding was all rumpled on the floor and the space extended between them forever over the cold wet sheets, it always seemed to her that this could never really happen in the first place. The swollen flesh on her and in her at the same time. Maybe there was such a thing as restoration, she thought. Why not?

She removed her sunglasses, smiled, and rubbed her eyes. Then she leaned over and tousled Heather's hair. Her head fell sideways, swayed a little under Marilyn's hand. The hair was long and smooth and clean. 'You got an extra brush?' she asked.

'Sure,' Heather replied looking up, 'why not.'

'Only I'm moving my sign to the picnic table,' Marilyn said. 'I'm not leaning down on the cement. It may be spring but the concrete is still cold and it is still hard and I, as you know, have been having a lot of trouble with my knees lately.'

Heather looked up again and Marilyn could see it in her eyes this time. She knows, Marilyn thought, already she knows too much.

'What is it,' Heather asked quietly.

'Oh nothing. I was just thinking about something that happened a long time ago, long ago and far away as they say in the fairy tales.'

'What happened to you, Mom?' Heather was examining her face.

'But before I start to paint I have to go inside,' Marilyn said, rising from her chair. She felt as if she needed to have a damn good cry is what it was, which seemed absolutely ridiculous to her now in the warm June sunlight and after such a long time.

MARLENE NOURBESE PHILIP

❧

BURN SUGAR

It don't come, never arrive, had not—for the first time since she leave, had left home; is the first, for the first time in forty years the Mother not stand-ing, had not stood over the aluminum bucket with her heavy belly whip-ping up the yellow eggs them and the green green lime-skin. 'People does buy cake in New York,' she say, the Mother had said, 'not make them.'

Every year it arrived, use to in time for Christmas or sometimes—a few time well—not till January; once it even come as late as in March. Wherever she is, happen to be, it come wrap up and tie up in two or three layers of brown wrapping paper, and tape up in a Peak Freans tin—from last Christmas—over-blacked black black from the oven. And it address on both sides—'just to make sure it get there,' she could hear the Mother saying—in the Mother funny printing (she could never write cursive she used to say). Air mail or sea mail, she could figure out the Mother's finances—whether she have money or not. When she cut the string she use to, would tear off the Scotch tape—impatient she would rip, rip off, rip the brown paper, prise off the lid, pause . . . sit back on she haunches and laugh—laugh she head off—the lid never match, never matched the tin, but it there all the same—black and moist. The cake.

The weeks them use to, would pass, passed—she eating the cake, would eat it—sometimes alone by sheself; sometimes she sharing, does share a slice with a friend. And then again—sometimes when she alone, is alone, she would, does cry as she eating—each black mouthful bringing up all kind of memory—then she would, does choke—the lump of food and memory blocking up, stick up in she throat—big and hard like a rock stone.

She don't know—when she begin to notice it she doesn't know, but once she has it always, was always there when she open the tin—faint—but it there, undeniable—musty and old it rise up, an odour of mouldiness and something else from the open tin making she nose, her nostrils twitch. Is like it cast a pall over she pleasure, shadowing her delight; it spoil, clouded the rich fruity black-cake smell, and every time she take a bit it there—in she mouth—hanging about it hung about her every mouthful. The Mother's advice was to pour some more make-sure-is-good-Trinidad rum on it. Nothing help, it didn't—the smell just there lingering.

And then she know, she knew that something on its annual journey to wherever she happened to be, something inside the cake does change, changed within the cake, and whether is the change that cause the funny smell, or the journey, the travel that cause the change that cause the funny smell . . . she don't know. . . .

It never use to, it didn't taste like this back home is what the first bite tell she—back back home where she hanging round, anxiously hanging about the kitchen getting in the Mother's way—underfoot—waiting for the baking to start—

'Wash the butter!' The Mother want to get her out of the way, and is like she feeling the feel of the earthenware bowl—cool, round, beige—the Mother push at her. Wash the butter, wash the butter, sit and wash the butter at the kitchen table, cover with a new piece of oilcloth for Christmas; wash the butter, and the sun coming through the breeze blocks, jumping all over the place dappling spots on she hand—it and the butter running competition for yellow. Wash the butter! Round and round . . . she pushing the lumps of butter round with a wooden spoon.

Every year she ask the same question—'Is why you have to do this?' and every year the Mother tell she is to get the salt out of the butter, and every year she washing the butter. The water don't look any different, it don't taste any different—if she could only see the salt leaving the butter. The Mother does catch she like this every year, and every year she washing the butter for hours, hours on end until is time to make the burn sugar.

Now! She stop. The Mother don't tell she this but she know, and the Mother know—it was understood between them. The coal-pot waiting with it red coals—the Mother never let she light it—and the iron pot waiting on the coal-pot, and the Mother waiting for the right time. She push her hand in the sugar bag—suddenly—one handful, two handful—and the white sugar rise up gentle gentle in the middle of the pot, two handfuls of white sugar rise gently . . . she had never, the Mother had never let she do it sheself, but to the last grain of sugar, the very last grain, she know how much does go into the pot.

She standing close close to the Mother, watching the white sugar; she know exactly when it going change—after she count to a hundred, she decide one year; another year she know for sure it wasn't going change while she holding her breath; and last year she close she eyes and know that when she open them, the sugar going change. It never once work. Every time she lose, was disappointed—the sugar never change when she expect it to, not once in all the years she watching, observing the Mother's rituals. Too quick, too slow, too late—it always catch she—by surprise—first the sugar turn sticky and brown at the edges, then a darker brown—by surprise—

smoke stinging, stings her eyes, tears run running down she face, the smell sharp and strong of burning sugar—by surprise—she don't budge, she stand still watching, watches what happening in the pot—by surprise—the white sugar completely gone leaving behind a thick, black, sticky mass like molasses—by surprise. If the pot stay on long enough, she wonder, would the sugar change back, right back to cane juice, runny and white . . . catching she—by surprise.

The Mother grab up a kitchen towel, grabs the pot and put it in the sink—all one gesture clean and complete—and it sitting there hissing and sizzling in the sink. The Mother open the tap and steam for so rise up and *brip brap*—just so it all over—smoke gone, steam gone, smoke and steam gone leaving behind this thick thick, black liquid.

She look down at the liquid—she use to call it she magic liquid; is like it have a life of it own—it own life—and the cake need it to make it taste different. She glance over at the Mother—maybe like she need the Mother to taste different. She wonder if the Mother need her like she need the Mother—which of them was essential to the other—which of them was the burn sugar?

She stick a finger in the pot and touch the burn sugar; turning she finger this way and that, she looking at it in the sunlight turning this way and that, making sure, she make sure you don't drop any of the burn sugar on the floor; closing she eyes she closes them, and touching she touch she tongue with her finger . . . gently, and she taste the taste of the burn sugar strong and black in its bitterness—it bitter—and she skin-up she face then smile—it taste like it should—strong, black and bitter it going make the cake taste like no other cake.

She hanging round again, watching and waiting and watching the Mother crack the eggs into the bucket—the aluminum bucket—and she dying to crack some in sheself—if she begged she got to crack a few but most of the time she just hanging, hung around watching and waiting and watching the Mother beat the eggs. Is like the Mother thick brown arm grow an appendage—the silver egg whisk—and she hypnotizing sheself watching the big arm go up and down scraping the sides of the bucket—a blur of brown and silver lifting up, lifts the deep yellow eggs—their pale yellow frothy Sunday-best tulle skirts—higher and higher in the bucket. The Mother stop and sigh, wipe she brow—a pause a sigh, she wipes her brow—and she throw in a piece of curly, green lime-skin, add a dash of rum—'to cut the freshness'—a curl of green lime-skin and a dash of rum. She don't know if the Mother know she was going to ask why, to ask her why the lime-skin—anticipating her question—or if she was just answering she own question, she don't know, but the arm continued, keep on beating as if it have a life of it own with a life of its own, grounded by the Mother's bulk which harness the sound of she own beat—the scrape, swish, and thump of her own beat.

She watching the Mother, watches her beat those eggs—how they rise up in the bucket, their heavy, yellow beauty driven by the beating arm; she remember the burn sugar and she wonder, wonders if change ever come gently . . . so much force or heat driving change before it. Her own change had come upon her gently . . . by surprise . . . in the night of blood . . . by surprise . . . over the months them as she watch her changes steal up on her . . . by surprise . . . the days of bloodcloth, the months that swell up her chest . . . by surprise . . . as she watched watching the swelling, budding breasts, fearful and frighten of what they mean, and don't mean. There wasn't no force there, or was there? too old and ancient and gradual for she or her to notice as she watch the Mother and wait, waiting to grow up and change into, but not like—not like she, not like her, not like . . . she watching . . . the Mother face shiny with sweat shines, she lips tie up tight tight with the effort of the beating arm, lips held in tight and she wondering, wonders whether she, the Mother, have any answers . . . or questions. Did she have any—what were they?

Nobody tell she but she hand over the bowl, the bowl of washed butter she pass to the Mother who pour off the water and put in the white sugar—granulated and white she add it to the lumpy yellow mass, and without a word the Mother pass it back to her. She hand too little to do it for long—cream the butter and sugar—her arm always grows too tired too soon, and then she does have to pass it back to the Mother. But once more, one more time—just before the Mother add the eggs, she does pass it back to her again for she to witness the change—surprise sudden and sharp all the way from she fingers right up she arm along she shoulder to she eyes that open wide wide, and she suck in her breath—indrawn—how smooth the texture—all the roughness smooth right out and cream up into a pale, yellow swirl. When she taste it not a single grain of sugar leave behind, is left to mar the smooth sweetness.

She want it to be all over now—quick quick, all this mixing and beating and mixing, but she notice the sound change now that the eggs meet the butter—it heavier and thicker, reminding her it reminds her of the Mother—she and the Mother together sharing in the Mother's sound.

She leans leaning over the bucket watching how the eggs and butter never want to mix, each resisting the other and bucking up against the Mother force. Little specks and flecks of butter, pale yellow in defiance; stand up to fight the darker yellow of the eggs them, and little by little they disappear until the butter give up and give in, yields—or maybe is the other way around—the eggs them give in to the butter. Is the Mother hand that win, the Mother's arm the victor in this battle of the two yellows.

The Mother add the dry fruit that soaking in rum and cherry brandy for months now, then the white flour; the batter getting thick thickens, stiffens its resistance to the Mother's hand, the beating arm, and all the time the Mother's voice encouraging and urging–'Have/to keep/beating/all the/time'–the words them heavy and rhythmical, keeping time with the strokes. The batter heavy and lumpy now, and it letting itself be pushed round and round the bucket–the Mother can only stir and turn now in spite of she own encouragement–but she refuse to let it alone, not giving it a minute's rest.

The Mother nod she head, and at last she know that *now* is the time–time for the burn sugar. She pick up the jar, holding it very carefully, and when the Mother nod again she begin to pour–she pouring the Mother stirring. The batter remain true to itself in how it willing to change–at first it turn from grey to brown–just like me she think, then it turn a dark brown like she sister, then an even darker brown–almost black–the colour of her brother, and all the time the Mother stirring. She empty the jar of burn sugar–her magic liquid–and the batter colour up now like she old grandmother–a seasoned black that still betray sometimes by whitesh flecks of butter, egg, and sugar, and the Mother arm don't stop beating and the batter turning in and on and over itself.

'How you know when it ready?'

'When the spoon can stand in it,' and to show what she mean, the Mother stick the spoon the batter and it stand up stiffs stiff.

Her spoon like the Mother's now stood at attention–stiff and alone in its turgid sea of black. It announced the cake's readiness for the final change of the oven. Was she ready? and was it the Mother's cake she now made? Or her own? Just an old family recipe–the cake had no other meaning–its preparation year after year only a part of painting the house, oiling the furniture, and making new curtains on the Singer machine that all together went to make up Christmas. She had never spoken to the Mother about it–about what, if anything, the cake and the burn sugar might mean . . .

It was its failure to arrive–the absence of the cake–even with its 'funny' smell that drove her to this understanding, this moment of epiphany as she now stood over her cheap, plastic bowl and watched the spoon. She looked down at her belly, flat and trim where the Mother's easily helped balance the aluminum bucket–not like, not like, not like her–she hadn't wanted to be like her, but she *was* trying to make the mother's black cake, and all those buckets of batter she had witnessed being driven through their changes were now here before her–challenging her. And she *was* different–from the Mother–as different perhaps as the burn sugar was from the granulated sugar, but of the same source. Here, over this bucket–it was a plastic bowl–

she met—they met and came together—to share in this old old ritual of trans-formation and metamorphosis.

The Mother would surely laugh at all this—all this fancy talk with words like 'transformation and metamorphosis'—she who had warned of change, yet was both change and constancy. 'Is only black cake, child, is what you carrying on so for?' she could hear the voice. They didn't speak the same language—except in the cake, but now the Mother was sitting look-ing at her make the cake.

'Look, Mammy—look, see how you do it—first, the most important thing is the burn sugar—the sweetness of the cake need that bitterness—you can't have black cake without it.' Mammy was smiling now,

'You was always a strange one.'

'Shut up, Mammy, and listen,' (gently of course) 'just listen—the burn sugar is something like we past, we history, and you know that smell I always tell you about?' Mammy nod her head, 'I now know what it is—is the smell of loneliness and separation—exile from family and home and tribe—even from the land, and you know what else, Mammy—is the same smell of —'

'Is only a cake, child—'

'The first ones—the first ones who come here rancid and rank with the smell of fear and death. And you know what else, Mammy? is just like that funny smell of the cake when I get it—the smell never leave—is always there with us—'

'Is what foolishness you talking, child—fear and death? Just make the cake and eat it.'

'But, Mammy, that is why I remember you making the cake—that is what the memory mean—it have to mean something—everything have to have a meaning—'

'Let me tell you something, girl,' Mammy voice was rough, her face tight tight—'some things don't have no meaning—no meaning at all, and if you don't know that you in for a lot of trouble. Is what you trying to tell me, child—that it have a meaning for we to be here—in this part of the world—the way we was brought here? That have a meaning? No, child'—the voice was gentler now—'no, child, you wrong and don't go looking for no meaning—it just going break you—'

'Mammy—'

But Mammy wasn't there, at least not to talk to. She looked down at the batter. The burn sugar she used was some she the Mother had made earlier that year, accompanied by the high-pitched whine of the smoke alarm. She had made the batter by hand, as much of it as she could, even adding the green green corkscrew of lime-skin, although according to Mammy 'these modern eggs never smell fresh like they suppose to—like those back home.'

When they were done she almost threw the cakes out. She had left them too long in the oven and a thick crust had formed around them; the insides were moist and tasted like they should—the bitter, sweet taste perfectly balanced by the deep, rich, black colour. But the crust had ruined them. Obviously she wasn't ready, and only the expense of the ingredients had prevented her from throwing them out immediately.

It was the Mother's advice that saved them. Following her instructions by phone she cut all the crusts off the cakes, then poured rum over them to keep them moist. She had smaller cakes now—not particularly attractive ones either, but they tasted like black cake should, and without that funny smell.

Was that hard crust a sign of something more significant than her newness at making the cake? Was there indeed no meaning to the memory, or the cake, or the funny smell? She wanted to ask the Mother—she almost did—but she knew the Mother would only laugh and tell her—'Cake is for eating not thinking about—eat it and enjoy it—stop looking for meaning in everything.'

She thanked the Mother, lowered the receiver slowly and said to herself—'You wrong, Mammy, you wrong—there have to—there have to be a meaning.'

MARGARET GIBSON

❧

THE BUTTERFLY WARD

Sometimes it can be beautiful inside this space. Most people, people who can ride on buses and streetcars and eat doughnuts for breakfast if and when they want and don't have to dial 0 on their phones to make a call would think that statement crazy. Maybe it is a bit crazy. Even phone calls cannot be simple here, everything twisted into complications but I am getting used to it now.

I have been here a month now on the neurological ward of a big hospital in Toronto. The biggest, I am told, with new wings that gleam and old ones that make me feel like a nun hiding in a bombed-out convent. I come from Kitchener, that is my home, but they sent me here. They, whoever *they* may be, said that the doctor working here on my case, Dr Carter, is the best neurologist in Ontario, maybe even all of Canada. The mysterious and secret *they* who have so neatly pigeon-holed my life. I wonder if I was supposed to be impressed with this news as my mother packed my suitcase and told me of all the wonderful little boutiques in Toronto, slipping in the famous name among the dried coloured flowers of the boutiques. My father stood in the doorway with his pipe in a reassuring mouth. I was not impressed. I had seen so many doctors for the secrets that dwelt inside my nebula that I was not. If a year or two ago they had told me of the famous Dr Carter in this huge city hospital in Toronto—then, I might have been impressed. Not now. I am a cynic, old and tangled in the opal of my mind. I was twenty-one last April, it is the end of May now. I came to this place—NEUROLOGICAL WARD, it was like that in bold letters, on the 28th of April and it is now May 30th. Yes, sometimes it is quite beautiful. I lie in my bed at night and creep into my nebula and watch fire and white matter like fine mists drifting past, I float with the clouds. There is no fire in there, my imagination has placed it thus so it can drift with the white mists. I have always loved beautiful things.

They have come to poke and pin Mrs Watson. She moans, no, no she cannot drink another quart of water and no more needles. Now, now they murmur softly. I am supposed to be asleep but I watch from the fine mists of my nebula, so beautiful and secret in there. I know this game and how to grit your teeth and pretend it doesn't matter that ten times in one night you are pinned with needles like a butterfly to a board or that you must drink a quart of water each time until it is like a poisonous liquid, a gas bloating up your stomach. Now, now the two nurses murmur softly, only two more to go, with their pins and poisonous liquid. One jabs her in the hip with the long, slender needle, pinned again, the other holds out the quart of water to her in a plastic jug. No, Mrs Watson whimpers, I feel sick to my stomach. Now, now they murmur. The pinned butterfly drinks the poisonous liquid, the two collectors of butterfly wings stand beside her board to make sure she drinks it all. They go. The pinned butterfly flutters and gasps and is free for another two hours. I know this game and how to play it. I have been the butterfly three times. The injections keep the liquid from pouring out, from escaping the body otherwise the doctors could not get a clear picture of the bloated nebula. Brain, to strangers to this place. I know this game.

Mrs Watson flutters and gasps trying her twisted wings. 'It's all right, Mrs Watson,' I murmur now from outside my nebula. I am lying in bed on the neurological ward and I must say to this woman that it is all right. She is forty but looks nearly sixty. I am twenty-one but look eighteen. I must say to this woman that it is all right. She has never been pinned on the butterfly board before nor drenched inside with the poisonous liquid bloating her stomach. She has only been here five days.

'Is that you, Kira?'

'Yes,' I answer softly. My mother is fond of Russian books and her greatest desire is to go to Russia someday and see the Kremlin and its turrets gleaming in the sun in white snow, thus the name Kira, which is Russian. At my conception visions of Russia and bells and snow going on forever and ever and the Kremlin shining in the sun were mingled with the sperm that made me, Kira. They lay in her womb ready for the sperm that would make me a Russian. Waiting, simply waiting unbeknownst to my father. The sperm came and the womb filled with Russia mingled with the sperm and received its new comrade, Kira. I have forgotten what it means but something very lovely I am sure. Mrs Watson whispers in the darkness, 'You are such a nice girl, Kira, so young. What are you doing here? Are you crazy?'

'No,' I say.

'They sent me here from a mental hospital. An O.H. I don't belong here, I didn't belong in that other place either. They said I cried all the time and got angry and threw things but I didn't! Liars, all of them! I don't do those things, you can see that for yourself. I thought the mental hospital was bad but this is worse. I'd rather have a shock treatment any time—zzz—burns out the brain. Does that scare you that I'm from a crazy joint?'

I can see her grey hair frizzled in the darkness like the zzz sound. 'No,'

I answer because it doesn't, nothing much does anymore.

'Then why are you here?' Her voice is curious, grasping for a reason she can borrow.

'I have fits sometimes and no-one knows why. The pills for epilepsy don't work for me. Maybe I'm a new breed of epileptic, I don't know.'

'They said I had fits and threw things and hurt people but I never did. Everyone lies, don't you forget it ever, everyone lies so they can get just what they want from you. They lie.' Her teeth look purple in the dark and tiny night lights.

'What do they want from you?' I ask.

Mrs Watson leans toward me from her bed, turning her head closer to me, her breath smells of the poisonous liquid. 'Money,' she whispers fiercely, 'money! I've written to my lawyers over and over again to let me out of the crazy house, to tell them how it is all a lie and a sham to get my money, but I know my lawyers never got those letters, never saw the truth. Otherwise I'd be out of there, out of here. The doctors at the crazy house opened them all and laughed and took more money from my estate, ripping my letters to bits, destroying vital information. Just take, take from my estate, laughing while they do it.' Mrs Watson's fierce whispers are filled with hate. I say nothing. I have never known a crazy person before, I am not sure of her map. 'I heard you been here a month, right?'

'Yes.'

'They . . . the staff, do they do this thing with needles and water often? I feel like I could throw up all over this bed but I can't.'

'That's because of the needles.'

'Well, do they do this often?'

What can I say? I have been pinned on the butterfly board three times and tomorrow comes the bigger board, the worst one. I do not want to tell her about what will happen tomorrow morning. They have pinned me to the butterfly board so often because the famous Dr Carter can find nothing. Maybe she will be lucky and they will find something in her nebula. 'No,' I finally answer, 'not often.'

'How often?'

A nurse with a flashlight beams it into our corner of the small ward. 'Kira, let Mrs Watson get some sleep, her next injection is in less than two hours. You know we like our patients to rest, sleep between injections.' The flashlight beam is gone and she with it. For a moment we do not speak. In fact I don't want to talk to Mrs Watson and her secret estate any longer. I have decided that I do not like her with her fierce whisper and teeth showing purple in the dark and her breath and her frizzy-zzz grey hair.

'How often?' she repeats.

Now I am mechanical in my answer but I will not tell her about tomorrow, I have decided that, I will not tell her. If she were my friend I would tell her but she is not. 'If they find what they're looking for in the picture of your brain maybe just once, maybe you will be lucky. If they don't find it they will do it again. Maybe three times.'

'Ahh God, you had it done three times?'

'Yes.'

'Ahhh God!' she moans. 'What happens in the morning, they told me I can't have any breakfast, what happens in the morning Kira?'

'They weigh you . . .' I say and let my voice trail off into a pretend sleep. Maybe I will really fall asleep.

'And then?' I do not answer, I breathe deeply as one does in sleep. 'And then?' Her hand, thin and veined and wretched-looking is pulling at the sleeve of my nightgown like an old bird's talon. I do not move or speak. 'And then?' Her voice is frantic, demanding. I say nothing, I am breathing deeply. She releases the sleeve of my blue cotton nightgown. I hear her whisper hatefully, 'Bitch! You little bitch! Let me tell you something, sleeping brat, sleeping little brat, I am the only sane person left in this whole damn world, little brat!' I am glad that I did not tell her what will happen in the morning, she is no friend of mine, she hates me because my veins do not bulge and I have never been to a crazy hospital. I belong to no private club. I am awake for her next injection, I hear the butterfly gasp and flutter and then I am asleep. The pill they gave me at nine o'clock has finally worked, my nebula turned dark with sleep. Drifting in the mists until morning.

It is a quarter to eight in the morning. Everyone in the small ward is awake, there are six beds in this room counting mine. Three on one side, three on the other. I am lying on my side waiting for my breakfast, pretending I do not hear Mrs Watson's demand and question over and over, 'And then?' I eat my milky scrambled eggs and cold toast and drink the coffee which is good and hot this morning. I brush my long hair then lean back against the two pillows with a lighted cigarette in one hand, my coffee cup in the other. Today I have no tests, I can smoke and drink coffee and watch the television my parents rented for me. The third day I was here a girl from some other part of the neurological wing in a wheelchair came into this small ward and screamed at me, 'Where did you get the TV! Who from?'

'From my parents,' I answered.

'Christ are you stupid!'

A nurse called her by her name, Linda, I think, and she wheeled herself out of the room giving me a hateful glance. I didn't know what she was talking about and I hated Toronto with its huge hospitals and the famous Dr Carter. I felt like crying. I asked a nurse to tell Dr Carter that I wanted to go home. The Cogitator came. 'This is just because you are unused to hospital routine. You've never been hospitalized before have you, Kira?'

'Only for a day and a night occasionally.'

The Cogitator, a woman called Dr Wells, patted my hand and told me that I would get used to it. She told me to call her Karen. Dr Karen Wells. She is in her late thirties and has nice legs and wears eyeshadow. She patted my hand that day and said, 'You'll get used to it.' She is chief Cogitator for Dr Carter. One sees Dr Carter only during the great pinning day or as he flies through the ward, white coat flapping, nodding to his charges, a group of new Dr Carters trailing behind him from bed to bed. He talks about you at your bedside as if you had merged with the pillow and the new Dr Carters fumble and ask and answer questions with reddening faces. Perhaps they sense their smallness, know already that they will never be a great and famous Dr Carter, only small Dr Carters. There is room for Greatness in only one on this ward.

They have weighed Mrs Watson. 'Gained nine pounds,' she says aloud to everyone in the small ward. 'Feel like I could burst open,' she says to Miss Smith who has Parkinson's disease. 'What do you think of that? After my money, all of them.' Miss Smith does not answer, only the tremors in her arms seem to weigh the related message and respond to it. Her face frozen in rigidity reveals nothing. 'Nine pounds on their vile water in one night,' she says again. 'The first time I gained ten pounds. Oh, how my nebula must have showed up clear and bright and bloated on their pictures! I ignore her. She pulls at my sleeve, I will not talk to her. 'Brat! Bitch!' she whispers even in daylight to me. I drink my coffee. If she were my friend. . . . She is not. At ten o'clock The Pinners with a touch of mania to them come and take Mrs Watson away. She is going to the big butterfly board but she does not know it. Not yet. 'I don't get angry or cry, ask that brat Kira! She knows. Thinks she's too good to talk to me. Ask her, that brat knows the truth!' Truth? She is asking The Pinners as they walk her from the small ward, 'What's going to happen? What's going to happen?' Her voice is plaintive. The Pinners do not answer, saying only, 'There, there,' and they are gone.

She said I knew the truth. I used to think I knew all there was to know about truth. I am slender and pleasant looking with long auburn hair and I graduated from high school with honours, in the top fifteen. That was a truth, the diploma and the cleverness. I went to the graduation dance with Adam, who was tall with husky shoulders and sky-blue eyes and soft brown hair, who had been telling me for the last year how much he loved me and that we should consummate our love. He wore a navy blue suit and a pale blue tie and I wore a long pink gown with a scoop neck and we danced all night together and drank a tepid fruit punch from a huge crystal bowl. Our love was never consummated. That was another truth. Adam finally gave up telling me how much he loved me, mouth aching from the word and left me. I didn't care too much.

I went to work in The Home for Retarded Children, that was a different kind of truth. There were mongoloids there and waterhead babies and the simply retarded, retarded beyond grasp or pain. Flies buzzed in the spring and summer in the playground where the children who were mobile went out to play. They constantly fell and cut and bruised themselves, the flies knew this and followed them, a dark buzzing cloud ready to light on the open wounds. The buzzing cloud followed them back into the Home when play period was over. Even after their wounds had been cleaned and bandaged a few flies still hovered with tenacity near the children's beds. Limbs of rubber, the waterheads. Some of them were quite beautiful, limbs of rubber, toes touching forehead. I felt no disgust or pity. I did feel compassion but more than that I felt necessary. That was another truth. 'Why do you work in a place that's so depressing and pays so poorly? You're so smart, get a better job,' everyone said to me. 'Go to university with your fine brain,' my mother said. They didn't know that I would simply be a numeral at university, perhaps a clever numeral but a numeral all the same. I could think of no other job that would make me feel as necessary. I tried to discuss this with my mother, this truth. I thought that she of all people having held Russia in her womb would understand. I was being a good proletarian working for the collective for a small amount of money per week. My mother had pointed out to me again and again since childhood the Mennonites when they came into town in their horse-drawn wagons, travelling with ease among cars and buses and pedestrians. 'Look how selfless they are.' She said it over and over again as we bought fruit and vegetables from the somberly dressed Mennonites. Mother, who should have understood but did not said, 'You should go to university. It's a very fine thing you are doing working at the Home but Kira you can't go on like that forever. Save your money and then you and I and your father, if he wants to, will go and see Russia next year and the next year you will go to university. It would be a shame to waste such a good brain. Study—study child psychology if you want. But don't waste that brain of yours Kira.'

'Russia?'

'Yes, the most beautiful country in the world. People for the people, green forests, all that snow, the Kremlin in winter . . .' She did not understand that there in Kitchener, Ontario, I was being a good proletarian. But I was doing it out of selfish reasons like a spy. It made me feel necessary.

I got a small apartment with a girl who was a beautician when I was nineteen. I filled the apartment with plants and flowers of all colours and sizes and watered them carefully and put plant pills in their soil before going to work at the Home. The beautician sat under the hairdryer each night for at least two hours, filing and polishing her nails as she sat there. Her hair was as brittle as dried twigs and the colour of straw in the sun. I was happy. That was a truth. It was when I was just twenty that I moved into the nebula, or that is to say it moved in on me. I would have a seizure and remember nothing afterward. 'A convulsion, kind of,' my roommate with the twig hair told the doctor. I had never thought about the brain, at least not my brain, despite my working in the Home—much less the nebula that had moved in on me. But that realization was only to come later, of the nebula. That was the newest truth, the next truth. I had e.e.g. after e.e.g. and still nothing, minor tests and finally this huge hospital in Toronto with the famous Dr Carter. 'The best in Ontario, maybe in Canada,' my mother had said. I was not impressed. My nebula. As I said, it can be beautiful inside this space.

I am dressed in pale blue brushed denim jeans and a blue cotton top. I sit propped up on my bed watching television and drinking coffee, no tests for me today. They came for Mrs Watson at ten o'clock, it is now ten-twenty, I know that for certain because the Phil Donahue Show is just beginning. Mrs Watson with her secret fortune is now pinned on the biggest butterfly board of them all. There is no anaesthesia for the dying butterfly. Yes, she will feel that this is dying. No anaesthesia, nothing can interfere with the test. She lies on the sterile table, hands clenched by her sides. Dr Carter will tell her to unclench her hands. Two long needles, one on either side of her face have been driven through her jawbone. Pinned. Dr Carter will tell her to lie perfectly still, the butterfly will lie pinned like that, still and dead for half an hour. Dr Carter and others will peer into her bloated brain but only Dr Carter will matter.

The first time I was the butterfly on the giant board, the pain of it—the sheer, smooth glass covering the butterfly board, from wing tip to wing tip, that first time it took The Pinners three tries before the giant pins settled properly into my jawbone. I thought perhaps my jawbone like my fits was different and unexplainable. The last two times however I was pinned in a neater fashion. I did not move, not the first, second, or third time. I did not cry. I threw up afterward each time, ten pounds of poisonous liquid down the toilet. The first time I sat beside the toilet after, sweating and holding my head in my hands, my long hair stank of vomit and my mother waited for me anxiously outside the washroom. We had been sitting in the cafeteria after the pinned butterfly had risen from the board and suddenly I knew I was going to be violently ill. Mother, kind and gentle, wanted to come with me. 'No, alone,' I managed to say.

'Kira, please.' I made it just in time to the washroom. It was there, I think, in that tidy, stinking cubicle that I perceived my brain as a nebula and it was then too that I knew what was in it and what they would never find. At first it was just an idea, a play toy in the long hours of white boredom, but as the tests went on and on, thrice the butterfly, my pain the smooth glass shield, it was no longer a toy. It is my escape. I am not a Mrs Watson, but when the night comes or I think I cannot bear another commercial for Brillo Pads or Mr Clean or when I have another e.e.g., I crouch in the mists of my nebula where it is beautiful and everything is calm, safer somehow in that beautiful misty space. 'You'll get used to it,' and Dr Karen Wells had patted my hand. It seems so very long ago now. This hospital in the big, shining car city, so many cars here, with streets of sparkling light at night, this city of Toronto where there are no Mennonites, just the famous Dr Carter who has become the next truth and with him the nebula. Is it the final truth? I am something of a novelty. They probe and pin and stick and pill and nothing changes, nothing works. I was always so ordinary before, simply Kira, a bright comrade born in an alien land but I adjusted, and my life read like a dull book, a simple map.

I think of my mother at home. Is she standing in front of the somberly dressed Mennonites buying their fruit and vegetables and marvelling at their selflessness? Soon I will get a letter from my father and he will write an amusing piece of poetry in it and tell me the latest news of everyone I have known and everyone he knows. He never runs out of words to fill sheets of paper with for my letters, the words brim over the pages like the tears in his eyes when I left. Tall, quiet Father, pipe in his reassuring mouth, gentle, tears in his eyes when I left for this huge monument to science and flesh. Mother finds it difficult to fill a single sheet of paper with words and yet it is she who comes here when I am pinned to the giant board, three times she has come; it is Father who cannot force himself to be witness. To what, I wonder? The Pinning, the aftermath of The Pinning of course. Tears brimmed up in his eyes when I left. Is it because of Russia, the land of the worker, the harsh land, the proletarian land, that my mother can come and bear witness like a good and sturdy comrade and my father cannot?

It is eleven o'clock, the Phil Donahue Show takes a commercial break. The Pinning has been over for ten minutes for Mrs Watson. Is she vomiting now? Weeping? Cursing the laughing doctors who opened her letters to her lawyers? I only vomited. Dr Carter himself said I was a very stoic person. Dr Karen Wells, chief Cogitator, beamed at me and so did the lesser Cogitators at these words for me, all for me, from the famous Dr Carter. Three times on the butterfly board and I have yet to weep. Is it that I am stoic or simply that I have the secret of my nebula and tell no-one. You see I have deduced what is wrong with my brain. Why don't I tell them? It would all be so simple. Would they think me high-strung giving in to stress? I'm not though, I am a sturdy comrade. I crouch in the mists of the nebula.

Mrs Watson has to be helped back to her bed, she is weeping and moaning, fingers tentatively exploring her aching, burning jawbone without actually touching it, sketching the pain of it in the air. 'I want all my personal belongings! I'm leaving your Dachau!' she screams. The nurses try to calm her down. 'There, there,' they say. It is their code word. 'Nazis!' she screams and begins to tear apart her bed. Pillows fall to the floor, a sheet tears, the night table topples over with a crash and the splinter of the glass ashtray. Pinned again. The slender, efficient needle plunges into her leg muscle. She sleeps. One nurse sighs and then turns to me smiling, 'How are you today, Kira?'

'I'm all right, a little bored I guess.'

'You can go down to the cafeteria or to the gift shop and buy some magazines, there's nothing scheduled for you today.' She means to be kind to this novelty, Kira-stoic.

'I probably will after lunch,' I reply. Two aides are straightening up the mess of Mrs Watson's bombed-out bed, removing the ripped sheet. Mrs Watson rolls like a piece of clay as they pull it out from under her, oblivious, her mind in a place of Not. Not anything, darkness is not even there. What strength in those thin bird-claw hands!

The next day is simple. I have another electroencephalograph. The needles are placed all over my scalp, little pin pricks, no pain. Blink. Stop. Deep breath. Stop. Fast shallow breathing. Stop. Deep, slow breathing. Stop. Blink rapidly. Stop. How used to all this I have become. Dr Wells patted my hand, 'You will get used to it.' Later after the e.e.g. is over I take a brief walk around the hospital block. It is now June. The June air is sweet and cool, a slight breeze caresses my hair and scalp where minutes ago it was covered with the little pin pricks of needles. I do not stay outside long. Soon I am back in the small ward watching the Mike Douglas Show. I drink a ginger ale and smoke. There is a comedian on and everyone in the TV audience laughs, even I laugh a little. It is June second, the beginning of my second month here. The nurse comes and gives Miss Smith a new pill to try, as if anything on earth could stop the small volcano in her arms and fingertips or smooth out the rigidity of her shoulder and face. I am given new pills to try out, grey with black little dots on them. I swallow the three round pills and soon my mind begins to feel heavy. My nebula fills with fat rain clouds. I sleep.

It is June the fifth. I received a long letter from my father today with an amusing poem in it and he ends by saying that he knows what the doctors are doing is right and that soon his Kira will be healthy and home.

I am to be pinned to the giant butterfly board again this morning, hands flat on the board, no flutter of wings. I could tell them quite simply that the thing that causes my fits is not a thing that a pill can cure. The amoeba. Yes, that is what it is. I knew that after my first pinning to the great board. It is nourishing itself on what they call my brain, enveloping the minute organisms held there. It floats in my nebula. It does not matter how many quarts of water or needles they give me at night to bloat my brain, everyone knows that an amoeba changes shape and because it is so change-able the famous Dr Carter will never catch it on his bloated-brain scans. Why do I not tell them this? They would not put me in a crazy house like Mrs Watson, who now wanders in a daze on a new drug, sometimes bump-ing into walls and furniture. No, not good stoic Comrade Kira. High strung and nervous under all the strain of it they would say kindly. Dr Karen Wells would simply pat my hand as she did on my third day here when she first told me I'd get used to it. Why don't I tell them that it is the amoeba eating away that is causing me to faint, have fits, and forget? Why not?

I am walking to the elevators with The Pinners now, in a few more min-utes I will be the butterfly, wing tip to wing tip pinned on the giant board. They will look and find nothing, the famous Dr Carter will shake his head in confusion. I feel no shiver in the pit of my stomach as I have on other Pinning days—this will be my fourth time on the giant board. Yes, I am get-ting used to it. I will lie pinned there as still as the dead butterflies in a col-lector's box, lovingly, carefully pinned. I will lie like that for half an hour and then my wing tips will flutter faintly and I will rise, the secret of the amoeba held within my lovely, fluttering wing tips, fluttering softly in the large Pinning Room. Everyone will smile. Poor butterfly. Yes, I am getting used to it. Perhaps that is the final truth of them all, the last.

ᖆ

THE KING OF SIAM

Jane is in Paris when the news comes: her mother is dead in the apple orchard in the Okanagan, where she and Jane's father have retired, supposedly at peace. And Jane remembers her mother dancing. Not with her father, Saturday night in the living room, after a discussion about how much hip she could use in the rhumba. He would be leading, driving her with both shoulders as one would a wheelbarrow. 'That much, no more,' he ruled. Her slim hip poked out; he put it back in its place, a stern man with a measuring eye.

'Here I go with my best foot backward,' her mother would say, waggishly, because the man always led, and his forward steps made her step out behind.

No, that is not what she remembers, but her mother dancing, alone, weekday mornings, letting loose, elbows pumping, her mouth a soundless smile. She looks like Mary Martin. The words she sings are Mary's: 'I'm gonna wash that man right outa my hair. . . .' The record spins in the dusty-bright air.

The house glares; the cloudless sky and the flat, snow-whitened lawns and streets bounce sunbeams through the picture windows. The beams explode geometrically again and again on motes of dust in the dry inside air, creating a painful brightness in all directions. Alone with the smallest child when the others have gone to school, her mother walks around in the forced-air heat with narrowed eyes, sometimes shading her brows with a forearm. The beige curtains are closed, to filter the light which could take two shades out of the upholstery in one season.

The house is a lightbox, her mother has two dimensions, like a paper doll glued onto sticks. The records are old ones in small jackets, the songs simple, like rhymes.

'Oh what a beautiful morning, oh what a beautiful day, I've got a wonderful feeling, everything's going my way.'

Every morning is the same. They have things to do. They will just put on a record while they work. They listen a few minutes and pretend to dust or sort tea towels but inevitably are seduced. First, certain pieces of furniture have to be moved, his stuffed footstool and the glass-topped coffee table with the three cones for legs. Then the choice—*Brigadoon? Carousel? The King and I?* They take off their shoes.

They are dancing. Not with each other, no, they move off into separate orbits; there in the veiled brilliance of the living room. Socks on the pink-beige carpet give shocks if they touch each other or the velvet chair. Bits of them arc through the hall mirror, and also in the glass of the picture frames. Cheap clichés these movements, but wildly sincere. The arched eyebrows, hands on knees, bug eyes for the benefit of the audience beyond the curtains fluttering over the forced-air vent. The faces out of which such words can come:

'I'm gonna wash that man right outa my hair, and send him on his way!'

Or the supple, breathy swaying, mouth slightly open:

'Some enchanted evening, you may see a stranger, you may see a stranger, across a crowded room . . .'

The room where such events can happen is somewhere else. But somewhere else is a place, a place you can get to, if you just keep going, going
    until
    it is not Jane, but just her mother dancing, Jane watching. Her mother fabulous and strong, her mother tough and funny. And Jane knows a kind of peace, almost holy. Her mother, the light, the music.

We are talking about the fifties, in the West. A growing city with a university, an industry; a small box house on a too wide street; her father working out of town on the oil rigs. The Oil Capital of Canada! Gateway to the North! But outside its boundaries, nowhere. West, but not coast, flattish, but not prairie, that was farther south. The American term 'Midwest,' conjuring visions of cornfields, did not apply. They call it parkland, but there were no parks, only a place where they sometimes went to see a herd of captive buffalo, brought back from near-extinction. During the gold rush, expeditions embarked from here for the Yukon; some lost their way; in all one hundred and twenty-eight people perished.

And there was the river, muscular, army-green, so wide it would lead Jane, years later, to scorn the Seine as puny. The North Saskatchewan's deep valley cut an S through the city, curling below Lolly Bacon, the treacherous toboggan hill, running straight under the High Level Bridge (One of the Seven Wonders of the World!) and looping the hill where stood the giant blue-roofed railway hotel. Then it straightened out to pass the refinery—when lit at night its scaffolds, arms and towers a fairy castle—and swept east, toward everything else.

In summer the family walked alongside the river, on a narrow path by the Outdoors Club, watching out for quicksand. In winter her father and the boys skied, on long light planks with leather lace-up boots. Jane stood by the back door looking after them down the walk. On either side the heaps of snow were piled over her head; she was too small to go out. Later, she went along, but she was clumsy and fell, and they were impatient.

Winter lasted from October to May. They were farther north than any other city of size except Moscow. In the depth of winter, the sun didn't come up until nine, and it was setting by four. Strange, then, it was not the dark she remembered, but the light. Winter days were dazzling: a clear sky and diamond sun on the packed dry snow, snowblindness as common as frostbite. And her mother dancing.

The rigs went south and so did they. Her mother's eyes went down, her back began to stoop. Something was wrong. Her mother seemed the victim of some terrible disease, consumed by things she wanted to be, or do, and couldn't. She never danced alone, only with him, her father, and it was not dancing anymore, it was just obedience. He worked in an office by then.

By the time her father comes home, her mother is trussed with an apron, hands sticky with flour and water, facing into the corner where the sink is. It is a fascinating corner; the mouse is said to live in the back of the cupboard. Jane feels kin to that mouse: she was a mouse in her dance recital, and her father calls her Mouse. There are windows above the sink, looking into the backyard, at the flowering crabapple tree which the waxwings visit in winter. Probably Jane is at the table drawing, invisible behind the door when her father pushes it open.

'Hi, honey.'

He comes up behind and slaps her bottom. Her mother stiffens, turning her face toward him for the kiss, but keeping the chin down.

'My hands,' she says, excusing herself. He opens the cupboard doors, taking a glass down with a hard clink, banging the door shut again, opening and shutting the refrigerator noisily. His movements are square, angry. He is already on his way back to the den, where he will sit and read the paper 'in peace.' Halfway down the hall his voice is louder.

'Kids out again?'

Her mother turns, whispers. 'Go see your father. Talk to him.'

She rises, looking down at her colouring book. The only thing that makes this bearable is that they are working together, mother and daughter. She knows she is an offering to forestall a perhaps inevitable wrath.

'Dad?'

'Is that you, Mouse?'

Still standing outside the door, not moving until requested to.

'Come in.'

She pushes open the door. His feet are closest to her, on the footstool in socks; wide, almost square feet, with toes that arch and curl as if by their own inclination. He is behind these feet leaning back in the armchair; the paper is folded in his lap. He has put down the paper. Now she must prove herself worthy of his attention.

She is invited up close, to sit on his lap. He gives her a rough hug; she ducks his face because of the scratchy whiskers. His head is like a bullet, his neck thick and pocked. Everything about him is strange and threatening. She is perched there when another faint tap comes on the door. Her mother, without the apron, with clean hands. There is a discreet change in his voice, and he sits up. 'I have work to do, girls.' They both slip out.

He doesn't want music on, music disturbs him at this hour. As dinner cooks Jane studies the record album. Anna and the King of Siam in sunset colours, before the flock of little round-faced children with blue-black hair.

'Shall we dance, On a bright cloud of music shall we fly? Shall we dance, shall we then say goodnight and mean goodbye?'

Anna was a beautiful, gentle woman who went to a strange land to look after the children. They were the King's children, not hers. The King was bald and mean, with blazing eyes and a very straight back, like Jane's father. He had unpredictable rages, he even put people to death if they displeased him. He was primitive, a brute. But Anna fell in love. Jane cannot understand what Anna sees in the King. And why did Anna go there in the first place? Reading closely, Jane discovers that Anna had another love, her true love, who died. Perhaps this was the case with her mother.

At five-thirty her father calls out his door about dinner—is it almost ready, or does someone want to get him another Scotch? Jane is sent to retrieve his glass. He has seated himself, by this time, at his desk and is working with a pencil and a ruler on large sheets of squared paper which roll up at the corners. She takes the glass to her mother, who pours more Scotch in it. By the time she reaches his door it happens. He cannot find the gum eraser.

'Nona! Nona!' he roars.

Now Jane is in the hall outside his door, and can see them both. In the kitchen her mother's head, ever ready for alarm, rises up like some deer's hearing distant gunfire. She pushes in the drawer where she is counting out table-napkins. Jane hates the panicky, hobbled sound of her mother's heels.

'What is it, dear?' sweetly, anxious.

'Who's been in this drawer? I told you not to let the kids at my things. Now I can't find my eraser.'

'I don't think they have been. I've told them so many times.'

Jane shrinks in the background. Has she taken the eraser? The accusation is so strong she thinks she must have.

His drawer slams.

'Oh, what's the point?' (bitterly, bitterly) 'I can't get anything done around here.'

After eating in silence, he pushes back his chair and announces that he has to go back to the office. Jane and her mother do the dishes together. After, her mother finds the eraser in the drawer, under a pile of envelopes. She reads to Jane, *The House at Pooh Corner*, before bed and she laughs, very hard, about Tigger falling out of the tree.

Jane lies awake in bed. Eventually her father comes home. His voice is still loud, and cross. Her mother murmurs, placating. They go to bed, in the room next to Jane. Jane doesn't want to hear the noises, so she sings to herself.

'Or perchance, when the *last leetle star* has leaved the sky, shall we still be together, with our arms around each other, and shall you be my new romance?'

Later the family found little to recommend these cities, little to remember. They moved to British Columbia, and her mother became more bitter, more crippled. Jane went away without regret. She didn't like ties, didn't want a man, never thought about it. She studied art, as her mother wished her to, and went to Paris. But she didn't paint. As she often said, she had nothing to paint. She worked, when she felt like it, writing features for Canadian newspapers. Her pieces always had some Canadian angle, that was how she sold them.

The day she learns that her mother has killed herself, not just died, passively, but died actively, by her own hand, all in the new blossoms of spring, Jane has lined up an interview with an artist. It is her father who telephones. Her father is sorry, he has been sorry for years, but he does not say so. And Jane, who thought she had forgiven him, is filled with hate. All she can think of is his impatience, the way he beat her mother down, the way her mother shrank. She puts down the telephone. Then, because Jane is alone and has nothing better to do, she goes to the interview.

The artist lives in the sixteenth district. Jane travels by Métro, getting off at the stop he named, turns up narrower streets than those she's passed through, and finds his door with a tiny gold nameplate. He greets Jane sternly, and turns his back. In the sitting room he brings a trolley, serves tea, and madeleines (à la Proust! he points out in a way not convivial but instructive). The artist is prairie Canadian, and very good; Jane wept in the gallery looking at his pictures. He shows her more. They are painted in egg tempera and are of people in empty rooms, of light from two windows hitting a corner, or sunglasses reflecting a flat horizon. She says she is from Edmonton. He was recently there.

'A terrible place full of awful people! And they all look just like you!'

The madeleines are crumbly and taste like dust. She mentions a few names.

'Oh yes! I saw him! He looks like he just came in from bashing baby seals. And the students! So lazy! All they ever asked me about was money. How much they could make as artists. Mind you, they were better than the faculty. These people, they were so lost, so ignorant. A dreadful, dreadful place.'

Something causes her to be polite, eager to please. She doesn't dare make her usual joke, that the North Saskatchewan is wider than the Seine.

'The only nice person in the whole city was a taxi driver. He drove me along the river valley,' says the artist.

'It's beautiful, isn't it?'

He glares and presses his lips together. 'You don't know Paris if you think that any other city is beautiful.'

Jane trips, stumbles from the staircase onto the sidewalk, turns this way and that in the crowded streets. The Métro stop is not where it was. She discovers another. She stares down at the rails in the tunnel. She reassesses the man's painting. They are unreasonable, relentless, unforgiving. There is a clinical coldness to them; but they have taught her something. They have made her see in terrible relief. The city is split into layers, levels one on top of each other. Gaps and improbabilities occur.

For instance, there on the dull shine of the train rail, a creature is moving. It has a familiar down-tilted, pear-shaped body and scaly tail. The rat looks her in the eye. It stands up on its hind legs as if to declare itself. Jane has never actually seen a rat before. There is a special program for rat control in Alberta, successful to an extraordinary degree.

Jane screams, clamping her hand on her mouth. She begins to tremble. She is falling apart, and on foreign soil. The train pulls into the station and the doors sigh open, with pressure. She enters the car with others. Parisians are so rude, they take the outside seat as if to dare you to climb over their knees to get to the other chair. She does. There is a boy sitting across from her. He has dirty, long hair and a huge Adam's apple. He leans forward in his chair, sensing weakness.

'You speak English?'

She stares straight ahead.

'Mademoiselle, you speak English.'

She does not answer.

'Français?'

She keeps staring, hoping to be taken for a deaf mute.

'Mademoiselle, you are American.'

That trips her into shaking her head.

'Not American; German, perhaps?'

The other passengers find this amusing. The young man slurs and leans, perhaps he is on drugs, he doesn't seem to be drunk. He puts his hand on her knee. He keeps asking her where she is from, he lists half the countries in Europe, but he really thinks she is English-speaking, and returns compulsively to 'America, America.' She shrinks in her seat. She is afraid to push him away, to push his hand off her knee; she thinks then he might leap on her.

The man who would not move over is watching. He cocks an eye as if to say, 'Why are you putting up with this? Why don't you fight back?' Women smirk. No one in the crowd will help her. They are waiting for her to speak. She cannot speak. Why should she expect them to defend her, if she can't defend herself? The only thing she can do is run away. The next time the train stops she springs over the man in the seat and out the door. People are laughing behind her. The hollow station magnifies her shame.

Jane walks, runs, sweating, through streets that are completely strange, not the Paris she knows. The faces around her are black; words from shopfront conversations fall around her ears like pebbles. The boy on the train has laid a curse on her: she understands no known language, she comes from nowhere. She carries on like this for a while, crying, while passersby look at her incuriously or not at all. When the tears are reduced to hiccups and shudders, she realizes that she is hungry and gathers her courage to enter a little restaurant. There at last, coffee before her, she becomes calm. She sits for a long time.

The man at a table by the window looks like the philosopher-king whose picture Jane has seen in the newspaper. He is very dark, with a beard, and a long, bony nose, long, narrow eyes. She looks past him at the street and recognizes a certain hare-lip newspaper vendor: there is the passage she calls Avenue des Crottes; around from that must be Square Saint-Sulpice. She has made her way back somehow to 'her' Paris. She smiles at her empty cup. She lifts her eyes. He is gazing at her.

They leave the café together. He corrects her French as they climb five floors to his room. As if he cares, as if he has been asking, she tells him she is from Canada. He is disappointed. He is crazy about things American, 'bask*ets*,' which turn out to be track shoes, and Broadway music. *West Side Story. South Pacific.* He has all the records. And a bottle of wine.

The sun is going down pale peach beyond the gummy grey windows.

She realizes that the light is wrong, there is a film on everything, the dirty air, the dusty desk top. There must be light. He plays records one after another. *Camelot, My Fair Lady*. Then, *The King and I*. She begins to sing the words. He knows them too, but not what they mean, he tests them in his mouth like unfamiliar candies. He rubs her nipples, hard, and they undress. His body is long and narrow and dark, with a rectangle of hair like a flag on his chest. When they make love, he is making love to America, but she doesn't care.

After, she gets up to dance, putting on his shirt. The philosopher—she doesn't even know his name, but somehow he is making all this possible—focuses a reading light on her. Tears slide over her cheeks, down her throat. By then she is stoned enough to forget about the rat and the terrible boy on the Métro, and the upbeat story she will have to write about the frightening artist—but not about her wasted, horribly dead mother, who has now turned into an ache running from the base of her rib on the left side right into her neck.

But Jane does not stop, she keeps on and she has all the moves, the snap wrists, the jammed-out hip, open mouth and fake innocent eyes; she is all those saucy heroines of the musicals. She is Nona, in the fifties, Nona in her lip-sync revolt.

'Oh, Mother, Mother, Mother,' she cries. It is all right to do it; the French understand these things. Didn't de Beauvoir write that Sartre himself cried out for his mother in sleep? She cries and she lets loose and she keeps going

until

it visits her again, that feeling of having no edges, nothing to defend, nothing to fear, that only-one-word-for-it peace from when she was four, or five, in the living room, watching her mother dance. And this peace is the gift, not the emptiness, not the ticket to leave. There was love, before the end. And Jane too may find it. She may even find it with the King of Siam.

JUDY FONG BATES

❧

MY SISTER'S LOVE

My sister's arrival in Canada had the effect of a cleaver, slicing up our lives. Three years earlier, my father had sponsored my mother and me to Canada. My mother had to leave my sister behind in Hong Kong because she was not my father's daughter. She was only twelve years old. My mother spent the next three years becoming a Canadian citizen. She learned the names of the provinces, and their respective capitals, and the pledge of allegiance to the Union Jack. Unfortunately, none of it really sounded like English. Even at age seven, I realized that the *lo fons* wouldn't understand the sounds she made.

When my mother saw my sister at the airport, she became a new person. Her tiredness fell away and there was a lightness in her body. Tears streamed down her face, yet she smiled and smiled. She stretched out her arms and ran toward her daughter. They locked each other in a tight embrace. Then my sister released herself. As she looked me up and down, her first words were, 'Your nose turns up too much, sort of like a pig.' My mother smiled with embarrassment and brushed it aside. I swallowed a lump in my throat.

We spent that night in my Uncle Eddy's house. They lived like the *lo fons*. Uncle Eddy operated a restaurant. He didn't live upstairs from it. His family lived in a proper house with living and dining rooms. My Aunt Lena didn't have to work. My mother told me that before Aunt Lena arrived, Uncle Eddy bought her a dresser for the bedroom, and filled it with lingerie, body lotions, and perfumes. That evening my mother, my sister, and I slept on a pull-out couch in the living room. My mother slept in the middle, her arms entwined around my sister.

The next day we went home to Cheatley on a Gray Coach bus. My mother and my sister sat together. I sat across from them, beside a large *lo fon* woman. It was a long journey, and I watched, as my sister fell asleep, her head gently resting on Mother's shoulder, her lips slightly parted and letting out small puffs of air.

My father met us at the bus stop in Cheatley. It was a town of 2000 people, too small to have a real station. An unmarried brother and sister managed a candy store that also sold ice cream, magazines, comics, and bus tickets. Each carrying a piece of luggage, we began to walk the two blocks to my father's hand laundry.

We must have made an odd-looking sight as we walked along the sidewalk. My father was a tiny man, barely five feet tall. Wrinkles were deeply engraved into his face. He tensely knitted his eyebrows so that two deep furrows formed in the middle of his forehead and extended to the bridge of his nose. He wore an oversized brown herringbone wool coat that had been left in the laundry by one of the customers, and a peaked brown wool cap. His steps were short and close together as he struggled with the weight of my sister's brown leather suitcase, trying to keep it from dragging on the sidewalk. He remained several steps ahead of us. Even when unencumbered, my father never walked with his head up. His eyes were always fixed on the ground.

Behind him, the three of us persevered against the March wind with our heads tucked into our chests, protecting ourselves from the sprays of snow. I wrestled with my share of my sister's bags and tried to keep pace with my mother walking in the middle. But after bumping into her several times she suggested that I walk behind. Mother and I were dressed in old winter coats given to us by one of the ladies from the Presbyterian church. They were shapeless and hung loosely on both of us. Mine had a belt that was tightly buckled, forming a skirt with deep folds around my waist. I was expected to grow into it. My sister wore a blue wool coat, tailor-made in Hong Kong, as smart as the one worn by the doctor's young wife. Her one free hand clutched the lapels together to keep the wind off her chest. And the wind whipped in every direction the previously obedient strands of her freshly permed hair.

My father, my mother, and I were all small and dark. My mother was round-faced and plump, while my father and I were thin and wiry. We both had high cheekbones and skin that stretched tautly around slightly protruding jaws. My hands were like my father's. They were large, with joints that were thickly knuckled and square at the fingertips.

Walking with us, my sister was tall, elegant, and exquisite. We were coarse, tough, and sinuous. Her face was a perfect oval with ivory skin, the texture of flower petals. But it was her hands that always captured people's attention. The palms were narrow and the long slender fingers ended in nails that glistened like water drops. When she held them together they reminded me of tendrils on a vine, seeking and wrapping—vulnerable and treacherous.

We passed the hardware store, turned a corner and came to my father's laundry, our home. My father set down the suitcase he was carrying and lifted the wooden latch on the panelled wooden door, then opened the heavier wooden door, the one with the glass window, and let us into the first room of the laundry. Because it was winter, we were greeted by a blast of sulphurous air from the coal burning stoves. My sister gasped. My father lifted the hinged portion of the handmade wooden counter that separated the work area from the customers. He awkwardly stepped aside as we filed past him. Silently we watched as my mother's smile tightened and her eyes grew large with anxiety, while her older daughter surveyed and assessed.

My sister glanced at the wooden shelves, stacked with brown paper bundles of finished laundry. We walked past a wooden table, the top thickly swathed with old blankets and sheets. At the edge of the table stood an iron, and beside it, a basin of water with a bamboo whisk resting inside. She pointed to two long horizontal rollers that were held up by a wooden frame. I explained that this was an ironing press. When my father bought the laundry, it was considered a real bonus, a true labour-saving device. When it was turned on, wrinkled bedding, tablecloths, tea towels, and pillowcases were fed between the humming, rotating rollers. Like magic they piled on the shelf underneath in smooth folds like sheets of molten lava. On ironing days my father stood at these tables from early morning until late at night. At the end of the day he rubbed *Tiger Balm* into his aching muscles.

My mother held open the red and yellow paisley curtain that concealed the washing room. The first thing that caught my sister's attention was the washing machine. It stood in a drainage pan in the middle of the floor. It was a monstrous steel barrel, held up horizontally by four posts, looking like some mythical headless beast. Along one wall was a row of three wooden tubs. Attached to the one at the end was a hand-cranked mangle, used to wring out water. Inside one tub was a four-legged wooden stand with an enamel basin. Above it hung a clothesline between two nails. Dangling down were three thin hand towels and facecloths. My sister's eyes moved slowly about the room. She swallowed as she looked at the four-burner coal stove with an oven. On the front burner was a large canning pot filled with hot water and holding a ladle. Beside the stove, on a wooden shelf covered in faded blue-and-white checked oilcloth, was a two-burner electric hotplate. The rings were finely cracked and the electric coils were recessed inside. In the corner, standing at attention, was a tall cylindrical water heater made of galvanized iron. Connected to it was a small coal burner. Hot water flowed from the taps only on washdays which were Mondays and Thursdays. Along the wall that led to the stairs were four straight-backed wooden chairs and a wooden table covered with the same faded, blue-checked oilcloth that was beneath the electric hotplate.

It seemed a long time before anyone spoke. Then I heard my mother's voice.

'Irene-*ah*, hang up Elder Sister's coat and take her upstairs. Show her where she'll sleep.'

After I hung up both our coats, I led my sister past the faded wallpaper of large yellow pansies, up the wooden stairs, and past the window whose frame was stuffed with rolls of rags, keeping out the winter air. We stood on a floor covered with a piece of worn and finely cracked linoleum, patterned with brown and blue paisleys. My sister set her suitcase down beside her. I pointed to a bed behind us. 'That's where Baba sleeps.' Then I pointed to a narrow room off the main one. 'You and Mah and I sleep in there.' A single bed was jammed against the end wall; at a right angle stood a bunk bed. Across from the bunk was a four-pane window. A flowered-print curtain, threaded with a string, was tied to a nail in each top corner of the wooden frame. She walked over and poked her head in the doorway. 'You can sleep in the bottom bunk; I sleep on the top.' My sister stood in the doorway, listening. I touched the large wooden dresser that stood opposite from my father's bed. 'This is where we keep our clothes. I use the bottom drawer. You can have the middle one. Baba and Mah use the small drawers at the top.'

'Well, if that isn't enough room, I can keep the rest in my suitcase.'

'Yeah,' I said. 'You can shove your suitcase under your bed.'

The next day when I returned home from school, I saw the photographer from the local newspaper in front of the laundry. My sister was standing beside a drift of snow and the man was taking her picture. By the time she started school two days later, her picture had appeared on the front page of the town paper.

For the few months that were left in that school year, my sister was in the grade eight class. But the following September, after her sixteenth birthday, the school placed her in grade seven. We never walked to school together. I remember often seeing her at recess, alone in a corner of the schoolyard. Our schoolyard was separated from the train tracks by a high wire-mesh fence. My sister always watched the trains whistle by as I played and laughed and talked with my friends.

While my sister was in Hong Kong, we lived on a diet of soup made from chicken bones, salted fish and pork, and dried vegetables. When she arrived, there was suddenly meat on the chicken bones, and fresh fruit on the table. My mother cooked my sister's favourite dishes. Lily picked at the food and rejected her efforts. My mother watched in despair as her daughter's unhappiness grew and seeped into our lives like a persistent mist. Lily longed for her friends in Hong Kong. She told me stories about her life there. With each telling our town became more dull, our home more meagre, our food more plain, our clothes more shabby. Even her new Canadian name, Lily, so evocative of her delicate beauty, and given to her by our neighbour across the road, did little to make her feel more at home.

Several month after Lily arrived, Mother decided to take us to Toronto to visit Uncle Eddy and Aunt Lena. Uncle Eddy took us for *dim sum* at a restaurant in Chinatown. Afterwards we shopped for groceries in the China Trading Store. The atmosphere at the store was always dusty and mysterious. The mingled, conflicting odours from the many packages of dried fish, shrimps, oysters, scallops, and mushrooms had a pungency that prickled the nostrils. The China Trading Store had glass cases along one wall. Inside were dried roots, seeds, and herbs that were carefully weighed on a hand-held scale before they were wrapped in white paper and sold. There were barrels containing 'thousand-year-old' eggs, and shelves of fresh fruit. On that particular day, there was displayed a small shipment of fresh lychees. No one in our family had had lychees since coming to Canada. My sister looked at them and touched them with her long white fingers. It was then that I noticed a man staring at us from a corner of the store. He was a tall, powerfully built man. His thick black hair was greased and combed straight back. He had a strong jaw and a nose that was slightly aquiline, unusual for a Chinese. His clothes were new and fashionable, his shoes black and polished. The other men in Chinatown were shabby, and their spirits were worn by living in the Gold Mountain. This man possessed a confidence that was enigmatic, predatory. His gaze fastened on my sister, and he watched as her hands picked up the lychees, and then put them back. My sister looked up and turned to meet his eyes. Then he suddenly walked toward us and shook hands with Uncle Eddy.

'Ah, Eddy, good to see you. How are you? How's business?'

'Not bad, not bad. And how about you, Tom?'

'The usual. And who are these two beautiful girls?' the man asked as his gaze once again fixed upon my sister.

'Yes, these are my two nieces, Lily and Irene. This is their mother, Chung *Tai Tai*. I'd like you to meet Tom Leung.' The man looked us over. Uncle Eddy went on proudly. 'They're visiting the big city. Later this afternoon they're leaving on the bus for Cheatley.'

Tom turned to my mother. 'Cheatley, I'm going that way myself. I can give you a lift.'

'Oh no. We don't want to take you out of your way. It would be too much trouble,' protested my mother.

Tom wouldn't hear of it, and that afternoon he made the first of many visits to our home.

In 1955, Tom Leung was forty-seven years old and a very wealthy man. He owned several restaurants in Chinatown, three houses, and a fancy car. However, he was still unmarried. Unlike other Chinese men his age, he had never returned to China to look for a wife. He had come to Canada as a young boy. A self-educated man, he moved with ease in the white man's world. He spoke English perfectly and he read their newspapers. When he joked with the *lo fons*, he laughed like an equal, throwing his head back with his mouth wide open. Other Chinese always came to him when they needed someone to fill out forms, or to read and answer letters from the government. In Chinatown, this gave him special status—a sense of power. This air of confidence, along with his flashing eyes and quick laughter, were like a magnet. But along with this expansive, easy charm, there was a shark-like quality that seemed to devour people.

A week after our ride home in Tom's car, he came to visit us. He drove up in a shiny sea-green car with gleaming chrome bumpers and a wraparound windshield. What impressed me most were his sunglasses. They were mirrors that rested on the bridge of his nose and reflected his world around him. What impressed my mother, though, were his gifts of food. He brought a barbecued duck, oranges, assorted *dim sum* from Chinatown, and lychees for Lily.

My mother was obviously flattered that a man with Tom's exalted reputation of wealth and influence should decide to visit us so soon.

'Ah, Leung *Sen Sun*, how are you? Come in. Come in. How good of you to come and visit. Sit down. Sit down.'

'My pleasure. Now that we're all in *Gam Sun* we must stick together. I've brought some small gifts for your family.'

'Oh, you needn't be so full of ceremony. Just come and visit.'

'No trouble at all.' Tom gave the bag of food to my mother, but first he took out the bag of lychees and handed them to my sister. Lily blushed, murmured thank you; she held Tom's gaze.

My father exchanged brief pleasantries with Tom and returned to work. Tom sat down on a wooden chair. Lily and I sat across from him. My mother placed the *dim sum* that Tom had bought on a plate, sliced some oranges, and filled a pot with water to boil for tea. I could tell by the way she fussed that she was embarrassed by the meagreness of our home. Tom looked at the unfinished plank floors, the dangling cords with the bare light bulbs, and the worn-out equipment for washing clothes. His eyes, though, always returned to rest on Lily's face.

Next Sunday, Tom visited our home again. Once more he offered gifts of steamed buns, barbecued meats, and fruit. But this time he had a stack of Chinese movie star magazines for Lily. 'Here, these are for you, Lily.'

'Ah, Leung *Sen Sun*, thank you so much. You have gone too far, too much trouble.' Lily beamed and shyly accepted the gift. She told Tom that Hung Bo Bo was her favourite singer and her favourite actress, and that she always went to her movies in Hong Kong.

'Perhaps next week, I could come and take you and your sister to China-town to see the movies. Chung *Tai Tai*, would you like to come as well?'

'I won't be able to come. Too much work in the laundry. It's very kind of you to invite the girls. You really shouldn't go to such expense.'

'Oh, Mah, it would be so much fun. I haven't seen a movie since I left Hong Kong. It's very kind of Leung *Sen Sun* to invite me and Irene.' Lily leaned eagerly forward in her chair, her hands clasped together in her lap. I hadn't seen her so excited since she arrived. From the dark look she shot in my direction, I knew that my wishes were not a consideration.

'Well then, it's settled. Next Sunday I'll come and take the girls for lunch in Chinatown, and then to the movies.' Tom sat back in his wooden chair and inhaled deeply on his cigarette. I watched the smoke come out of his mouth, curl upwards, slowly disappearing.

The next Sunday, Lily wore a blue-and-white striped full-skirted dress with a collar that tied in a bow at the front, and black slip-on flats on her feet. I wore a red shirt-waist dress with a gathered skirt and ruffles around the col-lar, and black patent leather shoes with buckles. Lily waited eagerly; I was resigned. That afternoon I rode alone in the back seat of Tom's car. At the movies, my sister sat in the middle.

After that day's outing, Tom came to visit us every Sunday. As Sunday came closer, I sensed Lily's swelling excitement and anticipation. On Saturday night she washed her hair and slept in curlers. Sunday morning she woke up singing and smiling. By the time I returned from Sunday school, Tom was at our house, engaging Lily in conversation and laughter.

Over the next few months Tom bought our family many gifts. He bought Lily a record player and records of Chinese music. One day he even came with a television. Mother and Lily greeted these gifts with delight and enthusiasm. My father muttered indecipherable comments under his breath and carried on with his work, his eyes always on the floor.

One day I returned home from Sunday school and found Tom and Lily speaking very seriously to my parents. Tom was earnestly explaining as he leaned forward in his chair, 'I wish to become Lily's godfather, her *kai yaah*. I could make life more comfortable for her and help towards her dowry when the time comes. As you know, I have no family of my own.'

'Leung *Sook* is already like an uncle, another father. He comes every Sunday and has been so good to us,' added Lily. Her face was radiant.

Mother was beaming, as if she couldn't believe the good fortune. 'Leung *Sook*, you honour us with your proposal. We would welcome you as a member of our family.'

My father mumbled agreement, as he sat perched uneasily at the edge of his stool. Tom rested comfortably back in his chair, one foot resting on the other knee. He smiled broadly and confidently as the smoke from his cigarette rose gently, vanishing into the air.

That evening over dinner, Tom, Lily, and Mother talked and laughed as they planned for a celebration banquet. My father and I quietly ate and exchanged glances.

After Lily and I went to bed that night, I woke up to the sound of loud voices. As Lily was softly, steadily breathing, I crept out of bed and crouched at the top of the stairs. I heard my father's voice.

'Something is not right. Tom is hiding his true feelings. They're not right. He's too close to her. I don't feel right about it.'

My mother hissed back in a loud whisper. 'Don't you see that he makes Lily happy? What can be wrong about his attention? He's old enough to be her father! She's just a teenager. He looks upon her as a daughter. Your suspicions are ridiculous.'

'I don't know. It just doesn't feel right.'

'Listen. He even said that he wants to be her godfather. You're just jealous that he's rich and successful! We should be honoured that he wants to help us. I'm not going to risk Lily's happiness. I'm going to bed.' My mother turned sharply. As she started up the stairs, I dashed back into the bedroom and scurried under my covers.

And so Tom continued to embrace our lives with his lavish gifts. Arrangements were made for a celebration banquet, making Tom's entry into our family official and respectable. Friends from Chinatown were invited. Everyone could see that Tom Leung had become Lily's godfather, her *kai yaah*. Everyone could see that his feelings were honourable. Lily was luminous, like a bride, in the new red silk dress that Tom had chosen for her. He sat proudly beside her, the smoke from his cigarette languidly floating above their heads. Mother sat at the banquet table and looked triumphantly at my father. Any nagging anxieties had been obviously banished to the corners of her mind.

In the months that followed, my father's gaze rarely left the floor. We were drowning in Tom's beneficence. He installed a bathtub and sink in the washroom upstairs so that we no longer had to wash in the wooden laundry tubs. He bought us a refrigerator. He even constructed a small addition to our house. His visits began to last for several days, until he became a per-

manent guest in the addition that he had built. He even took Lily away on
overnight weekend trips. One Sunday night, looking out the upstairs window, I saw Tom and Lily returning in Tom's car. Lily was asleep. Tom's arm
was around her and he kissed her gently on the lips to wake her up. When
I saw them get out of the car, I hurried into bed and pulled the covers over
my head. I never mentioned to anyone what I saw.

The following Wednesday, I had a headache at school and the teacher
let me come home early. I walked in the back door. My parents didn't know
I was there. As I peeked around the door to the work area, I saw my father
shove a letter in my mother's face.

'Read this. Read what Eddy's written. People are talking about your
daughter and her *kai yaah*. You've got to do something about this.' My father
spat out the words *kai yaah* like bile stuck his throat.

As my mother silently read the letter she started to cry. 'But Tom makes
Lily happy. Life here has been so hard for her. She hasn't made any friends
of her own. And he has spent so much money on us. What can we do?'

'Tom's feelings for Lily aren't those of a godfather. You know that. Stop
fooling yourself. Do you want Lily to marry Tom?'

'You know what I want for my daughters. I don't want them to be like
us. I want them to marry men, you know, educated, higher class. I want
them to be Canadians. Not helpless, like us.' My mother looked desperate.
'Tom has been so good to us. How can we tell him to go?'

'Well, if this keeps up, the talk in Chinatown will grow; Lily will have
no marriage prospects. And then what?'

My mother put the letter down on the ironing table, looked at my
father as she wiped her face, turned and left the room. I tiptoed out of the
house and crossed the road to call on a friend.

After that, the line of my mother's mouth changed. Her lips were
pressed tightly together with the corners tucked in, and the two tendons in
her neck stood out from her collar bone to her jaw. Her eyes, bewildered,
became moist whenever she looked at Lily and Tom.

The quarrelling between my parents grew worse. And it was over little
things. My father exploded one night because the soup wasn't hot enough.

'I've been working all day 'till I'm like a worn-out clog. And you can't
even come up with hot soup!'

One humid summer evening, while Lily and Tom were out for a drive
to escape the heat, my mother chased after my father as he ran into the
backyard. She pleaded with him. 'Tom has to leave this house. I know that
now. But I can't bring myself to do it. You have to do it.'

'But Lily is your daughter. You need to take charge.'

'I can't. Don't you see. Lily hates me. She hates me because I left her in Hong Kong, even though I had no choice. If I make Tom leave she'll hate me even more. You have to tell Tom to leave, for my sake, for the sake of our family.'

One afternoon in September, I returned home from school, went to my favourite corner and sat down on a squat wooden stool, opening a book of fairy tales I had borrowed from my teacher. The atmosphere felt different, clouds of tension and relief hanging in the air at the same time. My parents were silently working. My mother was preparing supper and my father was ironing clothes. A few minutes after I entered, Lily walked in. 'Where's *kai yaah*'s car? He's usually here by now.' Before anyone spoke, Lily understood. Panic and fear radiated from her eyes. She dashed upstairs to the small room that Tom had added. She saw the bed and opened the empty drawers of the dresser.

Lily came hurtling down the stairs. Mother was standing at the kitchen table, slicing vegetables for supper. Lily, her body rigid, walked over and faced her. Rage emanated from every pore in her body. Her words were like knives, slashing the air around her. 'Where is he? Why is his room empty?' In the silence that followed, I thought the air around us would explode. I wanted to fade into the flowered wallpaper, to become just a face, flat on the wall, staring out. Any movement would let them know I was there. I knew if I stayed perfectly still, I would become invisible.

Mother laid down the cleaver on its side, lifted her head and spoke. 'He had to leave, Lily. He had to leave on business. He's opening a new restaurant up north somewhere.'

Lily screamed, 'You're lying. He didn't have to go. You made him.' Her eyes shot toward my father. He stood in the adjoining ironing room with his back to her, pressing shirts, his arms moving like a robot's.

Mother implored, 'Lily, you've got to try and understand. Tom agreed to go. He wants you to have a life of your own. He wants you to marry a Chinese boy, close to your own age, someone who's educated, so you can be a real Canadian.' She reached into her apron pocket. 'Here, he left a letter for you.'

As Lily read Tom's letter, her disbelief gave way to tears. Then she walked into the ironing room, stopping a few feet from my father. Her rage and anguish rose from deep inside her, lacerating each of us. She glared at him as she spoke. 'You're the one who told him to go. You're the one who made him leave. I *hate* you. I *hate* everything about you. I *hate* this laundry. The *lo fons* come in here with their dirty clothes and laugh behind your back. And all you do is smile.'

My father carefully placed his iron on the table and turned, facing Lily as he spoke. 'Lily, Lily, I know this is hard. But it is for the best. Even Tom knows this.' He held out his arms toward her as he spoke. I could tell that he wanted to put them around her, but did not dare. Instead, she stood alone, covered her face with her hands, and wept, dropping Tom's letter on the floor. Mother walked over to her and lightly touched her shoulder. Lily immediately recoiled. My mother dropped her arm and took a step back. Lily stopped crying, straightened herself, and wiped her cheeks; staring all the while at my father and then our mother. Before my eyes my sister turned into stone; hard, cold, and impenetrable.

After that, I never saw Tom again. I don't know what happened to him. He never answered Lily's letters. I spent as much time away from home as possible. Any pleasures that I experienced with friends at school or at play, I hid when I came home. In the face of Lily's sorrow, I felt ashamed. What right had I to be happy? I grew more and more fearful of Lily. A glass of spilt milk, or my laughing too loud, unleashed in her a torrent of rage. She never spoke to my father again. At first he tried to make amends. He bought food that she liked. When he tried to engage her in conversation she never answered. She always turned her face away. We became accustomed to the silence. An invisible shroud encircled each of us and separated our lives.

Three years later, my mother arranged a marriage between Lily and a young Chinese man, an accountant, only four years older. He was tall and hollow-chested. His cheeks were severely pock-marked, his smile too eager. I remembered Lily at her wedding ceremony. Her eyes were glazed. The 'I do' was barely audible.

Afterwards at the reception, Lily sat, stone-faced, next to her husband at the head table. She watched the smoke from his cigarette coil slowly upwards, fading into the air.

CONNIE GAULT

❧

INSPECTION OF A SMALL VILLAGE

In a room defined by tables and windows the adulteress sits at her task. She has set herself the task to occupy her mind. The room is at the provincial archives; the adulteress is waiting for a folder of information on the town in which she was born. She has decided to stop treating herself like someone who may break with any breath she takes, but she holds herself delicately without realizing what she is doing and she sits very straight, with her hands in her lap and her head just so on her neck.

A slight young man slides the folder across the table toward her. He turns and disappears behind a swinging door without a word. This is a quiet room. Any words that are spoken by the half-dozen people distributed among the tables (with maximum space between them) are quiet words.

The folder contains the archives' local histories clippings file for the town in which she was born. Of the four items in the file, only one interests her enough that she picks it up and reads it. She holds the few pages of the badly typed report up to the fluorescent light that blankets the room, that cancels the light from the windows. She reads the words over and over and wills them to replace her thoughts. This is her task, this expulsion of her thoughts. It's a task appropriate to her dilemma, which is not so much that of being an adulteress as that of being sorry she is herself. She is young and has come against the fact of herself, a person born here, now. She thinks if she were a person born there, then, everything would be different. Given a choice, she'd be born French. Even better, she'd be born in a French movie. Those people really don't give a damn.

Report on a Systematic Inspection of the Village of Kerrody
July 8, 1958
Kerrody is a small thriving Village, busy by virtue of its central location in the southwest sector of Health Region No. 2. With an estimated population of 310, there are 119 houses standing and 5 new buildings under construction. Most of the single dwellings are small and well-maintained. This pleasant Village has no slum area to speak of, no corrupting influences. The outhouses are in good repair.

The report was written by the doctor who was the Regional Medical Health

Officer at the time. Likely he had no resemblance to the man the adulteress pictures; she sees a man with his elbows on the table at the Kerrody hotel and his head in his hands. A conscientious man. It is Dr Tolley she sees with his head in his hands. The adulteress has given her medical health officer the name Tolley because that is the name of the man who has made her heart sing. She doesn't really see him sitting at the table with his head in his hands so much as she feels the presence of his body, and 'heart sing' isn't the euphemism she first thought. She can't quite erase it.

Dr Tolley is sitting in the Kerrody hotel eating a chicken sandwich. He's not sitting with his head in his hands. Not yet. He has a report to write. A report that looks like seersucker from the sweat on his hands. No, he's not anxious yet. It's hot. It's a very hot day but his hands don't sweat.

Dr Tolley eats his sandwich and begins his report. He is new at his job but already he is determined to work as he goes while in the field and to spend as much time as possible with his wife when he's home. If Dr Tolley is ever inclined to be smug it is on two accounts, his efficiency and his great good fortune in marriage. He is humble enough to realize that neither have come to him through his own efforts to attain them. Rather, they have been by-products of his attempts to overcome his one real weakness, his fear that he isn't good enough. He fears not being good enough in his work and with women, and for the same reason: he harbours a slight but seemingly irremediable aversion to the human body. He became a physician to conquer the body and, like others equally pretentious, he has failed. The body, in all the thousands of manifestations that have passed before his eyes and under his hands, in spite of passing before his eyes and under his hands, has gone on being corrupted and insulted by disease and injury and abuse. The body in its most pristine forms displays its ugly potential. His wife has sensed his dilemma and protects him. She never dresses or undresses in front of him and always slips between their sheets in attire no one would remark on if the house caught fire and she had to stand on the lawn with their neighbours in the middle of the night watching it burn.

The adulteress tries to focus again on the words in the report, where no one's wife is mentioned. But the man named Tolley lingers. How has he made her heart sing? Only by wanting her body and by being unable to keep her from knowing. That's all it takes to make her heart sing, to set her mind ticking, timed for any moment, just say the word, look the look. Or say nothing, look nothing: think and she'll know.

Her doctor's head is in his hands. No, not yet. He is sitting with his pen poised, going over his thoughts. And his thoughts are all of the town in which the adulteress was born. That morning Dr Tolley walked up and down the back alleys of Kerrody. He spent more than an hour of a hot morning stepping in and out of outhouses, making notes on the night soil levels and swatting flies away from his face so that, forty years later, she will read his meticulous thoughts.

She almost believes this. She doesn't understand it—why in the world she's doing this, imagining him this way, but she almost believes it. She smiles to think of him holding his breath, stepping into yet another biffy in a time just before she was born, all for her, somehow.

Sewage and Slop

Except for seven houses in which modern sewage removal systems have been installed, and appear to be pumping satisfactorily, all the private dwellings in the Village continue to employ pit privies. My one concern with these privies, during a routing inspection, is in regard to night soil levels. When they reach approximately 4 feet from the surface, these nearly full pits become a dangerous source of fly breeding.

Dr Tolley is taking his lunch late. Yes, he's there, at the table, with his chicken sandwich and his crumpled report. He is the only person eating in the hotel, having just inspected the kitchen. The hotel owners knew he'd be coming sometime during the month as did the owners of the other premises he plans to inspect. He wanted to start by being strict but fair. He believes it's in the interest of everyone to provoke higher standards before he arrives rather than to make surprise visits and uncover poor conditions. He thinks about things like this even though he's only begun this job.

He underlines the word Hotel for his next heading and looks over his shoulder to be sure what he writes can't be seen by another. He is inclined to rate the hotel more highly than it deserves because he has become acquainted with the man and his wife who run it, but he can't know exactly what he will say until he writes it. He's learned that in writing, one thing can lead to another and that he might surprise himself, leaping from toilets to sinks to refrigerators, with an opinion he doesn't know he holds. In this way writing is like diagnosis. He was becoming a good diagnostician when he quit his medical practice; he was finding that by emptying his mind and letting his senses and intuition carry him, one thing invariably led to another. Unfortunately the end result was only briefly satisfying. What he won by successful diagnosis he often lost for lack of a cure.

She likes him so much, the young adulteress. Isn't that worth something?

Hotel

There is one hotel in the Village. Its sixteen rooms are of such small proportions (8' x 10') that they are not suitable for double occupancy. I am assured that they are usually

required by single guests. The bedrooms are adequately furnished and appear to be reg-
ularly cleaned. I am of the opinion that the comfort of guests could be increased by the
installation of louvred ventilation above each door.

Dr Tolley is of the private opinion that more than louvred ventilation will
be required if he is going to get to sleep tonight. The upstairs rooms have
already reached a temperature close to a hundred degrees. However, it's not
the hotel's fault he's arrived in a heat wave. Dr Tolley takes his handkerchief out of his breast pocket and wipes his face. Sweat is unbecoming to a
member of the medical profession and this poses a problem because he feels
he must wear a suit in the field and should remove his jacket only in his
own room, whatever the consequences to his personal comfort.

The cook, who is co-owner of the hotel with her husband, comes out of
the kitchen to clear his table. He slides his elbow across his report and declines
her offer of lemonade. He says he might drop in later for a cold drink.

The cook is a tall woman with a slouch that gives her more of a stomach than she should have for her weight. She stands close to him with her
hands clasped over her protruding apron. He notices that her hands are red
and rough and very clean and commends her on them.

'I just made pastry,' she says. 'It's always good for cleaning your fingernails.'

He can't tell if she's teasing him. Her face is deadpan. He slips the pages
of his report into his briefcase and excuses himself.

When he is outside walking down the one cement sidewalk, with the
sun high overhead and no more than inches of shade anywhere, the heat
sizzles on his skin. It feels hot enough to scorch the fabric of his suit. A wash
of sweat cascades from his back and chest and collects at his waistband.
Within seconds his waistband is soaked and his belt slides up and down,
chafing his middle. He ducks into the Red and White store. The difference
in light blinds him momentarily. He sighs as the impression of coolness
almost like a breeze floats over him.

'Everybody does that when they come in today,' the store owner says.
He is just like everybody else, Dr Tolley, just like any man doing his job the
best he can. This morning, after the outhouses, he went with the mayor to
visit the well, the village rest rooms, the nuisance ground and the cemetery.
On his list for the afternoon are the two general stores, the restaurant, the
meat market, the hairdresser's, the hospital, and the dairy, then he must
meet with the local medical practitioner. Up and down Main Street he will
walk on the shady side, once it develops, and he will smile into the heat, his
only obstacle. He mops his face good-naturedly now, in the Red and White
store, and grins. He is just like everybody else.

At the end of the afternoon, he hasn't quite accomplished all he set out to do. He decides to put off the dairy for the morning on his way out of town. This makes him a little early for his meeting with the town's only doctor, but he thinks that's preferable to being late. As he stands in the vestibule before the doctor's office, he mops his face for the hundredth time. His grin is weary, not much more than practice. He does not like Bob Berriman. Nevertheless, he's accepted his invitation to take supper with him.

People tend to accept Dr Berriman's invitations. The adulteress, sitting in the quiet room full of tables and windows, remembers this without knowing how she remembers.

They had planned to meet later, at the Chinese restaurant, but Dr Tolley is dropping in to see if his colleague will join him for a drink first at the hotel. He thinks a few ounces of whiskey will make supper bearable.

The vestibule is tiny and panelled with dark wood. Stairs to the second floor face the outside entrance. To Dr Tolley's right is the office door, closed because office hours are over. A square of wavy glass in the top of the door lets a faint shadowy light pass either way but doesn't allow him to see inside. He opens the door.

Directly in front of him a young woman is scrubbing the board floor on her hands and knees. She is wearing short shorts and a white cotton brassiere. He sees her from the side. He sees the tan and white wings of her breasts folded into the brassiere, and her raised, startled face. She has stopped her scrubbing and looked up, but not at Dr Tolley. She has raised her eyes to Dr Berriman, who leans against the receptionist's desk with his feet stretched before him, watching her. This tableau lasts only a second or two, then Bob Berriman, his face angry and red, crosses the room with his hand outstretched. He stands in front of the kneeling woman and shakes Dr Tolley's hand. His footprints remain on the wet floorboards.

'Ready early, are we?' he says. He scoops his jacket off a hook, takes Dr Tolley's elbow, and steers him out of the office. Dr Tolley has no opportunity for a second look. A second look isn't necessary.

Bob Berriman asks questions on the way to the hotel, questions about Dr Tolley's day which Dr Tolley answers. But not exactly as if nothing has happened. They drink their doubles at the hotel bar in silence. In the Chinese restaurant, where the service is quick, they discuss mutual acquaintances and Dr Tolley's wife (briefly, Dr Tolley doesn't like her name on Berriman's lips), and then the possibility of the townspeople adopting septic tanks in place of outhouses. They stretch the meal out with coffee until just after eight when their unexpressed mutual dislike overcomes the conversation and they part. With a long, bright evening before him and his hotel room unbearably hot, Dr Tolley takes his briefcase to the bar and makes himself busy.

He begins to write about the meat market. He writes that the chopping block was sweet and clean, that the display cases looked as if they had been scoured, that the standard of storage for both implements and meat was high. His pen skims the paper, describing the seemly and professional methods of the butcher in the operation of his shop.

He reports that conditions at the hairdresser in the village were found to be unsatisfactory.

. . . but it is to be hoped that what I discovered did not represent the usual custom. Neither formalin nor dettol were utilized for sterilizing scissors or combs and one must protest the practice of draping the same rather grimy cape over each unwary client.

Next Dr Tolley reports on the horrors of the pool hall toilet and the potentially risky practice of discarding hospital garbage in flimsy, insecure containers. And when he has finished that, he caps his pen and puts it down. It comes to him that maybe he has been putting too black an interpretation on the tableau he witnessed in Dr Berriman's office. Maybe the young woman removed her top in order to be cooler while she worked, not realizing that Berriman was still in the inner office, and Berriman came out and surprised her. Maybe she got up to put her top back on and Berriman said not to bother, she was as decently covered as she would have been at the beach and after all he was a doctor. Maybe she was a casual young woman and agreed. Maybe the fear he thought he felt in the room was his own fear.

Dr Tolley packs up his papers and takes himself to his room, away from the eyes of two old men who have been drinking coffee in the corner all evening, who have just switched to beer. His room is stifling; it is not possible to remain there.

The thermometer nailed to the hotel wall by the front door says eighty. He contemplated going out in his shirt sleeves, yet he is still dressed in his suit. Even though it's nearly midnight. He could meet someone. It's not for himself he wants to look respectable but for the office.

He strolls up and down the streets and alleys of the village, the same streets and alleys he travelled this morning. They look different in the dark but he hardly notices them; he might be anywhere.

The entire town can be walked in half an hour. In half an hour he turns up Main Street and heads for the hotel. An unexpected sound causes him to notice his surroundings. The sound is of a door opening. He is outside Berriman's office building. He watches as the door swings slowly back against the stucco and a figure steps out into the darkness. It is the young office cleaner. She is completely naked. He thinks that: completely naked. While he watches her walk toward him, he understands: it is a state that can be complete.

She is sleepwalking. Her eyes are open but unseeing. He backs out of her way. She passes close to him (smells of warm bedclothes) and turns to walk down the sidewalk. He follows her.

Now he sees everything in sharp focus, as in a dream. He sees the pock marks in the cement sidewalk and the pebbles in front of her feet, where her feet will land. He hears the soft pad of her bare soles on the cement. On the soles of his own feet, through his shoes, he believes he can feel the coolness and graininess of the cement surface, just as she feels it on her skin.

She passes under the street lamp on the corner. Her dark hair is for a second back lit then the light falls on her shoulders, on the curve of her buttocks and down her calves. She wears a paleness on her torso, like a transparent bathing suit. She walks easily and he walks behind her and the false fronts and cluttered signs and dusty windows of Kerrody roll past them and fall away.

There's only the gleam of the gravel road and the similar faint gleam of her skin. She walks. He follows. A beautiful quiet prevails. He's never been out in the night before, like this. He exhales; it's possible he's been holding his breath since leaving the town. With his breathing resumed, he starts to hear his brogues crunching down, scattering small stones, and the chirping of frogs, loud and exuberant as birds' singing. A splash. So they are near the slough, about a mile from town.

She stops, then turns and walks into the ditch.

Dr Tolley thinks: she will walk into the slough and drown herself. Then the absurdity of the situation strikes him. He has been following her as if part of her dream, as if a spectator in her dream, with no volition of his own—or as if the dream were his own, as if he had dreamed her and could only watch to see how his dream would end—while in fact he is a responsible medical doctor, a respectable married man, following a naked woman down a country road. Why hasn't he woken her gently, covered her decently and taken her home?

At the edge of the slough is a large rock where that morning, driving into the town, he saw two children fishing. She has climbed up onto that rock. He can just see her pale skin, the slip of water, dark shapes and the sky which, he suddenly notices, is crammed with stars. He has never seen so many stars, near and far, layers and layers of them from the brilliant to the distant almost unseeable. Just for a second he forgets who he is. Then is embarrassed for himself. How easily an atmosphere can fool a man into thinking nothing matters.

She is awake now, she has stepped down from the rock. She is climbing to the road from the ditch and hasn't yet seen him, and then sees him. The sound she makes is a whimper. His body responds with something like pity—a similar fear. Then he remembers who he is.

'I'm Dr Tolley, the Regional Health Inspector,' he says. They look into one another's faces. They both laugh. They laugh harder. It is so absurd, who he is. He takes off his suit jacket and hands it to her. They walk back to town silently. Dr Tolley allows himself to think of her breasts and belly and buttocks inside his suit jacket.

The door opens as they walk up the path to Berriman's office building. The young woman's husband stands in the vestibule watching them. Before they reach him, he turns and walks up the stairs, which are lit by a bare bulb above the landing. The young woman follows her husband and Dr Tolley follows her up into a suite of rooms.

'Excuse us,' the young man says politely to Dr Tolley. He leads his wife into their bedroom, closing the door behind them. A few seconds later he emerges with Dr Tolley's suit jacket.

'Thank you,' he says as he hands the jacket to Dr Tolley. Dr Tolley drapes it over his arm. The young man stands marooned in the centre of the room. Dr Tolley could introduce himself, which might be reassuring. He could talk in a clinical way about sleepwalking. He could explain how he'd happened on her. But it all seems superfluous. Without a word he walks out of the room and leaves the young couple behind.

In the morning he drinks a pot of coffee. He sits at his table in the hotel with his head in his hands. The couple who run the hotel speculate, in the kitchen, about what kind of night he had and how long he'll last in this job. He knows they'll be talking about him and doesn't care. All night he lay semi-conscious in a heat-drugged fugue.

He skips the dairy. No, he's much too conscientious to do that. He drives out and drags himself around the milk house, sniffing at the cans, bottles, filters, cooler, and milker, and then he drags himself around the stable and the yard. He is so grateful for the dairy's cleanliness and the remarkable absence of flies that he will give it his most glowing commendation.

Before he turns onto the highway to head home, Dr Tolley stops to remove his suit jacket. Another hot day is predicted and he can be forgiven, he thinks, for driving in his shirt sleeves in the privacy of his own car. He stops the car at the intersection and steps out to take his jacket off. Just for a second he appreciates the benevolent sky, his solitude. As is his usual practice, he folds the jacket with the lining facing outwards. When he gets into the car, he places the jacket on the passenger seat beside him and starts in third and stalls. That is the last time he will betray himself.

In the room of many tables and windows, the adulteress tries to remember the real story of the town in which she was born. She was very young when they moved away and has little memory of the 119 houses and the small businesses mentioned in the medical health officer's report. Her only vivid memory isn't even her own, it comes from a time before she was born, the memory of a story she heard many times of a short spell in her mother's life when her mother sleepwalked. The high point of the story is the time her mother escaped naked into the night. In the story, the adulteress's father discovered her mother was missing and hauled himself out of bed; pulled on his pants and a shirt, and followed her down Main Street. It was the adulteress's father who brought her mother home. Order was restored and anyone who was told the story laughed to think her mother—her shy young mother of all people—had walked naked through the dark streets where anyone might have seen her.

There is another memory that didn't get made into a story, a more shadowy memory that had to do with the doctor who owned the building they lived in, who had his office on the ground floor. The adulteress's mother cleaned the office for him in exchange for some money off the rent. But that was in a different time and place and the memory is too shadowy to get hold of.

She slips the report into its folder. She is thinking about her mother opening the door, stepping out. She thinks: I've inherited my mother's body. Forgetting where she is, she lifts her arms and stretches—her body is tired from sitting so long perusing those few pages. Across the room, a man looks up.

JANE URQUHART

～

THE DEATH OF ROBERT BROWNING

In December of 1889, as he was returning by gondola from the general vicinity of the Palazzo Manzoni, it occurred to Robert Browning that he was more than likely going to die soon. This revelation had nothing to do with either his advanced years or the state of his health. He was seventy-seven, a reasonably advanced age, but his physical condition was described by most of his acquaintances as vigorous and robust. He took a cold bath each morning and every afternoon insisted on a three-mile walk during which he performed small errands from a list his sister had made earlier in the day. He drank moderately and ate well. His mind was as quick and alert as ever.

Nevertheless, he knew he was going to die. He also had to admit that the idea had been with him for some time—two or three months at least. He was not a man to ignore symbols, especially when they carried personal messages. Now he had to acknowledge that the symbols were in the air as surely as winter. Perhaps, he speculated, a man carried the seeds of his death with him always, somewhere buried in his brain, like the face of a woman he is going to love. He leaned to one side, looked into the deep waters of the canal, and saw his own face reflected there. As broad and distinguished and cheerful as ever, health shining vigorously, robustly from his eyes—even in such a dark mirror.

Empty Gothic and Renaissance palaces floated on either side of him like soiled pink dreams. Like sunsets with dirty faces, he mused, and then, pleased with the phrase, he reached into his jacket for his notebook, ink pot and pen. He had trouble recording the words, however, as the chill in the air had numbed his hands. Even the ink seemed affected by the cold, not flowing as smoothly as usual. He wrote slowly and deliberately, making sure to add the exact time and the location. Then he closed the book and returned it with the pen and pot to his pocket, where he curled and uncurled his right hand for some minutes until he felt the circulation return to normal. The celebrated Venetian dampness was much worse in winter, and Browning began to look forward to the fire at his son's palazzo where they would be beginning to serve afternoon tea, perhaps, for his benefit, laced with rum.

A sudden wind scalloped the surface of the canal. Browning instinctively looked upwards. Some blue patches edged by ragged white clouds, behind them wisps of grey and then the solid dark strip of a storm front moving slowly up on the horizon. Such a disordered sky in this season. No solid, predictable blocks of weather with definite beginnings, definite endings. Every change in the atmosphere seemed an emotional response to something that had gone before. The light, too, harsh and metallic, not at all like the golden Venice of summer. There was something broken about all of it, torn. The sky, for instance, was like a damaged canvas. Pleased again by his own metaphorical thoughts, Browning considered reaching for the notebook. But the cold forced him to reject the idea before it had fully formed in his mind.

Instead, his thoughts moved lazily back to the place they had been when the notion of death so rudely interrupted them; back to the building he had just visited. Palazzo Manzoni. *Bello, bello* Palazzo Manzoni! The colourful marble medallions rolled across Browning's inner eye, detached from their home on the Renaissance façade, and he began, at once, to reconstruct for the thousandth time the imaginary windows and balconies he had planned for the building's restoration. In his daydreams the old poet had walked over the palace's swollen marble floors and slept beneath its frescoed ceilings, lit fires underneath its sculptured mantels and entertained guests by the light of its chandeliers. Surrounded by a small crowd of admirers he had read poetry aloud in the evenings, his voice echoing through the halls. *No R.B. tonight,* he had said to them, winking, *Let's have some real poetry.* Then, moving modestly into the palace's impressive library, he had selected a volume of Dante or Donne.

But they had all discouraged him and it had never come to pass. Some of them said that the façade was seriously cracked and the foundations were far from sound. Others told him that the absentee owner would never part with it for anything resembling a fair price. Eventually, friends and family wore him down with their disapproval and, on their advice, he abandoned his daydream though he still made an effort to visit it, despite the fact that it was now damaged and empty and the glass in its windows was broken.

It was the same kind of frustration and melancholy that he associated with his night dreams of Asolo, the little hill town he had first seen (and then only at a distance), when he was twenty-six years old. Since that time, and for no rational reason, it had appeared over and over in the poet's dreams as a destination on the horizon, one that, due to a variety of circumstances, he was never able to reach. Either his companions in the dream would persuade him to take an alternate route, or the road would be impassable, or he would awaken just as the town gate came into view, frustrated and out of sorts. 'I've had my old Asolo dream again,' he would tell his sister at breakfast, 'and it has no doubt ruined my work for the whole day.'

Then, just last summer, he had spent several months there at the home
of a friend. The house was charming and the view of the valley delighted
him. But, although he never once broke the well-established order that
ruled the days of his life, a sense of unreality clouded his perceptions. He
was visiting the memory of a dream with a major and important difference.
He had reached the previously elusive hill town with practically no effort.
Everything had proceeded according to plan. Thinking about this, under
the December sky in Venice, Browning realized that he had known since
then that it was only going to be a matter of time.

The gondola bumped against the steps of his son's palazzo.

Robert Browning climbed onto the terrace, paid the gondolier, and
walked briskly inside.

Lying on the magnificent carved bed in his room, trying unsuccessfully to
surrender himself to his regular pre-dinner nap, Robert Browning examined
his knowledge like a stolen jewel he had coveted for years; turning it first
this way, then that, imagining the reactions of his friends, what his future
biographers would have to say about it all. He was pleased that he had prudently written his death poem at Asolo in direct response to having received
a copy of Tennyson's 'Crossing the Bar' in the mail. How he detested that
poem! What *could* Alfred have been thinking of when he wrote it? He had
to admit, none the less, that to suggest that mourners restrain their sorrow,
as Tennyson had, guarantees the floodgates of female tears will eventually
burst open. His poem had, therefore, included similar sentiments, but without, he hoped, such obvious sentimentality. It was the final poem of his last
manuscript which was now, mercifully, at the printers.

Something for the biographers and for the weeping maidens; those who
had wept so copiously for his dear departed, though soon to be reinstated
wife. Surely it was not too much to ask that they might shed a few tears for
him as well, even if it was a more ordinary death, following, he winced to
have to add, a fairly conventional life.

How had it all happened? He had placed himself in the centre of some of
the world's most exotic scenery and had then lived his life there with the regularity of a copy clerk. A time for everything, everything in its time. Even when
hunting for lizards in Asolo, an occupation he considered slightly exotic, he
found he could predict the moment of their appearance; as if they knew he
was searching for them and assembled their modest population at the sound
of his footsteps. Even so, he was able to flush out only six or seven from a
hedge of considerable length and these were, more often than not, of the same
type. Once he thought he had seen a particularly strange lizard, large and
lumpy, but it had turned out to be merely two of the ordinary sort, copulating.

Copulation. What sad dirge-like associations the word dredged up from the poet's unconscious. All those Italians; those minstrels, dukes, princes, artists, and questionable monks whose voices had droned through Browning's pen over the years. Why had they all been so endlessly obsessed with the subject? He could never understand or control it. And even now, one of them had appeared in full period costume in his imagination. A duke, no doubt, by the look of the yards of velvet which covered his person. He was reading a letter that was causing him a great deal of pain. Was it a letter from his mistress? A draught of poison waited on an intricately tooled small table to his left. Perhaps a pistol or a dagger as well, but in this light Browning could not quite tell. The man paced, paused, looked wistfully out the window as if waiting for someone he knew would never, ever appear. Very, very soon now he would begin to speak, to tell his story. His right hand passed nervously across his eyes. He turned to look directly at Robert Browning who, as always, was beginning to feel somewhat embarrassed. Then the duke began:

> *At last to leave these darkening moments*
> *These rooms, these halls where once*
> *We stirred love's poisoned potions*
> *The deepest of all slumbers,*
> *After this astounds the mummers*
> *I cannot express the smile that circled*
> *Round and round the week*
> *This room and all our days when morning*
> *Entered, soft, across her cheek.*
> *She was my medallion, my caged dove,*
> *A trinket, a coin I carried warm,*
> *Against the skin inside my glove*
> *My favourite artwork was a kind of jail*
> *Our portrait permanent, imprinted by the moon*
> *Upon the ancient face of the canal.*

The man began to fade. Browning, who had not invited him into the room in the first place, was already bored. He therefore dismissed the crimson costume, the table, the potion housed in its delicate goblet of fine Venetian glass and began, quite inexplicably, to think about Percy Bysshe Shelley; about his life, and under the circumstances, more importantly, about his death.

Dinner over, sister, son and daughter-in-law, and friend all chatted with and later read to, Browning returned to his room with Shelley's death hovering around him like an annoying, directionless wind. He doubted, as he put on his nightgown, that Shelley had *ever* worn one, particularly in those dramatic days preceding his early demise. In his night-cap he felt as ridiculous as a humorous political drawing for *Punch* magazine. And, as he lumbered into bed alone, he remembered that Shelley would have had Mary beside him and possibly Clare as well, their minds buzzing with nameless Gothic terrors. For a desperate moment or two Browning tried to conjure a Gothic terror but discovered, to his great disappointment, that the vague shape taking form in his mind was only his dreary Italian duke coming, predictably, once again into focus.

Outside the ever calm water of the canal licked the edge of the terrace in a rhythmic, sleep-inducing manner; a restful sound guaranteeing peace of mind. Browning knew, however, that during Shelley's last days at Lerici, giant waves had crashed into the ground floor of Casa Magni, prefiguring the young poet's violent death and causing his sleep to be riddled with wonderful nightmares. Therefore, the very lack of activity on the part of the water below irritated the old man. He began to pad around the room in his bare feet, oblivious of the cold marble floor and the dying embers in the fireplace. He peered through the windows into the night, hoping that he, like Shelley, might at least see his double there, or possibly Elizabeth's ghost beckoning to him from the centre of the canal. He cursed softly as the night gazed back at him, serene and cold and entirely lacking in events—mysterious or otherwise.

He returned to the bed and knelt by its edge in order to say his evening prayers. But he was completely unable to concentrate. Shelley's last days were trapped in his brain like fish in a tank. He saw him surrounded by the sublime scenery of the Ligurian coast, searching the horizon for the boat that was to be his coffin. Then he saw him clinging desperately to the mast of that boat while lightning tore the sky in half and the ocean spilled across the hull. Finally, he saw Shelley's horrifying corpse rolling on the shoreline, practically unidentifiable except for the copy of Keats' poems housed in his breast pocket. *Next to his heart*, Byron had commented, just before he got to work on the funeral pyre.

Browning abandoned God for the moment and climbed beneath the blankets.

'I might at least have a nightmare,' he said petulantly to himself. Then he fell into a deep and dreamless sleep.

Browning awakened the next morning with an itchy feeling in his throat and lines from Shelley's *Prometheus Unbound* dancing in his head.

'Oh, God,' he groaned inwardly, 'now this. And I don't even *like*

Shelley's poetry anymore. Now I suppose I'm going to be plagued with it, day in, day out, until the instant of my imminent death.'

How he wished he had never, ever, been fond of Shelley's poems. Then, in his youth, he might have had the common sense *not* to read them compulsively to the point of total recall. But how could he have known in those early days that even though he would later come to reject both Shelley's life and work as being too impossibly self-absorbed and emotional, some far corner of his brain would still retain every syllable the young man had committed to paper. He had memorized his life's work. Shortly after Browning's memory recited *The crawling glaciers pierce me with spears / Of their moon freezing crystals, the bright chains / Eat with their burning cold into my bones*, he began to cough, a spasm that lasted until his sister knocked discreetly on the door to announce that, since he had not appeared downstairs, his breakfast was waiting on a tray in the hall.

While he was drinking his tea, the poem 'Ozymandias' repeated itself four times in his mind except that, to his great annoyance, he found that he could not remember the last three lines and kept ending with *Look on my works, ye Mighty, and despair*. He knew for certain that there were three more lines, but he was damned if he could recall even one of them. He thought of asking his sister but soon realized that, since she was familiar with his views on Shelley, he would be forced to answer a series of embarrassing questions about why he was thinking about the poem at all. Finally, he decided that *Look on my works, ye Mighty, and despair* was a much more fitting ending to the poem and attributed his lack of recall to the supposition that the last three lines were either unsuitable or completely unimportant. That settled, he wolfed down his roll, donned his hat and coat, and departed for the streets in hopes that something, anything, might happen.

Even years later, Browning's sister and son could still be counted upon to spend a full evening discussing what he might have done that day. The possibilities were endless. He might have gone off hunting for a suitable setting for a new poem, or for the physical characteristics of a duke by examining handsome northern Italian workmen. He might have gone, again, to visit his beloved Palazzo Manzoni, to gaze wistfully at its marble medallions. He might have gone to visit a Venetian builder, to discuss plans for the beautiful tower he had talked about building at Asolo, or out to Murano to watch men mould their delicate bubbles of glass. His sister was convinced that he had gone to the Church of S.S. Giovanni e Paolo to gaze at his favourite equestrian statue. His pious son, on the other hand, liked to believe that his father had spent the day in one of the few English churches in Venice, praying for the redemption of his soul. But all of their speculations assumed a sense of purpose on the poet's part, that he had left the house with a definite destination in mind, because as long as they could remember, he had never acted without a predetermined plan.

Without a plan, Robert Browning faced the Grand Canal with very little knowledge of what, in fact, he was going to do. He looked to the left, and then to the right, and then, waving aside an expectant gondolier, he turned abruptly and entered the thick of the city behind him. There he wandered aimlessly through a labyrinth of narrow streets, noting details; *putti* wafting stone garlands over windows, door knockers in the shape of gargoyles' heads, painted windows that fooled the eye, items that two weeks earlier would have delighted him but now seemed used and lifeless. Statues appeared to leak and ooze damp soot, window-glass was fogged with moisture, steps that led him over canals were slippery, covered with an unhealthy slime. He became peculiarly aware of smells he had previously ignored in favour of the more pleasant sensations the city had to offer. But now even the small roof gardens seemed to grow as if in stagnant water, winter chrysanthemums emitting a putrid odour, which spoke less of blossom than decay. With a kind of slow horror, Browning realized that he was seeing his beloved city through Shelley's eyes and immediately his inner voice began again: *Sepulchres where human forms / Like pollution nourished worms / To the corpse of greatness cling / Murdered and now mouldering.*

He quickened his steps, hoping that if he concentrated on physical activity his mind would not subject him to the complete version of Shelley's 'Lines Written Among the Euganean Hills.' But he was not to be spared. The poem had been one of his favourites in his youth and, as a result, his mind was now capable of reciting it to him, word by word, with appropriate emotional inflections, followed by a particularly moving rendition of 'Julian and Maddalo' accompanied by mental pictures of Shelley and Byron galloping along the beach at the Lido.

When at last the recitation ceased, Browning had walked as far as possible and now found himself at the edge of the Fondamente Nuove with only the wide flat expanse of the Laguna Morta in front of him.

He surveyed his surroundings and began, almost unconsciously, and certainly against his will, to search for the islanded madhouse that Shelley had described in 'Julian and Maddalo': *A building on an island; such a one / As age to age might add, for uses vile / A windowless, deformed and dreary pile.* Then he remembered, again against his will, that it was on the other side, near the Lido. Instead, his eyes came to rest on the cemetery island of San Michele whose neat white mausoleums and tidy cypresses looked fresher, less sepulchral than any portion of the city he had passed through. Although he had never been there, he could tell, even from this distance, that its paths would be raked and its marble scrubbed in a way that the rest of Venice never was.

Like a disease that cannot cross the water, the rot and mould of the city had never reached the cemetery's shore.

It pleased Browning, now, to think of the island's clean-boned inhabitants sleeping in their white-washed houses. Then, his mood abruptly changing, he thought with disgust of Shelley, of his bloated corpse upon the sands, how his flesh had been saturated by water, then burned away by fire, and how his heart had refused to burn, as if it had not been made of flesh at all.

Browning felt the congestion in his chest take hold, making his breathing shallow and laboured, and he turned back into the city, attempting to determine the direction of his son's palazzo. Pausing now and then to catch his breath, he made his way slowly through the streets that make up the Fondamente Nuove, an area with which he was completely unfamiliar. This was Venice at its most squalid. What little elegance had originally existed in this section had now faded so dramatically that it had all but disappeared. Scrawny children screamed and giggled on every narrow walkway and tattered washing hung from most windows. In doorways, sullen elderly widows stared insolently and with increasing hostility at this obvious foreigner who had invaded their territory. A dull panic began to overcome him as he realized he was lost. The disease meanwhile had weakened his legs, and he stumbled awkwardly under the communal gaze of these women who were like black angels marking his path. Eager to be rid of their judgemental stares, he turned into an alley, smaller than the last, and found to his relief that it was deserted and graced with a small fountain and a stone bench.

The alley, of course, was blind, went nowhere, but it was peaceful and Browning was in need of rest. He leaned back against the stone wall and closed his eyes. The fountain murmured *Bysshe, Bysshe, Bysshe* until the sound finally became soothing to Browning and he dozed, on and off, while fragments of Shelley's poetry moved in and out of his consciousness.

Then, waking suddenly from one of these moments of semi-slumber, he began to feel again that he was being watched. He searched the upper windows and the doorways around him for old women and found none. Instinctively, he looked at an archway which was just a fraction to the left of his line of vision. There, staring directly into his own, was the face of Percy Bysshe Shelley, as young and sad and powerful as Browning had ever known it would be. The visage gained flesh and expression for a glorious thirty seconds before returning to the marble that it really was. With a sickening and familiar sense of loss, Browning recognized the carving of Dionysus, or Pan, or Adonis, that often graced the tops of Venetian doorways. The sick old man walked towards it and, reaching up, placed his fingers on the soiled cheek. 'Suntreader,' he mumbled, then he moved out of the alley, past the black, disapproving women, into the streets towards a sizeable canal. There, bent over his walking stick, coughing spasmodically, he was able to hail a gondola.

All the way back across the city he murmured, 'Where have you been, where have you been, where did you go?'

Robert Browning lay dying in his son's Venetian palazzo. Half of his face was shaded by a large velvet curtain which was gathered by his shoulder, the other half lay exposed to the weak winter light. His sister, son, and daughter-in-law stood at the foot of the bed nervously awaiting words or signs from the old man. They spoke to each other silently by means of glances or gestures, hoping they would not miss any kind of signal from his body, mountain-like under the white bedclothes. But for hours now nothing had happened. Browning's large chest moved up and down in a slow and rhythmic fashion, not unlike an artificially manipulated bellows. He appeared to be unconscious.

But Browning was not unconscious. Rather, he had used the last remnants of his free will to make a final decision. There were to be no last words. How inadequate his words seemed now compared to Shelley's experience, how silly this monotonous bedridden death. He did not intend to further add to the absurdity by pontificating. He now knew that he had said too much. At this very moment, in London, a volume of superfluous words was coming off the press. All this chatter filling up the space of Shelley's more important silence. He now knew that when Shelley had spoken it was by choice and not by habit, that the young man's words had been a response and not a fabrication.

He opened his eyes a crack and found himself staring at the ceiling. The fresco there moved and changed and finally evolved into Shelley's iconography—an eagle struggling with a serpent. *Suntreader*. The clouds, the white foam of the clouds, like water, the feathers of the great wings becoming lost in this. *Half angel, half bird.* And the blue of the sky, opening now, erasing the ceiling, limitless so that the bird's wing seemed to vaporize. *A moulted feather, an eagle feather.* Such untravelled distance in which light arrived and disappeared leaving behind something that was not darkness. *His radiant form becoming less radiant.* Leaving its own natural absence with the strength and the suck of a vacuum. No alternate atmosphere to fill the place abandoned. *Suntreader.*

And now Browning understood. It was Shelley's absence he had carried with him all these years until it had passed beyond his understanding. *Soft star.* Shelley's emotions so absent from the old poet's life, his work, leaving him unanswered, speaking through the mouths of others, until he had to turn away from Shelley altogether in anger and disgust. The drowned spirit had outdistanced him wherever he sought it. *Lone and sunny idleness of heaven.* The anger, the disgust, the evaporation. *Suntreader, soft star.* The formless form he never possessed and was never possessed by.

Too weak for anger now, Robert Browning closed his eyes and relaxed his fists, allowing Shelley's corpse to enter the place in his imagination where once there had been only absence. It floated through the sea of Browning's mind, its muscles soft under the constant pressure of the ocean. Limp and drifting, the drowned man looked as supple as a mermaid, arms swaying in the current, hair and clothing tossed as if in a slow, slow wind. His body was losing colour, turning from pastel to opaque, the open eyes staring, pale, as if frozen by an image of the moon. Joints unlocked by moisture, limbs swung easy on their threads of tendon, the spine undulating and relaxed. The absolute grace of this death, that life caught there moving in the arms of the sea. Responding, always responding to the elements.

Now the drowned poet began to move into a kind of Atlantis consisting of Browning's dream architecture; the unobtainable and the unconstructed. In complete silence the young man swam through the rooms of the Palazzo Manzoni, slipping up and down the staircase, gliding down halls, in and out of fireplaces. He appeared briefly in mirrors. He drifted past balconies to the tower Browning had thought of building at Asolo. He wavered for a few minutes near its crenellated peak before moving in a slow spiral down along its edges to its base.

Browning had just enough time to wish for the drama and the luxury of a death by water. Then his fading attention was caught by the rhythmic bump of a moored gondola against the terrace below. The boat was waiting, he knew, to take his body to the cemetery at San Michele when the afternoon had passed. Shelley had said somewhere that a gondola was a butterfly of which the coffin was a chrysalis.

Suntreader. Still beyond his grasp. The eagle on the ceiling lost in unfocused fog. *A moulted feather, an eagle feather, well I forget the rest.* The drowned man's body separated into parts and moved slowly out of Browning's mind. The old poet contented himself with the thought of one last journey by water. The coffin boat, the chrysalis. Across the Laguna Morta to San Michele. All that cool white marble in exchange for the shifting sands of Lerici.

◄

FROM THE ANTHROPOLOGY OF WATER

The Wishing Jewel:
Introduction to Water Margins

> Brother (*noun*) associate, blood brother, cadet, colleague, fellow, frater, *frère, friar,* kinsman, sibling, soul brother, twin brother. *See* CLERGY, FRIEND, KINSHIP.
>
> *Roget*

My brother once showed me a piece of quartz that contained, he said, some trapped water older than all the seas in our world. He held it up to my ear. 'Listen,' he said, 'life and no escape.'

This was a favourite phrase of his at that time. He had dropped out of high school to do martial arts and his master liked to say 'life and no escape' when translating the Chinese word *qi*, which means 'breath' or 'energy' and is fundamental to good kicks. I remember we were down by the lake, it was sunset, fireboat clouds were lining up on the horizon. He was doing his Mountain Movements / Sea Movements exercises. 'Pervasive but you can't see it, physical but has no body.' His left foot flashed past my head. '*Qi* is like water, the master says, we float on the water when the level is right everything swims.' His right foot cut the air to ribbons. 'Put it in your mind you've got a wishing jewel.' It was cold sitting there in the November wind but I liked being with him. We had survived a lot together. It's true he hated me all through childhood—for my ugliness, he had explained simply, and this seemed reasonable enough. But around the age of fourteen hatred gave way to unexpected days of truce, perhaps because I caught up to him in school and was affable about doing his homework. Who cares why. A sun came out on my life. We spent a lot of time that winter driving around town in his truck listening to the radio and talking about Dad or sex. Well, he talked.

His stories were all about bad luck. It wasn't his fault that headlights got smashed, the school flunked him, his girlfriend thought she was pregnant, the police arrested him for driving naked on the beach. But good luck, he felt, was just around the corner. He was someone bound for happiness and he knew where to find it. He knew he was close. Very close. As I listened to him a sadness began in me that I have never quite put down. Still, it pleased me that he thought I was smart and asked my opinions about things. He called me Professor and gave me Roget's *Thesaurus* in the deluxe two-volume edition for Christmas. It is here beside me, volume one at least. He never got around to giving me volume two.

For some reason, he believed in me. 'She's going to be someone you know,' he said to my mother once. I heard this from her only after he was gone. It was late spring when he disappeared, for reasons having partly to do with the police, partly with my father—it doesn't matter now. Postcards came to us from farther and farther away, Vermont, Belgium, Crete, with long spaces of time in between them. No return address. Then very early one morning, about three years after he left, he called from Copenhagen (collect). I stood on the cold linoleum, listening to a voice that sounded like him in a padded costume. Layers and layers of hard times and resentment crusted on it. He had got his front teeth knocked out in a fight and needed a large sum for dentistry. He asked me to send money and not to tell Dad. After he hung up it took several moments to unclench my fingers from the telephone.

A card came from Copenhagen after I wired the money. He was on his way east, heading for China. Cards came from Paris and then from Marseilles— I remember that one, it was his birthday and he was buying drinks for everyone in the bar. A card came from Israel, rather sadder. A card came from Goa, mentioning heat and dirt and the monsoon delayed. Then no more cards came.

I don't reckon my brother ever got to China. So I made him a wishing jewel.

Water Margins:
An Essay on Swimming by My Brother

Friday 4:00 a.m. Not swimming.

Black motionless night. Bushes. The swimmer stands at the window. Ducks are awake down by the water's edge.

Friday 4:00 p.m. Swimming.

In late afternoon the lake is shaded. There is the sudden luxury of the places where the cold springs come flooding up around the swimmer's body from below like an opening dark green geranium of ice. Marble hands drift enormously in front of his face. He watches them move past him down into the lower water where red stalks float in dust. A sudden thin shaft of fish smell. No sleep here, the swimmer thinks as he shoots along through the utterly silent razor-glass dimness. One drop of water entirely awake.

Saturday 6:30 a.m. Swimming.

At dawn a small mist cool as pearls hangs above the lake. The water is dark and waits in its motionless kingdoms. Bars of light proceed diagonally in front of the swimmer as he moves forward following the motions of the strange white hands. Gold rungs slide past beneath. Red water plants waver up from the bottom in an attitude of plumes. How slow is the slow trance of wisdom, which the swimmer swims into.

Saturday 9:00 a.m. Swimming.

The swimmer prowls among the water lilies at the water's edge. Each has a different smell (orange, honey, milk, rot, clove, coin) like people. He is putting his nose into one calyx after another, wondering if they compete for him when an insect of the type called a darning needle rows into his eye-lashes. Rival suitor. The swimmer backpaddles and moves hugely on his way, through underwater courts of brides swaying the wonderful red feathers of their legs as lengths of visible secret. The water mounts pleasures at him through every doorway. Exposed. He swims off.

Sunday 8:00 a.m. Swimming.

A Sunday flood of hot lights pound down onto the black glass of the lake. The swimmer is grateful to escape underneath to where his dim water kingdom receives him. Silently. Its single huge gold nod. Who else ever knew me? the swimmer thinks. The hand with the wedding ring floats down past his face and disappears. No one.

Thursday 12:00 p.m. Swimming.

At noon the water is a cool bowl where the swimmer drops and darts away from the broiling air. He aligns himself and moves forward with his face in the water staring down at the bottom of the lake. Old, beautiful shadows are wavering steadily across it. He angles his body and looks up at the sky. Old, beautiful clouds are wavering steadily across it. The swimmer thinks about symmetries, then rotates himself to swim on his back staring at the sky. Could we be exactly wrong about such things as—he rotates again— which way is up? High above him he can feel the clouds watching his back, waiting for him to fall toward them.

Thursday 5:00 p.m. Swimming.

The swimmer lets himself fall out of the day heat and down through a gold bath of light deepening and cooling into thousands of evenings, thousands of Augusts, thousands of human sleeps. He is thinking of the light that sinks about her face in Leonardo's painting called *The Virgin of the Rocks.* Once he saw her kneeling by the water. Now he plunges along through the cold rock colours of the lake. Halos are coursing over the ridged mud of the bottom. He dives to get one. *If ever I forget my deep bond to you.*

Monday 5:30 a.m. Swimming.

Blue peaches are floating down onto the lake from under dawn cloud. The swimmer parts the water like a dancer peeling a leotard down her long opal leg. Sullen where he moves through its unlit depths—a smell of gasoline makes him stop and look around. A small silent rowboat is passing, two women in fishing hats studying him. Old ballerinas, he decides abruptly and dives out of sight.

Monday 12:00 p.m. Swimming.

Noon darkness clamps down on the lake. The water feels black enough to dye his skin. Its cold pressure. A strange greening on top of the water. The swimmer is trying to remember a sentence from Rilke about the world one beat before a thunderstorm—

Monday 6:00 p.m. Swimming.

Rain continues. The far hills are gun-coloured with ancient mist floating whitely before them. Chilly and concentrating hard the swimmer moves along just under the surface of the water, watching each drop hit the surface and bounce. Ping. Water on water. He is wondering how it would feel to be a voice in a medieval motet, not a person singing but a voice itself, all the liquors raining and unraining around it. Ping. Or to be a cold willow girl in the ancient hermit's embrace. High above him at the top of the sky, blood clouds are gathering like a wound behind flesh.

Monday 10:00 p.m. Not swimming.

Standing at the window the swimmer stares out through a stretching pitch-black wind toward the lake. He can feel it lift and turn like a sleeper in the same bed. Can hear the wind touch each link of its dreams in between. What does a lake dream? Ping.

Friday 4:00 a.m. Not swimming.

Staring. The lake lies like a silver tongue in a black mouth.

Friday 8:00 a.m. Swimming.

The storm has cleared. A blinding gold wind knocks hard waves flat across the swimmer's face as he plunges forward, trying to place himself in the trough of it but the diagonals shift and mock him. On the surface the water is navy blue and corrugated by wind. Spots of white foam crowd hectically up and down the waves. There is an urgency to it as if a telephone were ringing in the house. But there is no telephone in the house.

Friday 6:00 p.m. Swimming.

A dark blue wind is driving sunset home. The swimmer glances from under his arm at the shoreline where poplar trees are roaring with light and dropping their leaves to silver in the wind. With each stroke of his arm the swimmer exchanges this din for the silence beneath, his sliding green kingdom of hungers, monotonies, and empty penetrations. To open this treasury is not for one's father or brother or wife to decide. Oneself.

Wednesday 8:30 a.m. Swimming.

Small white bundles of mist are hurrying over the still surface of the lake. I wonder why I don't dream anymore, the swimmer is thinking as he inserts himself into the dark green glass. There were times he used to dream a lot. Now the nights are blank, except for intervals when he rises to look at the lake. And then behind his back he can feel the cat wake and observe him from its lit eyes. Not lifting his head. It is a very old cat (a gift from his brother) and seems to be dying. Before they go back to sleep he gives the cat a drink from a teacup of water in which he has dissolved some drops of honey. It eats little solid food nowadays but dreams well at night, so far as he can judge from its mutters and tiny thrashings. What unaccountable longings and hidden fears are swimming on fire in you? he wonders as he leans on the bed in the dark watching the small fur body. Almost everything physiologists know about the living brain has been learned from sleeping cats. Sleeping or waking, cat brains most resemble human brains in design. Cat neurons fire as intensely as human neurons, whether bombarded from without or from within. Lightly, lightly he touches its head where the suffering bones come haunting through old flesh. A glow enters his fingers, as if it were a pearl dreaming.

Wednesday 5:45 p.m. Swimming.

The lake is cool and rippled by an inattentive wind. The swimmer moves heavily through an oblique greenish gloom of underwater sunset, thinking about his dull life. Wondering why it doesn't bother him. It bothered everyone else including his father who died, his brother who left the country, and his wife who married again. 'Why don't you do something?' they would say. 'Call someone? What about Pons? What about Yevgeny? Don't you paint anymore?' The swimmer would glance out at the lake lying like a blue thigh in the open gold breeches of the noon sun and forget to answer. Only the cat does not question his lack of events. Where there is nothing to watch, it watches nothing. Perhaps I am the cat's dream, the swimmer thinks, breaking the surface.

Monday 5:00 a.m. Not swimming.

Watching from the window. When they are brand-new ballet shoes have this same sheen of pink and silver, as a lake glinting deep in the fringe of its leaves just before dawn. The cat stirs and groans. Behind its tight shut eyes millions of neurons are firing across the visual cortex. The swimmer bends down. A low rustle of longing sinks from the cat's small open mouth. Neurophysiologists think dreams begin in the brain stem, a box of night perched above the spinal column that also regulates such primitive functions as body temperature and appetite. The swimmer imagines himself dropping into the silent black water of that primitive lake. Shocks of fire flash and die above his head. The cold paints him. All at once he realizes it is not up to him, whether he drowns. Or why.

Friday 4:00 a.m. Not swimming.

The lake is a narrow fume of white mist still as a sleeping face in its dark bowl of leaves. One star hangs above. There is silver from it falling directly into the swimmer's eye. He glances at the cat asleep on the bed like a pile of dropped twigs. Looks back at the lake.

Friday 4:20 a.m. Swimming.

As he approaches the water's edge through soaked grasses he sees the mist open. He stops. Poised before him in the bluing air is a kingfisher heron almost as tall as himself. It is staring out over the lake. As the swimmer watches without breathing, the kingfisher totters profoundly forward from one red leg to another, then all of a sudden gathers itself and in a single pensive motion vanishes through a hole in the mist. The hole closes. The swimmer stands a moment, then drops, down through the dark blue mirror of the lake, to search for red legs and balancings and memories of the way people use love.

Saturday 8:00 a.m. Not swimming.

Robbed sentenced speechless. Bombarded like Sokrates by voices of law from within, the swimmer awakens suddenly feeling like the wrong side of a wing flipped up in the wind. The morning sun is hitting him straight in the eye. From where he lies he can see the lake like a flat plane of gold. A hardworking blue Saturday wind pushing white cloud rags into their places on the sky. The cat is gone.

Saturday 1:00 p.m. Not swimming.

A white eyelid of cloud has closed over the lake. The swimmer stands at the water's edge watching the surfaces of the water blacken and begin to move. Little starts of wind arrive from this direction and from that. Something is being loaded into the air from behind. The swimmer wonders about being struck by lightning. Who will feed the cat? Will his wife come to the funeral? Get hold of yourself, he thinks, but even in childhood he found Saturdays depressing, too porous, not like other days. He wonders where the cat has got to.

Saturday 3:00 p.m. Not swimming.

No storm yet. The air has the pressure and colour of fresh-cut granite. Black lake surface is moving, keeps moving, slightly, all over. As if some deep underwater clocks were being wound slowly into position for a moment of revelry. *That she and I may grow old together.* The swimmer turns and goes back up toward the house.

Saturday 5:00 p.m. Not swimming.

No storm. The water stares.

Thursday 7:30 a.m. Swimming.

White motionless mist and the steady screens of rain. A medieval city indicates itself ghostily on the opposite shore. The swimmer stands at the water's edge, listens, feels his ears fill with whiteness and time slip back a notch. He enters the water and begins to swim, placing himself between the black breasts of the water so that his stroke rolls him from wave to wave. The shore moves past. A mountain comes into view. In glimpses from under his arm the swimmer studies this unknown mountain. He sees huge blue pine trees and soaked rocks and white innards of mist hanging and trailing. From between roots a bit of fire. Beside this fire some strange and utterly simple soul keeping watch with its neck drawn into its shoulders. Nipples darken the paper robe. Roasting horse chestnuts and feeding them to something hunched on the log by its side. When the swimmer gets back to the house he finds the cat collapsed on the foot of the bed. Its wet fur smells vile.

Monday 4:30 p.m. Swimming.

A disconsolacy seeps out of the grey light and wanders on the grey water. Cold ripples in series move toward shore. Somewhere up the hill, a chainsaw chews into the air then stops. Silence comes lapping back. Shivering like a child the swimmer wades into the water. Childhood is nice in some ways, he thinks. Someone to hold a big towel and wrap you when you come out is nice. As he strikes off along the shore, grey waves slapping at his face, the swimmer thinks about his father holding out the big towel and bundling it around him and murmuring, 'Do your best, do your best' in his slightly wild way. The lake wind whipping at them.

Friday 8:45 a.m. Swimming.

The lake is a cold lead pane. Clouds and trees look saddened or dark. But underneath the water an odd verdigris glow is soaking out from somewhere. The swimmer swims along through rooms mysteriously lit as an early Annunciation. Stillness rushes everywhere. It is awake. It knows him and it cares nothing—yet to be known is not nothing. Sometimes the cat will look up suddenly with its eyes like two holes that pin him. *The world where we live is a burning house,* the eyes say. The swimmer glides deeper, thinking about the difference between fullness and emptiness. A few times it happened when he sat in the audience watching her dance that his wife's eyes came to rest on him—empty. He saw right to the back of her head. Modigliani would paint out the iris, which seemed to him too intimate.

Friday 10:00 p.m. Not swimming.

Over the unmoving black body of the lake the moon dreams its gold dream of life, as if it were alone in the world and what dreamer is not?

Sunday 10:30 p.m. Not swimming.

Freud learned about dreams from watching freshwater crabs which, he saw, were trying to disguise their twitches. The swimmer touches the cat ever so lightly on the bald spot in front of its ear. 'For some must watch,' he whispers. The cat is looking out from very far back in its eyes now, from a huge room where everything is running slowly away. On the other hand death, yes stealthy enough, ignores no one and never sleeps. The swimmer's tears run down his hand onto the bald spot quiet now. 'And some must sleep.' The soul of a cat is mortal. It does its best.

❧

NINETY-THREE MILLION MILES AWAY

At least part of the reason why Ali married Claude, a cosmetic surgeon with a growing practice, was so that she could quit her boring government job. Claude was all for it. 'You only have one life to live,' he said. 'You only have one kick at the can.' He gave her a generous allowance and told her to do what she wanted.

She wasn't sure what that was, aside from trying on clothes in expensive stores. Claude suggested something musical—she loved music—so she took dance classes and piano lessons and discovered that she had a tin ear and no sense of rhythm. She fell into a mild depression during which she peevishly questioned Claude about the ethics of cosmetic surgery.

'It all depends on what light you're looking at it in,' Claude said. He was not easily riled. What Ali needed to do, he said, was take the wider view.

She agreed. She decided to devote herself to learning, and she began a regimen of reading and studying, five days a week, five to six hours a day. She read novels, plays, biographies, essays, magazine articles, almanacs, the New Testament, *The Concise Oxford Dictionary*, *The Harper Anthology of Poetry*.

But after a year of this, although she became known as the person at dinner parties who could supply the name or date that somebody was snapping around for, she wasn't particularly happy, and she didn't even feel smart. Far from it, she felt stupid, a machine, an idiot savant whose one talent was memorization. If she had any *creative* talent, which was the only kind she really admired, she wasn't going to find it by armouring herself with facts. She grew slightly paranoid that Claude wanted her to settle down and have a baby.

On their second wedding anniversary they bought a condominium apartment with floor-to-ceiling windows, and Ali decided to abandon her reading regimen and to take up painting. Since she didn't know the first thing about painting or even drawing, she studied pictures from art books. She did know what her first subject was going to be—herself in the nude. A few months ago she'd had a dream about spotting her signature in the corner of a painting, and realizing from the conversation of the men who were admiring it (and blocking her view) that it was an extraordinary rendition of her naked self. She took the dream to be a sign. For two weeks she studied the proportions, skin tones, and muscle definitions of the nudes in her books, then she went out and bought art supplies and a self-standing, full-length mirror.

She set up her work area halfway down the living room. Here she had light without being directly in front of the window. When she was all ready to begin, she stood before the mirror and slipped off her white terry-cloth housecoat and her pink flannelette pyjamas, letting them fall to the floor. It aroused her a little to witness her careless shedding of clothes. She tried a pose: hands folded and resting loosely under her stomach, feet buried in the drift of her housecoat.

For some reason, however, she couldn't get a fix on what she looked like. Her face and body seemed indistinct, secretive in a way, as if they were actually well defined, but not to her, or not from where she was looking.

She decided that she should simply start, and see what happened. She did a pencil drawing of herself sitting in a chair and stretching. It struck her as being very good, not that she could really judge, but the out-of-kilter proportions seemed slyly deliberate, and there was a pleasing simplicity to the reaching arms and the elongated curve of the neck. Because flattery hadn't been her intention, Ali felt that at last she may have wrenched a vision out of her soul.

The next morning she got out of bed unusually early, not long after Claude had left the apartment, and discovered sunlight streaming oblique-ly into the living room through a gap between their building and the apart-ment house next door. As far as she knew, and in spite of the plate-glass windows, this was the only direct light they got. Deciding to make use of it while it lasted, she moved her easel, chair, and mirror closer to the window. Then she took off her housecoat and pyjamas.

For a few moments she stood there looking at herself, wondering what it was that had inspired the sketch. Today she was disposed to seeing her-self as not bad, overall. As far as certain specifics went, though, as to whether her breasts were small, for instance, or her eyes close together, she remained in the dark.

Did other people find her looks ambiguous? Claude was always calling her beautiful, except that the way he put it—'You're beautiful to me,' or 'I think you're beautiful'—made it sound as if she should understand that his taste in women was unconventional. Her only boyfriend before Claude, a guy called Roger, told her she was great but never said how exactly. When they had sex, Roger liked to hold the base of his penis and watch it going in and out of her. Once, he said that there were days he got so horny at the office, his pencil turned him on. (She felt it should have been his pencil sharpener.)

Maybe she was one of those people who are more attractive when they're animated, she thought. She gave it a try. She smiled and tossed her head, she tucked her hair behind her ears. She covered her breasts with her hands. Down her cleavage a drop of sweat slid haltingly, a sensation like the tip of a tongue. She circled her palms until her nipples hardened. She imagined a man's hands . . . not Claude's—a man's hands not attached to any particular man. She looked out the window.

In the apartment across from her she saw a man.

She leapt to one side, behind the drapes. Her heart pounded violently, as if something had thundered by. She stood there hugging herself. The drapes smelled bitter, cabbagey. Her right hand cupped her left breast, which felt like her heart because her pulse was in it.

After a moment she realized that she had started circling both of her palms on her nipples again. She stopped, astonished, then went on doing it but with the same sceptical thrill she used to get when she knew it wasn't *her* moving the ouija board. And then it was her feet that were moving involuntarily, taking her from behind the drapes into a preternatural brightness.

She went to the easel, picked up a brush and the palette and began to mix a skin colour. She didn't look at the window or at the mirror. She had the tranced sensation of being at the edge of a cliff. Her first strokes dripped, so she switched to dabbing at the canvass, producing what started to resemble feathers. Paint splashed on her own skin but she ignored it and went on dabbing, layer on layer until she lost the direct sun. Then she wet a rag in the turpentine and wiped her hands and her breasts and stomach.

She thought about the sun. That it is ninety-three million miles away and that its fuel supply will last another five billion years. Instead of thinking about the man who was watching her, she tried to recall a solar chart she had memorized a couple of years ago.

The surface temperature is six thousand degrees Fahrenheit, she told herself. Double that number and you have how many times bigger the surface of the sun is compared to the surface of the earth. Except that because the sun is a ball of hot gas, it actually has no surface.

When she had rubbed the paint off, she went into the kitchen to wash away the turpentine with soap and water. The man's eyes tracked her. She didn't have to glance at the window for confirmation. She switched on the light above the sink, soaped the dishcloth and began to wipe her skin. There was no reason to clean her arms, but she lifted each one and wiped the cloth over it. She wiped her breasts. She seemed to share in his scrutiny, as if she were looking at herself through his eyes. From his perspective she was able to see her physical self very clearly—her shiny, red-highlighted hair, her small waist and heart-shaped bottom, the dreamy tilt to her head.

She began to shiver. She wrung out the cloth and folded it over the faucet, then patted herself dry with a dish towel. Then, pretending to be examining her fingernails, she turned and walked over to the window. She looked up.

There he was, in the window straight across but one floor higher. Her glance of a quarter of an hour ago had registered dark hair and a white shirt. Now she saw a long, older face, a man in his fifties maybe. A green tie. She had seen him before this morning—quick, disinterested (or so she had thought) sightings of a man in his kitchen, watching television, going from room to room. A bachelor living next door. She pressed the palms of her hands on the window, and he stepped back into shadow.

The pane clouded from her breath. She leaned her body into it, flattening her breasts against the cool glass. Right at the window she was visible to his apartment and the one below, which had closed vertical blinds. 'Each window like a pill'ry appears,' she thought. Vaguely appropriate lines from the poems she had read last year were always occurring to her. She felt that he was still watching, but she yearned for proof.

When it became evident that he wasn't going to show himself, she went into the bedroom. The bedroom windows didn't face the apartment house, but she closed them anyway, then got into bed under the covers. Between her legs there was such a tender throbbing that she had to push a pillow into her crotch. Sex addicts must feel like this, she thought. Rapists, child molesters.

She said to herself, 'You are a certifiable exhibitionist.' She let out an amazed, almost exultant laugh, but instantly fell into a darker amazement as it dawned on her that she really was, she really *was* an exhibitionist. And what's more, she had been one for years, or at least she had been working up to being one for years.

Why, for instance, did she and Claude live here, in this vulgar low-rise. Wasn't it because of the floor-to-ceiling windows that faced the windows of the house next door?

And what about when she was twelve and became so obsessed with the idea of urinating on people's lawns that one night she crept out of the house after everyone was asleep and did it? Peed on the lawn of the townhouses next door, right under a streetlight, in fact.

What about two years ago, when she didn't wear underpants the entire summer? She'd had a minor yeast infection and had read that it was a good idea not to wear underpants at home, if you could help it, but she had stopped wearing them in public as well, beneath skirts and dresses, at parties, on buses, and she must have known that this was taking it a bit far, because she had kept it from Claude.

'Oh, my God,' she said wretchedly.

She went still, alerted by how theatrical that had sounded. Her heart was beating in her throat. She touched a finger to it. So fragile, a throat. She imagined the man being excited by one of her hands circling her throat.

What was going on? What was the matter with her? Maybe she was too aroused to be shocked at herself. She moved her hips, rubbing her crotch against the pillow. No, she didn't want to masturbate. That would ruin it.

Ruin what?

She closed her eyes, and the man appeared to her. She experienced a rush of wild longing. It was as if, all her life, she had been waiting for a long-faced, middle-aged man in a white shirt and green tie. He was probably still standing in his living room, watching her window.

She sat up, threw off the covers.

Dropped back down on the bed.

This was crazy. This really was crazy. What if he was a rapist? What if, right this minute, he was downstairs, finding out her name from the mail-box? Or what if he was just some lonely, normal man who took her display as an invitation to phone her up and ask her for a date? It's not as if she wanted to go out with him. She wasn't looking for an affair.

For an hour or so she fretted, and then she drifted off to sleep. When she woke up, shortly after noon, she was quite calm. The state she had worked herself into earlier struck her as overwrought. So, she gave some guy a thrill, so what? She was a bit of an exhibitionist. Most women were, she bet. It was instinctive, a side effect of being the receptor in the sex act.

She decided to have lunch and go for a walk. While she was making herself a sandwich she avoided glancing at the window, but as soon as she sat at the table she couldn't resist looking over.

He wasn't there, and yet she felt that he was watching her, standing out of the light. She ran a hand through her hair. 'For Christ's sake,' she reproached herself, but she was already with him. Again it was as if her eyes were in his head, although not replacing his eyes. She knew that he wanted her to slip her hand down her sweat pants. She did this. Watching his win-dow, she removed her hand and licked her wet fingers. At that instant she would have paid money for some sign that he was watching.

After a few minutes she began to chew on her fingernails. She was sud-denly depressed. She reached over and pulled the curtain across the win-dow and ate her sandwich. Her mouth, biting into the bread, trembled like an old lady's. 'Tremble like a guilty thing surprised,' she quoted to herself. It wasn't guilt, though. It wasn't frustration, either, not sexual frustration. She was acquainted with this bleached sadness—it came upon her at the height of sensation. After orgasms, after a day of trying on clothes in stores.

She finished her sandwich and went for a long walk in her new tore-ador pants and her tight black turtleneck. By the time she returned, Claude was home. He asked her if she had worked in the nude again.

'Of course,' she said absently. 'I have to.' She was looking past him at the man's closed drapes. 'Claude,' she said suddenly, 'am I beautiful? I mean not just to you. Am I empirically beautiful?'

Claude looked surprised. 'Well, yeah,' he said. 'Sure you are. Hell, I married you, didn't I? Hey!' He stepped back. 'Whoa!'

She was removing her clothes. When she was naked, she said, 'Don't think of me as your wife. Just as a woman. One of your patients. Am I beautiful or not?'

He made a show of eyeing her up and down. 'Not bad,' he said. 'Of course, it depends on what you mean by beautiful.' He laughed. 'What's going on?'

'I'm serious. You don't think I'm kind of . . . normal? You know, plain?'

'Of course not,' he said lovingly. He reached for her and drew her into his arms. 'You want hard evidence?' he said.

They went into the bedroom. It was dark because the curtains were still drawn. She switched on the bedside lamp, but once he was undressed he switched it off.

'No,' she said from the bed, 'leave it on.'

'What? You want it on?'

'For a change.'

The next morning she got up before he did. She had hardly slept. During breakfast she kept looking over at the apartment house, but there was no sign of the man. Which didn't necessarily mean that he wasn't there. She couldn't wait for Claude to leave so that she could stop pretend-ing she wasn't keyed-up. It was gnawing at her that she had overestimated or somehow misread the man's interest. How did she know? He might be gay. He might be so devoted to a certain woman that all other women repelled him. He might be puritanical, a priest, a Born-Again. He might be out of his mind.

The minute Claude left the apartment, she undressed and began work on the painting. She stood in the sunlight mixing colours, then sat on the chair in her stretching pose, looking at herself in the mirror, then stood up and, without paying much attention, glancing every few seconds at his win-dow, painted ribs and uplifted breasts.

An hour went by before she thought, He's not going to show up. She dropped into the chair, weak with disappointment, even though she knew that, very likely, he had simply been obliged to go to work, that his being home yesterday was a fluke. Forlornly she gazed at her painting. To her surprise she had accomplished something rather interesting: breasts like Picasso eyes. It is possible, she thought dully, that I am a natural talent.

She put her brush in the turpentine, and her face in her hands. She felt the sun on her hair. In a few minutes the sun would disappear behind his house, and after that, if she wanted him to get a good look at her, she would have to stand right at the window. She envisioned herself stationed there all day. You are ridiculous, she told herself. You are unhinged.

She glanced up at the window again.

He was there.

She sat up straight. Slowly she came to her feet. Stay, she prayed. He did. She walked to the window, her fingertips brushing her thighs. She held her breath. When she was at the window, she stood perfectly still. He stood perfectly still. He had on a white shirt again, but no tie. He was close enough that she could make out the darkness around his eyes, although she couldn't tell exactly where he was looking. But his eyes seemed to enter her head like a drug, and she felt herself aligned with his perspective. She saw herself—surprisingly slender, composed but apprehensive—through the glass and against the backdrop of the room's white walls.

After a minute or two she walked to the chair, picked it up and carried it to the window. She sat facing him, her knees apart. He was as still as a picture. So was she, because she had suddenly remembered that he might be gay, or crazy. She tried to give him a hard look. She observed his age and his sad, respectable appearance. And the fact that he remained at the window, revealing his interest.

No, he was the man she had imagined. I am a gift to him, she thought, opening her legs wider. I am his dream come true. She began to rotate her hips. With the fingers of both hands she spread her labia.

One small part of her mind, clinging to the person she had been until yesterday morning, tried to pull her back. She felt it as a presence behind the chair, a tableau of sensational, irrelevant warnings that she was obviously not about to turn around for. She kept her eyes on the man. Moving her left hand up to her breasts, she began to run and squeeze and to circle her fingers on the nipples. The middle finger of her right hand slipped into her vagina, as the palm massaged her clitoris.

He was motionless.

You are kissing me, she thought. She seemed to feel his lips, cool, soft, sliding and sucking down her stomach. You are kissing me. She imagined his hands under her, lifting her like a bowl to his lips.

She was coming.

Her body jolted. Her legs shook. She had never experienced anything like it. Seeing what he saw, she witnessed an act of shocking vulnerability.

It went on and on. She saw the charity of her display, her lavish reckless-ness and submission. It inspired her to the tenderest self-love. The man did not move, not until she had finally stopped moving, and then he reached up one hand—to signal, she thought, but it was to close the drapes.

She stayed sprawled in the chair. She was astonished. She couldn't believe herself. She couldn't believe him. How did he know to stay so still, to simply watch her? She avoided the thought that right at this moment he was proba-bly masturbating. She absorbed herself only with what she had seen, which was a dead-still man whose eyes she had sensed roving over her body the way that eyes in certain portraits seem to follow you around a room.

The next three mornings everything was the same. He had on his white shirt, she masturbated in the chair, he watched without moving, she came spectacularly, he closed the drapes.

Afterwards she went out clothes shopping or visiting people. Everyone told her how great she looked. At night she was passionate in bed, prompt-ing Claude to ask several times, 'What the hell's come over you?' but he asked it happily, he didn't look a gift horse in the mouth. She felt very lov-ing toward Claude, not out of guilt but out of high spirits. She knew better than to confess, of course, and yet she didn't believe that she was betraying him with the man next door. A man who hadn't touched her or spoken to her, who, as far as she was concerned, existed only from the waist up and who never moved except to pull his drapes, how could that man be count-ed as a lover?

The fourth day, Friday, the man didn't appear. For two hours she wait-ed in the chair. Finally she moved to the couch and watched television, keeping one eye on his window. She told herself that he must have had an urgent appointment, or that he had to go to work early. She was worried, though. At some point, late in the afternoon when she wasn't looking, he closed his drapes.

Saturday and Sunday he didn't seem to be home—the drapes were drawn and the lights off. Not that she could have done anything anyway, not with Claude there. On Monday morning she was in her chair, naked, as soon as Claude left the house. She waited until ten-thirty, then put on her toreador pants and white push-up halter-top and went for a walk. A con-soling line from *Romeo and Juliet* played in her head: 'He that is stricken blind cannot forget the precious treasure of his eyesight lost.' She was angry with the man for not being as keen as she was. If he was at his window tomorrow, she vowed she would shut her drapes on him.

But how would she replace him, what would she do? Become a table dancer? She had to laugh. Aside from the fact that she was a respectably married woman and could not dance to save her life and was probably ten years too old, the last thing she wanted was a bunch of slack-jawed, flat-eyed drunks grabbing at her breasts. She wanted one man, and she wanted him to have a sad, intelligent demeanour and the control to watch her without moving a muscle. She wanted him to wear a white shirt.

On the way home, passing his place, she stopped. The building was a mansion turned into luxury apartments. He must have money, she realized. An obvious conclusion, but until now she'd had no interest whatsoever in who he was.

She climbed the stairs and tried the door. Found it open. Walked in.

The mailboxes were numbered one to four. His would be four. She read the name in the little window. Dr Andrew Halsey.

Back at her apartment she looked him up under 'Physicians' in the phone book and found that, like Claude, he was a surgeon. A general surgeon, though, a remover of tumours and diseased organs. Presumably on call. Presumably dedicated, as a general surgeon had to be.

She guessed she would forgive his absences.

The next morning and the next, Andrew (as she now thought of him) was at the window. Thursday he wasn't. She tried not to be disappointed. She imagined him saving people's lives, drawing his scalpel along skin in beautifully precise cuts. For something to do she worked on her painting. She painted fish-like eyes, a hooked nose, a mouth full of teeth. She worked fast.

Andrew was there Friday morning. When Ali saw him she rose to her feet and pressed her body against the window, as she had done the first morning. Then she walked to the chair, turned it around and leaned over it, her back to him. She masturbated stroking herself from behind.

That afternoon she bought him a pair of binoculars, an expensive, powerful pair, which she wrapped in brown paper, addressed and left on the floor in front of his mailbox. All weekend she was preoccupied with wondering whether he would understand that she had given them to him and whether he would use them. She had considered including a message—'For our mornings' or something like that—but such direct communication seemed like a violation of a pact between them. The binoculars alone were a risk.

Monday, before she even had her housecoat off, he walked from the rear of the room to the window, the binoculars at his eyes. Because most of his face was covered by the binoculars and his hands, she had the impression that he was masked. Her legs shook. When she opened her legs and spread her labia, his eyes crawled up her. She masturbated but didn't come and didn't try to, although she put on a show of coming. She was so devoted to his appreciation that her pleasure seemed like a siphoning of his, an early, childish indulgence that she would never return to.

It was later, with Claude, that she came. After supper she pulled him onto the bed. She pretended that he was Andrew, or rather she imagined a dark, long-faced, silent man who made love with his eyes open but who smelled and felt like Claude and whom she loved and trusted as she did Claude. With this hybrid partner she was able to relax enough to encourage the kind of kissing and movement she needed but had never had the confidence to insist upon. The next morning, masturbating for Andrew, she reached the height of ecstasy, as if her orgasms with him had been the fantasy, and her pretences of orgasm were the real thing. Not coming released her completely into his dream of her. The whole show was for him—cunt, ass, mouth, throat offered to his magnified vision.

For several weeks Andrew turned up regularly, five mornings a week, and she lived in a state of elation. In the afternoons she worked on her painting, without much concentration though, since finishing it didn't seem to matter anymore in spite of how well it was turning out. Claude insisted that it was still very much a self-portrait, a statement Ali was insulted by, given the woman's obvious primitivism and her flat, distant eyes.

There was no reason for her to continue working in the nude, not in the afternoon, but she did, out of habit and comfort and on the outside chance that Andrew might be home and peeking through his drapes. While she painted she wondered about her exhibitionism, what it was about her that craved to have a strange man look at her. Of course, everyone and everything like to be looked at to a certain degree, she thought. Flowers, cats, anything that preened or shone, children crying, 'Look at me!' Some mornings her episodes with Andrew seemed to have nothing at all to do with lust. They were completely display, wholehearted surrender to what felt like the most inaugural and genuine of all desires, which was not sex but which happened to be expressed through a sexual act.

One night she dreamed that Andrew was operating on her. Above the surgical mask his eyes were expressionless. He had very long arms. She was also able to see, as if through his eyes, the vertical incision that went from between her breasts to her navel, and the skin on either side of the incision folded back like a scroll. Her heart was brilliant red and perfectly heart-shaped. All of her other organs were glistening yellows and oranges. Somebody should take a picture of this, she thought. Andrew's gloved hands barely appeared to move as they wielded long, silver instruments. There was no blood on his hands. Very carefully, so that she hardly felt it, he prodded her organs and plucked at her veins and tendons, occasionally drawing a tendon out and dropping it into a petri dish. It was as if he were weeding a garden. Her heart throbbed. A tendon encircled her heart, and when he pulled on it she could feel that its other end encircled her vagina, and the uncoiling there was the most exquisite sensation she had ever experienced. She worried that she would come and that her trembling and spasms would cause him to accidentally stab her. She woke up coming.

All day the dream obsessed her. It *could* happen, she reasoned. She could have a gall bladder or an appendicitis attack and be rushed to the hospital and, just as she was going under, see that the surgeon was Andrew. It could happen.

When she woke up the next morning, the dream was her first thought. She looked down at the gentle swell of her stomach and felt sentimental and excited. She found it impossible to shake the dream, even while she was masturbating for Andrew, so that instead of entering *his* dream of her, instead of seeing a naked woman sitting in a pool of morning sun, she saw her sliced-open chest in the shaft of his surgeon's light. Her heart was what she focused on, its fragile pulsing, but she also saw the slower rise and fall of her lungs, and the quivering of her other organs. Between her organs were tantalizing crevices and entwined swirls of blue and red—her veins and arteries. Her tendons were seashell pink, threaded tight as guitar strings.

Of course she realized that she had the physiology all wrong and that in a real operation there would be blood and pain and she would be anaesthetized. It was an impossible, mad fantasy. She didn't expect it to last. But every day it became more enticing as she authenticated it with hard data, such as the name of the hospital he operated out of (she called his number in the phone book and asked his nurse) and the name of the surgical instruments he would use (she consulted one of Claude's medical texts), and as she smoothed out the rough edges by imagining, for instance, minuscule suction tubes planted here and there in the incision to remove every last drop of blood.

In the mornings, during her real encounters with Andrew, she became increasingly frustrated until it was all she could do not to quit in the middle, close the drapes or walk out of the room. And yet if he failed to show up she was desperate. She started to drink gin and tonics before lunch and to sunbathe at the edge of the driveway between her building and his, knowing he wasn't home from ten o'clock on, but lying there for hours, just in case.

One afternoon, light-headed from gin and sun, restless with worry because he hadn't turned up the last three mornings, she changed out of her bikini and into a strapless cotton dress and went for a walk. She walked past the park she had been heading for, past the stores she had thought she might browse in. The sun bore down. Strutting by men who eyed her bare shoulders, she felt voluptuous, sweetly rounded. But at the pit of her stomach was a filament of anxiety, evidence that despite telling herself otherwise, she knew where she was going.

She entered the hospital by the Emergency doors and wandered the corridors for what seemed like half an hour before discovering Andrew's office. By this time she was holding her stomach and half believing that the feeling of anxiety might actually be a symptom of something very serious.

'Dr Halsey isn't seeing patients,' his nurse said. She slit open a manila envelope with a lion's head letter opener. 'They'll take care of you at Emergency.'

'I have to see Dr Halsey,' Ali said, her voice cracking. 'I'm a friend.'

The nurse sighed. 'Just a minute.' She stood and went down a hall, opening a door at the end after a quick knock.

Ali pressed her fists into her stomach. For some reason she no longer felt a thing. She pressed harder. What a miracle if she burst her appendix! She should stab herself with the letter opener. She should at least break her fingers, slam them in a drawer like a draft dodger.

'Would you like to come in?' a high, nasal voice said. Ali spun around. It was Andrew, standing at the door.

'The doctor will see you,' the nurse said impatiently, sitting back behind her desk.

Ali's heart began to pound. She felt as if a pair of hands were cupping and uncupping her ears. His shirt was blue. She went down the hall, squeezing past him without looking up, and sat in the chair beside his desk. He shut the door and walked to the window. It was a big room. There was a long expanse of old green and yellow floor tiles between them. Leaning his hip against a filing cabinet, he just stood there, hands in his trouser pockets, regarding her with such a polite, impersonal expression that she asked him if he recognized her.

'Of course I do,' he said quietly.

'Well—' Suddenly she was mortified. She felt like a woman about to sob that she couldn't afford the abortion. She touched her fingers to her hot face.

'I don't know your name,' he said.

'Oh. Ali. Ali Perrin.'

'What do you want, Ali?'

Her eyes fluttered down to his shoes—black, shabby loafers. She hated his adenoidal voice. What did she want? What she wanted was to bolt from the room like the mad woman she suspected she was. She glanced up at him again. Because he was standing with his back to the window, he was outlined in light. It made him seem unreal, like a film image superimposed against a screen. She tried to look away, but his eyes held her. Out in the waiting room the telephone was ringing. What do *you* want, she thought, capitulating to the pull of her perspective over his, seeing now, from across the room, a charming woman with tanned, bare shoulders and blushing cheeks.

The light blinked on his phone. Both of them glanced at it, but he stayed standing where he was. After a moment she murmured. 'I have no idea what I'm doing here.'

He was silent. She kept her eyes on the phone, waiting for him to speak. When he didn't, she said, 'I had a dream . . .' She let out a disbelieving laugh. 'God.' She shook her head.

'You are very lovely,' he said in a speculative tone. She glanced up at him, and he turned away. Pressing his hands together, he took a few steps along the window. 'I have very much enjoyed our . . . our encounters.'

'Oh, don't worry,' she said. 'I'm not here to—'

'However,' he cut in, 'I should tell you that I am moving into another building.'

She looked straight at him.

'This weekend, as a matter of fact.' He frowned at his wall of framed diplomas.

'This weekend?' she said.

'Yes.'

'So,' she murmured. 'It's over, then.'

'Regrettably.'

She stared at his profile. In profile he was a stranger—beak-nosed, round-shouldered. She hated his shoes, his floor, his formal way of speaking, his voice, his profile, and yet her eyes filled and she longed for him to look at her again.

Abruptly he turned his back to her and said that this apartment was in the east end, near the beach. He gestured out the window. Did she know where the yacht club was?

'No,' she whispered.

'Not that I am a member,' he said with a mild laugh.

'Listen,' she said, wiping her eyes. 'I'm sorry.' She came to her feet. 'I guess I just wanted to see you.'

He strode like an obliging host over to the door.

'Well, goodbye,' she said, looking up into his face.

He had garlic breath and five-o'clock shadow. His eyes grazed hers. 'I wouldn't feel too badly about anything,' he said affably.

When she got back to the apartment the first thing she did was take her clothes off and go over to the full-length mirror, which was still standing next to the easel. Her eyes filled again because without Andrew's appreciation or the hope of it (and despite how repellant she had found him) what she saw was a pathetic little woman with pasty skin and short legs.

She looked at the painting. If *that* was her, as Claude claimed, then she also had flat eyes and crude, wild proportions.

What on earth did Claude see in her?

What had Andrew seen? 'You are very lovely,' Andrew had said, but maybe he'd been reminding himself. Maybe he'd meant 'lovely when I'm in the next building.'

After supper that evening she asked Claude to lie with her on the couch, and the two of them watched TV. She held his hand against her breast. 'Let this be enough,' she prayed.

But she didn't believe it ever would be. The world was too full of surprises, it frightened her. As Claude was always saying, things looked different from different angles and in different lights. What this meant to her was that everything hinged on where you happened to be standing at a given moment, or even on who you imagined you were. It meant that in certain lights, desire sprang up out of nowhere.

ELIZABETH HAY

❧

THE FRIEND

She was thirty, a pale beautiful woman with long blond hair and high cheek-bones, small eyes, sensuous mouth, an air of serenity and loftiness—superi-ority—and under that, nervousness, insecurity, disappointment. She was tired. There was the young child who woke several times a night. There was Danny who painted till two in the morning, then slid in beside her and coaxed her awake. There was her own passivity. She was always willing, even though she had to get up early, and always resentful, but never out loud. She complied. In conversation she was direct and Danny often took part, but in bed, apparently, she said nothing. She felt him slide against her, his hand between her legs, its motion the reverse of a woman wiping her-self, back to front instead of front to back. She smelled paint—the air of the poorly ventilated attic where he worked—and felt his energetic weariness and responded with a weary energy of her own.

He didn't speak. He didn't call her by any name (during the day he called her Moe more often than Maureen). He reached across her and with practised efficiency found the Vaseline in the bedside drawer.

I met her one afternoon on the sidewalk outside the neighbourhood gro-cery store. It was sunny and it must have been warm—a Saturday in early June. Our section of New York was poor and Italian, and we looked very different from the dark women around us. The friendship began with that shorthand—shortcut to each other—an understanding that goes without say-ing. I had a small child too.

A week later, at her invitation, I walked the three blocks to her house and knocked on the front door. She opened a side door and called my name. 'Beth,' she said, 'this way.' She was dressed in a loose and colourful quilted top and linen pants. She looked composed and bohemian and from another class.

Inside there was very little furniture: a sofa, a chest, a rug, Danny's paintings on the wall. He was there. A small man with Fred Astaire's face and an ingratiating smile. Once he started to talk, she splashed into the con-versation, commenting on everything he said and making it convoluted out of what I supposed was a desire to be included. Only later did I realize how much she insisted on being the centre of attention, and how successfully she became the centre of mine.

We used to take our kids to the only playground within walking distance. It was part of a school yard that marked the border between our neighbourhood and the next. The pavement shimmered with broken glass, the kids were wild and unattended. We pushed our two on the swings and kept each other company. She said she would be so mad if Danny got AIDS, and I thought about her choice of words—'so mad'—struck by the understatement.

I learned about sex from her the way girls learn about sex from each other. In this case the information came not in whispered conversations behind a hedge, but more directly and personally than anything I might have imagined at the age of twelve. In those days the hedge was high and green and the soil below it dark, a setting at once private, natural, and fenced off. This time everything was in the open. I was the audience, the friend with stroller, the mild-mannered wide-eyed listener who learned that breastfeeding brought her to the point of orgasm, that childbirth had made her vagina sloppy and loose, that anal sex hurt so much she would sit on the toilet afterwards, bracing herself against the stabs of pain.

We were in the playground (that sour, overused, wrongly used, hardly playful patch of pavement) and she said she was sore and told me why. When I protested on her behalf she said, 'But I might have wanted it. I don't know. I think I did want it in some way.'

I can't remember her hands, not here in this small cool room in another country and several years after the fact. I remember watching her do many things with her hands; yet I can't remember what they looked like. They must have been long, slender, pale unless tanned. But they don't come to mind the way a man's might and I suppose that's because she didn't touch me. Or is it because I became so adept at holding her at bay? I remember her lips, those dry thin Rock Hudson lips.

One evening we stood on the corner and she smiled her fleeting meaningful smiles, looking at me with what she called her northern eyes (they were blue and she cried easily) while her heartbreak of a husband put his arm around her. What will become of her, I wondered, even after I found out.

She was standing next to the stove and I saw her go up in flames: the open gas jets, the tininess of the room, the proximity of the children—standing on chairs by the stove—and her hair. It slid down her front and fell down her back. She was making pancakes that were obviously raw. She knew they were raw, predicted they would be, yet did nothing about it. Nor did I. I just poured on lots of syrup and said they were good.

I saw her go up in flames, or did I wish it?

In the beginning we saw each other almost every day and couldn't believe how much the friendship had improved our lives. A close, easy intensity which lasted in that phase of its life for several months. My husband talked of moving–an apartment had come open in a building where we had friends–but I couldn't imagine moving away from Maureen.

It was a throwback to girlhood, the sort of miracle that occurs when you find a friend with whom you can talk about everything.

Maureen had grown up rich and poor. Her family was poor, but she was gifted enough to receive scholarships to private schools. It was the private school look she had fixed on me the first time we met, and the poor background she offered later. As a child she received nothing but praise, she said, from parents astonished by their good fortune: They had produced a beautiful and brilliant daughter while everything else went wrong: car accidents, sudden deaths, mental illness.

Danny's private school adjoined hers. They met when they were twelve and he never tried to hide his various obsessions. She could never say that she had never known.

In the spring her mother came to visit. The street was torn up for repairs, the weather prematurely hot, the air thick with dust. Maureen had spread a green cloth over the table and set a vase of cherry blossoms in the middle. I remember the shade of green and the lushness of the blossoms because the sight was so out of character: everything about Maureen was usually in scattered disarray.

Her mother was tall, and more attractive in photographs than in person. In photographs she was still, in person she darted about, high-strung, high-pitched, erratic. Her rapid murmur left the same impression: startling in its abnormality, yet apparently normal. After years of endless talking about the same thing she now made the sounds that people heard: they had stopped up their ears long ago.

She talked about Maureen. How precocious she had been as a child, reading by the age of four and by the age of five memorizing whole books.

'I remember her reading a page, and I told her to go and read it to Daddy. She said, "With or without the paper?" Lots of children can read at five, even her sister was reading at five, but few have Maureen's stamina. She could read for hours, and adult books. I had to put Taylor Caldwell on the top shelf.'

A photograph of the child was tacked to the wall in Danny's studio. She was seated in a chair wearing one of those very short summer dresses we used to wear that ended well above bare round knees. Her face was unfor-

gettable. It was more than beautiful. It had a direct, knowing, almost luminous look produced by astonishingly clear eyes and fair, fair skin. Already
she knew enough not to smile.

'That's her,' said Danny. 'There she is.'

The beautiful kernel of the beautiful woman.

She had always imagined bodies firmer than hers but not substantially different. She had always imagined Danny with a boy.

I met the lover without realizing it. It was late summer, we were at their
house in the country, a shaded house beside a stream—cool, green, quiet—
the physical manifestation of the serenity I once thought she possessed. A
phrase in a movie review: her wealth so old it had a patina. Maureen's tension so polished it had a fine sheen.

All weekend I picked her long hairs off my daughter's sweater and off
my own. I picked them off the sheet on the bed. I picked blackberries,
which left hair-like scratches on my hands.

My hands felt like hers. I looked down at my stained fingers and they
seemed longer. I felt the places where her hands had been, changing dia-
pers, buttoning shirts, deep in tofu and tahini, closing in on frogs which she
caught with gusto. Swimming, no matter how cold.

I washed my hands and lost that feeling of being in contact with many
things. Yet the landscape continued—the scratches if not the smells, the sight
of her hands and hair.

An old painter came to visit. He parked his station wagon next to the
house and followed Danny into his studio in the barn. Maureen and I went
off with the kids to pick berries. It was hot and humid. There would be rain
in the night and again in the morning. We followed a path through the
woods to a stream where the kids splashed about while Maureen and I dan-
gled our feet over the bank. Her feet were long and slender, mine were wide
and short. We sent ripples of water towards the kids.

She told me that Henry—the painter's name was Henry—was Danny's
mentor, they had known each other for years and he was a terrible alcoholic.
Then she leaned so close her shoulder touched mine. One night last summer
Danny had come back from Henry's studio and confessed—confided—that
he had let the old man blow him. Can you believe it? And she laughed—
giddy—flushed—excited—and eager, it seemed, to impress me with her sexual openness and to console herself with the thought that she had impressed
me. A warm breeze blew a strand of her hair into my face. I brushed it away
and it came back—ticklish, intimate, warm and animal-like. I didn't find it
unpleasant, not at the time.

We brought the berries back to the house, and late in the afternoon the two men emerged to sit with us on the veranda. Henry was whiskery, gallant, shy. Maureen talked a great deal and laughed even more. Before dark, Henry drove away.

She knew. It all came out the next spring and she pretended to be horrified, but she knew.

That night sounds woke me: Danny's low murmur, Maureen's uninhibited cries. I listened for a long time. It must have occurred to me then that the more gay he was, the more she was aroused.

I thought it was someone come to visit. But the second time I realized it was ice falling. At midday, icicles fall from the eavestrough into the deep snow below.

And the floor which I keep sweeping for crumbs? There are no crumbs. The sound comes from the old linoleum itself. It crackles in the cold.

Often I wake at one or two in the morning, overheated from the hot water bottle, the three blankets, the open sleeping bag spread on top. In my dreams I take an exam over and over again.

In the morning I go down in the socks I've worn all night to turn up the heat and raise the thin bamboo blind through which everyone can see us anyway. I make coffee, then scald milk in a hand-beaten copper pot with a long handle. Quebec has an expression for beating up egg whites: *monter en neige*. Milk foams up and snow rises.

Under the old linoleum old newspapers advertise an 'equipped one bedroom at Lorne near Albert' for $175. Beside the porch door the linoleum has broken away and you can read mildew, dust, grit, *Ottawa Citizen*, May 1, 1979. The floor is a pattern of squares inset with triangles and curlicues in wheat shades of immature to ripe. Upstairs the colours are similar but faded; and flowers, petals.

During the eclipse last month I saw Maureen when I saw the moon. I saw my thumb inch across her pale white face.

I have no regrets about this. But I have many thoughts.

We pushed swings in the playground while late afternoon light licked at the broken glass on the pavement. New York's dangers were all around us, as was Maureen's fake laugh. She pushed William high in the swing, then let out a little trill each time he came swooping back.

It was the time of Hedda Nussbaum. We cut out the stories in the newspaper and passed them back and forth—photographs of Hedda's beaten face, robust husband, abused and dead daughter. It had been going on for so long. Hedda had been beaten for thirteen years, the child was seven years old.

In the playground, light licked at the broken glass and then the light died and we headed home. Often we stopped for tea at Maureen's. Her house always had a loose and welcoming atmosphere which hid the sharp edge of need against which I rubbed.

She began to call before breakfast, dressing me with her voice, her worries, her anger, her malleability. Usually she was angry with Danny for staying up so late that he was useless all day, of no help in looking after William, while she continued to work to support them, to look after the little boy in the morning and evening, to have no time for herself. But when I expressed anger on her behalf she defended him . . .

Similarly with the stomach pains. An ulcer, she suggested, then made light of the possibility when I took it seriously.

She would ask, 'Is this all? Is this going to be my contribution?' She was referring to her brilliant past and her sorry present: her pedestrian job, the poor neighbourhood, her high-maintenance husband when there were any number of men she could have married, any number she said. Motherhood gave her something to excel at. She did everything for her son—dressed him, fed him, directed every moment of play. 'Is this all right, sweetie? Is this? What about this? Then, sweetie pie, what do you want?'

Sweetie pie wanted what he got. His mother all to himself for a passionately abusive hour, then peace, affection. During a tantrum she would hold him in her lap behind a closed door, then emerge half an hour later with a small smile. 'That was a short one. You should see what they're like sometimes.'

Even when Danny offered to look after him, even when he urged her to take a long walk, she refused. Walked, but briefly, back and forth on the same sidewalk, or up and down the same driveway. Then returned out of a sense of responsibility to the child. But the child was fine.

At two years he still nursed four or five times a night and her nipples were covered with scabs. 'But the skin there heals so quickly,' she said.

We moved to the other side of the city and the full force of it hit me. I remember bending down under the sink of our new apartment, still swallowing a mouthful of peanut butter, to cram s.o.s. pads into the hole—against the mouse, taste of it, peanut butter in the trap. Feel of it, dry and coarse under my fingers. Look of it, out of the corner of my eye a small dark slipper. Her hair always in her face, and the way I was ratting on her.

It got to the point where I knew the phone was going to ring before it rang. Instead of answering, I stood there counting. Thirty rings. Forty. Once I told her I thought she had called earlier, I was in the bathroom and the phone rang forever. Oh, she said, I'm sorry, I wasn't even paying attention. Then I saw the two of us: Maureen mesmerized by the act of picking up a phone and holding it for a time; and me, frantic with resentment at being swallowed whole.

'Why is she so exhausting?' I asked my husband. Then answered my own question. 'She never stops talking and she always talks about the same thing.'

But I wasn't satisfied with my answer. 'She doesn't want solutions to her problems. That's what is so exhausting.'

And yet that old wish—a real wish—to get along. I went to bed thinking about her, woke up thinking about her and something different, yet related, the two mixed together in a single emotion. I had taken my daughter to play with her friend Joyce, another girl was already there and they didn't want Annie to join them. I woke up thinking of my daughter's rejection, my own various rejections, and Maureen.

It seemed inevitable that he would leave her—clear that he was gay and therefore inevitable that he would leave her. He was an artist. To further his art he would pursue his sexuality. But I was wrong; he didn't leave her. And neither did I.

Every six months he had another gay attack and talked, thought, drew penises. Every six months she reacted predictably and never tired of her reactions, her persistence taking on huge, saintly proportions. As for me, I never initiated a visit or a call, but I didn't make a break. As yielding as she was, and she seemed to be all give, Danny and I were even more so.

Tensions accumulated—the panic as she continued to call and I continued to come when called, though each visit became more abrasive, more insulting, as though staged to show who cared least: You haven't called me, you never call me, you think you can make up for your inattention with this visit but I'll show you that I don't care either: the only reason I'm here is so that my son can play with your daughter.

We walked along the river near her country place. William was on the good tricycle, my daughter on the one that didn't work. Maureen said, 'I don't think children should be forced to share. Do you? I think kids should share when they want to share.'

Her son would not give my daughter a turn the whole long two-hour walk beside the river—with me pointing out what? Honeysuckle. Yes, honeysuckle. Swathes of it among the rocks. And fishermen with strings of perch. I stared out over the river, unable to look at Maureen and not arguing; I couldn't find the words.

With each visit there was the memory of an earlier intimacy, and no interest in resurrecting it. Better than nothing. Better than too much. And so it continued, until it spun lower.

We were sitting on the mattress on the floor of Danny's studio in front of a wall-sized mirror. Around us were his small successful paintings and his huge failures. He insisted on painting big, she said, because he was so small. 'I really think so. It's just machismo.'

How clear-eyed she was.

I rested my back against the mirror, Maureen faced it. She glanced at me, then the mirror, and each time she looked in the mirror she smiled slightly. Her son was there. He wandered off and then it became clear that she was watching herself.

She told me she was pregnant again. It took two years to persuade Danny, 'and now he's even more eager that I am,' smiling at herself in the mirror.

Danny got sick. I suppose he had been sick for months, but I heard about it in the spring. Maureen called in tears. 'The shoe has dropped,' she said.

He was so sick that he had confessed to the doctors that he and Henry— old dissipated Henry whose cock had slipped into who knows what—had been screwing for the last five years. Maureen talked and wept for thirty minutes before I realized that she had no intention of leaving him, or he of leaving her. They would go on. The only change, and this wasn't certain, was that they wouldn't sleep together. They would go to their country place in June and stay all summer.

I felt cheated, set up, used. 'Look, you should *do* something,' I said. 'Make some change.'

She said, 'I know. But I don't want to precipitate anything. Now isn't the time.'

She said it wasn't AIDS.

Her lips dried out like tangerine sections separated in the morning and left out all day. She nursed her children so long that her breasts turned into small apricots, and now I cannot hold an apricot in my hand and feel its soft loose skin, its soft non-weight, without thinking of small spent breasts—little dugs.

She caught hold of me, a silk scarf against an uneven wall, and clung.

Two years later I snuck away. In the weeks leading up to the move, I thought I might write to her afterwards, but in the days immediately before, I knew I would not. One night in late August when the weather was cool and the evenings still long, we finished packing at nine and pulled away in the dark.

We turned right on Broadway and rode the traffic in dark slow motion out of the city, north along the Hudson, and home.

In Canada I thought about old friends who were new friends because I hadn't seen them for such a long time. And newer friends who were old friends because I'd left them behind in the other place. And what I noticed was that I had no landscape in which to set them. They were portraits in my mind (not satisfying portraits either, because I couldn't remember parts of their bodies; their hands, for instance, wouldn't come to mind). They were emotion and episode divorced from time and place. Yet there was a time—the recent past, and a place—a big city across the border.

And here was I, where I had wanted to be for as long as I had been away from it—home—and it didn't register either. In other words, I discovered that I wasn't in a place. I was the place. I felt populated by old friends. They lived in my head amid my various broodings. Here they met again, going through the same motions and different ones. Here they coupled in ways that hadn't occurred really. And here was I, disloyal but faithful, occupied by people I didn't want to see and didn't want to lose.

September came and went, October came and went, winter didn't come. It rained in November, it rained again in December. In January a little snow fell, then more rain.

Winter came when I was asleep. One morning I looked out at frozen puddles dusted with snow. It was very cold. I stepped carefully into the street and this is what I saw. I saw the landscape of friendship. I saw Sunday at four in the afternoon. I saw childhood panic. People looked familiar to me, yet they didn't say hello. I saw two people I hadn't seen in fifteen years, one seated in a restaurant, the other skating by. I looked at them keenly, waiting for recognition to burst upon them, but it didn't.

Strangers claimed to recognize me. They said they had seen me before, some said precisely where. 'It was at a conference two years ago.' Or, 'I saw you walk by every day with your husband last summer. You were walking quickly.'

But last summer Ted and I had been somewhere else.

The connections were wistful, intangible, maddening. Memory tantalized before it finally failed. Yet as much as memory failed, those odd, unhinged conjunctures helped. Strange glimmerings and intense looks were better than nothing.

The last time I saw Maureen, she was wearing a black-and-white summer dress and her teeth were chattering. 'Look at me,' she said, her mouth barely able to form the words, her lower jaw shaking. 'It's not that cold.'

We were in the old neighbourhood. The street was dark and narrow with shops on either side, and many people. I was asking my usual questions, she was doing her best to answer them.

'Look,' she said again, pointing to her lips which were shaking uncontrollably.

I nodded, drew my jacket tight, mentioned how much warmer it had been on the way to the café, my voice friendly enough but without the intonations of affection and interest, the rhythms of sympathy, the animation of friendship. In the subway we felt warm again. She waited for my train to come, trying to redeem and at the same time distance herself. I asked about Danny and she answered. She talked about his job, her job, how little time each of them had for themselves. She went on and on. Before she finished I asked about her children. Again she talked.

'I don't mean to brag,' she said, helpless against the desire to brag, 'but Victoria is so verbal.'

Doing to her children and for herself what her mother had done to her and for herself.

'So verbal, so precocious. I don't say this to everyone,' listing the words that Victoria already knew.

She still shivered occasionally. She must have known why I didn't call anymore, aware of the reasons while inventing others in a self-defence that was both pathetic and dignified. She never asked what went wrong. Never begged for explanations (dignified even in her begging: her persistence as she continued to call and extend invitations).

We stood in the subway station—one in a black-and-white dress, the other in a warm jacket—one hurt and pale, the other triumphant in the indifference which had taken so long to acquire. We appeared to be friends. But a close observer would have seen how static we were, rooted in a determination not to have a scene, not to allow the other to cause hurt. Standing, waiting for my train to come in.

DIONNE BRAND

❧

PHOTOGRAPH

My grandmother has left no trace, no sign of her self. There is no photo-graph, except one which she took with much trouble for her identity card. I remember the day that she had to take it. It was for voting, when we got Independence; and my grandmother, with fear in her eyes, woke up that morning, got dressed, put on her hat, and left. It was the small beige hat with the lace piece for the face. There was apprehension in the house. My grandmother, on these occasions, the rare ones when she left the house, pat-ted her temples with limacol. Her smelling salts were placed in her purse. The little bottle with the green crystals and liquid had a pungent odour and a powerful aura for me until I was much older. She never let us touch it. She kept it in her purse, now held tightly in one hand, the same hand which held her one embroidered handkerchief.

That morning we all woke up and were put to work getting my grand-mother ready to go to the identity card place.

One of us put the water to boil for my grandmother's bath; my big sis-ter combed her hair and the rest of us were dispatched to get shoes, petti-coat, or stockings. My grandmother's mouth moved nervously as these events took place and her fingers hardened over ours each time our clum-sy efforts crinkled a pleat or spilled scent.

We were an ever growing bunch of cousins, sisters, and brothers. My grandmother's grandchildren. Children of my grandmother's daughters. We were seven in all, from time to time more, given to my grandmother for safekeeping. Eula, Kat, Ava, and I were sisters. Eula was the oldest. Genevieve, Wil, and Dri were sister and brothers and our cousins. Our mothers were away. Away-away or in the country-away. That's all we knew of them except for their photographs which we used tauntingly in our bat-tles about whose mother was prettier.

Like the bottle of smelling salts, all my grandmother's things had that same aura. We would wait until she was out of sight, which only meant that she was in the kitchen since she never left the house, and then we would try on her dresses or her hat, or open the bottom drawer of the wardrobe where she kept sheets, pillowcases and underwear, candles and candlesticks, boxes of matches, pieces of cloth for headties and dresses and curtains, black cake and wafers, rice and sweetbread, in pillow cases, just in case of an emergency. We would unpack my grandmother's things down to the bottom of the drawer, where she kept camphor balls, and touch them over and over again. We would wrap ourselves in pieces of cloth, pretending we were African queens; we would put on my grandmother's gold chain, pretending we were rich. We would pinch her black cakes until they were down to nothing and then we would swear that we never touched them and never saw who did. Often, she caught us and beat us, but we were always on the lookout for the next chance to interfere in my grandmother's sacred things. There was always something new there. Once, just before Christmas, we found a black doll. It caused commotion and rare dissension among us. All of us wanted it so, of course, my grandmother discovered us. None of us, my grandmother said, deserved it and on top of that she threatened that there would be no Santa Claus for us. She kept the doll at the head of her bed until she relented and gave it to Kat, who was the littlest.

We never knew how anything got into the drawer, because we never saw things enter the house. Everything in the drawer was pressed and ironed and smelled of starch and ironing and newness and oldness. My grandmother guarded them often more like burden than treasure. Their depletion would make her anxious; their addition would pose problems of space in our tiny house.

As she rarely left the house, my grandmother felt that everyone on the street where we lived would be looking at her, going to take her picture for her identity card. We felt the same too and worried as she left, stepping heavily, yet shakily down the short hill that lead to the savannah, at the far end of which was the community centre. My big sister held her hand. We could see the curtains moving discreetly in the houses next to ours, as my grandmother walked, head up, face hidden behind her veil. We prayed that she would not fall. She had warned us not to hang out of the windows looking at her. We, nevertheless, hung out of the windows gawking at her, along with the woman who lived across the street, whom my grandmother thought lived a scandalous life and had scandalous children and a scandalous laugh which could be heard all the way up the street when the woman sat old blagging with her friends on her veranda. We now hung out of the windows keeping company with 'Tante,' as she was called, standing with her hands on her massive hips looking and praying for my grandmother. She did not stop, nor did she turn back to give us her look; but we knew that the minute she returned our ears would be burning, because we had joined Tante in disgracing my grandmother.

The photograph from that outing is the only one we have of my grandmother and it is all wrinkled and chewed up, even after my grandmother hid it from us and warned us not to touch it. Someone retrieved it when my grandmother was taken to the hospital. The laminate was now dull and my grandmother's picture was grey and creased and distant.

As my grandmother turned the corner with my sister, the rest of us turned to lawlessness, eating sugar from the kitchen and opening the new refrigerator as often as we wanted and rummaging through my grandmother's things. Dressed up in my grandmother's clothes and splashing each other with her limacol, we paraded outside the house where she had distinctly told us not to go. We waved at Tante, mincing along in my grandmother's shoes. After a while, we grew tired and querulous; assessing the damage we had done to the kitchen, the sugar bowl, and my grandmother's wardrobe, we began assigning blame. We all decided to tell on each other. Who had more sugar than whom and who was the first to open the cabinet drawer where my grandmother kept our birth certificates.

We liked to smell our birth certificates, their musty smell and yellowing water-marked coarse paper was proof that my grandmother owned us. She had made such a fuss to get them from our mothers.

A glum silence descended when we realized that it was useless quarrelling. We were all implicated and my grandmother always beat everyone, no matter who committed the crime.

When my grandmother returned we were too chastened to protest her beating. We began to cry as soon as we saw her coming around the corner with my sister. By the time she hit the doorstep we were weeping buckets and the noise we made sounded like a wake, groaning in unison and holding onto each other. My grandmother, too tired from her ordeal at the identity card place, looked at us scornfully and sat down. There was a weakness in her eyes which we recognized. It meant that our beating would be postponed for hours, maybe days, until she could regain her strength. She had been what seemed like hours at the identity card place. My grandmother had to wait, leaning on my sister and having people stare at her, she said. All that indignity and the pain which always appeared in her back at these moments, had made her barely able to walk back to the house. We, too, had been so distraught that we did not even stand outside the house jumping up and down and shouting that she was coming. So at least she was spared that embarrassment. For the rest of the day we quietly went about our chores, without being told to do them and walked lightly past my grandmother's room, where she lay resting in a mound, under the pink chenille.

We had always lived with my grandmother. None of us could recollect our mothers, except as letters from England or occasional visits from women who came on weekends and made plans to take us, eventfully, to live with them. The letters from England came every two weeks and at

Christmas with a brown box full of foreign-smelling clothes. The clothes smelled of a good life in a country where white people lived and where bad-behaved children like us would not be tolerated. All this my grandmother said. There, children had manners and didn't play in mud and didn't dirty everything and didn't cry if there wasn't any food and didn't run under the mango trees, grabbing mangoes when the wind blew them down and walked and did not run through the house like warrahoons and did not act like little old niggers. Eula, my big sister, would read the letters to my grand-mother who, from time to time, would let us listen. Then my grandmother would urge us to grow up and go away too and live well. When she came to the part about going away, we would feel half-proud and half-nervous. The occasional visits made us feel as precarious as the letters. When we misbehaved, my grandmother often threatened to send us away-away, where white men ate Black children, or to quite-to-quite in the country.

Passing by my grandmother's room, bunched up under the spread, with her face tight and hollow-cheeked, her mouth set against us, the spec-tre of quite-to-quite and white cannibals loomed brightly. It was useless try-ing to 'dog back' to her she said, when one of my cousins sat close to her bed, inquiring if she would like us to pick her grey hairs out. That was how serious this incident was. Because my grandmother loved us to pick her grey hairs from her head. She would promise us a penny for every ten which we could get by the root. If we broke a hair, that would not count, she said. And, if we threw the little balls of her hair out into the yard for the wind, my grandmother became quite upset since that meant that birds would fly off with her hair and send her mad, send her mind to the four corners of the earth, or they would build a nest with her hair and steal her brain. We never threw hair in the yard for the wind, at least not my grand-mother's hair and we took on her indignant look when we chastised each other for doing it with our own hair. My cousin Genevieve didn't mind though. She chewed her long front plait when she sucked on her thumb and saved balls of hair to throw to the birds. Genevieve made mudpies under the house, which we bought with leaf money. You could get yellow mudpies or brown mudpies or red mudpies, this depended on the depth of the hole under the house and the wash water which my grandmother threw there on Saturdays. We took my grandmother's word that having to search the four corners of the earth for your mind was not an easy task, but Genevieve wondered what it would be like.

There's a photograph of Genevieve and me and two of my sisters someplace. We took it to send to England. My grandmother dressed us up, put my big sister in charge of us, giving her 50 cents tied up in a handker-chief and pinned to the waistband of her dress, and warned us not to give her any trouble. We marched to Wong's Studio on the Coffee, the main road in our town, and fidgeted as Mr Wong fixed us in front of a promenade scene to take our picture. My little sister cried through it all and sucked her fingers. Nobody knows that it's me in the photograph, but my sisters and Genevieve look like themselves.

Banishment from my grandmother's room was torture. It was her room, even though three of us slept beside her each night. It was a small room with two windows kept shut most of the time, except every afternoon when my grandmother would look out of the front window, her head resting on her big arms, waiting for us to return from school. There was a bed in the room with a headboard where she kept the bible, a bureau with a round mirror, and a washstand with a jug and basin. She spent much of her time here. We too, sitting on the polished floor under the front window talking to her or against the foot of the bed, if we were trying to get back into her favour or beg her for money. We knew the smell of the brown varnished wood of her bed intimately.

My grandmother's room was rescue from pursuit. Anyone trying to catch anyone would pull up straight and get quiet, if you ducked into her room. We read under my grandmother's bed and, playing catch, we hid from each other behind the bulk of her body.

We never received that licking for the photograph day, but my grandmother could keep a silence that was punishment enough. The photograph now does not look like her. It is grey and pained. In real, she was round and comfortable. When we knew her she had a full lap and beautiful arms, her cocoa brown skin smelled of wood smoke and familiar.

My grandmother never thought that people should sleep on Saturdays. She woke us up 'peepee au jour' as she called it, which meant before it was light outside, and set us to work. My grandmother said that she couldn't stand a lazy house, full of lazy children. The washing had to be done and dried before three o'clock on Saturday when the baking would begin and continue until the evening. My big sister and my grandmother did the washing, leaning over the scrubbing board and the tub and when we others grew older we scrubbed the clothes out, under the eyes of my grandmother. We had to lay the soap-scrubbed clothes out on the square pile of stones so that the sun would bleach them clean, then pick them up and rinse and hang them to dry. We all learned to bake from the time that our chins could reach the table and we washed dishes standing on the bench in front of the sink. In the rainy season, the washing was done on the sunniest days. A sudden shower of rain and my grandmother would send us flying to collect the washing off the lines. We would sit for hours watching the rain gush through the drains which we had dug, in anticipation, around the flower garden in front of the house. The yellow brown water lumbered unsteadily through the drains rebuilding the mud and forming a lake at the place where our efforts were frustrated by a large stone.

In the rainy season, my big sister planted corn and pigeon peas on the right side of the house. Just at the tail end of the season, we planted the flower garden. Zinnias and jump-up-and-kiss-me, which grew easily, and xora and roses which we could never get to grow. Only the soil on one side of the front yard was good for growing flowers or food. On the other side a sour-sop tree and an almond tree sucked the soil of everything, leaving the ground sandy and thin, and pushed up their roots, ridging the yard, into a hill. The almond tree, under the front window, fed a nest of ants which lived in one pillar of our house. A line of small red ants could be seen making their way from pillar to almond tree, carrying bits of leaves and bark.

One Saturday evening, I tried to stay outside playing longer than allowed by my grandmother, leaning on the almond tree and ignoring her calls. 'Laugh and cry live in the same house,' my grandmother warned, threatening to beat me when I finally came inside. At first I only felt the bite of one ant on my leg but, no sooner, my whole body was invaded by thousands of little red ants biting my skin blue crimson. My sisters and cousins laughed, my grandmother, looking at me pitiably, sent me to the shower; but the itching did not stop and the pains did not subside until the next day.

I often polished the floor on Saturdays. At first, I hated the brown polish-dried rag with which I had to rub the floors, creeping on my hands and knees. I hated the corners of the room which collected fluff and dust. If we tried to polish the floor without first scrubbing it, my grandmother would make us start all over again. My grandmother supervised all these activities when she was ill, sitting on the bed. She saw my distaste for the rag and therefore insisted that I polish over and over again some spot which I was sure that I had gone over. I learned to look at the rag, to notice its layers of brown polish, its waxy shines in some places, its wetness when my grandmother made me mix the polish with kerosene to stretch its use. It became a rich object, all full of continuous ribbing and working, which my grandmother insisted that I do with my hands and no shortcuts of standing and doing it with the heel of my foot. We poor people had to get used to work, my grandmother said. After polishing, we would shine the floor with more rags. Up and down, until my grandmother was satisfied. Then the morris chairs, whose slats fell off every once in a while with our jumping, had to be polished and shined, and the cabinet, and all put back in their place.

She wasted nothing. Everything turned into something else when it was too old to be everything. Dresses turned into skirts and then into underwear. Shoes turned into slippers. Corn, too hard for eating, turned into meal. My grandmother herself never wore anything new, except when she went out. She had two dresses and a petticoat hanging in the wardrobe for those times. At home, she dressed in layers of old clothing, half-slip over dress, old socks, because her feet were always cold, and slippers, cut out of old shoes. A safety pin or two, anchored to the front of her dress or the hem of her skirt, to pin up our falling underwear or ruined zippers.

My grandmother didn't like it when we changed the furniture around. She said that changing the furniture around was a sign to people that we didn't have any money. Only people with no money changed their furniture around and around all the time. My grandmother had various lectures on money, to protect us from the knowledge that we had little or none. At night, we could not drop pennies on the floor, for thieves may be passing and think that we did have money and come to rob us.

My grandmother always said that money ran through your hands like water, especially when you had so many mouths to feed. Every two or three weeks money would run out of my grandmother's hands. These times were as routine as our chores or going to school or the games which we played. My grandmother had stretched it over stewed chicken, rice, provisions and macaroni pie on Sundays, split peas soup on Mondays, fish and bake on Tuesdays, corn meal dumplings and salt cod on Wednesdays, okra and rice on Thursdays, split peas, salt cod, and rice on Fridays, and pelau on Saturdays. By the time the third week of the month came around my grandmother's stretching would become apparent. She carried a worried look on her face and was more silent than usual. We understood this to be a sign of lean times and times when we could not bother my grandmother or else we would get one of her painful explanations across our ears. Besides it really hurt my grandmother not to give us what we needed, as we all settled with her into a depressive hungry silence.

At times we couldn't help but look accusingly at her. Who else could we blame for the gnawing pain in our stomachs and the dry corners of our mouths. We stared at my grandmother hungrily, while she avoided our eyes. We would all gather around her as she lay in bed, leaning against her or sitting on the floor beside the bed, all in silence. We devoted these silences to hope—hope that something would appear to deliver us, perhaps my grandfather, with provisions from the country—and to wild imagination that we would be rich some day and be able to buy pounds of sugar and milk. But sweet water, a thin mixture of water and sugar, was all the balm for our hunger. When even that did not show itself in abundance, our silences were even deeper. We drank water, until our stomachs became distended and nautical.

My little sister, who came along a few years after we had grown accus-

tomed to the routine of hunger and silence, could never grasp the importance of these moments. We made her swear not to cry for food when there
wasn't any and, to give her credit, she did mean it when she promised. But
the moment the hungry silence set in, she began to cry, begging my grandmother for sweet water. She probably cried out of fear that we would never
eat again, and admittedly our silences were somewhat awesome, mixtures
of despair and grief, made potent by the weakness which the heavy hot sun
brought on in our bodies.

We resented my little sister for these indiscretions. She reminded us that
we were hungry, a thought we had been transcending in our growing asceti-
cism, and we felt sorry for my grandmother having to answer her cries.
Because it was only then that my grandmother relented and sent one of us
to borrow a cup of sugar from the woman across the street, Tante. One of
us suffered the indignity of crossing the road and repeating haltingly whatever words my grandmother had told her to say.

My grandmother always sent us to Tante, never to Mrs Sommard who
was a religious woman and our next door neighbour, nor to Mrs Benjamin
who had money and was our other next door neighbour. Mrs Sommard
only had prayers to give and Mrs Benjamin, scorn. But Tante, with nothing, like us, would give whatever she could manage. Mrs Sommard was a
Seventh Day Adventist and the only time my grandmother sent one of us
to beg a cup of something, Mrs Sommard sent back a message to pray. My
grandmother took it quietly and never sent us there again and told us to
have respect for Mrs Sommard because she was a religious woman and
believed that God would provide.

Mrs Sommard's husband, Mr Sommard, took two years to die. For the
two years that he took to die the house was always brightly lit. Mr
Sommard was so afraid of dying that he could not sleep and didn't like it
when darkness fell. He stayed awake all night and all day for two years and
kept his wife and daughter awake too. My grandmother said he pinched
them if they fell asleep and told them that if he couldn't sleep, they shouldn't
sleep either. How this ordeal squared with Mrs Sommard's religiousness,
my grandmother was of two minds about. Either the Lord was trying Mrs
Sommard's faith or Mrs Sommard had done some wickedness that the Lord
was punishing her for.

The Benjamins, on the other side, we didn't know where they got their
money from, but they seemed to have a lot of it. For Mrs Benjamin sometimes told our friend Patsy not to play with us. Patsy lived with Mrs
Benjamin, her grandmother; Miss Lena, her aunt and her grandfather, Mr
Benjamin. We could always smell chicken that Miss Lena was cooking from
their pot, even when our house fell into silence.

The Benjamins were the reason that my grandmother didn't like us running down into the backyard to pick up mangoes when the wind blew them down. She felt ashamed that we would show such hunger in the eyes of people who had plenty. The next thing was that the Benjamins' rose mango tree was so huge, it spread half its body over their fence into our yard. We felt that this meant that any mangoes that dropped on our side belonged to us and Patsy Benjamin and her family thought that it belonged to them. My grandmother took their side, not because she thought that they were right, but she thought that if they were such greedy people, they should have the mangoes. Let them kill themselves on it, she said. So she made us call to Mrs Benjamin and give them all the rose mangoes that fell in our yard. Mrs Benjamin thought that we were doing this out of respect for their status and so she would often tell us with superiority to keep the mangoes, but my grandmother would decline. We, grudgingly, had to do the same and, as my grandmother warned us, without a sad look on our faces. From time to time, we undermined my grandmother's pride, by pretending not to find any rose mangoes on the ground, and hid them in a stash under the house or deep in the backyard under leaves. Since my grandmother never ventured from the cover and secrecy of the walls of the house, or that area in the yard hidden by the walls, she was never likely to discover our lie.

Deep in the backyard, over the drain which we called the canal, we were out of range of my grandmother's voice, since she refused to shout, and the palms of her hands, but not her eyes. We were out of reach of her broomstick which she flung at our fleeing backs or up into one of the mango trees where one of us was perched, escaping her beatings.

Deep in the back of the yard, we smoked sponge wood and danced in risqué fashion and uttered the few cuss words that we knew and made up calypsos. There, we pretended to be big people with children. We put our hands on our hips and shook our heads, as we had seen big people do, and complained about having so much children, children, children to feed.

My grandmother showed us how to kill a chicken, holding its body in the tub and placing the scrubbing board over it leaving the neck exposed, then with a sharp knife quickly cut the neck, leaving the scrubbing board over the tub. Few of us became expert at killing a chicken. The beating of the dying fowl would frighten us and the scrubbing board would slip whereupon the headless bird would escape, its warm blood still gushing, propelling its body around and around the house. My grandmother would order us to go get the chicken, which was impossible since the direction that the chicken took and the speed with which it ran were indeterminate. She didn't like us making our faces up in distaste at anything that had to do with

eating or cleaning or washing. So, whoever let the chicken escape or whoever refused to go get it would have to stand holding it for five minutes until
my grandmother made a few turns in the house, then they would have to
pluck it and gut it and wrap the feathers and innards in newspaper, throwing it in the garbage. That person may well have to take the garbage out for
a week. If you can eat, my grandmother would say, you can clean and you
shouldn't scorn a life.

One day we found a huge balloon down in the backyard. It was the
biggest balloon we'd ever had and it wasn't even around Christmas time.
Patsy Benjamin, who played through her fence with us, hidden by the rose
mango tree from her aunt Lena, forgot herself and started shouting that it
was hers. She began crying and ran complaining to her aunt that we had
stolen her balloon. Her aunt dragged her inside and we ran around our
house fighting and pulling at each other, swearing that the balloon belonged
to this one or that one. My grandmother grabbed one of us on the fourth
or fifth round and snatched the balloon away. We never understood the
cause for this, since it was such a find and never quite understood my
grandmother muttering something about Tante's son leaving his 'nastiness'
everywhere. Tante herself had been trying to get our attention, as we raced
round and round the house. This was our first brush with what was called
'doing rudeness'. Later, when my big sister began to menstruate and stopped
hanging around with us, we heard from our classmates that men menstruat-
ed too and so we put two and two together and figured that Tante's son's
nastiness must have to do with his menstruation.

On our way home from school one day, a rumour blazed its way
through all the children just let out from school that there was a male sanitary napkin at the side of the road near the pharmacy on Royal Road. It was
someone from the Catholic girl's school who started it and troupe after
troupe of school children hurried to the scene, to see it. The rumour spread
back and forth, along the Coffee, with school children corroborating and tes-
tifying that they had actually seen it. By the time we got there, we only saw
an empty brown box which we skirted, a little frightened at first, then
pressed in for a better view. There really wasn't very much more to see and
we figured that someone must have removed it before we got there.
Nevertheless, we swore that we had seen it and continued to spread the
rumour along the way, until we got home, picking up the chant which was
building as all the girls whipped their fingers at the boys on the street singing,
'Boys have periods TOOOOOO!' We couldn't ask my grandmother if men
had periods, but it was the source of weeks of arguing back and forth.

When my period came, it was my big sister who told me what to do.
My grandmother was not there. By then, my mother had returned from

England and an unease had fallen over us. Anyway, when I showed my big sister, she shoved a sanitary napkin and two pins at me and told me not to play with boys anymore and that I couldn't climb the mango tree anymore and that I shouldn't fly around the yard anymore either. I swore everyone not to tell my mother when she got home from work but they all did anyway and my mother with her air, which I could never determine since I never looked her in the face, said nothing.

My mother had returned. We had anticipated her arrival with a mixture of pride and fear. These added to an uncomfortable sense that things would not be the same, because in the weeks preceding her arrival my grandmother revved up the old warning about us not being able to be rude or disobey anymore, that we would have to be on our best behaviour to be deserving of this woman who had been to England, where children were not like us. She was my grandmother's favourite daughter too, so my grandmother was quite proud of her. When she arrived, some of us hung back behind my grandmother's skirt, embarrassing her before my mother who, my grandmother said, was expecting to meet well brought up children who weren't afraid of people.

To tell the truth, we were expecting a white woman to come through the door, the way my grandmother had described my mother and the way the whole street that we lived on treated the news of my mother's return, as if we were about to ascend in their respect. The more my grandmother pushed us forward to say hello to my mother, the more we clung to her skirts until she finally had to order us to say hello. In the succeeding months, my grandmother tried to push us toward my mother. She looked at us with reproach in her eyes that we did not acknowledge my mother's presence and her power. My mother brought us wieners and fried eggs and mashed potatoes, which we had never had before, and said that she longed for kippers, which we did not know. We enjoyed her strangeness but we were uncomfortable under her eyes. Her suitcase smelled strange and foreign and for weeks despite our halting welcome of her, we showed off in the neighbourhood that we had someone from away.

Then she began ordering us about and the wars began.

Those winters in England, when she must have bicycled to Hampstead General Hospital from which we once received a letter and a postcard with her smiling to us astride a bicycle, must have hardened the smile which my grandmother said that she had and which was dimly recognizable from the photograph. These winters, which she wrote about and which we envied as my sister read them to us, she must have hated. And the thought of four ungrateful children who deprived her of a new dress or stockings to travel London, made my mother unmerciful on her return.

We would run to my grandmother, hiding behind her skirt, or dive for the sanctuary of my grandmother's room. She would enter, accusing my grandmother of interfering in how she chose to discipline 'her' children. We were shocked. Where my mother acquired this authority we could not imagine. At first my grandmother let her hit us, but finally she could not help but intervene and ask my mother if she thought that she was beating animals. Then my mother would reply that my grandmother had brought us up as animals. This insult would galvanize us all against my mother. A back answer would fly from the child in question who would, in turn, receive a slap from my grandmother, whereupon my grandmother would turn on my mother with the length of her tongue. When my grandmother gave someone the length of her tongue, it was given in a low, intense, and damning tone, punctuated by chest beating and the biblical, 'I have nurtured a viper in my bosom.'

My mother often became hysterical and left the house, crying what my grandmother said were crocodile tears. We had never seen an adult cry in a rage before. The sound in her throat was a gagging yet raging sound, which frightened us, but it was the sight of her tall threatening figure which cowed us. Later, she lost hope that we would ever come around to her and she began to think and accuse my grandmother of setting her children against her. I recall her shoes mostly, white and thick, striding across the tiny house.

These accusations increased and my grandmother began to talk of dying and leaving us. Once or twice, my mother tried to intervene on behalf of one or the other of us in a dispute with my grandmother. There would be silence from both my grandmother and us, as to the strangeness of this intervention. It would immediately bring us on side to my grandmother's point of view and my mother would find herself in the company of an old woman and some children who had a life of their own—who understood their plays, their dances, gestures, and signals, who were already intent on one another. My mother would find herself standing outside these gestures into which her inroads were abrupt and incautious. Each foray made our dances more secretive, our gestures subterranean.

Our life stopped when she entered the door of the house, conversations closed in mid-sentence and elegant gestures with each other turned to sharp asexual movements.

My mother sensed these closures since, at first, we could not hide these scenes fast enough to escape her jealous glance. In the end, we closed our scenes ostentatiously in her presence. My grandmother's tongue lapping over a new story or embellishing an old one would become brusque in, 'Tell your mother good evening.' We, telling my grandmother a story or receiving her assurance that when we get rich, we would buy a this or a that, while picking out her grey hairs, would fall silent. We longed for when my mother stayed away. Most of all we longed for when she worked nights. Then we could sit all evening in the grand darkness of my grandmother's stories.

When the electricity went out and my grandmother sat in the rocking chair, the wicker seat bursting from the weight of her hips, the stories she spun, no matter how often we heard them, languished over the darkness whose thickness we felt, rolling in and out of the veranda. Some nights the darkness, billowing about us would be suffused by the perfume of lady-of-the-night, a white, velvet, yellow, orchid-like flower which grew up the street in a neighbour's yard. My grandmother's voice, brown and melodic, about how my grandfather, 'Yuh Papa, one dark night, was walking from Ortoire to Guayaguayare . . .'

The road was dark and my grandfather walked alone with his torch light pointed toward his feet. He came to a spot in the road, which suddenly chilled him. Then, a few yards later, he came to a hot spot in the road, which made him feel for a shower of rain. Then, up ahead, he saw a figure and behind him he heard its footsteps. He kept walking, the footsteps pursued him dragging a chain, its figure ahead of him. If he had stopped, the figure, which my grandfather knew to be a legahoo, would take his soul; so my grandfather walked steadily, shining his torchlight at his feet and repeating psalm twenty-three, until he passed the bridge by the sea wall and passed the savannah, until he arrived at St Mary's, where he lived with my grandmother.

It was in the darkness on the veranda, in the honey chuckle back of my grandmother's throat, that we learned how to catch a soucouyant and a lajabless and not to answer to the 'hoop! hoop! hoop!' of duennes, the souls of dead children who were not baptized, come to call living children to play with them. To catch a soucouyant, you had to either find the barrel of rain water where she had left her skin and throw pepper in it or sprinkle salt or rice on your doorstep so that when she tried to enter the house to take your blood, she would have to count every grain of salt or rice before entering. If she dropped just one grain or miscounted, she would have to start all over again her impossible task and in the mornings she would be discovered, distraught and without her skin on the doorstep.

When we lived in the country before moving to the street, my grandmother had shown us, walking along the beach in back of the house, how to identify a duenne foot. She made it with her heel in the sand and then, without laying the ball of her foot down, imprinted her toes in the front of the heel print.

Back in the country, my grandmother walked outside and up and down the beach and cut coconut with a cutlass and dug, chip-chip, on the beach and slammed the kitchen window one night just as a mad man leapt to it to try to get into the house. My grandmother said that, as a child in the country, my mother had fallen and hit her head, ever since which she had been pampered and given the best food to eat and so up to this day she was very moody and could go off her head at the slightest. My mother took this liberty whenever she returned home, skewing the order of our routines in my grandmother.

It seemed that my grandmother had raised more mad children than usual, for my uncle was also mad and one time he held up a gas station which was only the second time that my grandmother had to leave the house, again on the arm of my big sister. We readied my grandmother then and she and my big sister and I went to the courthouse on the Promenade to hear my uncle's case. They didn't allow children in, but they allowed my big sister as my grandmother had to lean on her. My uncle's case was not heard that morning, so we left the court and walked up to the Promenade. We had only gone a few steps when my grandmother felt faint. My sister held the smelling salts at her nostrils, as we slowly made our way as inconspicuously as we could to a bench near the bandstand. My grandmother cried, mopping her eyes with her handkerchief and talked about the trouble her children had caused her. We, all three, sat on the bench on the Promenade near the bandstand, feeling stiff and uncomfortable. My grandmother said my uncle had allowed the public to wash their mouth in our family business. She was tired by then and she prayed that my mother would return and take care of us, so that she would be able to die in peace.

Soon after, someone must have written my mother to come home, for we received a letter saying that she was finally coming.

We had debated what to call my mother over and over again and came to no conclusions. Some of the words sounded insincere and disloyal, since they really belonged to my grandmother, although we never called her by those names. But when we tried them out for my mother, they hung so cold in the throat that we were discouraged immediately. Calling my mother by her given name was too presumptuous, even though we had always called all our aunts and uncles by theirs. Unable to come to a decision we abandoned each other to individual choices. In the end, after our vain attempts to form some word, we never called my mother by any name. If we needed to address her we stood about until she noticed that we were there and then we spoke. Finally, we never called my mother.

All of the words which we knew belonged to my grandmother. All of them, a voluptuous body of endearment, dependence, comfort, and infinite knowing. We were all full of my grandmother, she had left us full and empty of her. We dreamed in my grandmother and we woke up in her, bleary-eyed and gesturing for her arm, her elbows, her smell. We jockeyed with each other, lied to each other, quarrelled with each other and with her for the boon of lying close to her, sculpting ourselves around the roundness of her back. Braiding her hair and oiling her feet. We dreamed in my grandmother and we woke up in her, bleary-eyed and gesturing for her lap, her arms, her elbows, her smell, the fat flesh of her arms. We fought, tricked each other for the crook between her thighs and calves. We anticipated where she would sit and got there before her. We bought her achar and paradise plums.

My mother had walked the streets of London, as the legend went, with one dress on her back for years, in order to send those brown envelopes, the stamps from which I saved in an old album. But her years of estrangement had left her angry and us cold to her sacrifice. She settled into fits of fury. Rage which raised welts on our backs, faces, and thin legs. When my grandmother had turned away, laughing from us, saying there was no place to beat, my mother found room.

Our silences which once warded off hunger now warded off her blows. She took this to mean impudence and her rages whipped around our silences more furiously than before. I, the most ascetic of us all, sustained the most terrible moments of her rage. The more enraged she grew, the more silent I became, the harder she hit, the more wooden, I. I refined this silence into a jewel of the most sacred sandalwood, finely-grained, perfumed, mournful yet stoic. I became the only inhabitant of a cloistered place carrying my jewel of fullness and emptiness, voluptuousness and scarcity. But she altered the silences profoundly.

Before, with my grandmother, the silences had company, were peopled by our hope. Now, they were desolate.

She had left us full and empty of her. When someone took the time to check, there was no photograph of my grandmother, no figure of my grandmother in layers of clothing and odd-sided socks, no finger stroking the air in reprimand, no arm under her chin at the front window or crossed over her breasts waiting for us.

My grandmother had never been away from home for more than a couple of hours and only three times that I could remember. So her absence was lonely. We visited her in the hospital every evening. They had put her in a room with eleven other people. The room was bare. You could see underneath all the beds from the doorway and the floors were always scrubbed with that hospital smelling antiseptic which reeked its own sickliness and which I detested for years after. My grandmother lay in one of the beds nearest the door and I remember my big sister remarking to my grandmother that she should have a better room, but my grandmother hushed her saying that it was alright and anyway she wouldn't be there for long and the nurses were nice to her. From the chair beside my grandmother's bed in the hospital you could see the parking lot on Chancery Lane. I would sit with my grandmother, looking out the window and describing the scene to her. You could also see part of the wharf and the gulf of Paria which was murky where it held to the wharf. And St Paul's Church, where I was confirmed, even though I did not know the catechism and only mumbled when Canon Farquar drilled us in it.

Through our talks at the window my grandmother made me swear that I would behave for my mother. We planned, when I grew up and went away, that I would send for my grandmother and that I would grow up to be something good, that she and I and Eula and Ava and Kat and Genevieve would go to Guayaguayare and live there forever. I made her promise that she would not leave me with my mother.

It was a Sunday afternoon, the last time that I spoke with my grandmother. I was describing a bicycle rider in the parking lot and my grandmother promised to buy one for me when she got out of hospital.

My big sister cried and curled herself up beneath the radio when my grandmother died. Genevieve's face was wet with tears, her front braid pulled over her nose, she, sucking her thumb.

When they brought my grandmother home, it was after weeks in the white twelve-storey hospital. We took the curtains down, leaving all the windows and doors bare, in respect for the dead. The ornaments, doilies, and plastic flowers were removed and the mirrors and furniture covered with white sheets. We stayed inside the house and did not go out to play. We kept the house clean and we fell into our routine of silence when faced with hunger. We felt alone. We did not believe. We thought that it was untrue. In disbelief, we said of my grandmother, 'Mama can't be serious!'

The night of the wake, the house was full of strangers. My grandmother would never allow this. Strangers, sitting and talking everywhere, even in my grandmother's room. Someone, a great aunt, a sister of my grandmother, whom we had never seen before, turned to me sitting on the sewing machine and ordered me in a stern voice to get down. I left the room, slinking away, feeling abandoned by my grandmother to strangers.

I never cried in public for my grandmother. I locked myself in the bathroom or hid deep in the backyard and wept. I had learned as my grandmother had taught me, never to show people your private business.

When they brought my grandmother home the next day, we all made a line to kiss her goodbye. My littlest sister was afraid; the others smiled for my grandmother. I kissed my grandmother's face hoping that it was warm.

JANICE KULYK KEEFER

❧

GOING OVER THE BARS

for Stella Karpus

*Breathe out, breathe in, breathe out, breathe in. In must always follow out for the whole
business to go on at all. Even if it feels like rubbing your lungs back and forth along a
grater, even if you have to throw yourself into the effort, the way you once threw yourself
into an office assignment or a piece of housework. Out, in, breathe out, breathe in*

For a moment, it feels as though she's swinging, abandoning her body to a
plank of wood, ropes burning the palms of her hands—a surge of air. *Oh I
do think it's the pleasantest thing / Ever a child can do.* An old rhyme, misremem-
bered. Once she knew it by heart, once she'd spent whole afternoons swinging at the park, hanging her head back till her hair swept the ground, the
whole world upside down as she aimed her toes at the sky.

Up in the air and over the trees / Till I can see so far. Words going back and
forth, in and out of her head as if she were eight years old and swinging so
high she gets dizzy. Never so high that she'd lose control and go sailing over
the bars. Some mornings she'd find the ropes of the swings wound crazily
around the crossbar—someone's gone over, she'd think, and back away, avoiding the swings for the rest of that day, and perhaps a whole week after. *Byrd
Ellen went widdershins around a church, and no one caught sight of her again on God's
good earth.* Going over the bars she'd fly right off, and never come back at all.

Breathe out, breathe in, breathe out, breathe in. Dizzy. It's because of the medicine fraying the links between nerve and brain. But how can it stop her
from feeling the scrape of their feet down the thinning tunnels of her blood,
the way they jostle against her bones? Her bones, bitten to harsh lace.
There are holes under the scars which were her breasts, yet still they keep
on, voracious, racing from one watering hole to another. But they are nearly done for, those insatiable travellers. Soon they'll find themselves without
a destination, never mind a road to take them there. Her blood and bones
will suddenly give out like a bridge suspended over a gorge, swaying, snapping as they rush across. *Breathe out, breathe in, breathe out, breathe in.*

Who decided it was best for them to bring her here? Her husband has
arranged for her bed to face the window; he's arranged for the window to
look out onto a garden, but when she does manage to open her eyes she

can only stare at the ceiling. At home she'd look up to find rivers crackling an endless plain; the canals of Mars were there, and bruises from the moon's sallow face. A map, a reassurance like her doctor's jokes, the press of her husband's hand, the trusting incomprehension of her children. But here the ceiling is a mirror showing skin like lumps of powdered ivory. The travellers themselves are white, devouring her with stiff, colourless lips. She thinks of plagues passing over the face of the land: locusts, sirocco winds. There is a drought inside her; arteries, veins turned into skeleton leaves, a fringe unravelling.

Trees, she thinks, have the best of death, their flesh compact, burning clear and dry. She remembers them in winter, black-haired skeletons against a blank of sky. Or well and truly dead: branches polished beyond all possibility of bud or leaf—petrified lightning against blue summer air. And the way the leaves slough off—the leathery smell, the not unpleasant sourness of their decay. Flesh is a nicer word than meat. Once she'd felt shamed by its sheer, sickened sprawl inside of her; now there is almost nothing left of it, they have worn it down with their rats' feet, rats' mouths, rats the size and speed of tigers. *Breathe out, breathe in.*

It's this shifting an iron bar from one hand to the other, the weight of air that makes her lungs ache. It's the funeral scent of the flowers; iris clogged in its caul, tulips reeling on worm-soft stems. Today he's come in unexpectedly; he should be at work, should be with the children. He's here, now, because he knows the flowers make it impossible for her to find her breath, to throw it out again, lift up her hands to catch it back.

He takes the flowers and the vase away. Now she won't have to hear the noise the tulips make as their petals distend, the hiss as the iris shrivels. Now she will be able to hear her breath coming in, going out, the slow, unsteady creak of a swing. . . . It takes him a long time to get rid of the flowers and return to her bed, to his waiting. Once he'd waited for her at airports and hotels, waited for her to finish dressing the children or undressing herself. Now he waits for the moment when a line fine as a hair will sever his life from hers. *Out, in. Breathe in after out, out after in, or the swing will stop, altogether*

Death may be an accomplishment of which we're all capable. Dying—at least, her kind of dying—is another matter. It is loss of control. Not surrender, but loss: progressive, irreversible, absolute. Out of an infinitude of cells all perfectly ordered and obedient, one becomes malignant, *disposed to rebel, disaffected, malcontent.* One cell deserting the ranks, changing itself, creating another in its own likeness. And that other spawns another, and another. Functions not so dissimilar to her own: to eat, to reproduce. To journey:

metastasis. Her body an unknown continent discovered, devoured by travellers who burn so many bridges that there's no road back, nothing to go on to. They trespass on the routes of her blood and brain; they tunnel her bones. And her body answers back by closing shop, boarding the windows, locking the doors of whatever's left unvisited. They call it failure—her kidneys are failing, her liver and spleen. Her body an examination paper with Xs piling up.

At first she'd dismissed the disaffected and rebellious cells. 'I'm not giving an inch, not half an inch—you think you can do as you please, change as you will, but I'm not letting even one of you get your way.' Her friends had applauded her spirit; she was a fighter and a winner; she wouldn't walk but swagger through the shadow valley. But something—not her friends, not her family, not even her own bravado—let her down. She'd had to switch tactics, lecture them the way she might have lived to lecture her children in another ten years. 'What you're doing is stupid, useless—can't you understand? Like it or not, I'm the one in authority here—you have to play by my rules.' At last, she'd tried reason. 'Don't you see that you're eating the hand that feeds you? If I'm gone, how will you travel, where will you go? It's completely illogical—in nobody's interest, surely you must understand.'

And then she'd refused all parley—they were no longer rebels but an invading army. *Exterminate all the brutes!* They had been scalped, torched, drowned with chemicals. Five, three, perhaps only one escaped the assaults that poisoned her, as well. Fleeing to undefended ground, pitching camp and recruiting forces, sending out vanguards to occupy still farther reaches of a land lush, helpless as grass. That was the point at which her doctor had stopped joking and her husband's hand had not seemed quite so firm when it grasped her own. Her children's clear and perfect faces became smudged when they looked at her; how could she help them when she couldn't even save herself? She'd spoken one last time, not to rebels or a victorious army, but to an unimaginable horde of travellers. 'I see, now. You're not invading me; my body sent you, it has even kindly provided you with an itinerary. You may not even know that you're destroying yourselves by killing me— you may not even care. It's not you who are making me die. My body's committing suicide, and I'm given nothing at all to say in the matter. My body has simply stopped talking to me.'

After the first operation he'd brought her home, put her in the spare bedroom, the one where they'd hung the old, bleached-out curtains with their tenuous patterns of gazebos, lovers, and gardens. She was content. Here she could rest; here she could save something from the wreckage, knit up the forces of something she could now call, with all formality, her soul. This was the occasion to read Dante, to listen to nothing but Bach. But the print scratched her eyes, the notes blurred into one inchoate adagio. Very well, she would shut eyes, shut ears, draw the curtains so that the lovers drowned in the muggy light that struggled through the lining. She would lie in a square white bed, enwomb herself, unfold the truth of everything she'd been taught, everything she'd wanted to be true. All the birthing and growing and coupling for which the cells first joined themselves: whipcord sperm, moon-faced egg—this counted for nothing. Only this malignant birth was real, parthenogenesis of rebel cells. Born to die, this was the truth her body uncovered under all its layers of skin, muscle, bone grown fragile as tissue paper.

Yet it meant nothing. Knowing brought no peace, no certainty, no end of wanting. When her children came into her room she still stretched out her arms to hold them. Holding them too long, too tight, breathing in the bread-and-butter scents of their skin and hair. They were very good, they let her hold them—they were afraid of her. It was the truth, though her husband denied it. He wasn't concerned with what was true, only with the angles of belief, measured by love's geometry. He was quite clear, quite confident in this: he wasn't dying.

Everything she'd known and felt, watched and thought through, everything she'd expected to have to hand—a rod, a staff to keep her place, guarding whatever ground she'd gained—she'd lost it. And her dying brought no revelation, only confirmation of obscurity. But she wouldn't give in to it. If she'd lost control of what was happening to her body, and why, she could at least dictate the how and where. She would *not* be taken from her home, dragged over the border from pain to stupor, dumped into a gleaming terminal where strangers would speak to her only in charts and graphs, syringes, intravenous bags. But in the end she was taken, dragged, and dumped. Then *she* was lectured to and reasoned with: *You need special drugs, special care. Your husband can't cope anymore. It's become too hard on the children.* The ambulance attendants were angels, substandard issue; they lifted her as clumsily as if they'd been using wings, not hands. She couldn't refuse them with her body, which had refused her orders for so long, now; how could she refuse them with her mind, bumbling slow, soft circles round a wick of morphine.

Once out of nature I will never take / My bodily form from any living thing. What made the poet think he'd be given any say in the matter? Metempsychosis, her soul sidling into the body of a dog, a cat, a rat—or perhaps just such another one as she, a body that will suddenly and for no reason whatsoever turn on itself after thirty years of working perfectly, the cells unfathomably obedient, so many of them reciting their messages word for word, relaying the codes through blood and tissue and across placental seas. Her children carry her body inside them the way she once carried theirs. Her body and its switch, the mind, but not her soul, psyche, *pneuma*–whatever it is that lifts her onto the wooden plank–pull it back, back, and then release her into an arc of air. *Breathe out, breathe in*

Those who hold that the soul perishes with the body are consigned to fire, on the authority of a great poet. And yet she could never acquiesce to an eternity of bliss, that potpourri of rose and fire. She cannot even think of angels except as white cockatiels, talons and tail feathers clipped, twisting their heads to the side of short, arthritic necks and croaking *holy, holy, holy*. She has read about accidental Lazari expiring momentarily on operating tables, pacing vestibules of foggy light before their lives click on again. Do we at least get the afterlife we desire? Or does it depend on whether we perform our deaths the way we should? She is as nervous about this as she was about piano recitals, passing exams, taking off her clothes for her first lover. And yet it seems so simple–all she has to do when the time comes is to assume transparency. Her soul will weigh no more than a scrap of cellophane, than breath on a mirror. It will float out of her body the way paper rushes up the flue of a chimney, the way children jump off a swing in full sail.

Breathe in, breathe out. . . . Her husband visits after work, every day–he has stopped bringing the children; they are staying with their aunt in a different part of the city. He brings her their crayon drawings, stick figures drawn with the simplicity that certainty inspires: a circle and five lines = a body. Crayon lines cannot be erased, but only scratched away, and even if the colour's gone, a line will remain like a cut that's bled dry. She had held her daughters, sung to them, bathed them, scolded them for their four and two years of life; they will remember her, at worst, as a stick-figure pinned to a square white bed; at best, as a temporary cradle of arms and breasts and lap. She told him, as soon as she knew, that he should remarry. They were drinking the bottle of *Liebfraumilch* he had bought on the way home from the doctor's (Chekhov's physician had ordered *him* champagne). 'A wife for you, a mother for the children'–she'd said she didn't want him to play Heathcliffe to her Cathy. He'd made a face that wasn't even a passable imitation of Olivier.

I am incomparably above and beyond you all. These will be her last words, if she has voice enough to speak them, and if anyone happens to be there to hear. Such things happen–everyone dies alone, though some are fortunate enough to have an audience. For it will be a show–of confidence, of unconcern, of panic or simply transformed energies; the effort her body now expends in crumpling and uncrumpling the paper bags of her lungs, sending her blood on its sluggish rounds, dispensing endless hospitality to footsore, hungry tumours, will go into lighting sure, slow fires of decay. Malignant cells and healthy—*All are punished.*

Breathe out, breathe in. She'd thought to go about her dying with a certain style. At first she'd entertained illusions the way you do the kind of guest you're certain to impress. But it came to nothing. She remembered a film she once saw, an image of a large, moon-faced woman cradling a death's-head in a muslin bonnet. But no *magna mater* has come to offer her the breast. Death and the maiden? He's stood her up—she hasn't caught so much as a glimpse of his spindle-shanks, a twirl of his scythe. Perhaps because she has no flowers to give Him, having twice rolled the stone away to bring her children out. They haven't yet learned to mourn the death of a pet—now they will be marked forever: 'Their mother died when they were very young.' A letter of introduction to *Herr Angst.*

Her husband holds her hands. They are an arrangement of bones—doesn't he fear they will fall apart in his hands, a game of pick-up sticks? Her husband pays his calls and she knows his presence in the way she knows that Saturn and Jupiter orbit the sun: invisibly, at an incalculable distance. *Breathe out, breathe in, swing up, swing down, hold tight to the ropes, hold tight.* . . . He is holding her hands and bending his face towards her, eyes wide open like the tulips she made him throw away. Murmurings, measurements, a jigger of morphine. Shaking out the long, fine hair she no longer has; running to the swings at the end of the park.

Incomparably above and beyond. He leans in over her, asking her what it is she wants, can he get her anything, is she in pain? How to tell him she feels nothing save the rush of air against her face as she swings higher, higher. She is somewhere between body and mind—it is too difficult to explain and she has lost her voice, just as she's lost the ability to curl her fingers round even a child's hand, to return a pressure. *Breathe out, breathe in.* But she wants him to understand this being in-between. It is something like looking at colour transparencies whose outlines haven't quite meshed, so there's a gap between where the line is drawn and the colour begins. A gap. Not absence, and certainly not an abyss, but just an unexpected space to slip through. Like that possibility, high up on a swing, of pumping so hard you go up and over the bars.

She'd never been able to do it as a child, and she'd forbidden her own children to try. Because they would break bones, smash skulls, end up in hospital. *Swing up, swing down, swing harder, higher.* She's been so stupid to have left it behind her, left it so long as if it were shameful, a childish thing. When she'd taken her own children to the playground she'd avoided the swings, sitting instead on a corner of the sand-box or patrolling the rim of the paddling pool, trying not to get splashed. Now she doesn't care if any-one sees her like this, alone and free, head down and her long hair brush-ing the ground. The world turned upside down, a sky of packed earth with stones for stars.

Swinging back and forth, higher and higher till the bars creak and groan. *Over the wall, and up in the trees / Till I can see so far.* She can see every-thing now; the cracked ceiling over her head pulls back, like flesh from the sides of a wound. It shows whatever it is that lies in the gap between out-line and colour. Dante, Bach, *Mehr Licht.* But all that fills her head now is a children's rhyme. *Out, in, out.* The swing comes up to its highest point; she's gripping the rope so tight it tears her hands. Something splits inside, a hair-line crack; something fiery, clear as glass spills out. *In, out. Out.*

Over the bars

JUDITH KALMAN

❧

THE COUNTY OF BIRCHES

My mother, Sári, met my father, Gábor, in a schoolhouse in September 1945. She sat with the women at the back of the schoolroom that smelled of dust and dry leaves and a trace of chalk, like ash. The evocation of ash was almost sensual. Powdery and soft as child's hair, and that unreal. Murmuring was subdued, because of those who weren't there.

The young men improvising the Rosh Hashanah service sat up front behind a lectern. One by one they stood to read the prayers they knew by heart, avoiding the eyes of those who had gathered.

'And this one?' Sári whispered. 'Who is the one pulling his ear like a sidelock? Kramer, you say, from Nyirbátor? And the one with red hair . . . ?'

She had drifted to her first husband's county when she had found no one of her own in Beregszász. In any event, the conference in Yalta had traded her hometown to the Soviets. She left while the boundaries were just dotted and pencilled in, as empty-handed as she'd arrived. What could she have taken that would have survived the war, a bolt of cloth from her mother's shop?

'What about this one, the big one? Weisz? Weisz, you say. What Weisz? Which Weisz? From where—Vaja? The Vaja Weiszes? No.' No. János had never mentioned any relations from that village.

Sári Friedlander Weisz shared Gábor's name by marriage. She would have passed him over like the rest had she not learned from the other women that he was head of local JOINT, where those who came back sought assistance. Gábor Weisz was the man to see about finding János.

Sári observed him reading. The voice tuneless but proficient, round head nodding to an age-old cadence, thick fingers turning the page ahead of his words, just like any old-fashioned davening Jew. He couldn't have been more different from her János. Weisz. The same name, and from the same county. It was a cruel coincidence that another Weisz, but of no shared blood, belonged to this sad scrap of earth.

The town of Nyiregyháza where Sári met Gábor is named for the birch tree, like many of the cities and hamlets of the plain in northeastern Hungary. This flatland is actually more distinguished by the acacias that grow profusely in its sandy soil than by anything we North Americans would recognize as birch. Nonetheless, my father's region abounds in tributes to the white-barked tree. The Nyírség, it is called—the state of being birch—and its towns reflect this birchness in name if nothing else: Nyírmada, Nyírgyulaj, Nyírbátor, Nyírvásvári, Nyírmegges, Nyírjákó, Nyírvaja. The birch names are as ubiquitous as they are unpronounceable in English.

I begin here, when, after the service, Gábor passed through the congregation clasping hands. Round-faced Gábor, his nose long and sorrowful, his brown eyes initially shrinking from something so lovely as this woman with hair she threw back like a mare tossing its mane, accepted the hand Sári held out first. Sári Friedlander Weisz deliberately flaunted her hair as though it had grown thick and rich, long and dark, out of defiance. Her inborn vanity had not been expunged by near death from gas and starvation. She was a woman who had grown back hardier and harder, like a rosebush pruned close to the quick. Her hair had been fair before it was shaved.

I imagine myself conceived when my mother, tossing back her hair, felt my father's eyes upon her. Light-sensitive eyes that had sworn off joy. Deeply impressionable, they drank in her hair, brown and unfettered like his first wife Miri's had been only in the privacy of their bedroom, and her legs like a doe's slim and long, and her hand outstretched like a man's.

I begin at this point when my father's heart rekindles, though theoretically I go back further, before the great conflagration that reduced the numbers of his family from over a hundred to fewer than twenty, to the very beginning in fact of what we know of his ancestry, the pious vagabond without a surname called Itzig the Jew, which may have been a name generic to every Jew in the countryside. Itzig the Jew dragging his caftan in the dust of the Hungarian countryside at the end of the eighteenth century. I also hark back to the vineyards where my mother grew up and she and her six siblings played hide and seek, though it was forbidden to touch or trample the valuable fruit. (Among seven children, there are always a few young and small enough to wriggle belly down along the furrows, and fast enough to flee the raised fists of the field hands when they are discovered.) The story really starts with them, because who my parents once were and where they came from is a sum I repeatedly figure, trying to calculate how it adds up to me and my sister.

Like any child, most of all I care about the *I*. The I that clamours to speak for itself. This I owes less to the piety of generations of orthodox Jews or to the mercantile candour that characterized my mother's family than it does—its very inception—to the war that wedded them and to which it became a reluctant heir.

I knew this war like I knew the pale hand that held the spoon to my mouth. A hand moderately proportioned, distinguished by its smoothness and the incipient arthritic swell of its knuckles. I felt these joints when I played with her wedding band, working the ring up and over the first knuckle. Even the second one arched slightly, causing the ring to skin its surface. I have always known the war like I knew the impatient withdrawal of that hand if food was not taken quickly enough or if the ring slipped and fell from my stubby fingers. I have never not known of the war, though I don't recall hearing about it for the first time any more than I remember the first chime of my mother's voice or kiss of fresh air.

The war came to me with all that is good. It dawned on me like my own sweet flesh and buds of toes and the bright gold band that lay on the soft pads of my palm.

My mother's marriage, the one before Gábor, was hardly more than a courtship. Promenading arm-in-arm along the *korzo*, she in her smart suit and box hat, her military man uniformed, they made a decorative couple. People mated during the disastrous decade. People stepped out and showed off. They would wake up one day and the nightmare would be over. A beautiful girl like Sári, her parents reasoned, would need to be married. My mother dwelt on that, the promenading, the handsome figure they cut as a pair. It was all she had to tell us, all there was to that match.

And that on her wedding night she was slipped under the wire of the labour camp. She'd say that matter-of-factly. On her three-week honeymoon she was smuggled into the camp nightly. *Under the wire of the labour camp.*

Sári, my mother, who would squirm away impatiently whenever Gábor gave her fanny a friendly pat. Sári who, kissing me goodnight, would pull both my arms from under the bedclothes and press them firmly over the blankets, admonishing me to keep them that way. Sári who educated me early in the decorum of intimacy with the cryptic warning, 'Remember, it's always the man who takes and the woman who gives.' Her stance was prudish and ingenuous, as though she had never been touched by men's hands.

Yet every night for three weeks, she had allowed herself to be smuggled onto János's pallet. Risking military discipline, they made a love that must have been memorable. Love, among the coughs and groans and gases of male strangers. He waited for her in the dark beside the wire fence he and his friends had clipped and disguised, then pulled her through the dark into the barracks that smelled of boots and sweat. This young woman who had accepted his kisses coquettishly, always drawing back, who had lived sheltered in her parents' home, never exposed to danger. In that animal kingdom of men and their fear of death, I assume he used humour to disarm her. *Humour.* Because what we knew about my mother's first husband, we had heard from Gábor.

My father described János Weisz as a professional soldier, an officer in fact, who had served as captain in the Magyar army. Stripped by the so-called 'Jewish Laws' of his rank and career, János Weisz was conscripted into the labour service in the fall of 1941, just like Gábor and his brother Bandi, agronomists by profession, and their lawyer-brother Miklós. They were thrown together with village boys so poor and unschooled my father and his brothers had to take them in hand, show them what part of the boot to polish, simple village Jews whose main skill was the practice of Jewish tradition. János Weisz became their natural leader. When the actual sergeant turned out to be a Hungarian peasant much like themselves, pulled from his hut and put in charge of a regiment, no one questioned the authority of János Weisz over the ragtail band. The military officer was relieved to lie low in the local café.

The first labour service bore little resemblance to what would follow. As the war progressed, licence with life was taken increasingly. But when the labour service was first established, Hungarian Jews were emboldened to believe that if this was all that was going to happen—this and their restriction from professions and owning land—if what was to be taken from them fell short of breath, they could bear it. Labour service would kill Bandi in the copper mines of Bor and abandon János Weisz on the Russian front, but it saved my father from Buchenwald.

Gábor respected János Weisz. János was not a big man, but his military bearing gave him stature. He was younger than Gábor but, Gábor said, you could see that he was a man of the world, not easily intimidated. My father was impressed by the distance János Weisz kept from the rest of them, for the sake of authority.

Enlistment took place a few weeks before Jewish New Year. For many of the men in the troop this would be their first Rosh Hashanah away from home. Business and education had led Jews of the monied class out into the world, but it was usual for poor Jews of the countryside to live their lives in one village. Observance of the High Holy Days was through prayer and strict abstention from work. The village Jews assumed that the Lord would see to it that His Law, as intrinsic as the laws of nature, would prevail. Tension mounted as the High Holy Days approached and the Lord had not indicated what they should do.

János Weisz became aware that the poor Jews in his company had started looking on him as the unlikely instrument of the Lord. They were fearful and uncertain, bowed beneath centuries of religious tradition and cowed by secular authority. János Weisz knew the ways of their military and Christian masters. They didn't accept him as a real Jew; he was too worldly, too tainted by outside influences. But in his own way he was enough like them to understand their dilemma. János Weisz grew aloof. He withdrew and ate alone, giving no indication of how he would direct them on upcoming Rosh Hashanah.

Gábor and his brothers were orthodox Jews, but their God appreciated extenuating circumstances. They would risk His wrath before that of their taskmasters. Gábor sympathized with János Weisz, whose authority was unofficial at best. The slightest leniency on János Weisz's part, or suggestion that he was sparing the Jews, might unleash upon them all some devil sent to teach them a lesson, and on himself a personal penalty. But when a delegation begged Gábor to appeal to János Weisz to permit them to observe the Holy Day with respect, Gábor could not bring himself to refuse. He saw their beardless faces and heads shaved in military fashion, so incongruous with the pious stoop of their shoulders and bends of their noses and melancholy eyes, and he felt for them a deep pity. These people were helpless without their customs.

On *erev* Rosh Hashanah, the eve of the holiday, Gábor approached János Weisz. The mood in the barracks was heavy with dread. János Weisz was losing his patience. Had someone died here? Which one of them had been beaten recently, or received a bullet in the head? Which one of them had passed a day without eating? What were these fools mooning about? Did they not realize? Did they not know that Jews elsewhere in Europe were dying? Now here was Gábor Weisz, a man of good sense who should know better; what did Weisz expect of him?

'János,' Gábor began, 'the men are deeply distressed at having to work and desecrate this Holy Day.'

'Is that so?' The reply was curt and impassive. 'Let them make their apologies to the Lord then.'

Gábor was surprised and offended. He was a man of social standing, accustomed to respect in the Jewish community. Shrugging, he returned to the others.

Rosh Hashanah dawned, a day like any other. And as on any other day, János Weisz marched his men into the woods.

Ten days later, on Yom Kippur, no one appealed to the Jew in János Weisz. True, Gábor recalled, the mood among the company was funereal. But no one suggested observing the Day of Days. Those who chose would fast and pray while they worked.

János Weisz called up his company on Yom Kippur and marched them out. Each man carried his axe and his pack. At home, they would have walked the shortest distance to *shul*. They would have spent the day in prayer neither drinking nor eating until the first star appeared in the heavens. This Yom Kippur morning was cold and clear. The sun rose in a cloudless sky, brightening the firmament. Ordinarily it would have been the kind of fall day they might have liked being outside. The trees would wear long shadows; the men would take in the cold air, and watch clouds of breath affirm that they were alive. But because it was Yom Kippur, the boots marched into the forest bearing them like husks.

The discontent, unvoiced, was nonetheless pronounced. Day after day their company of Jews had felled timber to meet a daily quota. The military officer had come out once or twice to keep up a semblance of command, but regularly he was more than content to leave the company's direction to Weisz. Far from the front, and performing menial back-up services, their company had received only tertiary attention from the authorities. All Rosh Hashanah day they had wielded their axes. And if János Weisz had called just a fifteen-minute break for them to respectfully say a few prayers, there would have been none to know the difference. When his men looked at János Weisz, they did not see his military training. That meant nothing to them. What they saw was an apostate Jew, and he affected them with horror.

At noon of the holiest day of the year, János Weisz gave the order to stop. The axes ceased swinging. The men looked up. No one pulled bread from his pack. János Weisz barked, 'Quota met! Company, dismissed!' The men stood irresolutely, unsure of what was meant by the command. Clearly they had not achieved the day's requirement. 'Dismissed!' János Weisz shouted again.

Gábor summoned his two younger brothers. Arms around each other, they turned to face east to the Holy Land, as did each member of the company. Then, not daring to murmur their prayers aloud, they began to sway to an ingrained measure. Some had hats; others tore leaves from the trees to cover their heads, not to appear bareheaded before the Lord.

Outside, under the sun and among the trees, they celebrated the Holy One, praised be He. Gábor said later that the sun's rays had poured over them. In all his life, he never had—and never would again—feel so tangibly the presence of God. As a boy in the synagogue of his paternal grandfather he had not felt so near to the Deity. Nagyapa Weisz with his prophet's face and passion had awed the boy with the force of his faith. Yet here in the woods, in the open air, Gábor felt the Creator in His element. Gábor felt loved by God.

'What do you mean, Apu?' I asked, hearing this story for the third or fourth time. 'What do you mean, "loved by God"? How did He love you different from the others? Why you, Apu, why did God love you and not János Weisz or Bandi-bácsi or Miklós-bácsi, or your wife Miri-néni or your baby Clárika?'

'I don't say God loved only me, where do you get that?' he answered testily. 'I say that I felt at that moment that indeed God loved me. He loved us all to pour His glory over us. To let us worship Him so purely out in the open amid His creations. He could only love us to create for us such a wonderful moment. Terror and sorrow and loss transformed into the glory of God. He must have loved us to create for us such a moment. And I felt He loved me. That He was there with me, beside me, warming me with the breath of His love.'

While the company of Jews prayed, János Weisz struck his axe. Throughout the afternoon, he maintained a steady rhythm. That is how the sergeant found them. From a distance, a single axe stroke did not sound thin. But as the sergeant neared it would have become evident that not everyone could be working. Even so, he was taken by surprise at the sight awaiting him when he came through the trees. Men scattered in the woods, swaying silently, lost in their own private worlds like inmates in an asylum for lunatics. One madman swinging an axe. A company of mindless mutes, facing east, swaying on its heels.

The sergeant was a thick-armed peasant. Having neither money nor education nor aristocratic name, he would never have reached the rank of officer in normal times. Some officers with little experience compensated with excessive brutality.

'Weisz! What's the meaning of this?' he demanded.

János Weisz had laid down his axe, Gábor said. He stood smartly at attention to answer his commanding officer.

'Sir,' he said distinctly and without hesitation, 'the men are overworked, Sir. They need to rest.'

'And who decided this? Who said they are tired? Who gave them permission to rest?'

'I did, Sir.'

Stalled by the authority in his subordinate's response, the sergeant wavered indecisively until he was struck by a baffling observation.

'On their feet! They rest on their feet?'

'Yes, Sir,' said János Weisz without blinking or expression. 'That's how they rest, Sir—Jews. Like horses.'

'*Like horses*,' Gábor said. 'János Weisz said "like horses".' And Gábor would chuckle slyly. He was not a man given to laughter. When he did laugh, it was always with some guilt. '*Like horses*. Do you see?' Not one of us enjoyed the joke more than Gábor. It was always fresh for him.

No one had laughed in the woods. No one moved for some moments. The silence was complete, palpable with the sense of impending reprisal. But the sergeant retreated without comment.

My mother listened quietly whenever Gábor told us the story of the Yom Kippur woods. She never said impatiently, as she did to so many of my father's anecdotes, 'We know that one already.' The rapt way in which I followed Gábor's tales usually made her fidget or get up to make a phone call. But she would listen to this story, told always the same way, ending always with Gábor's chuckle, 'Like horses.' My mother recognized the humour. She knew the man who wooed a young bride inside a barracks that was a portico to death, the man who could find something funny in these circumstances. At the time she had understood János's recklessness as ardour, but Gábor's story showed a man who defied the inexorable march of history by slowing it down a few paces. As Gábor wove the scene of the Erdelyi Woods, Sári listened. So this was the man who had pleasured her in the dark. This was the man with whom she might have spent her life.

Gábor survived four labour services altogether. It was during a discharge, as he was about to board the train that would take him home to where his wife, Miri, and their child had moved to be with his parents, that his path literally crossed that of his fellow serviceman. János Weisz was disembarking. He had been called up to re-enlist. The two men greeted each other warmly, hands clasping in the steaming stench and roar of the station.

And how have you fared in these lousy times?

They had not been close, not friends. After the Yom Kippur episode, János Weisz had maintained his reserve. But when they met in the Nagyvárad train station, János and Gábor felt a warmth for each other that might have blossomed into friendship in another clime. They shook hands, and Gábor clapped the other man's shoulder.

'So, you're on your way then. Do you know where they're sending you?'

'Who knows anything?' János replied. 'But you're going home. That's what matters. Look, I'm not doing so bad. Let me show you.'

Gábor was anxious to board. At home they were waiting for him. Miri had written that the child, Clárika, had started to read since he'd last seen her. She had taught herself her letters, and not yet four years old. They would be waiting in the carriage sent to meet his train.

János Weisz pulled something from his breast pocket. Grinning, he handed it to Gábor.

'She's a beauty, isn't she? We've just been engaged.'

Gábor said he didn't take much notice of the photograph. It was a studio shot that revealed little more than a pretty face. He glanced at the photograph of Sári Friedlander courteously. He was glad for János Weisz. You had to go on living, believing that one day the world would turn itself right side up.

'I wish you one hundred and twenty years of happiness,' Gábor said, using a Yiddish expression.

They had parted, one going home and the other away, one east and the other west. But they didn't end up at different destinations. Inscrutable the ways of the Lord that bestowed and denied, filled a moment with meaning and discarded human life. Their paths eventually met rather than crossed. They joined at the woman who would bear their name.

János Weisz returned to Hungary from the Soviet Union in June of 1948, when my sister, Lili, was seven months old. Sári and Gábor had known of his whereabouts for a short while. They were lovers at the time János was traced to a camp for prisoners of war, as the first prisoners were released by the Russians and began to trickle home, bringing with them the names of others.

Sári lost her bearings when János wrote to say he was coming home. She had given him up with the others for dead. How could he be alive if everyone else who had belonged to her was done for or gone? She had been deserted by everyone. Mamuka. Apuka. Her sisters, too: Toni, Netti, Erzsike, all her older sisters dead. Her brother Laci had escaped to England to avoid the labour service draft. Izi, her other brother, was pioneering in Palestine. Only Sári and her youngest sister, Cimi, remained. The dead were all dead. They were a vast collective. She was numb at the thought of them. Them, the solid crowd of them. When János broke from the ranks of the dead, the whole company crumpled into separate, excruciating parts.

Gábor and Sári weren't married. Without death certificates for their spouses, they could not legally marry for seven years. This allowed for the lost to be found, the departed to return, for time to sort the living from the dead. They were not officially joined, and now János was said to be alive when Sári considered someone else in every way her husband.

She had no idea what her parents would have had her do. No one had taught her the rules for this contingency. Where were Mamuka and Apuka when she needed their guidance most? How could they have left her? What would they tell her was right? Right for her. Right for János, and right for this man they had never met but who looked to her as a plant looks up at the sun and drinks the rain. She was distracted by rage and loss. Cimi was no help. Cimi was starving somewhere in the south of the country, with a Chassidic boy she had picked up like a stray cat. Sári screamed at Gábor to keep away.

Gábor found a rabbi—most likely a reasonable proxy, a young man who was once a rabbinical student, perhaps—and they built a *chupah*, the ceremonial canopy used in Jewish weddings. He told Sári: What did the state matter? They would be joined as Jews, they would become man and wife in the eyes of the Lord.

'And János?'

Gábor, essentially a conservative man, did not even attempt to overlook the affront to decency posed by his displacement of János. János was his burden, another twist of fate to Gábor's right arm.

'János will know it couldn't be helped,' he sighed.

Sári married Gábor, older than her by thirteen years, the same age difference there had been between Sári and her eldest sister, Toni, in whose house she used to set the table and rock the baby. She would care for her own children as she had learned to nurse that baby who had been in Sári's girlhood the best of toys. Gábor had lost a child too, also a little girl. Sári saw in Gábor someone who might span the chasm between her parents and her present. He was the bridge she crossed to bind the broken pieces of her life.

János had written for the first time from the Soviet Union. He wrote three identical letters, sending them in care of the JOINT offices in Budapest, in Munkács, and in Nyiregyháza, the places Sári would most likely have gone back to. Sári responded, telling him of her new circumstances. She asked for his forgiveness.

No further news came from János until just before his return journey. Lili was a newborn. Sári wrote back that it was no use. But János persisted. He wrote that in the black pit of his deprivations he had thought of her and the darkness that had woven them together. He was coming home to her and to the baby, it didn't matter whose. He wanted her and he wanted the baby and he wanted them to begin. They had never had the chance to even start their life together. They'd never known what it was like to live as man and wife.

She answered that she was now the wife of another.

He wrote a last time once he was back in the country. János said he bore Sári no ill. The man she had favoured was a decent man, János recognized that. He wished them well.

As children Lili and I knew of our parents' first spouses as we knew of all their lost relatives. The card came every holiday season from another world, somewhere called Argentina: 'Best wishes, János.' It was Gábor who responded, not Sári, signing on behalf of us all.

It puzzled me, the Nyirség, the county where my parents met. Why was it named for birches? When I asked him, Gábor would shrug. No, he would say, birches could never have grown there. Acacias were indigenous. Acacias in the Nyirség, the county of birches. The Nyirség became for me a place of mind against which our real acacia world would never measure up.

Gábor and Sári were plain people, something belied in the storybook concurrence of their encounter. They worked, raised their children, tended their garden, socialized little. They cared about family, tradition, and security. But their story was heroic. This discrepancy irked me. The circumstances of their past imbued them with a grandeur that didn't fit. They were ennobled by tragic events, and elevated further when these events were shaped through telling. Gábor's stories grafted meaning to their lives. There was a point always to his anecdotes, as though history has form we have only to uncover. Caught up in the story, I learned to expect meaning that makes sense of time.

Gábor often said that the finger of God pointed him the way out of each brush with death—the finger of God, because he was not an intuitive man, nor one given to notions beyond reason, and because he would never attribute to himself any special good sense that was not shared by other members of his family. Gábor believed in the finger of God, because he had to explain somehow the chance of his survival. And I believed in it too; otherwise why was I here? What I figured was that for some reason or other *I* had to happen. Those people and their world must have been misconceived. God had made a mistake, brushed off the chalkboard, and begun again. Otherwise the tally didn't add up. My father depicted an earlier world that was a golden era of wealth and community and insoluble family bonds. The glory, and most of the happiness, predated me. Only cataclysm could have brought about my parents' union. And whatever for? Why would that have been?

There's a photograph of me before we left Hungary. I am standing in a field, on unsteady legs wrapped in ribbed leggings. I am hatless, and my few wisps of hair have been gathered in a spout on top of my head. My expression wavers between a frown and a smile. I have been crying, says my mother, because I don't want to be photographed. The long grasses of the field bend in the breeze. I still have it in my hand, she says, the gold wedding band she has given me to distract me from my tears. It is there in the picture, although we can't see it clutched in my plump paw. It is our last unglimpsed knowledge of its whereabouts. I know it, feel it pressed into the soft folds of my skin. It brings the tentative smile to my face. The gold in my hand is the sun emerging from my clouded features. I am last to have it, the ring that binds my mother and my father, before I let it slip into the dense wild grasses.

༕

FIVE SMALL ROOMS
(A MURDER MYSTERY)

I have learned not to underestimate the power of rooms, especially a small room with unequivocal corners, exemplary walls, and well-mannered windows divided into many rectangular panes. I like a small room without curtains, carpets, misgivings, or ghosts.

I. SMALL ROOM WITH PEARS

I like a room painted in a confident full-bodied colour. I steer clear of pastels because they are, generally speaking, capricious, irresolute, and frequently coy. Blue is a good colour for a small room, especially if it is of a shade called Tidal Pool, Tropical Sea, Azure, Atoll, or Night Swim.

I once painted a room a shade of blue called Rainy Day. I find a rainy day to be a fine thing on occasion, particularly after an unmitigated stretch of gratuitous sunshine. In that blue room, I kept a stock of umbrellas ready at hand just in case. This was the first room I had ever painted all by myself. For years I had believed that painting a room was a task I could never master, a task better left to professionals or men. After I finished painting this room, I was as proud of myself as if I had discovered the Northwest Passage.

This room had many outstanding features including lots of large cupboards and a counter ample enough to perform surgery on if necessary. In the cupboards I kept all kinds of things: dresses that no longer fit or flattered me, a bird's nest I'd found in the park when I was six, a red and white lace negligee, the program from a musical version of *Macbeth*, several single socks and earrings, instruction manuals for a radio, a blow-dryer, and a lawn mower that I no longer owned, a package of love letters tied up with a black satin ribbon. No matter how many secrets I stowed in these cupboards, they never filled up.

Often I found myself wandering into the blue room in the middle of the night. I would stand naked staring into the refrigerator at three in the morning, until the cold air gave me goose bumps and my nipples got hard. It was a very old refrigerator which sometimes chirped like a distant melancholy cricket. I was searching not for food so much as for memories, motives, an alibi: how it looked, how it happened, when.

I would reach into the refrigerator and pull out a chunk of ham, a chicken leg, a slice of cheese, or some fruit. Pears were my favourite. Imagine the feel of the sweet gritty flesh on your tongue, the voluptuous juice on your chin. Pears are so delicate. My fingertips made bruises on their thin mottled skin.

This was nothing like 'The Love Song of J. Alfred Prufrock': *Shall I part my hair behind? Do I dare to eat a peach? / I shall wear white flannel trousers, and walk upon the beach. / I have heard the mermaids singing, each to each.* Peaches I am not fond of. Their fuzz gives me shivers like fingernails on a chalkboard. The colour of their flesh close to the pit is too much like that of meat close to the bone. My consumption of pears had nothing to do with daring or indecision. It was strictly a matter of pure pleasure, which always comes as a great relief. At that point in my life I'd had no dealings with mermaids and did not expect to. I am tone deaf and, much as I admire a good body of water, I have never learned to swim.

As for the women who come and go, they are not likely to be talking of Michelangelo.

II. SMALL ROOM WITH SEASHELLS

Later there was another small blue room, this one painted in a shade called Atlantis because it was situated on the very edge of the ocean. In this room I enjoyed the omnipresent odour of salt water and the ubiquitous sound of the surf. These struck me as two things I would never grow tired of.

This room was very sturdy, with support beams as substantial and steadfast as tree trunks. The windows were recessed deep into the thick outer walls. These walls were solid straight through, not hollow in the middle like most. They put me in mind of chocolate Easter bunnies, how the best bunnies are the solid ones, how cheated you feel when biting into a hollow one only to discover it is just a thin shell of chocolate around a rabbit-shaped pocket of sweet empty air.

Here I often wandered out to the beach in the middle of the night. I did not wear white flannel trousers and I never heard the mermaids singing. I had no desire to disturb the universe. I simply stood there with my toes in the ocean and my head in the sky. The hair on my arms stood up in the moonlight. I studied the constellations and thought about words like *firmament, nebula,* and *galactic cannibalism.* I had to keep reminding myself that some of the stars I was seeing were already dead. I had trouble at first with the whole notion of light-years, with time as a function of distance, speed, and illumination, rather than as simply the conduit from then to now.

On cloudy nights, when I could not pursue the perfection of my theory of stars, I turned instead to collecting the miscellaneous offerings which the ocean so munificently deposited at my feet.

I gathered seashells by the fistful, listened for the ocean in each of them, and it was always there, like the same moon seen from every continent, the same God petitioned in every prayer. From the sand I plucked moon shells, harp shells, angel wings, helmets, goblets, butterflies, cockles, and tusks. Less plentiful and so of course more desirable were the sundial and chambered nautilus shells. I'd read somewhere once how the young cephalopod at first lives in the centre of its shell but as it grows larger, it must move forward, sealing off each chamber behind itself. This would be like shutting a door and having it permanently locked behind you.

The seashells, like the stars, were long dead, the beautiful cast-off husks of the ugly mollusks that had made them. Only these pretty skeletons had survived, just as it was only the light of the stars that could still reach me. I thought long and hard about chambers, skeletons, a series of small rooms, the missing bodies of seashells and stars.

There were other things too offered up by the sea: tangled balls of fishing line, plastic bags, a bracelet, a knife. A pair of panty hose, a set of keys, a bathing suit, and several used condoms. Pieces of driftwood like bones, coils of seaweed like entrails. One night I found a water-bloated copy of a murder mystery called *Dead Dead Double Dead*. The last five pages were missing. This, I could not help but think, was hitting a little too close to home.

Apparently the ocean, in addition to being a weighty and ambivalent symbol of dynamic forces, transitional states, the collective unconscious, chaos, creation, and universal womanhood in all its benevolent and heinous incarnations, was also the repository of all lost things. I had long ago wondered what happened to those socks that went into the washing machine and never came out.

At this time I still believed that I could summon up my former self whenever I was ready, that I could gather up my innocence and step back into it like an old pair of shoes. Now I began to see this was no longer true. Eventually I realized that in this small room I was forever in danger of drowning or being swallowed by a sea monster. This epiphany marked the end of my blue period.

III. SMALL ROOM WITH CATS

Various shades of brown are good for small rooms too. Brown imparts a sense of serenity, solidity, and security. Imagine lying down on a bed of warm soil. Imagine being buried alive and liking it. I am partial to any colour of brown that looks like coffee with milk in it or any shade that is named after food: Honey Nut, Bran Muffin, Caramel Chip, or Indian Corn. In a small room painted a colour called Pumpkin Loaf, I always felt full. Sometimes in the morning I thought I could smell the sweet bread baking.

In this room there were tables but no chairs. Clearly the importance of chairs has been overestimated. I quickly got over my atavistic longings for them. Soon enough I could hardly imagine what I'd ever deemed to be indispensable about chairs. Like so many other things I once thought I could never live without, chairs, once I got used to their absence, proved to be just another habit, a knee-jerk reflex like flinching, apologizing, or falling in love. The only time I seriously missed them was when I wanted to sit down and tie my shoes. This was like wishing for a man when you want to clean out the eavestrough or open a new jar of pickles.

There were also many shelves in this brown room, tidy well-spaced shelves like boxes built right into the wall. Some of them still bore items left behind by some former fugitive tenant. There was a pink lampshade which, in a happier time, I might have put on my head. There were some pale yellow bed sheets, soft from many washings, stained with the bodily fluids of long-gone strangers. No matter where you go, you are always leaving incriminating tidbits of evidence behind you.

There was a stack of old *National Geographic* magazines. Everyone has a pile of these stashed away somewhere. There were also several empty picture frames propped up on the shelves and hammered to the walls. I carefully cut photographs from the magazines and stuck them in these frames. I selected several panoramic views of jungles, mountains, fields of wheat. I chose skies without clouds, seas without boats, landscapes without figures. I changed these pictures often so as not to feel that I was just treading water or running in place.

Here I kept cats for company. I like the look of a small room with two cats in it. I tried to emulate the way they can settle themselves anywhere like boneless shape-shifting pillows and how, when falling from a great height, they will almost always land on their feet. I was impressed too by their apparently infinite ability to adapt, the way they can live well anywhere: in an alley, a barn, a palace, or a small brown room with tables and shelves, no chairs.

I told my cats stories of other cats, famous cats, tenacious cats, heroic cats, miraculous cats who found their way home again after travelling through endless miles of wilderness, fording rivers, scaling canyons, leaping tall buildings with a single bound. My cats curled around me and purred. It is not true that cats only purr when they're happy. They also do it when they're worried or in pain.

In my time I have been accused of many things: jealousy, arrogance, selfishness, viciousness, laziness, bitterness, and lust. Also infidelity, inclemency, insanity, immorality, and pride. I have been called reckless, heartless, shameless, malicious, sarcastic, demanding, domineering, cold-blooded, and cruel. The cats, of course, knew none of this and did not care to ask. They were

well aware of the perils of curiosity, the trials and tribulations of being misunderstood. There is always someone who will be offended by a cat's enthusiasm for killing. Think of the way they play with their prey and then, once
it is sufficiently dead, how they always eat the head first, often swallowing it
whole. Think of the way they leave the hearts behind, those slimy little
lumps drawing flies in the driveway. Myself, I do not find this distasteful.
There is always someone who will tell you that your instincts are wrong.
Outside, the sweet yellow fog pressed against the windowpanes.

IV. SMALL ROOM WITH MOTH

Most kinds of green paint, as you would expect, are named after pastoral
scenes and growing things: Meadow, Pasture, Orchard, Leaf, Broccoli,
Asparagus, Spinach, and Dill. In a small room painted a shade called Forest
Lane, the air was always moist, emitting an intimate odour of new growth
and decay. The light was leafy and diffuse, like a green glaze on my skin.
The ceiling was done in Maiden of the Mist, a humid colour much like that
of the sky on a hazy August afternoon. If I stared at this ceiling for too long,
I found I could not catch my breath.

Where the walls met the ceiling there were curves instead of straight
lines and angles. The tops of the windows and doorway were vaulted too.
I enjoyed these arches the way you enjoy a symphony, your whole body
thrilling at the crescendo's inevitable approach. I like a good old-fashioned
symphony, the way it stirs the blood. At this point in my life I knew I was
ripe for a transformation.

In this room there were many solid wooden benches, the purpose of
which was never clear. Perhaps the room had once been the meeting place
of a secret cult whose members would sit on these benches in rows of black
cloaks and hoods, worshipping their various devils and gods, planning their
next move. Arranged upon these mysterious benches was an impressive
assortment of cookware, metal pots and bowls of many sizes, some battered, some smooth. Perhaps these had been used to boil the sacrificial vir-
gins or lambs. My desires both to cook and to eat having been dislodged by
the heat and my overactive imagination, I filled these vessels with flowers
instead of stew, sacrificial or otherwise. In this green room I ate only raw
green things: lettuce, celery, sweet peppers, and limes.

Here I did not wander at night. I still went to bed not knowing what I
had been accused of but this uncertainty no longer tormented me. I had
only two bad dreams during my sojourn in this green room. The first was
of having my head shrivelled to the size of a small sweet pepper, then sliced
in half and served upon a big green platter. The second was of having my
body covered with a fine white powder and then pinned still wriggling to

the wall. It was not a green wall. It was a red wall. I slept flat on my back with the windows open and a candle burning on the floor beside me.

Moths flew in through the open windows, misguided emissaries from the unbridled night. The patterns on their wings were written in a language I did not yet understand. They came from miles around, unable to resist the sweet deadly pull of the flame any more than I could ever resist a ripe pear, a good murder mystery, or a man who said he could save me. Moths, like humans, engage in complicated courtship rituals which involve elaborate dances and sudden dazzling flights. It was hard to determine whether they were courting each other or the promise of a hot dramatic death. I could have reached up from my bed and touched them. But as a child I was told you must never touch a moth because if that fine powder is rubbed off its wings, it will die. Outside, I thought I heard voices but I was mistaken.

I did not touch the moths. They died anyway. In the morning I would find their corpses littering the floor around my guttered candle. Their beautiful wings were scorched, their feathery antennae fried, that magic powder turned to ash. There was a lesson to be learned here, something about fortitude and the purification of the soul by fire. Either that or the moths were simply too stupid to survive. Some people believe that white moths are actually the souls of the dead and that if a black moth flies into a house, it means that someone who lives there will die within the year.

Looking back on my own life, it is hard to determine which was the moth and which was the flame. In these matters, there is no such thing as black and white.

V. SMALL ROOM WITH CLOCKS

I have learned to be wary of the purples which have names like Dazzle, Delusion, Charade, Mirage, and Masquerade. When I first painted this small room a shade of purple called New Year's Eve, it was easy to fool myself into believing that here I could make time stand still. I imagined myself poised in the middle of the countdown to midnight. All around me expectant voices chanted: *Ten nine eight seven six five.* Then they stopped. Thousands of upturned faces gaped incredulously as the silver ball hung there and dropped no farther. Like the boy with his finger in the dike, I believed I could hold back time by the sheer forces of will, desire, and good intentions. I was encouraged by the knowledge that ancient sailors without clocks had navigated solely by instinct and fortuity.

This room, like the others, has large windows divided into many rectangular panes, thick walls solid straight through, built-in shelves filled with an efficient array of cookware, several sturdy tables, and no chairs. I see now that I am beginning to repeat myself.

In an old barrel with wooden slats and rusted iron bands I found two large clocks, identical in every way. Under normal circumstances, I appreciate an accurate clock but here I tried not to dwell on the fact that these two clocks kept impeccable time.

It was winter. Christmas was coming. I hung clusters of purple glass baubles from the ceiling on strands of invisible thread. This was meant to be festive. Outside, it should have been snowing. But in this part of the world at this time of the year it rains instead.

Each night as dusk fell, I liked to sit on the edge of the table closest to the windows. I would roll up my shirt sleeves, eat my toast, and sip my sweet milky tea. Sometimes it was raining, cold drops on black asphalt. On Christmas Eve, children sang carols in the street, their faces and their voices cherubic under red and green umbrellas in the rain. I was smug, thinking myself exempt from the passage of time, the wretched welter of loneliness, the annoying need to question, insist, or explain. Despite all the evidence against me, I was not afraid. It was easy enough to be brave with these purple walls wrapped like the robes of royalty around me.

On New Year's morning I awoke to the sound of a million calendars turning their pages in the wind. I was forced to acknowledge the unbearable sweetness of being. You can run but you can't hide.

Now I find myself watching the clocks instead of the rain-sprinkled street. Their faces are impassive but their hands are always in motion. All mechanical clocks depend on the slow controlled release of power. Like the ticking of the clocks, there is a refrain in my head all day long now: *Be careful. Be careful. Be careful.* Sometimes it is only background noise and I am not actually hearing it. But then, if I pay attention to it even for an instant, it drives everything else right out of my head. This is like the way mothers are always warning their rambunctious children: *Be careful, don't fall. Be careful, don't bump your head. Be careful, it's hot. Be careful, it's sharp. Be careful, it's dark.*

When I need to hear a human voice instead of this carnivorous ticking of my brain and the clocks, I talk to the walls. Talking to the walls is not necessarily a bad thing, not if they are good strong walls, perfectly perpendicular, freshly painted, cool and smooth when you press your fevered lips against them. Purple walls in particular can convince you that everything you are telling them is brilliant, witty, and profound.

Time, they say, heals all wounds. Unless of course the wounds were fatal in the first place. He is not Lazarus. He will not rise from the dead. Even time has its limits. Do not expect that your life will follow the orderly unfolding of beginning, middle, and end. Once upon a time our hearts were innocent, generous, and sweet, oh so sweet, sweet hearts. It is time to make it clear that, although hell indeed hath no fury like a woman scorned, still I did not leave his heart to draw flies in the driveway. I did not eat his head first. I did not swallow it whole.

It is time to turn my back on the seduction of these small rooms. It is time to address the issues and answer the charges. It is time to go home: home, where the walls are white and the hearts are black. Oh, do not ask, 'Where is it?' *Let us go and make our visit.*

It is time to make it clear that I did not kill him. But yes, oh yes, I wanted to.

LINDA SVENDSEN

❧

WHITE SHOULDERS

My oldest sister's name is Irene de Haan and she has never hurt anybody. She lives with cancer, in remission, and she has stayed married to the same undemonstrative Belgian Canadian, a brake specialist, going on thirty years. In the family's crumbling domestic empire, Irene and Peter's union has been, quietly, and despite tragedy, what our mother calls the lone success.

Back in the late summer of 1984, before Irene was admitted into hospital for removal of her left breast, I flew home from New York to Vancouver to be with her. We hadn't seen each other for four years, and since I didn't start teaching ESL night classes until mid-September, I was free, at loose ends, unlike the rest of her family. Over the past months, Peter had used up vacation and personal days shuttling her to numerous tests, but finally had to get back to work. He still had a mortgage. Their only child, Jill, who'd just turned seventeen, was entering her last year of high school. Until junior high, she'd been one of those unnaturally well-rounded kids—taking classes in the high dive, water ballet, drawing, and drama, and boy-hunting in the mall on Saturdays with a posse of dizzy friends. Then, Irene said, overnight she became unathletic, withdrawn, and bookish: an academic drone. At any rate, for Jill and Peter's sake, Irene didn't intend to allow her illness to interfere with their life. She wanted everything to proceed as normally as possible. As who wouldn't.

In a way, and this will sound callous, the timing had worked out. Earlier that summer, my ex-husband had been offered a temporary teaching position across the country, and after a long dinner at our old Szechuan dive, I'd agreed to temporarily revise our custody arrangement. With his newfound bounty, Bill would rent a California town house for nine months and royally support the kids. 'Dine and Disney,' he'd said.

I'd blessed this, but then missed them. I found myself dead asleep in the middle of the day in Jane's lower bunk, or tuning in late afternoons to my six-year-old son's, and Bill's, obsession, *People's Court*. My arms ached when I saw other women holding sticky hands, pulling frenzied children along behind them in the August dog days. So I flew west. To be a mother again, I'd jokingly told Irene over the phone. To serve that very need.

▸

Peter was late meeting me at the airport. We gave each other a minimal hug, and then he shouldered my bags and walked ahead out into the rain. The Datsun was double-parked, hazards flashing, with a homemade sign taped on the rear window that said STUD. DRIVER. 'Jill,' he said, loading the trunk. 'Irene's been teaching her so she can pick up the groceries. Help out for a change.' I got in, he turned on easy-listening, and we headed north towards the grey mountains.

Irene had been in love with him since I was a child; he'd been orphaned in Belgium during World War II, which moved both Irene and our mother. He'd also reminded us of Emile, the Frenchman in *South Pacific*, because he was greying, autocratic, and seemed misunderstood. But the European charm had gradually worn thin; over the years, I'd been startled by Peter's racism and petty tyranny. I'd often wished that the young Irene had been fondled off her two feet by a breadwinner more tender, more local. Nobody else in the family agreed and Mum had even hinted that I'd become bitter since the demise of my own marriage.

'So how is she?' I finally asked Peter.

'She's got a cold,' he said, 'worrying herself sick. And other than that, it's hard to say.' His tone was markedly guarded. He said prospects were poor; the lump was large and she had the fast-growing, speedy sort of cancer. 'But she thinks the Paki quack will get it when he cuts,' he said.

I sat with that. 'And how's Jill?'

'Grouchy,' he said. 'Bitchy.' This gave me pause, and it seemed to have the same effect on him.

We pulled into the garage of the brick house they'd lived in since Jill's birth, and he waved me on while he handled the luggage. The house seemed smaller now, tucked under tall Douglas firs and fringed with baskets of acutely pink geraniums and baby's breath. The back door was open, so I walked in; the master bedroom door was ajar, but I knocked first. She wasn't there. Jill called, 'Aunt Adele?' and I headed back down the hall to the guest-room, and stuck my head in.

A wan version of my sister rested on a water bed in the dark. When I plunked down I made a tiny wave. Irene almost smiled. She was thin as a fine chain; in my embrace, her flesh barely did the favour of keeping her bones company. Her blondish hair was quite short, and she looked ordinary, like a middle-aged matron who probably worked at a bank and kept a no-fail punch recipe filed away. I had to hold her, barely, close again. Behind us, the closet was full of her conservative garments—flannel, floral—and I understood that this was her room now. She slept here alone. She didn't frolic with Peter anymore, have sex.

'Don't cling,' Irene said slowly, but with her old warmth. 'Don't get melodramatic. I'm not dying. It's just a cold.'

'Aunt Adele,' Jill said.

I turned around; I'd forgotten my niece was even there, and she was sitting right on the bed, wedged against a bolster. We kissed hello with loud smooch effects—our ritual—and while she kept a hand on Irene's shoulder, she stuttered answers to my questions about school and her summer. Irene kept an eye on a mute TV—the US Open—although she didn't have much interest in tennis; I sensed, really, that she didn't have any extra energy available for banter. This was conservation, not rudeness.

Jill looked different. In fact, the change in her appearance and demeanour exceeded the ordinary drama of puberty; she seemed to be another girl—shy, unsure, and unable to look me in the eye. She wore silver wire glasses, no makeup, jeans with an oversize kelly-green sweatshirt, and many extra pounds. Her soft straw-coloured hair was pulled back with a swan barrette, the swan's eye downcast. When she passed Irene a glass of water and a pill, Irene managed a swallow, then passed it back, and Jill drank, too. To me, it seemed she took great care, twisting the glass in her hand, to sip from the very spot her mother's lips had touched.

Peter came in, sat down on Jill's side of the bed, and stretched both arms around to raise the back of his shirt. He bared red, hairless skin, and said, 'Scratch.'

'But I'm watching tennis,' Jill said softly.

'But you're my daughter,' he said. 'And I have an itch.'

Peter looked at Irene and she gave Jill a sharp nudge. 'Do your poor dad,' she said. 'You don't even have to get up.'

'But aren't I watching something?' Jill said. She glanced around, searching for an ally.

'*Vrouw*,' Peter spoke up. 'This girl, she doesn't do anything except mope, eat, mope, eat.'

Jill's shoulders sagged slightly, as if all air had suddenly abandoned her body, and then she slowly got up. 'I'll see you after, Aunt Adele,' she whispered, and I said, 'Yes, sure,' and then she walked out.

Irene looked dismally at Peter; he made a perverse sort of face—skewing his lips south. Then she reached over and started to scratch his bare back. It was an effort. 'Be patient with her, Peter,' she said. 'She's worried about the surgery.'

'She's worried you won't be around to wait on her,' Peter said, then instructed, 'Go a little higher.' Irene's fingers crept obediently up. 'Tell Adele what Jill said.'

Irene shook her head. 'I don't remember.'

Peter turned to me. 'When Irene told her about the cancer, she said, "Don't die on me, Mum, or I'll kill you." And she said this so serious. Can you imagine?' Peter laughed uninhibitedly, and then Irene joined in, too, although her quiet accompaniment was forced. There wasn't any recollected pleasure in her eyes at all; rather, it seemed as if she didn't want Peter to laugh alone, to appear as odd as he did. 'Don't die or I'll kill you,' Peter said.

Irene had always been private about her marriage. If there were disagreements with Peter, and there had been—I'd once dropped in unannounced and witnessed a string of Christmas lights whip against the fireplace and shatter—they were never rebroadcast to the rest of the family; if she was ever discouraged or lonely, she didn't confide in anyone, unless she kept a journal or spoke to her own God. She had never said a word against the man.

The night before Irene's surgery, after many earnest wishes and ugly flowers had been delivered, she asked me to stay late with her at Lion's Gate Hospital. The room had emptied. Peter had absconded with Jill—and she'd gone reluctantly, asking to stay until I left—and our mother, who'd been so nervous and sad that an intern had fed her Valium from his pocket. 'Why is this happening to her?' Mum said to him. 'To my only happy child.'

Irene, leashed to an IV, raised herself to the edge of the bed and looked out at the parking lot and that kind Pacific twilight. 'That Jill,' Irene said. She allowed her head to fall, arms crossed in front of her. 'She should lift a finger for her father.'

'Well,' I said, watching my step, aware she needed peace, 'Peter's not exactly the most easygoing.'

'No,' she said weakly.

We sat for a long time, Irene in her white gown, me beside her in my orange-and-avocado track suit, until I began to think I'd been too tough on Peter and had distressed her. Then she spoke. 'Sometimes I wish I'd learned more Dutch,' she said neutrally. 'When I met Peter, we married not speaking the same language, really. And that made a difference.'

She didn't expect a comment—she raised her head and stared out the half-open window—but I was too shocked to respond anyway. I'd never heard her remotely suggest that her and Peter's marriage had been less than a living storybook. 'You don't like him, do you?' she said. 'You don't care for his Belgian manner.'

I didn't answer; it didn't need to be said aloud. I turned away. 'I'm probably not the woman who can best judge these things,' I said.

Out in the hall, a female patient talked on the phone. Irene and I both listened. 'I left it in the top drawer,' she said wearily. 'No. The *bedroom*.' There was a pause. 'The desk in the hall, try that.' Another pause. 'Then ask Susan where she put it, because I'm tired of this and I need it.' I turned as she hung the phone up and saw her check to see if money had tumbled back. The hospital was quiet again. Irene did not move, but she was shaking; I found it difficult to watch this and reached out and took her hand.

'What is it?' I said. 'Irene.'

She told me she was scared. Not for herself, but for Peter. That when she had first explained to him about the cancer, he hadn't spoken to her for three weeks. Or touched her. Or kissed her. He'd slept in the guestroom, until she'd offered to move there. And he'd been after Jill to butter his toast, change the sheets, iron his pants. Irene had speculated about this, she said, until she'd realized he was acting this way because of what had happened to him when he was little. In Belgium. Bruges, the war. He had only confided in her once. He'd said all the women he'd ever loved had left him. His mother killed, his sister. 'And now me,' Irene said. 'The big C which leads to the big D. If I move on, I leave two children. And I've told Jill they have to stick together.'

I got off the bed. 'But, Irene,' I said, 'she's not on earth to please her father. Who can be unreasonable. In my opinion.'

By this time, a medical team was touring the room. The junior member paused by Irene and said, 'Give me your vein.'

'In a minute,' she said to him, 'please,' and he left. There were dark areas, the colour of new bruises, under her eyes. 'I want you to promise me something.'

'Yes.'

'If I die,' she said, 'and I'm not going to, but if I do, I don't want Jill to live with you in New York. Because that's what she wants to do. I want her to stay with Peter. Even if she runs to you, send her back.'

'I can't promise that,' I said. 'Because you're not going to go anywhere.'

She looked at me. Pale, fragile. She was my oldest sister, who'd always been zealous about the silver lining in that cloud; and now it seemed she might be dying, in her forties—too soon—and she needed to believe I could relieve her of this burden. So I nodded, *Yes.*

໙

When I got back, by cab, to Irene and Peter's that night, the house was dark. I groped up the back steps, ascending through a hovering scent of honeysuckle, stepped inside, and turned on the kitchen light. The TV was going—some ultra-loud camera commercial—in the living room. Nobody was watching. 'Jill?' I said. 'Peter?'

I wandered down the long hall, snapping on switches: Irene's sickroom, the upstairs bathroom, the master bedroom, Peter's domain. I did a double-take; he was there. Naked, lying on top of the bed, his still hand holding his penis—as if to keep it warm and safe—the head shining. The blades of the ceiling fan cut in slow circles above him. His eyes were vague and didn't turn my way; he was staring up. 'Oh, sorry,' I whispered, 'God, sorry,' and flicked the light off again.

I headed back to the living room and sat, for a few seconds. When I'd collected myself, I went to find Jill. She wasn't in her downstairs room, which seemed typically adolescent in its decor—Boy George poster, socks multiplying in a corner—until I spotted a quote from Rilke, in careful purple handwriting, taped to her long mirror: 'Beauty is only the first touch of terror we can still bear.'

I finally spotted the light under the basement bathroom door.

'Jill,' I said. 'It's me.'

'I'm in the bathroom,' she said.

'I know,' I said. 'I want to talk.'

She unlocked the door and let me in. She looked tense and peculiar; it looked as if she'd just thrown water on her face. She was still dressed in her clothes from the hospital—and from the day before, the kelly-green sweat job—and she'd obviously been sitting on the edge of the tub, writing. There was a Papermate, a pad of yellow legal paper. The top sheet was covered with verses of tiny backward-slanting words. There was also last night's pot of Kraft Dinner on the sink.

'You're all locked in,' I said.

She didn't comment, and when the silence stretched on too long I said, 'Homework?' and pointed to the legal pad.

'No,' she said. Then she gave me a look and said, 'Poem.'

'Oh,' I said, and I *was* surprised. 'Do you ever show them? Or it?'

'No,' she said. 'They're not very good.' She sat back down on the tub. 'But maybe I'd show you, Aunt Adele.'

'Good,' I said. 'Not that I'm a judge.' I told her Irene was tucked in and that she was in a better, more positive frame of mind. More like herself. This seemed to relax Jill so much, I marched the lie a step further. 'Once your mum is out of the woods,' I said, 'your father may lighten up.'

'That day will never come,' she said.

'Never say never,' I said. I gave her a hug—she was so much bigger than my daughter, but I embraced her the same way I had Jane since she was born: a hand and a held kiss on the top of the head.

She hugged me back. 'Maybe I'll come live with you, Auntie A.'

'Maybe,' I said, mindful of Irene's wishes. 'You and everybody,' and saw the disappointment on her streaked face. So I added, 'Everything will be all right. Wait and see. She'll be all right.'

And Irene was. They claimed they'd got it, and ten days later she came home, earlier than expected. When Peter, Jill, and I were gathered around her in the sickroom, Irene started cracking jokes about her future prosthetic fitting. 'How about the Dolly Parton, hon?' she said to Peter. 'Then I'd be a handful.'

I was surprised to see Peter envelop her in his arm; I hadn't ever seen him offer an affectionate gesture. He told her he didn't care what size boob she bought, because breasts were for the hungry babies—not so much for the husband. 'I have these,' he said. 'These are mine. These big white shoulders.' And he rested his head against her shoulder and looked placidly at Jill; he was heavy, but Irene used her other arm to bolster herself, hold him up, and she closed her eyes in what seemed to be joy. Jill came and sat by me.

Irene took it easy for the next few days; I stuck by, as did Jill, when she ventured in after school. I was shocked that there weren't more calls, or cards, or visitors except for Mum, and I realized my sister's life was actually very narrow, or extremely focused: family came first. Even Jill didn't seem to have any friends at all; the phone never rang for her.

Then Irene suddenly started to push herself—she prepared a complicated deep-fried Belgian dish; in the afternoon, she sat with Jill, in the Datsun, while Jill practised parallel parking in front of the house and lobbied for a mother-daughter trip to lovely downtown Brooklyn for Christmas. And then, after a long nap and little dinner, Irene insisted on attending the open house at Jill's school.

We were sitting listening to the band rehearse, a *Flashdance* medley, when I became aware of Irene's body heat—she was on my right—and asked if she might not want to head home. She was burning up. 'Let me get through this,' she said. Then Jill, on my other side, suddenly said in a small tight voice, 'Mum.' She was staring at her mother's blouse, where a bright stitch of scarlet had shown up. Irene had bled through her dressing. Irene looked down. 'Oh,' she said. 'Peter.'

On the tear to the hospital, Peter said he'd sue Irene's stupid 'Paki bugger' doctor. He also said he should take his stupid wife to court for loss of sex. He should get a divorce for no-nookie. For supporting a one-tit wonder. And on and on.

Irene wasn't in any shape to respond; I doubt she would have anyway.

Beside me in the back seat, Jill turned to stare out the window; she was white, sitting on her hands.

I found my voice. 'I don't think we need to hear this right now, Peter,' I said.

'Oh, Adele,' Irene said warningly. Disappointed.

He pulled over, smoothly, into a bus zone. Some of the people waiting for the bus weren't pleased. Peter turned and faced me, his finger punctuating. 'This is my wife, my daughter, my Datsun.' He paused. 'I can say what the hell I want. And you're welcome to walk.' He reached over and opened my door.

The two women at the bus shelter hurried away, correctly sensing an incident.

'I'm going with Aunt—' Jill was barely audible.

'No,' said Irene. 'You stay here.'

I sat there, paralysed. I wanted to get out, but didn't want to leave Irene and Jill alone with him; Irene was very ill, Jill seemed defenceless. 'Look,' I said to Peter, 'forget I said anything. Let's just get Irene there, okay?'

He pulled the door shut, then turned front, checked me in the rearview one last time—cold, intimidating—and headed off again. Jill was crying silently. The insides of her glasses were smeared; I shifted over beside her and she linked her arm through mine tight, tight. Up front, Irene did not move.

They said it was an infection which had spread to the chest wall, requiring antibiotics and hospital admission. They were also going to perform more tests.

Peter took off with Jill, saying that they both had to get up in the morning.

Before I left Irene, she spoke to me privately, in a curtained cubicle in Emergency, and asked if I could stay at our mother's for the last few days of my visit; Irene didn't want to hurt me, but she thought it would be better, for all concerned, if I cleared out.

And then she went on; her fever was high, but she was lucid and fighting hard to stay that way. Could I keep quiet about this to our mother? And stop gushing about the East to Jill, going on about the Statue of Liberty and the view of the water from the window in the crown? And worry a little more about my own lost children and less about her daughter? And try to be more understanding of her husband, who sometimes wasn't able to exercise control over his emotions? Irene said Peter needed more love, more time; more of her, God willing. After that, she couldn't speak. And, frankly, neither could I.

I gave in to everything she asked. Jill and Peter dropped in together during the evening to see her; I visited Irene, with Mum, during the day when Peter was at work. Our conversations were banal and strained—they didn't seem to do either of us much good. After I left her one afternoon, I didn't know where I was going and ended up at my father's grave. I just sat there, on top of it, on the lap of the stone.

The day before my New York flight, I borrowed my mother's car to pick up a prescription for her at the mall. I was window-shopping my way back to the parking lot, when I saw somebody resembling my niece sitting on a bench outside a sporting goods store. At first, the girl seemed too dishevelled, too dirty-looking, actually, to be Jill, but as I approached, it became clear it was her. She wasn't doing anything. She sat there, draped in her mother's London Fog raincoat, her hands resting on her thickish thighs, clicking a barrette open, closed, open, closed. It was ten in the morning; she should have been at school. In English. For a moment, it crossed my mind that she might be on drugs: this was a relief; it would explain everything. But I didn't think she was. I was going to go over and simply say, *Yo, Jill, let's do tea*, and then I remembered my sister's frightening talk with me at the hospital and thought, *Fuck it. Butt out, Adele*, and walked the long way round. I turned my back.

One sultry Saturday morning, in late September—after I'd been back in Brooklyn for a few weeks—I was up on the roof preparing the first lessons for classes, when the super brought a handful of mail up. He'd been delivering it personally to tenants since the box had been ripped out of the entrance wall. It was the usual stuff and a thin white business envelope from Canada. From Jill. I opened it: *Dearlingest* (sic) *Aunt Adele, These are my only copies. Love, your only niece, Jill. P.S. I'm going to get a job and come see you at Easter.*

There were two. The poems were carefully written, each neat on their single page, with the script leaning left, as if blown by a stiff breeze. 'Black Milk' was about three deaths: before her beloved husband leaves for war, a nursing mother shares a bottle of old wine with him, saved from their wedding day, and unknowingly poisons her child and then herself. Dying, she rocks her dying child in her arms, but her last conscious thought is for her husband at the front. Jill had misspelled wedding; she'd put weeding.

'Belgium' described a young girl ice skating across a frozen lake—Jill had been to Belgium with her parents two times—fleeing an unnamed pursuer. During each quick, desperate glide, the ice melts beneath her until, at the end, she is underwater: 'In the deep cold / Face to face / Look, he comes now / My Father / My Maker.' The girl wakes up; it was a bad dream. And then her earthly father appears in her bed and, 'He makes night / Come again / All night,' by covering her eyes with his large, heavy hand.

I read these, and read them again, and I wept. I looked out, past the steeples and the tar roofs, where I thought I saw the heat rising, toward the green of Prospect Park, and held the poems on my lap, flat under my two hands. I didn't know what to do; I didn't know what to do right away; I thought I should wait until I knew clearly what to say and whom to say it to.

❧

In late October, Mum phoned, crying, and said that Irene's cancer had not been caught by the mastectomy. Stray cells had been detected in other areas of her body. Chemotherapy was advised. Irene had switched doctors; she was seeing a naturopath. She was paying big money for an American miracle gum, among other things.

Mum also said that Jill had disappeared for thirty-two hours. Irene claimed that Jill had been upset because of a grade—a C in Phys. Ed. Mum didn't believe it was really that; she thought Irene's condition was disturbing Jill, but hadn't said that to Irene.

She didn't volunteer any information about the other member of Irene's family and I did not ask.

In November, Bill came east for a visit and brought the children, as scheduled; he also brought a woman named Cheryl Oak. The day before Thanksgiving, the two of them were invited to a dinner party, and I took Graham and Jane, taller and both painfully shy with me, to Central Park. It was a crisp, windy night. We watched the gi-normous balloons being blown up for the Macy's parade and bought roasted chestnuts, not to eat, but to warm the palms of our hands. I walked them back to their hotel and delivered them to the quiet, intelligent person who would probably become their stepmother, and be good to them, as she'd obviously been for Bill. Later, back in Brooklyn, I was still awake—wondering how another woman had succeeded with my husband and, now, my own little ones—when Irene phoned at 3 a.m. She told me Jill was dead. 'There's been an accident,' she said.

A few days later, my mother and stepfather picked me up at the Vancouver airport on a warm, cloudy morning. On the way to the funeral, they tried to tell me, between them—between breakdowns—what had happened. She had died of hypothermia; the impact of hitting the water had most likely rendered her unconscious. She probably hadn't been aware of drowning, but she'd done that, too. She'd driven the Datsun to Stanley Park—she'd told Irene she was going to the library—left the key in the ignition, walked not quite to the middle of the bridge, and hoisted herself over the railing. There was one eyewitness: a guy who worked in a video store. He'd kept saying, 'It was like a movie. I saw this little dumpling girl just throw herself off.'

The chapel was half-empty, and the director mumbled that that was unusual when a teenager passed on. Irene had not known, and neither had Mum, where to reach Joyce, our middle sister, who was missing as usual; Ray, our older brother, gave a short eulogy. He stated that he didn't believe in any God, but Irene did, and he was glad for that this day. He also guessed that when any child takes her own life, the whole family must wonder why, and probably do that forever. The face of my sister was not to be borne. Then we all sang 'The Water Is Wide,' which Jill had once performed in an elementary-school talent show. She'd won Honourable Mention.

After the congregation dispersed, Peter remained on his knees, his head in his hands, while Irene approached the casket. Jill wore a pale pink dress and her other glasses, and her hair was pinned back, as usual, with a barrette—this time, a dove. Irene bent and kissed her on the mouth, on the forehead, then tugged at Jill's lace collar, adjusting it just so. It was the eternal mother's gesture, that finishing touch, before your daughter sails out the door on her big date.

I drank to excess at the reception; we all did, and needed to. Irene and I did not exchange a word; we just held each other for a long minute. From a distance, and that distance was necessary, I heard Peter talking about Belgium and memories of his childhood. On his fifth birthday, his sister, Kristin, had sent him a pencil from Paris, a new one, unsharpened, and he had used it until the lead was gone and it was so short he could barely hold it between his fingers. On the morning his mother was shot, in cold blood, he'd been dressing in the dark. The last thing she had said, to the Germans, was, 'Don't hurt my little boy.' This was when Mum and I saw Irene go to him and take his hand. She led him down the hall to his bedroom and closed the door behind them. 'Thank God,' Mum said. 'Thank God, they have each other. Thank God, she has him.'

And for that moment, I forgot about the despair that had prompted Jill to do what she did, and my own responsibility and silence, because I was alive and full of needs, sickness, and dreams myself. I thought, *No, I will never tell my sister what I suspect, because life is short and very hard*, and I thought, *Yes, a bad marriage is better than none*, and I thought, *Adele, let the sun go down on your anger, because it will not bring her back*, and I turned to my mother. 'Yes,' I said. 'Thank God.'

ARITHA VAN HERK

❧

IN VISIBLE INK

It is May. In the ordinary world, beyond these ridges of ice, beyond the edge of the Arctic Ocean, below the tree line, below the imaginary dashes of the Arctic Circle, it is spring: all the snow gone, the cold vanished in wait for next year's winter, and the sun a long light retiring into evening. This is the time of blackthorn winter, a metaphorical cold of the second week in May, unreal as this freezing surround is not.

It is the second week of May and I am sitting on the back of a komatik riding over the frozen Arctic Ocean. Everywhere that my eye reaches is dazzling snow, implacable ice, a white/blue/white/blue configuration of polar sea. The blue is not water but old, old ice, ice that has floed and shifted, that continually grinds against itself, that has never thawed, that will not melt for years. To the far edges of my seeing is frozen ocean, no skating smooth expanse but choppy with ridges, broken, a nordic goddess's tumbled cake pans.

I am travelling over this broken water, chopped and corrugated and firm as ground. The komatik I ride is not a comfortable mode of transportation. The traditional Inuit sledge, pulled by a snarling avid snowmobile, it bounces and bangs, rises precariously over icy ledges to slam down on the snow beyond. I am jarred to the very bone, the komatik creaking and groaning through this rutted and unpolished ice whose ironbound surface breaks and breaks.

And yet, in this distant, eerie world of ice, unwriting and unwritten, merely a cipher of human bone and blood, I am inexplicably, immeasurably happy: because I am finally free of words.

The Inuit make little distinction between land and water. In the extreme Arctic, living with an ocean that cracks open into water for only a few short months a year, they move from land to ice and ice to land with assurance of both's accessibility, opportunity for food and water and even shelter. For the Inuit, *the land* does not end where ocean begins: it only begins there. The ocean and its creatures are still the primary source of their survival. It is to the sea, its bountifulness, that the people of the north go. Inland is no preferred concept. There is ice and there is land. They are both, despite their fundamental difference, covered with snow. They are both consummate enpagements, intagli in the white of this endless folio.

May is relatively warm—between twenty and ten below—and the Arctic sun keeps itself up for twenty-four hours, although it drops low on the horizon between ten at night and two in the morning. May is a good month for hunting seal, which come onto the ice to bask beside their holes. It is a good month to travel, before the ice breaks up. And I am travelling, by snowmobile and komatik, from Resolute Bay on Cornwallis Island to Grise Fiord (the most northerly of Canadian communities), on Ellesmere Island. Only Eureka and Alert lie farther north than Grise Fiord, and they are white man's stations (not settlements because no one lives there permanently), one a weather station and the other an army base.

You, reader, are entitled to wonder why I am doing this.

This journey's conditions are no more luxurious than riding in a komatik is comfortable. In order to stay warm, I wear five layers of clothing, I huddle beneath a caribou skin, and at night, I sleep on that same caribou skin. The clothing I wear is of Inuit design, my kamiks warmer than any southern boot could imagine itself. Still, it is significantly below zero and wind intensifies the cold. Out on the open ice, the Arctic temperature prods every nerve, every bone. A reminder of where I am, and that who I am does not matter a writ in this cryptically enduring world.

I am not motivated by destination, although I appear to be enacting a journey: travelling between Resolute Bay and Grise Fiord. But departure and arrival are of no consequence. The six hundred odd kilometres we meander, the five days and nights we spend moving around Dungeness Point on Cornwallis Island, up Wellington Channel, across Devon Island, down Viks Fiord to Bear Bay, then across Jones Sound to South Cape on Ellesmere Island may offer the illusion of travel, but are essentially the measurements of measurement-obsessed man in the south. I know that when I return to my home in Calgary I will be bombarded with questions of measurement: how long did the trip take? how far did you go? how cold was it? Such determinations are meaningless here; they are completely effaced by the articulation of each moment's essense, this hereness, this nowness, and nothing else. I am suspended in an Arctic, not near Arctic or high Arctic but extreme Arctic, beyond all writing and its romance, beyond the intellectual comprehension or the geographical experience of most of those people calling themselves Canadians. I am simply here, reduced to *being*, breathing the ice-crystal air through my nose and into my lungs, stamping my feet against the granular snow to revive my circulation. I am at last beyond language, at last literately invisible.

Which is, reader, I confess, the state I ideally wish to attain. Finally, finally, in a life dominated by language, I am to some degree free of it, of having to speak and read and write. If you have read *Places Far From*

Ellesmere, you know that the time I spent at Lake Hazen in the northern part of Ellesmere Island taught me unreading, the act of dismantling a text past all its previous readings and writings. The landscape there, its delicious remoteness, calm unmeasurability, catalysed my reading act into something beyond reading, enabling me to untie all the neatly laced up expectations of words and their printing, their arrangement on the page, the pages bound together into a directive narrative, that then refused to be static, but turned and began to read back, to read me, to unread my very reading and my personal geography. But reader, that was summer, however brief.

And yes, I always want to go farther, push back another boundary, cross another invisible line. Yes, reader, what I am about to confess is heresy, but I long, finally, to escape the page, to escape ink and my own implacable literacy, altogether.

Yes, I am anxious about reading, that I will always have something (enough) to read, that I will always have satisfying words for company, that I will never be stranded without a book, an addiction to reading the intimacies of language caressed by others. I am anxious about writing, that I will always find words to articulate my intellectual transgressions, the ideas I circle and circle, watching and writing. I force the two together, write about my reading, read my writing, refuse to function without one or the other implicated in some way, even if only silently, secretly, in my head. The conspiracies of bibliophilism. I book my world, I word all possible collisions and encounters, I am enslaved to language, and I enslave my experience to language. Visible ink.

But reader, I am not complaining, not in distress. I do not dismiss language as primary and pivotal function, nor do I subscribe to the naive temptations of anti-intellectualism. Literacy is a powerful talisman; I do not decry its magic, and I hold it the most precious skill of my life. My reading and writing sustain me beyond sustenance: they are both life and livelihood. Thus important enough for me to recognize that I should deprive–hardly even possible!–myself of them, even for a short time, to understand more completely their consequence in my life.

So reader, I have freed myself from words–at least, written and read words. For the first time since I learned to read at the age of five (and I am thirty-seven now) I am spending five days without reading a word, holding my breath. Although I took books with me to Resolute Bay, muttered and mumbled and weighted them in my hand and turned them upside-down, I am now on the frozen reaches of the Arctic Ocean with no signs to signify for me, invisibled to print. And while the pedant will argue that there is always oral and mental language, that we carry our signs and their signifiers with us, that I am reading this Arctic I am suspended in; while you may be right that I struggle to find some corresponding signs to articulate my experience, ultimately this page of Arctic is not written or read by insignificant me. No, it (agent) reads and writes me. I am its text, impressionable, inscribable, desirous of contamination, a page open to its tattoo, marking.

How to describe or even begin to evoke this landscape? Reader, it occupies the realm of magic, a terrifying ecstasy. The world *is* beauty without adornment, beyond imagined possibility into almost hallucinatory beguilement. Here is a strange combination of mirage-like airiness and abiding perpetuity, a lapidification of fluidity both physically daunting and terrifyingly lovely. So thin, so meagre language seems in its capacity to re-cite this sublimity. Overwhelmed by this daunting and indifferent and resplendent Arctic, my paltry language is finally insufficient. I am merely filled with a wonder beyond wonder, invisibled by awe.

When we bump off Cornwallis Island and onto the ice, Resolute Bay quickly fades to a visual handful of coloured dust. No boundary crossed, a seemingly limitless surface tempting entrance, we are reduced to infinitesimal punctuation marks. The wind against my stinging face adjuratory breath, cold suffusing time.

Young seal sunning on the ice are still furry and gaze pure curiosity. Their open holes blue circles indiscernible in the blue snow around them, camouflaged as their black bodies are not. They slip into those apertures as slickly as their bodies' shape, phocine. The rough zigzagging of our path, ice blocks like chunks of cake thrust into blue and green pressure ridges. The komatik slams itself over a crease, then rises again and on a quick turn drives itself up against a huge block of ice, the runner stuck fast on either side. The snowmobile crescendoes fruitlessly, we climb out and back the komatik off, then push, heave it over the ridge. Right wooden runner cracked by the impact. Keep going, and at the next smooth spot we stop, Pijamini neatly saws a plywood piece to fit, nails from a tin, hammers the runner back to strength. Rough ice. Push more than we ride, climbing in and out of the komatik an ordeal wearing so many clothes, the cold cold, the sun hot. Bannock dipped in hot tea. And again buckled ice, huge scrawling chunks that we inconceivably thread, intricate reading of passage a reminder that we are not travelling but static, finally arrested here, in the ice-landscape. And polar bear tracks, crossing before our tracks, lines of intersection conspicuous for their rarity (Wiebe, *Playing Dead* 50), but here not rare, a veritable highway for the golden-white sovereign (*Thalarctus maritimus*) patrolling the broken ridges for absent-minded or sleeping seal. Stunningly huge, full-muscled and furred, moving effortlessly through the rough ice. Slows, walks, looks at us, scoops snow with his mouth, ambles away. Tracks, tracks, one bear days ago, a mother and two cubs a few hours ago, tracks, tracks, the creases of their padded feet clear as character, imprinted on the snow. Markings: claw marks on the ice side of an iceberg. And tracks, tracks, polar bear tracks followed by fox tracks, following the possibility of dozing seal, their flipper marks around ocean breathing holes. Our komatik tracks following themselves into tracklessness and invisibility. Writings of passage. Pressure ridges, lines where the ocean meets itself and forces its own force upwards. The tide under the ice, currents below solidity. Colophons.

I sleep on this cryptic and indifferent ocean. No hull between us, only solid solid ice, and the thin sail of a double-walled tent. Below me a down sleeping bag, then caribou skin, then foamy, then tent floor, then four inches of snow, then six feet of ice, then five hundred feet of freezing polar water cold as a fist; yet rich with fish, seal, whales, shrimp. They bump their noses against my sleeping skin, this sleep without dreams, without sign or reference, measureless and deep. Here or now invisible and unfathomable. Only sleeping. Written into sleep.

The komatik creaks and groans like an old ship battling high seas. Made of wood now (once bones and moss, skin and sinew and ice), but still lashed together only with rope, no nails. Pliable and resilient, it seems almost supple in its tracking of the snowmobile, giving into the jarring tilts and plunges of the fractured ice. And land no smoother in its dips and curves, banks under the runners, Devon Island wet and heavy with snow, even the cliffs jagged, and the sharp hooves of the elegant caribou, fleet as a sentence, a distant conjunction. Muskoxen lower their heads at us over a hill, then turn and drag their tracks away. Moss under the snow, and rock, screelings of gravel, emerging to stark cliffs as encarved as Egypt's Abu Simbel and then ice again, a different phonation, ringing faintly under our runners.

There is hoarfrost on the snow, crystals of snow growing on snow, dazzling yellow and blue under the sun. Intricate, delicate rime of a cryological aesthetic, blades sometimes an inch long, and every frostflake exquisite construction. And patches of ice-fog, the contours of land and ice surreal disappearance, the komatik floating silently through silence, and I see grain elevators, caragana hedges, the parkland around the Battle River miraged onto this arctic. Reader, I have almost left myself behind, and in this ice-fog read my own erasure, written and engraved past, the language I am slave to made invisible. We drift eerily, and I cannot be sure if I sleep or wake, if we are suspended or moving. Still, when I lean over the komatik's side, the air rushes against my face, and I hear the steady hiss of the runners along the snow, another passing.

Sundogs refract on either side of the glaring sun that my dark glasses cannot diminish. An omen surely, a reading of the snow and its polar perhelion, constituent activity. Warning or blessing, guide or direction? No sign. A polar body, coordinate, codeclination? Where am I? Vanished, effaced, unwritten. Invisibled.

Yes, reader, I have cited space and measurement, time and quotidian gesture, all in vain. I cannot read these reaches. I have no language for *arctic*, impossible to convey to you the sensation of stepping from a sleeping bag warm with night breath into an eagerly frigid weatherglass. I cannot measure polar bear tracks, or describe to you the habits of sunning seals. I am quite simply unable to write of or through this polar spell. Instead, it inscribes me, takes over my cullible imagination and its capacity for words: invents me for its own absent-minded pleasure. Effaces my referentiality, a transformation without continuity or chronology. I am re-invented by a great white page. Not *isolation* but complete invisibility, all causes and destinations blurred by causes other to causalities I believe I know.

And now know I do not know.

Even more extreme is the illusion of absence that is truly presence, tremendous presence, with no need to articulate itself narcissistically, being so much a *hereness*. This space, this landscape, this temperature, question all *document* and instead document me, without reference to an other; decipherable as glass I am, and fragile as any silenced voice, a tracement of arctic essence. No comparisons possible, no contrast available for measurement or ruler for diversity. This north is the gauge, and all else divergence. I am effaced, become an enunciative field, a page untouched by pen, no archive and no history. Happily.

Ah reader, what discourse is this? A snowmobile's diminished whine? The snowhiss of runners, the creak and groan of a labouring komatik, bouncing over what is not a smooth page of snow but a rough-toothed, jagged dimension, continually broken and interrupted by itself? As I am now, profoundly interrupted, disinherited of all that locates my literate self. Lost to text and language, become finally merely a text to be written. A flimsy alphabet. I could believe I have found the north in my own head (Wiebe, *Playing Dead* 113).

No, it has found me.

I wake in the morning to Pijamini's voice talking on the radio in the cooktent. He talks to Annie, whose husband he is, in Grise Fiord. The soft, throaty Inuktitut syllables bridge sleep and wakefulness, and signifying morning—or is it afternoon, or evening? Time not measureable either, we seem to be getting up around two in the afternoon and travelling all night, but watches mean and matter nothing. Pijamini's voice speaks me into existence, creates my ears again. Huskily sibilant, his language in its rhythmic rise and fall delineates both where and who I am, unwritten here on the thick blue ice of the Arctic Ocean. Pijamini is short and solid, almost tiny, but his strength is powerfully obvious, despite his age, sixty-four, he says with a grin. He is the leader, the most experienced person on this becalmed journey, and I ride in the komatik pulled by his snowmobile. How well he reads this invisible world, his body itself a signage, *polar* and *north* contained in his posture. He climbs icebergs to survey his north, then unerringly proceeds through the most impenetrable of ice fields.

He understands and speaks very simple (what does that mean, uncomplicated, uncluttered?) English, but he is at first shy, silent. Only after hours of pushing the komatik over rough ice, after I sight the first polar bear, does he say a word to me. I am ashamed that I use this rough, barbaric language, ashamed that I can speak to him only in the coldness of English, that I know no Inuktitut. I do not want to speak English with him, I want to talk to him in *his* language, the language of this overwhelming snowworld. I say nothing, smile only, push the komatik when it gets stuck. And then, in a sudden moment of desire, I ask him the Inuit word for sun. He tells me, pokerfaced, a little curiously, and when I repeat it, he laughs. My epiglottal Dutch for once give me some pronunciative advantage. 'You speak good Inuktitut,' he says. 'Very good.'

Reader, even invisibled to language, one makes what signs one can. I placed my dwarfed foot in the foot-writing left by a polar bear. I circle every iceberg three times, on my right, reading myself a spell. And Pijamini names his world for me: cloud, sun, falling snow, snow on the ground, ice, bear, tracks, caribou, muskox, sundogs, iceberg, seal. He names his family to me, his seven children and their children. He names the points, the promontories, the edges of the islands as we pass. I repeat his namings, carefully shaping my mouth and tongue around their inflections and contours, and Pijamini laughs. 'Very good, very good. You should come to Grise Fiord, study Inuktitut.' He gives me *his* words, and thus names me, writes my invisible and unlanguaged self into his archaeology. I am written, finally, with that nomadic language.

Reader, reading you, I know you want me to put those words down here, reveal their magic incantation. Never. They are Pijamini's words, not mine, and if I was able to hear them and to mimic them, it was only through his agency. I will not raid them, or repeat them beyond the Arctic sea, beyond the secret worlds of ice. They gave me a reading, read me in that space where I, trying to read anew, was finally written. Reader, this amulet of the first and most final of all crypto-frictions is that one can be disappeared and re-written in a language beyond one's own. Herein resides the ultimate illusion of text: you are not reading me but writing, not me but yourself; you are not reading writing but being read, a live text in a languaging world.

And yes, reader, in this cold May where I am finally freed from words, I am given a different text to carry south with me, to this oh so visible place full of words shouting everywhere, demanding to be read. In the silence after text dies, I will hear, somewhere in my buried polar ear, the soft Inuit voice of Pijamini naming the world in Inuktitut, and laughing.

SHREE GHATAGE

❧

DEAFNESS COMES TO ME

Deafness comes to me, takes you away.

I look at my door again and again. The curtain hangs stiff. You do not come.

Ever since the lizard fell on my bed two weeks ago, it is as though, come nightfall, the wall with the wooden door that connects me to the rest of the house becomes a backdrop, a theatrical prop; my room, a stage. Mine is the only name in the list of players for there are no wings, no dramatic entrances, no well-timed exits.

I turn to the window, run my hands up and down iron bars. My fingers stumble on a crack. Even though my nails are short I don't give up. Like black petals falling off a crumbling rose, smooth peels of stripped paint settle softly on the floor.

The crescent moon dangles, a reflective pendant around the neck of a reclining sky. It is the gold chandrakor you gave me so many years ago, twelve days after our son was born, when we both remarked how, on that auspicious night, the full moon dimmed attending stars with its molten radiance. Like your face, you said, running rough thumbs along my smooth edges, undoing the clasp of my new chain, you must shine only for me. Earlier, I had worn a moss green sari with vermilion border. Go and change, you commanded, when you saw me in the hall, two crimson roses in my hair, ready to greet our guests who were coming for the naming ceremony. I smiled to myself. Wore off-white raw silk with tumeric border instead. Even then eyes followed me everywhere that night. But you didn't notice, didn't know that happiness is hard to conceal.

I look up at the doorway. You are not there.

This time it began the night the lizard that makes her home in the terrace garden outside my window lost her footing, fell on my bed. Landed on her back so I could see bleached underbelly, slightly bloated, rubbery, smooth. Zana flicked her off my razai, chased her along the floor. She was halfway up the wall when Zana's bristle broom found her. I quickly lifted the neckline of my gown up to my eyebrows, averted my eyes. Even then I could see the tail squirming and thrashing long after it had been severed from her body. And I knew without being told that my horoscope entered its inauspicious period the very moment that tail lay still.

So I wasn't surprised next morning when I awakened to a frantic bird pecking at my scalp. Large, black wings flapped against my ears, splayed claws gouged my eyes. I couldn't move. The roar of the wings, it was as if my head was trapped inside a drug-crazed dombari's drum.

Next thing I knew, Zana was pinning my hands to my sides, her calm eyes willing mine to take control. After two minutes she must have seen the terror there subside, for she moved away, closed the window above my head.

'That bird attacked me, Zana, that crow was inside my room! You shouldn't have left the terrace door open!'

Zana walked to the door that leads out on the terrace, threw open its double shutters. Arms flailing, she shooed away the crow which I couldn't see, now that my window was shut. She bent over, stepped back in with something in her hands. When she saw I was looking her way she quickly covered whatever it was with the front of her sari.

'Bring it here! Don't *you* start hiding things from me.' My voice must have been harsh, on the verge of something I know not what, for she came directly to my bed, held out an object that left a trail on the floor. A nest. Inside, three cracked eggs, albumen oozing out of shallow crevices like polluted water.

'Why did the crow attack me, Zana, why? I didn't do that!'

Zana laid the nest on the windowsill. Stood at the terrace door, small eyes darting, searching for the high, collapsible steel awning that hadn't been opened for over six months. Turning to me, she pointed upwards. No doubt broken straws still hung from the spot where the nest must have lodged.

She handed me a comb from my night table then walked towards the door that connects me to the rest of the house, holding the disintegrating nest that had so recently cocooned life.

I looked away from the terrace and that's when I saw you standing in the doorway, yellow curtain flowers nodding in your wake. You moved aside for Zana, walked towards me, your shoulders with the single mole exactly centred between their blades, broad, high colour in your cheeks. You were shaking your head from side to side. But your eyes! They were the gentlest I'd ever seen them. Your lips started to move, then stopped, your mouth slightly open so I could see the two bottom teeth that I know are sharp, the ones that lean inward. You didn't say anything, just ran your fingertips up and down my face, following their trail with your eyes. You were dressed for the office.

When Zana returned, you left.

Deafness comes to me, takes you away.

She brought with her a large basin of water, some cotton wool rolled in brown paper, a small hand towel. She sat beside me and holding my chin steady with one hand, started cleaning my face and neck with the other. She showed me the wet wad of cotton. It was bloodied.

'Her claws,' I said. 'Why didn't you come sooner, Zana?' She said nothing, continued to clean me until the basin turned pink. She then dried my face. Carefully applied Cibazol to raw stinging cuts.

'The crow wasn't inside the room,' Zana moved her lips slowly, thumbs interlocked, fingers flapping. She was shaking her head, pointing at the floor. Zana looks at my eyes when she speaks to me, the only person who does that besides you. She never raises her tone either. I can tell. 'The crow wasn't inside,' she repeated.

'How do you explain the scratches on my face then?' I said, suddenly complacent. She held my hands in hers, ran the balls of her thumbs along my fingernails. She took a clean slate from under my mattress, started writing: 'As soon as I heard your screams I rushed in. You were slapping, scratching your head, face, neck, ears—I thought a bee must have strayed from its hive—Then I saw the crow's shadow on your bed, to-ing and fro-ing across your head. Heard raucous cawing—'

'Are you telling me it was a shadow?' I touched her hand lightly.

She finished writing, handed me the slate. 'I'm trying to think how you could have been mistaken.' Zana is the only person who tries to explain my actions. Like me, she knows there is always logic in everything I do. Strangeness, maybe, unpredictability, yes, but always logic.

She got off my bed and opened the window she'd previously shut. The sun crept in, still high enough in the sky to crawl through my window that way. This time the shadow on my crumpled bedding was the elongated shadow of iron bars.

She removed a nail cuter from the top drawer of the dressing table. Then slid the cut nails into a small envelope she made with a scrap of paper. While she gathered all her cleaning things together, she was shaking her head from side to side. Just the way you had earlier on. The first time I'd seen either of you do that.

Deafness comes to me, takes you away.

It's a fortnight since that ill-omened lizard fell on my bed. I am too afraid to ask the astrologer how long this period will continue for I fear he will shake his head too.

I keep constant vigil at my doorway. You do not come.

Oh, you come during the day, when Zana is in the room, when Dr Gupta visits, when Balu is mopping the floors. When our relatives crowd around me, chatter all at once, hold up cloudy slates, make sure that I understand they are doing their best to keep me informed. You may have lost your hearing, their eyes say, but that doesn't mean you should stop living. When Zana sees my fingernails begin to rake my scalp, when I slump back against propped pillows, she suggests everyone go to the dining room where tea is laid out. They quickly get off my bed, rush to the door.

But you never come alone. Never when bright stars nail soft sky with hard, piercing brilliance, when the moon waxes and wanes according to her mood.

'Do not get so agitated!' Dr Gupta wrote with heavy hand across the chalkboard on my wall, on the morning that grief-stricken crow fluttered helplessly outside my window, 'Not much was lost when you lost your hearing. Believe me when I say there is nothing left in this world that is worthy of your ears!'

Just as he'd finished writing, you walked in. And I thought you'd already left for work. Dr Gupta took you aside, turned his back to me. When I saw your eyes leave his face, rove the walls, I knew right away what the doctor must have said: 'Delusions! Why she should be suffering delusions I do not know. I think I will increase the dosage.'

No! I wanted to call out to you. Don't listen to him! It is not delusions which make me confused. Just fear. Fear of a universe without sound. Fear of facing a sea of babbling mouths. Fear of losing you.

There is so much I want to say. But you do not come to me, not anymore, not the way you used to when our troubles began. Then, my frustration was your frustration, your ache, mine. I held you close as you said— your mouth pressed against my ear for I was only hard of hearing then—'We must get another specialist to examine you. What all the rest are saying is simply not plausible. I've never heard of such a thing happening before! You develop high fever, the doctor prescribes antibiotics, and you become—'

'Don't say it!' I said, turning my head swiftly, covering your mouth with mine. I ran my fingertips through your hair. I could feel your exhaustion. I was exhausted too. In less than two minutes you were asleep, warm breath fanning my neck, our ankles tightly intertwined. I felt your body take shape under my palms, your flesh warm, malleable to my touch. I heard you then. Your voice gay, confident, as you held our Dilip for the first time: 'I felt it in my bones,' you said. 'On the day of our engagement, the moment you handed me that sweetened cup of tea: Only *you* would give me a son.' Oblivious to Matron who stood in the corner, meticulously folding soft mulmul kerchiefs into tiny triangles. She, who had seen hundreds of women giving birth to hundreds of sons, couldn't help but smile at your words.

The tightness in your voice, possessive, jealous. 'I don't want him in my house ever again. I don't care that his wife is your childhood friend. Did you see how he couldn't keep his eyes off you?'

And another: lazy, languorous, expansive, exaggerating. 'Your breasts are a deeply quenching two-wave ocean,' your mouth reflected moist moon-shine, 'each wave perfectly capped, gently cresting, one just a little bit high-er than the other.'

It was that last voice I kept hearing yesterday afternoon, after Zana handed me your message. 'I finally got through to Dilip just now,' you'd dic-tated on the phone. 'He'll be here in two days. I know his coming will be a tonic for you. I'll see you tomorrow morning. I have a meeting tonight and I don't know how late I'll be.'

I twisted the paper in my hands.

It is not my son I need. It is you. I need you.

I must have fallen asleep then for when I woke the room was smaller, the walls squatter, the ceiling loomed like a vault. Purplish-red shadows stretched interminably, the sunshine dropped lustreless to my floor. I turned the fan to full speed. Hotter air swirled around me faster. I began to feel wet. That's when I took off my sari, pulled at the hooks on my blouse, loosened the drawstrings of my petticoat.

I don't know what they told you when you returned home last night. Balu and the cook.

Zana repeated to me what Balu told her. He said he walked into my room with my afternoon tea and found me at the window, 'unclothed.' (I doubt 'unclothed' is what Balu said but that's how Zana put it.) He told her he shouted for the cook who came running, wrapped me carefully in sheets. Zana cried and cried because she wasn't at home when 'it' happened. 'I had to go to the tailor,' she scribbled, 'but I could have gone some other time.'

I patted her back. 'Don't cry! The cook was very gentle, really. She even chose my favourite colour when she brought me a dry sari. Mauve. Look at it, Zana. Do I not look beautiful? Stop crying! Just tell him to come and see me when he comes home. I will not let Dr Gupta examine me without him.'

But Dr Gupta was waiting outside my room, already too long. He took my pulse, listened to my chest, wrote out a prescription. He kept scratching his arm vigorously, first the left, then the right. Left, right. Then suddenly, he lunged towards the duster that lay alongside my chalkboard and rubbed out what he'd written there two weeks ago.

Deafness came to me, took you away.

My wall with its connecting door is an abandoned prop. Curtain flow-ers lose colour as night enters the dark quarter. I want to tear them down: the curtain, the door, the wall. Want to call out to you. Come to me, come back. I'm sorry for yesterday afternoon. I forgot your note said you would be late coming home. I just wanted you to see me, all of me, that's all. Not the way I once was but the way I still am. I wanted you to see me. I want-ed you to see.

LYNN COADY

~

A GREAT MAN'S PASSING

'Oh may my heart's truth
Still be sung
On this high hill in a year's turning.'

People who didn't know, and that was mostly tourists, thought that the
Sloane house, about a hundred feet backed up from the main road, had to
be deserted. They didn't even think this in a conscious way. They
processed it the way drivers process the things they see on a long, empty
country road. House. Cow. Mailbox. Deserted house. It never occurred to
anyone that such a place could be inhabited.

But it was, and the truth is, it had become so decrepit precisely because
of how inhabited it was. This never occurred to anyone either. No one
thought that a house could gradually be destroyed by how lived in it was.
People passed the Sloane house and thought: deserted. That house has no
one looking after it. The people who drove by the Sloane house and
thought that were the kind of people who assumed that if there was somebody living in a home, it was automatically being looked after.

But it wasn't, because the overriding concern of the Sloane family was
looking after itself. And if the passing tourists had been aware of the size of
the Sloane family, they would understand why there was no time for looking after anything else.

Bess never thought that the Sloane house was deserted because she had
always known better. In the summers, when she and her parents would
drive by on the way to Gramma and Grampa's, Bess would shout, There's
the Sloane house, because it was a landmark that told her they were almost
to the farm, and also because she had been in it before, and, in her little-girl
consciousness, this fact made the house hers.

She knew the Sloanes, too, she knew the name of every single child living
in that house. So they were hers, too. The youngest was Terry, then Margaret,
then Mary Catherine. Then came some boys. Robert and Angus and Roland,
who was Bess' age. Then they started getting older than her. Dougal and Jn'-
Pat. Ann Rose. At that point they reached an age where the names came easier than the faces. Elizabeth. David. Ian. Joseph. Carrie and Stephen. That was

it. Bess bragged to her friends about knowing so big a family.

We go down there every month, almost, she would say. We bring them our old clothes and other stuff. Mary Catherine always gets my old clothes and whatever toys I'm sick of. There's babies and clothes everywhere, in every room. And one of the boys has a weird eye. It don't go right. He wears glasses a hundred feet thick. His name is Angus but they call him Cookie cause his eyes make him look like the Cookie Monster.

At that point, Maureen MacEachern would always try to steal away a little bit of Bess' spotlight. I know! she'd say. Cause my mom is always filling up garbage bags with all of our old stuff and giving them to your Mom to give to them.

Yeah, but you've never been there. I've been in the house and I know them. Dad says they're my third cousins. So I've got fifteen third cousins.

It made Bess mad because Maureen had so much to brag about already, why did she have to take what Bess had. She had lived in the nicest house in town and her dad was deputy-mayor. Bess' dad was on the town council. Their families went on vacations and camping trips together. Plus, Maureen had five brothers and two sisters. That was a pretty big family, too, but it wasn't the same.

Bess had never known what Mr Sloane did, and she hardly even knew what he looked like. He was never there when they came to drop off their garbage bags, or, maybe he was, but had just been obscured by children. Mrs Sloane was always there, her stomach perpetually large because it never had a chance to get small again. She and Mom would talk, she would say, Thank you so much, Ellen, you are always thinking of us, to Mommy. The little girls would follow Bess around and ask her questions and try to show her things while the boys would yell at her and make fun of her and try to get her to chase them. Sometimes she would and sometimes she wouldn't. One time she was chasing Cookie, and he scrambled up onto the trunk of one of the rusted old automobiles that were sprawled alongside of the house. So Bess had reached out and grabbed Cookie by the belt of his pants, and down the pants came, and Cookie's underwear had the silliest patterns and most lurid colours on them that Bess ever could have imagined. Embarrassed more by the shorts than by the fact that she had pulled a boy's pants right off of him, she turned away and pretended to be interested in what the little girls had been trying to tell her ever since she'd arrived. When she looked back, Cookie was returning, hoisting up his pants with a little smile. He didn't care. He wanted her to chase him some more.

When Bess got older, and it began to seem like less of a treat to go see Gramma and Grampa on the weekends, it also became less of an adventure to drop off bags at the Sloanes, which had been par for the course during such visits, just as it had been par for the course to do things like swinging on the thick rope with the hook on the end of it in the barn, which Grampa said never to do and Dad always said, O, go ahead and do it anyway. Like attending mass on Sundays at the small Catholic church down the road where you would always see Mrs Sloane with what Daddy called 'her litter' and Mom would say in the awed, quiet voice that she used when saying prayers with Bess, That woman makes it to church every Sunday. All this was part of the adventure. But when Bess got older it became part of the routine. That's the problem with getting older, Bess thought.

And now, living here in her childhood vacationland, everything was different altogether, and it was strange that she had seen more of the Sloanes when she was a child and living in town, than she did now that she was an adult and living only a few miles down the road. Every once in a while Mommy would say to her something like, Jn'-Pat Sloane's supposed to be getting married. A little girl from the Forks. Cameron, I believe.

And Bess would have to think for a minute before honing in on his identity. He's the dark one?

They're all dark, Bessie. Except for Angus and Ann Rose.

No, I know which one you mean. Which Cameron girl?

Dad would say, Pregnant, I suppose.

Oh, let's not be cynical, Bess would reply.

And every time Mommy would share some Sloane tidbit of news with Bess, she would always bring the topic to a close with the words: Poor MaryKate. Which was Mrs Sloane's first name. Every time something happened to one of the Sloane children, Mommy always spoke as if it had in some deeper, more significant way, to Mrs Sloane. But as far as Bess knew, Mommy hardly ever saw Mrs Sloane anymore. And there they were, just a few miles down the road.

Mid-Fall, Bess had a job. There had been no getting around it. It had fallen into her lap, such a rare thing that to refuse would have been like showing your middle finger to God just when he was in a good mood. The man who owned the Bonnie Prince Inn was an American named Rufus Bank, who asked that you call him Ruf. He had come to Daddy in the summer wanting to know where he could catch trout, and so Dad asked the man over for dinner and took him behind the house and down the side of the hill and they fished about a mile upriver from where Dad's gaspreaux trap was set up. Everyone but the American knew that there wouldn't be any trout, but they also knew that he would be just as satisfied if he caught even one bony gaspreaux, which he did, and he was. They came back up to the house and fried the fish up for Mr Bank's dinner. With it, he drank one of Bess' beer.

'You people have a paradise here, do you know that?' said Ruf, looking around at them all with good-hearted reproach, as though perhaps they were guilty of not knowing it. 'I've wanted to live here all my life. When the Bonnie Prince came up for sale, I said to myself, there's my retirement. Right there. Couldn't believe my luck.' He looked at Bess and he told her that she couldn't have picked a better spot in which to raise her little boy. Then he looked at Dylan, chomping on a pork-chop bone in his high-chair. Bess looked at him too.

In the winters, Ruf had to close the Bonnie Prince, but he left the lounge open for the locals. The previous owner hadn't done that, and if you wanted to get drunk, you either had to drive to Inverness, or go to one of the dances in the South-West Hall, or stay home. Bess had gone to one of the dances, once, in the early summer, with her second cousin. Meg, who was trying to help her to feel welcome. When they arrived outside the Hall, Bess said to Meg, Is it an outdoor dance in this weather? Because it looked as though everyone had gathered out in front instead of inside. Then Bess saw that the crowd was standing in a circle and in the middle of the circle one young man was jumping up and down on another man's head. Meg parked the car close by and the two of them sat in it, passing a bottle of rum back and forth until the fight was over.

'That was Dougal Sloane,' Meg commented, capping the rum and dropping it back into her purse.

'Who?'

'The guy who won.'

'He's gotten big,' Bess said after a moment.

But now there was Ruf's lounge to go to, and he had painted it, and installed a fulltime DJ and every other weekend a band from Blues Mills called 'Ryder' would play there. Also, Ruf had changed the name from the uncomplicated 'Bonnie Prince Inn Lounge' to 'Red Ruf's' because, he said, he had used to have red hair and he noticed that everyone 'around here' had nicknames and that was one of the things he loved about the place. Bess was to learn that the best way to endear yourself to the American was to refer to him affectionately as Red Ruf, as often as you could get away with.

Red Ruf had offered Bess a job because Daddy had asked him to during one of their fishing trips. Daddy wanted Bess to be clear about that.

'There we were in our hip-waders and Ruf's going on about the lounge and how there'll be people coming in from as far away as Whycocomah once he gets his whatdayacallit sound system installed and he's pretty damn sure he's going to be needing some extra staff to help serve the liquor up, and I say, well goddamnit, Ruf, our Bessie's been looking for a job ever since she landed here and the little fella started getting more independent. I know she'd appreciate getting off the welfare. It's been hard on her, you know, what with the little guy . . .'

Lies. Bess hadn't minded the welfare so much at all. It had kept Dylan clothed and fed all summer long, and she earned her own keep by working at home and helping with Gramma and Grampa. Best of all, it allowed for her to be with him every moment, and so Bess, although she heard things on the radio about Welfare Queens, and talk that the government would no longer tolerate her kind of inertia, could not feel guilty about her own reluctance to enter the workforce. She knew this was a great sin in her society, but didn't quite understand why. She saw men on television who said that all they wanted to do was work. They would do anything, clean out toilets, mop floors, but they could not withstand the ignominy of welfare. They said they felt degraded.

All Bess knew was that Dylan was being fed and that she was able to spend as much time with him as she needed, which was all the time. It seemed to her that, if there had to be a government, this was the kind of thing it was supposed to be doing for people. Daddy said that this was naive.

'You have to participate. You can't just live off the sweat of honest, working people.'

'I'm an honest working person, too.'

'You're a hippie that thinks the world owes you something . . .' she saw him stop himself, and filled in the rest. Going around having babies thinking the government's gonna look after them. Free love and all that. He's talking about himself, him and me, Bess thought, smouldering as she always did when she thought about the two of them, playing tug of war and if one person lets go of the taut rope the other will suddenly go flying. As if I am not cleaning up your mother's pasty yellow poo every night, spoon-feeding her curds and potatoes. As if I have not conceded to raise my boy in a funeral home, with the two corpses propped up in front of the TV set, one saying a rosary, the other smoking a cigarette. As if I couldn't have stayed away if I wanted to. As if I still couldn't go.

Ruf didn't know about any of this. All Ruf knew was that he was giving a job to someone who needed it.

'That's very nice of you, Mr Bank,' stunned Bess had said into the phone when he called up with his offer.

'Oh, well,' said Ruf. 'It's nice to know that I can do some good around here, what with the unemployment situation and everything. It's nice to know that I'm not just here for myself, that I can make a little bit of a difference to some of the people—if you know what I mean. You know—you people are my neighbours, now, and I want to help you in any way I can.'

'That's very nice of you,' Bess said again, beginning to panic, looking down at Dylan who was on the floor in front of her playing with her shoe. How long will he want me to work, she wondered. How many hours out of the day? Then there was the fact that she had always thought that the last job she would ever choose for herself would be that of a bartender.

But there was no saying no, there simply wasn't, and she didn't. While she had been talking on the phone to Ruf, the members of her family had all quietly materialized, and when she looked up they were standing there with smiles, as if she had just opened a gift from the three of them.

'Who was that, now?' asked Daddy, smiling most of all.

So now Bess had a job, and even though that was more than could be said for the rest of the family, they still seemed to possess a sort of moral high ground that she would never be able to attain. She thought that it was probably because they were old, and had all worked hard in the past. A million years ago Auntie Marg was a nurse and Dad had done a lot of different things before having enough money to buy a hotel/restaurant, and becoming the kind of upstanding citizen who sits on town councils, and then losing the hotel/restaurant a few years later and not being that kind of citizen anymore. Then Daddy became disillusioned and didn't do much and said that if he couldn't do things his way, he wouldn't do anything at all. And then he lost the house and he said that it was just as well because Mumma and The Boss were getting on and needing someone to take care of themselves and the farm full-time anyway. Plus, moving to the farm meant no mortgage, no rent. 'Now I do what I goddamn well please,' Bess had heard him say to Red Ruf Bank.

But Bess was young and had to work. It was, Dad said, 'a shame' for her not to work, and worse for her not to want to. After Red Ruf's phone call, Bess had been cranky all day and drank all the beer that was in the fridge. She looked outside at the dead, empty field which no snow had had the decency to come and bury yet. In a way, the job had come at a good time, she supposed, with winter on the way and the snow piled up at the doors and windows and no way for her and Dylan to escape down to the river for a swim or even out to the field because Bess hated snow and the idea of plodding along in the wet cold stuff just for the hell of it made no sense to her. So that meant more time spent indoors, but more time spent indoors meant more time in the funeral home, so maybe it would be a good thing to have somewhere to go. Mommy had said, 'It will be good for you to get out.'

What irked her, though, was the momentousness of it all. Mommy making a special Bess-got-a-job dinner that night, and Daddy telling the stories of how he had wrangled the offer out of Red Ruf, reeling him in as they stood in the middle of the river with the pathos of Bess' 'situation.' Bess having to think about what she was going to wear for the first time in months, and everybody happy for her, happy that she was going to be serving up Moosehead to head-stomping pulp-cutters and cod-jiggers. And it wasn't even that. Just happy that she was going to be doing something. Not understanding that time is going to go by and that days are going to pass whether you are doing something or doing nothing. And when you are doing nothing, they go by just as quick, if not quicker—a fact that people who are always doing something will not believe if you tell it to them.

The first two shifts she did for Red Ruf, she had to go to and sit in the employees bathroom and cry because she was wondering what Dylan was doing. She imagined Mommy and Aunt Marg gleefully following him around with aprons full of cookies to be offered in case he fell down and hurt himself or threw some kind of tantrum. It's like being in love, she thought to herself, rubbing her eyes unrestrainedly because she was unused to wearing make-up and forgot that she would be smudging black mascara and blue powder all over her stupid head. Washing her face, she thought, It is, but it isn't.

The next couple of shifts she did were on the weekend, and Bess got her first taste of culture shock, the shock of someone who has been in hiding for over a year, and suddenly finds herself the centre of a large, oddly unsociable party where people seemed to expect more from her than drinks. They wanted to banter, they wanted her to smile and chat and learn their first names and tell them where she was from and who her father was. It seemed that most of them would rather talk to her than the people they were with.

Sometimes, Red Ruf would show up with the intention of helping her at the bar, but most of the time he forgot about that and ended up perching on one of the stools and holding a sort of court among the locals. Most of the locals loved him. He was afforded the status of a 'character' because he was rich and American. This was something you could tell Red Ruf had always longed for but had never been able to attain when he had lived among other rich Americans.

There were awkward moments, like when she noticed her second cousin Meg there with all of her brothers and didn't know if she should speak to the brothers, who were virtually strangers, in the way people are expected to speak to relatives that they haven't spoken to for ages, or, if she should just behave toward them the same way as she did everyone else in the bar. She prayed that Meg would come up to the bar with the brothers in tow and initiate some kind of dialogue that would take the onus off of Bess, but things never happen that way. The first time Bess noticed that her cousins were in the lounge, Meg hadn't even seen Bess working the bar and they went right past her, to a table. Then, a little later, one of the older brothers who, Bess was pretty sure was called Findlay, came up to get beers for everybody and looked right through her. Bess took his order, began setting the beer down in front of him, and, watching the beer bottles very closely, said, 'Do you remember me, Findlay?'

When she looked up, she saw that his gaze had focused in on her a little, even though his face hadn't changed.

'Of course I do, Bess,' he said, and then he took his beer and returned to his table. Bess thought about it for a while before coming to the realization that she had forgotten all about the completely familiarizing power of gossip. Findlay had probably been hearing so much about Bess all throughout the summer from his sister Meg and father Alistair—who liked to talk about anything as often as possible—that it was impossible for him to have lost track of her existence in the way that she had of his, and of so many other people that her parents insisted she knew, and remembered fondly.

When the Sloanes began popping up, Bess had been expecting pretty much the same treatment she'd received from Meg's brothers, who, she could tell right away, had listened intently to every opinion their father Alistair had espoused regarding Bess. She had a pretty good idea as to what these opinions were, because he had also espoused them to Bess numerous times over the summer when he would be sitting across from her at the dinner table tossing back some of Aunt Marg's whiskey after he and Daddy had come up from the trap. In any case, Bess was not bothered with what Alistair's sons thought, she was only relieved to know that she wasn't going to have to be friendly toward them as she had at first feared. As the weekend shifts went by, she came to see from their consistent sponging of drinks and groping of randomly passing arses that they were only slimmed-down, less shambling versions of Alistair, and this made it easy to be unconcerned by them.

But late into one evening, Findlay came weaving up to the bar to have a rare word with her. 'How's she going?' he initiated.

'Good Findlay, how're you?'

'Well well well. She's talking to me,'

'And you're talking to me.'

'I never thought you'd lower yourself,'

'Say hi to Alistair next time you see him.'

'Don't you say nothin about Daddy.'

'Okay,'

'Okay. Some good, you.'

'What—Findlay—what's the problem?'

But Findlay gave her a look as though to say that it was hopeless trying to talk to her, she was too low, or too high, or something ignoble like that, and he shambled away. Whoo, big confrontation, Bess thought, mopping beer up off the counter. But she was grimacing, because it hasn't been good. You people are my neighbours, now.

The first night that she noticed the Sloanes had begun to frequent Red Ruf's, was one time when somebody hollered, 'Foit!' and everybody in the lounge bolted for the door.

'Oh my gosh,' said Red Ruf, gazing out one of the windows, 'Maybe you'd better call the police, Bessie. I don't think I want this kind of thing going on.'

'What's happening?' said Bess, having to stay behind the bar.

'Some young lad's kicking a man's head in out there.'

At that moment, Cookie Sloane hurried in from outside. Bess thought that he had only grown about a foot since the time she had pulled down his pants. Otherwise, he looked completely the same, peering through his thick glasses like they were fog.

'Don't call the mounties,' he said, rushing over the bar. 'Okay, Bessie? Please? The guy was a fucking arsehole. Dougal will finish up in just a bit. Okay?'

'Okay,' said Bessie, forgetting to consult with Ruf.

Cookie smiled, all dirty teeth—'God love ya, dear!'—and ran back outside.

Dougal and Cookie sat on barstools beside one another, Dougal with his head down, looking at his beer, smiling very happily at all the things Cookie was saying to Bess about him.

'He's just a big idiot,' Cookie was saying. 'Stupid as mine and your arses put together. That's what he is. Doesn't know how to do anything except pummel the shit out of some poor bastard who doesn't know how to keep his tongue in his head. Isn't that right you hopeless fucking dumbie?'

'Yes,' said Dougal, smiling.

'How you been, Bessie?' Cookie went on without blinking. When you looked into his freaky eyes through the thickness of those glasses, you expected his voice to sound like it was coming from a mile away. 'Are you good? Mummy told me you was living down here now, up at Ian and Lizzie's place. She said you got knocked up and have a little boy, now. That can be tough, eh? Same thing happened to Ann Rose and Elizabeth, but they're living together in town and doing okay. Sort of a joint effort. Still, it gets me cross. I'm saying to Mary Catherine all the time, Now don't you fuck! I don't care how bored you get, don't do it, it's not all that much fun anyhow and it gives a lot of stupid bastards something to talk about and a person to feel superior to. But I suppose the girls've gotta get their rocks off somehow, too, that's only fair. Somebody told me that girls don't like it, and I used to think that was true but then I had a girlfriend and Jesus Mary and Joseph, how we used to go at it. It was always her wanting to. She's gone, now, though, up to Halifax to study the nursing. She wanted me to write letters but I'm no damn good at it. How's your Grammie and Grampie, Bess? Christ Almighty, they must be getting up there, eh? You Mum's help-ing to take care of them, my mum was saying. My mum says your mums a saint, did you know that? She's always saying what a saint your mum is, and how you guys always used to help us out. I always remember, we'd see you and your mother driving up in the station wagon and it was just like fucking Christmas. The girls would go into hysterics and Mary Catherine would always have to have a lay-down after you left. Anyways, I know I talk too much, but someone's gotta make up for the wordless idiotic won-der over here. I'll have another beer, Bessie, me mouth is pretty dry. That was a good fight, though, you have to admit. The guy didn't look too bad. Listen, Bessie, how are you, though, dear, how are you really?'

With Cookie—and it hadn't been like this with anyone else since she had arrived in the late Spring—it was just like picking up where they had left off. Like any second he would jump up and pull her hair and say, blah, blah, dumb old ugly old stupid old Bess, there she is, and she, delighted, would jump up too and chase him all over the yard until they got so tired that one of them would gasp, 'Times,' and then, after they had rested, Bess would abruptly scream, 'Off times!' and pounce on him. She had not felt as if she could feel like that again in a very long time.

Bess saw Cookie at Red Ruf's almost every weekend, usually with Dougal in tow. Although they caused no more fights, Red Ruf sometimes frowned in a worried, slightly disappointed way when he came in to hold court and spotted Bess haunched over the bar, straining to hear one of Cookie's obser-vations, blatantly ignoring an older patron down on the far end, one of Ruf's own courtiers.

'You know those boys?' he wondered to her one day, in an almost laughably casual tone. Bess had been watching Cookie with glee, out on the dance floor with one of the local girls. Cookie was, by his own admission, 'A dancing fucking fool,' and whenever he wasn't huddled on a barstool beside Dougal, he would sweep into the crowd and descend upon any one of the girls, every one of whom loved him, and lead them, shaking their hips and clapping their hands, out onto the floor where Cookie would commence to stomp up and down in his workboots, shaking his frail blonde head in ecstasy and pausing every now and again to adjust his glasses.

'Which boys?'

'The boys who started that fight,' Ruf said pointedly. He referred to it as 'that fight,' because it was the first one ever to occur at Red Ruf's and there was no doubt in his mind that if it hadn't been for that first fight, none of the other ones that broke out regularly each weekend would ever have come about.

'Cookie and Dougal. They're great guys, Red Ruf. Look at Cookie out there. I don't think you'd get any women in here if it wasn't for him.'

Ruf squinted out at the dance floor with all the ill-concealed befuddlement that all big men demonstrate when they see women obviously enjoying themselves with the kind of man that Cookie was. It made Bess laugh out loud, which made Ruf jump and stare at her. As if Cookie was a man at all and not a sexless little sprite who made you feel as if he valued your company over everyone else's and told you everything as though it were the greatest of secrets and talked dirtier than anyone you've ever met, yet with an absolute innocence.

'You like that little fella, Bessie?' Ruf asked, turning his squint her way.

'He's adorable.'

'I don't know,' said Ruf, big white head swivelling back toward the dance floor. 'The first time I saw him and his lunkhead brother in here I kinda figured he was what your Dad would call a shit-disturber.'

Bess folded her arms cooly and gazed off in the same direction as Ruf. 'They're my cousins,' she said.

'Oh, Bessie, dear,' he said, jumping again. 'Why don't you set yourself up with a beer, dear.'

Bess smiled, setting herself up with a beer. Ruf had yet to understand that everybody was cousins.

One night Bess arrived from work to find the funeral home minus one ghoul. Gramma sat on her side of the room, rocking in time with her prayers to the virgin and Mommy sat close beside her on a chair she had brought out from the kitchen, nodding at the garbled prayers and watching Dylan play with trucks. The television was on, babbling news. Bess came in and leaned against Gramps's empty chair, the stink of ancient smoke and piss emanating from its fibres. On the floor beside it sat the emptied stewed tomato can which he used to hork his old-man's juice into. Beside that was a pack of matches. Dylan came up and wrapped his body around Bess' leg.

'Took him to the hospital, did they?'

'Yes God love the poor soul.'

'When was this?'

'Around suppertime.'

'Poor Ian,' said Gramma to nobody. 'Croc a nian, scat a nean,'—which was a song about salt cod that recently she had been mistaking for the Our Father.

He was in the hospital about a week, Dad and Aunt Marg usually with him, Mommy alone with the baby and the invalid. At supper one night, Gramma spit out a mouthful of potatoes and curds and said, 'Ach, poor Daddy. Dyin of the cancer, you know.'

Aunt Marg cleaned up the mouthful with a dishtowel, pressing her lips together. 'He doesn't have the cancer, Mumma.'

Gramma spit again, at the air. 'If he's dying, he must have the cancer. We won't be able to bury him here, he'll give cancer to everybody, all the relatives. Bury him on the mainland.'

'He's not dying, Mumma,' said Aunt Marg. 'He won't give his cancer to anyone.'

Bess believed this, that he wasn't dying. He never died, and neither did she. Both of them had been going in and out of the hospital for as long as she could remember. Even when she was a little girl everyone considered them too old to live. 'This is it,' everyone always said, not happy and not sad. Grim. Just grim, and determined. But they never died, and Bess was positive they never would.

Saturday night she made a mistake that fated Sunday morning into being a bad one. She had been setting herself up with beers during most of her shift as Red Ruf often invited her to do so, and when the time came to take off her apron and accept a lift home from him, Cookie, instead, instructed her to sit at a table with himself and Dougal, down a few, and they would take her home in a bit. Loving Cookie and Dougal as she did, this seemed at first a reasonable idea, but once she got out from behind the bar and in the centre of the crowd, the culture shock resurfaced and everything was terrible again. All of Cookie's many friends approached the table to talk to him, and when they saw Bess there, they tried to talk to her too. Sometimes Cookie went off to dance, but the friends stayed, talking to Bess and asking her questions. She knew them all remotely from working the bar, but now felt that this pleasant remoteness had been ruined. There would be no more of these people coming up, smiling at her, asking for a beer and saying please, and no more of Bess obliging them with another smile and they going away.

Cookie, indicating the dance floor, said to her at one point, 'Let's get on out there for Jesus' sake,' and she thought that she might as well, but once Bess found herself standing there across from Cookie doing his sweaty workboot stomp, she felt very large and vivid with the lights flashing on her and the music all around, and so she reached over to pull on Cookie's sleeve and tell him that she was going to sit back down again. He nodded and bounded off toward the tables to get someone else.

And it was terrible because she had no way home except for Cookie and Dougal's father's fish truck parked outside. When she had told Ruf, no thanks, she'd be staying, he blinked at her in a kind of lost way and then said, Alright, pulling on his jacket. She saw now that she should've gone home when Ruf offered his customary lift, like she always did–that would've been the right thing to do because now she was trapped with all these people and the road home was three miles long, unlit and lined on either side with woods. And, this was what always happened, the more nervous she got, the faster she finished her beer. Dougal, who sat always at the table, smiling, never getting up to dance or do anything except go to the men's room, looked over at her accumulation of empties and commented that she was 'quite the Jesus partier,'

Cookie bounded over, sweaty, and sat down. He leaned over and punched Bess on the shoulder, 'Wouldn't even gimme a dance!' He laughed like it was a joke, which was a trick of his Bess had come to know. He used it when he sensed somebody was uncomfortable. Just saying things and laughing at them, but making you feel as if you were actually the funny one, the clever wit. She smiled and shrugged and told him she was sorry as though what she had done was natural and excusable. They all pretended this.

On the other side of her, her second cousin Findlay thumped into a chair.

'Findlay ya crazy cocksucker,' Cookie yelled above the music.

'Meg's wonderin how you're doing,' he said, leaning toward Bess.

'Oh, is Meg here?' Bess stretched her neck and peered into the crowd.

'Oh, is Meg here?' Findlay repeated, pretending to look desperately around.

'Oh for Christ's sake.' Bess, who was now drunk, said.

'Now what's that supposed to mean. Eh? We been here all night, looking y' right in the eye. I wonder what yer Dad would say, hearin you turnin up yer nose at Alistair's kids.'

'Here's a beer for ya, Findlay,' said Cookie.

'I don't suppose you'd lower yourself to dance.'

'No thanks,' Bess answered helplessly.

'Turned me down too, jeezless teaser!' shouted Cookie, still holding out Findlay's beer. 'Walked right off the dance floor, me standing there with my dick in my hand! Trying to make me look silly or something is my guess,'

'That's about what I figured.' Findlay attempted to stand up, and, after a few minutes, succeeded at it, finally accepting the extended bottle. 'Cookie,' he said, pointing with it, 'You don't talk to me, you little fairy bastard.'

Dougal stood up, still smiling.

'Oh, no, no, no,' Bess shouted, shaking her head extravagantly.

But Findlay had already lumbered hastily off toward his table, wherever that was. And Bess got up and went behind the bar to use the phone. She called her father who said that they hadn't even known where she was and here's the poor little fella squalling for his mother and nobody knowing what the Jesus to tell him, had to let him cry himself to sleep and Mommy pacing the floor half in tears and everybody worried sick to death about the Boss until finally I decide to give Ruf a call and, Oh my! She's out drinking with the Sloanes, Alec, didn't you know? Didn't she even call?

Daddy, won't you come get me please?

So Sunday morning was fated to be a bad one. Bess woke at around six in the morning, the sun still pale, and stayed awake even though she had several semi-dreams which were about ridiculous things like walking across the yard with the dumb chickens that her grandparents used to keep, scurrying behind her thinking she would feed them, and then turning abruptly around and running at them, causing them all to cluck and scatter hysterically. On the other side of the room, the little boy breathed with comfortable steadiness. Bess tried to convince herself that, because of the dreams, she was really asleep, unaware of any headache.

At around eight o'clock, the house came awake, the first stirrings taking place in the bathroom down the hall and then extending into the kitchen downstairs. Bess had a brief dream about their dead black steer Uncle Remus, who tried to kill her in the summer and Daddy and Alistair had to shoot it. In the dream she got Uncle Remus mixed up with Candy, their pony, and she was standing alongside of Uncle Remus out in the middle of the field, stroking his nose and feeding him a carrot. Uncle Remus chewed on the carrot thoughtfully before looking up at Bess and saying, Well, of course you must understand why. And Bess was embarrassed for him and stroked his nose furiously. Of course, of course, don't give it another thought.

Downstairs, the phone rang. It was their line, one long and two short, and she heard Marg scurry to answer it. Dylan turned over, sighing, would be awake soon wanting Bess to play and watch the sparse Sunday morning cartoons. Things were quiet downstairs for a little while, maybe a half an hour, and then Bess could hear Mommy clear her throat, get up from a chair, and cross the floor. Then Bess heard her feet on the staircase, creak, creak, and she cleared her throat again. She was coming up very deliberately, to wake up Bess. Bess heard her coming down the hall, pushing aside the already half-open door. Dylan turning over again and probably opening his eyes and looking at her as she sat down on the edge of Bess' bed. Mommy touching her shoulder and clearing her throat a third time and then leaning over to kiss Bess soft on the cheek which was the way she had woken Bess up since the beginning of everything.

'I have some bad news.'

'Grampa's dead.'

'An hour ago. Daddy says we're going to wake him here.'

Bess sat up. 'Jesus Christ.' Dylan was awake and smiling at her.

Mommy ran her thin hands through her short hair. 'I know,' she said. 'We're going to have to start the cleaning today, as soon as you're dressed.'

MaryKate Sloane brought six plates of sandwiches and two large bowls of potato salad. She also brought a banana bread and a cinnamon loaf and two tins full of biscuits. She also brought a bottle of rye and a bottle of scotch, which she presented to Auntie Marg.

'I couldn't remember, Margaret, was it the Jack Daniel's you liked? Or the Johnnie Walker?'

'It's the Johnnie Walker dear. God love you. It all goes down the same hole, in any case.'

She had pulled up wedged between Cookie and Dougal in her husband's fish truck. When they got out, Bess saw that the back was full of boxes with food in them, and her daughter Mary Catherine had ridden back there too, partly to hold the boxes in place but mostly because there was no room in the front. She sat primly on top of a box, wearing a jacket that certainly couldn't have kept her warm enough during the ride, and high heels, and smoothing down a black skirt. Bess was very pleased to see her for some reason, and wanted to stay close to her the whole time she was there and ask her questions about how she was doing in school and whatever else she was up to these days.

'We're here to help, not as guests,' Mrs Sloane said. 'Not that we don't want to pay our respects to Ian, God love his soul, but anything you need done, you tell me or one of the boys or Mary and we'll see to it. Now you get back to your guests and we'll serve this here food up.'

'Don't be so foolish, MaryKate,' Aunt Marg protested.

'No, no, no,' said Mrs Sloane, picking up one of the boxes that Dougal had hefted from the truck. 'Let me see. This is the pickles. I'll need some little bowls, unless you'd just like to serve them in the jars.'

Daddy had hired a fiddler to sit in the corner with a drink at his feet and play mournful Scotch/Irish tunes. He had not actually been hired, Daddy had called him up with the request and offered to pay him for it, but, because he was an old friend of the family, the fiddler refused. The fiddler was actually a celebrity of sorts and most of the guests considered it something of an event, having him there. He was an old man in a wheelchair with a sagging pink face and pure white hair and black, fifties-style glasses. He had a deep, resonating voice and was known to be a story-teller. Someone from Ontario had once included him in a book of maritime folklore, and now he was widely considered a sage. He remembered Bess' father as a little boy, he'd told her once.

Bess was in a state of nervous irritation. She had never seen so many people in the house at once. For the last three days, the place was full, morning and night as many of them were relatives from Boston and Ontario with no other place to stay. The corpse was laid out in the living room, the first thing she saw in the morning when she got up, the last when she went to bed at night. She worried about Dylan, about his psyche and all that, even though he appeared to be having the time of his life, and it was all Bess could do to keep him away from the coffin, from poking philosophically at its contents. It was Cookie, usually, who would intercept him at just the last minute, sweeping him up and away just as the baby was about to experiment with one of Grampa's eyelids. Cookie would take him off into a corner somewhere and bounce him up and down on his knee, singing,

> . . . A deedle deedle dump
> diddle dump diddle dump
> A deedle deedle dump
> Deedle dump dump dump!

—And on the last 'dump' he would abruptly open his legs, dropping Dylan through the gap. Dylan loved this.

There were relatives like most people had flies in the summer. Cousins and uncles. No aunts except for Marg and a couple of great-ones, arriving with a child or grandchild supporting either arm, wearing black fur coats purchased over forty years ago, and freakish little black hats with veils that had to be pinned into their webby hair if they were to remain in place. The aunts sat in a corner on either side of Gramma's chair, fingering black rosaries, and guiding her through the correct number of Our Fathers and Hail Marys. The procession stopped by her chair to kiss her before heading to the coffin.

'God bless his dear soul, Elizabeth.'

'Well, he's in a better place now, God love him.'

'Yes God love his soul.'

'He's happy now, dear. No need to cry for poor Ian.'

'No God bless him.'

Bess had never in her life heard Gramma so lucid, let alone so gracious. Something had come back to her. The procession moved away from her chair murmuring My God what a woman.

Daddy and the uncles sat in another corner of the living room, drinking coffee and looking extremely sober. Some were Dad's uncles and some were his brothers. They were all reformed, watching the youngsters soak it up with pity and contempt, the contempt, of course, for the young, and the pity for themselves.

Uncle Roddie's children, for instance, were something of a mess. They had all grown up in Ontario and visited as children in the summers. They were all older than Bess, and she could remember worshipping them with their clothes and cigarettes. They had been young in the sixties, and so the girls were very independent, one wearing a brushcut. They drank beer and were exotic. Now they were all members of the Liberal party, which still made them exotic, and a little dangerous, in Daddy's eyes. Daddy had always been wary of Roddie's girls. What do you do with girls like that, he always wanted to know. The fact that only one of them had ever gotten married seemed to prove whatever point he was trying to make.

Most of Roddie's kids were in the civil service, but one had gone to art school and now worked in the Museum of Civilization. They were still the way they had been, independent and open-minded, arguing with Daddy about the French. Whenever they visited, they would do things like buy a case of Alexander Keith's and go to square dances and Judique on the Floor Days and all the other festivals. They would come back to the house and sit in the kitchen with their Keith's and start all their sentences with 'Jesus, Mary and Joseph,' and 'Lord t'undering Jesus.' They would play their Rankin Family and Rita MacNeil tapes.

But now they were a mess because Grampa had died and they remembered things about him that Bess didn't, or so she supposed. One of them plunked down beside Bess on the couch and asked her how she was holding up and she said fine.

'You were with him right up until the end.'

'Yes.'

'Last time I was down was five years ago, I think. God, maybe more. I never had a chance to get down. At home, we always would talk about it, spending maybe a month out of the summer, visiting all the relatives just like we used to. What was he like?'

'He wasn't like much of anything. I mean, he was pretty old.'

'Ah, Bessie, you don't remember him like I do. What a man. What a great man. The stories he used to tell. But a simple man, you know?'

But I've lived with him almost all my life, Bess wished to say. Then she felt she was being callous all of a sudden and got up to get Auntie Marg, very dignified and controlled with her hand around her glass, because she would be able to talk to the cousins the way they wanted to be talked to. Bess penanced herself by fetching drinks for everybody and bringing the more distracted ones plates of food.

'Sit down, sit down, Bessie,' said MaryKate Sloane. 'Mary Catherine and the boys are taking care of all that.'

'No, no, no,' said Bess.

Cookie, in fact, was sitting at the dining room table with a scotch alongside of him, picking at a tray of squares. 'Sit down for the love of Christ, Bessie. Wait, fix yourself a drink first.'

She sat down, feeling a tingling in her legs. He didn't say anything while she took her first sip.

'That's a nice buck your Dad's got hanging outside,' Cookie finally remarked. 'Got it on the weekend, did he?'

'No, just the other day,' she said, thinking for the first time about the gutted deer, swinging in the wind upside down from the big, leafless maple, with a red, open gash down its front. Everybody had forgotten about it. She thought that it probably wasn't a thing to have outside of a wake, but she wasn't sure. Nobody had said anything until now.

'Season finished Saturday,' Cookie pointed out.

'I know,' said Bess, 'but there was nothing to be done. Daddy looked out into the field early the other morning and it was just standing there.'

'No shit!'

'Yes he nearly killed himself going for the rifle.'

'Were you there, did you see it go down?'

'Oy, yes. Alistair was asleep on the couch because he had passed out the night before and Daddy was hollering for him to get up.'

'Did he get up?'

'He got up just in time to see Daddy shoot it.'

It had been just like the time with Uncle Remus. Men running to and fro, hollering to each other. Except Uncle Remus had been crazy and the buck just stood there the whole time, in the morning frost.

'Well I'll be jiggered.' said Cookie, leaning back.

'Do you think anybody noticed it, Cookie?'

'The deer? Jesus, yes, she looks great.'

Daddy wandered in and put his coffee cup down on the table. He examined the trays for something good.

'I was just saying to Bessie that's a hell of a nice deer you got out there,' Cookie told him.

'Thank you Angus,' Daddy said, picking up a square. 'You tell your mother to sit down and have a bite to eat, now. There's no need to her going to all this trouble.'

'She don't mind at all, but I'll go see if I can bring her a bite,' Cookie got up apologetically and went to find his mother, and Daddy sat down in his spot.

'Glad to see you're enjoying yourself,' he said, indicating Bess' drink.

'I'm taking a break, here.'

'What's all this with the little Sloane fella?'

'Cookie's nice.'

'Cookie's nice, is he? Weird little eyeball bastard. Ruf says you're just as thick as thieves, you and the Sloane boys. I said to him, I hope that's not right, Ruf, I honestly do.'

'What's wrong with the Sloanes?' she said to him pointedly.

He held up his hands. 'MaryKate's a saint and I'd never say a word against her, now.'

'Well, what the hell?'

'Don't let me hear about you running all over hell with those boys, that's all I'm saying.'

'I don't. I never do anything.'

'Drunk til all hours with the Boss on his deathbed.'

And what was there to say to that? There was nothing to say. The times when Bess was angriest were always the times when there was nothing to say. When Daddy told an unfair truth and made it so that there was nothing to say. She got up and went to find Cookie so that she could make a joke out of it.

Later, she was to feel sorry, getting angry and getting up like that so that she could be away from him. She felt sorry watching him move among all the people that he was so unused to with nothing to defend himself but an empty coffee mug and a napkin with a brownie on it. He wore a grey wool sweater that stretched over his belly, and a tie stuffed down inside of it, so you could only see the knot. His father was dead. The problem was, Bess kept having to remind herself of that, that today was an especially bad day for him, and that all of his anger was justified today. And it was basically her fault. She knew that he was the angriest man in the world and that it was her fault. That his father had died, and that he was poor and then not poor and then poor again, that he had been an alcoholic but then got to a point where he had to quit, and so quit, all by himself, without any help from AA or anyone. It was her fault because she had done nothing the right way. She had done nothing in her life to make any of it worthwhile.

Red Ruf Bank, looking like a large, grey baby in his dark suit and with his combed-down hair, got on well with Leland MacEachern when both of them put in an appearance on the last day of the wake, Leland and his wife and daughter Maureen in tow, Maureen probably having been dragged along because she was the closest in his family to Bess' age, and since they had played together on all the camping and fishing trips that their families had gone on all those years ago, both families assumed that they were friends.

It was rather an awesome thing, Leland coming to pay his respects, because he was now an MLA in the Conservative government and you sometimes saw him on television. After he had spoken quietly to Gramma, holding her hand all the while, and knelt down beside the corpse to pay his respects, he stood chatting with Ruf and Daddy and all the men, and his wife and Maureen stood with the women, Bess trying to think of something to say to Maureen, who had grown very sleek and stylish, in a conservative kind of way.

'How's your little boy?' Maureen wanted to know.

'He's very good.'

Mrs MacEachern turned her head and said, 'Oh, that reminds me, Ellen, we brought a bag down for those people you used to help, remember?'

'The Sloanes.'

'The Sloanes! But I was just thinking that there may be one or two things in there to fit Bess' little one. David's boy Peter outgrows his things faster than we can buy them, so everything's practically unused!'

And, before Bess had time to think about it, she had answered enthusiastically, that this was great, and she couldn't wait to look through the bag. She was momentarily enchanted by the thought of Dylan in new clothes, which he needed, but after she had stood there listening to the women talk for a little while, the feeling wore off. She had just turned to resume her search for Cookie, when she realized that he was approaching with Dylan in one arm and fresh scotch for Bess.

'Do you want to know something funny?' she said to him, relieving him of both Dylan and the drink. 'Every now and again I find myself having a good time.'

'It's all this free booze,' said Cookie. 'Do *you* want to know something funny? You know that wire fence in the playground of the Forks school?' Bess shook her head and reminded him that they hadn't gone to school together. 'Oh, yeah. Well there's this fence in behind the school that they put there to keep all the little bastards from running off into the woods at recess. Anyways, every day at recess and lunch, I used to go and talk to the fence.'

'Talk to the fence.'

'Yes, that fence was my Jesus best friend. And I gave him a name too. Jaimeson.'

'Oh, yeah.'

'Maybe if little Dilly here goes to school at the Forks, he'll take to talking to Jaimeson too.'

'I hope to God he doesn't.'

Maureen MacEachern, Bess saw, was observing them for lack of anything else to do. Bess looked at her and said, 'Oh, this is Dylan,' jostling the boy in her arms to draw Maureen's attention.

'What a sweetie,' said Maureen, 'Oooh what a sweetie,' she poked at his nose. Cookie stood there, smiling, trying to see through his glasses.

'This here,' added Bess, hastily putting her free arm around Cookie and towering over him, also spilling a little bit of her drink, 'is my husband.'

'Is that right?'

'His name,' said Bess, 'is Red Angus John-Dougal Sloane McFeely.'

'But he doesn't even have red hair!' said Maureen.

'No, I know. They call him that because his great uncle once had an Irish setter.'

Bess put Dylan down and let him run.

A moment later, she explained to Cookie, who hadn't even questioned, 'Daddy figures you and me are going to run away together.'

'Actually, you can't blame me, most men are afraid of that,' he said, looking thoughtful. 'Me running off with their women. I'm a known snatch-sniffer.'

Bess couldn't believe it, this at the poor old bastard's wake. She had to run to the bathroom, it was so funny.

NOTES ON AUTHORS

❧

EDNA ALFORD (b. 1947). Born and raised in Turtleford, Saskatchewan, she was educated at the University of Saskatchewan. In 1975 she co-founded the literary magazine *Dandelion*, and she is currently associate director of the Writing Studio at the Banff Centre for the Arts. Alford has published two collections of short fiction, *A Sleep Full of Dreams* (1981) and *The Garden of Eloise Loon* (1986). In 1988 she was awarded the Marion Engel Award. She edited, with Claire Harris, the anthology *Kitchen Talk: Contemporary Women's Prose and Poetry* (1992).

MARGARET ATWOOD (b. 1939). Born in Ottawa, Margaret Eleanor Atwood moved with her family to Sault Ste Marie in 1945, and to Toronto a year later. She was educated at the University of Toronto, Radcliffe College, and Harvard University. Beginning with *Double Persephone* (1961), she has published more than a dozen collections of poetry; the most recent is *Morning in the Burned House* (1995). Her first novel, *The Edible Woman* (1969), was followed by *Surfacing* (1972), *Lady Oracle* (1976), *Life Before Man* (1979), *Bodily Harm* (1981), *The Handmaid's Tale* (1985), *Cat's Eye* (1988), *The Robber Bride* (1993), and *Alias Grace* (1996). In addition, she has published five collections of short fiction—*Dancing Girls* (1977), *Murder In the Dark* (1983), *Bluebeard's Egg* (1983), *Wilderness Tips* (1991), and *Good Bones* (1992)—and three of criticism: *Survival: A Thematic Guide to Canadian Literature* (1972), *Second Words: Selected Critical Prose* (1982), and *Strange Things: The Malevolent North in Canadian Literature* (1995). Atwood has received numerous honours, including the Governor General's Award (twice), the Molson Prize (1981), Companion of the Order of Canada (1981), the Government of France's Chevalier dans l'Ordre des Arts et des Lettres (1994), and the Giller Prize for Fiction (1996).

HIMANI BANNERJI (b. 1942). Born in Bangladesh when it was still part of India, she was educated at Visva Bharati University, Santiniketan, and Jadavpur University, West Bengal, where she also taught English. She immigrated to Canada in 1969 to pursue graduate studies at the University of Toronto and is now Professor of Sociology at York University. Her recent publications include *Thinking Through* (1995); *Returning the Gaze: Essays on Racism, Feminism, and Politics* (1993), which she edited; *Writing on the Wall: Essays on Culture and Politics* (1993); and *Unsettling Relations: The University as a Site of Feminist Struggle* (1991), which she co-edited. She has also published two collections of poetry, *A Separate Sky* (1982) and *Doing Time* (1986), as well as a children's novel, *Coloured Pictures* (1991). Her stories, essays, and poems have appeared in many literary and academic journals.

JUDY FONG BATES (b. 1949). Born in China, she came to Canada as a child and grew up in several small Ontario towns. She now lives in Toronto. Bates's stories have been broadcast on CBC radio and have appeared in *Fireweed*, *This Magazine*, and *Canadian Forum*. Her collection *China Dog: And Other Tales from a Chinese Laundry* was published in 1997.

SANDRA BIRDSELL (b. 1942). Sandra Bartlette was born in Hamiota and raised in Morris, Manitoba. After living for many years in Winnipeg, she now teaches English at Capilano College in North Vancouver. She began publishing her stories in western journals such as *Grain, Capilano Review, NeWest Review,* and *Prairie Fire.* Her first book, *Night Travellers* (1982), a collection of stories set in the fictional town of Agassiz, won the Gerald Lampert Memorial Award. It was followed by *Ladies of the House* (1984), stories linked to the first collection through interrelated storylines about the Lafrenière family; in 1987 the two collections were reissued in one volume as *Agassiz Stories.* Birdsell has written two novels: *The Missing Child* (1987) won the W.H. Smith/*Books in Canada* First Novel Award, and *The Chrome Suite* (1992) won the McNally Robinson Award for Manitoba Book of the Year. She won the Marion Engel Award in 1993, and in 1997 she published *The Two-Headed Calf,* a collection of stories, and *The Town That Floated Away,* a children's book.

DIONNE BRAND (b. 1953). Born in Trinidad, Brand immigrated to Canada in 1970. She studied at the University of Toronto and the Ontario Institute for Studies in Education, and was a founding member and editor of *Our Lives,* the first Black women's newspaper in Canada. She has published six volumes of poetry: *Earth Magic* (1978), a collection for children; *Primitive Offensive* (1982); *Winter Epigrams and Epigrams to Ernesto Cardenal in Defense of Claudia* (1983); *Chronicles of the Hostile Sun* (1984); *No Language Is Neutral* (1990); and *Land to Light On* (1997), which won a Governor Genera's Award. In addition, she is the author of a collection of short fiction, *Sans Souci and Other Stories* (1988); a collection of essays, *Bread Out of Stone: Recollections, Sex, Recognitions, Race, Dreaming, Politics* (1994); and two novels, *In Another Place, Not Here* (1996) and *At the Full and Change of the Moon* (1999).

BETH BRANT (DEGONWADONTI) (b. 1941). A Bay of Quinte Mohawk from the Tyendinaga Territory in Ontario, Brant started to write at the age of forty. Since then she has published two books of short stories, *Mohawk Trail* (1985) and *Food and Spirits* (1991), as well as *Writing as Witness: Essay and Talk* (1994), *A Gathering of Spirit: Writing and Art by Indian Women* (1984) and *I'll Sing Till the Day I Die: Conversations with Tyendinaga Elders* (1995). A founder of Turtle Grandmothers, a group that assists and gathers information about Native women writers, she has often taught creative writing and has published widely in literary magazines, including those focusing on gay and lesbian issues.

BONNIE BURNARD (b. 1945). Born in Saskatchewan, Burnard now lives in Ontario. In 1983 several of her stories appeared in the anthology *Coming Attractions*; others have been published in literary magazines, broadcast on radio, and dramatized for television. Her collection *Women of Influence* (1988) won the Commonwealth Award for Best First Book, *Casino and Other Stories* (1994) was named Saskatchewan Book of the Year, and in 1995 she won the Marion Engel Award. Her first novel *A Good House* was published in 1999. The fiction editor of the prairie literary periodical *Grain* from 1982 to 1986, she also edited the short-fiction anthologies *The Old Dance: Love Stories of One Kind or Another* (1986) and *Stage Line: Stories by Men* (1995).

SHARON BUTALA (b. 1940). Sharon Le Blanc was born in northern Saskatchewan, near the village of Nipawin. She received a B.A. in English and Art at the University of Saskatchewan and a decade later obtained a B.Ed. With her second husband, Peter Butala, she lives on a cattle ranch in southwest Saskatchewan. She has published two collections of short stories, *Queen of the Headaches* (1985) and *Fever* (1990), and six novels:

Country of the Heart (1984), *The Gates of the Sun* (1986), *Luna* (1988), *Upstream: 'Le pays d'en haut'* (1991), *The Fourth Archangel* (1992), and *The Garden of Eden* (1998), a sequel to *Country of the Heart*. *The Perfection of the Morning* (1994) and *Coyote's Morning Cry* (1995) are collections of essays.

ANNE CARSON (b. 1950). Born in Toronto, Carson was educated at the University of Toronto and has taught at the University of Calgary, Princeton University, and Emory University in Atlanta, Georgia; she is currently professor of classics at McGill University in Montreal. Widely published in American journals, including *Grand Street* and *The New Yorker*, she is the author of *Eros the Bittersweet: An Essay* (1986); *Short Talks* (1995), a collection of prose poems later included in *Plainwater: Essays and Poetry* (1995); and *Glass, Irony and God: Essays and Poetry* (1995). In 1996 she won the Lannan Literary Award, a $50,000 prize given by the Lannan Foundation in Los Angeles.

JOAN CLARK (b. 1934). Born in Liverpool, Nova Scotia, Joan MacDonald studied drama at Acadia University and education at the University of Alberta. She married Jack Clark, an engineer with the Royal Canadian Air Force, and went with him to Winisk, Hudson Bay. Living in Alberta for twenty years, she was president of the Writers' Guild of Alberta and editor (with Edna Alford) of *Dandelion*, the province's first literary magazine. She first made her name as a children's writer, publishing short fiction and poetry in literary magazines. Her first adult book was the short-story collection *From a High Thin Wire* (1982). It was followed by a novel, *The Victory of Geraldine Gull* (1988), inspired by her early experiences in Hudson Bay. A second story collection, *Swimming Toward the Light*, was published in 1990, she won the Marion Engel Award in 1991, and a second novel, *Eiriksdottir: A Tale of Dreams and Luck*, appeared in 1994. She currently resides in Newfoundland.

LYNN COADY (b. 1970). Coady was raised by her adoptive family in Port Hawkesbury, Cape Breton, and educated at Carleton University in Ottawa. Now living in Vancouver, she is the author of three plays and a screenplay as well as a novel, *Strange Heaven* (1998). Her stories have appeared in journals including *The Antigonish Review*, *The Fiddlehead*, *Free Magaine*, and *Other Voices*, and in the anthology *Fiddlehead Gold*. Her first collection of stories *Play the Monster Blind* will appear in 2000.

MARIAN ENGEL (1933–85). Marian Passmore was born in Toronto and grew up in the smaller Ontario cities of Sarnia, Galt, and Hamilton. Educated at McMaster and McGill universities, she studied French literature at Aix-en-Provence, France, and taught for a while in Cyprus. In 1964 she returned to Canada, where she married Howard Engel (from whom she was later divorced) and made Toronto her home. In addition to radio scripts, journalism, two books for children, and two collections of short stories—*Inside the Easter Egg* (1975) and *The Tattooed Woman*, which appeared posthumously in 1985—she wrote seven novels: *No Clouds of Glory* (1968), re-issued in 1974 as *Sara Bastard's Notebook*; *The Honeyman Festival* (1970); *Monodromos* (1973), reissued in 1975 as *One Way Street*; *Joanne* (1975); *Bear* (1976), which won a Governor General's Award; *The Glassy Sea* (1978); and *Lunatic Villas* (1981). Her correspondence with Hugh MacLennan was published as *Dear Marian, Dear Hugh* (1995), edited by Christl Verduyn.

CYNTHIA FLOOD (b. 1940). Born in Toronto, she was educated at the University of Toronto and the University of California, Berkeley, and in 1969 she moved to Vancouver.

Her stories have appeared in several anthologies, as well as literary journals including *Fireweed*, *Queen's Quarterly*, *Room of One's Own*, and *Wascana Review*. She has published two collections of stories, *The Animals In Their Elements* (1987) and *My Father Took a Cake to France* (1992), the title story of which won the $10,000 Journey Prize in 1990. In addition, Flood won the Western Magazine Award for Fiction in 1993.

MAVIS GALLANT (b. 1922). Born Mavis de Trafford Young in Montreal and educated in Canada and the United States, she worked for the National Film Board and the Montreal *Standard*. Following a brief marriage to John Gallant, in 1950 she moved to Paris, where she has lived ever since. Although Gallant has published two novels, *Green Water, Green Sky* (1959) and *A Fairly Good Time* (1970), she is best known for her shorter fiction, collected in *The Other Paris* (1956); *My Heart Is Broken* (1959); *The Pegnitz Junction* (1973); *The End of the World and Other Stories* (1973); *From the Fifteenth District* (1979); *Home Truths* (1981), which won a Governor General's Award; *Overhead in a Balloon: Stories of Paris* (1985); *In Transit* (1988); *Across the Bridge* (1993); *The Moslem Wife and Other Stories* (1994); and *The Selected Stories* (1996). A number of her essays and book reviews are collected in *Paris Notebooks: Essays and Reviews* (1986).

CONNIE GAULT (b. 1949). Born in Central Butte, Saskatchewan, Gault has lived in Ontario, Quebec, Alberta, and British Columbia, and is a former fiction editor of the literary magazine *Grain*. She has published two plays, *Sky* (1989) and *The Soft Eclipse* (1990), and two story collections, *Some of Eve's Daughters* (1986) and *Inspection of a Small Village* (1996). Her plays have been produced across Canada, and a number of her radio dramas have been broadcast on the CBC and the BBC World Service.

SHREE GHATAGE (b. 1957). Born in Bombay, India, she now lives in St John's, Newfoundland. Among the journals in which Ghatage's stories have appeared are *Canadian Fiction Magazine*, *Antigonish Review*, *Grain*, and *The Malahat Review*. The winner of three awards in the Newfoundland and Labrador Arts and Letters Competition, she published her first book, *Awake When All the World Is Asleep*, in 1997.

MARGARET GIBSON (b. 1948). Margaret Gibson was born and raised in Toronto, where she still lives. Her formal education ended at grade ten because of mental illness, which has become the central theme of her writing. She has published four story collections: *The Butterfly Ward* (1976), the first edition of which was published under her married name, Gilboord, and won the City of Toronto Award; *Considering Her Condition* (1978); *Sweet Poison* (1993); and *The Fear Room* (1996). Her first novel, *Opium Dreams*, appeared in 1997. Her story 'Making It' was the basis for the film *Outrageous!*

KATHERINE GOVIER (b. 1948). Born in Edmonton and educated at the University of Alberta, Govier taught creative writing at York University in Toronto from 1982 to 1986. In addition to five novels—*Random Descent* (1979), *Going Through the Motions* (1982), *Between Men* (1987), *Hearts of Flame* (1991), and *Angel Walk* (1996)—she has published three story collections, *Fables of Brunswick Avenue* (1985), *Before and After* (1989), and *The Immaculate Conception Photography Gallery* (1994), and a travel anthology, *Without a Guide* (1994). She received the Marion Engel Award in 1997.

BARBARA GOWDY (b. 1950). Born in Windsor, Ontario, she studied theatre at York University in Toronto. She worked for the publisher Lester & Orpen Dennys and was later a reporter on the TVOntario literary program *Imprint*. Gowdy's first book, a collection of poems and stories entitled *The Rabbit and the Hare* (1982), was followed by the novels *Through the Green Valley* (1988), *Falling Angels* (1989), *Mister Sandman* (1995), and *The White Bone* (1998). She won the Marion Engel Award in 1996, and the title story of her collection *We So Seldom Look on Love* (1992) was adapted as the prize-winning film *Kissed*.

ELISABETH HARVOR (b. 1936). Erica Elisabeth Arendt Deichmann was born in Saint John, New Brunswick. Beginning nurse's training in 1954, she left nine months before graduation and married Stig Harvor. After a year and a half in Europe the couple settled in Ottawa; they were divorced in 1977. In 1983 Harvor enrolled at Concordia University, obtaining an M.A. in 1986. She has published three volumes of short stories: *Women and Children* (1973), which was revised and reissued as *Our Lady of All the Distances* (1991); *If Only We Could Drive Like This Forever* (1988); and *Let Me Be the One* (1996). *Fortress of Chairs* (1992), a selection of poetry, won the Gerald Lampert Memorial Award. A second volume of poetry, *The Long Cold Green Evenings of Spring*, was published in 1997.

ELIZABETH HAY (b. 1951). Hay was born in Owen Sound, Ontario. She has travelled widely and worked for many years as a broadcaster and documentary producer for CBC Radio. She has published two 'documentary novels', *The Only Snow in Havana* (1992) and *Captivity Tales: Canadians in New York* (1993), and two collections of short fiction, *Crossing the Snow Line* (1989) and *Small Change* (1997).

JANETTE TURNER HOSPITAL (b. 1942). Janette Turner was born in Melbourne, Australia, and educated at the University of Queensland. With her husband, Clifford George Hospital, she moved in 1967 to the US and in 1971 to Kingston, Ontario. In addition to six novels—*The Ivory Swing* (1982), *The Tiger in the Tiger Pit* (1983), *Borderline* (1985), *Charades* (1988), *The Last Magician* (1992), and *Oyster* (1996)—she has written three collections of short stories: *Dislocations* (1986), *Isobars* (1990), *Collected Stories* (1995); a crime thriller, *A Very Proper Death* (1990), published under the name Alex Juniper; and a novella, *L'Envolée* (1995), published in French.

ISABEL HUGGAN (b. 1943). Born in Kitchener, Ontario, she grew up in nearby Elmira, received a B.A. from the University of Western Ontario in 1965, and has lived, with her husband, in Kenya, France, and the Philippines. Huggan has published two collections of short stories: *The Elizabeth Stories* (1984) and *You Never Know* (1993). She also contributed an essay, 'Notes from the Philippines' to *Writing Away: the PEN Canada Travel Anthology* (1994), edited by Constance Rooke.

E. PAULINE JOHNSON (TEKAHIONWAKE) (1861–1913). Johnson was born on the Six Nations Reserve, the daughter of a Mohawk chief and his English wife. A gifted performer, she established her reputation with public readings for which she often dressed in Native costume. Her first volume of poems, *The White Wampum* (1895), was followed by *Canadian Born* (1903) and *Flint and Feather* (1912). *Legends of Vancouver* (1911) is a collection of mythic narratives inspired by her friend Chief Joe Capilano. *The Shagganappi* (1912) and *The Moccasin Maker* (1913) contain mostly short didactic stories.

JUDITH KALMAN (b. 1954). Born in Budapest and educated at Concordia University in Montreal and the University of Windsor, Kalman now lives in Toronto, where she works as an editor of language arts books for children. Her stories have appeared in *Saturday Night*, *Queen's Quarterly*, *Grain*, *Descant*, and *Prairie Fire*, as well as the anthology *Celebrating Canadian Women*. The winner of the 1995 Tilden Canadian Literary Award and both the Gold Medal and the President's Medal at the 1996 National Magazine Awards, she published her first book, *The County of Birches*, in 1998.

JANICE KULYK KEEFER (b. 1953). Janice Kulyk was raised in Toronto and studied at the University of Toronto and the University of Sussex in England. After spending a year in France, she and her husband settled in Nova Scotia. Her first books were collections of poetry, *White of the Lesser Angels* (1986), and short fiction, *The Paris–Napoli Express* (1986). Among her other publications are two more story collections, *Transfigurations* (1987) and *Travelling Ladies* (1990); two volumes of criticism, *Under Eastern Eyes: A Critical Reading of Maritime Fiction* (1987) and *Reading Mavis Gallant* (1989); three novels, *Constellations* (1988), *Rest Harrow* (1992), and *The Green Library* (1996); and a memoir *Honey and Ashes: A Story of Family* (1998).

MARGARET LAURENCE (1926–87). Jean Margaret Wemys was born in Neepawa, Manitoba—the inspiration for the prairie town of Manawaka in her fiction. Her parents died when she was young and she was brought up by an aunt. After graduating in 1947 from United Collegein Winnipeg, she worked as a reporter for the *Winnipeg Citizen*. She married Jack Laurence in 1947 and moved with him to England in 1949; they lived in Africa from 1950 to 1957, returning to Canada and living in Vancouver from 1957 to 1962. After separating from her husband in 1962, she lived in England for ten years before returning to Canada and settling in Lakefield, Ontario, where she died. Laurence's African writings include a novel, *This Side Jordan* (1960); a collection of stories, *The Tomorrow-Tamer* (1962); and a memoir, *The Prophet's Camel Bell* (1963). The first of her Manawaka novels was *The Stone Angel* (1964); it was followed by *A Jest of God* (1966), *The Fire Dwellers* (1966), and *The Diviners* (1974), which won a Governor General's Award. *A Bird in the House* (1970) is a collection of linked semi-autobiographical stories. Laurence also published several books for children and a number of magazine articles, collected in *Heart of a Stranger* (1976).

L.M. MONTGOMERY (1874–1942). Born at Clifton (now New London), Prince Edward Island, Lucy Maud Montgomery was raised by her maternal grandparents after her widowed father moved to Saskatchewan. Her first novel, *Anne of Green Gables* (1908), gained her international recognition. Marrying the Rev. Ewan Macdonald in 1911, she continued to pursue her writing career, producing seven sequels: *Anne of Avonlea* (1909), *Anne of the Island* (1915), *Anne's House of Dreams* (1917), *Rainbow Valley* (1919), *Rilla of Ingleside* (1921), *Anne of Windy Poplars* (1936), and *Anne of Ingleside* (1939). In addition she published several collections of short stories, including *The Story Girl* (1911) and *Further Chronicles of Avonlea* (1920); the series *Emily of New Moon* (1923), *Emily Climbs* (1925), and *Emily's Quest* (1927); and two adult novels, *The Blue Castle* (1926) and *A Tangled Web* (1931), as well as *Pat of Silver Bush* (1933), *Mistress Pat* (1935), and *Jane of Lantern Hill* (1937). A volume of her poetry, *The Watchman and Other Poems*, appeared in 1916, and several prose collections were published posthumously.

ALICE MUNRO (b. 1931). Alice Laidlaw was born and grew up in the southwestern Ontario town of Wingham. After marrying James Munro in 1951 she moved to Vancouver and then to Victoria, British Columbia, where she began publishing her short stories in magazines. After her divorce in 1976, she returned to live in Clinton, another southwestern Ontario town, with her second husband. Her first collection, *Dance of the Happy Shades*

(1968), won a Governor General's Award, and her only novel, *Lives of Girls and Women* (1971), received the Canadian Booksellers Award. A second collection, *Something I've Been Meaning to Tell You* (1974), was followed by *Who Do You Think You Are?* (1978), which also won a Governor General's Award. Her other collections are *The Moons of Jupiter* (1982), *The Progress of Love* (1986), *Friend of My Youth* (1990), and *Open Secrets* (1994). *Selected Stories* (1996) is a collection of twenty-eight stories from earlier books. Munro has also written a number of radio scripts, and her television play 'How I Met My Husband' was published in the collection *The Play's the Thing* (1976), edited by Tony Gifford.

P.K. PAGE (b. 1909). Patricia Kathleen Page was born at Swanage in the south of England and came to Canada with her family in 1919, settling in Red Deer, Alberta. She published her first poems while living in Montreal in the early 1940s, and her first collection, *As Ten as Twenty*, in 1946. In 1950 she married William Arthur Irwin. Her second collection, *The Metal and the Flower* (1954), won a Governor General's Award. Other well-known volumes include *Cry Ararat* (1967); *Evening Dance of the Grey Flies* (1981), the centre-piece of which, the futurist story 'Unless the Eye Catch Fire', is the subject of a forthcoming film; *The Glass Air: Selected Poems* (1985), which also includes drawings and two essays; *Brazilian Journal* (1987); and *Hologram: A Book of Glosas* (1994). Page has also written two books of fairy tales for children, *A Flask of Sea Water* (1989) and *The Goat that Flew* (1993). Her only novel, *The Sun and the Moon* (1944), originally published under the name Judith Cape, was reissued under her own name in 1973 in *The Sun and the Moon and Other Fictions*.

MARLENE NOURBESE PHILIP (b. 1947). Born in Moriah, Tobago, Marlene Irma Philip adopted the name Nourbese and now signs her work M. Nourbese Philip. In 1967 she earned a B.Sc. from the University of the West Indies and immigrated to Canada. After studying political science and law at the University of Western Ontario, she practised immigration and family law in Toronto until 1982, when she turned to writing full-time. She has published three collections of poetry, *Thorns* (1980), *Salmon Courage* (1983), and *She Tries Her Tongue, Her Silence Softly Breaks* (1989), which won the Casa de las Americas Prize for English-Caribbean poetry; a novel for young people, *Harriet's Daughter* (1988); a narrative in poetry and prose, *Looking for Livingstone: An Odyssey of Silence* (1991); and three collections of essays, *Frontiers: Essays and Writings on Racism and Culture* (1992), *Showing Grit: Showboating North of the 44th Parallel* (1993), and *A Genealogy of Resistance: Essays* (1997).

JANE RULE (b. 1931). Born in Plainfield, New Jersey, Jane Vance Rule grew up in various parts of the American mid-west and in California. Moving to Vancouver in 1956, she taught from time to time at the University of British Columbia. In 1976 she settled on Galiano Island, British Columbia, where she now makes her home. Her first novel, *Desert of the Heart* (1964), which is set in Reno, Nevada, and explores a developing lesbian relationship, became the basis for the 1986 film *Desert Hearts*. Rule published six other novels— *This Is Not for You* (1970), *Against the Season* (1971), *The Young In One Another's Arms* (1977), *Contract With the World* (1980), *Memory Board* (1987), and *After the Fire* (1989)— before declaring her retirement from writing (partly because of severe arthritis). Her short stories have been published in three collections, *Themes for Diverse Instruments* (1975), *Outlander* (1981), and *Inland Passage* (1985). She is also the author of *Lesbian Images* (1975)— a study of such writers as Radclyffe Hall, Colette, and Vita Sackville West—and a collection of essays, *A Hot-Eyed Moderate* (1985).

DIANE SCHOEMPERLEN (b. 1954). Born in Thunder Bay, Ontario, she graduated from Lakehead University in 1976 and now lives in Kingston, Ontario. Shoemperlen has published six books of short fiction: *Double Exposures* (1984); *Frogs and Other Stories* (1986), which won the Writers Guild of Alberta Award; *Hockey Night In Canada* (1987), the title story of which was made into a 30-minute television play; *The Man of My Dreams* (1990); *Hockey Night In Canada and Other Stories* (1991); and *Forms of Devotion: Stories and Pictures* (1998), which won a Governor General's Award; and a novel *The Language of Love: A Novel in 100 Chapters* (1994),

GAIL SCOTT (b. 1945). Born in Ottawa, Scott grew up in a bilingual community in eastern Ontario and studied at Queen's University in Kingston, Ontario, and the Université de Grenoble in France. Scott was a founding editor of the alternative political publication *The Last Post* (1970), the feminist magazine *Des Luttes et des rires des femmes* (1970s), and the French-language cultural magazine *Spirale* (1979–83). Her publications include a collection of short stories, *Spare Parts* (1981); a collection of essays, *Spaces Like Stairs* (1989); and three novels, *Heroine* (1988), *Main Brides* (1993), and *My Paris* (1999).

CAROL SHIELDS (b. 1935). Carol Warner was born in Oak Park, Illinois, and educated in Indiana and at the University of Ottawa. In 1957 she married Donald Hugh Shields, and she became a Canadian citizen in 1971. She now lives in Winnipeg and teaches at the University of Manitoba. Shields has published poetry, short stories, and literary criticism—a revision of her thesis was published as *Susanna Moodie: Voice and Vision* (1972)—as well as plays for radio and the stage, but she is best known as a novelist. Her first novel, *Small Ceremonies* (1976), won the Canadian Authors' Association Award. Among her other novels are *The Box Garden* (1977), *Happenstance* (1980), *A Fairly Conventional Woman* (1982), *Swann: A Mystery* (1987), *The Republic of Love* (1992), and *The Stone Diaries* (1993), which won a Governor General's Award in Canada and the Pulitzer Prize for Fiction in the US. Her most recent novel, *Larry's Party* (1997), was awarded the Orange Prize. Her short stories have been collected in *Various Miracles* (1985) and *The Orange Fish* (1989).

ELIZABETH SPENCER (b. 1921). Born in Carrollton, Mississippi, Spencer travelled to Italy on a Guggenheim Fellowship in 1956 and then to Montreal, where she taught creative writing at Concordia University between 1958 and 1986. She is the author of seven novels—*Fire in the Morning* (1948), *This Crooked Way* (1951), *The Voice at the Back Door* (1956), *No Place for an Angel* (1967), *The Snare* (1972), *The Salt Line* (1984), and *The Night Travellers* (1991)—and two novellas—*The Light in the Piazza* (1960) and *Knights and Dragons* (1965). She has also published five collections of short stories: *Ship Island and Other Stories* (1968), *The Stories of Elizabeth Spencer* (1981), *Marilee* (1981), *Jack of Diamonds and Other Stories* (1988), and *On the Gulf* (1991).

LINDA SVENDSEN (b. 1954). Born and raised in the Vancouver area, she studied at the University of British Columbia and Columbia and Stanford universities in the United States. After a period in New York City she returned to Vancouver, where she teaches creative writing at UBC. Svendsen's short fiction has appeared in magazines such as the *Atlantic Monthly* and *Saturday Night*, and has been anthologized in *Best Canadian Stories*. Her collection *Marine Life* was published in 1992. In 1990 she edited the anthology *Words We Call Home: Celebrating Canadian Writing at UBC*.

SUSAN SWAN (b. 1945). Born in Midland, Ontario, she studied English at McGill

University in Montreal and worked for a time as a journalist. She now teaches at York University in Toronto. Her three novels are *The Biggest Modern Woman of the World* (1983), *The Last of the Golden Girls* (1989), and *The Wives of Bath* (1993). Swan has also published two collections of short stories: *Unfit for Paradise* (1982) and *Stupid Boys Are Good to Relax With* (1996).

AUDREY THOMAS (b. 1935). Audrey Grace Callahan was born in Binghamton, New York, and educated at Smith College in the US and St Andrews University in Scotland. She married Ian Thomas in 1958 and the couple immigrated to Canada in 1959. From 1964 to 1966 she lived in Ghana, where her husband was teaching. Returning to Vancouver, Thomas published her first collection of stories, *Ten Green Bottles* (1967). After separating from her husband in 1972 she made her home on Galiano Island, British Columbia. Thomas's other works include *Mrs Blood* (1970); two related novellas in one volume, *Munchmeyer and Prospero on the Island* (1971); *Songs My Mother Taught Me* (1973); *Blown Figures* (1974); *Ladies and Escorts* (1977); *Latakia* (1979); *Real Mothers* (1981); *Two in the Bush and Other Stories* (1981); *Goodbye Harold, Good Luck* (1986); *The Wild Blue Yonder* (1990); *Graven Images* (1993); and *Coming Down From Wa* (1995). Thomas has also written numerous radio plays and won many prizes, including the Ethel Wilson Fiction Prize (three times) and the Marian Engel Award.

CATHARINE PARR TRAILL (1802–99). Born in Kent, England, Catharine Strickland immigrated to Canada in 1832 with her husband, Thomas Traill, and settled near present-day Lakefield, Ontario. Of her numerous books, many of them for children, the best-known is *The Backwoods of Canada: Being Letters From the Wife of an Emigrant Officer, Illustrative of the Domestic Economy of British America* (1836). In 1868 Traill combined her text with paintings by Susanna Moodie's daughter, Agnes Fitzgibbon, in *Canadian Wild Flowers*. Her most significant work as a naturalist, *Studies of Plant Life in Canada; or, Gleanings from Forest, Lake and Plain*, appeared in 1885. A number of sketches and stories of bush life that originally appeared in British and Canadian magazines have been collected in *Forest and Other Gleanings: The Fugitive Writings of Catharine Parr Traill* (1994).

JANE URQUHART (b. 1949). Born Jane Carter in Little Long Lac, Ontario, she was educated at the University of Guelph and married the painter Tony Urquhart in 1976. Her first books were three poetry collections: *I'm Walking in the Garden of His Imaginary Palace* (1982), *False Shuffles* (1982), and *The Little Flowers of Madame de Montespan* (1984). Her first book of fiction, *The Whirlpool* (1986), won France's Prix du Meilleur Livre Étranger. It was followed by a collection of short stories, *Storm Glass* (1987), and two novels, *Changing Heaven* (1990) and *Away* (1993), for which Urquart was named co-winner of the 1994 Trillium Award. In the same year she won the Marian Engel Award. Her most recent novel, *The Underpainter* (1997), won a Governor General's Award.

ARITHA VAN HERK (b. 1954). Born in Wetaskiwin, Alberta, she grew up on her family's farm, studied at the University of Alberta, and has taught at the University of Calgary since 1983. Her novel *Judith* (1978), which received the Seal First Novel Award, was followed by *The Tent Peg* (1981) and *No Fixed Address: An Amorous Journey* (1986), which won the Howard O'Hagan Prize for Best Novel in Alberta. *Places Far From Ellesmere: A Geografictione: Explorations on Site* (1991) combines elements of autobiography, travel, fiction, and criticism. In addition, van Herk has published two collections of essays, *In Visible*

Ink: Crypto-Frictions (1991) and *A Frozen Tongue* (1992) and edited several anthologies, including *Alberta Re/Bound* (1990) and *Boundless Alberta* (1993). Her most recent novel is *Restlessness* (1998).

MEEKA WALSH (b. 1943). Based in Winnipeg, she has been the editor of the international arts magazine *Border Crossings* since 1993. In 1989 she published *Ordinary Magic: Intervals in a Life* (1989), a book of journals, and in 1995 she edited *Don Reichert: A Life in Work*. Her stories have appeared in such literary magazines as *Descant*, *The Malahat Review*, *Canadian Fiction Magazine*, and *Prairie Fire*. *The Garden of Earthly Intimacies* (1996) is her first book of short fiction.

EMMA LEE WARRIOR (b. 1941). A member of the North Peigan (Blackfoot) band, Emma Lee Warrior grew up on the Peigan Reserve in southern Alberta, close to the American border. She was educated in a boarding school there and at the University of Washington, where she trained as a counsellor. Her stories and poems have appeared in *Wicazo Sa*, *Canadian Fiction Magazine*, A *Gathering of Spirit*, *Harper's Anthology of Twentieth Century Native American Poetry*, and *An Anthology of Canadian Native Literature in English* (2nd ed.,1998).

SHEILA WATSON (1909–98). Born Sheila Doherty in New Westminster, British Columbia, she married the poet Wilfred Watson in 1941 and taught at the University of Alberta from 1961 to 1975. Her celebrated novel *The Double Hook* appeared in 1959, and her uncollected prose was published as a special number of the journal *Open Letter* (1975). *Four Stories* (1979) was followed by *Five Stories* (1984) and a second novel, *Deep Hollow Creek*, which although written in the 1930s was not published until 1992.

HELEN WEINZWEIG (b. 1915). Born in Poland, Helen Tenenbaum moved to Toronto at the age of nine and married the composer John Weinzweig in 1940. She published her first novel, *Passing Ceremony*, in 1973, at the age of fifty-seven. Her second novel, *Basic Black with Pearls* (1980), won the City of Toronto Book Award. A collection of short stories, *A View from the Roof*, appeared in 1989.

ETHEL WILSON (1888–1980). Ethel Davis Bryant was born at Port Elizabeth, South Africa, and orphaned at the age of ten. Sent to live with her grandmother in Vancouver, she was educated in Canada and Britain and worked as a teacher for several years before marrying Dr Wallace Wilson in 1921. Her writing career began relatively late, with short stories published in the *New Statesman and Nation* in the late 1930s. Her first novel, *Hetty Dorval*, appeared in 1947. It was followed by three more novels—*The Innocent Traveller* (1949), *Swamp Angel* (1954), and *Love and Salt Water* (1956)—as well as two novellas published under the title *The Equations of Love* (1952). The majority of Wilson's short stories are collected in *Mrs Golightly and Other Stories* (1961).

RACHEL WYATT (b. 1929). Born in Bradford, England, Wyatt studied nursing in London before immigrating to Canada in 1957 with her husband and children. She began writing radio drama in the early 1970s; more than seventy-five of her radio plays have been produced by the CBC, and thirty by the BBC. In addition to five novels—*The String Box* (1970), *The Rosedale Hoax* (1977), *Foreign Bodies* (1982), *Time in the Air* (1985), and *Mona Lisa Smiled a Little* (1999)—she has published a book-length sequence of short stories, *The Day Marlene Dietrich Died* (1995). She has also written two stage plays, *Geometry* (1983) and *Chairs and Tables* (1984), and in 1995 she wrote a stage adaptation of Adele Wiseman's novel *Crackpot*.

INDEX